CHOIR

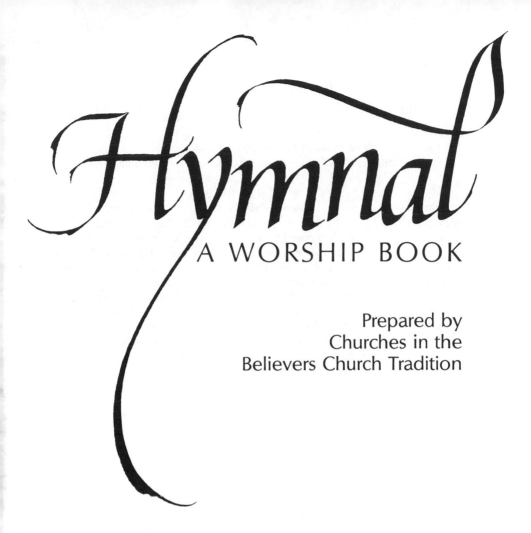

Hymnal
A WORSHIP BOOK

Prepared by
Churches in the
Believers Church Tradition

Brethren Press
Elgin, Illinois

Faith and Life Press
Newton, Kansas

Mennonite Publishing House
Scottdale, Pennsylvania

Hymnal: A Worship Book

Library of Congress Catalog Card Number: 92-81937
Printed in the United States of America
Cover Design: Gwen Stamm
Typography: Midwest Engraving, Russell Springs, Kentucky
Printer: Quebecor Printing/Hawkins, Kingsport, Tennessee

Cover symbol: The lamb in the midst of briars is a traditional Anabaptist symbol. It illustrates the suffering Lamb of God, who calls the faithful to obedient service. Since in the past it has been used to represent unity among believers, it is an appropriate symbol for this cooperatively produced hymnal.

5   6   7   8   9   10   01   00   99   98   97   96

INTRODUCTION

Congregational singing is an essential part of worship in the Church of the Brethren, the General Conference Mennonite Church, and the Mennonite Church in North America. Our singing reveals much about who we have been and who we are as Anabaptists and Pietists. *Hymnal: A Worship Book* was prepared with the goal of continuing and expanding our singing tradition.

The creative activity of the Holy Spirit through music and poetry has nurtured our life of faith. Our singing has been shaped by hymns created throughout the centuries of Christian history and expanded by hymns set in contemporary idioms. The presence of African-American, Asian, Native American, Hispanic, and African hymns deepens our sense of unity in Christ through the Spirit. We share a rich hymnic legacy with many Christians, past and present.

The responsive readings, prayers, ceremonies, and scripture readings included also span the range of Christian history and experience. They help us speak with distinctive and powerful voices our deepest desires, needs, and joys. As our worship bridges the past and embraces the present, we glimpse what we may become in the future.

The title *A Worship Book* reveals that we have conceived of this book as a guide and resource for worship. The hymns and worship resources have been ordered according to their probable or potential use in a congregation's worship cycle. The needs of Sunday morning worship received primary attention, but resources are provided for other significant congregational occasions. We not only attended to the structure of worship actions in our selections, but to the various dynamics, moods, styles, and sentiments of these actions as well.

Two other books offer support for worship and music leaders using this book. The *Hymnal Accompaniment Handbook* contains essays introducing the styles of music new to our traditions, performance suggestions for many hymns and resources, and accompaniments. The *Hymnal Companion* provides detailed histories about the people and circumstances that produced the hymns and resources found in *Hymnal: A Worship Book;* beneath each hymn is The Hymnal Project's best determination of the first appearance of the hymn's text and music.

Our purpose in undertaking the task of producing this worship book was to be part of the Spirit's ongoing activity. We offer *Hymnal: A Worship Book* to our people with the hope that our worship will be enriched and that we will be strengthened in faith. We pray that through it the Spirit will lead us deeper into the wondrous mystery of God.

Rebecca Slough, Managing Editor
On behalf of the Members of The Hymnal Project

HYMNAL PROJECT PERSONNEL

HYMNAL PROJECT CHAIR

Nancy Rosenberger Faus	1986-1992
Mary Oyer	1984-1986

CHURCH OF THE BRETHREN

* Harold Bowser, Text Committee	1988-1991
* Robert Durnbaugh, Publishers Committee	1984-1992
* Nancy Rosenberger Faus, Text Committee	1984-1987
Nadine Pence Frantz, Worship Committee	1987-1992
Joan Fyock, Music Committee	1984-1991
Jill Zook-Jones, Worship Committee	1985-1987
Christine Michael, Worship Committee	1984-1985
Kenneth Morse, Text Committee	1984-1990
Jerry Peterson, Marketing Committee	1988-1992
* Robin Risser Mundey, Music Committee	1984-1991
* Jimmy Ross, Worship Committee	1984-1991

GENERAL CONFERENCE MENNONITE CHURCH

John Gaeddert, Worship Committee	1989-1990
* Marilyn Houser Hamm, Music Committee	1984-1991
Harris Loewen, Text Committee	1984-1990
* Dietrich Rempel, Publishers Committee	1984-1992
* John Rempel, Worship Committee	1984-1991
Mark Regier, Marketing Committee	1990-1992
* Orlando Schmidt, Text Committee	1984-1991
J. W. Sprunger, Worship Committee	1984-1988
George Wiebe, Music Committee	1984-1990

MENNONITE CHURCH

* A. Don Augsburger, Worship Committee	1984-1989
* Tony Brown, Text Committee	1984-1990
Pauline Kennel, Text Committee	1984-1986
* Marlene Kropf, Worship Committee	1989-1992
* Laurence Martin, Publishers Committee	1984-1992
* Shirley Martin, Text Committee	1986-1991
* Kenneth Nafziger, Music Committee	1984-1992
Mary Oyer, Music Committee	1984-1989
Rebecca Slough, Worship Committee	1984-1989
J. W. Sprunger, Marketing Committee	1988-1992

*indicates Hymnal Council member

CHURCHES OF GOD CONTRIBUTORS
Robert Asel, Dale Brougher, Stephen Dunn, Everett Falk, Barbara Chong Gossard, J. Harvey Gossard, David Green, Marilyn Rayle Kern, Jean Leathers, Robert Stephenson, Joyce Thornton

MENNONITE BRETHREN CHURCH CONTRIBUTORS
Clarence Hiebert, Jacob Klaassen, Larry Warkentin

STAFF

Rebecca Slough, Managing Editor	1989-1992
Kenneth Nafziger, Music Editor	1989-1992
Lani Wright, Administrative Secretary	1986-1992
Joan Fyock, Research Associate	1985-1992
Mary Oyer, Project Manager	1987-1989
Robert Bowman, Executive Director	1984-1987
Dan Shenk, Copy Editor for Fifth Printing	1993-1995

TOPICAL INDEXERS: John David Bowman, Margaret Franz, Estella Horning, Del Keeney, Eleanor Loewen, Joyce Wyse.

PROOFREADERS: Doug Basinger, Anita Breckbill, David Breckbill, Jeremy Nafziger, Linda Richer, Uli Schorn-Hoffert, Grete Stenersen.

CONTRIBUTORS TO FIFTH PRINTING: Marlene Kropf, Wendy McFadden, Ken Nafziger, Rebecca Slough, Lani Wright.

TABLE OF CONTENTS

What is this place

KOMT NU MET ZANG 98. 98. 966

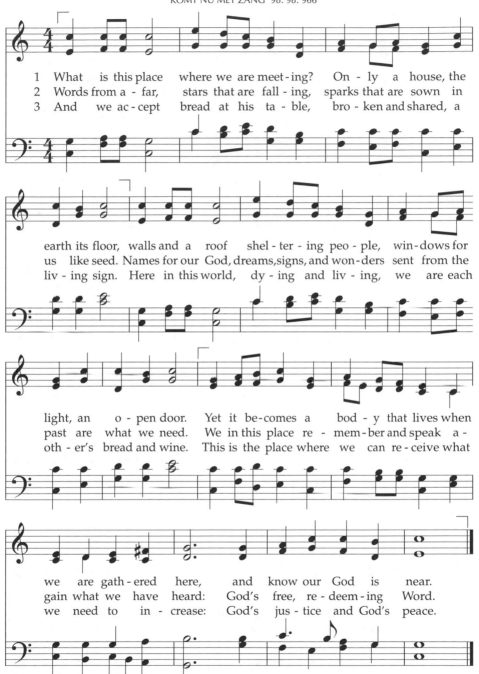

1 What is this place where we are meet-ing? On-ly a house, the
2 Words from a-far, stars that are fall-ing, sparks that are sown in
3 And we ac-cept bread at his ta-ble, bro-ken and shared, a

earth its floor, walls and a roof shel-ter-ing peo-ple, win-dows for
us like seed. Names for our God, dreams, signs, and won-ders sent from the
liv-ing sign. Here in this world, dy-ing and liv-ing, we are each

light, an o-pen door. Yet it be-comes a bod-y that lives when
past are what we need. We in this place re-mem-ber and speak a-
oth-er's bread and wine. This is the place where we can re-ceive what

we are gath-ered here, and know our God is near.
gain what we have heard: God's free, re-deem-ing Word.
we need to in-crease: God's jus-tice and God's peace.

Text: Huub Oosterhuis, *Zomaar een dak boven wat hoofden,* 1968; tr. David Smith, ca. 1970
Music: *Nederlandtsche Gedenckclanck,* 1626; harmonized by B. Huijbers, 1968

2 In thy holy place we bow

77. 77. 87. 87

1 In thy ho - ly place we bow, per - fumes sweet to
2 Ho - ly light doth fill this place; Spir - it, light our
3 On thy ho - ly bread we feed, hun - ger nev - er

heav - en rise, while our gold - en cen - sers glow with the
way to guide. In the pres - ence of thy face sin and
more to know. Thou sup - pli - est all our need; Sav - ior,

fire of sac - ri - fice. Saints low bend - ing, prayers as -
dark - ness ne'er can hide. Heav - en's gleam - ing, full - ness
whith - er shall we go? Ne'er for - sak - ing, here par -

cend-ing, ho - ly lips and hands im - plore, faith be - liev - ing
stream-ing, life and truth for all are found; light per - vad - ing,
tak - ing bread our souls to sat - is - fy; here a - bid - ing

Text: S. F. Coffman, 1901, *Church and Sunday School Hymnal, Supplement,* 1911, alt.
Music: J. D. Brunk, *Church and Sunday School Hymnal, Supplement,* 1911

and re - ceiv - ing grace from thee whom we a - dore.
nev - er fad - ing, light - ing all the world a - round.
and con - fid - ing, we shall nev - er want nor die.

Create my soul anew 3

MT. EPHRAIM SM

1 Cre - ate my soul a - new, else all my
2 De - scend, ce - les - tial Fire, and seize me
3 Let joy and wor - ship spend the rem - nant

wor - ship's vain. This wretch - ed heart will
from a - bove! Wrap me in flames of
of my days, and to my God my

ne'er prove true till it ____ be formed a - gain.
pure de - sire, a sac - ri - fice to love.
soul as - cend in sweet ____ per - fumes of praise!

Text: Isaac Watts, *Horae Lyricae,* 1706
Music: Benjamin Milgrove, *Sixteen Hymns ...,* 1769

4 Unto thy temple, Lord, we come

ROCKINGHAM OLD LM

1 Un - to thy tem - ple, Lord, we come with thank - ful
2 the com - mon home of rich and poor, of bond and
3 And dwell thou with us in this place, thou and thy
4 May thy whole truth be spo - ken here, thy gos - pel

hearts to wor - ship thee, and pray that this may
free, and great and small; large as thy love for -
Christ, to guide and bless. Here make the well - springs
light for - ev - er shine, thy per - fect love cast

be our home un - til we touch e - ter - ni - ty;
ev - er - more, and warm and bright and good to all.
of thy grace like foun - tains in the wil - der - ness.
out all fear, and hu - man life be - come di - vine.

Text: Robert Collyer, 1866, *The River of Life*, 1873
Music: *Supplement to Psalmody*, ca. 1780; arranged by Edward Miller, 1790

There is a place of quiet rest

McAFEE CM with refrain

1 There is a place of qui - et rest, near to the heart of God,
2 There is a place of com - fort sweet, near to the heart of God,
3 There is a place of full re - lease, near to the heart of God,

a place where sin can - not mo - lest, near to the heart of God.
a place where we our Sav - ior meet, near to the heart of God.
a place where all is joy and peace, near to the heart of God.

Refrain

O Je - sus, bless'd Re - deem - er, sent from the heart of God,

hold us, who wait be - fore thee, near to the heart of God.

Text: Cleland B. McAfee, 1901, *The Choir Leader,* 1903
Music: Cleland B. McAfee, 1901, *The Choir Leader,* 1903

6 Here in this place

GATHER US IN Irregular

1 Here in this place, new light is stream-ing, now is the dark-ness
2 We are the young – our lives are a mys - t'ry, we are the old– who
3 Here we will take the wine and the wa - ter, here we will take the
4 Not in the dark of build-ings con - fin - ing, not in some heav-en,

van-ished a - way. See, in this space, our fears and our dream-ings,
yearn for your face. We have been sung through - out all of his - t'ry,
bread of new birth. Here you shall call your sons and your daugh-ters,
light years a - way, but here in this place, the new light is shin-ing;

brought here to you in the light of this day.
called to be light to the whole hu - man race.
call us a - new to be salt for the earth.
now is the king - dom, now is the day.

Gath - er us in – the lost and for - sak - en, gath - er us in – the
Gath - er us in – the rich and the haugh-ty, gath - er us in – the
Give us to drink the wine of com - pas - sion, give us to eat the
Gath - er us in – and hold us for - ev - er, gath - er us in – and

blind and the lame. Call to us now, and we shall a - wak - en,
proud and the strong. Give us a heart so meek and so low - ly,
bread that is you. Nour-ish us well, and teach us to fash-ion
make us your own. Gath - er us in – all peo - ples to - geth - er,

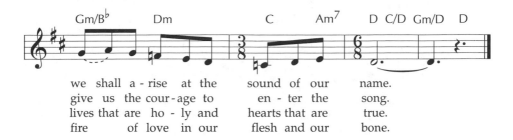

we shall a - rise at the   sound of our   name.
give us the cour-age to   en - ter the   song.
lives that are ho - ly and   hearts that are   true.
fire   of love in our   flesh and our   bone.

Here, O Lord, your servants gather 7

TOKYO 75. 75 D

1 Here, O Lord, your   ser - vants gath - er,   hand we link with hand.
2 Man - y are the tongues we speak,   scat-tered are the lands,
3 Na - ture's se - crets   o - pen wide,   chang - es nev - er cease.
4 Grant, O God, an   age re-newed,   filled with death-less love.

Look-ing toward our   Sav - ior's cross,   joined in love we   stand.
yet   our hearts are   one in God,   one in love's de - mands.
Where, oh where, can   wea - ry souls   find the source of   peace?
Help us   as we   work and pray,   send us from a - bove

As   we seek the   realm of God,   we u - nite to   pray:
E'en in dark-ness   hope ap - pears,   call - ing age and   youth.
Un - to   all those   sore dis-tressed,   torn by end-less strife,
truth and cour - age,   faith and pow - er   need - ed in our   strife.

Je - sus, Sav - ior,   guide our   steps,   for you are the   way.
Je - sus, Teach - er,   dwell with   us,   for you are the   truth.
Je - sus, Heal - er,   bring your   balm,   for you are the   life.
Je - sus, Mas - ter,   be our   way,   be our truth, our   life!

8 Brethren, we have met to worship

HOLY MANNA 87. 87 D

1 Breth-ren, we have met to wor-ship and a - dore the
2 Sis - ters, will you come and help us? Mo - ses' sis - ters
3 Is there here a trem-bling jail - er, seek-ing grace and
4 Let us love our God su - preme-ly, let us love each

Lord our God. Will you pray with all your pow - er
aid - ed him. Will you help the trem - bling mourn - ers
filled with fears? Is there here a weep - ing Ma - ry
oth - er, too. Let us love and pray for sin - ners

while we try to preach the word? All is vain un -
who are strug - gling hard with sin? Tell them all a -
pour - ing forth a flood of tears? Breth - ren, join your
till our God makes all things new. Christ will call us

less the Spir - it of the ho - ly One comes down. Breth-ren,
bout the Sav - ior. Tell them that he will be found. Sis - ters,
cries to help them, sis - ters, let your prayers a - bound! Pray, oh
home to heav-en, at his ta - ble we'll sit down. Christ will

Text: *The Columbian Harmony*, 1825
Music: *The Columbian Harmony*, 1825

Jesus A, Nahetotaetanome 9
(Jesus Lord, how joyful you have made)
Irregular

pray, and ho - ly man - na will be show-ered all a-round.
pray, and ho - ly man - na will be show-ered all a-round.
pray, that ho - ly man - na will be scat-tered all a-round.
gird him - self and serve us with sweet man - na all a-round.

Je - sus A, Na-he-to-tae-ta-no-me tseh-ma-no'-ee'-
Je - sus Lord, how joy-ful you have made us to come to-geth-

to - va - tse - me - no-to, tse-'o-noo-me-me-no-to.
er here with you now! In your mer-cy you have called us.

"Na-nee-hoo-ve me-o-'o," tsex-he-še-me-no-to.
You say, "I am the way." We hear you call us.

Neh-pa-ve-a-me-otše-še-meno ne-me-o-ne-va!
We ask you, "Come lead us day by day." We fol-low your way.

Text: John Heap of Birds, *Jesus Nahetotaetanome*; tr. David Graber and others, *Tsese-Ma'heone-Nemetòtose*, 1982
         Copyright ©1982 Mennonite Indian Leaders' Council
Music: Plains Indian

10 Jesus, we want to meet

Irregular

Leader
1 Je - sus, we want to meet on this thy
2 We kneel in awe and fear on this thy
3 Thy bless - ing, Lord, we seek on this thy
4 Our minds we ded - i - cate on this thy

Leader
ho - ly day. We gath - er 'round thy throne
ho - ly day, pray God to teach us here
ho - ly day. Give joy of thy vic - to - ry
ho - ly day, heart and soul con - se - crate

All ... **Leader**
on this thy ho - ly day. Thou art our
on this thy ho - ly day. Save us and
on this thy ho - ly day. Through grace a - lone
on this thy ho - ly day. Ho - ly Spir - it,

heav'n - ly friend, hear our prayers as they as - cend.
cleanse our hearts, lead and guide our acts of praise,
are we saved. In thy flock may we be found.
make us whole. Bless the ser - mon in this place,

All
Look in - to our hearts and minds to - day, on this thy ho - ly day.
and our faith from seed to flow - er raise, on this thy ho - ly day.
Let the mind of Christ a - bide in us on this thy ho - ly day.
and as we go, lead us, Lord; we shall be thine ev - er - more.

Text: A. T. Olajide Olude; tr. Biodun Adebesin, versified by Austin C. Lovelace
English translation and versification copyright ©1964 Abingdon Press
Music: Nigerian melody; adapted by A. T. Olajide Olude

Sweet hour of prayer

SWEET HOUR LMD

1 Sweet hour of prayer, sweet hour of prayer, that calls me from a world of care, and bids me at my Fa-ther's throne make all my wants and wish-es known; in sea-sons of dis-tress and grief, my soul has of-ten found re-lief, and oft es-caped the tempt-er's snare, by thy re-turn, sweet hour of prayer!

2 Sweet hour of prayer, sweet hour of prayer, the joys I feel, the bliss I share, of those whose anx-ious spir-its burn with strong de-sires for thy re-turn! With such I has-ten to the place where God my Sav-ior shows his face, and glad-ly take my sta-tion there, and wait for thee, sweet hour of prayer!

3 Sweet hour of prayer, sweet hour of prayer, thy wings shall my pe-ti-tion bear to him whose truth and faith-ful-ness en-gage the wait-ing soul to bless. And since he bids me seek his face, be-lieve his word and trust his grace, I'll cast on him my ev-'ry care, and wait for thee, sweet hour of prayer!

Text: anonymous, *The New York Observer*, 1845
Music: William B. Bradbury, *Cottage Melodies*, 1859

12 Come, let us all unite to sing

GOD IS LOVE 83. 83. 8884 with refrain

1 Come, let us all u-nite to sing, God is love. Let heav'n and
2 O tell to earth's re-mot-est bound, God is love. In Christ we
3 How hap-py is our por-tion here, God is love. His prom-is-

earth their prais-es bring, God is love. Let ev-'ry soul from
have re-demp-tion found, God is love. His blood has washed our
es our spir-its cheer, God is love. He is our sun and

sin a-wake, let ev-'ry heart sweet mu-sic make, and sing with
sins a-way, his Spir-it turned our night to day, and now we
shield by day, our help, our hope, our strength and stay; he will be

Refrain

us for Je-sus' sake, for God is love.
can re-joice to say that God is love. God is love! God is
with us all the way, our God is love. God is love!

love! Come, let us all u-nite to sing that God is love.
God is love!

Text: anonymous, attributed to Howard Kingsbury, *Complete Compendium of Revival Music*, 1876
Music: Edmund S. Lorenz, *Notes of Triumph: for the Sunday School*, 1886

Blessed Jesus, at your word   13

LIEBSTER JESU, WIR SIND HIER 78. 78. 88

1 Bless-ed Je-sus, at your word we are gath-ered
2 All our knowl-edge, sense, and sight lie in deep-est
3 Glo-rious Lord, your-self im-part! Light of light from

all to hear you. Let our hearts and souls be stirred
dark-ness shroud-ed, till your Spir-it breaks our night
God pro-ceed-ing, o-pen lips and ears and heart,

now to seek and love and fear you. By your gos-pel
with your beams of truth un-cloud-ed. You a-lone to
help us by your Spir-it's lead-ing. Hear the cry your

pure and ho-ly teach us, Lord, to love you sole-ly.
God can win us, you must work all good with-in us.
church now rais-es; Lord, ac-cept our prayers and prais-es!

Text: Tobias Clausnitzer, "Liebster Jesu, wir sind hier," *Altdorffisches Gesangbüchlein,* 1663; tr. Catherine Winkworth,
         Lyra Germanica, Series II, 1858, alt.
Music: Johann R. Ahle, *Neue geistliche auf die Sonntage ... Andachten,* 1664

14 Come, we that love the Lord

WE'RE MARCHING TO ZION SM extended with refrain

1 Come, we that love the Lord, and let our joys be known. Join
2 Let those re-fuse to sing who nev-er knew our God, but
3 The hill of Zi-on yields a thou-sand sa-cred sweets, be-
4 Then let our songs a-bound, and ev-'ry tear be dry. We're

in a song with sweet ac-cord, join in a song with sweet ac-
chil-dren of the heav'n-ly King, but chil-dren of the heav'n-ly
fore we reach the heav'n-ly fields, be-fore we reach the heav'n-ly
march-ing thro' Im-man-uel's ground, we're march-ing thro' Im-man-uel's

cord, and thus sur - round the throne, and thus sur-round the throne.
King may speak their joys a-broad, may speak their joys a-broad.
fields, or walk the gold-en streets, or walk the gold-en streets.
ground, to fair - er worlds on high, to fair-er worlds on high.

and thus sur-round the throne, and thus sur-round the throne.
may speak their joys a-broad, may speak their joys a - broad.
or walk the gold-en streets, or walk the gold - en streets.
to fair-er worlds on high, to fair - er worlds on high.

Text: Isaac Watts, *Hymns and Spiritual Songs,* 1707, alt.; refrain by Robert Lowry
Music: Robert Lowry, 1867, *Silver Spray,* 1868

Refrain

We're march - ing to Zi - on, beau-ti-ful, beau-ti-ful Zi - on. We're
We're march-ing on to Zi - on,

march - ing up - ward to Zi - on, the beau-ti-ful cit-y of God.
Zi - on, Zi - on,

O Prince of peace 15
10 10. 10 10

1 O Prince of peace, O ho-ly God and King, to fel-low-
2 O Lord, we know you love us one and all, wheth-er from

ship to-day with you we come. All na-tions of the earth re-joice and
West or East we come to you. All of one faith we hear your sov-'reign

sing to sanc-ti - fy and glo-ri-fy your name.
call. O Je-sus Christ, you are our guide and stay.

Text: Saptayaadi; tr. Lawrence M. Yoder, *International Songbook,* Mennonite World Conference, 1978
Music: Javanese melody
    Text and music copyright ©1978 Mennonite World Conference

16 God is here among us

WUNDERBARER KÖNIG 668. 668. 33. 66

1 God is here a - mong us; let us all a - dore him, and with
2 Come, a - bide with - in me; let my soul, like Ma - ry, be thine
3 Glad - ly we sur - ren - der earth's de - ceit - ful trea - sures, pride of

awe ap - pear be - fore him. God is here with - in us; soul, in
earth - ly sanc - tu - ar - y. Come, in - dwell - ing Spir - it, with trans-
life, and sin - ful plea - sures. Glad - ly, Lord, we of - fer thine to

si - lence fear him, hum - bly, fer - vent - ly draw near him. Now his own
fig - ured splen - dor; love and hon - or will I ren - der. Where I go
be for - ev - er, soul and life and each en - deav - or. Thou a - lone

who have known God in wor - ship low - ly yield their spir - its whol - ly.
here be - low, let me bow be - fore thee, know thee, and a - dore thee.
shalt be known Lord of all our be - ing, life's true way de - cree - ing.

Text: Gerhard Tersteegen, "Gott ist gegenwärtig," *Geistliches Blumengärtlein*, 1729; tr. *The Hymnal 1940*, alt.
Music: *Alpha und Omega, Glaub- und Liebesübung*, 1680

We gather together

KREMSER 12 11. 12 11

1 We gath - er to - geth - er to ask the Lord's bless - ing.
2 Be - side us to guide us, our God with us join - ing,
3 We all do ex - tol thee, thou Lead - er tri - um - phant,

He chas - tens and has - tens his will to make known.
or - dain - ing, main - tain - ing his king - dom di - vine.
and pray that thou still our de - fend - er wilt be.

The wick - ed op - press - ing now cease from dis - tress - ing.
So from the be - gin - ning the fight we were win - ning;
Let thy con - gre - ga - tion es - cape trib - u - la - tion.

Sing prais - es to his name, he for - gets not his own.
thou, Lord, wast at our side, all glo - ry be thine!
Thy name be ev - er praised! O Lord, make us free!

Text: *Nederlandtsche Gedenckclanck*, 1626; tr. Theodore Baker, *Dutch Folk Songs*, 1917
Music: *Nederlandtsche Gedenckclanck*, 1626; melody adapted by Edward Kremser, *Sechs altniederländische Volkslieder*, 1877

18 Before Jehovah's aweful throne

WATTS LM

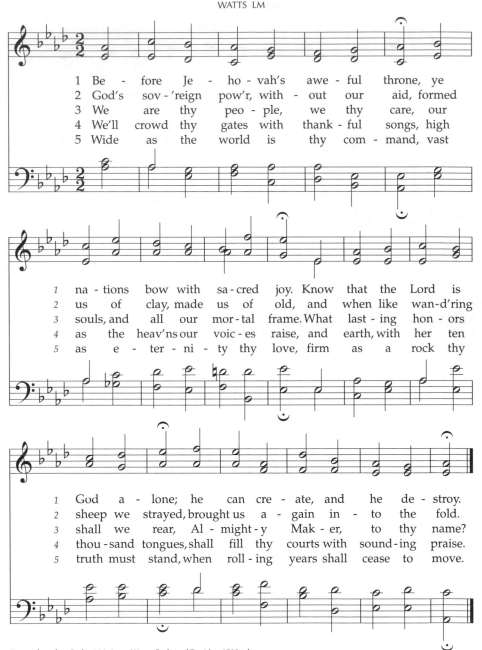

1 Be - fore Je - ho - vah's awe - ful throne, ye
2 God's sov - 'reign pow'r, with - out our aid, formed
3 We are thy peo - ple, we thy care, our
4 We'll crowd thy gates with thank - ful songs, high
5 Wide as the world is thy com - mand, vast

1 na - tions bow with sa - cred joy. Know that the Lord is
2 us of clay, made us of old, and when like wan-d'ring
3 souls, and all our mor - tal frame. What last - ing hon - ors
4 as the heav'ns our voic - es raise, and earth, with her ten
5 as e - ter - ni - ty thy love, firm as a rock thy

1 God a - lone; he can cre - ate, and he de - stroy.
2 sheep we strayed, brought us a - gain in - to the fold.
3 shall we rear, Al - might - y Mak - er, to thy name?
4 thou - sand tongues, shall fill thy courts with sound - ing praise.
5 truth must stand, when roll - ing years shall cease to move.

Text: based on Psalm 100, Isaac Watts, *Psalms of David...*, 1719, alt.
Music: J. D. Brunk, 1910, *Church and Sunday School Hymnal, Supplement,* 1911

Open now thy gates of beauty 19

UNSER HERRSCHER (NEANDER) 87. 87. 77

1 O - pen now thy gates of beau - ty, Zi - on; let me
2 Gra - cious God, I come be - fore thee, come thou al - so
3 Speak, O God, and I will hear thee; let thy will be

en - ter there, where my soul, in joy - ful du - ty,
un - to me. Where we find thee and a - dore thee,
done in - deed. May I un - dis - turbed draw near thee

waits for One who an - swers prayer. Oh, how bless - ed
there a heav'n on earth must be. To my heart O
while thou dost thy peo - ple feed. Here of life the

is this place, filled with sol - ace, light, and grace!
en - ter thou, let it be thy tem - ple now.
foun - tain flows, here is balm for all our woes.

Text: Benjamin Schmolck, "Tut mir auf die schöne Pforte," *Kirchen-Gefährte*, 1732; tr. Catherine Winkworth, *Chorale Book for England*, 1863, alt.
Music: Joachim Neander, *Alpha und Omega, Glaub- und Liebesübung*, 1680

Come and see

Irregular

1 "Come and see, come and see, I am the way and the truth," said he.
2 Ky - ri - e, Ky - ri - e, Ky - ri - e e - le - i-son.

"Fol - low me, fol - low me, come as a child, O come and see."
Chris - te, Chris - te, Chris - te e - le - i - son.

3 Chris - te, Chris - te, a - do - ra - mus te.

(melody)

3 Ky - ri - e, Ky - ri - e, Ky - ri - e e - le - i-son.

Al - le - lu - ia, Ky - ri - e e - le - i - son.*

Chris - te, Chris - te, Chris - te e - le - i - son.*

*Translation: Christ, we adore you. Alleluia, Lord, have mercy.
        Lord, have mercy. Christ, have mercy.

Text: based on John 1, Marilyn Houser Hamm, 1974, *Sing and Rejoice*, 1979
Music: Marilyn Houser Hamm, 1974, *Sing and Rejoice*, 1979
        Text and music copyright ©1974 Marilyn Houser Hamm

All praise to our redeeming Lord 21

RESIGNATION (JENKS) CM

1 All praise to our re-deem-ing Lord, who joins us by his grace, and bids us, each to each re-stored, to-geth-er seek his face.

2 He bids us build each oth-er up, and gath-ered in-to one, to our high call-ing's glo-rious hope, we hand in hand go forth.

3 The gift which he on one be-stows, we all de-light to prove; the grace through ev-'ry ves-sel flows, in pur-est streams of love.

4 We all par-take the joy of one, the com-mon peace we feel, a peace to world-ly minds un-known, a joy un-speak-a-ble.

5 The kiss of peace to each we give, a pledge of Chris-tian love, in love, while here on earth we'll live, in love we'll dwell a-bove.

Text: Charles Wesley, *Hymns for those that seek …* (Sts. 1-4), 1747, *The Brethren's Hymn Book* (St. 5), 1867
Music: Stephen Jenks, *The Brethren's Tune and Hymn Book*, 1872

22 Lord Jesus Christ, be present now

HERR JESU CHRIST, DICH ZU UNS WEND LM

1 Lord Je - sus Christ, be pres - ent now, our hearts in true de - vo - tion bow. Thy Spir - it send with grace di - vine, and let thy truth with - in us shine.

2 Un - seal our lips to sing thy praise, our souls to thee in wor - ship raise. Make strong our faith, in - crease our light that we may know thy name a - right,

3 till we with saints in glad ac - cord sing, "Ho - ly, ho - ly is the Lord!" and in the light of heav'n a - bove shall see thy face and know thy love.

4 All glo - ry to the Fa - ther, Son, and Ho - ly Spir - it, Three - in - One! To thee, O bless - ed Trin - i - ty, be praise through-out e - ter - ni - ty!

Text: "Herr Jesu Christ, dich zu uns wend," *Pensum Sacrum* (Sts. 1-3), 1648, *Cantionale Sacrum* (St. 4), 1651; tr. Catherine Winkworth,
        Chorale Book for England, 1863, alt.
Music: *Cantionale Germanicum*, 1628

23   Hear thou our prayer, Lord

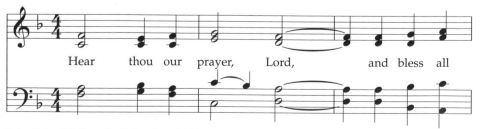

Hear thou our prayer, Lord, and bless all

Text: Nelson T. Huffman, *The Brethren Hymnal*, 1951
Music: Nelson T. Huffman, *The Brethren Hymnal*, 1951

souls that wait be - fore thee. A - men

Grace to you and peace   24

Canon

Grace to you and peace from God the Fa - ther, and the Lord

Je - sus Christ, a - men.

Text: based on Romans 1 :7, KJV
Music: Alice Parker, 1962, *The Mennonite Hymnal*, 1969
        Copyright ©1962 Alice Parker

Jesus, stand among us   25
WEM IN LEIDENSTAGEN 65. 65

1 Je - sus, stand a - mong us in your ris - en pow'r.
2 Breathe the Ho - ly Spir - it in - to ev - 'ry heart.

Let this time of wor - ship be a hal - lowed hour.
Bid the fears and sor - rows from each soul de - part.

Text: William Pennefather, *Original Hymns and Thoughts in Verse*, 1873
Music: Friedrich Filitz, *Vierstimmiges Choralbuch*, 1847

26 Holy Spirit, come with power

BEACH SPRING 87. 87D

1 Ho-ly Spir-it, come with pow-er, breathe in-to our
2 Ho-ly Spir-it, come with fi-re, burn us with your
3 Ho-ly Spir-it, bring your mes-sage, burn and breathe each

ach-ing night. We ex-pect you this glad ho-ur, wait-ing
pres-ence new. Let us as one might-y cho-ir sing our
word a-new deep in-to our tir-ed liv-ing till we

for your strength and light. We are fear-ful, we are
hymn of praise to you. Burn a-way our wast-ed
strive your work to do. Teach us love and trust-ing

ail-ing, we are weak and self-ish too. Break up-
sad-ness and en-flame us with your love. Burst up-
kind-ness, lend our hands to those who hurt. Breathe up-

Text: Anne Neufeld Rupp, 1970, alt.
        Copyright ©1970 Anne Neufeld Rupp
Music: attributed to B. F. White, *Sacred Harp*, 1844; harmonized by Joan A. Fyock
        Harmonization copyright ©1989 Joan A. Fyock

on your con-gre-ga-tion, give us vig - or, life a - new.
on your con-gre-ga-tion, give us glad - ness from a - bove.
on your con-gre-ga tion and in - spire us with your word.

Come, O Creator Spirit, come 27
VENI CREATOR SPIRITUS LM

1 Come, O Cre - a - tor   Spir - it, come,   and make with - in   our
2 O   Com - fort - er, that   name is thine,   of God most high the
3 Our sens - es   with thy   light in - flame,   our hearts to heav'n - ly
4 May we   by   thee the   Fa - ther learn,   and know the Son, and

hearts thy home.   To   us   thy   grace   ce - les - tial give,
gift   di - vine;   the well   of   life,   the   fire of love,
love re - claim,   our bod - ies'   poor   in - fir - mi - ty
thee dis - cern,   who art   of   both,   and   so   a - dore

who   of thy   breath-ing   move and live.
our   souls' a - noint - ing   from a - bove.
with strength per - pet - ual   for - ti - fy.
in   per - fect   faith for - ev - er - more.   A - men

Text: anonymous, *Veni Creator Spiritus*, 9th c.; tr. Robert Bridges, *Yattendon Hymnal*, 1899
Music: Plainsong, 4th c.

28 Breathe upon us, Holy Spirit

SHOWALTER 87. 87D

1 Breathe up - on us, Ho - ly Spir - it, as a - dor - ing-
2 Thou art pure and thou art ho - ly; Je - sus, make us
3 Now re - ceive us, as re - pen - tant to thy heart of
4 Here shall love, like sa - cred in - cense, up - ward mount to

ly we bow at these al - tars, pure and sa - cred, pay - ing
more like thee. Thou art meek and thou art low - ly; so may
love we fly. Par - don all our sin and fol - ly, lead us
thy great throne, from the cleans - ed heart and con - science of a

thee our sol - emn vow. All our fee - ble grac - es quick - en
we thy chil - dren be. Shed a - broad thy love with - in us,
to thy - self on high. Oh, these hearts need thy re - fin - ing,
peo - ple all thine own. Hum - ble are the gifts we bring thee,

with the streams of thy sweet grace, and make glo - rious
fill our souls with light di - vine. Ho - ly Spir - it,
and the cleans - ing of thy blood! Con - se - crate and
and up - on thine al - tar lay, yet be gra - cious

Text: Elisha A. Hoffman, 1899, *The Brethren Hymnal,* 1901
Music: J. Henry Showalter, 1899, *The Brethren Hymnal,* 1901

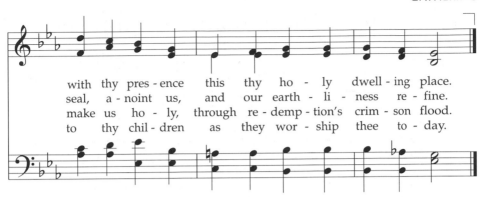

with thy pres-ence this thy ho-ly dwell-ing place.
seal, a-noint us, and our earth-li-ness re-fine.
make us ho-ly, through re-demp-tion's crim-son flood.
to thy chil-dren as they wor-ship thee to-day.

Like the murmur of the dove's song 29

BRIDEGROOM 87. 87. 6

Unison

1 Like the mur-mur of the dove's song, like the chal-lenge of her
2 To the mem-bers of Christ's bod-y, to the branch-es of the
3 With the heal-ing of di-vi-sion, with the cease-less voice of

flight, like the vi-gor of the wind's rush, like the
Vine, to the church in faith as-sem-bled, to her
prayer, with the pow'r to love and wit-ness, with the

new flame's ea-ger might: come, Ho-ly Spir-it, come.
midst as gift and sign: come, Ho-ly Spir-it, come.
peace be-yond com-pare: come, Ho-ly Spir-it, come.

Text: Carl P. Daw, Jr., *The Hymnal 1982*, 1985
        Copyright ©1982 Hope Publishing Co.
Music: Peter Cutts, 1969
        Copyright ©1969 Hope Publishing Co.

30 Spirit divine, inspire our prayers

GRÄFENBURG (NUN DANKET ALL') CM

1 Spir - it di - vine, in - spire our prayers, and make our hearts your home. De - scend with all your gra - cious pow'rs — O come, great Spir - it, come!

2 Come as the light – re - veal our need, our hid - den fail - ings show, and lead us in those paths of life in which the right - eous go.

3 Come as the fire, and cleanse our hearts with pur - i - fy - ing flame. Let our whole life an of - f'ring be to our Re - deem - er's name.

4 Come as the dew, and gent - ly bless this con - se - crat - ed hour. May bar - ren souls re - joice to know your life - cre - at - ing pow'r.

5 Come as the dove, and spread your wings, the wings of peace - ful love, and let your church on earth be - come bless'd as the church a - bove.

6 Come as the wind, with rush - ing sound and pen - te - cos - tal grace, that all the world with joy may see the glo - ry of your face.

Text: Andrew Reed, *Evangelical Magazine*, 1829; revised in *Hymns for Today's Church*, 1982
           Copyright ©1982 Hope Publishing Co.
Music: Johann Crüger, *Praxis Pietatis Melica*, 5th ed., 1653

Wind who makes all winds

FALCONE 77.77D

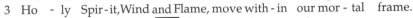

1 Wind who makes all winds that blow–gusts that bend the sap-lings low,
2 Fire who fuels all fires that burn – suns a-round which plan-ets turn,
3 Ho - ly Spir-it, Wind and Flame, move with-in our mor-tal frame.

gales that heave the sea in waves, stir-rings in the mind's deep caves –
bea - cons mark-ing reefs and shoals, shin-ing truth to guide our souls –
Make our hearts an al-tar pyre. Kin - dle them with your own fire.

aim your breath with stead-y pow'r on your church, this day, this hour.
come to us as once you came; burst in tongues of sa-cred flame!
Breathe and blow up - on that blaze till our lives, our deeds, and ways

Raise, re - new the life we've lost, Spir-it God of Pen-te - cost.
Light and Pow-er, Might and Strength, fill your church, its breadth and length.
speak that tongue which ev - 'ry land by your grace shall un-der - stand.

Text: Thomas H. Troeger, *The Christian Ministry,* 1983
Copyright ©1983, 1985 Oxford University Press, Inc.
Music: Carol Doran, 1985, *New Hymns for the Lectionary,* 1986; harmonized in four parts by Carol Doran, 1988
Copyright ©1985 Oxford University Press, Inc.

32 Our Father God, thy name we praise

NUN FREUT EUCH 87. 87. 887

1 Our Fa-ther God, thy name we praise, to thee our hymns ad-
2 Touch, Lord, the lips that speak for thee; set words of truth be-
3 Lord, make thy pil-grim peo-ple wise, the gos-pel mes-sage
4 As with each oth-er here we meet, thy grace a-lone can

dress-ing, and joy-ful-ly our voic-es raise, thy faith-ful-ness con-
fore us, that we may grow in con-stan-cy, the light of wis-dom
know-ing, that we may walk with light-ened eyes in grace and good-ness
feed us, as here we gath-er at thy feet we pray that thou wilt

fess-ing. As-sem-bled by thy grace, O Lord, we
o'er us. Give us this day our dai-ly bread; may
grow-ing. The right-eous must thy pre-cepts heed; thy
heed us. The pow'r is thine, O Lord di-vine, the

seek fresh guid-ance from thy word. Now grant a-new thy bless-ing.
hun-gry souls a-gain be fed; may heav'n-ly food re-store us.
word a-lone sup-plies their need, from heav'n their suc-cor flow-ing.
king-dom and the rule are thine. May Je-sus Christ still lead us!

Text: Leenaerdt Clock, 16th-17th c., *O Gott Vater, wir loben dich, Ausbund,* 17th c.; tr. Ernest A. Payne, 1956, *British Baptist Hymn Book,* 1962, alt.
Translation copyright ©1956 Ernest A. Payne
Music: *Geistliche Lieder,* 1535

O Gott Vater

AUS TIEFER NOT 87. 87. 887

O Gott Va - ter,
die du, O Herr,

wir lo - ben
so gnä - dig -

dich, und dei - ne Gü -
lich, an uns neu hast

te prei - sen:
be - wie - sen,

und hast uns,

Herr, zu - sam - men

g'führt, uns zu

er - mah - nen durch

dein Wort, gib uns

Ge - nad zu die - sem.

Text: Leenaerdt Clock, 16th-17th c.; *Ausbund*, 17th c.
Music: based on the notations of J. W. Yoder in *Amische Lieder*, 1940, and Olen F. Yoder in *Ausbund Songs with Notes*, 1984
        Adapted to current singing east of Goshen, Ind., by Mary K. Oyer

34 When the morning stars together

WEISSE FLÄGGEN 87. 87D

1 When the morn-ing stars to-geth-er their Cre-a-tor's
2 When in syn-a-gogue and tem-ple voic-es raised the
3 Voice and in-stru-ment, in un-ion through the ag-es,
4 Lord, we bring our gift of mu-sic; touch our lips and

glo-ry sang, and the an-gel host all shout-ed till with
psalm-ists' songs, of-fer-ing the a-do-ra-tion which a-
spoke your praise. Plain-song, tune-ful hymns, and an-thems told your
fire our hearts, teach our minds and train our sens-es, fit us

joy the heav-ens rang, then your wis-dom and your great-ness
lone to you be-longs, when the sing-ers and the cym-bals
faith-ful, gra-cious ways. Choir and or-ches-tra and or-gan
for this sa-cred art. Then with skill and con-se-cra-tion

their ex-ul-tant mu-sic told, all the beau-ty
with the trum-pet made ac-cord, glo-ry filled the
each a sa-cred of-f'ring brought, while, in-spired by
we would serve you, Lord, and give all our pow'rs to

and the splen - dor which your might - y works un - fold.
house of wor - ship, and all knew your pres - ence, Lord.
your own Spir - it, po - et and com - pos - er wrought.
glo - ri - fy you, and in serv - ing ful - ly live.

Text: Albert F. Bayly, ca.1966
    Copyright ©1969 Oxford University Press
Music: anonymous, *Tochter Sion*, 1741

Many and great, O God   35

LACQUIPARLE Irregular

1 Man - y and great, O God, are your works,
2 Grant un - to us com - mun - ion with you,

Mak - er of earth and sky. Your hands have
O star - a - bid - ing One. Come un - to

set the heav - ens with stars; your fin - gers spread the
us and dwell with us; with you are found the

moun - tains and plains. Lo, at your word the wa - ters were
gifts of life. Bless us with life that has no

formed; deep seas o - bey your voice.
end, e - ter - nal life with you.

Text: Joseph R. Renville, *Dakota Dowanpi Kin (Odowan Wowapi)*,1846; paraphrased by Francis Philip Frazier, 1929, alt.
    Alteration copyright © South Dakota Conference, United Church of Christ
Music: Plains Indian melody, *Dakota Odowan*, 1879

36 God of our strength

GOD OF OUR STRENGTH LM with refrain

1 God of our strength, en-throned a-bove, the source of life, the
2 To thee we lift our joy-ful eyes, to thee on wings of
3 God of our strength, from day to day di-rect our thoughts and
4 God of our strength, on thee we call. God of our hope, our

fount of love, O let de-vo-tion's sa-cred flame
faith we rise. Come thou, and let thy courts on earth
guide our way. Oh, may our hearts u-nit-ed be
light, our all, thy name we praise, thy love a-dore,

our souls a-wake to praise thy name.
ring out thy praise in days of mirth.
in sweet com-mun-ion, Lord, with thee.
our rock, our shield, for-ev-er-more.

Refrain

God of our strength,

we wait on thee, our sure de-fense for-ev-er be.

Text: Fanny J. Crosby, 1882, *Baptist Hymnal*, 1883
Music: William H. Doane, *Baptist Hymnal*, 1883

Praise to the Lord, the Almighty 37

LOBE DEN HERREN 14 14. 47. 8

1 Praise to the Lord, the Al - might - y, the King of cre - a -
2 Praise to the Lord, who o'er all things so won-drous-ly reign -
3 Praise to the Lord, who doth pros-per thy work and de - fend
4 Praise to the Lord, oh, let all that is in me a - dore

tion! O my soul, praise him, for he is thy health and sal -
eth, shel - ters thee un - der his wings, yea, so gent - ly sus -
thee. Sure - ly his good - ness and mer - cy shall dai - ly at -
him! All that hath life and breath, come now with prais - es be -

va - tion! All ye who hear, now to God's tem - ple draw
tain - eth. Hast thou not seen how thy heart's wish - es have
tend thee. Pon - der a - new what the Al - might - y can
fore him! Let the "a - men" sound from God's peo - ple a -

near. Join me in glad ad - o - ra - tion.
been grant - ed in what he or - dain - eth?
do, as with his love he be - friends thee.
gain; glad - ly for - ev - er a - dore him.

Text: Joachim Neander, "Lobe den Herren, den mächtigen König der Ehren," *Alpha und Omega, Glaub- und Liebesübung,* 1680;
        tr. Catherine Winkworth, *Chorale Book for England,* 1863, alt.
Music: *Erneuerten Gesangbuch,* 1665

38 The Lord is in his holy temple

The Lord is in his ho - ly tem - ple. Let all the earth keep

si - lence, keep si - lence be - fore him. A - men

Text: Habakkuk 2:20, KJV
Music: Edwin O. Excell, *International Praise*, 1902

39 Lord of the worlds above

LENOX 66. 66. 88 extended

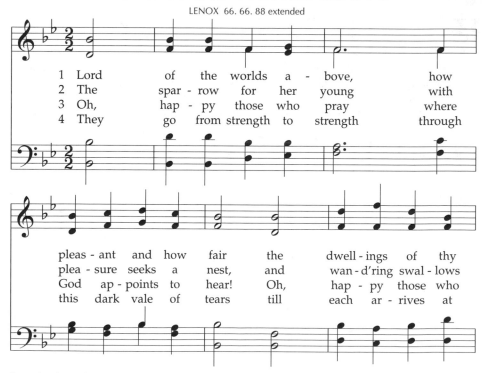

1 Lord of the worlds a - bove, how
2 The spar - row for her young with
3 Oh, hap - py those who pray where
4 They go from strength to strength through

pleas - ant and how fair the dwell - ings of thy
plea - sure seeks a nest, and wan - d'ring swal - lows
God ap - points to hear! Oh, hap - py those who
this dark vale of tears till each ar - rives at

Text: based on Psalm 84, Isaac Watts, *Psalms of David...*, 1719
Music: Lewis Edson, Sr., *The Chorister's Companion*, 1782 or 1783

40 Jesus Christ, God's only Son

PRAISE AND PRAYER 77. 77. 77

1 Je - sus Christ, God's on - ly Son, praise and hon - or
2 Lift, O Lord, thy gra - cious face, give us of thy
3 Bless, O Lord, this church of thine, which thou with thy

be to thee! Thou the great en - thron - ed One,
ho - ly peace. May the light of thy sweet grace
blood didst buy. Fill us with thy grace di - vine;

'round whom throngs of an - gels be. Man - y thou-sand
in our midst, Lord, nev - er cease. Lead thy lambs, we
'twas for us that thou didst die. Thou hast cho - sen

watch - ers there lift up joy - ful praise and prayer.
hum - bly pray, in and out, day af - ter day.
us to be con - se - crat - ed, Lord, to thee.

Text: Alexander Mack, Jr., *Etliche liebliche und erbauliche Lieder*, 1788; tr. Ora W. Garber, *The Brethren Hymnal*, 1951
Music: Nevin W. Fisher, *The Brethren Hymnal*, 1951

Come, thou Almighty King

ITALIAN HYMN 664. 6664

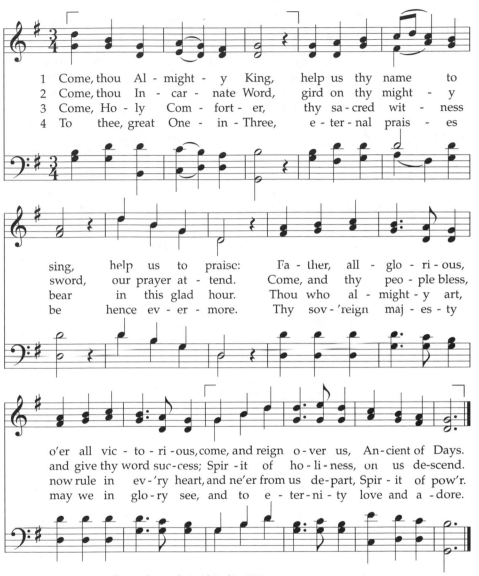

1 Come, thou Al - might - y King, help us thy name to
2 Come, thou In - car - nate Word, gird on thy might - y
3 Come, Ho - ly Com - fort - er, thy sa - cred wit - ness
4 To thee, great One - in - Three, e - ter - nal prais - es

sing, help us to praise: Fa - ther, all - glo - ri - ous,
sword, our prayer at - tend. Come, and thy peo - ple bless,
bear in this glad hour. Thou who al - might - y art,
be hence ev - er - more. Thy sov - 'reign maj - es - ty

o'er all vic - to - ri - ous, come, and reign o - ver us, An - cient of Days.
and give thy word suc-cess; Spir - it of ho - li - ness, on us de-scend.
now rule in ev - 'ry heart, and ne'er from us de-part, Spir - it of pow'r.
may we in glo - ry see, and to e - ter - ni - ty love and a -dore.

Text: anonymous, tract in *Collection of Hymns for Social Worship,* 1757
Music: Felice de Giardini, *Collection of Psalm and Hymn Tunes,* 1769

42 All people that on earth do dwell

OLD HUNDREDTH LM

1 All peo - ple that on earth do dwell, sing
2 Know that the Lord is God in - deed. With -
3 Oh, en - ter then his gates with praise. Ap -
4 For why? the Lord our God is good. His

to the Lord with cheer - ful voice. Him serve with mirth, his
out our aid he did us make. We are his flock, he
proach with joy his courts un - to. Praise, laud, and bless his
mer - cy is for - ev - er sure. His truth at all times

praise forth tell, come ye be - fore him and re - joice.
doth us feed, and for his sheep he doth us take.
name al - ways, for it is seem - ly so to do.
firm - ly stood, and shall from age to age en - dure.

Text: based on Psalm 100, William Kethe, 1561, *The Psalms of David in Meeter,* 1650
Music: Louis Bourgeois, *Genevan Psalter,* 1551

Christ is our cornerstone

DARWALL'S 148th 66. 66. 88

1 Christ is our cor - ner - stone, on him a - lone we build. With his true saints a - lone the courts of heav'n are filled. On his great love our hopes we place of pres - ent grace and joys a - bove.

2 Oh, then with hymns of praise these hal - lowed courts shall ring. Our voic - es we will raise, the Three - in - One to sing, and thus pro - claim in joy - ful song both loud and long that glo - rious name.

3 Here, gra - cious God, do thou for - ev - er - more draw nigh. Ac - cept each faith - ful prayer, and mark each sup - pliant sigh. In co - pious shower on all who pray each ho - ly day thy bless - ings pour!

4 Here may we gain from heav'n the grace which we im - plore, and may that grace, once giv'n, be with us ev - er - more, un - til that day when all the bless'd to end - less rest are called a - way!

Text: anonymous, *Angularis fundamentum lapis,* 6th-7th c.; tr. John Chandler, *Hymns of the Primitive Church,* 1837, alt.
Music: John Darwall, *New Universal Psalmodist,* 1770

44 When in our music God is glorified

ENGELBERG 10 10. 10 4

Unison

1 When in our mu - sic God is glo - ri - fied,
2 How of - ten, mak - ing mu - sic, we have found
3 So has the church, in lit - ur - gy and song,
4 And did not Je - sus sing a psalm that night
5 Let ev - 'ry in - stru-ment be tuned for praise!

1 and ad - o - ra - tion leaves no room for pride,
2 a new di - men - sion in the world of sound,
3 in faith and love, through cen - tu - ries of wrong,
4 when ut - most e - vil strove a - gainst the Light?
5 Let all re - joice who have a voice to raise!

1 it is as though the whole cre - a - tion cried
2 as wor - ship moved us to a more pro - found
3 borne wit - ness to the truth in ev - 'ry tongue,
4 Then let us sing, for whom he won the fight:
5 And may God give us faith to sing al - ways

1-4

5

1-4 al - le - lu - ia! 5 al - le - lu - ia!

Text: Fred Pratt Green, 1972, *The Hymn*, 1973
Copyright ©1972 Hope Publishing Co.
Music: Charles V. Stanford, *Hymns Ancient and Modern*, 1904

I cannot dance, O Love

MAGDEBURG 76. 76D

1 I can-not dance, O Love, un-less you lead me on.
2 Love is the mu-sic 'round us, we glide as birds in air,
3 O bless-ed Love, your circ-ling u-nites us, God and soul.

gladness

I can-not leap in glad-ness un-less you lift me up. From
en-twin-ing, soul and bod-y, your wings hold us with care. Your
From the be-gin-ning, your arms em-brace and make us whole. Hold

love to love we cir-cle, be-yond all knowl-edge grow, for
Spir-it is the harp-ist and all your chil-dren sing; her
us in steps of mer-cy from which you nev-er part, that

when you lead we fol-low, to new worlds you can show.
hands the cur-rents 'round us, your love the gold-en strings.
we may know more ful-ly the danc-es of your heart.

fol-low,

Text: based on the writings of Mechthild of Magdeburg, Jean Janzen, 1991
            Copyright ©1991 Jean Wiebe Janzen
Music: Alice Parker, 1991
            Copyright ©1991 Alice Parker

46 I sing the mighty power of God

ELLACOMBE CMD

1 I sing the might-y pow'r of God, that made the moun-tains rise,
2 I sing the good-ness of the Lord, that filled the earth with food.
3 There's not a plant or flow'r be - low, but makes thy glo - ries known,

that spread the flow - ing seas a - broad and built the loft - y skies.
God formed the crea - tures with a word, and then pro - nounced them good.
and clouds a - rise, and tem - pests blow, by or - der from thy throne.

I sing the wis - dom that or - dained the sun to rule the day.
Lord, how thy won - ders are dis - played, wher - e'er I turn my eye,
While all that bor - rows life from thee is ev - er in thy care,

The moon shines full at God's com - mand and all the stars o - bey.
if I sur - vey the ground I tread, or gaze up - on the sky!
there's not a place where we can flee but God is pres - ent there.

Text: Isaac Watts, *Divine and Moral Songs for Children*, 1715, alt.
Music: *Gesangbuch der Herzogl*, 1784; harmonized by William H. Monk, *Hymns Ancient and Modern, Appendix*, 1868

Earth and all stars

EARTH AND ALL STARS 4 5 7D with refrain

1 Earth and all stars! loud rush-ing plan-ets sing to the
2 Hail, wind, and rain! loud blow-ing snow-storm sing to the
3 Trum-pet and pipes! loud clash-ing cym-bals sing to the
4 En-gines and steel! loud pound-ing ham-mers sing to the
5 Knowl-edge and truth! loud sound-ing wis-dom sing to the

1 Lord a new song! Oh, vic-to-ry! Loud hosts of heav-en
2 Lord a new song! Flow-ers and trees! loud rus-tling dry leaves
3 Lord a new song! Harp, lute, and lyre! loud hum-ming cel-los
4 Lord a new song! Lime-stone and beams! loud build-ing work-ers
5 Lord a new song! Daugh-ter and son! loud prais-ing mem-bers

sing to the Lord a new song!

Refrain

God has done mar-ve-lous things. I too, I

too sing prais-es with a new song!

Text: Herbert Brokering, 1964, *Twelve Folksongs and Spirituals,* 1968, alt.
Music: Jan Bender
Text and music copyright ©1968 Augsburg Publishing House

48 All creatures of our God and King

LASST UNS ERFREUEN LM with alleluias

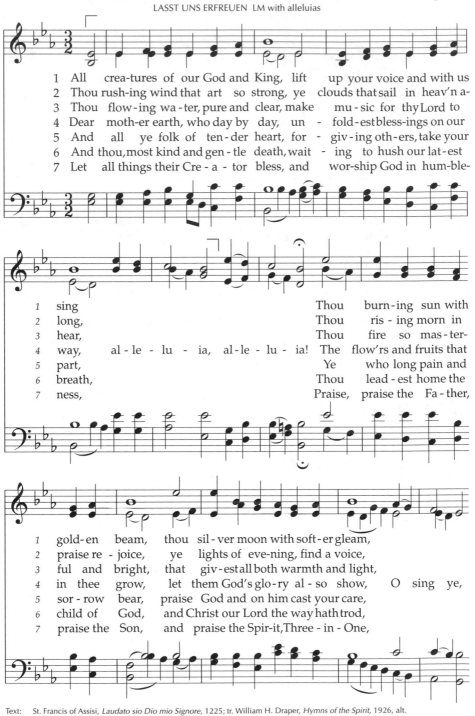

1 All crea-tures of our God and King, lift up your voice and with us
2 Thou rush-ing wind that art so strong, ye clouds that sail in heav'n a-
3 Thou flow-ing wa-ter, pure and clear, make mu-sic for thy Lord to
4 Dear moth-er earth, who day by day, un - fold-est bless-ings on our
5 And all ye folk of ten-der heart, for - giv-ing oth-ers, take your
6 And thou, most kind and gen-tle death, wait - ing to hush our lat-est
7 Let all things their Cre-a-tor bless, and wor-ship God in hum-ble-

1 sing   Thou burn-ing sun with
2 long,   Thou ris-ing morn in
3 hear,   Thou fire so mas-ter-
4 way, al-le-lu-ia, al-le-lu-ia! The flow'rs and fruits that
5 part,   Ye who long pain and
6 breath,   Thou lead-est home the
7 ness,   Praise, praise the Fa-ther,

1 gold-en beam, thou sil-ver moon with soft-er gleam,
2 praise re-joice, ye lights of eve-ning, find a voice,
3 ful and bright, that giv-est all both warmth and light,
4 in thee grow, let them God's glo-ry al-so show, O sing ye,
5 sor-row bear, praise God and on him cast your care,
6 child of God, and Christ our Lord the way hath trod,
7 praise the Son, and praise the Spir-it, Three-in-One,

Text: St. Francis of Assisi, *Laudato sio Dio mio Signore*, 1225; tr. William H. Draper, *Hymns of the Spirit*, 1926, alt.
        Copyright ©1927, renewed J. Curwen & Sons, Ltd., London
Music: *Kirchengesangbuch*, Cologne, 1623; adapted and harmonized by Ralph Vaughan Williams, *The English Hymnal*,
        1906, simplified
        Harmonization copyright © Oxford University Press, London

O sing ye, al-le - lu - ia, al-le - lu - ia, al-le - lu - ia!

From all that dwell below the skies 49

DUKE STREET LM

1 From all that dwell be - low the skies let the Cre -
2 In ev - 'ry land be - gin the song, to ev - 'ry
3 Your loft - y themes, O mor - tals, bring, in songs of
4 E - ter - nal are your mer - cies, Lord. E - ter - nal

a - tor's praise a - rise! Let the Re - deem - er's
land the strains be - long. In cheer - ful sounds all
praise di - vine - ly sing. The great sal - va - tion
truth at - tends your word. Your praise shall sound from

name be sung through ev - 'ry land by ev - 'ry tongue.
voic - es raise, and fill the world with loud - est praise.
loud pro - claim, and shout for joy the Sav - ior's name.
shore to shore, till suns shall rise and set no more.

Text: based on Psalm 117 (Sts. 1-2), Isaac Watts, *Psalms of David…*, 1719, alt., *A Pocket Hymn-Book* (Sts. 3-4), ca. 1781
Music: attributed to John Hatton, *Psalm and Hymn Tunes,* 1793

50 Praise the Lord, sing hallelujah

PRAISE JEHOVAH 87. 87D with refrain

1 Praise the Lord, sing hal - le - lu - jah, from the heav-ens praise his
2 Let them praise the Lord Cre - a - tor; they were made at his com-
3 All you fruit - ful trees and ce - dars, ev - 'ry hill and moun-tain

name! Praise the Lord, our great Cre - a - tor; all his
mand. God es - tab - lished them for - ev - er, his de-
high, creep - ing things and beasts and cat - tle, birds that

an - gels, praise pro - claim. All his hosts, to - geth - er
cree shall ev - er stand. From the earth O praise your
in the heav - ens fly, kings of earth and all you

praise him, sun and moon and stars on high. Praise the
Mak - er, rag - ing seas, you crea - tures all, fire and
peo - ple, rul - ers great, earth's judg - es all; praise his

Text: based on Psalm 148; adapted by William J. Kirkpatrick, *The Book of Psalms,* 1871, alt.
Music: William J. Kirkpatrick, ca. 1893

51 Let the whole creation cry

LLANFAIR 77. 77 with alleluias

1 Let the whole cre - a - tion cry
2 Praise God, heav'n-ly hosts a - bove,
3 Rul - ers bow-ing to the Lord,
4 Men and wom-en, young and old,

al - le - lu - ia!

"Glo - ry to the Lord on high!"
ev - er bright and fair in love!
proph-ets burn - ing with the word,
raise the an - them man - i - fold,

al - le - lu - ia!

Heav'n and earth, a - wake and sing,
Sun and moon, up - lift your voice,
those to whom the arts be - long,
And let chil - dren's hap - py hearts,

al - le - lu - ia!

"God is God and reigns su - preme,"
Night and stars, in God re - joice,
join the rush - ing of the song,
in this wor - ship bear their parts,

al - le - lu - ia!

Text: based on Psalm 148, Stopford A. Brooke, *Christian Hymns,* 1881, alt.
Music: Robert Williams, 1817, *Peroriaeth Hyfryd,* 1837

Praise the Lord

SAKURA Irregular

1 Praise the Lord, praise the Lord,
2 Thanks to God, thanks to God,
3 Glo - ry to God, glo - ry to God,

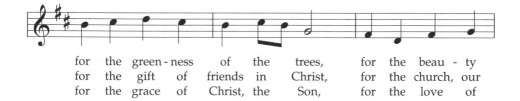

for the green-ness of the trees, for the beau - ty
for the gift of friends in Christ, for the church, our
for the grace of Christ, the Son, for the love of

of the flow'rs, for the blue - ness of the sky,
house of faith, for the gift of won - drous love,
par - ent God, for the com - fort and the strength

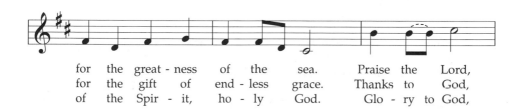

for the great - ness of the sea. Praise the Lord,
for the gift of end - less grace. Thanks to God,
of the Spir - it, ho - ly God. Glo - ry to God,

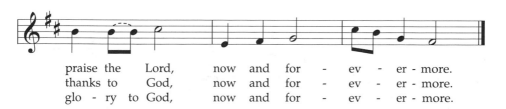

praise the Lord, now and for - ev - er - more.
thanks to God, now and for - ev - er - more.
glo - ry to God, now and for - ev - er - more.

Text: Nobuaki Hanaoka, 1980, *Hymns from the Four Winds*, 1983
          Copyright ©1980 Nobuaki Hanaoka
Music: traditional Japanese melody
          Transcription copyright ©1983 assigned to Abingdon Press

53 God of the earth, the sky, the sea

ST. CATHERINE LM with refrain

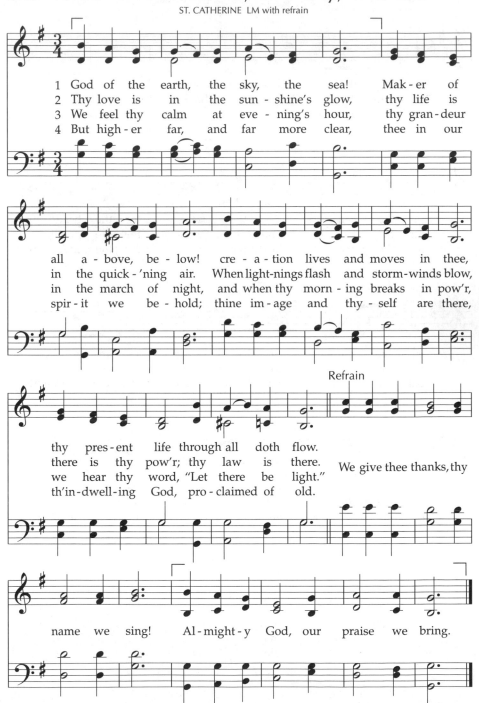

1 God of the earth, the sky, the sea! Mak-er of
2 Thy love is in the sun-shine's glow, thy life is
3 We feel thy calm at eve-ning's hour, thy gran-deur
4 But high-er far, and far more clear, thee in our

all a-bove, be-low! cre-a-tion lives and moves in thee,
in the quick-'ning air. When light-nings flash and storm-winds blow,
in the march of night, and when thy morn-ing breaks in pow'r,
spir-it we be-hold; thine im-age and thy-self are there,

Refrain

thy pres-ent life through all doth flow.
there is thy pow'r; thy law is there.   We give thee thanks, thy
we hear thy word, "Let there be light."
th'in-dwell-ing God, pro-claimed of old.

name we sing! Al-might-y God, our praise we bring.

Text: Samuel Longfellow, *Hymns of the Spirit,* 1864, alt.
Music: Henri F. Hemy, *Crown of Jesus Music,* 1864; adapted by James G. Walton, *Plainsong Music for the Holy Communion Office,* 1874

Praise the Lord who reigns above 54

AMSTERDAM 76. 76. 77. 76

1 Praise the Lord who reigns a-bove, and keeps a court be-low.
2 Cel - e-brate th'e - ter - nal God with harp and psal - ter - y,
3 God, in whom they move and live, let ev - 'ry crea - ture sing,

Praise the ho - ly Lord of love, and all God's great - ness show.
tim - brels soft and cym - bals loud in no - blest praise a - gree.
glo - ry to their Mak - er give, and grate - ful hom - age bring.

Praise the Lord for no - ble deeds, praise the Lord for match-less pow'r.
Praise the Lord with tune - ful string, all the reach of heav'n - ly art,
Hal-low'd be the Name be - neath, as in heav'n on earth a - dored.

God from whom all good pro - ceeds let earth and heav'n a - dore.
all the pow'rs of mu - sic bring, the mu - sic of the heart.
Praise the Lord in ev - 'ry breath, let all things praise the Lord!

Text: based on Psalm 150, Charles Wesley, *A Collection of Psalms and Hymns,* 1743, alt.
Music: *Neues Geistreiches Gesangbuch,* 1704; adapted by John Wesley, *Foundery Collection,* 1742

55 Cantemos al Señor
(Let's sing unto the Lord)

ROSAS 67. 68D with refrain

1 Can - te - mos al Se - ñor   un him - no de a - le -
2 Can - te - mos al Se - ñor   un him - no de a - la -
1 Let's sing un - to the Lord   a hymn of glad re -
2 Let's sing un - to the Lord   a hymn of a - do -

grí - a,   un cán - ti - co de a - mor   al na -
ban - za   que ex - pre - se nues - tro a - mor,   nues - tra
joic - ing.   Let's sing a hymn of love,   join - ing
ra - tion,   ex - press un - to the Lord   our

cer el nue - vo dí - a.   El hi - zo el cie - lo el
fe y nues - tra es - pe - ran - za.   En to - da la crea -
hearts and hap - py voic - es.   God made the sky a -
songs of faith and hope.   Cre - a - tion's broad dis -

mar,   el sol y las es - tre - llas   y
ción   pre - go - na su gran - de - za,   a -
bove,   the stars, the sun, the o - ceans.   Their
play   pro - claims the work of gran - deur,   the

vio en e - llos bon - dad,   pues sus o - bras e - ran
sí nues - tro can - tar   va a - nun - cian - do su be -
good - ness does pro - claim   the glo - ry of God's
bound - less love of One   who bless - es us with

Text: based on Psalm 19, Carlos Rosas; tr. Roberto Escamilla, Elise Eslinger, and George Lockwood IV, 1983
Translation copyright ©1989 The United Methodist Publishing House
Music: Carlos Rosas
Text (Spanish) and music copyright ©1976 Resource Publications, Inc.

Dm   C

be - llas.   ¡A - le - lu - ya!
lle - za.
name.   Al - le - lu - ia!
beau - ty.

B♭   A⁷   Gm

¡A - le - lu - ya!   Can - te - mos al   Se -
Al - le - lu - ia!   Let's sing un - to the

Dm   A⁷   Dm

ñor.   ¡A - le - lu - ya!
Lord.   Al - le - lu - ia!

Coda after final stanza

Gm   Dm   A⁷   Dm

Can - te - mos al Se - ñor.   ¡A - le - lu - ya!
Let's sing un - to the Lord.   Al - le - lu - ia!

Awake, arise, O sing a new song 56

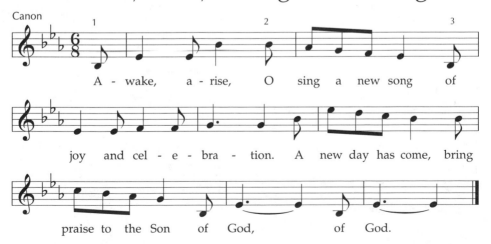

Canon   1   2   3

A - wake, a - rise, O sing a new song of

joy and cel - e - bra - tion. A new day has come, bring

praise to the Son of God, of God.

Text: Marna Leasure
Music: Marna Leasure
Text and music copyright ©1975 Choristers Guild

57 Come and give thanks to the Giver

BAY HALL 10 7. 10 7 with refrain

1 Come and give thanks to the
2 All that has o - pened and
3 Moun - tains, deep o - ceans, and
4 Let us give care to this

Giv - er of life; all that we have is from God.
all that have wings ride the wide cur - rents of earth.
for - ests of trees, sing the glad mu - sic of God.
wealth from a - bove. May ev - 'ry spir - it em - brace

Gath - er the flow - ers and fruits of the land,
Seed, sprout, and har - vest, all fish - es and beasts,
Join with the stars and the plan - ets in space;
trea - sures of earth and of all hu - man love,

lift up their fra - grance with song.
blend in a con - cert of praise.
dark - ness and light, clap your hands!
ten - der - ly hold - ing God's gifts.

Refrain (Harmony)

All life, all love flows from Cre - a - tor - God.

Text: Jean Janzen, 1991
          Copyright ©1991 Jean Wiebe Janzen
Music: Michael Dawney, 1973, Hymns for Celebration, 1974
          Copyright ©1973 Michael Dawney

Earth is one ho-ly gift; life is one ho-ly breath.

This is the day 58

OTO JEST DZIEŃ Irregular

This is the day that the Lord has made.

Let us be glad and re-joice in it.

Al-le-lu-ia, al-le-lu-ia!

Text: based on Psalm 118, *Liturgia Godzin*, Vol. 3, Poznań, 1982
Music: André Gouzes, O.P.; arranged by Jacek Gałuszka, O.P.
Copyright ©1989 Atelier de Musique Liturgique

59 Sing praise to God who reigns

MIT FREUDEN ZART 87. 87. 88. 7

1 Sing praise to God who reigns a-bove, the God of all cre - a - tion, the God of pow'r, the God of love, the God of our sal - va - tion. With heal - ing balm my soul is filled, and ev - 'ry faith - less

2 What in al-might - y pow'r was made, God's gra-cious mer-cy keep - eth. By morn-ing glow or eve-ning shade, God's watch-ful eye ne'er sleep - eth. With - in the shel - ter of God's might, lo! all is just, and

3 Our God is nev - er far a - way, through - out all grief dis - tress - ing, an ev - er - pres - ent help and stay, our peace, and joy, and bless - ing. As with a moth - er's ten - der hand, God gent - ly leads the

4 Then all my glad-some way a - long, I sing a - loud thy prais - es, that all may hear the grate - ful song my voice un - wea - ried rais - es: Be joy - ful in the Lord, my heart! Both soul and bod - y,

Text: Johann J. Schütz, "Sei Lob und Ehr dem höchsten Gut," *Christliches Gedenckbüchlein*, 1675; tr. Frances E. Cox, *Hymns from the German*, 1864, alt.
Music: adapted from GENEVA 138, *Genevan Psalter*, 1547, Bohemian Brethren's *Kirchengeseng*, 1566

mur - mur stilled.
all   is   right.   To   God all praise and   glo - ry!
cho - sen band.
bear your part!

Songs of praise the angels sang 60

MONKLAND 77. 77

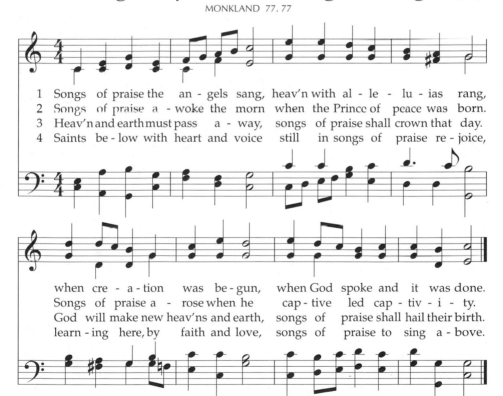

1 Songs of praise the   an - gels sang, heav'n with al - le - lu - ias rang,
2 Songs of praise a - woke the morn when the Prince of peace was born.
3 Heav'n and earth must pass   a - way, songs of praise shall crown that day.
4 Saints be - low with heart and voice   still   in songs of praise re - joice,

when cre - a - tion   was be - gun,   when God spoke and it was done.
Songs of praise a - rose when he   cap - tive led cap - tiv - i - ty.
God will make new heav'ns and earth, songs of   praise shall hail their birth.
learn - ing here, by   faith and love, songs of   praise to sing a - bove.

Text: James Montgomery, in Thomas Cotterill's *Selection of Psalms and Hymns,* 1819, alt.
Music: John Antes, *Hymn Tunes of the United Brethren,* 1824; adapted by John B. Wilkes, *Hymns Ancient and Modern,* 1861

61 Let all creation bless the Lord

LOBT GOTT DEN HERREN 87. 87. 887

1 Let all cre-a-tion bless the Lord, till heav'n with
2 All liv-ing things up-on the earth, green fer-tile
3 O men and wom-en ev-'ry-where, lift up a

praise is ring - ing. Sun, moon, and stars, peal out a
hills and moun - tains, sing to the God who gave you
hymn of glo - ry. Let all who know God's stead-fast

chord, stir up the an - gels' sing - ing. Sing, wind and
birth! Be joy-ful, springs and foun - tains, lithe wa-ter-
care tell out sal - va - tion's sto - ry. No tongue be

rain! Sing, snow and sleet! Make mu - sic, day, night, cold, and heat!
life, bright air-borne birds, wild rov-ing beasts, tame flocks and herds!
si - lent – sing your part, you hum-ble souls and meek of heart!

Text: based on the *Benedicite*, Carl P. Daw, Jr., *A Year of Grace*, 1990
Copyright ©1990 Hope Publishing Co.
Music: Melchior Vulpius, *Ein schön geistlich Gesangbuch*, 1609

Ex - alt the God who made you.

Who is so great a God 62

THE GREAT PROKEIMENON Irregular

Who is so great a God as our God?

Thou art the God who do-est won - ders. Thou art the

God who do-est won - ders. The God, the

God, the God who do - est won - ders.

Text: from Russian Orthodox liturgy
Music: Dimitri S. Bortniansky

63 Praise, my soul, the God of heaven

LAUDA ANIMA (ANDREWS) 87. 87. 87

1 Praise, my soul, the God of heav-en! To the throne your trib-ute raise. Ran - somed, healed, re - stored, for - giv-en, who, like us, should sing God's praise? Al - le - lu - ia! Al - le - lu - ia!

2 Praise the Lord for grace and fa - vor to all peo - ple in dis - tress. Praise God, still the same as ev - er, slow to chide, and swift to bless. Al - le - lu - ia! Al - le - lu - ia!

3 Fa - ther - like, God tends and spares us, well our fee - ble frame God knows. Moth - er - like, God gent - ly bears us, res - cues us from all our foes. Al - le - lu - ia! Al - le - lu - ia!

4 An - gels in the height a - dor - ing, you be - hold God face to face. Saints tri - um - phant, now a - dor - ing, gath - ered in from ev - 'ry race, al - le - lu - ia! al - le - lu - ia!

Text: based on Psalm 103, Henry F. Lyte, *The Spirit of the Psalms,* 1834, alt.
Music: Mark Andrews; arranged by Nevin W. Fisher, *The Brethren Hymnal,* 1951

Praise our Mak - er all our days.
Glo - rious now God's faith - ful - ness.
Wide - ly yet God's mer - cy flows.
praise with us the God of grace.

Asithi: Amen
(Sing amen)

64

A - si - thi: A - men, si - ya - ku - du - mi - sa. A - si - thi:
Sing a - men: A - men, we praise your name, O Lord. Sing a - men:

A - men, si - ya - ku - du - mi - sa. A - si - thi: A - men, Ba - ba,
A - men, we praise your name, O Lord. Sing a - men: A - men, a - men,

a - men, Ba - ba, a - men, si - ya - ku - du - mi - sa.
a - men, a - men, a - men, we praise your name, O Lord.

Text: South African hymn
Music: S. C. Molefe

65 Praise, my soul, the King of heaven

BENEDIC ANIMA 87. 87. 87

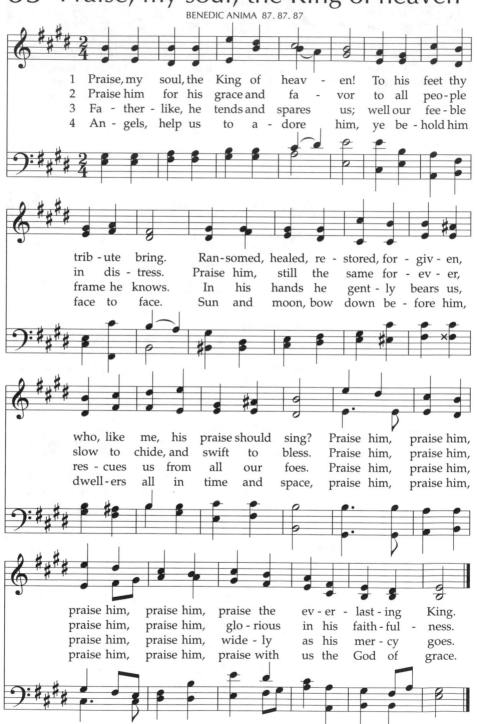

1 Praise, my soul, the King of heav - en! To his feet thy
2 Praise him for his grace and fa - vor to all peo - ple
3 Fa - ther - like, he tends and spares us; well our fee - ble
4 An - gels, help us to a - dore him, ye be - hold him

trib - ute bring. Ran-somed, healed, re - stored, for - giv - en,
in dis - tress. Praise him, still the same for - ev - er,
frame he knows. In his hands he gent - ly bears us,
face to face. Sun and moon, bow down be - fore him,

who, like me, his praise should sing? Praise him, praise him,
slow to chide, and swift to bless. Praise him, praise him,
res - cues us from all our foes. Praise him, praise him,
dwell - ers all in time and space, praise him, praise him,

praise him, praise him, praise the ev - er - last - ing King.
praise him, praise him, glo - rious in his faith - ful - ness.
praise him, praise him, wide - ly as his mer - cy goes.
praise him, praise him, praise with us the God of grace.

Text: based on Psalm 103, Henry F. Lyte, *The Spirit of the Psalms,* 1834, alt.
Music: John Goss, *The Supplemental Hymn and Tune Book,* 1869

O worship the King

66

LYONS 10 10. 11 11

1 O   wor-ship the   King,   all   glo-rious a-bove,
2 O   tell   of   his   might,   O   sing   of   his   grace,
3 Thy   boun-ti-ful   care,   what   tongue can   re-cite?
4 Frail   chil-dren of   dust,   and   fee-ble   as   frail,

O   grate-ful-ly   sing   his   pow-er and his   love;
whose   robe   is   the   light,   whose   can-o-py   space.
It   breathes   in   the   air,   it   shines   in   the   light,
in   thee   do   we   trust,   nor   find   thee to   fail;

our   Shield   and   De-fend-er,   the   An-cient   of   Days,
His   char-iots   of   wrath the   deep   thun-der-clouds   form,
it   streams from   the   hills,   it   de-scends   to   the   plain,
thy   mer-cies how   ten-der,   how   firm   to   the   end,

pa-vil-ioned in   splen-dor, and   gird-ed   with   praise.
and   dark   is   his   path   on   the   wings   of   the   storm.
and   sweet-ly   dis-tills   in   the   dew   and the   rain.
our   Mak-er,   De-fend-er,   Re-deem-er, and   Friend!

Text: based on Psalm 104, Robert H. Grant, *Christian Psalmody*, 1833
Music: *Sacred Melodies,* Vol. 2, 1815

67 Sing hallelujah, praise the Lord

BECHLER 86. 86. 88. 86

1 Sing hal-le-lu-jah, praise the Lord, sing with a cheer-ful voice. Ex-
2 There we to all e - ter-ni - ty for nev-er-end-ing days shall

alt our God with one ac-cord, and in his name re - joice. Ne'er
sing in per-fect har-mo - ny to God our Sav-ior's praise. Christ

cease to sing, thou ran-somed host, praise Fa - ther, Son, and Ho - ly Ghost, un -
hath re-deemed us by his blood, and made us kings and priests to God. For

til in realms of end - less light your prais-es shall u - nite.
us, for us, the Lamb was slain; praise ye the Lord! A - men!

Text: John Swertner, *English Moravian Hymnbook*, 1789
Music: John C. Bechler, before 1822

O come, loud anthems let us sing 68

SALISBURY LM with refrain

1 O come, loud anthems let us sing, loud thanks to
2 In - to his pres - ence let us haste, to thank him
3 The depths of earth are in his hand, her se - cret
4 Oh, let us to his courts re - pair, and bow with

our Al - might - y King, for we our voic - es high should
for his fa - vors past, to him ad - dress, in joy - ful
wealth at his com - mand, the strength of hills that reach the
ad - o - ra - tion there, down on our knees, de - vout - ly

Refrain

raise, when our sal - va - tion's rock we praise.
songs, the praise that to his name be - longs. Great is the
skies, sub - ject - ed to his em - pire lies.
all, be - fore the Lord, our Mak - er, fall.

Lord! What tongue can frame an e - qual hon - or to his name?

Text: based on Psalm 95, Nahum Tate and Nicholas Brady, *New Version of the Psalms of David,* 1696; refrain by Isaac Watts
Music: anonymous, "Haydn" in Lowell Mason's *Boston Handel and Haydn Society Collection ...,* 1822

69 The Lord is King

SO LANGE JESUS BLEIBT LM

1 The Lord is King, O praise his name, o'er all the
2 Oh, see the might-y hand of God, his love and
3 This shall the song for-ev-er be of saints be-
4 O Star that lights the pil-grim's way! Our Lord of

earth his grace pro-claim! From age to age, from day to
mer-cy chang-eth not! His blood and right-eous-ness a-
fore the crys-tal sea: O Christ, that on the cross hath
lords, our hope and stay! The Head to whom we hom-age

day, his won-ders grow more glo-rious-ly.
vail, his grace and par-don nev-er fail!
bled, hath safe-ly through life's val-ley led.
bring, the Rock to which our faith may cling!

1 So lange Jesus bleibt der Herr,
wird's alle Tage herrlicher.
So war's, so ist's, so wird es sein
bei seiner gläubigen Gemein.

2 Es bleibt bei dem bekannten Wort
von Zeit zu Zeit, von Ort zu Ort:
Christi Blut und Gerechtigkeit
bleibt der Gemeinde Schmuck und Kleid.

3 Das Psalmlied am krystallnen Meer,
das Losungswort vom kleinen Heer
ist: Eines hat uns durchgebracht,
Lamm Gottes, dass du warst geschlacht.

4 Du bist und bleibest unser Herr,
der Leitstern deiner Wanderer,
der Deinen teures Oberhaupt,
dem keiner Feinde Macht sie raubt.

Text: Nicolaus L. von Zinzendorf, *So lange Jesus bleibt der Herr,* 1742; tr. Esther C. Bergen, *The Hymn Book* (Canadian Mennonite Brethren), 1960
Translation copyright ©1959 Esther C. Bergen
Music: oral tradition of Russian Mennonites; written form from *Gesangbuch,* 1955

Immortal, invisible, God only wise 70

ST. DENIO (JOANNA) 11 11. 11 11

1 Im - mor - tal, in - vis - i - ble, God on - ly wise,
2 Un - rest - ing, un - hast - ing, and si - lent as light,
3 To all, life thou giv - est, to both great and small.
4 Great God of all glo - ry, great God of all light,

in light in - ac - ces - si - ble, hid from our eyes,
nor want - ing, nor wast - ing, thou rul - est in might,
In all life thou liv - est, the true Life of all.
thine an - gels a - dore thee, all veil - ing their sight.

most bless - ed, most glo - rious, the An - cient of Days,
thy jus - tice like moun - tains high soar - ing a - bove
We blos - som and flour - ish as leaves on the tree,
All praise we would ren - der; O help us to see

al - might - y, vic - to - rious, thy great name we praise.
thy clouds which are foun - tains of good - ness and love.
and with - er and per - ish, but naught chang - eth thee.
'tis on - ly the splen - dor of light hid - eth thee.

Text: Walter C. Smith, *Hymns of Christ and the Christian Life*, 1867, alt.
Music: Welsh melody, *Caniadau y Cyssegr*, 1839

71 Joyful, joyful, we adore thee

HYMN TO JOY 87. 87D

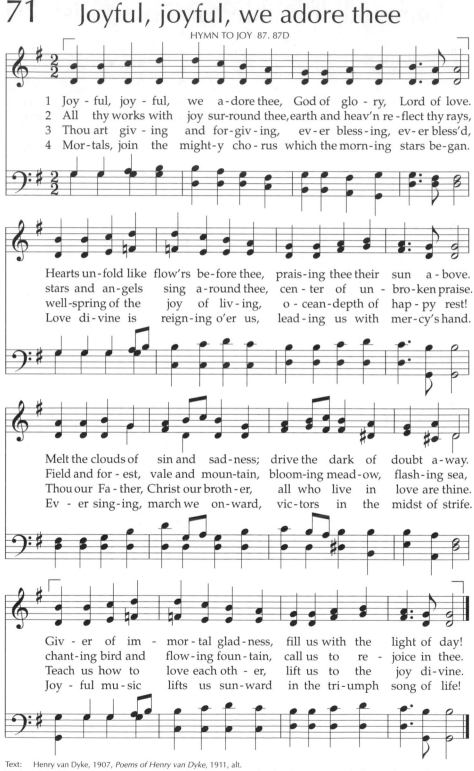

1 Joy - ful, joy - ful, we a - dore thee, God of glo - ry, Lord of love.
2 All thy works with joy sur - round thee, earth and heav'n re - flect thy rays.
3 Thou art giv - ing and for - giv - ing, ev - er bless - ing, ev - er bless'd,
4 Mor - tals, join the might - y cho - rus which the morn - ing stars be - gan.

Hearts un - fold like flow'rs be - fore thee, prais - ing thee their sun a - bove.
stars and an - gels sing a - round thee, cen - ter of un - bro - ken praise.
well - spring of the joy of liv - ing, o - cean - depth of hap - py rest!
Love di - vine is reign - ing o'er us, lead - ing us with mer - cy's hand.

Melt the clouds of sin and sad - ness; drive the dark of doubt a - way.
Field and for - est, vale and moun - tain, bloom - ing mead - ow, flash - ing sea,
Thou our Fa - ther, Christ our broth - er, all who live in love are thine.
Ev - er sing - ing, march we on - ward, vic - tors in the midst of strife.

Giv - er of im - mor - tal glad - ness, fill us with the light of day!
chant - ing bird and flow - ing foun - tain, call us to re - joice in thee.
Teach us how to love each oth - er, lift us to the joy di - vine.
Joy - ful mu - sic lifts us sun - ward in the tri - umph song of life!

Text: Henry van Dyke, 1907, *Poems of Henry van Dyke*, 1911, alt.
Music: adapted from Ludwig van Beethoven, 1823; based on adaptation by Edward Hodges, *Trinity Collection of Church Music*, 1864

When all thy mercies, O my God 72

GENEVA CM

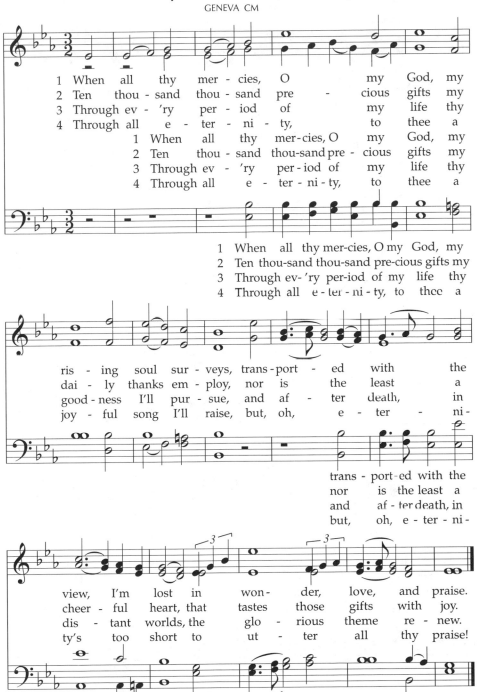

1 When all thy mer - cies, O my God, my
2 Ten thou - sand thou - sand pre - cious gifts my
3 Through ev - 'ry per - iod of my life thy
4 Through all e - ter - ni - ty, to thee a

1 When all thy mer-cies, O my God, my
2 Ten thou - sand thou-sand pre - cious gifts my
3 Through ev - 'ry per - iod of my life thy
4 Through all e - ter - ni - ty, to thee a

1 When all thy mer-cies, O my God, my
2 Ten thou-sand thou-sand pre-cious gifts my
3 Through ev-'ry per-iod of my life thy
4 Through all e - ter - ni - ty, to thee a

ris - ing soul sur - veys, trans - port - ed with the
dai - ly thanks em - ploy, nor is the least a
good - ness I'll pur - sue, and af - ter death, in
joy - ful song I'll raise, but, oh, e - ter - ni -

trans - port - ed with the
nor is the least a
and af - ter death, in
but, oh, e - ter - ni -

view, I'm lost in won - der, love, and praise.
cheer - ful heart, that tastes those gifts with joy.
dis - tant worlds, the glo - rious theme re - new.
ty's too short to ut - ter all thy praise!

Text: Joseph Addison, *The Spectator*, 1712
Music: John Cole, *Ecclesiastical Harmony*, 1805; version from the Funk brothers' *Harmonia Sacra*, 12th ed., 1867

73 Make music to the Lord most high

BISHOPTHORPE CM

1 Make music to the Lord most high whose
2 Lord, when we see all you have done our
3 The god-less mind will nev-er know, be-
4 For-ev-er, Lord, you are su-preme. Your
5 How like the ce-dar and the palm the
6 To fruit-ful age they still pro-claim the

1 praise is our de-light. We sing your love as
2 songs of joy re-sound. Your hand-i-work, how
3 cause its sense is void: that though the wick-ed
4 throne re-mains on high, while reb-els meet e-
5 right-eous stand se-rene. They flour-ish in the
6 Lord who makes them new— our God, in whom no

1 day be-gins, your faith-ful-ness by night.
2 vast it is, your coun-sels, how pro-found!
3 spread like grass, they all shall be de-stroyed.
4 ter-nal doom and e-vil-do-ers die.
5 house of God, their leaves are fresh and green.
6 wrong is found, my Rock, for-ev-er true.

Text: based on Psalm 92, Christopher Idle, 1981, *The Book of Praises*, 1987
Copyright ©1990 Hope Publishing Co.
Music: attributed to Jeremiah Clarke, *Select Portions of the Psalms of David*, ca. 1780

We would extol thee

GENEVA 124 (OLD 124th) 10 10. 10 10 10

1 We would ex-tol thee, ev-er-bless-ed Lord. Thy ho-ly
2 Age shall to age pass on the end-less song, tell-ing the
3 Thou, Lord, art gra-cious, mer-ci-ful to all, nigh to thy

name for-ev-er be a-dored. Each day we live to
won-ders which to thee be-long, thy might-y acts with
chil-dren when on thee they call. Slow un-to an-ger,

thee our psalm we raise. Thou, God and Sov-'reign, wor-thy of our
joy and fear re-late. Laud we thy glo-ry while on thee we
pit-i-ful and kind, thou to com-pas-sion ev-er art in-

praise, great and un-search-a-ble art all thy ways.
wait, glad in the knowl-edge of thy love so great.
clined. We love thee with our heart and strength and mind.

Text: based on Psalm 145, *The Psalms of David in Meeter*, 1650; altered by Nichol Grieve, *The Scottish Metrical Psalter of 1650: A Revision*, 1940
Copyright ©1940 T&T Clark, Ltd.
Music: Louis Bourgeois, *Genevan Psalter*, 1551; harmonization adapted from Claude Goudimel, *Les Pseaumes ...*, 1565

75 Heilig, heilig, heilig
(Holy, holy, holy)

65. 65D

1,2 Hei - lig, hei - lig, hei - lig, hei - lig ist der Herr!
1,2 Ho - ly, ho - ly, ho - ly, ho - ly is the Lord!

Hei - lig, hei - lig, hei - lig, hei - lig ist nur Er!
Ho - ly, ho - ly, ho - ly, ho - ly God a - lone!

1 Er, der nie be - gon - nen, Er, der im - mer war,
2 All - macht, Wun - der, Lie - be, al - les rings - um - her!
1 God, who, un - cre - at - ed, God who al - ways was,
2 Might - y, won - drous, lov - ing, cir - cled 'round with awe;

e - wig ist und wal - tet, sein wird im - mer - dar.
Hei - lig, hei - lig, hei - lig, hei - lig ist der Herr!
end - less - ly ex - alt - ed, reign for - ev - er - more.
ho - ly, ho - ly, ho - ly, ho - ly is the Lord.

Text: Johann P. Neumann; tr. John D. Rempel
          Translation copyright ©1990 John D. Rempel
Music: Franz Schubert, *Gesänge zur Feier des heiligen Opfer der Messe*, 1826

Je louerai l'Eternel
(Praise, I will praise you, Lord)

PRAISING/ADORING
76

1 Je loue-rai l'E-ter-nel de tout mon coeur, je
1 Praise, I will praise you, Lord,
2 Love, I will love you, Lord with all my heart. O
3 Serve, I will serve you, Lord

ra-con-te-rai tou-tes tes mer-veilles, je chan-te-rai ton
God, I will tell the won-ders of your ways, and glo-ri-fy your

nom. Je loue-rai l'E-ter-nel de tout mon coeur, je
name. Praise, I will praise you, Lord, with all my heart. In
Love,
Serve,

fe-rai de toi le su-jet de ma joie. Al-le-lu-ia!
you I will find the source of all my joy. Al-le-lu-ia!

Text: based on Psalm 9:1-2, Claude Fraysse, 1975; tr. Kenneth I. Morse, 1988, *Hymnal Sampler,* 1989
   Translation copyright ©1989 The Hymnal Project
Music: Claude Fraysse, 1975; harmonized by Alain Bergèse, 1976
   Text (French) and music copyright ©1976 Alain Bergèse

77 God of many names

MANY NAMES 55. 88 with refrain

1 God of man-y names, gath-ered in-to One, in your glo-ry
God of hov-'ring wings, Womb and Birth of time, joy-ful-ly we
2 God of Jew-ish faith, ex-o-dus and law, in your glo-ry
God of Je-sus Christ, Rab-bi of the poor, joy-ful-ly we
3 God of wound-ed hands, Web and Loom of love, in your glo-ry
God of man-y names, gath-ered in-to One, joy-ful-ly we

1 come and meet us, Mov-ing, end-less-ly Be-com-ing,
sing your prais-es, Breath of life in ev-'ry peo-ple—
2 come and meet us, joy of Mir-i-am and Mo-ses!
sing your prais-es, cru-ci-fied, a-live for-ev-er—
3 come and meet us, Car-pen-ter of new cre-a-tion.
sing your prais-es, Mov-ing, end-less-ly Be-com-ing—

Refrain

Hush, hush, hal-le-lu-jah, ha-le-lu-jah! Shout, shout, hal-le-

lu-jah, hal-le-lu-jah! Sing, sing, hal-le-lu-jah, hal-le-lu-

Text: Brian Wren, 1985, *Praising a Mystery*, 1986
Music: William P. Rowan, 1985, *Praising a Mystery*, 1986

jah! Sing, God is love, God is love! love!

Ehane he'ama
(Father God, you are holy)

78

Irregular

E - ha - ne he - 'a - ma, Vo - voa - he - to HE - E!
Fa - ther God, you are ho - ly, you're the First One HE - E!*

Ne - 'a-nohene - se - va - ta - me - na - no ne - ne-
Let your love come on down and touch your chil - dren

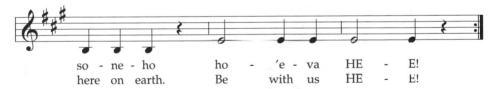

so - ne - ho ho - 'e - va HE - E!
here on earth. Be with us HE - E!

Je - sus A, ne - 'e-va - voo - me - me - no HE - E!
Je - sus, we call you; watch o - ver us HE - E!

*The exclamation "HE-E!" is pronounced "Hay-ay!"

Text: Harvey Whiteshield, *Ehane He'ama Vovoaheto;* tr. David Graber and others, *Tsese-Ma'heone-Nemeotôtse,* 1982
   Copyright ©1982 Mennonite Indian Leaders' Council
Music: Plains Indian melody

79 Lord, with devotion we pray

HILLERY 78. 10 7 with refrain

1 Lord, with de - vo - tion we pray; now look thou up - on us with
2 Let all that seek thee re - joice – oh, let them be glad in the
3 Thou art my hope, O my God; yea, thou art my trust from my

love. While we a - dore thee and hon - or thy name,
Lord. Let such as love thy sal - va - tion sing praise –
youth. Thou art my ref - uge, my for - tress, my rock –

Refrain

grant us thy smiles from a - bove.
thou hast the fall - en re - stored! Oh, great is the Lord! Thy
Lord, thou art wis - dom and truth!

name shall en - dure! Let heav-en and earth, oh, let all sing thy praise! Oh,

Text: Edyth Hillery Hay, *Hymnal: Church of the Brethren*, 1925, alt.
Music: Edyth Hillery Hay, alt.; harmonized by J. Henry Showalter, *Hymnal: Church of the Brethren*, 1925

great is the Lord, thy name shall en-dure, for thou art the joy of my days!

O bless the Lord, my soul 80

VIGIL SM

1 O bless the Lord, my soul! God's
2 God clothes you with great love, up-
3 Love's mer - cy bear in mind when
4 God par - dons all your sin, pro -
5 Then bless God's ho - ly name, whose

1 grace to you pro - claim, and all that is with -
2 holds you with the truth, and like the ea - gle
3 you are plagued with wrong. God's an - ger will be
4 longs your fee - ble breath, heals all your sick - ness,
5 grace has made you whole, whose lov - ing - kind - ness

1 in me join to bless God's ho - ly name.
2 God re - news the vig - or of your youth.
3 slow to rise; Love's pa - tience stretch - es long.
4 ev - 'ry pain, and saves you from your death.
5 crowns your days; O bless the Lord, my soul!

Text: based on Psalm 103, James Montgomery, in Thomas Cotterill's *Selection of Psalms and Hymns*, 1819; altered by
        Jean Janzen, 1991
        Copyright ©1991 Jean Wiebe Janzen
Music: *St. Alban's Tune Book*, 1865

81 Oh, for a thousand tongues to sing

LYNGHAM CM extended

1 Oh, for a thou - sand tongues to sing my
2 My gra - cious Mas - ter and my God, as -
3 Glo - ry to God and praise and love be

great Re - deem - er's praise, my great Re - deem - er's praise,
sist me to pro - claim, as - sist me to pro - claim,
ev - er, ev - er given, be ev - er, ev - er given,

the glo - ries of my God and King,
to spread through all the earth a - broad
by saints be - low and saints a - bove,

the tri - umphs of his grace, the
the hon - ors of thy name, the
the church in earth and heav'n, the

the tri - umphs of his grace, the tri - umphs of his
the hon - ors of thy name, the hon - ors of thy ...
the church in earth and heav'n, the church in earth and ...

Text: Charles Wesley, 1739, *Hymns and Sacred Poems,* 1740
Music: Thomas Jarman, *Sacred Music,* 1803

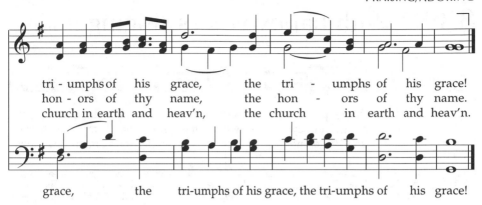

tri - umphs of his grace, the tri - umphs of his grace!
hon - ors of thy name, the hon - ors of thy name.
church in earth and heav'n, the church in earth and heav'n.

grace, the tri-umphs of his grace, the tri-umphs of his grace!

Great God, how infinite art thou 82

WINDSOR CM

1,5 Great God, how in - fi - nite art thou! How
2 Thy throne e - ter - nal ag - es stood, ere
3 E - ter - ni - ty, with all its years, stands
4 Our lives through var - ious scenes are drawn, and

poor and weak are we! Let the whole race of
seas or stars were made. Thou art the ev - er -
pres - ent in thy view. To thee there's noth - ing
vexed with tri - fling cares, while thine e - ter - nal

crea - tures bow, and pay their praise to thee.
liv - ing God, were all the na - tions dead.
old ap - pears; great God, there's noth - ing new.
thought moves on thine un - dis - turbed af - fairs.

Text: Isaac Watts, *Hymns and Spiritual Songs*, 1707
Music: *The Second Booke … of M. William Damon*, 1591

83 With happy voices singing

FAITHFUL 76. 76D

1 With hap-py voic-es sing-ing, thy chil-dren, Lord, ap-
2 For though no eye be-holds thee, no hand thy touch may
3 And shall we not a-dore thee, with more than joy-ous

pear, their joy-ous prais-es bring-ing in an-thems full and
feel, thy u-ni-verse un-folds thee, thy star-ry heav'ns re-
song, and live in truth be-fore thee, all beau-ti-ful and

clear. For skies of gold-en splen-dor, for az-ure roll-ing
veal. The earth and all its glo-ry, our homes and all we
strong? Lord, bless our souls' en-deav-or thy ser-vants true to

sea, for blos-soms sweet and ten-der, O Lord, we wor-ship thee.
love, tell forth the won-drous sto-ry of One who reigns a-bove.
be, and through all life, for-ev-er, to live our praise to thee.

Text: William G. Tarrant, 1888, *Supplement to Essex Hall Hymnal*, 1892
Music: adapted from J. S. Bach, Cantata No. 68, 1735

Oh, that I had a thousand voices 84

O DASS ICH TAUSEND ZUNGEN HÄTTE 98. 98. 88

1 Oh, that I had a thou-sand voic - es to praise my God with thou-sand tongues! My heart, which in the Lord re - joic - es, would then pro - claim in grate-ful songs to all, wher - ev - er I might be, what great things God has done for me!

2 O all you pow'rs that God im-plant - ed, a - rise, keep si - lence now no more. Put forth the strength that God has grant - ed! Your no-blest work is to a - dore! O soul and bod - y, join to raise with heart-felt joy our Mak-er's praise!

3 You for - est leaves so green and ten - der that dance for joy in sum - mer air, you mead - ow grass - es, bright and slen - der, you flow'rs so fra-grant and so fair, you live to show God's praise a - lone; join me to make God's glo - ry known!

4 All crea-tures that have breath and mo - tion, that throng the earth, the sea, the sky, come, share with me my heart's de - vo - tion, help me to sing God's prais - es high! My ut-most pow'rs can nev - er quite de-clare the won - ders of God's might!

5 Cre - a - tor, hum - bly I im - plore you to lis - ten to my earth - ly song un - til that day when I a - dore you, when I have joined the an - gel throng, and learned with choirs of heav'n to sing e - ter - nal an - thems to my King!

Text: Johann Mentzer, "O dass ich tausend Zungen hätte," *Neues Geistreiches Gesangbuch*, 1704; tr. *The Lutheran Hymnal*, 1941, alt.
        Translation copyright ©1941 Concordia Publishing House
Music: Johann B. König, *Harmonischer Liederschatz*, 1738

85 Now thank we all our God

NUN DANKET ALLE GOTT 67. 67. 66. 66

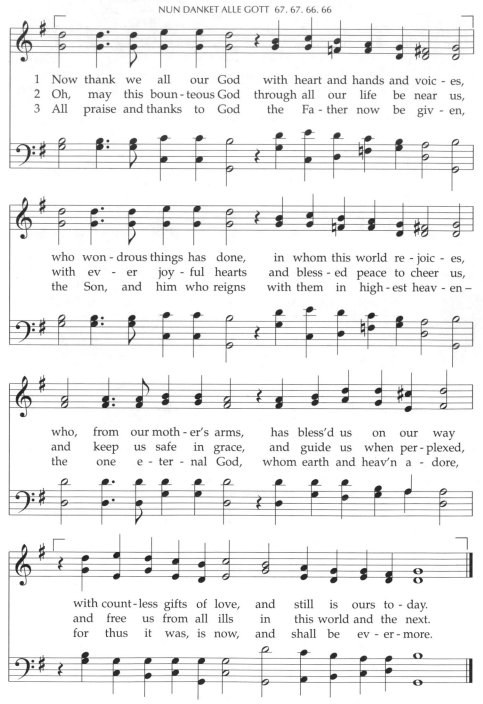

1 Now thank we all our God with heart and hands and voic - es,
2 Oh, may this boun - teous God through all our life be near us,
3 All praise and thanks to God the Fa - ther now be giv - en,

who won - drous things has done, in whom this world re - joic - es,
with ev - er joy - ful hearts and bless - ed peace to cheer us,
the Son, and him who reigns with them in high - est heav - en –

who, from our moth - er's arms, has bless'd us on our way
and keep us safe in grace, and guide us when per - plexed,
the one e - ter - nal God, whom earth and heav'n a - dore,

with count - less gifts of love, and still is ours to - day.
and free us from all ills in this world and the next.
for thus it was, is now, and shall be ev - er - more.

Text: Martin Rinckart, *Jesu Hertz-Büchlein*, 1636; tr. Catherine Winkworth, *Lyra Germanica*, Series II, 1858, alt.
Music: Johann Crüger, *Praxis Pietatis Melica*, 4th ed., 1647

Now thank we all our God   86

NUN DANKET ALLE GOTT 67. 67. 66. 66

1 Now thank we all our God with heart and hands and voic - es,
2 Oh, may this boun-teous God through all our life be near us,
3 All praise and thanks to God the Fa - ther now be giv - en,

who won-drous things has done, in whom this world re - joic - es,
with ev - er joy - ful hearts and bless - ed peace to cheer us,
the Son, and him who reigns with them in high - est heav - en —

who, from our moth - er's arms, has bless'd us on our way
and keep us safe in grace, and guide us when per - plexed,
the one e - ter - nal God, whom earth and heav'n a - dore,

with count - less gifts of love, and still is ours to - day.
and free us from all ills in this world and the next.
for thus it was, is now, and shall be ev - er - more.

Text: Martin Rinckart, *Jesu Hertz-Buchlein,* 1636; tr. Catherine Winkworth, *Lyra Germanica,* Series II, 1858, alt.
Music: Johann Crüger, *Praxis Pietatis Melica,* 4th ed., 1647; harmonized by Felix Mendelssohn, Symphony No. 2, *Lobgesang,*
Opus 52, 1840

87 Great is the Lord

GREAT IS THE LORD 10 9954 with refrain

Refrain

Great is the Lord, he is ho-ly and just, by his pow-er we trust in his love. Great is the Lord, he is faith-ful and true, by his mer-cy he proves he is love.

1 Great is the Lord, and wor-thy of glo-ry! Great is the Lord, and wor-thy of praise.
2 Great are you, Lord, and wor-thy of glo-ry! Great are you, Lord, and wor-thy of praise.

Text: Michael W. Smith and Deborah D. Smith, 1982
Music: Michael W. Smith and Deborah D. Smith, 1982
Text and music copyright ©1982 and this arrangement ©1992 Meadowgreen Music Co.

Bb/C   F   Bb/C   D   G   G/F   E   Am

Great is the Lord; now lift up your voice, now lift up your voice:
Great are you, Lord; I lift up my voice, I lift up my voice:

Dm   Dm7/G   G   G7   1 Am   Am/G   2 C

Great   is the Lord!   Lord!
Great   are you, Lord!   Lord!

Still, I search for my God   88

WASDIN PANG IPAAD   Irregular

1 Still,   I search for my God.   In si - lence, I
2 Come,   lis - ten to the trees,   the green fields, the
3 Yes,   I am filled with peace,   for I feel the

mar - vel at the u - ni - verse,   the world it con -
riv - ers and the morn - ing breeze,   the birds of the
pres - ence of the Lord my God.   Your praise I will

tains,   the beau - ty,   the har - mo - ny!   Cre -
air   all sing - ing   their Mak - er's praise.   Cre -
sing,   my Mak - er,   Cre - a - tor of all,   be -

a - tor of such per - fec - tion,   who else could it be?
a - tor of count - less won - ders,   who else could it be?
cause when I think of your works,   joy reigns in my heart.

Text: Francisco F. Feliciano, 1977, *Hymns from the Four Winds*, 1983
Music: Francisco F. Feliciano, 1977, *Hymns from the Four Winds*, 1983
Text and music copyright ©1983 Francisco F. Feliciano

89 For the beauty of the earth

DIX 77.77.77

1 For the beau-ty of the earth, for the glo-ry
2 For the beau-ty of each hour of the day and
3 For the joy of ear and eye, for the heart and
4 For the joy of hu-man love, broth-er, sis-ter,
5 For thy church that ev-er-more lift-eth ho-ly

1 of the skies, for the love which from our birth
2 of the night, hill and vale and tree and flow'r,
3 mind's de-light, for the mys-tic har-mo-ny
4 par-ent, child, friends on earth and friends a-bove,
5 hands a-bove, of-f'ring up on ev-'ry shore

1 o-ver and a-round us lies:
2 sun and moon and stars of light:
3 link-ing sense to sound and sight: Lord of all, to
4 for all gen-tle thoughts and mild:
5 her pure sac-ri-fice of love:

thee we raise this our hymn of grate-ful praise.

Text: Folliott S. Pierpoint, *Lyra Eucharistica*, 1864
Music: Conrad Kocher, *Stimmen aus dem Reiche Gottes,* 1838; adapted by William H. Monk, *Hymns Ancient and Modern,* 1861

For the fruit of all creation

90

FIRSTFRUITS 84. 84. 888. 4

1 For the fruit of all cre - a - tion, thanks be to God.
2 In the just re - ward of la - bor, God's will is done.
3 For the har - vest of the Spir - it, thanks be to God.

For the gifts to ev - 'ry na - tion, thanks be to God. For the
In the help we give our neigh - bor, God's will is done. In our
For the good we all in - her - it, thanks be to God. For the

plow - ing, sow - ing, reap - ing, si - lent growth while we are sleep - ing, fu - ture
world-wide task of car - ing for the hun - gry and de - spair - ing, in the
won - ders that as - tound us, for the truths that still con - found us, most of

needs in earth's safe - keep - ing, thanks be to God.
har - vests we are shar - ing, God's will is done.
all, that love has found us, thanks be to God.

Text: Fred Pratt Green, *Methodist Recorder,* 1970, alt.
Copyright ©1970 Hope Publishing Co.
Music: Bradley P. Lehman, 1991
Copyright ©1991 Bradley P. Lehman

91 Praise to God, immortal praise

PRAYER 77.77
Part 1 of Barbauld poem

1 Praise to God, im - mor - tal praise, for the
2 For the bless - ings of the field, for the
3 Clouds that drop re - fresh - ing dews, suns that
4 all that spring, with boun - teous hand, scat - ters
5 these, great God, to thee we owe, Source whence

1 love that crowns our days. Boun - teous Source of
2 stores the gar - dens yield, for the joy which
3 gen - ial heat dif - fuse, flocks that whit - en
4 o'er the smil - ing land; all that lib - 'ral
5 all our bless - ings flow; and for these our

1 ev - 'ry joy, let thy praise our tongues em - ploy.
2 har - vests bring, grate - ful prais - es now we sing.
3 all the plain, yel - low sheaves of rip - ened grain,
4 au - tumn pours from her o - ver - flow - ing stores.
5 souls shall raise grate - ful vows and sol - emn praise.

Text: Anna L. Barbauld, *Hymns for Public Worship*, 1772, alt.
Music: Asahel Abbot, *The Devotional Harmonist*, 1850

Lord, should rising whirlwinds 92

ORIENTIS PARTIBUS 77. 77
Part 2 of Barbauld poem

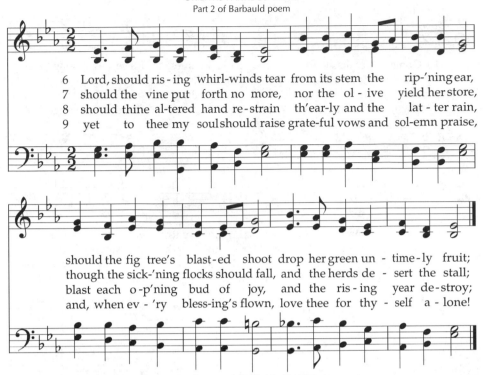

6 Lord, should rising whirlwinds tear from its stem the rip-'ning ear,
7 should the vine put forth no more, nor the olive yield her store,
8 should thine altered hand restrain th'early and the latter rain,
9 yet to thee my soul should raise grateful vows and solemn praise,

should the fig tree's blasted shoot drop her green untimely fruit;
though the sick-'ning flocks should fall, and the herds desert the stall;
blast each op'ning bud of joy, and the rising year destroy;
and, when ev-'ry blessing's flown, love thee for thyself alone!

Text: based on Habakkuk 3:17-18, Anna L. Barbauld, *Hymns for Public Worship*, 1772
Music: Pierre de Corbeil; harmonized by Richard Redhead, *Church Hymn Tunes, Ancient and Modern*, 1853

Lord, bless the hands 93

Canon

Lord, bless the hands that share with us.

And bless the hearts that care for us. Now hear this

simple prayer from us. A - men. A - men.

Text: M. Andrew Murray, 1974, *The Brethren Songbook*, 1975
Music: Teresa R. Murray, 1974, *The Brethren Songbook*, 1975

94 Come, ye thankful people

ST. GEORGE'S WINDSOR 77. 77D

1 Come, ye thank-ful peo-ple, come! Raise the song of har-vest home. All is safe-ly gath-ered in ere the win-ter storms be-gin. God, our Mak-er, doth pro-vide for our need to be sup-plied. Come to God's own

2 All the world is God's own field, fruit un-to God's praise to yield; wheat and tares to-geth-er sown, un-to joy or sor-row grown. First the blade and then the ear, then the full corn shall ap-pear. Lord of har-vest,

3 For the Lord our God shall come, and shall take the har-vest home, from the field shall in that day all of-fens-es purge a-way, giv-ing an-gels charge at last in the fire the tares to cast, but the fruit-ful

4 Then, O church tri-um-phant, come. Raise the song of har-vest home. All are safe-ly gath-ered in, free from sor-row, free from sin; there for-ev-er pur-i-fied in God's pres-ence to a-bide. Come, ten thou-sand

Text: Henry Alford, *Psalms and Hymns*, 1844, alt.
Music: George J. Elvey, *A Selection of Psalm and Hymn Tunes*, 1858

tem - ple, come. Raise the song of har - vest home.
grant that we whole - some grain and pure may be.
ears to store in God's gar - ner ev - er - more.
an - gels, come! Raise the song of har - vest home.

Praise God, the Source of life   95

DEUS TUORUM MILITUM LM

Praise God, the Source of life and birth. Praise God, the

Word who came to earth. Praise God the Spir - it,

ho - ly Flame. All glo - ry, hon - or to God's name.

Text: Ruth C. Duck, ca. 1986, *Touch Holiness,* 1990
          Copyright ©1990 The Pilgrim Press
Music: French church melody, *Grenoble Antiphoner,* 1753

96 We plow the fields and scatter

WIR PFLÜGEN 76. 76D with refrain

1 We plow the fields and scat-ter the good seed on the land,
2 You on-ly are the Mak-er of all things near and far.
3 We thank you, then, Cre - a - tor, for all things bright and good,

but it is fed and wa - tered by God's al-might-y hand.
You paint the way-side flow - er, you light the eve-ning star.
the seed-time and the har - vest, our life, our health, our food.

God sends the snow in win - ter, the warmth to swell the grain,
The winds and waves o - bey you, by you the birds are fed;
Ac - cept the gifts we of - fer, for all your love im - parts,

the breez - es and the sun - shine, and soft re-fresh-ing rain.
much more to us, your chil - dren, you give our dai - ly bread.
and what you most would wel-come, our hum - ble, thank-ful hearts.

Text: Matthias Claudius, "Wir pflügen und wir streuen," *Paul Erdmann's Fest*, 1782; tr. Jane M. Campbell, *Garland of Song*, 1861, alt.
Music: attributed to Johann A. P. Schulz, *Lieder für Volksschulen mit Musik*, 1800

From the hands

97

CLOVIS Irregular

Canon

From the hands of your earth and the lap

of your sky, your gifts are poured on us each day.

Your arms sur-round us with your care; ac-cept our love and

thanks, we pray. A - men, a - men, a - men.

Text: Jean Janzen, 1990
Copyright ©1991 Jean Wiebe Janzen
Music: Larry Warkentin, 1990
Copyright ©1991 Larry Warkentin

98 Sing to the Lord of harvest

WIE LIEBLICH IST DER MAIEN 76. 76D

1 Sing to the Lord of har-vest, sing songs of love and praise.
2 By him the clouds drop fat-ness, the des-erts bloom and spring,
3 Heap on his sa-cred al-tar the gifts his good-ness gave,
4 To God the great Cre-a-tor, who made us "ver-y good,"

With joy-ful hearts and voic-es your al-le-lu-ias raise!
the hills leap up in glad-ness, the val-leys laugh and sing.
the gold-en sheaves of har-vest, the souls Christ died to save.
to Christ, who, when we wan-dered, re-stored us with his blood,

By him the roll-ing sea-sons in fruit-ful or-der move.
He fill-eth with his full-ness all things with large in-crease,
Your hearts lay down be-fore him when at his feet you fall,
and to the Ho-ly Spir-it, who doth up-on us pour

Sing to the Lord of har-vest a song of hap-py love.
he crowns the year with good-ness, with plen-ty, and with peace.
and with your lives a-dore him who gave his life for all.
re-fresh-ing dews and sun-shine, be praise for-ev-er-more.

Text: John S. B. Monsell, *Hymns of Love and Praise*, 2nd ed., 1866, alt.
Music: Johann Steurlein; adapted by Healey Willan, 1958
Copyright ©1969 Concordia Publishing House

We praise thee, O God

REVIVE US AGAIN 11 11 with refrain

1 We praise thee, O God, for the Son of thy love,
2 We praise thee, O God, for thy Spir - it of light,
3 All glo - ry and praise to the Lamb that was slain,
4 We praise thee, O God, for the joy thou hast giv'n
5 Re - vive us a - gain, fill each heart with thy love.

1 for Je - sus who died, and is now gone a - bove.
2 who has shown us our Sav - ior and scat - tered our night.
3 who has borne all our sins, and doth cleanse ev - 'ry stain.
4 to thy saints in com - mun - ion, these fore - tastes of heav'n.
5 May each soul be re - kin - dled with fire from a - bove.

Refrain

Hal - le - lu - jah! Thine the glo - ry, hal - le - lu - jah! A - men!

Hal - le - lu - jah! Thine the glo - ry, re - vive us a - gain.

Text: William P. Mackay, 1863, revised in *New Praises of Jesus*, ca. 1867
Music: attributed to John J. Husband, ca. 1815, *New Praises of Jesus*, ca. 1867

100 Praise him, praise him

ALLEN 12 10. 12 10. 11 10 with refrain

1 Praise him, praise him! Je-sus, our bless-ed Re - deem-er! Sing, O
2 Praise him, praise him! Je-sus, our bless-ed Re - deem-er! For our
3 Praise him, praise him! Je-sus, our bless-ed Re - deem-er! Heav'n-ly

earth, his won-der-ful love pro - claim! Hail him, hail him!
sins he suf-fered and bled and died. He our rock, our
por - tals loud with ho-san-nas ring! Je - sus, Sav - ior,

high - est arch-an-gels in glo - ry! Strength and hon - or
hope of e - ter-nal sal - va - tion, hail him, hail him!
reign - eth for-ev - er and ev - er! Crown him, crown him!

give to his ho - ly name! Like a shep - herd, Je-sus will
Je - sus, the cru - ci - fied. Sound his prais - es, Je-sus who
proph-et, and priest, and King! Christ is com - ing, o - ver the

Text: Fanny J. Crosby, *Bright Jewels for the Sunday School*, 1869
Music: Chester G. Allen, *Bright Jewels for the Sunday School*, 1869

guard his chil-dren. In his arms he car-ries them all day long.
bore our sor-rows, love un-bound-ed, won-der-ful, deep, and strong.
world vic-to-rious. Pow'r and glo-ry un-to the Lord be-long.

Refrain

Praise him! praise him! tell of his ex-cel-lent great-ness.

Praise him! praise him! ev-er in joy-ful song.

Alleluia

101

Al-le-lu-ia, al-le-lu-ia, al-le-lu - ia. Al-le-lu-ia, al-le-lu-ia, al-le-lu - ia!

102   To God be the glory

TO GOD BE THE GLORY 11 11. 11 11 with refrain

1 To   God be the glo-ry, great things he hath done, so loved he the
2 Oh,   per-fect re-demp-tion, the pur-chase of blood, to ev-'ry be-
3 Great things he hath taught us, great things he hath done, and great our re-

world that he   gave us his   Son, who yield-ed his   life an a-
liev-er the prom-ise of   God. The   vil-est of-fend-er who
joic-ing through Je-sus the   Son, but   pur-er, and high-er, and

tone-ment for   sin, and o-pened the   life-gate that   all may go   in.
tru-ly be-lieves, that mo-ment from Je-sus a   par-don re-ceives.
great-er will   be   our won-der, our trans-port, when Je-sus we   see.

Refrain

Praise the Lord, praise the Lord, let the   earth hear his   voice! Praise the

Text: Fanny J. Crosby, *Brightest and Best*, 1875
Music: William H. Doane, *Brightest and Best*, 1875

Lord, praise the Lord, let the peo-ple re-joice! O come to the Fa-ther, through

Je-sus the Son, and give him the glo-ry, great things he hath done.

Jubilate Deo omnis terra 103

Canon

Ju-bi-la-te De-o om-nis ter-ra.

Ser-vi-te Do-mi-no in lae-ti-ti-a.*

Al-le-lu-ia, al-le-lu-ia, in lae-ti-ti-a.

Al-le-lu-ia, al-le-lu-ia, in lae-ti-ti-a!

*Translation: Rejoice in the Lord, all lands. Serve the Lord with gladness. Alleluia!

Text: based on Psalm 100, *Music from Taizé*, Vol. I, 1978, 1980, 1981
Music: Jacques Berthier, 1980, *Music from Taizé*, Vol. I, 1978, 1980, 1981
        Text and music copyright ©1982 Les Presses de Taizé (France). Used by permission of G.I.A. Publications, Inc.

104 Of the Father's love begotten

DIVINUM MYSTERIUM 87. 87. 877

```
1 Of    the    Fa-ther's love  be-got  -  ten,      ere  the worlds
2 By    his    word was   all   cre-at  -  ed.      He  com-mand-
3 This  is     he whom seers in  old    time     chant-ed  of
4 O     ye heights of heav'n, a-dore    him,       an-gel  hosts,
```

```
be-gan    to   be,    he   is  Al-pha and O-me-ga,  he the Source,
ed   and 'twas done. Earth and sky andbound-less o-cean,  u-ni-verse
with one    ac-cord, whom the voic-es  of the proph-ets  prom-ised in
his  prais-es   sing. Pow'rs,do-min-ions, fall be-fore  him,  and ex-tol
```

```
the  End-ing he,   of  the things that  are  and have _____ been,
of  Three-in-One.  All that sees the moon's soft ra  -  diance,
their faith-ful word. Now he shines, the  long-ex-pect  -  ed.
our  God    and King.  Let  no tongue on earth keep si  -  lent,
```

```
and  that  fu-ture years shall see,   ev-er-more and ev-er-more!
all  that breathes be-neath the sun,  ev-er-more and ev-er-more!
Let  cre-a-tion praise its Lord,      ev-er-more and ev-er-more!
ev-'ry voice in  con-cert ring,       ev-er-more and ev-er-more!
```

Text: Aurelius Clemens Prudentius, *Corde natus ex Parentis*; tr. John M. Neale, *The Hymnal Noted,* 1851, and Henry W. Baker,
         Hymns Ancient and Modern, 1861
Music: Plainsong, 13th c., *Piae Cantiones ...,* 1582

Christ, we do all adore thee 105

Irregular

Christ, we do all a - dore thee, and we do praise thee for - ev - er.

Christ, we do all a - dore thee, and we do praise thee for - ev - er,

for on the ho - ly cross hast thou the world from sin re - deem - ed.

Christ, we do all a - dore thee, and we do praise thee for - ev - er.

(instrument)

Christ, we do all a - dore thee.

Text: *Adoramus te Christe;* English version by Theodore Baker, *The Seven Last Words of Christ,* 1899
Music: Théodore Dubois, *The Seven Last Words of Christ,* 1867

106 All hail the power of Jesus' name

CORONATION CM extended

1 All hail the pow'r of Je - sus' name! Let an - gels pros - trate fall. Bring forth the roy - al di - a - dem, and crown him Lord of all! Bring forth the roy - al di - a - dem, and crown him Lord of all!

2 Ye cho - sen seed of Is - rael's race, ye ran - somed of the fall, hail him who saves you by his grace, and crown him Lord of all! Hail him who saves you by his grace, and crown him Lord of all!

3 Let ev - 'ry kin - dred, ev - 'ry tribe, on this ter - res - trial ball, to him all maj - es - ty as - cribe, and crown him Lord of all! To him all maj - es - ty as - cribe, and crown him Lord of all!

4 Oh, that with yon - der sa - cred throng we at his feet may fall! We'll join the ev - er - last - ing song, and crown him Lord of all! We'll join the ev - er - last - ing song, and crown him Lord of all!

Text: Edward Perronet, *Gospel Magazine*, 1779-1780; revised by John Rippon, *Selection of Hymns*, 1787
Music: Oliver Holden, 1792, *Union Harmony*, 1793

Blessed Savior, we adore thee 107

GLORIOUS NAME 87. 87 with refrain

1 Bless-ed Sav-ior, we a-dore thee, we thy love and grace pro-claim.
2 Great Re-deem-er, Lord and Mas-ter, Light of all e-ter-nal days,
3 From the throne of heav-en's glo-ry to the cross of sin and shame,
4 Come, O come, im-mor-tal Sav-ior, come and take thy roy-al throne.

Thou art might-y, thou art ho-ly, glo-rious is thy match-less name!
let the saints of ev-'ry na-tion sing thy just and end-less praise!
thou didst come to die a ran-som, guilt-y sin-ners to re-claim!
Come, and reign, and reign for-ev-er, be the king-dom all thine own!

Refrain

Glo - ri-ous, glo - ri-ous,

Glo-rious is thy name, O Lord! Glo-rious is thy name, O Lord!

1

2

glo-rious is thy name, O Lord! name, O Lord!

Text: Baylus B. McKinney, *Teacher*, 1942
Music: Baylus B. McKinney, *Teacher*, 1942
Text and music copyright © Broadman Press

108 Blessing and honor and glory

AMERICAN HYMN 10 10. 10 10 extended

1 Bless-ing and hon-or and glo-ry and pow'r, wis-dom and
2 Sound all the heav-en! Re-sound with his name! Ring all the
3 Ev-er as-cend-ing the song and the joy, ev-er de-
4 Give we the glo-ry and praise to the Lamb! Take we the

rich-es and strength ev-er-more, of-fer to Christ who our
earth with his glo-ry and fame! O-cean and moun-tain, stream,
scend-ing the love from on high; bless-ing and hon-or and
robe and the harp and the palm. Sing we the song of the

bat-tle has won, whose are the king-dom, the crown, and the
for-est, and flow'r ech-o his prais-es and tell of his
glo-ry and praise – this is the theme of the hymns that we
Lamb who was slain, dy-ing in weak-ness but ris-ing to

throne, whose are the king-dom, the crown, and the throne!
pow'r, ech-o his prais-es and tell of his pow'r.
raise, this is the theme of the hymns that we raise.
reign, dy-ing in weak-ness but ris-ing to reign!

Text: Horatius N. Bonar, *Hymns of Faith and Hope, Third Series,* 1866, alt.
Music: Matthias Keller, 1865, *Common Service Book,* 1917

I will praise the Lord

109

87. 87 with refrain

1 I will praise the Lord my glo - ry, I will praise the Lord my light.
2 I will praise the Lord my proph-et, ho - ly priest, and right-eous King.
3 I will praise the Lord my shep-herd, keep-er, pas - ture, door, and fold.
4 I will love the Lord my Sav-ior, all the rem - nant of my days,

He my cloud by day to cov - er, he my fire to guide by night.
With the an - gels who a - dore him, "Ho - ly, ho - ly," I will sing.
O'er the lone - ly hills he sought me, when the night was dark and cold.
and will sing through end - less ag - es, on - ly my Re-deem-er's praise.

Refrain

I will praise you with my whole heart, will praise you, O Lord.

I will be glad and re - joice in you, O Lord Most High.

Text: Daniel W. Whittle, 1890, *Gospel Hymns, No. 6*, 1891, alt.
Music: James McGranahan, 1890, *Gospel Hymns, No. 6*, 1891

110 Oh, for a thousand tongues to sing

AZMON CM

1 Oh, for a thou - sand tongues to sing my
2 Je - sus! the name that charms our fears, that
3 He speaks, and lis - t'ning to his voice new
4 My gra - cious Mas - ter and my God, as -
5 Glo - ry to God and praise and love be

1 great Re - deem - er's praise, the glo - ries of my
2 bids our sor - row cease, 'tis mu - sic to the
3 life the dead re - ceive, the mourn - ful, bro - ken
4 sist me to pro - claim, to spread through all the
5 ev - er, ev - er giv'n by saints be - low and

1 God and King, the tri - umphs of his grace.
2 sin - ner's ears, 'tis life, and health, and peace.
3 hearts re - joice, the hum - ble poor be - lieve.
4 earth a - broad the hon - ors of thy name.
5 saints a - bove, the church in earth and heav'n.

Text: Charles Wesley, 1739, *Hymns and Sacred Poems,* 1740
Music: Carl G. Gläser; arranged by Lowell Mason, *Modern Psalmist,* 1839

O praise the gracious power   111

CHRISTPRAISE RAY SM with refrain

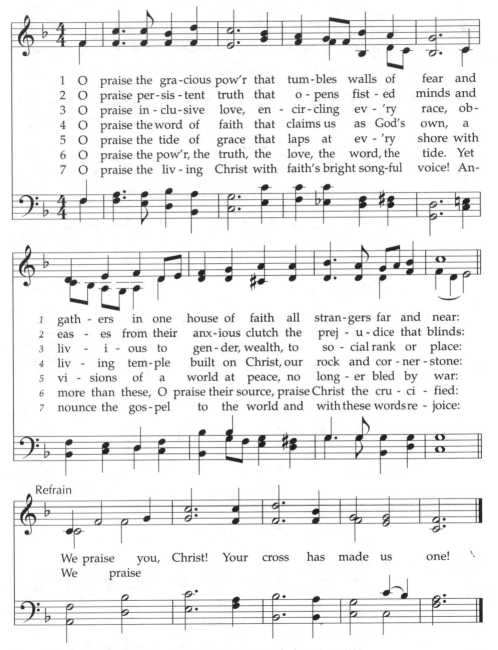

1 O praise the gra-cious pow'r that tum-bles walls of fear and
2 O praise per-sis-tent truth that o-pens fist-ed minds and
3 O praise in-clu-sive love, en-cir-cling ev-'ry race, ob-
4 O praise the word of faith that claims us as God's own, a
5 O praise the tide of grace that laps at ev-'ry shore with
6 O praise the pow'r, the truth, the love, the word, the tide. Yet
7 O praise the liv-ing Christ with faith's bright song-ful voice! An-

1 gath-ers in one house of faith all stran-gers far and near:
2 eas-es from their anx-ious clutch the prej-u-dice that blinds:
3 liv-i-ous to gen-der, wealth, to so-cial rank or place:
4 liv-ing tem-ple built on Christ, our rock and cor-ner-stone:
5 vi-sions of a world at peace, no long-er bled by war:
6 more than these, O praise their source, praise Christ the cru-ci-fied:
7 nounce the gos-pel to the world and with these words re-joice:

Refrain

We praise you, Christ! Your cross has made us one!
We praise

Text: based on Ephesians 2:11-14, Thomas H. Troeger, 1984, *New Hymns for the Lectionary,* 1986
Music: Carol Doran, 1984, *New Hymns for the Lectionary,* 1986
Text and music copyright ©1984 Oxford University Press, Inc.

112 O Lord, our Lord, how majestic

HOW MAJESTIC IS YOUR NAME Irregular

O Lord, our Lord, how ma-jes-tic is your name in all the

earth. O Lord, our Lord, how ma-jes-tic is your

name in all the earth. O Lord

O Lord, our Lord, ———

O our Lord, we praise your name. O We

Lord ———

mag-ni-fy your name, O Lord, we mag-ni-fy your

Text: based on Psalm 8, Michael W. Smith, 1981
Music: Michael W. Smith, 1981; arranged by Martha Hershberger, 1990
        Text and music copyright ©1981 and this arrangement ©1990 Meadowgreen Music Co.

name, Prince of peace, might-y God, O Lord God Al-

might - y. O y.

O Christe Domine Jesu 113

O Chris - te Do - mi - ne Je - su,* O

Chris - te Do - mi - ne Je - su! O

*Translation: O Christ, Lord Jesus

Text: Jacques Berthier, *Music from Taizé*, Vol. II, 1982, 1983, 1984
Music: Jacques Berthier, *Music from Taizé*, Vol. II, 1982, 1983, 1984

114
In thee is gladness

IN DIR IST FREUDE 55. 7D 55. 55. 9 D

1 In thee is glad - ness a - mid all sad - ness, Je - sus,
By thee are giv - en the gifts of heav - en, thou the
2 If he is ours we fear no pow - ers, nor of
He sees and bless - es in worst dis - tress - es, he can

1 sun - shine of my heart! 1 Our souls thou wak - est,
true Re - deem - er art! Our hearts are pin - ing
2 earth, nor sin, nor death. 2 Where - fore the sto - ry,
change them with a breath! We shout for glad - ness,

1 our bonds thou break - est, who trusts thee sure - ly hath built se -
to see thy shin - ing, dy - ing or liv - ing to thee are
2 tell of his glo - ry, with heart and voic - es all heav'n re -
tri - umph o'er sad - ness, love thee and praise thee, and still shall

1 cure - ly, and stands for - ev - er: Hal - le - lu - jah!
cleav - ing, naught can us sev - er: Hal - le - lu - jah!
2 joic - es in him for - ev - er: Hal - le - lu - jah!
raise thee glad hymns for - ev - er: Hal - le - lu - jah!

Text: Johann Lindemann, "In dir ist Freude," *Decades Amorum Filii Dei*, 1594, 1596; tr. Catherine Winkworth, *Lyra Germanica*,
        Series II, 1858
Music: adapted from Giovanni G. Gastoldi, *Balletti*, 1591

Jesus, thou mighty Lord

115

DOANE 64. 64D

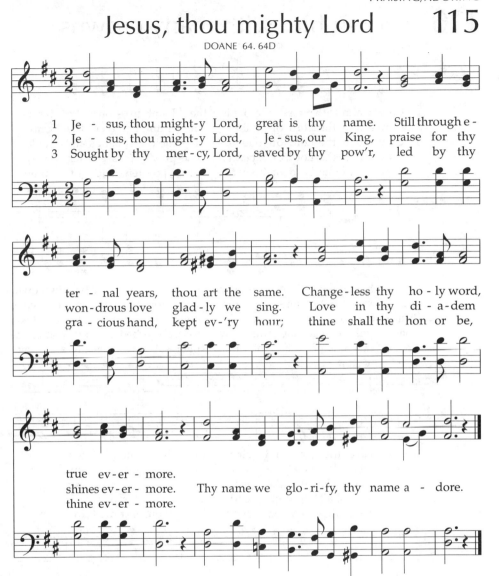

1 Je - sus, thou might-y Lord, great is thy name. Still through e -
2 Je - sus, thou might-y Lord, Je - sus, our King, praise for thy
3 Sought by thy mer-cy, Lord, saved by thy pow'r, led by thy

ter - nal years, thou art the same. Change-less thy ho - ly word,
won - drous love glad - ly we sing. Love in thy di - a - dem
gra - cious hand, kept ev-'ry hour; thine shall the hon or be,

true ev - er - more.
shines ev - er - more. Thy name we glo - ri-fy, thy name a - dore.
thine ev - er - more.

Text: Fanny J. Crosby, *Baptist Hymnal*, 1883
Music: William H. Doane, *Baptist Hymnal*, 1883

116 Crown him with many crowns

DIADEMATA SMD

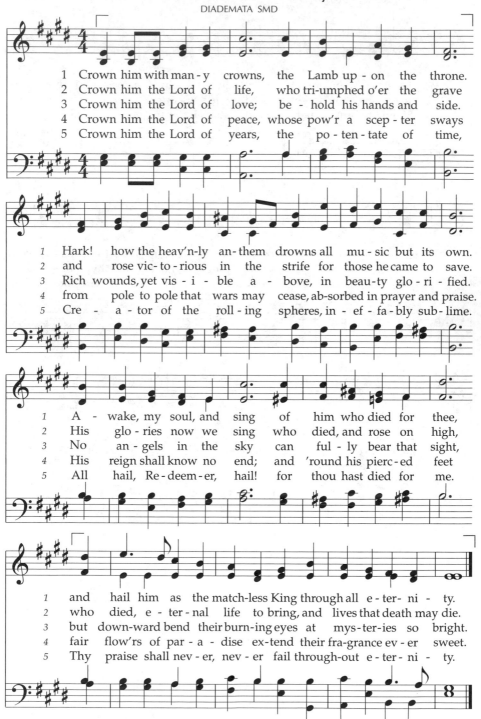

1 Crown him with man-y crowns, the Lamb up-on the throne.
2 Crown him the Lord of life, who tri-umphed o'er the grave
3 Crown him the Lord of love; be-hold his hands and side.
4 Crown him the Lord of peace, whose pow'r a scep-ter sways
5 Crown him the Lord of years, the po-ten-tate of time,

1 Hark! how the heav'n-ly an-them drowns all mu-sic but its own.
2 and rose vic-to-rious in the strife for those he came to save.
3 Rich wounds, yet vis-i-ble a-bove, in beau-ty glo-ri-fied.
4 from pole to pole that wars may cease, ab-sorbed in prayer and praise.
5 Cre-a-tor of the roll-ing spheres, in-ef-fa-bly sub-lime.

1 A-wake, my soul, and sing of him who died for thee,
2 His glo-ries now we sing who died, and rose on high,
3 No an-gels in the sky can ful-ly bear that sight,
4 His reign shall know no end; and 'round his pierc-ed feet
5 All hail, Re-deem-er, hail! for thou hast died for me.

1 and hail him as the match-less King through all e-ter-ni-ty.
2 who died, e-ter-nal life to bring, and lives that death may die.
3 but down-ward bend their burn-ing eyes at mys-ter-ies so bright.
4 fair flow'rs of par-a-dise ex-tend their fra-grance ev-er sweet.
5 Thy praise shall nev-er, nev-er fail through-out e-ter-ni-ty.

Text: Matthew Bridges (Sts. 1,3-5), *Hymns of the Heart*, 2nd ed., 1851, Godfrey Thring (St. 2), *Hymns and Sacred Lyrics*, 1874
Music: George J. Elvey, *Hymns Ancient and Modern, Appendix*, 1868

Fairest Lord Jesus

117

CRUSADERS' HYMN 568. 558 (Irregular)

1 Fair - est Lord Je - sus, rul - er of all na - ture, O thou of
2 Fair are the mead - ows, fair - er still the wood - lands, robed in the
3 Fair is the sun - shine, fair - er still the moon - light, and all the

God and Ma - ry's Son, thee will I cher - ish,
bloom - ing garb of spring. Je - sus is fair - er,
twin - kling, star - ry host. Je - sus shines bright - er,

thee will I hon - or, thou, my soul's glo - ry, joy, and crown.
Je - sus is pur - er, who makes the woe - ful heart to sing.
Je - sus shines pur - er than all the an - gels heav'n can boast.

4 Beautiful Savior,
  Lord of all the nations,
  Son of God and Son of Man,
  glory and honor,
  praise, adoration,
  now and forevermore be thine.

Text: "Schönster Herr Jesu!" *Gesangbuch* (Sts. 1,3), Münster, 1677, Heinrich A.H.von Fallersleben (St. 2), *Schlesische Volkslieder*, 1842, anonymous (St. 4); tr. anonymous, *Church Chorals and Choir Studies* (Sts. 1-3), 1850, alt., Joseph A. Seiss, *Sunday School Book for the Use of Evangelical Lutheran Congregations* (St. 4), 1873

Music: *Schlesische Volkslieder*, 1842; harmonized by Richard S. Willis, *Church Chorals and Choir Studies*, 1850

118 Praise God from whom

DEDICATION ANTHEM (606)

*Alternate phrases: Praise God from whom all blessings flow, praise God all creatures here below, praise God
above, ye heav'nly host

Text: Thomas Ken, *A Manual of Prayers ...*, 1695; altered 1709
Music: Lowell Mason's *Boston Handel and Haydn Society Collection ...*, 9th ed., 1830

*Alternate phrase: O praise our God, bless'd Three-in-One.

Praise God from whom 119

OLD HUNDREDTH LM

A Praise God from whom all bless - ings flow; praise
B Praise God from whom all bless - ings flow; in

him all crea - tures here be - low; praise him a - bove ye
heav'n a - bove and earth be - low; one God three per - sons

heav'n - ly host; praise Fa - ther, Son, and Ho - ly Ghost.
we a - dore. To God be praise for - ev - er - more. A - men

SPANISH

A la Divina Trinidad,
todos unidos alabad,
con alegría y gratitud,
su amor y gracia celebrad.

KOREAN

Manboke keunwon hananim
on bakseong chansong drigo
Jeo cheonsayeo chansonghasei,
chansong seongbu, seogja,
   seongryoung.

HAUSA

Mai bayarwa ne Allahnmu,
yabe shi, ku 'yan Adam duk.
Yabe shi, ku Mala'iku
uba da Da da Ruhu, daya. Amin

CHINESE

Thi^{n}ē bānpang bānkok bānbîn.
Kèng pài Siōngtè, Pē, Kiá^{n}, Sèng-Sîn.
Oló Samūi itthé Siōngthè.
Chunmiâ liûhoân titkàu bānsè.

Text A: Thomas Ken, *A Manual of Prayers ...*, 1695
Text B: based on Thomas Ken's doxology; revised in *Hymns for Today's Church*, 1982
         Copyright ©1982 Hope Publishing Co.
Music: Louis Bourgeois, *Genevan Psalter*, 1551

120 Holy, holy, holy

NICAEA 11 12. 12 10

1 Ho-ly, ho-ly, ho - ly! Lord God Al - might - y!
2 Ho-ly, ho-ly, ho - ly! All the saints a - dore thee,
3 Ho-ly, ho-ly, ho - ly! Though the dark-ness hide thee,
4 Ho-ly, ho-ly, ho - ly! Lord God Al - might - y!

Ear - ly in the morn - ing our song shall rise to thee.
cast-ing down their gold - en crowns a - round the glass - y sea;
though the eye made blind by sin thy glo - ry may not see,
All thy works shall praise thy name, in earth, and sky, and sea.

Ho - ly, ho - ly, ho - ly! Mer - ci - ful and might - y!
cher - u - bim and ser - a - phim fall - ing down be - fore thee,
on - ly thou art ho - ly; there is none be - side thee,
Ho - ly, ho - ly, ho - ly! Mer - ci - ful and might - y!

God in three per - sons, bless - ed Trin - i - ty!
which wert, and art, and ev - er - more shalt be.
per - fect in pow'r, in love, and pur - i - ty.
God in three per - sons, bless - ed Trin - i - ty!

Text: Reginald Heber, *A Selection of Psalms and Hymns for the Parish Church of Banbury*, 1826
Music: John B. Dykes, *Hymns Ancient and Modern*, 1861

Holy God, we praise thy name 121

GROSSER GOTT, WIR LOBEN DICH 78. 78. 77

1 Ho - ly God, we praise thy name. Lord of all, we
2 Hark, the loud ce - les - tial hymn, an - gel choirs a -
3 Lo! the ap - os - tol - ic train join thy sa - cred
4 Ho - ly Fa - ther, ho - ly Son, Ho - ly Spir - it,

bow be - fore thee. All on earth thy scep - ter claim;
bove are rais - ing. Cher - u - bim and ser - a - phim,
name to hal - low. Proph - ets swell the glad re - frain,
three we name thee, though in es - sence on - ly one,

all in heav'n a - bove a - dore thee. In - fi - nite thy
in un - ceas - ing cho - rus prais-ing, fill the heav'ns with
and the white - robed mar - tyrs fol - low, and, from morn till
un - di - vid - ed God we claim thee, and a - dor - ing

vast do - main, ev - er - last - ing is thy reign.
sweet ac - cord: Ho - ly, ho - ly, ho - ly Lord.
set of sun, through the church the song goes on.
bend the knee, while we own the mys - ter - y.

Text: anonymous, *Te Deum laudamus*, late 4th c.; Clarence A. Walworth's English translation (1853) based on
Ignaz Franz's German translation (ca. 1774) of *Te Deum laudamus*, alt.
Music: *Katholisches Gesangbuch*, Vienna, 1774

122 All glory be to God on high

ALLEIN GOTT IN DER HÖH 87. 87. 887

1 All glo - ry be to God on high and
2 O Fa - ther, for your lord - ship true we
3 Lord Je - sus Christ, the on - ly Son of
4 O Ho - ly Spir - it, per - fect gift, who

thanks to him for - ev - er! What - ev - er Sa - tan's
give you praise and hon - or. We wor - ship you; we
God, cre - a - tion's Au - thor, Re - deem - er of your
brings us con - so - la - tion, to men and wom - en

host may try, God foils their dark en - deav - or.
trust in you; we give you thanks for - ev - er.
wan - d'ring ones, and Source of all true plea - sure:
saved by Christ as - sure your in - spi - ra - tion.

He bends his ear to ev - 'ry call, and of - fers peace,
Your will is per - fect, and your might re - lent - less - ly
O Lamb of God, O Lord di - vine, con - form our lives
Through sick - ness, need, and bit - ter death, grant us your warm,

Text: Nicolaus Decius, *Allein Gott in der Höh*, 1522, *Gesang Buch*, 1525; tr. Gilbert Doan, 1978
        Translation copyright ©1978 *Lutheran Book of Worship*
Music: Nicolaus Decius, 1522, *Deutsche Evangelische Messe*, 1524

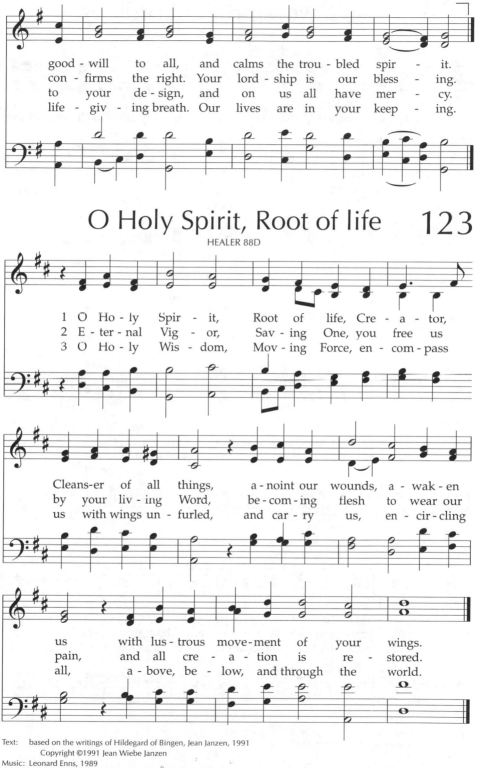

good - will to all, and calms the trou - bled spir - it.
con - firms the right. Your lord - ship is our bless - ing.
to your de - sign, and on us all have mer - cy.
life - giv - ing breath. Our lives are in your keep - ing.

O Holy Spirit, Root of life 123

HEALER 88D

1 O Ho - ly Spir - it, Root of life, Cre - a - tor,
2 E - ter - nal Vig - or, Sav - ing One, you free us
3 O Ho - ly Wis - dom, Mov - ing Force, en - com - pass

Cleans - er of all things, a - noint our wounds, a - wak - en
by your liv - ing Word, be - com - ing flesh to wear our
us with wings un - furled, and car - ry us, en - cir - cling

us with lus - trous move - ment of your wings.
pain, and all cre - a - tion is re - stored.
all, a - bove, be - low, and through the world.

Text: based on the writings of Hildegard of Bingen, Jean Janzen, 1991
Copyright ©1991 Jean Wiebe Janzen
Music: Leonard Enns, 1989
Copyright ©1989 Leonard Jacob Enns

124 O worship the Lord

BEAUTY OF HOLINESS Irregular with refrain

1,2,3 O wor-ship the Lord in the beau-ty of ho-li-ness, in the

beau-ty of ho-li-ness, in the beau-ty of ho-li-ness.

Glo - ry to the Fa - ther, a - bound - ing in mer - cy!
Glo - ry be to Je - sus, our gra - cious Re - deem - er!
Glo - ry to the Spir - it, the ho - ly re - veal - er!

Be joy - ful, all ye peo - ple, and mag - ni - fy the Lord God!
We praise him, for he loved us, and brought a great sal - va - tion.
Sing prais - es to the Spir - it, to the Fa - ther, and the Sav - ior.

Text: Robert Lowry, *Royal Diadem for the Sunday School*, 1873, alt.
Music: Robert Lowry, *Royal Diadem for the Sunday School*, 1873

Refrain

Oh, glo - ry hal - le - lu - jah, hal - le - lu - jah, hal - le - lu - jah,

O come be-fore his pres - ence and glo - ri - fy his name.

To God, with the Lamb 125

EDGEFIELD LM extended

Canon

To God, with the Lamb and the Dove, all

hon - or and praise we com - mend. As is, was in truth, and in love, and

shall be the world with-out end, and shall be the world with-out end.

Text: Christopher Smart, *A Translation ... Adapted to the Divine Service,* 1765
Music: *Sacred Harp,* 1844

126 How wondrous great

AWEFUL MAJESTY CM

1 How won-drous great, how glo-rious bright must our Cre-
2 Our soar-ing spir-its up-ward rise un-to the
3 Our rea-son stretch-es all its wings, and climbs a-
4 While all the heav'n-ly pow'rs con-spire e-ter-nal

a- tor be, who dwells a-midst the
burn- ing throne. There would we see the
bove the skies. But still how far be-
praise to bring, let faith in hum-ble

daz-zling light of vast e-ter-ni- ty.
bless-ed Three and the al-might-y One.
neath God's feet our mor-tal knowl-edge lies!
notes a-dore, the glo-rious Mys-t'ry sing.

Text: Isaac Watts, *Hymns and Spiritual Songs*, Book II, 1707-1709, alt.
Music: Joseph Funk's *Genuine Church Music*, 4th ed., 1847; arranged by Alice Parker, 1967
        Copyright ©1967 Lawson-Gould, Inc.

127 Glory be to the Father

Glo-ry be to the Fa-ther, and to the Son, and to the

Text: anonymous (Greek hymn), *Gloria Patri*, early Christian doxology
Music: Christopher Meineke, *Music for the Church*, 1844

Ho - ly Ghost. As it was in the be - gin-ning, is now, and

ev - er shall be, world with-out end. A - men, a - men.

Create in me a clean heart 128

TONUS REGIUS

1 Create in me a clean heart, O God,
2 Cast me not away from thy pres - ence,
3 Restore unto me the joy of thy sal - va - tion,

and renew a right spirit with - in me.
and take not thy Ho - ly Spir - it from me.
and uphold me with thy free Spir - it.

Text: Psalm 51:10-12, KJV
Music: *The Common Service Book and Hymnal,* 1917

129 Fire of God, undying Flame

NUN KOMM, DER HEIDEN HEILAND 77. 77

1 Fire of God, un - dy - ing Flame,
2 Breath of God, that swept in pow'r
3 Strength of God, your might with - in
4 Truth of God, your pierc - ing rays
5 Love of God, your grace pro - found

1 Spir - it who in splen - dor came, let your heat my
2 in the pen - te - cos - tal hour, ho - ly Breath, be
3 con - quers sor - row, pain, and sin. For - ti - fy from
4 pen - e - trate my se - cret ways. May the light that
5 knows not ei - ther age or bound. Come, my heart's own

1 soul re - fine, till it glows with love di - vine.
2 now in me source of vi - tal en - er - gy.
3 e - vil's art all the gate - ways of my heart.
4 shames my sin guide me ho - lier paths to win.
5 guest to be; dwell for - ev - er - more in me.

Text: Albert F. Bayly, 1947, *Rejoice, O God*, 1950
          Copyright © Oxford University Press, London
Music: *Geystliche Gesangk Buchleyn*, 1524; harmonized by Melchior Vulpius

O God of mystery and might 130

O GOD OF MYSTERY LM

1 O God of mys-ter-y and might, great Mov-er
2 Lord, set our ears to lis-ten - ing for rea-sons
3 O God of ten - der-ness and trust, whose ways are
4 From pride and pre - tense set us free to walk in

of the stars in flight, a - lert our hearts to ap - pre -
in each sea-son's spring, and teach our minds to med - i -
mer - ci - ful and just, lest we be o - ver-come with
truth's in - teg - ri - ty. O grant us grace to reach, to

hend the si - lent wit - ness-es you send.
tate long - er on love, while pas - sions wait.
gain bind us in - to each oth - er's pain.
give, to touch the dream by which we live.

Text: Kenneth I. Morse, 1970, *Messenger,* 1971, alt.
Music: Wilbur E. Brumbaugh, 1970, *Messenger,* 1971, alt.
Text and music copyright ©1970 Church of the Brethren General Board

131 When in the hour of deepest need

WENN WIR IN HÖCHSTEN NÖTEN SEIN LM

1 When in the hour of deep - est need we know not
2 our com - fort then is this a - lone: that we may
3 For you have made a prom - ise true to par - don
4 And so we come, O God, to - day, and all our
5 Oh, from our sins hide not your face. Ab - solve us
6 So we with all our hearts each day to you our

1 where to look for aid. When days and nights of
2 meet be - fore your throne and cry to you, O
3 those who flee to you, through him whose name a -
4 woes be - fore you lay, for sore - ly tried, cast
5 through your bound - less grace! Be with us in our
6 glad thanks - giv - ing pay, then walk o - be - dient

1 anx - ious thought no help or coun - sel yet have brought,
2 faith - ful God, for res - cue from our sor - ry lot.
3 lone is great, our Sav - ior and our ad - vo - cate.
4 down, we stand, per - plexed by fears on ev - 'ry hand.
5 an - guish still! Free us at last from ev - 'ry ill!
6 to your word, and now and ev - er praise you, Lord.

Text: Paul Eber, *Wenn wir in höchsten Nöten sein*, 1560, *Naw Betbüchlein*, 1566; tr. Catherine Winkworth,
        Lyra Germanica, Series II, 1858, alt.
Music: adapted from LES COMMANDEMENS DE DIEU, *La forme des prières ...*, 1545, *Das Gebet Josaphat*, 1567

Holy Spirit, Storm of love 132

STORM 77.77.77

1 Ho - ly Spir - it, Storm of love, break our self - pro -
2 Show us, in his tor - tured flesh, earth's Cre - a - tor
3 Show us how this dy - ing love en - tered, bore, and
4 Thus con - vic - ted, claimed, and called – freed as Christ, we
5 news that Je - sus is a - live, as his peo - ple

1 tect - ing walls. Bring us out and show us
2 on dis - play, bro - ken by af - fairs of
3 un - der - stood all our deep, un - con - scious
4 free - ly choose, washed in love, re - born, re -
5 of the dove, go - ing out in praise and

1 why, na - ked - ly up - on the cross, o - pen
2 state, drink - ing hor - ror, pain and grief, arch - ing
3 drives, each ex - ploit - ing, e - vil thread wo - ven
4 named, do - ing jus - tice, know - ing God, may we
5 prayer, meet the e - vils of our time and the

[1-4] [5]

1 to the wind and sky, Je - sus waits and Je - sus calls.
2 in the winds of hate, giv - ing love and life a - way.
3 through our na - tions' lives, all our life a - part from God.
4 wit - ness un - a - shamed, con - fi - dent to give good news;
5 de - mons of de - spair with for - giv - ing, liv - ing love.

Text: Brian Wren, 1985, *Praising a Mystery*, 1986
Copyright ©1986 Hope Publishing Co.
Music: Bradley P. Lehman, 1991
Copyright ©1991 Bradley P. Lehman

133 Out of the depths I cry to you

AUS TIEFER NOT (DE PROFUNDIS) 87. 87. 887

1 Out of the depths I cry to you; O Lord, now hear me
2 All things you send are full of grace. You crown our lives with
3 It is in God that we shall hope, and not in our own
4 My soul is wait-ing for the Lord as one who longs for

call - ing. In-cline your ear to my dis-tress in spite of
fa - vor. All our good works are done in vain with-out our
mer - it. We rest our fears in God's good Word and trust the
morn - ing. No watch-er waits with great-er hope than I for

my re-bel-ling. Do not re-gard my sin-ful deeds. Send me
Lord and Sav - ior. We praise the God who gives us faith and saves
Ho - ly Spir - it, whose prom-ise keeps us strong and sure. We trust
Christ's re-turn-ing. I hope as Is-rael in the Lord, who sends

the grace my spir - it needs; with-out it I am noth - ing.
us from the grip of death; our lives are in God's keep - ing.
the ho - ly sig - na-ture of hope be-yond all mea - sure.
re - demp-tion through the Word. Praise God for end-less mer - cy.

Text: based on Psalm 130, Martin Luther, 1523-1524, "Aus tiefer Not schrei ich zu dir," *Etlich Christlich Lieder*, 1524;
        tr. Gracia Grindal, *Lutheran Book of Worship*, 1978, alt.
        Translation copyright ©1978 *Lutheran Book of Worship*
Music: attributed to Martin Luther, *Geystliche Gesangk Buchleyn*, 1524; harmonized by The Hymnal Project
        Harmonization copyright ©1990 The Hymnal Project

Babylon streams received our tears 134

LLEF LM

1 Bab - y - lon streams re - ceived our tears: Zi - on, the
2 Our cap - tors laughed, "Per - form your praise! Mer - ri - ly
3 So help us, God, you may de - stroy our work - ing
4 Re - mem - ber, Lord, the aw - ful day vi - o - lent
5 God give you e - vil for re - ward. Bless'd be the

1 ho - ly cit - y, gone. Ex - iles, we cried be -
2 dance, Je - ru - sa - lem!" How could we chant the
3 hands if we de - ny; strike our mouths mute if
4 E - dom cursed your folk, "Bab - y - lon, break Je -
5 one who brings your fall. Bab - y - lon great – your

1 neath the trees. Harps hung in si - lence man - y years.
2 Lord God's songs while we were crushed by hea-thens' ways?
3 we ne - glect to make your cit - y our chief joy.
4 ru - sa - lem! Raze to the ground, strip her a - way!"
5 seed be smashed! Ven-geance shall come from God our Lord.

Text: based on Psalm 137, Calvin Seerveld, 1982, *Psalter Hymnal,* 1987
Copyright ©1982 Calvin Seerveld
Music: Griffith H. Jones, *Gemau Mawl,* 1890

135 God, whose purpose is to kindle

BAPTISM BY FIRE 87. 87D

1 God, whose pur-pose is to kin-dle, now ig-nite us with your fire.
2 God, who still a sword de-liv-ers ra-ther than a pla-cid peace,
3 God, who in your ho-ly gos-pel wills that all should tru-ly live,

While the earth a - waits your burn-ing, with your pas-sion
with your sharp-ened word dis-turb us, from com-pla-cen-
make us sense our share of fail-ure, our tran-quil-i-

us in-spire. O - ver-come our sin - ful calm-ness,
cy re-lease! Save us now from sat - is-fac-tion,
ty for-give. Teach us cour-age as we strug-gle

stir us with your sav - ing name. Bap-tize with your
when we pri-vate - ly are free, yet are un-dis-
in all lib-er - at-ing strife. Lift the small-ness

Text: based on Luke 12:49, D. Elton Trueblood, *The Incendiary Fellowship*, 1967, alt.
          Copyright ©1967 David Elton Trueblood. Reprinted by permission of HarperCollins Publishers, Inc.
Music: Esther Wiebe, 1968
          Copyright ©1968 Esther Wiebe

fi - ery Spir - it, crown our lives with tongues of flame.
turbed in spir - it by our neigh - bor's mis - er - y.
of our vi - sion by your own a - bun-dant life.

From the depths of sin 136

FROM THE DEPTHS 87. 87

1 From the depths of sin and sad - ness,
2 If you, Lord, re - cord our sin - ning,
3 For the Lord my heart is wait - ing,

I have called un - to the Lord.
who could then be - fore you stand?
for God's Word I hope and wait.

Be not deaf to my poor plead - ing,
But with you there is for - give - ness,
More than watch - ers wait for sun - rise,

in your mer - cy, hear my voice. voice.
you shall ev - er be re - vered. vered.
I am wait - ing for the Lord. Lord.

Text: based on Psalm 130, Willard F. Jabusch, ca. 1966, alt.
        Copyright ©1966 Willard F. Jabusch
Music: Russian folk melody; harmonized by Harris J. Loewen
        Harmonization copyright ©1988 Harris J. Loewen

137 · Forgive our sins as we forgive

DETROIT CM

1 "For - give our sins as we for - give," you
2 How can your par - don reach and bless the
3 In blaz - ing light your cross re - veals the
4 Lord, cleanse the depths with - in our souls and

taught us, Lord, to pray, but you a - lone can
un - for - giv - ing heart that broods on wrongs and
truth we dim - ly knew: what triv - ial debts are
bid re - sent - ment cease. Then, bound to all in

grant us grace to live the words we say.
will not let old bit - ter - ness de - part?
owed to us, how great our debt to you.
bonds of love, our lives will spread your peace.

Text: Rosamond E. Herklots, *100 Hymns for Today*, 1969, and *Hymns and Songs*, 1969
        Copyright ©1969 Oxford University Press, London
Music: *Supplement to the Kentucky Harmony*, 1820; harmonized by Alice Parker
        Harmonization copyright ©1991 Alice Parker

Let God, who called the worlds 138

CHURCH TRIUMPHANT LM

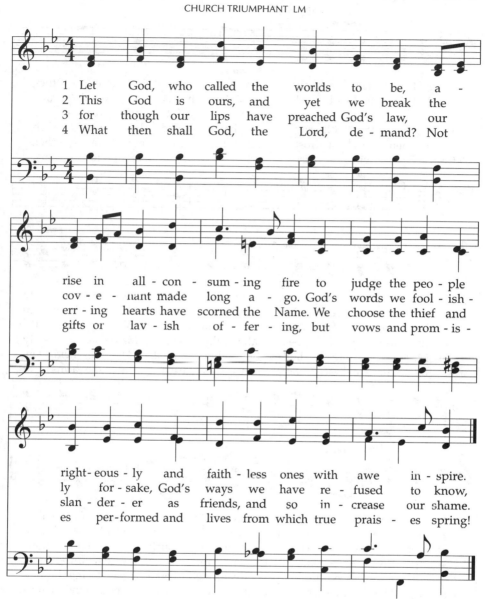

1 Let God, who called the worlds to be, a-
2 This God is ours, and yet we break the
3 for though our lips have preached God's law, our
4 What then shall God, the Lord, de-mand? Not

rise in all-con-sum-ing fire to judge the peo-ple
cov-e-nant made long a-go. God's words we fool-ish-
err-ing hearts have scorned the Name. We choose the thief and
gifts or lav-ish of-fer-ing, but vows and prom-is-

right-eous-ly and faith-less ones with awe in-spire.
ly for-sake, God's ways we have re-fused to know,
slan-der-er as friends, and so in-crease our shame.
es per-formed and lives from which true prais-es spring!

Text: based on Psalm 50, David Mowbray, *Psalms for Today,* 1990
Copyright ©1989 Hope Publishing Co.
Music: J. W. Elliott, *Church Hymns with Tunes,* 1874

139 Far, far away from my loving father

RESTORATION (I WILL ARISE) 10 8. 87

1 Far, far a - way from my lov - ing fa - ther,
2 Fain had I fed on the husks a - round me,
3 I will a - rise, though faint and wea - ry,
4 "Fa - ther," I'll say, "I have sinned be - fore thee,
5 Then I a - rose and came to my fa - ther.
Refrain: I will a - rise and go to Je - sus,

1 I had been wan - d'ring, way - ward, wild, fear - ing on - ly
2 till to my - self I came, and said, "Plen - ty have my
3 home to my fa - ther I will go. Woe is me that
4 no more may I be called thy son. Make me on - ly
5 Mer - cy a - maz - ing! Love un - known! He be - held me,
Refrain: he will em - brace me in his arms. In the arms of

1 lest his an - ger o - ver - take his sin - ful child.
2 fa - ther's ser - vants, per - ish I for want of bread."
3 e'er I wan - dered, ah, that I such need should know.
4 as thy ser - vant, pit - y me, a wretch un - done!"
5 ran, em - braced me, par - doned, wel - comed, called me "son!"
Refrain: my dear Sav - ior, oh, there are ten thou - sand charms.

Text: anonymous, in Philip P. Bliss's *Gospel Songs,* 1874
Music: American folk melody, *Southern Harmony,* 1835, alt.

Open, Lord, my inward ear 140

WHISPER 76. 76. 77. 76

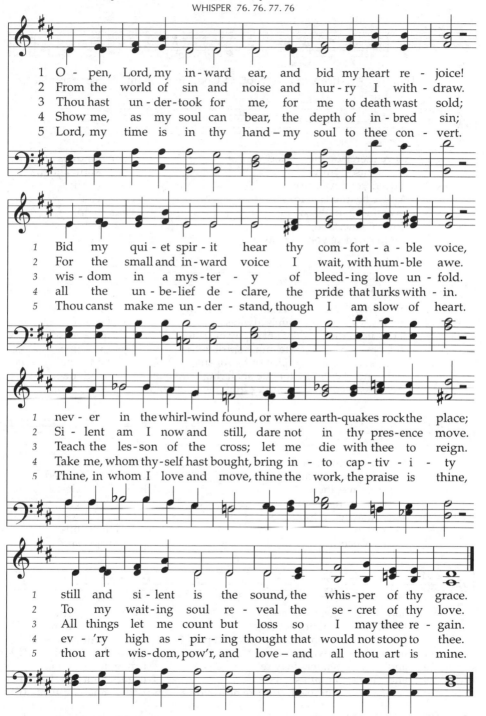

1 O - pen, Lord, my in-ward ear, and bid my heart re - joice!
2 From the world of sin and noise and hur - ry I with - draw.
3 Thou hast un - der-took for me, for me to death wast sold;
4 Show me, as my soul can bear, the depth of in - bred sin;
5 Lord, my time is in thy hand – my soul to thee con - vert.

1 Bid my qui - et spir - it hear thy com - fort - a - ble voice,
2 For the small and in-ward voice I wait, with hum - ble awe.
3 wis - dom in a mys-ter - y of bleed-ing love un - fold.
4 all the un - be-lief de - clare, the pride that lurks with - in.
5 Thou canst make me un - der - stand, though I am slow of heart.

1 nev - er in the whirl-wind found, or where earth-quakes rock the place;
2 Si - lent am I now and still, dare not in thy pres-ence move.
3 Teach the les-son of the cross; let me die with thee to reign.
4 Take me, whom thy-self hast bought, bring in - to cap-tiv - i - ty
5 Thine, in whom I love and move, thine the work, the praise is thine,

1 still and si - lent is the sound, the whis-per of thy grace.
2 To my wait-ing soul re - veal the se - cret of thy love.
3 All things let me count but loss so I may thee re - gain.
4 ev - 'ry high as - pir - ing thought that would not stoop to thee.
5 thou art wis-dom, pow'r, and love – and all thou art is mine.

Text: Charles Wesley, *Hymns and Spiritual Songs,* 1742
Music: Bradley P. Lehman, 1991

141 The sacrifice you accept, O God

Refrain   Irregular

The sac-ri-fice you ac-cept, O God, is a hum-ble spir-it.

1 Have mercy on me, O God, in   your kindness;
2 My offenses, truly   I know them;
3 Indeed you love truth in   the heart;
4 A pure heart create for me,   O God,
5 Give me again the joy of   your help.
6 O rescue me, God,   my helper,
7 For in sacrifice you take no   de - light,

1 in your com - passion blot out my   of - fense.
2 my sin is always   be - fore me.
3 then in the secret of my heart teach   me wisdom.
4 put a steadfast spirit with -   in me.
5 With a spirit of fervor sus -   tain me,
6 and my tongue shall ring out your   good-ness.
7 burnt offering from me you would   re - fuse;

1 O wash me more and more   from my guilt
2 Against you, you alone,   have I sinned.
3 O purify me, then I   shall be clean.
4 Do not cast me away   from your presence,
5 that I may teach transgres -   sors your ways
6 O Lord, o -   pen my lips
7 my sacrifice, a   con - trite spirit.

1 and cleanse me   from my sin.
2 What is evil in your sight   I have done. (R)
3 O wash me, and I shall be pur -   er than snow.
4 nor de - prive me of your   Ho - ly Spirit. (R)
5 and sinners may re -   turn to you.
6 and my mouth shall de -   clare your praise. (R)
7 A humbled, contrite heart you   will not spurn. (R)

Text: based on Psalm 51; tr. Ladies of the Grail
       Copyright ©1985 Ladies of the Grail (England). Used by permission of G.I.A. Publications, Inc.
Music: David C. Isele
       Copyright ©1979 G.I.A. Publications, Inc.

Brothers and sisters of mine 142

MINE ARE THE HUNGRY 11 11. 11 11

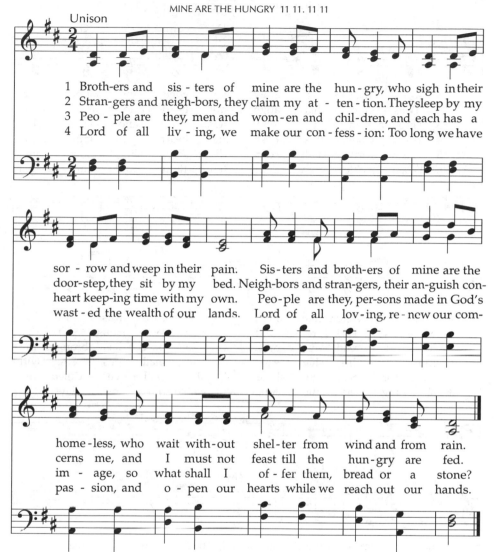

Unison

1 Broth-ers and sis-ters of mine are the hun-gry, who sigh in their
2 Stran-gers and neigh-bors, they claim my at-ten-tion. They sleep by my
3 Peo-ple are they, men and wom-en and chil-dren, and each has a
4 Lord of all liv-ing, we make our con-fess-ion: Too long we have

sor-row and weep in their pain. Sis-ters and broth-ers of mine are the
door-step, they sit by my bed. Neigh-bors and stran-gers, their an-guish con-
heart keep-ing time with my own. Peo-ple are they, per-sons made in God's
wast-ed the wealth of our lands. Lord of all lov-ing, re-new our com-

home-less, who wait with-out shel-ter from wind and from rain.
cerns me, and I must not feast till the hun-gry are fed.
im-age, so what shall I of-fer them, bread or a stone?
pas-sion, and o-pen our hearts while we reach out our hands.

Text: Kenneth I. Morse, *The Brethren Songbook*, 1974
Music: Wilbur E. Brumbaugh, *The Brethren Songbook*, 1974
Text and music copyright ©1974 Church of the Brethren General Board

143 Amazing grace

NEW BRITAIN (AMAZING GRACE) CM

1 A - maz - ing grace! how sweet the sound, that
2 'Twas grace that taught my heart to fear, and
3 Through man - y dan - gers, toils, and snares, I
4 Yes, when this flesh and heart shall fail, and
5 The earth shall soon dis - solve like snow, the
6 When we've been there ten thou - sand years, bright

1 saved a wretch like me! I once was lost, but
2 grace my fears re - lieved. How pre - cious did that
3 have al - read - y come. 'Tis grace has brought me
4 mor - tal life shall cease, I shall pos - sess, with -
5 sun for - bear to shine; but God, who called me
6 shin - ing as the sun, we've no less days to

1 now am found, was blind, but now I see.
2 grace ap - pear the hour I first be - lieved.
3 safe thus far, and grace will lead me home.
4 in the vail, a life of joy and peace.
5 here be - low, will be for - ev - er mine.
6 sing God's praise than when we'd first be - gun.

Text: John Newton (Sts. 1-5), *Olney Hymns,* 1779, *A Collection of Sacred Ballads* (St. 6), 1790
Music: American folk melody, *Virginia Harmony,* 1831; adapted and harmonized by Edwin O. Excell, 1900

SPANISH

Sublime gracia del Señor,
que a un pecador salvó;
perdido andaba, él me halló,
su luz me rescató.

Su gracia me enseñó a vencer,
mis dudas disipó.
¡Qué gozo siento en mi ser!
Mi vida él cambió.

Peligros, lucha y aflicción,
los he tenido aquí;
su gracia siempre me libró,
consuelo recibí.

Y cuando en Sión por siglos mil
brillando esté cual sol,
yo cantaré por siempre allí
a Cristo el Salvador.

NORTHERN OJIBWAY

Kihcishawencikewin
kaapimaaci´ ikoyaan
Ninkakippiinkwenaapan hsa
Nookom itahsh niwaap

Ninkiihsekis imaa nte 'ink
Oshawencikewin tahsh
ninkii 'oncipisaa' nentam
ehtepweyentamaan

CHEYENNE

Jesus ne-ta-vo-ve-ho-ne
Tse´-oh-ke-a-me-otsé-haetsé,
Tse´-oh-ke-vo-voh-néhe-še-haetsé oe-šeevá!
Ha-hoo, ne-ta-he-toné.

KOREAN

Na gateun jaein salisin,
joo eun hye nollawa
Irutdeon saing myoung chazatgo,
kwang myoung eul ōdōtne.

Keun jae-ak-eseo gunzisin,
joo eun hey gomawa
Na cheo-um middeun geu-si-gan
gui hago guihada.

Izekkert naega san-gutdo,
joo ni-me eunhyera
Tto na-reul jangcha bonhyangei
indo hae joosiri.

Keokiseo uri youngwonhi,
joo ni-me eunhyero
hai cheorum balge salmyounseo,
joo chanyang harira.

HAUSA

Alherin Ubangijina
abin mamaki ne.
Yesu ya ba jininsa
pansar mai zunbi.

Tun ranar da na tuba fa,
alherinsa 'na nan.
Alheri kuwa zai kai ni can
wurin Ubangiji.

Ya raina, kar ka manta dai
da duk alherinsa
abu duk da ke cinkina
ya yabi sunansa.

Kyrie eleison

ORTHODOX KYRIE

144

Ky - ri-e e-lei - son.*   Ky - ri-e e-lei - son.

Ky - ri-e e-le - i - son.

*Translation: Lord, have mercy.

Text: Greek litany
Music: Russian Orthodox liturgy

145 There's a wideness in God's mercy

WELLESLEY 87. 87

1 There's a wide - ness in God's mer - cy,
2 There is wel - come for the sin - ner,
3 But we make God's love too nar - row
4 For the love of God is broad - er
5 If our love were but more sim - ple

1 like the wide - ness of the sea. There's a kind - ness
2 and more grac - es for the good. There is mer - cy
3 by false lim - its of our own, and we mag - ni -
4 than the mea - sures of the mind, and the heart of
5 we should rest up - on God's word, and our lives would

1 in God's jus - tice, which is more than lib - er - ty.
2 with the Sav - ior, there is heal - ing in his blood.
3 fy its strict - ness with a zeal God will not own.
4 the E - ter - nal is most won - der - ful - ly kind.
5 be il - lu - mined by the pres - ence of our Lord.

Text: Frederick W. Faber, *Oratory Hymns*, 1854, *Hymns*, 1862, alt.
Music: Lizzie S. Tourjée, *Hymnal of the Methodist Church with Tunes*, 1878

O Lamb of God all holy 146

O LAMM GOTTES 77. 77. 778

1 O Lamb of God all ho - ly! who on the cross didst suf - fer,
2 O Lamb of God all ho - ly! who on the cross didst suf - fer,
3 O Lamb of God all ho - ly! who on the cross didst suf - fer,

and pa - tient still and low - ly, thy - self to scorn didst of - fer.
and pa - tient still and low - ly, thy - self to scorn didst of - fer.
and pa - tient still and low - ly, thy - self to scorn didst of - fer.

Our sins by thee were tak - en, or hope had us for -
Our sins by thee were tak - en, or hope had us for -
Our sins by thee were tak - en, or hope had us for -

sak - en. Have mer - cy on us, O Je - sus!
sak - en. Have mer - cy on us, O Je - sus!
sak - en. Thy peace be with us, O Je - sus!

Text: based on *Agnus Dei*, Nicolaus Decius, ca.1522, "O Lamm Gottes unschuldig," *Geystlyke Leder,* 1531; tr. Arthur T. Russell,
        German Hospital Collection (Sts. 1-2), 1848, *Psalms and Hymns* (St. 3), 1851
Music: based on a Gregorian melody, Nicolaus Decius, *Christliche Kirchen-Ordnung,* 1542

147 Oh, how wondrous the grace

RICHES OF GRACE 98. 98 with refrain

1 Oh, how won-drous the grace of our God, how
2 We were sunk in the ru-ins of sin, but
3 We are saved by the grace of our God, and are

sweet and how joy-ous the thought, that Christ ran-somed our
swift-ly he came to our aid. O'er our foes he did
kept by his pow-er and love. All our sins washed a-

souls with his blood, for us he sal-va-tion has bought!
vic-to-ry win, for us, peace with God he has made.
way in the blood, each day we his faith-ful-ness prove.

Refrain

Oh, how deep are the rich-es of grace, how great is the

Text: Mrs. W. J. Kennedy, *The Brethren Hymnal,* 1901
Music: J. Henry Showalter, *The Brethren Hymnal,* 1901

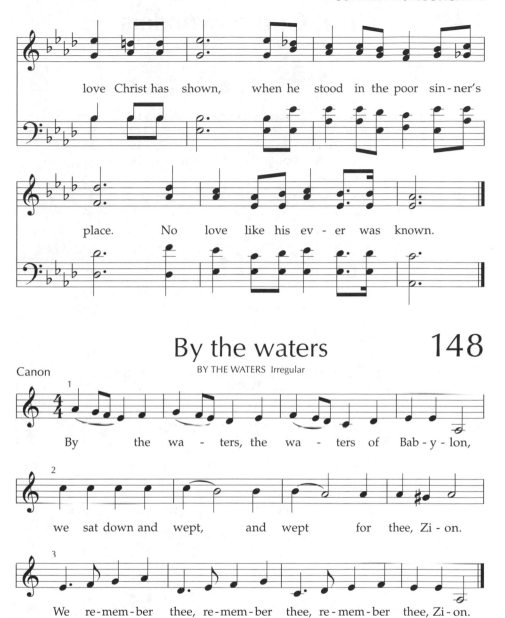

love Christ has shown, when he stood in the poor sin-ner's

place. No love like his ev - er was known.

By the waters

148

Canon

BY THE WATERS Irregular

1

By the wa - ters, the wa - ters of Bab-y-lon,

2

we sat down and wept, and wept for thee, Zi - on.

3

We re-mem-ber thee, re-mem-ber thee, re-mem-ber thee, Zi-on.

Text: based on Psalm 137:1
Music: Philip Hayes, *The Muses' Delight: Catches, Glees, Canzonets, and Canons,* 1786, adapted

149 Great God of wonders

SOVEREIGNTY 88. 888 with refrain

1 Great God of won-ders! All thy ways dis-
2 In won-der lost, with trem-bling joy we
3 Par-don—from an of-fend-ed God! Par-
4 Oh, may this strange, this match-less grace, this

play the at-tri-butes di-vine;
take the par-don of our God —
don—for sins of deep-est dye!
God-like mir-a-cle of love,

but count-less acts of par-d'ning grace be-
par-don for crimes of deep-est dye, a
Par-don—be-stowed through Je-sus' blood! Par-
fill the wide earth with grate-ful praise, as

yond thine oth—er won-ders shine, be-
par-don bought with Je-sus' blood, a
don—that brings the reb-el nigh! Par-
now it fills the choirs a-bove,

Text: Samuel Davies, *Hymns Adapted to Divine Worship*, 1769
Music: John Newton, *The Pilgrim*, 2nd ed., 1839

yond thine oth - er won - ders shine.
par - don bought with Je - sus' blood.
don — that brings the reb - el nigh!
now it fills the choirs a - bove!

Refrain

Who is a par - d'ning God like thee?

Or who has grace so rich and

free, or who has grace so rich and free?

150 Wonderful grace of Jesus

WONDERFUL GRACE 76. 76. 76. 12 with refrain

1 Won - der - ful grace of Je - sus, great - er than all my sin;
2 Won - der - ful grace of Je - sus, reach - ing to all the lost,
3 Won - der - ful grace of Je - sus, reach - ing the most de - filed,

how shall my tongue de - scribe it, where shall its praise be - gin?
by it I have been par - doned, saved to the ut - ter - most.
by its trans - form - ing pow - er mak - ing me God's dear child,

Tak - ing a - way my bur - den, set - ting my spir - it free,
Chains have been torn a - sun - der, giv - ing me lib - er - ty,
pur - chas - ing peace and heav - en for all e - ter - ni - ty,

for the won - der - ful grace of Je - sus reach - es me.
for the won - der - ful grace of Je - sus reach - es me.
for the won - der - ful grace of Je - sus reach - es me.

Refrain

the match - less grace of Je - sus,
Won - der - ful the match - less grace of Je - sus, deep - er

151 Marvelous grace of our loving Lord

MARVELOUS GRACE 99. 99 with refrain

1 Mar-vel-ous grace of our lov-ing Lord, grace that ex-ceeds our
2 Sin and de-spair, like the sea waves cold, threat-en the soul with
3 Mar-vel-ous, in-fi-nite, match-less grace, free-ly be-stowed on

sin and our guilt, yon-der on Cal-va-ry's mount out-poured,
in-fi-nite loss. Grace that is great-er, yes, grace un-told,
all who be-lieve. You that are long-ing to see his face,

Refrain

there where the blood of the Lamb was spilt. Grace, grace,
points to the ref-uge, the might-y cross. Mar-vel-ous grace,
will you this mo-ment his grace re-ceive?

God's grace, grace that will par-don and cleanse with-in. Grace,
in-fi-nite grace, Mar-vel-ous

Text: Julia H. Johnston, *Hymns Tried and True*, 1911
Music: Daniel B. Towner, 1910, *Hymns Tried and True*, 1911

grace, God's grace, grace that is great-er than all our sin.
grace, in-fi-nite grace,

Kyrie 152
TAIZÉ KYRIE

Ky - ri - e, Ky - ri - e, e - le - i - son.*

*Translation: Lord, have mercy.
Text: Greek litany
Music: Jacques Berthier, *Music from Taizé*, Vol. I, 1978, 1980, 1981
Copyright ©1978, 1980, 1981 Les Presses de Taizé (France). Used by permission of G.I.A. Publications, Inc.

O Christ, the Lamb of God 153
CHRISTE, DU LAMM GOTTES Irregular

1,2,3 O Christ, the Lamb of God, who takes a - way the sin

of the world, have mer - cy on us. grant us your peace.

Text: based on John 1:29, *Agnus Dei*
Music: *Kirchenordnung*, Braunschweig, 1528; setting adapted from Joachim Decker, 1604

154 This is my Father's world

TERRA BEATA SMD

1 This is my Fa-ther's world, and to my lis-t'ning ears all
2 This is my Fa-ther's world, the birds their car-ols raise, the
3 This is my Fa-ther's world. Oh, let me ne'er for - get that

na - ture sings, and 'round me rings the mu - sic of the spheres.
morn - ing light, the lil - y white de - clare their Mak-er's praise.
though the wrong seems oft so strong God is the rul - er yet.

This is my Fa-ther's world, I rest me in the thought of
This is my Fa-ther's world, he shines in all that's fair. In the
This is my Fa-ther's world, the bat - tle is not done. Je -

rocks and trees, of skies and seas—his hand the won-ders wrought.
rus - tling grass I hear him pass, he speaks to me ev-'ry-where.
sus who died shall be sat - is - fied, and earth and heav'n be one.

Text: Maltbie D. Babcock, *Thoughts for Every-Day Living,* 1901
Music: Franklin Sheppard, *Alleluia,* 1915

O God, great womb

155

BIXEL LM

1 O God, great womb of won-drous love, your
2 O hearth, O heart-beat of the whole, your
3 O fire, O fir-ma-ment and sea, your
4 O si-lent soul, O mind and strength, your
5 Now come with rest, O Sab-bath sun, O

1 Spir-it mov-ing on the deep did wake a world with-
2 dark light dance be-gan the times, the days and sea-sons,
3 seeth-ing fer-ment's en-er-gy called forth a whirl-ing
4 cen-ter did con-ceive and bear its male and fe-male
5 sanc-tu-ar-y, sa-cred home, we groan till all is

1 in your-self, a puls-ing, light-ed world, from sleep.
2 sec-onds, years, the ag-es' rhy-thms and the rhymes.
3 waltz of life, each plant and crea-ture and its seed.
4 im-age-self – two hu-man forms, one breath to share.
5 grown com-plete, ful-filled, at peace, O great sha-lom.

Text: Harris J. Loewen, *Assembly Songs*, 1983
Copyright ©1983 Harris J. Loewen
Music: James W. Bixel, *Assembly Songs*, 1983
Copyright ©1983 James W. Bixel

156 All things bright and beautiful

ROYAL OAK 76. 76 with refrain

*Guitar chords for unison singing only

Text: Cecil F. Alexander, *Hymns for Little Children,* 1848, alt.
Music: English melody, 17th c., *The Dancing Master,* 1686; adapted by Martin Shaw, 1915
        Harmonization copyright ©1955, renewed 1983 John Ribble

Lord, our Lord, your glorious name 157

BINGHAM 77.77

1 Lord, our Lord, your glo - rious name all your
2 In - fant voic - es chant your praise, tell - ing
3 Moon and stars in shin - ing height night - ly
4 Who are we that we should share in your
5 With do - min - ion crowned, we stand o'er the
6 Lord, our Lord, in all the earth, yours the

1 won - drous works pro - claim, in the heav'ns with ra - diant
2 of your glo - rious ways, weak - est means work out your
3 tell their Mak - er's might. When I view the heav'ns a -
4 love and ten - der care – raised to an ex - alt - ed
5 crea - tures of your hand, all to you sub - jec - tion
6 Name of match - less worth. In the heav'ns with ra - diant

1 signs ev - er - more your glo - ry shines.
2 will, might - y en - e - mies to still.
3 far, then I know how small we are.
4 height, crowned with hon - or in your sight?
5 yield, in the sea and air and field.
6 signs ev - er - more your glo - ry shines.

Text: based on Psalm 8, *Psalter,* 1912, alt.
Music: Dorothy H. Sheets, 1983, *The Hymnal 1982,* 1985
          Copyright ©1983 Dorothy Howell Sheets

158 Since o'er thy footstool

MAGNIFICENCE 86. 86. 88

1 Since o'er thy foot-stool here be-low such
2 If night's blue cur-tain of the sky – with
3 The daz-zling sun at noon-day hour – as
4 Oh, how shall these dim eyes en-dure that

ra-diant gems are strewn, oh, what mag-nif-i-cence must glow,
thou-sand stars in-wrought, hung like a roy-al can-o-py
from a flam-ing vase fling-ing o'er earth the gold-en show'r
noon of liv-ing rays, or how our spir-its, so im-pure,

great God, a-bout thy throne! So bril-liant here these
with glit-t'ring dia-monds fraught – be, Lord, thy tem-ple's
till vale and moun-tain blaze – but shows, O Lord, one
up-on thy glo-ry gaze! A-noint, O Lord, a-

drops of light – there the full o-cean rolls, how bright!
out-er veil, what splen-dor at the shrine must dwell!
beam of thine, what, then, the day where thou dost shine!
noint our sight, and fit us for that world of light.

Text: William A. Muhlenberg, *A Collection of Psalms and Hymns ...*, 2nd ed., 1837
Music: Asa B. Everett, *A Collection of Psalms and Hymns ...*, 2nd ed., 1837

All beautiful the march of days 159

FOREST GREEN CMD

1 All beau-ti-ful the march of days, as sea-sons come and go.
2 O'er white ex-pans-es spar-kling pure the ra-diant morns un - fold.
3 O thou from whose un - fath-omed law the year in beau-ty flows,

The hand that shaped the rose hath wrought the crys-tal of the snow,
The sol-emn splen-dors of the night burn bright-er through the cold.
thy - self the vi - sion pass-ing by in crys-tal and in rose,

hath sent the hoar-y frost of heav'n, the flow-ing wa-ters sealed,
Life mounts in ev-'ry throb-bing vein, love deep-ens 'round the hearth,
day un - to day doth ut -ter speech, and night to night pro - claim,

and laid a si-lent love-li-ness on hill and wood and field.
and clear-er sounds the an - gel hymn, "Good will and peace on earth."
in ev-er-chang-ing words of light, the won-der of thy name.

Text: Frances Whitmarsh Wile, *Unity Hymns and Carols*, revised ed. 1911
Music: traditional English melody; arranged by Ralph Vaughan Williams, *The English Hymnal*, 1906
Arrangement copyright © Oxford University Press, London

160 God created heaven and earth

TOA-SIA 77.77

1 God cre - at - ed heav'n and earth, all things per - fect
2 Let us praise God's mer - cy great! All our needs that
3 God is one, will ev - er be. I - dols are mere
4 But God's grace be - yond com - pare saves us all from

brought to birth. God's great pow'r made
love a - wait; God who fash - ions
van - i - ty; hand - made gods of
death's de - spair. So earth's crea - tures

dark and light, earth re - volv - ing day and night.
all that lives, to each one a bless - ing gives.
wood and clay can - not help us when we pray.
small and great give thanks for that bless - ed state.

Text: traditional Taiwanese hymn; tr. Boris and Clare Anderson, *Hymns from the Four Winds,* 1983
Translation copyright ©1983 Boris and Clare Anderson
Music: Taiwanese melody

We give thanks unto you

161

Irregular

1 We give thanks un-to you, O God of might,
2 From of old you have led your peo - ple in faith,
3 You de - liv - ered the ones who called un - to you,
4 You have o - pened the sea and brought your peo - ple through,
5 You re - mem - ber your prom - ise age to age,

for your love is nev - er end - ing;

1 we give thanks un - to you, the God of gods,
2 you have shown your com - pas - sion, strength, and love,
3 from bond - age to free - dom, you brought them forth,
4 brought them in - to a land that flows with life,
5 you show mer - cy on those of low de - gree,

for your love is nev - er end - ing.

Text: based on Psalm 136, Marty Haugen, *Shepherd Me, O God*, 1986
Music: Marty Haugen, *Shepherd Me, O God*, 1986
Text and music copyright ©1988 G.I.A. Publications, Inc.

162 The God of Abraham praise

LEONI 66. 84D

1 The God of A-brah'm praise. All prais-ed be the Name,
2 God's Spir-it flow-ing free, high - surg-ing where it will –
3 God has e-ter-nal life im - plant-ed in the soul.

who was, and is, and is to be, is still the same;
in proph-et's word it spoke of old – is speak-ing still.
God's love shall be our strength and stay, while ag - es roll.

the one e-ter-nal God, ere all that now ap - pears,
Es-tab-lished is God's law, and change-less it shall stand,
Praise to the liv-ing God! All prais - ed be the Name,

the First, the Last, be - yond all thought through time - less years!
deep writ up-on the hu-man heart, on sea, or land.
who was, and is, and is to be, is still the same!

Text: *Yigdal* prayer (Jewish doxology), 14th c.; translated and paraphrased by Max Landsberg and Newton Mann, ca. 1885, alt.
Music: Hebrew melody; transcribed by Meyer Leoni, ca. 1770

Obey my voice

163

OBEY MY VOICE Irregular

O - bey my voice, and I will be your God, and
ye shall be my peo - ple, and walk in
all the ways I have com - mand - ed you, that it may be
well with you and I will be your God. O - bey my
voice, and I will be your God, and ye shall
be my peo - ple.

Text: based on Jeremiah 7:23, KJV
Music: Sheilagh Nowacki, 1970, *Festival of the Holy Spirit Song Book*, 1972
        Copyright ©1972 Sheilagh Nowacki

164 When Israel was in Egypt's land

1 When Is-rael was in E-gypt's land, let my peo-ple
2 "Thus saith the Lord," bold Mo-ses said, let my peo-ple
3 No more shall they in bond-age toil, let my peo-ple
4 The Lord told Mo-ses what to do, let my peo-ple
5 They jour-neyed on at God's com-mand, let my peo-ple
6 Oh, let us all from bond-age flee, let my peo-ple

1 go; op-pressed so hard they could not stand,
2 go; "If not, I'll smite your first-born dead,"
3 go; let them come out with E-gypt's spoil,
4 go; to lead the childr'n of Is-rael through,
5 go; and came at length to Ca-naan's land,
6 go; and let us all in Christ be free,

let my peo-ple go. Go down, Mo-ses, 'way down in

E-gypt land. Tell old Phar-aoh, let my peo-ple go.

Text: African-American spiritual
Music: African-American spiritual

165 A mighty fortress is our God

EIN FESTE BURG 87. 87. 66. 66. 7

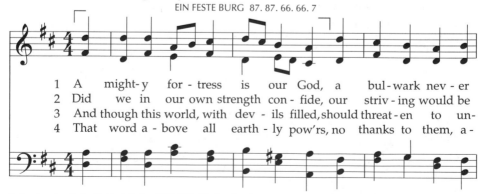

1 A might-y for-tress is our God, a bul-wark nev-er
2 Did we in our own strength con-fide, our striv-ing would be
3 And though this world, with dev-ils filled, should threat-en to un-
4 That word a-bove all earth-ly pow'rs, no thanks to them, a-

Text: based on Psalm 46, Martin Luther, 1527-1529, "Ein feste Burg ist unser Gott," *Geistliche Lieder*, 1529, 1531;
        tr. Frederick H. Hedge, 1852
Music: Martin Luther, 1529, *Geistliche Lieder*, 1529, 1531

fail - ing. Our help-er he a - mid the flood of mor-tal
los - ing, were not the right Man on our side, the Man of
do us, we will not fear, for God hath willed his truth to
bid - eth. The Spir-it and the gifts are ours, through him who

ills pre - vail - ing, for still our an-cient foe doth
God's own choos - ing. Dost ask who that may be? Christ
tri - umph through us. The prince of dark-ness grim, we
with us sid - eth. Let goods and kin-dred go, this

seek to work us woe. His craft and pow'r are great, and
Je - sus, it is he! Lord Sab - a - oth, his name, from
trem - ble not for him. His rage we can en - dure, for
mor - tal life al - so. The bod - y they may kill, God's

arm'd with cru - el hate, on earth is not his e - qual.
age to age the same, and he must win the bat - tle.
lo, his doom is sure. One lit - tle word shall fell him.
truth a - bid - eth still. His king-dom is for - ev - er.

166   I'll praise my Maker

NASHVILLE 888. 888

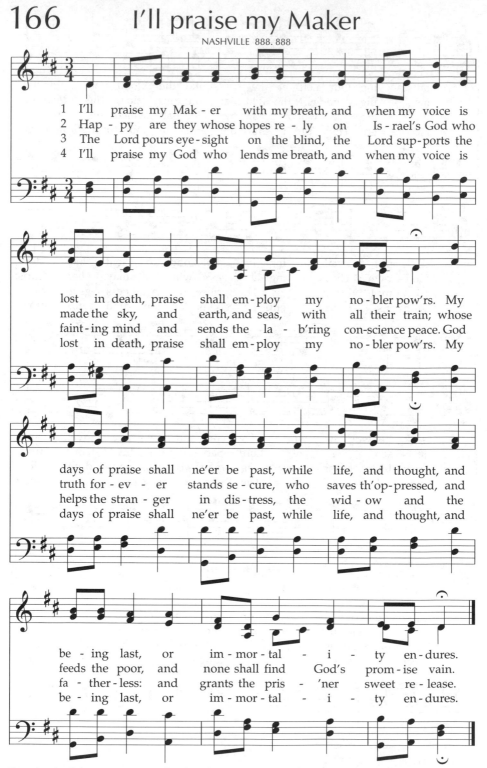

1 I'll praise my Mak - er with my breath, and when my voice is
2 Hap - py are they whose hopes re - ly on Is - rael's God who
3 The Lord pours eye - sight on the blind, the Lord sup - ports the
4 I'll praise my God who lends me breath, and when my voice is

lost in death, praise shall em - ploy my no - bler pow'rs. My
made the sky, and earth, and seas, with all their train; whose
faint - ing mind and sends the la - b'ring con - science peace. God
lost in death, praise shall em - ploy my no - bler pow'rs. My

days of praise shall ne'er be past, while life, and thought, and
truth for - ev - er stands se - cure, who saves th'op - pressed, and
helps the stran - ger in dis - tress, the wid - ow and the
days of praise shall ne'er be past, while life, and thought, and

be - ing last, or im - mor - tal - i - ty en - dures.
feeds the poor, and none shall find God's prom - ise vain.
fa - ther - less: and grants the pris - 'ner sweet re - lease.
be - ing last, or im - mor - tal - i - ty en - dures.

Text: based on Psalm 146, Isaac Watts, *Psalms of David ...*, 1719, alt.
Music: Lowell Mason, *The Choir, or Union Collection of Church Music*, 1832

For God so loved us

GOTT IST DIE LIEBE 10 9 with refrain

1 For God so loved us, he sent the Sav - ior. For God so
2 He sent the Sav - ior, the bless'd Re - deem - er. He sent the
3 He bade me wel - come; oh word of mer - cy. He bade me
4 Glo - ry and hon - or, O Love e - ter - nal, to thee be

loved us, and loves me too.
Sav - ior to set me free.
wel - come; oh voice di - vine.
giv - en while life shall last.

Refrain

Love so un - end - ing,

I'll sing thy prais - es. God loves his chil - dren, loves e - ven me.

1 Gott ist die Liebe, lässt mich erlösen.
Gott ist die Liebe, er liebt auch mich.

2 Ich lag in Banden der schnöden Sünde,
ich lag in Banden und konnt nicht los.

3 Er sandte Jesum, den treuen Heiland,
er sandte Jesum und macht mich los.

4 Jesus, mein Heiland, gab sich zum Opfer,
Jesus, mein Heiland, büsst meine Schuld.

Refrain:
Drum sag ich noch einmal:
Gott ist die Liebe,
Gott ist die Liebe,
er liebt auch mich.

Text: August Rische, *Gott ist die Liebe*; tr. Esther C. Bergen (Sts. 1-3), *The Youth Hymnary*, 1956, copyright ©1956 Faith and Life Press
The Hymn Book (St. 4 and refrain), 1960
Translation (St. 4 and refrain) copyright ©1960 *The Hymn Book*
Music: Thüringer melody, ca. 1840

168 Creating God, your fingers trace

CHRISTOPHER DOCK LM with refrain

Cre-at-ing God,

1 Cre - at - ing God, your fin - gers trace the
2 Sus - tain - ing God, your hands up - hold earth's
3 Re - deem - ing God, your arms em - brace all
4 In - dwell - ing God, your gos - pel claims one

bold de - signs of far-thest space. Let sun and moon and
mys - t'ries known or yet un - told. Let wa - ter's fra - gile
now op - pressed for creed or race. Let peace, de - scend - ing
fam - 'ly with a bil - lion names. Let ev - 'ry life be

stars and light and what lies hid - den praise your might.
blend with air, en - a - bling life, pro - claim your care.
as the dove, make known on earth your heal - ing love.
touched by grace un - til we praise you face to face.

Refrain

God   God
God Cre - a - tor! God Sus - tain - er!

Text: Jeffery W. Rowthorn, 1974, *The Hymn*, 1979
        Copyright ©1979 The Hymn Society. Refrain copyright © Philip K. Clemens
Music: Philip K. Clemens, 1982, *Assembly Songs*, 1983
        Copyright ©1983 Philip K. Clemens

Dwell - er - in - us! Heal - ing Love! Re - deem - ing God!

I to the hills will lift my eyes 169

DUNDEE CM

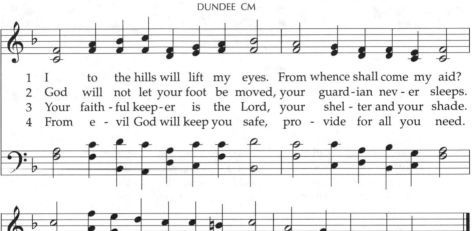

1 I   to   the hills will lift my eyes. From whence shall come my aid?
2 God will not let your foot be moved, your   guard-ian nev-er sleeps.
3 Your faith - ful keep-er is the Lord, your   shel - ter and your shade.
4 From   e - vil God will keep you safe, pro - vide for all you   need.

My   help is from the Lord a - lone, who heav'n and earth has made.
God's watch-ful and un-slum-b'ring care pro - tects and safe-ly keeps.
'Neath sun or moon, by day or night, you   shall not be a - fraid.
Your go-ing out, your com-ing in, God will for - ev - er lead.

Text: based on Psalm 121, *Psalter,* 1912, alt.
Music: *The CL Psalmes of David,* 1615

170 The King of love my shepherd is

ST. COLUMBA 87. 87

1 The King of love my shep - herd is, whose
2 Where streams of liv - ing wa - ter flow my
3 Per - verse and fool - ish oft I strayed, but
4 In death's dark vale I fear no ill with
5 And so through all the length of days thy

1 good - ness fail - eth nev - er. I noth - ing lack if
2 ran - somed soul he lead - eth, and, where the ver - dant
3 yet in love he sought me, and on his shoul - der
4 thee, dear Lord, be - side me; thy rod and staff my
5 good - ness fail - eth nev - er. Good Shep - herd, may I

1 I am his, and he is mine for - ev - er.
2 pas - tures grow, with food ce - les - tial feed - eth.
3 gent - ly laid, and home, re - joic - ing, brought me.
4 com - fort still, thy cross be - fore to guide me.
5 sing thy praise with - in thy house for - ev - er.

Text: based on Psalm 23, Henry W. Baker, *Hymns Ancient and Modern, Appendix*, 1868
Music: Irish melody, *Irish Church Hymnal*, 1873 or 1874

How lovely is your dwelling 171

76. 76. 776

1 How love-ly is your dwell-ing, O God, my hope and strength.
2 How bless'd are those whose trav-els are strength-ened by your hand,
3 Look on me, God of good-ness, you are my sun and shield.

My spir-it longs for shel-ter, my flesh cries out for home,
who pass through dark-ened val-leys and find re-fresh-ing springs.
One day with-in your house-hold is what I most de-sire.

where e-ven swal-lows nest-ing be-side your
Your rains fall soft as kind-ness on all your
O guide me in your mer-cy a-long my

al-tar rest-ing are ev-er prais-ing you.
faith-ful pil-grims un-til they come to you.
lone-ly path-way; O bring me safe-ly home.

Text: based on Psalm 84, Jean Janzen, 1991
Copyright ©1991 Jean Wiebe Janzen
Music: Heinrich Schütz, *Psalmen Davids ...*, 1628

172 O come, O come, Immanuel

VENI EMMANUEL LM with refrain

1 O come, O come, Im - man - u - el, and ran-som cap-tive
2 O come, thou Rod of Jes - se, free thine own from Sa - tan's
3 O come, thou Day-spring, come and cheer our spir - its by thine
4 O come, thou Key of Da - vid, come and o - pen wide our
5 O come, thou Wis - dom from on high, and or - der all things
6 O come, De - sire of na - tions, bind all peo - ples in one

1 Is - ra - el, that mourns in lone - ly ex - ile
2 tyr - an - ny. From depths of hell thy peo - ple
3 ad - vent here. Dis - perse the gloom - y clouds of
4 heav'n - ly home. Make safe the way that leads on
5 far and nigh. To us the path of knowl - edge
6 heart and mind. Bid en - vy, strife, and quar - rels

1 here, un - til the Son of God ap - pear.
2 save, and give them vic - t'ry o'er the grave.
3 night, and death's dark shad - ow put to flight.
4 high, and close the path to mis - er - y.
5 show, and cause us in thy ways to go.
6 cease. Fill the whole world with heav - en's peace.

Refrain

Re - joice! Re - joice! Im - man -

u - el shall come to thee, O Is - ra - el.

Text: anonymous, ca. 6th-7th c., *Veni, veni Emmanuel*, 12th c.; tr. John M. Neale (Sts. 1-4), *Medieval Hymns and Sequences*, 1851, Henry Sloane Coffin (Sts. 5-6), *Hymns of the Kingdom of God*, 1916
Music: Trope melody, 15th c.

Savior of the nations, come 173

NUN KOMM, DER HEIDEN HEILAND 77. 77

1 Sav - ior of the na - tions, come!
2 Not by hu - man flesh and blood,
3 Won - drous birth! Oh, won - drous child
4 Now your low - ly man - ger bright

Vir - gin's son, here make your home! Mar - vel now, O
by the Spir - it of our God was the Word of
of the vir - gin un - de - filed! Hu - man and di -
hal - lows night with new - born light. Let no night this

heav'n and earth, that the Lord chose such a birth.
God made flesh, wom - an's off - spring, pure and fresh.
vine in one, ea - ger now his race to run!
light sub - due, let our faith shine ev - er new.

Text: Attributed to Ambrose of Milan; tr. Martin Luther, *Nun komm, der Heiden Heiland,* 1523, *Eyn Enchiridion,* 1524;
         tr. William M. Reynolds (Sts. 1-2), *Hymns Original and Selected,* 1851, Martin L. Seltz (Sts. 3-4), *Worship Supplement* to
         The Lutheran Hymnal, 1969, alt.
         Translation (Sts. 3-4) copyright ©1969 Concordia Publishing House
Music: *Geystliche Gesangk Buchleyn,* 1524; harmonized by Melchior Vulpius

174 Bless'd be the God of Israel

WEBB 76. 76D

1 Bless'd be the God of Is - rael, who comes to set us free,
2 Now from the house of Da - vid a child of grace is giv'n,
3 On pris - on - ers of dark - ness the sun be - gins to rise,

who vis - its and re - deems us, and grants us lib - er - ty!
a Sav - ior comes a - mong us to raise us up to heav'n.
the dawn - ing of for - give - ness up - on the sin - ner's eyes,

The proph - ets spoke of mer - cy, of free - dom and re - lease;
Be - fore him goes the her - ald, fore - run - ner in the way,
to guide the feet of pil - grims a - long the paths of peace.

God shall ful - fill the prom - ise to bring our peo - ple peace.
the proph - et of sal - va - tion, the har - bin - ger of day.
O bless our God and Sav - ior with songs that nev - er cease!

Text: based on Luke 1:68-79, Michael A. Perry, *Psalm Praise*, 1973
Copyright ©1973 Hope Publishing Co.
Music: George J. Webb, 1830, *The Odeon*, 1837

O Savior, rend the heavens 175

O HEILAND, REISS DIE HIMMEL AUF LM

1 O Sav - ior, rend the heav - ens wide! Come down, come
2 O Day-spring, dew from heav - en send. As gen - tle
3 O earth, in flow - 'ring bud be seen, clothe hill and
4 Here dread - ful doom up - on us lies. Death looms so
5 There will we all our prais - es bring ev - er to

1 down with might - y stride. Un - bar the gates, the
2 dew, O Son, de - scend. Drop down, you clouds, and
3 dale in garb of green. O earth, bring forth this
4 grim be - fore our eyes. O come, lead us with
5 thee, our Sav - ior King. There will we laud thee

1 doors break down; un - bar the way to heav - en's crown.
2 tor - rents bring, to Ja - cob's line rain down a King.
3 Blos - som rare; O Sav - ior, rise from mead - ow fair.
4 might - y hand from ex - ile to our prom - ised land.
5 and a - dore for - ev - er and for - ev - er - more.

Text: Friedrich von Spee, "O Heiland, reiss die Himmel auf," *Gesangbuch,* Köln, 1623; tr. Martin L. Seltz, 1965,
           The Mennonite Hymnal, 1969, alt.
           Translation copyright ©1965 Martin L. Seltz
Music: *Gesangbuch,* Augsburg, 1666; harmonized by Esther Wiebe
           Harmonization copyright ©1964 Esther Wiebe

176 Comfort, comfort, O my people

GENEVA 42 (FREU DICH SEHR) 87. 87. 77. 88

1 Com - fort, com - fort, O my peo - ple, speak of peace, now
2 Hark, the voice of one who's cry - ing in the des - ert
3 O make straight what long was crook - ed, make the rough - er

says our God. Com - fort those who sit in dark - ness,
far and near, bid - ding all to full re - pen - tance
plac - es plain. Let your hearts be true and hum - ble,

mourn - ing 'neath their sor - rows' load. Speak un - to Je - ru - sa -
since the king - dom now is here. O that warn - ing cry o -
as be - fits his ho - ly reign. For the glo - ry of the

lem of the peace that waits for them. Tell of all the
bey! Now pre-pare for God a way. Let the val - leys
Lord now o'er earth is shed a - broad. And all flesh shall

Text: based on Isaiah 40, Johannes Olearius, "Tröstet, tröstet, meine Lieben," *Geistliche Singe-kunst,* 1671; tr. Catherine Winkworth, *Chorale Book for England,* 1863, alt.

Music: Louis Bourgeois, *Genevan Psalter,* 1551; harmonization adapted from Claude Goudimel, *Les Pseaumes ...,* 1565

sins I cov - er,   and   that war - fare now is o - ver.
rise to meet him and the hills bow down to greet him.
see the to - ken that his word is nev - er bro - ken.

Creator of the stars of night 177

CONDITOR ALME SIDERUM LM

1 Cre - a - tor of the stars of night, your peo - ple's
2 In sor - row that the an - cient curse should doom to
3 When this old world drew on t'ward night, you came, but
4 At your great name, O Je - sus, now all knees must
5 Come in your ho - ly might, we pray, re - deem us
6 To God Cre - a - tor, God the Son, and God the

1 ev - er - last - ing light, O Christ, Re - deem - er of us all,
2 death a u - ni - verse, you came, O Sav - ior, to set free
3 not in splen - dor bright, not as a mon - arch, but the child
4 bend, all hearts must bow. All things on earth with one ac - cord,
5 for e - ter - nal day. De - fend us while we dwell be - low
6 Spir - it, Three - in - One, praise, hon - or, might, and glo - ry be

1 we pray you hear us when we call.
2 your own in glo - rious lib - er - ty.
3 of Ma - ry, bless - ed moth - er mild.
4 like those in heav'n, shall call you Lord.
5 from all as - saults of our dread foe.
6 from age to age e - ter - nal - ly.

Text: anonymous, *Conditor alme siderum*, 9th c.; tr. *The Hymnal 1940*, alt.
          Translation copyright ©1985 The Church Pension Fund
Music: Plainsong

178 Come, thou long-expected Jesus

HYFRYDOL 87. 87D

1 Come, thou long - ex - pect - ed Je - sus! born to set thy
2 Born thy peo - ple to de - liv - er, born a child, and

peo - ple free, from our fears and sins re - lease us,
yet a King, born to reign in us for - ev - er,

let us find our rest in thee. Is - rael's strength and con - so -
now thy gra - cious king - dom bring. By thine own e - ter - nal

la - tion, hope of all the earth thou art, dear de -
Spir - it, rule in all our hearts a - lone. By thine

Text: Charles Wesley, *Hymns for the Nativity of Our Lord,* 1744
Music: Rowland H. Prichard, ca. 1830, *Cyfaill y Cantorion,* 1844; arranged by Ralph Vaughan Williams, *The English Hymnal,* 1906,
        adapted 1951, *BBC Hymn Book*
        Arrangement copyright © Oxford University Press, London

sire of ev - 'ry na - tion, joy of ev - 'ry long-ing heart.
all - suf - fi - cient mer - it, raise us to thy glo - rious throne.

Blessed be the Lord   179

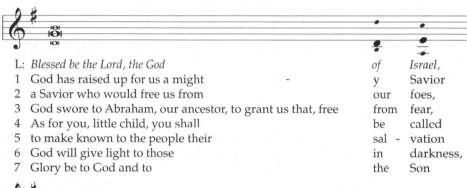

L: *Blessed be the Lord, the God*   *of*   *Israel,*
1 God has raised up for us a might - y Savior
2 a Savior who would free us from our foes,
3 God swore to Abraham, our ancestor, to grant us that, free from fear,
4 As for you, little child, you shall be called
5 to make known to the people their sal - vation
6 God will give light to those in darkness,
7 Glory be to God and to the Son

who has visited the people and re - deemed them. (to Stanza 1)
1 in the house of   David, the Lord's   servant,   as was promised by the
2 from the hands of   all who   hate us.   So God's love for our
3 and saved from the   hands of our   foes,   we might serve in
4 a prophet of   God, the Most   High.   You shall go a -
5 through the for - giveness of their   sins,   the loving-kindness of the
6 those who dwell in the   shadow of   death,   and guide us into the
7 and to the   Holy   Spirit,   as it was in the beginning, is

1 lips of   holy ones,   those who were the   prophets from of old –
2 parents is ful - filled   and the holy   covenant re - membered.
3 holiness and   justice   all the days of our   life in the holy   Presence.
4 head of the   anointed One   to prepare a   way be - fore him,
5 heart of our   God   who visits us like the   dawn from on   high.
6 way of   peace,   guide us into the   way of   peace.
7 now, and ever   shall be,   world without   end. A - men.

Text: Luke 1:68-79; tr. Ladies of the Grail
      Copyright ©1963 Ladies of the Grail (England). Used by permission of G.I.A. Publications, Inc.
Music: Abbey Notre Dame du Tamié
      Music copyright ©1980 Trappist Abbey of Tamié

180 The angel Gabriel

GABRIEL'S MESSAGE Irregular

1 The an - gel Ga - bri - el from heav - en came, his
2 "For known as bless - ed moth - er thou shalt be, all
3 Then gen - tle Ma - ry meek - ly bowed her head, "To

wings as drift - ed snow, his eyes as flame.
gen - er - a - tions laud and hon - or thee.
me be as it pleas - eth God," she said.

"All hail," said he, "thou low - ly maid - en Ma - ry,
Thy son shall be Im - man - u - el by seers fore - told,
"My soul shall laud and mag - ni - fy his ho - ly name."

most high - ly fa - vored la - dy," glo - ri - a!

Text: Sabine Baring-Gould, *University Carol Book*, 1923
Music: Basque carol; arranged by C. Edgar Pettman, *University Carol Book*, 1961
      Text and music arrangement copyright ©1961 H. Freeman & Co./International Music Publications

My soul proclaims with wonder 181

WALNUT 76. 76 with refrain

Refrain/Unison

My soul pro-claims with won - der the great-ness of the Lord,

Fine

re - joic - ing in God's great - ness my spir - it is re - stored.

1 To me has God shown fa - vor, to one the world thought frail,
2 God's mer - cy shields the faith - ful and saves them from de - feat,
3 The might - y have been van - quished the low - ly lift - ed up.
4 To A - bra-ham's de - scen-dants, the Lord will stead-fast prove,

D.C.

and ev - 'ry age will ech - o the an - gel's first "All hail."
with strength that turns to scat - ter the proud in their con - ceit.
The hun - gry find a - bun-dance, the rich, an emp - ty cup.
for God has made with Is - rael a cov - e - nant of love.

Text: based on Luke 1:46-55, Carl P. Daw, Jr., 1986, *Songs of Rejoicing*, 1989
         Copyright ©1987 Hope Publishing Co.
Music: J. Harold Moyer, 1990
         Copyright ©1991 The Hymnal Project

182 Oh, how shall I receive thee

ST. THEODULPH (VALET WILL ICH DIR GEBEN) 76. 76D

1 Oh, how shall I re - ceive thee, how meet thee on thy way,
2 Love caused thine in - car - na - tion; Love brought thee down to me.
3 Thou com - est, Lord, with glad - ness, in mer - cy and good will,

bless'd hope of ev - 'ry na - tion, my soul's de - light and stay?
Thy thirst for my sal - va - tion pro - cured my lib - er - ty.
to bring an end to sad - ness and bid our fears be still.

O Je - sus, Je - sus, give me now by thine own pure light
Oh, love be - yond all tell - ing, that led thee to em - brace,
We wel - come thee, our Sav - ior; come gath - er us to thee,

to know what - e'er is pleas - ing and wel - come in thy sight.
in love, all love ex - cel - ling, our lost and trou - bled race.
that in thy light e - ter - nal our joy - ous home may be.

Text: based on Matthew 21:9, Paul Gerhardt, "Wie soll ich dich empfangen," *Praxis Pietatis Melica,* 5th ed., 1653; tr. Arthur T. Russell,
         Psalms and Hymns, 1851, alt.
Music: Melchior Teschner, 1613, *Ein andächtiges Gebet ...,* 1615

On Jordan's banks the Baptist's cry 183

WINCHESTER NEW LM

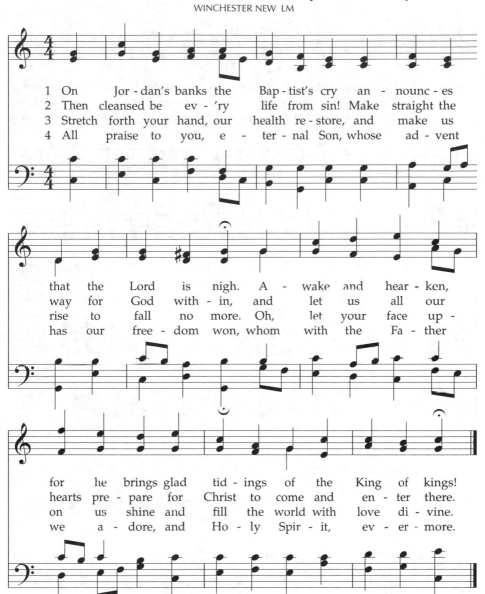

1 On Jor-dan's banks the Bap-tist's cry an-nounc-es
2 Then cleansed be ev-'ry life from sin! Make straight the
3 Stretch forth your hand, our health re-store, and make us
4 All praise to you, e-ter-nal Son, whose ad-vent

that the Lord is nigh. A-wake and hear-ken,
way for God with-in, and let us all our
rise to fall no more. Oh, let your face up-
has our free-dom won, whom with the Fa-ther

for he brings glad tid-ings of the King of kings!
hearts pre-pare for Christ to come and en-ter there.
on us shine and fill the world with love di-vine.
we a-dore, and Ho-ly Spir-it, ev-er-more.

Text: Charles Coffin, "Jordanis oras praevia," *Hymni Sacri* and *Paris Breviary,* 1736; tr. John Chandler (Sts. 1-3),
         Hymns of the Primitive Church, 1837, alt., *Hymns Ancient and Modern* (St. 4), 1861, alt.
Music: *Musicalisch Handbuch ...,* 1690; arranged by William H. Havergal, *Old Church Psalmody,* 1847

184 Hark! the glad sound

COMMUNION CMD

1 Hark! the glad sound! The Sav-ior comes! the Sav-ior prom-ised long!
2 He comes the pris-'ners to re-lease, in Sa-tan's bond-age held.
3 His sil-ver trum-pets pub-lish loud the ju-b'lee of the Lord.

Let ev-'ry heart pre-pare a throne, and ev-'ry voice a song.
The gates of brass be-fore him burst, the i-ron fet-ters yield.
Our debts are all re-mit-ted now, our her-i-tage re-stored.

On him the Spir-it large-ly poured, ex-erts its sa-cred fire,
He comes the bro-ken heart to bind, the bleed-ing soul to cure,
Our glad ho-san-nas, Prince of peace, thy wel-come shall pro-claim,

wis-dom and might and zeal and love, his ho-ly breast in-spire.
and with the trea-sures of his grace to en-rich the hum-ble poor.
and heav'n's e-ter-nal arch-es ring with thy be-lov-ed name.

Text: Philip Doddridge, 1735, *Translations and Paraphrases*, 1745
Music: "Robinson" in John Wyeth's *Repository of Sacred Music, Part Second*, 1813; harmonized by J. Harold Moyer, 1965
Harmonization copyright ©1969 Faith and Life Press/Mennonite Publishing House

Hail to the Lord's anointed 185

FARMER 76. 76D

1 Hail to the Lord's a - noint - ed, great Da - vid's great - er Son!
2 He comes with jus - tice sure - ly to those who suf - fer wrong,
3 He shall come down like show - ers up - on the fruit - ful earth.
4 To him shall prayer un - ceas - ing and dai - ly vows as - cend,

Hail in the time ap - point - ed, his reign on earth be - gun!
to help the poor and need - y, and bid the weak be strong,
Love, joy, and hope, like flow - ers, spring in his path to birth.
his king - dom still in - creas - ing, a king - dom with - out end.

He comes to break op - pres - sion, to set the cap - tives free,
to give them songs for sigh - ing, their dark - ness turn to light,
Be - fore him, on the moun - tains, shall peace, the her - ald, go,
The tide of time shall nev - er his cov - e - nant re - move.

to take a - way trans - gres - sions, and rule in eq - ui - ty.
whose souls, con - demned and dy - ing, are pre - cious in his sight.
and right - eous - ness, in foun - tains, from hill to val - ley flow.
His name shall stand for - ev - er; that name to us is Love.

Text: based on Psalm 72, James Montgomery, *Evangelical Magazine*, 1822
Music: John Farmer, 1892

186 Fling wide the door, unbar the gate

MACHT HOCH DIE TÜR 88. 88. 88. 66

1 Fling wide the door, un-bar the gate! The King of glo-ry comes in state; the Lord of lords and King of kings, the Sav-ior of the world who brings his great sal-va-tion to the earth. So raise a shout of ho-ly mirth and

2 He is the Rock of our be-lief, the heart of mer-cy's gen-tle self. His king-ly crown is ho-li-ness, his scep-ter is his love-li-ness; he brings our sor-rows to an end. Now glad-ly praise our King and friend, and

3 Oh, hap-py towns and bless-ed lands that live by their true King's com-mands, and bless-ed be the hearts he rules, the hum-ble plac-es where he dwells. He is the right-ful Son of bliss who fills our lives and makes us his, Cre-

4 Come, Lord, our Sav-ior, Je-sus Christ, our hearts are o-pen wide in trust. O show us now your love-ly grace, up-on our sor-rows shine your face, and let your Ho-ly Spir-it guide our jour-ney in your grace so wide. We

Text: based on Psalm 24, Georg Weissel, "Macht hoch die Tür," *Preussische Fest-Lieder*, 1642; tr. Gracia Grindal,
        Lutheran Book of Worship, 1978
        Translation copyright ©1978 Lutheran Book of Worship
Music: *Neues Geistreiches Gesangbuch*, 1704

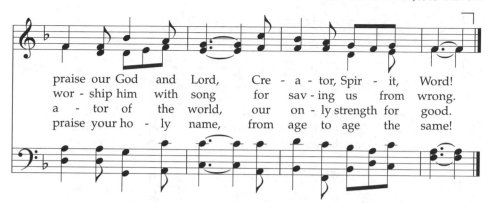

praise our God and Lord, Cre - a - tor, Spir - it, Word!
wor - ship him with song for sav - ing us from wrong.
a - tor of the world, our on - ly strength for good.
praise your ho - ly name, from age to age the same!

Let the heavens be glad 187

Canon   Irregular

1 Let the heav'ns be glad and the earth re -
      for - ests shout, let them sing, let them

joice. Let the sea and all with-in it roar. Let
shout; ev - 'ry path made straight be-fore the Lord. With

fields and all they bear be thrilled be-fore the Lord, the
joy - ful sound, with danc - ing down up-on the earth, the

Lord is come. 2 Let the
Lord is   come.

Text: based on Psalm 96:11-13, John B. Foley, S.J.
Music: John B. Foley, S.J., 1975
          Text and music copyright ©1977 John B. Foley, S.J., and New Dawn Music

188 Sleepers, wake

WACHET AUF 898. 898. 664. 88

1 "Sleep-ers, wake!" A voice as-tounds _____ us. The shout of ram-
2 Zi - on hears the night-watch sing - ing. Her heart with joy-
3 Lamb of God, the heav'ns a-dore _____ you. Let saints and an-

part guards sur-rounds us: "A-wake, Je-ru-sa-lem, a-rise!"
ful hope is spring-ing. She wakes and hur-ries through the night.
gels sing be-fore you, as harps and cym-bals swell the sound.

Mid - night's peace their cry has bro - ken, their ur-gent sum-
Forth he comes, the Bride-groom glo - rious in strength of grace,
Twelve great pearls, the cit - y's por - tals: through them we stream

mons clear-ly spo - ken: "The time has come, O maid-ens wise!
in truth vic - to - rious; her star is ris'n, her light grows bright.
to join th'im-mor - tals as we with joy your throne sur-round.

Text: Philipp Nicolai, "Wachet auf, ruft uns die Stimme," *Appendix to Freuden-Spiegel des ewigen Lebens,* 1599; tr. Carl P. Daw, Jr., and others, alt.
Translation copyright©1982 Hope Publishing Co.
Music: Philipp Nicolai, *Appendix to Freuden-Spiegel des ewigen Lebens,* 1599

Rise up, and give us light. The Bride - groom is in sight.
Now come, most wor - thy Lord, God's Son, In - car - nate Word.
No eye has known the sight, no ear heard such de - light.

Al - le - lu - ia! Your lamps pre - pare and has - ten there,
Al - le - lu - ia! We fol - low all in - to the hall
Al - le - lu - ia! There - fore we sing to greet our King.

that you the wed - ding feast may share."
to join the wed - ding fes - ti - val.
For - ev - er let our prais - es ring.

189 To us a Child of hope is born

ZERAH CM extended

1 To us a Child of hope is born, to us a
2 His name shall be the Prince of peace, for - ev - er-
3 His pow'r, in - creas - ing, still shall spread, his reign no

Son is giv'n. Him shall the tribes of earth o - bey,
more a - dored, the Won - der - ful, the Coun - sel - or,
end shall know. Jus - tice shall guard his throne a - bove,

him all the hosts of heav'n, him shall the tribes of
the great and might - y Lord, the Won - der - ful, the
and peace a - bound be - low, jus - tice shall guard his

earth o - bey, him all the hosts of heav'n.
Coun - sel - or, the great and might - y Lord.
throne a - bove, and peace a - bound be - low.

Text: based on Isaiah 9:6-7, John Morison, *Scottish Paraphrases*, 1781
Music: Lowell Mason, *Occasional Psalm and Hymn Tunes*, 1836

'Twas in the moon of wintertime 190

JESOUS AHATONHIA 86. 86. 88 with refrain

1 'Twas in the moon of win-ter-time, when all the birds had
2 With-in a lodge of bro-ken bark the ten-der babe was
3 The ear-liest moon of win-ter-time is not so round and
4 O chil-dren of the for-est free, O seed of Man-i-

fled, the might-y Git-chi Man-i-tou* sent an-gel choirs in-
found, a rag-ged robe of rab-bit skin en-wrapped his beau-ty
fair as was the ring of glo-ry on the help-less in-fant
tou, the ho-ly child of earth and heav'n is born to-day for

stead. Be-fore their light the stars grew dim, and
'round. But as the hunt-er braves drew nigh, the
there. The chiefs from far be-fore him knelt with
you. Come kneel be-fore the ra-diant boy who

Refrain

won-d'ring hunt-ers heard the hymn:
an-gel-song rang loud and high:
gifts of fox and beav-er pelt.   Je-sus your King is born,
brings you beau-ty, peace, and joy.

Je-sus is born, in ex-cel-sis glo-ri-a.

*Translation: the mighty Lord of all the world

Text: Jean de Brébeuf, *Estennial de tsonue Jesous ahatonhia*, ca. 1643; tr. J. E. Middleton, 1926
            Translation copyright © Frederick Harris Music Co., Ltd.
Music: French folk melody

191 O little town of Bethlehem

ST. LOUIS 86. 86. 76. 86

1 O lit - tle town of Beth - le - hem, how still we see thee lie!
2 For Christ is born of Ma - ry, and gath - ered all a - bove,
3 How si - lent - ly, how si - lent - ly, the won - drous gift is giv'n!
4 O ho - ly Child of Beth - le - hem, de - scend to us, we pray,

A - bove thy deep and dream - less sleep the si - lent stars go by.
while mor - tals sleep, the an - gels keep their watch of won - d'ring love.
So God im - parts to hu - man hearts the bless - ings of the heav'ns.
cast out our sin, and en - ter in, be born in us to - day!

Yet in thy dark streets shin - eth the ev - er - last - ing light;
O morn - ing stars, to - geth - er pro - claim the ho - ly birth!
No ear may hear his com - ing, but in this world of sin,
We hear the Christ - mas an - gels the great glad tid - ings tell.

the hopes and fears of all the years are met in thee to - night.
and prais - es sing to God the King, and peace to all the earth!
where meek souls will re - ceive him still the dear Christ en - ters in.
O come to us, a - bide with us, our Lord Im - man - u - el!

Text: Phillips Brooks, 1868, *The Church Porch* ..., 1874
Music: Lewis H. Redner, 1868, *The Church Porch* ..., 1874

On this day earth shall ring 192

PERSONENT HODIE 666. 66 with refrain

1 On this day earth shall ring
2 His the doom, ours the mirth,
3 God's bright star, o'er his head,
4 On this day an - gels sing;

with the song chil-dren sing to the Lord, Christ our King,
when he came down to earth. Beth - le - hem saw his birth;
wise men three to him led. Kneel they low by his bed,
with their song earth shall ring, prais-ing Christ, heav-en's King,

born on earth to save us; him the Fa - ther gave us.
ox and ass be - side him from the cold would hide him.
lay their gifts be - fore him, praise him and a - dore him.
born on earth to save us; peace and love he gave us.

Refrain

Id - e - o - o - o, id - e - o - o - o,

id - e - o glo - ri - a in ex - cel - sis De - o!*

*Translation: Therefore, glory to God in the highest!

Text: *Piae Cantiones* ..., 1582; tr. Jane M. Joseph
          Translation copyright © J. Curwen & Sons, Ltd., London
Music: German melody, 1360, *Piae Cantiones* ..., 1582

193 Silent night, holy night

STILLE NACHT Irregular

1 Si - lent night, ho - ly night! All is calm, all is bright
2 Si - lent night, ho - ly night! Shep - herds quake at the sight,
3 Si - lent night, ho - ly night! Son of God, Love's pure light,
4 Si - lent night, ho - ly night! Won - drous star, lend thy light.

'round yon vir - gin moth-er and child! Ho - ly In - fant, so ten-der and mild,
glo - ries stream from heav-en a - far, heav'n-ly hosts sing, "Al-le-lu - ia!
ra - diant, beams from thy ho-ly face with the dawn of re - deem-ing grace,
With the an - gels let us sing "Al - le-lu - ia" to our King,

sleep in heav-en-ly peace, sleep in heav-en-ly peace.
Christ the Sav - ior is born, Christ the Sav - ior is born."
Je - sus, Lord, at thy birth, Je - sus, Lord, at thy birth.
"Christ the Sav - ior is born, Christ the Sav - ior is born."

1 Stille Nacht! Heilige Nacht!
Alles schläft, einsam wacht
nur das traute hoch heilige Paar.
"Holder Knabe im lockigen Haar,
schlaf in himmlischer Ruh',
schlaf in himmlischer Ruh'!"

2 Stille Nacht! Heilige Nacht!
Hirten erst kundgemacht.
Durch der Engel Halleluja
tönt es laut von fern und nah:
Christ, der Retter ist da,
Christ, der Retter ist da!

3 Stille Nacht! Heilige Nacht!
Gottes Sohn, o wie lacht
Lieb' aus deinem göttlichen Mund,
da uns schlägt die rettende Stund':
Christ, in deiner Geburt.
Christ, in deiner Geburt.

4 Stille Nacht! Heilige Nacht,
die der Welt Heil gebracht;
aus des Himmels goldenen Höhn,
uns der Gnade Fülle laßt sehn:
Jesum in Menschengestalt,
Jesum in Menschengestalt.

Text: Joseph Mohr, "Stille Nacht, Heilige Nacht," 1818, *Leipziger Gesangbuch*, 1838; tr. John F. Young, *The Sunday School Service and Tune Book*, 1863
Music: Franz Gruber, 1818, *Leipziger Gesangbuch*, 1838

Away in a manger

CRADLE SONG 11 11. 11 11

194

1 A - way in a man - ger, no crib for a
2 The cat - tle are low - ing, the ba - by a -
3 Be near me, Lord Je - sus, I ask thee to

bed, the lit - tle Lord Je - sus laid down his sweet
wakes, but lit - tle Lord Je - sus no cry - ing he
stay close by me for - ev - er, and love me, I

head. The stars in the bright sky looked down where he
makes. I love thee, Lord Je - sus! Look down from the
pray. Bless all the dear chil - dren in thy ten - der

lay, the lit - tle Lord Je - sus a - sleep on the hay.
sky, and stay by my side un - til morn - ing is nigh.
care, and fit us for heav - en to live with thee there.

Text: anonymous, *Little Children's Book* ... (Sts. 1-2), 1885, *Vineyard Songs* (St. 3), 1892
Music: William J. Kirkpatrick, *Around the World with Christmas*, 1895; arranged by Joan A. Fyock
            Arrangement copyright ©1989 Joan A. Fyock

195 It came upon a midnight clear

CAROL CMD

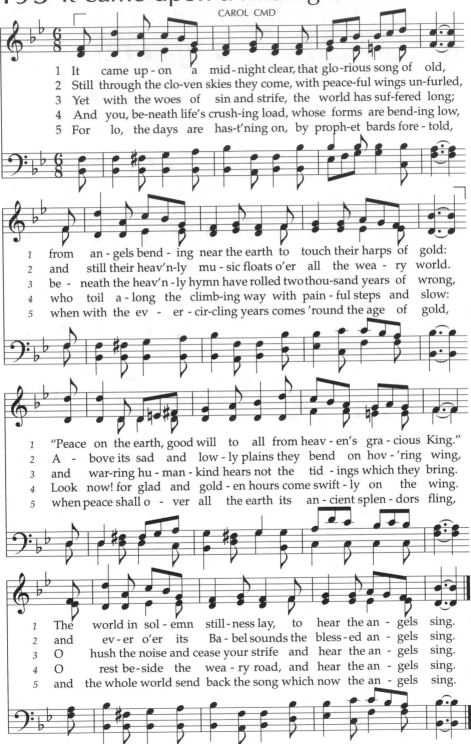

1 It came up-on a mid-night clear, that glo-rious song of old,
2 Still through the clo-ven skies they come, with peace-ful wings un-furled,
3 Yet with the woes of sin and strife, the world has suf-fered long;
4 And you, be-neath life's crush-ing load, whose forms are bend-ing low,
5 For lo, the days are has-t'ning on, by proph-et bards fore-told,

1 from an-gels bend-ing near the earth to touch their harps of gold:
2 and still their heav'n-ly mu-sic floats o'er all the wea-ry world.
3 be-neath the heav'n-ly hymn have rolled two thou-sand years of wrong,
4 who toil a-long the climb-ing way with pain-ful steps and slow:
5 when with the ev-er-cir-cling years comes 'round the age of gold,

1 "Peace on the earth, good will to all from heav-en's gra-cious King."
2 A-bove its sad and low-ly plains they bend on hov-'ring wing,
3 and war-ring hu-man-kind hears not the tid-ings which they bring.
4 Look now! for glad and gold-en hours come swift-ly on the wing.
5 when peace shall o-ver all the earth its an-cient splen-dors fling,

1 The world in sol-emn still-ness lay, to hear the an-gels sing.
2 and ev-er o'er its Ba-bel sounds the bless-ed an-gels sing.
3 O hush the noise and cease your strife and hear the an-gels sing.
4 O rest be-side the wea-ry road, and hear the an-gels sing.
5 and the whole world send back the song which now the an-gels sing.

Text: Edmund H. Sears, *Christian Register*, 1849, alt.
Music: Richard S. Willis, *Church Chorals and Choir Studies*, 1850

While shepherds watched 196

WINCHESTER OLD CM

1 While shep - herds watched their flocks by night, all
2 "Fear not," said he, for might - y dread had
3 "To you, in Da - vid's town, this day is
4 "The heav'n - ly Babe you there shall find to
5 Thus spoke the ser - aph and forth - with ap -
6 "All glo - ry be to God on high and

1 seat - ed on the ground, the an - gel of the
2 seized their trou - bled mind. "Glad tid - ings of great
3 born of Da - vid's line the Sav - ior, who is
4 hu - man view dis - played, all hum - bly wrapped in
5 peared a shin - ing throng of an - gels prais - ing
6 to the earth be peace, good - will hence-forth from

1 Lord came down, and glo - ry shone a - round.
2 joy I bring to you and hu - man - kind.
3 Christ the Lord, and this shall be the sign:
4 swath - ing bands, and in a man - ger laid."
5 God, and thus ad - dressed their joy - ful song:
6 heav - en to be - gin and nev - er cease!"

Text: based on Luke 2:8-14, Nahum Tate, *A Supplement to the New Version of the Psalms*, 1700, alt.
Music: Thomas Est's *The Whole Booke of Psalmes ...*, 1592

197 Angels we have heard on high

GLORIA 77. 77 with refrain

1 An - gels we have heard on high, sing - ing sweet - ly through the night,
2 Shep - herds, why this ju - bi - lee? Why these songs of hap - py cheer?
3 Come to Beth - le - hem and see him whose birth the an - gels sing.
4 See him in a man - ger laid whom the an - gels praise a - bove.

and the moun - tains in re - ply ech - o - ing their brave de - light.
What great bright - ness did you see? What glad tid - ings did you hear?
Come, a - dore on bend - ed knee Christ, the Lord, the new - born King.
Ma - ry, Jo - seph, lend your aid, while we raise our hearts in love.

Refrain

Glo - - - ri - a

in ex - cel - sis De - o, glo -

Text: *Nouveau Recueil de Cantiques*, 1855; tr. anonymous, altered by Earl Marlatt, *New Church Hymnal*, 1937
Music: traditional French carol, *Nouveau Recueil de Cantiques*, 1855

- ri - a   in ex - cel - sis   De - o.

Let our gladness have no end 198

NARODIL SE KRISTUS PÁN 74. 74. 666

1 Let our glad-ness have no end,   hal - le - lu - jah!
2 See, the love-liest bloom-ing Rose,   hal - le - lu - jah!
3 In - to flesh is made the Word,   hal - le - lu - jah!

for to earth did Christ de-scend.   Hal - le - lu - jah!   On this day God
from the branch of Jes - se grows.   Hal - le - lu - jah!
Christ, our ref -uge and our Lord.   Hal - le - lu - jah!

gave   us   Christ, the Son, to save   us,   Christ, the Son, to save   us.

Text: *Kancional*, 1602; tr. anonymous
Music: Bohemian carol, 15th c.; harmonized by Richard Hillert, *The Lutheran Hymnal*, 1941
Setting copyright ©1978 *Lutheran Book of Worship*

199 The first Noel, the angel did say

THE FIRST NOEL Irregular with refrain

1 The first No - el, the an - gel did say, was to
2 They look - ed up and saw a star shin-ing
3 And by the light of that same star three
4 This star drew nigh to the North - west, o'er
5 Then en - tered in those wise men three, full

1 cer - tain poor shep-herds in fields as they lay — in fields where
2 in the East, be - yond them far, and to the
3 wise men came from coun - try far. To seek for a
4 Beth - le - hem it took its rest, and there it
5 rev - 'rent - ly up - on the knee, and of - fered

1 they lay keep - ing their sheep, on a cold win - ter's
2 earth it gave great light, and so it con -
3 king was their in - tent, and to fol - low the
4 did both stop and stay, right o - ver the
5 there in his pres - ence, their gold — and

Refrain

1 night that was so deep.
2 tin - ued both day and night.
3 star wher - ev - er it went. No - el, No - el, No -
4 place where Je - sus lay.
5 myrrh and frank - in - cense.

Text: English carol, *Some Ancient Christmas Carols ...*, 2nd ed., 1823
Music: English carol, *Christmas Carols*, 1833; harmonized by John Stainer, 1871

el, No - el, born is the King of Is - ra - el.

Where is this stupendous Stranger? 200

McRAE 87. 87

1 Where is this stu - pen - dous Stran - ger? Proph - ets,
2 O most Might - y, O most Ho - ly, far be -
3 Oh, the mag - ni - tude of meek - ness! worth from
4 God all - boun - teous, all - cre - a - tive, whom no

shep - herds, kings, ad - vise! Lead me to my Mas - ter's
yond the ser - aph's thought, art thou then so mean and
worth im - mor - tal sprung! Oh, the strength of in - fant
ills from good dis - suade, is in - car - nate and a

man - ger, show me where my Sav - ior lies.
low - ly as un - heed - ed proph - ets thought?
weak - ness, if e - ter - nal is so young!
na - tive of the ver - y world he made.

Text: Christopher Smart, *Hymns and Spiritual Songs …*, 1765, alt.
Music: Joan A. Fyock, 1989
       Copyright ©1989 Joan A. Fyock

201 Hark! the herald angels sing

MENDELSSOHN 77.77D

1 Hark! the her-ald an-gels sing, "Glo-ry to the new-born King!
2 Christ, by high-est heav'n a-dored; Christ, the ev-er - last-ing Lord,
3 Hail, the heav'n-born Prince of peace! Hail, the Sun of right-eous-ness!

Peace on earth, and mer-cy mild, God and sin-ners rec - on-ciled!"
late in time be - hold him come, off-spring of the vir-gin's womb.
Light and life to all he brings, ris'n with heal-ing in his wings.

Joy - ful all ye na-tions, rise, join the tri-umph of the skies,
Veiled in flesh the God-head see, hail th'In-car-nate De - i - ty;
Mild he lays his glo-ry by, born that we no more may die,

with th'an-gel - ic host pro-claim, "Christ is born in Beth-le-hem."
pleased with us in flesh to dwell; Je - sus, our Im - man-u - el!
born to raise us from the earth, born to give us sec-ond birth.

Text: Charles Wesley and others, *Hymns and Sacred Poems*, 1739, alt.
Music: Felix Mendelssohn, 1840; adapted by William H. Cummings, 1855, *Congregational Hymn and Tune Book*, 1857

Hark! the her-ald an-gels sing, "Glo-ry to the new-born King!"

The virgin Mary had a baby boy 202

Irregular with refrain

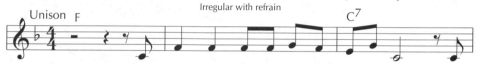

Unison F

1 The vir - gin Ma - ry had a ba - by boy, the
2 The an - gels sang when the ba - by born, the
3 The wise men saw when the ba - by born, the

vir - gin Ma - ry had a ba - by boy, the vir - gin Ma - ry had a
an - gels sang when the ba - by born, the an - gels sang when the
wise men saw where the ba - by born, the wise men went where the

ba - by boy,
ba - by born, and they say that his name was Je - sus.
ba - by born,

Refrain F

He come from the glo - ry, he come from the glo-rious king-dom.

Oh, yes! be - liev - er! Oh, yes! be - liev - er!

He come from the glo - ry, he come from the glo-rious king-dom.

Text: West Indian carol, from the *Edric Conner Collection of West Indian Spirituals*
Music: West Indian carol, from the *Edric Conner Collection of West Indian Spirituals*
Text and music copyright ©1945 Boosey & Co., Ltd.; copyright renewed

203 Break forth, O beauteous heavenly

ERMUNTRE DICH 87. 87. 88. 77

1 Break forth, O beau-teous heav'n-ly light, and
2 This night of won-der, night of joy, was
3 Come, dear-est child, in-to our hearts, and

ush-er in the morn - ing. O shep-herds, shrink not
born the Christ, our broth - er. He comes, not might-y
leave your crib be - hind you! Let this be where the

with af - fright, but hear the an-gel's warn - ing. This
to de-stroy, to bid us love each oth - er. How
new life starts for all who seek and find you. To

child, now weak in in - fan-cy, our con - fi - dence and
could he quit his king - ly state for such a world of
you be hon - or, thanks, and praise, for all your gifts this

Text: Johann Rist, "Ermuntre dich, mein schwacher Geist," *Himmlische Lieder,* 1641; tr. John Troutbeck (St. 1), ca. 1885,
Fred Pratt Green (Sts. 2-3), 1986
Translation (Sts. 2-3), copyright ©1989 Hope Publishing Co.
Music: Johann Schop, *Himmlische Lieder,* 1641; harmonized by J. S. Bach, *Christmas Oratorio,* 1734

joy shall be, the power of Sa - tan
greed and hate? What deep hu - mil - i -
time of grace. Come con - quer and de -

break - ing, our peace e - ter - nal mak - ing.
a - tion se - cured the world's sal - va - tion!
liv - er this world, and us, for - ev - er.

Gloria

GLORIA III

204

Canon 1 Dm Gm C F 2 Dm Gm C F

Glo - ri - a, glo - ri - a, in ex - cel - sis De - o!

3 Dm Gm C F 4 Dm Gm C F

Glo - ri - a, glo - ri - a, al - le - lu - ia, al - le - lu - ia!

Music: Jacques Berthier, *Music from Taizé*, Vol. I, 1978, 1980, 1981

205 From heaven above to earth I come

VOM HIMMEL HOCH LM

1 From heav'n a - bove to earth I come to
2 To you this night is born a child of
3 This is the Christ, God's Son most high, who
4 Wel - come to earth, O no - ble Guest, through
5 My heart for ver - y joy now leaps. My
6 "Glo - ry to God in high - est heav'n, who

1 bear good news to ev - 'ry - one. Glad tid - ings of great
2 Ma - ry, cho - sen vir - gin mild. This new - born child, of
3 hears your sad and bit - ter cry. He will him - self your
4 whom this sin - ful world is bless'd! You turned not from our
5 voice no long - er si - lence keeps. I, too, must join the
6 un - to us a Son has giv'n." With an - gels sing in

1 joy I bring to all the world, and glad - ly sing:
2 low - ly birth, shall be the joy of all the earth.
3 Sav - ior be and from all sin will set you free.
4 needs a - way! How can our thanks such love re - pay?
5 an - gel - throng to sing with joy his cra - dle - song.
6 joy - ful mirth – a glad new year to all the earth!

Text: Martin Luther, "Vom Himmel Hoch," *Geistliche Lieder,* Wittenberg, 1535; tr. Catherine Winkworth, *Lyra Germanica,*
          Series I, 1855, and composite translation by Inter-Lutheran Commission on Worship, 1978
          Translation copyright ©1978 *Lutheran Book of Worship.* Used by permission of Augsburg Fortress
Music: *Geistliche Lieder,* Leipzig, 1539

Infant holy, Infant lowly

206

W ŻŁOBIE LEŻY 87. 87. 88. 77

1 In - fant ho - ly, In - fant low - ly, for his bed a cat - tle stall;
2 Flocks were sleep-ing, shep-herds keep-ing vi-gil till the morn-ing new,

ox - en low - ing, lit - tle know - ing Christ the babe is Lord of all.
saw the glo - ry, heard the sto - ry — tid-ings of a gos-pel true.

Swift-ly wing-ing an-gels sing-ing, bells are ring-ing, tid-ings bring-ing:
Thus re-joic-ing, free from sor-row, prais-es voic-ing, greet the mor-row:

Christ the babe is Lord of all, Christ the babe is Lord of all!
Christ the babe was born for you, Christ the babe was born for you!

Text: Polish carol; tr. Edith M. G. Reed, *Music and Youth*, 1925, *Panpipes*, 1925
Music: Polish folk melody; adapted by A. E. Rusbridge
Harmonization copyright © Rosalind Rusbridge

207

Niño lindo
(Child so lovely)

CARACAS Irregular with refrain

Estribillo (Refrain)

Ni - ño lin - do, an - te ti me rin - do, ni - ño
Child so love - ly, here I kneel be - fore you, child so

lin - do, e - res tú mi Dios. Ni - ño lin - do,
love - ly, you are Christ, my God. Child so love - ly,

an - te ti me rin - do; ni - ño lin - do,
here I kneel be - fore you, child so love - ly,

e - res tú mi Dios. Dios. Fine
you are Christ, the Lord. Lord.

1 E - sa tu her - mo -
2 La vi - da, bien
1 You have heav - en's
2 All my life, my

1 su - ra; e - se tu can - dor, el al - ma me ro - ba,
2 mí - o, y el al - ma tam - bién; te o - frez - co, gus - to - so,
1 beau - ty, and God's pur - i - ty, steal - ing my de - vo - tion,
2 dar - ling, and my soul, as well; this is what I of - fer,

1 el al - ma me ro - ba, me ro - ba el a - mor.
2 te o - frez - co, gus - to - so, ren - di - do a tus pies.
1 steal - ing my af - fec - tion, steal - ing all my soul.
2 of - fer joy - ous - ly fall - ing at your feet.

D.C.

Text: Venezuelan hymn; tr. George Lockwood IV, 1987, *The United Methodist Hymnal,* 1989
English translation copyright ©1989 The United Methodist Publishing House
Music: Venezuelan melody

Love came down at Christmas 208

LOVE INCARNATE 67. 67 with refrain

1 Love came down at Christ - mas, love all love - ly,
2 Wor - ship we the God - head, love in - car - nate,
3 Love shall be our to - ken, love be yours and

love di - vine. Love was born at Christ - mas –
love di - vine. Wor - ship we our Je - sus –
love be mine, love to God and neigh - bor,

Refrain

star and an - gels gave the sign.
what shall be our sa - cred sign? Sing no - el,
love for prayer and gift and sign. Sing no-

sing no - el, sing no - el.
el, sing no - el.

Text: Christina G. Rossetti, *Time Flies: A Reading Diary,* 1885; revised in *Hymns for Today's Church,* 1982
Copyright ©1982 Hope Publishing Co.
Music: C. Edgar Pettman, *University Carol Book,* 1923

209 Oh, how joyfully

O SANCTISSIMA 557. 447

1 Oh, how joy-ful-ly, oh, how hope-ful-ly, waits the
2 Oh, how joy-ful-ly, oh, how peace-ful-ly, sleeps the
3 Oh, how joy-ful-ly, oh, how thank-ful-ly, wakes the

earth on Christ-mas eve! Love comes heal - ing, God re-
earth on Christ-mas night! Sins are cov - ered, grace dis-
earth on Christ-mas morn! God has spo - ken, death is

veal - ing. Friends, be joy - ful and be - lieve!
cov - ered. In our dark - ness shines the light!
bro - ken. Al - le - lu - ia! Christ is born!

1 O du fröhliche,
O du selige,
gnadenbringende Weihnachtszeit!
Welt ging verloren;
Christ ist geboren:
Freue, freue dich, O Christenheit!

2 O du fröhliche,
O du selige,
gnadenbringende Weihnachtszeit!
Christ ist erschienen,
uns zu versühnen,
Freue, freue dich, O Christenheit!

3 O du fröhliche,
O du selige,
gnadenbringende Weihnachtszeit!
Himmlische Heere
jauchzen dir Ehre.
Freue, freue dich, O Christenheit!

Text: Johannes D. Falk (St. 1), *Auserlesene Werke*, 1819, Heinrich Holzschuher (Sts. 2-3); tr. Harris J. Loewen, re-envisioned by
        Brian Wren, 1990
        Copyright ©1990 Hope Publishing Co.

Music: *The European Magazine and London Review*, 1792; arranged by Robert Shaw and Alice Parker, 1953
        Arrangement copyright ©1953, renewed G. Schirmer, Inc.

Good Christian friends, rejoice 210

IN DULCI JUBILO 66. 77. 78. 55

1 Good Chris-tian friends, re - joice, with heart and soul and voice.
2 Good Chris-tian friends, re - joice, with heart and soul and voice.
3 Good Chris-tian friends, re - joice, with heart and soul and voice.

Give ye heed to what we say: Je - sus Christ is born to - day!
Now ye hear of end - less bliss; Je - sus Christ was born for this!
Now ye need not fear the grave; Je - sus Christ was born to save!

Ox and ass be - fore him bow, and he is in the man - ger now.
He has o - pened heav-en's door, and we are bless'd for - ev - er-more.
Calls you one and calls you all, to gain his ev - er - last - ing hall.

Christ is born to - day! Christ is born to - day!
Christ was born for this! Christ was born for this!
Christ was born to save! Christ was born to save!

Text: *In dulci jubilo*, 14th c.; tr. John M. Neale, *Carols for Christmastide,* 1853, alt.
Music: *Geistliche Lieder,* 1535; harmonized by Robert L. Pearsall

211 Lo, how a Rose e'er blooming

ES IST EIN ROS' 76. 76. 676

1 Lo, how a Rose e'er bloom-ing from ten-der stem has sprung!
2 I - sa-iah 'twas fore-told it, the Rose I have in mind.
3 Flow-er, whose fra-grance ten - der with sweet-ness fills the air,

Of Jes-se's lin-eage com - ing as saints of old have sung.
With Ma - ry we be - hold it, the vir - gin moth - er kind.
dis - pel in glo-rious splen-dor the dark-ness ev - 'ry - where.

It came, a flow'r - et bright, a - mid the
To show God's love a - right, she bore to
True man, yet ver - y God, from sin and

cold of win - ter, when half-spent was the night.
us a Sav - ior, when half-spent was the night.
death he saves us, and light-ens ev - 'ry load.

Text: anonymous, *Es ist ein Ros' entsprungen* (Sts. 1-2), *Alte Catholische Geistliche Kirchengeseng*, 1599, Friedrich Layritz (St. 3),
    Liederschatz, 1832; tr. Theodore Baker (Sts. 1-2), 1894, Harriet K. Spaeth (St. 3), 1875, *The Hymnal 1940*, alt.
Music: *Alte Catholische Geistliche Kirchengeseng*, 1599; harmonized by Michael Praetorius, *Musae Sionae, VI*, 1609

O come, all ye faithful

212

ADESTE FIDELES Irregular

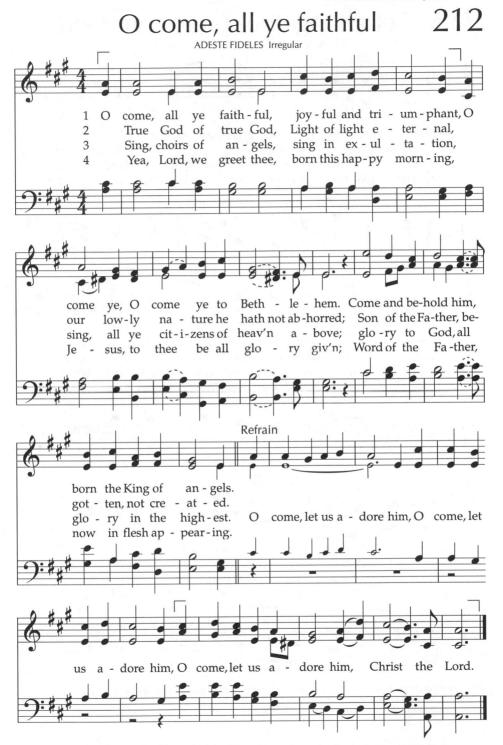

1 O come, all ye faith-ful, joy-ful and tri-um-phant, O
2 True God of true God, Light of light e-ter-nal,
3 Sing, choirs of an-gels, sing in ex-ul-ta-tion,
4 Yea, Lord, we greet thee, born this hap-py morn-ing,

come ye, O come ye to Beth-le-hem. Come and be-hold him,
our low-ly na-ture he hath not ab-horred; Son of the Fa-ther, be-
sing, all ye cit-i-zens of heav'n a-bove; glo-ry to God, all
Je-sus, to thee be all glo-ry giv'n; Word of the Fa-ther,

born the King of an-gels.
got-ten, not cre-at-ed.
glo-ry in the high-est. O come, let us a-dore him, O come, let
now in flesh ap-pear-ing.

Refrain

us a-dore him, O come, let us a-dore him, Christ the Lord.

Text: John F. Wade, ca. 1743, *Adeste fideles laeti triumphantes*, Office de St. Omer (Sts.1,3-4), 1822, Etienne J. F. Borderies
(St. 2), 1822; tr. Frederick Oakeley and others (Sts. 1,3-4), 1841, alt., William Mercer (St. 2), 1854
Music: attributed to John F. Wade, ca. 1743, *Essay on the Church Plain Chant*, 1782

213 Let all together praise our God

LOBT GOTT, IHR CHRISTEN CM extended

1 Let all to-geth-er praise our God up-on the loft-y
2 Christ lays a-side his maj-es-ty and seems as noth-ing
3 Be-hold the won-der-ful ex-change our Lord with us doth
4 The glo-rious gates of par-a-dise the an-gel guards no

throne, for God un-locks the heav'ns to-day and
worth, and takes on him a ser-vant's form, who
make! Lo, he as-sumes our flesh and blood, and
more. This day a-gain those gates un-fold; with

gives to us a Son, and gives to us a Son.
made the heav'n and earth, who made the heav'n and earth.
we of heav'n par-take, and we of heav'n par-take.
praise our God a-dore, with praise our God a-dore!

Text: Nicolaus Hermann, *Lobt Gott, ihr Christen alle gleich,* ca.1554, *Die Sonntags Evangelia über das gantze Jahr,* 1560;
        tr. Arthur T. Russell, *Psalms and Hymns,* 1851
Music: Nicolaus Hermann, *Ein Christlicher Abentreien,* 1554; harmonized by J. S. Bach, Cantata No. 151, 1725

Morning Star, O cheering sight 214

HAGEN 77. 33. 7

1 Morn-ing Star, O cheer-ing sight! Ere thou cam'st how
2 Morn-ing Star, thy glo-ry bright far ex-cels the
3 Thy glad beams, thou Morn-ing Star, cheer the na-tions
4 Morn-ing Star, my soul's true light, tar-ry not, dis-

dark earth's night! Morn-ing Star, O cheer-ing sight! Ere thou
sun's clear light. Morn-ing Star, thy glo-ry bright far ex-
near and far. Thy glad beams, thou Morn-ing Star, cheer the
pel my night. Morn-ing Star, my soul's true light, tar-ry

cam'st how dark earth's night! Je-sus mine, in me shine; in me
cels the sun's clear light. Je-sus be, con-stant-ly, con-stant-
na-tions near and far. Thee we own, Lord a-lone, Lord a-
not, dis-pel my night. Je-sus mine, in me shine; in me

shine, Je-sus mine. Fill my heart with light di-vine.
ly, Je-sus be more than thou-sand suns to me.
lone, thee we own our great Sav-ior, God's dear Son.
shine, Je-sus mine. Fill my heart with light di-vine.

Text: Johann Scheffler, 1657; tr. Bennet Harvey, Jr., 1885
Music: Francis F. Hagen, 1836

215 What Child is this

GREENSLEEVES 87. 87. 68. 67

1 What Child is this, who, laid to rest, on Ma - ry's
2 Why lies he in such mean es - tate where ox and
3 So bring him in - cense, gold, and myrrh, come, peas - ant,

lap is sleep - ing, whom an - gels greet with an - thems
ass are feed - ing? Good Chris - tian, fear, for sin - ners
king, to own him. The King of kings sal - va - tion

sweet, while shep - herds watch are keep - ing? This, this is
here the si - lent Word is plead - ing. Nails, spear shall
brings, let lov - ing hearts en - throne him. Raise, raise the

Christ the King, whom shep - herds guard and an - gels sing.
pierce him through, the cross be borne for me, for you.
song on high; the vir - gin sings her lul - la - by.

Text: William C. Dix, *The Manger Throne*, ca.1865
Music: traditional English melody

Haste, haste to bring him laud,
Hail, hail the Word-made-flesh, the babe, the son of Ma-ry!
Joy, joy for Christ is born,

Christ, whose glory fills the skies 216
LUX PRIMA 77. 77. 77

1 Christ, whose glo - ry fills the skies, Christ, the true, the on - ly light,
2 Dark and cheer-less is the morn un - ac - com - pan - ied by thee.
3 Vis - it, then, this soul of mine. Pierce the gloom of sin and grief.

Sun of right-eous-ness, a - rise, tri - umph o'er the shades of night.
Joy - less is the day's re - turn till thy mer - cy's beams I see.
Fill me, Ra-dian - cy di - vine. Scat - ter all my un - be - lief.

Day-spring from on high, be near; Day-star, in my heart ap-pear.
Till they in-ward light im - part, glad my eyes and warm my heart.
More and more thy - self dis-play, shin-ing to the per - fect day.

Text: Charles Wesley, *Hymns and Sacred Poems,* 1740
Music: Charles F. Gounod, *The Hymnary,* 1872

217 When Christ's appearing

ERHALT UNS, HERR LM

1 When Christ's ap - pear - ing was made known, King Her - od
2 The east - ern sag - es saw from far and fol - lowed
3 With - in the Jor - dan's sa - cred flood the heav'n - ly
4 And oh, what mir - a - cle di - vine, when wa - ter
5 For this his glad e - piph - a - ny, all glo - ry

1 trem - bled for his throne. But he who of - fers
2 on his guid - ing star. By light their way to
3 Lamb in meek - ness stood, that he, of whom no
4 red - dened in - to wine! He spoke the word, and
5 un - to Je - sus be, whom with the Fa - ther

1 heav'n - ly birth seeks not the king - doms of this earth.
2 light they trod, and by their gifts con - fessed their God.
3 sin was known, might cleanse his peo - ple from their own.
4 forth it flowed in streams that na - ture ne'er be - stowed.
5 we a - dore, and Ho - ly Ghost for - ev - er - more.

Text: Coelius Sedulius, *Hostis Herodes impie,* 5th c.; tr. *The Hymn Book* (St. 1), 1971, composite translation, including
John M. Neale (Sts. 2-5)
Translation (St. 1) copyright ©1971 *The Hymn Book*
Music: attributed to Martin Luther, *Geistliche Lieder,* 1543

As with gladness men of old 218

DIX 77.77.77

1 As with glad-ness men of old did the guid-ing
2 As with joy-ful steps they sped, Sav-ior, to thy
3 As they of-fered gifts most rare at thy cra-dle
4 Ho-ly Je-sus, ev-'ry day keep us in the
5 In the heav'n-ly coun-try bright need they no cre-

1 star be-hold, as with joy they hailed its light,
2 low-ly bed, there to bend the knee be-fore
3 rude and bare, so may we with ho-ly joy,
4 nar-row way, and, when earth-ly things are past,
5 at-ed light; thou its light, its joy, its crown,

1 lead-ing on-ward, beam-ing bright; so, most gra-cious
2 thee whom heav'n and earth a-dore; so may we with
3 pure and free from sin's al-loy, all our cost-liest
4 bring our ran-somed souls at last where they need no
5 thou its sun which goes not down. There for-ev-er

1 Lord, may we ev-er-more be led to thee.
2 will-ing feet ev-er seek thy mer-cy seat.
3 trea-sures bring, Christ, to thee, our heav'n-ly King.
4 star to guide, where no clouds thy glo-ry hide.
5 may we sing al-le-lu-ias to our King.

Text: William C. Dix, ca. 1858, *Hymns of Love and Joy*, ca. 1860
Music: Conrad Kocher, *Stimmen aus dem Reiche Gottes*, 1838; adapted by William H. Monk, *Hymns Ancient and Modern*, 1861

219 Bright and glorious is the sky

DEJLIG ER DEN HIMMEL BLAA 77. 88. 77

1 Bright and glo-rious is the sky, ra-diant are the
2 Sag-es from the East a-far, when they saw this
3 Him they found in Beth-le-hem, yet he wore no
4 Guid-ed by the star, they found him whose praise the
5 As a star, God's ho-ly word leads us to our

1 heav-ens high where the gold-en star is shin-ing,
2 won-drous star, went to find the King of na-tions
3 di-a-dem. They but saw a maid-en low-ly
4 ag-es sound. We too have a star to guide us
5 King and Lord. Bright-ly from its sa-cred pag-es

1 all its rays to earth in-clin-ing, lead-ing to the
2 and to of-fer their ob-la-tions un-to him as
3 with an in-fant pure and ho-ly rest-ing in her
4 that for-ev-er will pro-vide us with the light to
5 shall this light through-out the ag-es shine up-on our

1 new-born King, lead-ing to the new-born King.
2 Lord and King, un-to him as Lord and King.
3 lov-ing arms, rest-ing in her lov-ing arms.
4 find our Lord, with the light to find our Lord.
5 path of life, shine up-on our path of life.

Text: Nikolai F. S. Grundtvig, 1810, *Sandsigeren,* 1811; tr. Jens C. Aaberg and *Service Book and Hymnal,* 1958
        Translation copyright ©1958 *Service Book and Hymnal*
Music: Danish melody, ca.1840, *Melodier til den af Roeskildes ...,* 1853

Worship the Lord in the beauty 220

WAS LEBET, WAS SCHWEBET 12 10. 12 10

1,5 Wor - ship the Lord in the beau - ty of ho - li - ness,
2 Low at his feet lay your bur - den of care - ful - ness,
3 Fear not to en - ter his courts in the slen - der - ness
4 these, though we bring them in trem - bling and fear - ful - ness,

bow down be - fore him, his glo - ry pro - claim.
high on his heart he will bear it for you,
of the poor wealth you would count as your own.
he will ac - cept for the Name that is dear,

Gold of o - be - dience and in - cense of low - li - ness
com - fort your sor - rows, and an - swer your prayer - ful - ness,
Truth in its beau - ty, and love in its ten - der - ness –
morn - ings of joy give for eve - nings of tear - ful - ness,

bring and a - dore him; the Lord is his name!
guid - ing your steps in a way that is true.
these are the of - f'rings to bring to his throne;
trust for our trem - bling, and hope for our fear.

Text: John S. B. Monsell, *Hymns of Love and Praise*, 1st ed., 1863, alt.
Music: *Manuscript Chorale Book*, 1754

221 Hail the bless'd morn

STAR IN THE EAST 11 10. 11 10D

1 Hail the bless'd morn, see the great Me - di - a - tor
2 Shall we not yield him, in cost - ly de - vo - tion,
3 Vain - ly we of - fer each am - ple ob - la - tion,

down from the re - gion of glo - ry de - scend!
fra - grance of E - dom and of - f'rings di - vine,
vain - ly with gifts would his fa - vor se - cure.

Shep - herds, go wor - ship the babe in the man - ger,
gems of the moun - tain and pearls of the o - cean,
Rich - er by far is the heart's ad - o - ra - tion,

lo, for his guard the bright an - gels at - tend.
myrrh from the for - est or gold from the mine?
dear - er to God are the prayers of the poor.

Text: Reginald Heber, *Christian Observer*, 1811, alt.
Music: *Southern Harmony*, 1835; harmonized by Alice Parker
Harmonization copyright ©1990 Alice Parker

222 How brightly beams the morning

WIE SCHÖN LEUCHTET DER MORGENSTERN 887. 887. 4 12 8

1 How bright-ly beams the morn-ing star! What sud-den ra -
2 Come, heav'n-ly Bride-groom, Light di-vine, and deep with-in
3 Oh, let the harps break forth in sound! Our joy be all

diance from a - far, a - glow with grace and mer - cy!
our hearts now shine. There light a flame un - dy - ing!
with mu - sic crowned, our voic - es rich - ly blend - ing!

Of Ja - cob's race, King Da-vid's son, our Lord and Mas -
In your one bod - y let us be as liv - ing branch -
For Christ goes with us all the way, to-day, to - mor -

Text: Philipp Nicolai, "Wie schön leuchtet der Morgenstern," *Appendix to Freuden-Spiegel des ewigen Lebens,* 1599; composite translation by Inter-Lutheran Commission on Worship, 1978, alt.
Translation copyright ©1978 *Lutheran Book of Worship.* Reprinted by permission of Augsburg Fortress
Text (German) from *Gesangbuch mit Noten,* ca.1905
Music: Philipp Nicolai, *Appendix to Freuden-Spiegel des ewigen Lebens,* 1599

ter, you have won our hearts to serve you on - ly!
es of a tree, your life our lives sup - ply - ing.
row, ev - 'ry day! His love is nev - er - end - ing!

Low - ly, ho - ly! great and glo - rious, all vic - to - rious,
Now, though dai - ly earth's deep sad - ness may per - plex us
Sing out! Ring out! Ju - bi - la - tion! Ex - ul - ta - tion!

rich in bless - ing! Rule in might, o'er all pos - sess - ing!
and dis - tress us, yet with heav'n - ly joy you bless us.
Tell the sto - ry! Great is he, the King of glo - ry!

1 Wie schön leucht't uns der Morgenstern
voll Gnad' und Wahrheit von dem Herrn,
aus Juda aufgegangen!
Du Davids Sohn aus Jakobs Stamm,
mein König und mein Bräutigam,
nur du bist mein Verlangen:
Lieblich, freundlich, schön und mächtig,
groß und prächtig, reich an Gaben,
hoch und wundervoll erhaben!

2 O meine Perl' und werthe Kron',
du Gottes- und des Menschen Sohn,
ein hochgeborner König!
Du bist des Herzens schönste Blum';
dein süßes Evangelium
ist lauter Milch und Honig.
Ich dein! Du mein! Hosianna!
Himmlisch Manna, das wir essen!
Deiner kann ich nicht vergessen.

3 Wie bin ich doch so herzlich froh,
daß mein Freund ist das A und Ω,
der Anfang und das Ende!
Er nimmt mich, deß bin ich gewiß,
zu Seinem Preis in's Paradies,
d'rauf fass' ich seine Hände.
Amen, Amen! Komm, du schöne
Freudenkrone, bleib' nicht lange,
daß ich ewig dich umfange.

223

Woman in the night

CANDLE 55. 55 with refrain

1 Wom-an in the night, spent from giv-ing birth,
2 Wom-an in the crowd, creep-ing up be-hind,
3 Wom-an at the well, ques-tion the Mes-siah.
4 Wom-an at the feast, let the right-eous stare.
5 Wom-an in the house, nur-tured to be meek,
6 Wom-en on the road, wel-comed and re-stored,
7 Wom-en on the hill, stand when men have fled!
8 Wom-en in the dawn, care and spic-es bring;

1 guard our pre-cious light; peace is on the earth!
2 touch-ing is al-lowed; seek and you will find!
3 Find your friends and tell; drink your heart's de-sire!
4 Come and go in peace; love him with your hair!
5 leave your se-cond place; lis-ten, think, and speak!
6 trav-el far and wide; wit-ness to the Lord!
7 Christ needs lov-ing still, though your hope is dead.
8 ear-li-est to mourn, ear-li-est to sing!

Refrain

Come and join the song, wom-en, chil-dren, men. Je-sus

Text: Brian Wren, 1982, *Faith Looking Forward,* 1983
Copyright ©1983 Hope Publishing Co.
Music: Marilyn Houser Hamm, 1990
Copyright ©1990 Marilyn Houser Hamm

makes us free to live a - gain!

The kingdom of God   224

MUSTARD SEED 13 13. 85

1 The   king-dom of God is   like a grain of   mus-tard   seed.
2 For   when it is sown, it   grows in - to   the   larg - est   plant,
3 It   grows   so birds can   rest in-side   its   crown of   leaves,
4 And   so   we can lik - en   it   to seeds which make   a   tree

When it   is sown   in the   earth it   is   the small - est   seed.
great - er than all   of the   herbs and grows in - to   a   tree.
deep in   its shad - ows a -   way from   e - vil things that   prey.
larg - er than all   of the   trees from just the small - est   seed.

It   is   like the king-dom of God   and a   mys   -   ter - y.

Text: based on Mark 4:30-34, Gracia Grindal, *Singing the Story*, 1983
Music: Austin C. Lovelace, 1987, *Hymnal Supplement II*, 1987

225 The glory of these forty days

ERHALT UNS, HERR LM

1 The glo - ry of these for - ty days we cel - e -
2 A - lone and fast - ing Mo - ses saw the lov - ing
3 So Dan - iel trained his mys - tic sight, de - liv - ered
4 Then grant that we, like them, be true, con - sumed in

brate with songs of praise, for Christ, by whom all
God who gave the law. And to E - li - jah,
from the li - on's might. And John, the Bride - groom's
fast and prayer with you. Our spir - its strength - en

things were made, him - self has fast - ed and has prayed.
fast - ing, came the steed and char - i - ots of flame.
friend, be - came the her - ald of Mes - si - ah's name.
with your grace, and give us joy to see your face.

Text: attributed to Gregory the Great, *Clarum decus jejunii*, 11th c.; tr. Maurice F. Bell, *The English Hymnal*, 1906, alt.
Translation copyright © Oxford University Press, London
Music: attributed to Martin Luther, *Geistliche Lieder*, 1543

You are salt for the earth   226

BRING FORTH THE KINGDOM Irregular

1 You   are   salt for the   earth,   O   peo - ple,
2 You   are   a light on the   hill,   O   peo - ple,
3 You   are   a seed of the   word,   O   peo - ple,
4 We   are   a bless'd and a   pil - grim   peo - ple,

salt   for   the   king - dom of God!   Share   the   fla - vor of
light   for   the   cit - y of God!   Shine   so   ho - ly and
bring   forth   the   king - dom of God!   Seeds   of   mer - cy and
bound   for   the   king - dom of God!   Love   our   jour - ney and

life,   O   peo - ple: life   in   the   king - dom of   God!
bright,   O   peo - ple: shine   for   the   king - dom of   God!
seeds   of   jus - tice,   grow   in   the   king - dom of   God!
love   our   home - land: love   is   the   king - dom of   God!

Bring   forth   the   king - dom of   mer - cy,   bring   forth   the

king - dom of peace.   Bring   forth   the   king - dom of   jus - tice,

bring   forth   the   cit - y of God!

Text: Marty Haugen, 1985, *Gather*, 1988
Music: Marty Haugen, 1985, *Gather*, 1988
Text and music copyright ©1986 G.I.A. Publications, Inc.

227

Two fishermen

LEAVE ALL THINGS BEHIND CMD with refrain

1 Two fish - er - men, who lived a - long the Sea of
2 And as he walked a - long the shore 'twas James and
3 O Si - mon Pe - ter, An - drew, James, and John be -
4 And you, good Chris - tians, one and all who'd fol - low

Gal - i - lee, stood by the shore to cast their nets
John he'd find, and these two sons of Zeb - e - dee
lov - ed one, you heard Christ's call to speak good news
Je - sus' way, come leave be - hind what keeps you bound

in - to an age - less sea. Now Je - sus watched them
would leave their boats be - hind. Their work and all they
re - vealed to God's own Son. Su - san - na, Ma - ry,
to trap - pings of our day, and lis - ten as he

from a - far, then called them each by name.
held so dear they left be - side their nets.
Mag - da - lene who trav - eled with your Lord,
calls your name to come and fol - low near,

It changed their lives, these sim - ple men; they'd nev - er
Their names they'd heard as Je - sus called; they came with -
you min - is - tered to him with joy for he is
for still he speaks in var - ied ways to those his

be the same.
out re - gret.
God a - dored.
call will hear.

"Leave all things you have and

come and fol - low me, and come and fol - low me."

Our Father who art in heaven 228

1 Our Father who art in heaven, hallowed be thy name.
2 Give us this day our dai - ly bread,
3 And lead us not into temptation, but deliver us from evil,

Thy kingdom come, thy will be done on earth as it is in heaven.
and forgive us our sins, as we forgive them that sin against us.
for thine is the kingdom, and the power, and the glory, for - ever. A - men

Text: Matthew 6:9-13
Music: anonymous

229 Tú has venido a la orilla
(Lord, you have come to the lakeshore)

PESCADOR DE HOMBRES* Irregular with refrain

1 Tú has ve-ni-do a la o-ri-lla, no has bus-
2 Tú sa-bes bien lo que ten-go; en mi
1 Lord, you have come to the lake-shore look-ing
2 You know so well my pos-ses-sions; my boat

ca-do ni a sa-bios ni a ri-cos, tan só-lo
bar-ca no hay o-ro ni es-pa-das, tan só-lo
nei-ther for wealth-y nor wise ones. You on-ly
car-ries no gold and no weap-ons; but nets and

quie-res que yo te si-ga.
re-des y mi tra-ba-jo.
asked me to fol-low hum-bly.
fish-es — my dai-ly la-bor.

Estribillo (Refrain)

Se-ñor, me has mi-ra-do a los o-jos y son-
O Lord, with your eyes you have searched me, kind-ly

rien-do has di-cho mi nom-bre. En la a-
smil-ing, have spo-ken my name. Now my

re-na he de-ja-do mi bar-ca; jun-to a
boat's left on the shore-line be-hind me; by your

*Original title

Text: Cesáreo Gabaraín, *Dios con Nosotros*, 1979; tr. Gertrude C. Suppe, George Lockwood IV, and Raquel Gutiérrez-Achon, 1987
    Translation copyright ©1989 The United Methodist Publishing House
Music: Cesáreo Gabaraín, *Dios con Nosotros*, 1979
    Text (Spanish) and music copyright ©1979 Cesáreo Gabaraín. Published by OCP Publications

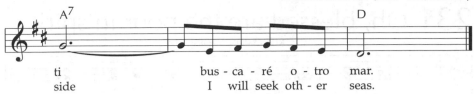

ti   bus - ca - ré   o - tro   mar.
side   I   will   seek   oth - er   seas.

3   Tú necesitas mis manos,
     mi cansancio que a otros descanse,
     amor que quiera seguir amando.
     (Estribillo)

3   You need my hands, full of caring,
     through my labors to give others rest,
     and constant love that keeps on loving.
     (Refrain)

4   Tú, pescador de otros mares,
     ansia eterna de almas que esperan,
     amigo bueno, que así me llamas.
     (Estribillo)

4   You, who have fished other oceans,
     ever longed-for by souls who are waiting,
     my loving friend, as thus you call me.
     (Refrain)

Blessed are the persecuted 230

Irregular with refrain

1 Bless - ed are the   per - se - cut - ed,   for Je - sus Christ   is
2 Bless - ed are they   who are hun - gry   in spir - it,   for   the
3 Bless - ed are the   pure in heart,   for Je - sus Christ   is
4 Bless - ed are they   who are thirst - y   in spir - it,   for   the

Refrain

liv - ing with-in them.
Lord lives with-in them.
liv - ing with-in them.
Lord lives with-in them.

Great will be their re - ward,   they shall be

giv'n a crown,   when the Lord   comes   from heav'n to meet them.

Text: based on Matthew 5; adapted by Esther C. Bergen
        Copyright ©1990 Mennonite World Conference
Music: Tonga melody (Zambia)

231 Oh, blessed are the poor in spirit

KONTAKION Irregular

1 Oh, bless - ed are the poor in spirit,
3 Oh, bless - ed are the meek,
5 Oh, bless - ed are the merciful,
7 Oh, bless - ed are the peacemakers,
9 Oh, bless - ed are you when the world re - viles you and persecutes you,

1 for theirs is the kingdom of heav - en.
3 for they shall in - her - it the earth.
5 for they shall obtain mer - cy.
7 for they shall be called the chil - dren of God.
9 and utters all manner of evil against you falsely for my sake.

2 Oh, bless - ed are those who mourn,
4 Oh, bless - ed are those who hunger and thirst af - ter righteousness,
6 Oh, bless - ed are the pure in heart,
8 Oh, bless - ed are those who are perse - cut - ed for righteousness' sake,
10 Re - joice and be ex - ceedingly glad,

2 for they shall be com - fort - ed.
4 for they shall be sat - is - fied.
6 for they shall see God.
8 for theirs is the kingdom of heav - en.
10 for great is your reward in heav - en.

Text: based on Matthew 5:3-12
Music: Russian Orthodox liturgy; adapted by Richard Proulx

Christ upon the mountain peak 232

MOUNTAIN PEAK 78. 78 with alleluia

1 Christ up-on the moun-tain peak stands a-lone in
2 Trem-bling at his feet we saw Mo-ses and E-
3 Swift the cloud of glo-ry came; God, pro-claim-ing
4 This is God's be-lov-ed Son! Law and proph-ets

glo-ry blaz-ing. Let us, if we dare to speak,
li-jah speak-ing. All the proph-ets and the law
in its thun-der Je-sus as the Son by name!
fade be-fore him. First and Last and on-ly One,

with the saints and an-gels praise him. Al-le-lu - ia!
shout through them their joy-ful greet-ing. Al-le-lu - ia!
Na-tions, cry a-loud in won-der. Al-le-lu - ia!
let cre-a-tion now a-dore him. Al-le-lu - ia!

Text: Brian Wren, 1962, *English Praise,* 1975, alt.
        Copyright ©1977 Hope Publishing Co.
Music: Bradley P. Lehman, 1984
        Copyright ©1984 Bradley P. Lehman

233 Joyful is the dark

JOYFUL DARK 55 10. 65 10

1 Joy-ful is the dark, ho-ly, hid-den God,
2 Joy-ful is the dark spir-it of the deep,
3 Joy-ful is the dark, shad-owed, sta-ble floor;
4 Joy-ful is the dark cool-ness of the tomb,
5 Joy-ful is the dark depth of love di-vine,

1 roll-ing cloud of night be-yond all nam - ing,
2 wing-ing wild-ly o'er the world's cre - a - tion,
3 an - gels flick-er, God on earth con - fes - sing,
4 wait-ing for the won-der of the morn - ing.
5 roar-ing, loom-ing thun-der-cloud of glo - ry,

1 maj-es-ty in dark - ness, en-er-gy of
2 silk-en sheen of mid - night, plum-age black and
3 as with ex-ul - ta - tion Ma-ry, giv-ing
4 Nev-er was that mid - night touched by dread and
5 ho-ly, haunt-ing beau - ty, liv-ing, lov-ing

1 maj-es-ty in dark - ness, en-er-gy of love,
2 silk-en sheen of mid - night, plum-age black and bright,
3 as with ex-ul - ta - tion Ma-ry, giv-ing birth,
4 Nev-er was that mid - night touched by dread and gloom;
5 ho-ly, haunt-ing beau - ty, liv-ing, lov-ing God.

Text: Brian Wren, 1986, *Bring Many Names*, 1989
Copyright ©1989 Hope Publishing Co.
Music: Philip K. Clemens, 1991
Copyright ©1991 Philip K. Clemens

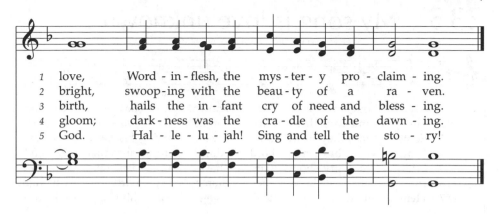

1. love,   Word - in - flesh, the   mys - ter - y pro - claim - ing.
2. bright,   swoop-ing with the   beau - ty of a   ra - ven.
3. birth,   hails the in - fant   cry of need and bless - ing.
4. gloom;   dark - ness was the   cra - dle of the dawn - ing.
5. God.   Hal - le - lu - jah! Sing and tell the sto - ry!

When Jesus wept, the falling tear 234

WHEN JESUS WEPT LM

Canon

When Je - sus wept, the fall - ing tear

in mer - cy flowed be - yond all bound.

When Je - sus groaned, a trem - bling fear

seized all the guilt - y world a - round.

Text: William Billings, *The New England Psalm Singer*, 1770
Music: William Billings, *The New England Psalm Singer*, 1770

235 My song is love unknown

LOVE UNKNOWN 66. 66. 448

1 My song is love un - known, my Sav-ior's love for
2 He came from heav - en's throne sal - va - tion to be-
3 Some - times they crowd his way and his sweet prais - es
4 Why, what has my Lord done to cause this rage and
5 With an - gry shouts they have my dear Lord done a -
6 In life, no house, no home my Lord on earth might
7 Here might I stay and sing of him my soul a -

1 me: love to the love - less shown that they might love - ly
2 stow. But they re-fused, and none the longed-for Christ would
3 sing, re - sound-ing all the day ho - san - nas to their
4 spite? He made the lame to run, and gave the blind their
5 way. A mur - der - er they save, the Prince of life they
6 have. In death, no friend - ly tomb, but what a stran - ger
7 dores. Nev - er was love, dear King, nev - er was grief like

1 be. But who am I, that for my sake
2 know. This is my friend, my friend in - deed,
3 King. Then "cru - ci - fy" is all their breath,
4 sight. What in - jur - ies! yet these are why
5 slay! Yet will - ing - ly he bears the shame
6 gave. What may I say? Heav'n was his home,
7 yours! This is my friend in whose sweet praise

Text: Samuel Crossman, *The Young Man's Meditations, or some few Sacred Poems ...*, 1664; revised in *Hymns for Today's Church*, 1982
        Copyright ©1982 Hope Publishing Co.
Music: John N. Ireland, *Songs of Praise*, 1925
        Copyright ©1925 John Ireland Trust, London

1 my Lord should take frail flesh and die?
2 who at my need his life did spend.
3 and for his death they thirst and cry.
4 the Lord most high so cruel - ly dies.
5 that through his name all might be free.
6 but mine the tomb where - in he lay.
7 I all my days could glad - ly spend.

O love, how deep, how broad 236
DEO GRACIAS LM

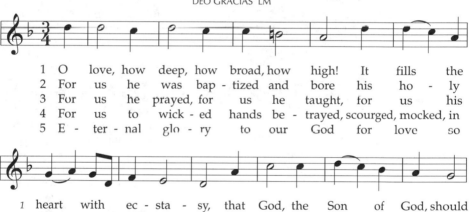

1 O love, how deep, how broad, how high! It fills the
2 For us he was bap - tized and bore his ho - ly
3 For us he prayed, for us he taught, for us his
4 For us to wick - ed hands be - trayed, scourged, mocked, in
5 E - ter - nal glo - ry to our God for love so

1 heart with ec - sta - sy, that God, the Son of God, should
2 fast, and hun-gered sore. For us temp - ta - tion sharp he
3 dai - ly works he wrought, by words and signs and ac - tions
4 pur - ple robe ar - rayed, he bore the shame - ful cross and
5 deep, so high, so broad; the Trin - i - ty whom we a -

1 take our mor - tal form for mor - tals' sake.
2 knew, for us the tempt - er ov - er - threw.
3 thus still seek - ing not him - self, but us.
4 death, for us at length gave up his breath.
5 dore for - ev - er and for - ev - er - more.

Text: attributed to Thomas à Kempis, 15th c.; tr. Benjamin Webb, *The Hymnal Noted*, 1851, alt.
Music: English melody, 15th c.

237 All glory, laud, and honor

ST. THEODULPH (VALET WILL ICH DIR GEBEN) 76. 76 with refrain

Refrain

All glo-ry, laud, and hon-or to thee, Re-deem-er, King,

Fine

to whom the lips of chil-dren made sweet ho-san-nas ring.

1 Thou art the King of Is-rael and Da-vid's roy-al Son,
2 The com-pa-ny of an-gels is prais-ing thee on high,
3 The peo-ple of the He-brews with palms be-fore thee went;
4 To thee be-fore thy pas-sion, they sang their hymns of praise;
5 Thou didst ac-cept their prais-es, ac-cept the prayers we bring,

D.C.

1 who in the Lord's name com-eth, the King and bless-ed one.
2 and we, with all cre-a-tion, in cho-rus make re-ply.
3 our praise and prayer and an-thems be-fore thee we pre-sent.
4 to thee, now high ex-alt-ed, our mel-o-dy we raise.
5 who in all good de-light-est, thou good and gra-cious King.

Text: Theodulph of Orleans, "Gloria, laus, et honor," ca. 820; tr. John M. Neale, *The Hymnal Noted*, 1851
Music: Melchior Teschner, 1613, *Ein andächtiges Gebet ...*, 1615

Hosanna, loud hosanna 238

ELLACOMBE 76. 76D

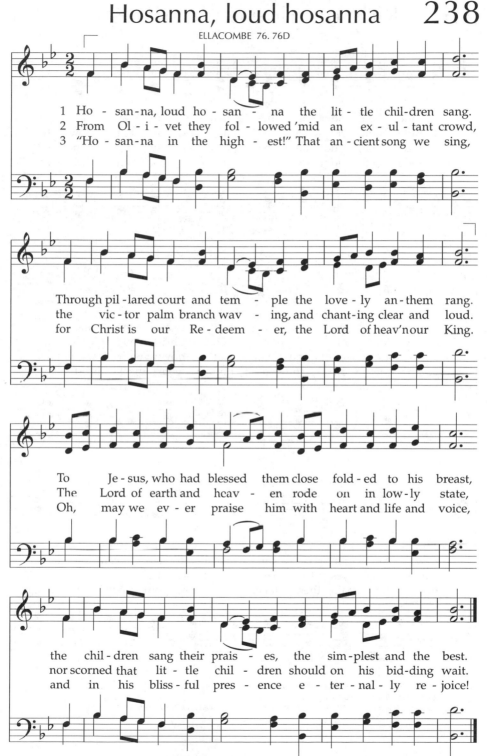

1 Ho - san-na, loud ho - san - na the lit - tle chil-dren sang.
2 From Ol - i - vet they fol - lowed 'mid an ex - ul - tant crowd,
3 "Ho - san-na in the high - est!" That an - cient song we sing,

Through pil -lared court and tem — ple the love - ly an -them rang.
the vic - tor palm branch wav - ing, and chant-ing clear and loud.
for Christ is our Re - deem - er, the Lord of heav'n our King.

To Je - sus, who had blessed them close fold - ed to his breast,
The Lord of earth and heav - en rode on in low-ly state,
Oh, may we ev - er praise him with heart and life and voice,

the chil - dren sang their prais — es, the sim -plest and the best.
nor scorned that lit - tle chil - dren should on his bid-ding wait.
and in his bliss - ful pres - ence e - ter - nal - ly re - joice!

Text: Jeannette Threlfall, *Sunshine and Shadow*, 1873, alt.
Music: *Gesangbuch* ..., Württemberg, 1784; harmonized by William H. Monk, *Hymns Ancient and Modern, Appendix*, 1868

239 Ride on, ride on in majesty

WINCHESTER NEW LM

1 Ride on, ride on in maj - es - ty, as all the
2 Ride on, ride on in maj - es - ty, in low - ly
3 Ride on, ride on in maj - es - ty – the an - gel
4 Ride on, ride on in maj - es - ty, in low - ly

crowds "Ho - san - na!" cry, through wav - ing branch - es
pomp ride on to die. O Christ, your tri - umph
arm - ies of the sky look down with sad and
pomp ride on to die. Bow your meek head to

slow - ly ride, O Sav - ior, to be cru - ci - fied.
now be - gin with cap - tured death and con - quered sin!
won - d'ring eyes to see th'ap - proach - ing sac - ri - fice.
mor - tal pain, then take, O God, your pow'r and reign.

Text: Henry H. Milman, *Hymns*, 1827; revised in *Hymns for Today's Church*, 1982
         Copyright ©1982 Hope Publishing Co.
Music: *Musicalisch Handbuch* ..., 1690; arranged by William H. Havergal, *Old Church Psalmody*, 1847

Go to dark Gethsemane   240

REDHEAD NO. 76 (GETHSEMANE) 77. 77. 77

1 Go to dark Geth - sem - a - ne, ye that feel the
2 Fol - low to the judg - ment hall, view the Lord of
3 Cal - v'ry's mourn - ful moun - tain climb: There, a - dor - ing

tempt - er's pow'r. Your Re - deem - er's con - flict see,
life ar - raigned. Oh, the worm - wood and the gall!
at his feet, mark that mir - a - cle of time,

watch with him one bit - ter hour. Turn not from his
Oh, the pangs his soul sus - tained! Shun not suf - f'ring,
God's own sac - ri - fice com - plete. "It is fin - ished!"

griefs a - way. Learn of Je - sus Christ to pray.
shame, or loss. Learn of him to bear the cross.
hear the cry. Learn of Je - sus Christ to die.

Text: James Montgomery, *Christian Psalmist*, 1825
Music: Richard Redhead, *Church Hymn Tunes, Ancient and Modern*, 1853

241 'Tis midnight, and on Olive's brow

OLIVE'S BROW LM

1 'Tis mid-night, and on Ol-ive's brow the
star is dimmed that late-ly shone. 'Tis mid-night; in the
gar-den now the suf-f'ring Sav-ior prays a-lone.

2 'Tis mid-night, and from all re-moved, Im-
man-uel wres-tles 'lone with fears. E'en that dis-ci-ple
whom he loved heeds not his Mas-ter's grief and tears.

3 'Tis mid-night, and for oth-ers' guilt the
Man of sor-rows weeps in blood. Yet he who hath in
an-guish knelt is not for-sak-en by his God.

Text: William B. Tappan, *Poems*, 1822
Music: William B. Bradbury, *The Shawm*, 1853

Stay with me 242

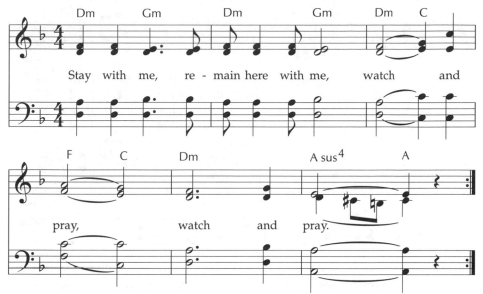

Stay with me, re-main here with me, watch and pray, watch and pray.

Text: based on Matthew 26:36-46, *Music from Taizé,* Vol. II, 1982, 1983, 1984
Music: Jacques Berthier, *Music from Taizé,* Vol. II, 1982, 1983, 1984
        Text and music copyright ©1982 Les Presses de Taizé (France). Used by permission of G.I.A. Publications, Inc.

Before the cock crew twice 243
HALLGRIM 65. 65

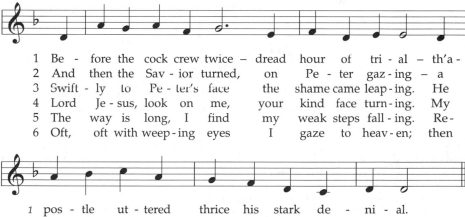

1 Be - fore the cock crew twice – dread hour of tri - al – th'a -
2 And then the Sav - ior turned, on Pe - ter gaz - ing – a
3 Swift - ly to Pe - ter's face the shame came leap - ing. He
4 Lord Je - sus, look on me, your kind face turn - ing. My
5 The way is long, I find my weak steps fall - ing. Re -
6 Oft, oft with weep - ing eyes I gaze to heav - en; then

1 pos - tle ut - tered thrice his stark de - ni - al.
2 look di - vine, that yearned with love a - maz - ing.
3 had de - nied such grace, and went forth weep - ing.
4 soul with ag - o - ny of sin is burn - ing!
5 turn, un - to my mind your grace re - call - ing.
6 at your look, a - rise re - stored, for - giv - en.

Text: Hallgrim Pjetursson, *Fimmtiu Passiusalmar,* 1659; tr. Charles V. Pilcher, 1921, *Icelandic Meditations on the Passion,* 1923
        Translation copyright © F. E. Pilcher
Music: Lawrence F. Bartlett, *The Australian Hymn Book,* 1977
        Copyright ©1977 Lawrence F. Bartlett

244 Alone thou goest forth

BANGOR CM

1 A - lone thou go - est forth, O Lord, in
2 Our sins, not thine, thou bear - est, Lord. Make
3 This is earth's dark - est hour, but thou dost
4 Give us com - pas - sion for thee, Lord, that

sac - ri - fice to die. Is this thy sor - row
us thy sor - row feel, till through our pit - y
light and life re - store. Then let all praise be
as we share this hour, thy cross may bring us

naught to us who pass un - heed - ing by?
and our shame love an - swers Love's ap - peal.
giv - en thee who liv - est ev - er - more!
to thy joy and res - ur - rec - tion pow'r.

Text: Peter Abelard, 12th c.; tr. F. Bland Tucker, 1938, *The Hymnal 1940*
Translation copyright ©1938 F. Bland Tucker. Used by permission of The Church Pension Fund
Music: *Compleat Melody or Harmony of Zion,* 1734

At the cross, her vigil keeping 245

STABAT MATER 887. 887

1 At the cross, her vi - gil keep - ing, stood the mourn - ful
  through her soul of joy be - reav - ed, bowed with sor - row
2 Who up - on that moth - er gaz - ing, in her an - guish
  Who, of Christ's dear moth - er think - ing, while her son that
3 For his peo - ple's sins chas - tis - ed, she be - held her
  saw him then from judg - ment tak - en, and in death by
4 Near your cross, O Christ, a - bid - ing, grief and love my
  By your sav - ing cross up - hold me, in your dy - ing,

1 moth - er weep - ing, where he hung, the dy - ing Lord,
  deep - ly griev - ed, passed the sharp and pierc - ing sword.
2 so a - maz - ing, born of wom - an, would not weep?
  cup is drink - ing, would not share her sor - row deep?
3 son de - spis - ed, scourged, and crowned with thorns en - twined,
  all for - sak - en, till his spir - it he re - signed.
4 heart di - vid - ing, I with her would take my place.
  Christ, en - fold me, with the death - less arms of grace.

Text: attributed to Jacopone da Todi, *Stabat Mater dolorosa*, 13th c.; tr. Edward Caswall and others, alt.
Music: *Gesangbuch*, Mainz and Frankfurt, 1661
      Arrangement copyright © Oxford University Press, London

246 Why has God forsaken me?

SHIMPI 77. 77

1 "Why has God for - sak - en me?" cried our Sav - ior
2 At the tomb of Laz - a - rus Je - sus wept with
3 As his life ex - pired, our Lord placed him - self with -
4 Mys - t'ry shrouds our life and death but we need not

from the cross as he shared the lone - li - ness
o - pen grief. Grant us, Lord, the tears which heal
in God's care. At our dy - ing, Lord, may we
be a - fraid, for the mys - t'ry's heart is love,

of our deep - est grief and loss.
all our pain and un - be - lief.
trust the love which con - quers fear.
God's great love which Christ dis - played.

Text: Bill Wallace, *Something to Sing About*, 1981
         Copyright ©1981 W. L. Wallace
Music: Taihei Sato, 1981
         Copyright ©1983 Taihei Sato

247 Jesus, remember me

Je - sus, re - mem - ber me   when you come in - to your king - dom.

Je - sus, re - mem - ber me   when you come in - to your king - dom.

Text: based on Luke 23:42, Taizé community, 1981, *Music from Taizé*, Vol. I, 1978, 1980, 1981
Music: Jacques Berthier, 1981, *Music from Taizé*, Vol. I, 1978, 1980, 1981
         Text and music copyright ©1981 Les Presses de Taizé (France). Used by permission of G.I.A. Publications, Inc.

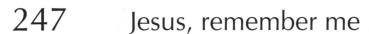

My God, my God, why 248

1 My God, my God, why have you for - saken me?
3 Yet you are the ho - ly One,
5 All who see me laugh me to scorn;
7 They stare and gloat over me;

1 and are so far from my
  cry and from the words of my dis - tress?
3 en - throned up-on the prais-es of Israel.
5 they curl up their lips and wag their heads, saying,
7 they divide my garments
  among them; they cast lots for my clothing.

2 O my God, I cry in the
  daytime but you do not answer;
4 Our ancestors put their trust in you;
6 "Commit your cause to the Lord; let God deliver –
8 Be not far a - way, O Lord;

2 by night as well, but I find no rest.
4 they trusted, and you de - livered them.
6 let the one be rescued in whom God de - lights."
8 you are my strength; has - ten to help me.

Text: based on Psalm 22
Music: Edward J. Hopkins, *The Hymnal 1940*
Copyright ©1982 The Church Pension Fund

249 Calvary

Irregular

Refrain

Cal - va - ry, Cal - va - ry, Cal - va -

ry, Cal - va - ry, Cal - va - ry, Cal - va -

Fine

ry, sure - ly he died on Cal - va - ry.

1 Ev - 'ry time I think a - bout Je - sus, ev - 'ry time I
2 Don't you hear the ham - mer ring - ing? Don't you hear the
3 Don't you hear him call - ing his Fa - ther? Don't you hear him
4 Don't you hear him say, "It is fin - ished"? Don't you hear him
5 Je - sus fur - nished my sal - va - tion. Je - sus fur - nished
6 Sin - ner, do you love my Je - sus? Sin - ner, do you

1 think a - bout Je - sus, ev - 'ry time I think a - bout Je - sus,
2 ham - mer ring - ing? Don't you hear the ham - mer ring - ing?
3 call - ing his Fa - ther? Don't you hear him call - ing his Fa - ther?
4 say, "It is fin - ished"? Don't you hear him say, "It is fin - ished"?
5 my sal - va - tion. Je - sus fur - nished my sal - va - tion.
6 love my Je - sus? Sin - ner, do you love my Je - sus?

D.C.

Sure - ly he died on Cal - va - ry.

Text: African-American spiritual
Music: African-American spiritual

Beneath the cross of Jesus 250

ST. CHRISTOPHER 76. 86. 86. 86

1 Be - neath the cross of Je - sus I fain would take my stand,
2 Up - on that cross of Je - sus mine eyes at times can see
3 I take, O cross, thy shad - ow for mine a - bid - ing place.

the shad - ow of a might - y rock with - in a wea - ry land,
the ver - y dy - ing form of One who suf - fered there for me.
I ask no oth - er sun - shine than the sun - shine of his face.

a home with - in the wil - der - ness, a rest up - on the way
And from my smit - ten heart with tears two won - ders I con - fess;
Con - tent to let the world go by, to know no gain nor loss;

from the burn - ing of the noon - tide heat, and the bur - den of the day.
the won - ders of re - deem - ing love and my un - wor - thi - ness.
my sin - ful self my on - ly shame, my glo - ry all the cross.

Text: Elizabeth C. Clephane, *Family Treasury*, 1872, alt.
Music: Frederick C. Maker, *Bristol Tune Book*, 1881

251 How shallow former shadows

THE THIRD MELODY CMD

1 How shal-low for - mer shad-ows seem be-side this great re - verse,
2 This is no mid - day fan - ta - sy, no flight of fe - vered brain.
3 Yet deep with-in this dark-ness lives a Love so fierce and free,

as dark - ness swal - lows up the light of all the u - ni-verse.
With ven-geance aw - ful, grim, and real, cha - os is come a - gain.
that arcs all voids and – risk su-preme! — em-brac - es ag - o - ny.

Cre - a - tion shiv - ers at the shock, the tem - ple rends its veil.
The hands that formed us from the soil are nailed up - on the cross.
Its per - fect test - a-ment is etched in i - ron, blood, and wood.

A pal - lid still - ness sti - fles time and na-ture's mo-tions fail.
The Word that gave us life and breath ex-pires in ut - ter loss.
With awe we glimpse its true im - port and dare to call it good.

Text: Carl P. Daw, Jr., *A Year of Grace,* 1990
        Copyright ©1990 Hope Publishing Co.
Music: Thomas Tallis, *The Whole Psalter Translated into English Metre,* ca. 1567

O sacred Head, now wounded 252

HERZLICH TUT MICH VERLANGEN 76. 76D

1 O sa - cred Head, now wound - ed, with grief and shame weighed down,
2 O no - blest Brow and dear - est, in oth - er days the world
3 What thou, my Lord, hast suf - fered was all for sin - ners' gain.
4 What lan - guage shall I bor - row to thank thee, dear - est Friend,
5 Be near when I am dy - ing, O show thy cross to me,

1 now scorn - ful - ly sur - round - ed with thorns, thine on - ly crown!
2 all feared when thou ap - pear - edst; what shame on thee is hurled!
3 Mine, mine was the trans - gres - sion, but thine the dead - ly pain.
4 for this thy dy - ing sor - row, thy pit - y with - out end?
5 and for my res - cue, fly - ing, come, Lord, and set me free!

1 O sa - cred Head, what glo - ry, what bliss till now was thine!
2 How art thou pale with an - guish, with sore a - buse and scorn.
3 Lo, here I fall, my Sav - ior! 'Tis I de - serve thy place.
4 O make me thine for - ev - er, and should I faint - ing be,
5 These eyes, new faith re - ceiv - ing, from Je - sus shall not move,

1 Yet, though de - spised and gor - y, I joy to call thee mine.
2 How does that vis - age lan - guish, which once was bright as morn!
3 Look on me with thy fa - vor, vouch - safe to me thy grace.
4 Lord, let me nev - er, nev - er out - live my love to thee.
5 for all who die be - liev - ing, die safe - ly, through thy love.

Text: anonymous, based on *Salve caput cruentatum,* 13th c., Paul Gerhardt, "O Haupt voll Blut und Wunden,"
         Praxis Pietatis Melica, 1656; tr. James W. Alexander, revised in *The Breaking Crucible,* 1861
Music: Hans L. Hassler, *Lustgarten neuer Deutscher Gesäng,* 1601; harmonized by J. S. Bach, *Passion According to St. Matthew,* 1729

253 Alas! and did my Savior bleed?

MARTYRDOM (AVON) CM

1 A - las! and did my Sav - ior bleed? And
2 Was it for sins that I have done he
3 Well might the sun in dark - ness hide, and
4 But drops of grief can ne'er re - pay the

did my Sov - 'reign die? Would he de - vote that
groaned up - on the tree? A - maz - ing pit - y,
shut its glo - ries in, when Christ, the might - y
debt of love I owe. Here, Lord, I give my -

sa - cred head for sin - ners such as I?
grace un - known, and love "be - yond de - gree!
Mak - er, died for his own crea - tures' sin.
self a - way; 'tis all that I can do.

Text: Isaac Watts, *Hymns and Spiritual Songs,* Book II, 1707, alt.
Music: Hugh Wilson; adapted by Robert A. Smith, *Sacred Music,* 1825

Ah, holy Jesus

254

HERZLIEBSTER JESU 11 11 11. 5

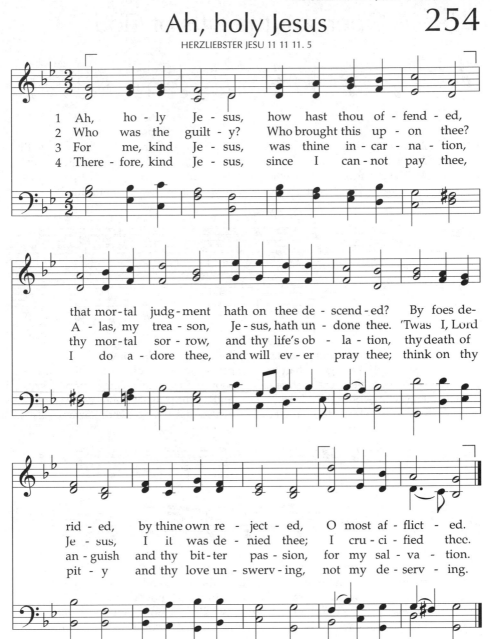

1 Ah, ho-ly Je-sus, how hast thou of-fend-ed,
2 Who was the guilt-y? Who brought this up-on thee?
3 For me, kind Je-sus, was thine in-car-na-tion,
4 There-fore, kind Je-sus, since I can-not pay thee,

that mor-tal judg-ment hath on thee de-scend-ed? By foes de-
A-las, my trea-son, Je-sus, hath un-done thee. 'Twas I, Lord
thy mor-tal sor-row, and thy life's ob-la-tion, thy death of
I do a-dore thee, and will ev-er pray thee; think on thy

rid-ed, by thine own re-ject-ed, O most af-flict-ed.
Je-sus, I it was de-nied thee; I cru-ci-fied thee.
an-guish and thy bit-ter pas-sion, for my sal-va-tion.
pit-y and thy love un-swerv-ing, not my de-serv-ing.

Text: Johann Heermann, "Herzliebster Jesu," *Devoti Musica Cordis,* 1630; tr. Robert Bridges, *Yattendon Hymnal,* 1899, alt.
Music: Johann Crüger, *Newes vollkömliches Gesangbuch,* Vol. II, 1640

255 Open are the gifts of God

SONG 13 77. 77

1 O - pen are the gifts of God, gifts of
2 Love that gives, gives ev - er - more, gives with
3 Drained is love in mak - ing full, bound in
4 There - fore he who shows us God help - less
5 Here is God: no mon - arch he, throned in

1 love to mind and sense; hid - den is love's ag - o -
2 zeal, with ea - ger hands, spares not, keeps not, all out -
3 set - ting oth - ers free, poor in mak - ing man - y
4 hangs up - on the tree, and the nails and crown of
5 eas - y state to reign; here is God, whose arms of

1 ny, love's en - deav - or, love's ex - pense.
2 pours, ven - tures all, its all ex - pends.
3 rich, weak in giv - ing pow'r to be.
4 thorns tell of what God's love must be.
5 love, ach - ing, spent, the world sus - tain.

Text: W. H. Vanstone, *The Risk of Love*, 1978
Copyright © J. W. Shore
Music: Orlando Gibbons, *Hymnes and Songs of the Church*, 1623

Sing, my tongue, the song   256
PANGE LINGUA 87. 87. 87

1 Sing, my tongue, the song of tri - umph,   tell   the   sto - ry
2 Thir - ty years a - mong us dwell - ing,   his   ap - point - ed
3 He en - dured the nails, the spit - ting,   vin - e - gar and
4 Faith - ful cross, thou sign of tri - umph,   now   for   us   the
5 Thus the scheme of our sal - va - tion   was   of   old   in
6 Un - to God be praise and glo - ry: to   the   Fa - ther

1 far and wide.   Tell of dread and fi - nal bat - tle,
2 time ful - filled,   born for this, he met his Pas - sion,
3 spear and reed.   From that ho - ly bod - y bro - ken
4 no - blest tree,   none in fo - liage, none in blos - som,
5 or - der laid   that the man - i - fold de - ceiv - er's
6 and the Son,   to th'e - ter - nal Spir - it hon - or

1 sing of Sav - ior cru - ci - fied,   how, up - on the cross a
2 this the Sav - ior free - ly willed.   On the cross the Lamb is
3 blood and wa - ter forth pro - ceed.   Earth and stars and sky and
4 none in fruit thine e - qual be;   sweet - est wood and sweet - est
5 art by art might be out - weighed,   and the lure the foe put
6 now and ev - er - more be done;   praise and glo - ry in the

1 vic - tim van - quish - ing in   death he died.
2 lift - ed, where his pre - cious   blood he spilled.
3 o - cean by that flood from   stain are freed.
4 i - ron, sweet - est weight is   hung on thee.
5 for - ward in - to means of   heal - ing made.
6 high - est, while un - end - ing   ag - es run. A - men

Text: Venatius Fortunatus, "Pange lingua gloriosi praelium certaminis," 569; composite translation *The Hymnal 1982*
        (Sts. 2,4-5), 1985
        Translation (Sts. 2,4-5) copyright ©1982 The Church Pension Fund
Music: Sarum plainsong

257 Were you there

WERE YOU THERE Irregular

Were you there when they cru - ci - fied my Lord? Were you
there when they cru - ci - fied my Lord? Oh! _____
Some - times it caus - es me to trem - ble, trem - ble, trem - ble.
Were you there when they cru - ci - fied my Lord?

2 Were you there when they nailed him to the tree?
3 Were you there when they pierced him in the side?
4 Were you there when they laid him in the tomb?
5 Were you there when he rose up from the dead?

Text: African-American spiritual, *Old Plantation Hymns,* 1899
Music: African-American spiritual, revised in *Folk Songs of the American Negro,* 1907

258 Man of sorrows

MAN OF SORROWS 77. 78

1 "Man of sor - rows," what a name   for the Son of   God who came,
2 Bear - ing shame and scoff - ing rude,   in my place con - demned he stood,
3 He was lift - ed up to die.   "It is fin - ished" was his cry.
4 When he comes, our glo - rious King,   all his ran - somed home to bring,

Text: Philip P. Bliss, *International Lessons Monthly,* 1875
Music: Philip P. Bliss, *International Lessons Monthly,* 1875

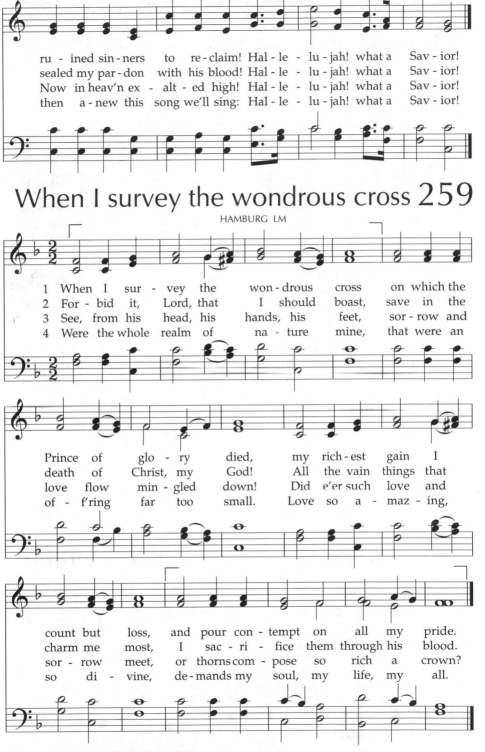

ru - ined sin-ners to re-claim! Hal - le - lu - jah! what a Sav - ior!
sealed my par-don with his blood! Hal - le - lu - jah! what a Sav - ior!
Now in heav'n ex - alt - ed high! Hal - le - lu - jah! what a Sav - ior!
then a - new this song we'll sing: Hal - le - lu - jah! what a Sav - ior!

When I survey the wondrous cross 259

HAMBURG LM

1 When I sur - vey the won - drous cross on which the
2 For - bid it, Lord, that I should boast, save in the
3 See, from his head, his hands, his feet, sor - row and
4 Were the whole realm of na - ture mine, that were an

Prince of glo - ry died, my rich - est gain I
death of Christ, my God! All the vain things that
love flow min - gled down! Did e'er such love and
of - f'ring far too small. Love so a - maz - ing,

count but loss, and pour con - tempt on all my pride.
charm me most, I sac - ri - fice them through his blood.
sor - row meet, or thorns com - pose so rich a crown?
so di - vine, de - mands my soul, my life, my all.

Text: Isaac Watts, *Hymns and Spiritual Songs*, 1707
Music: Lowell Mason, 1824, *Boston Handel and Haydn Society Collection ...*, 3rd ed., 1825

260 When I survey the wondrous cross

LM

1 When I sur - vey the won - drous cross
2 For - bid it, Lord, that I should boast,
3 See, from his head, his hands, his feet,
4 Were the whole realm of na - ture mine,

on which the Prince of glo - ry died, my rich - est
save in the death of Christ, my God! All the vain
sor - row and love flow min - gled down! Did e'er such
that were an of - f'ring far too small. Love so a -

gain I count but loss, and pour con -
things that charm me most, I sac - ri -
love and sor - row meet, or thorns com -
maz - ing, so di - vine, de - mands my

tempt on all my pride.
fice them through his blood.
pose so rich a crown?
soul, my life, my all.

Text: Isaac Watts, *Hymns and Spiritual Songs*, 1707
Music: African hymn melody

261 I will sing the Lord's high triumph

TYDDYN LLWYN 87. 87. 877

1 I will sing the Lord's high tri - umph, rul - ing
2 By the storm and at the moun - tain, grace and
3 Who is like the God of Is - rael, faith - ful,
4 Praise our God, who in his thun - der led a

Text: based on Exodus 15, Christopher Idle, 1975, revised 1987, *Psalms for Today*, 1990
Copyright ©1990 Hope Publishing Co.
Music: Evan Morgan

earth and sky and sea. God, my strength, my song, my
judg - ment both are shown. All who planned his peo - ple's
ho - ly, throned a - bove? Stretch-ing out the arm of
na - tion through the sea. Praise the one whose blood re -

glo - ry, my sal - va - tion now is he. Through the
ru - in pow'r di - vine has o - ver - thrown. Na - tions
an - ger, yet he guides us by his love. To our
leased us from our deep - er slav - er - y. Al - le -

wa - ters, through the wa - ters, God has brought us lib - er -
trem - ble, na - tions trem - ble; God has made his mer - cy
home - land, to our home - land, God will see us safe - ly
lu - ia, al - le - lu - ia, Christ is ris - en — we are

ty, God has brought us lib - er - ty.
known, God has made his mer - cy known.
move, God will see us safe - ly move.
free! Christ is ris - en — we are free!

262 At the Lamb's high feast

SONNE DER GERECHTIGKEIT 77. 77 with alleluia

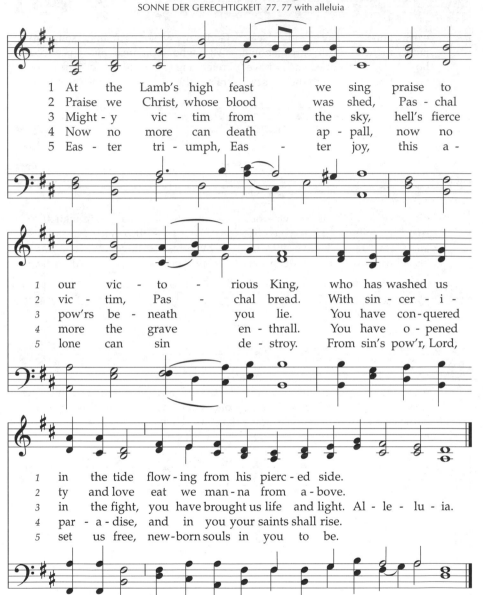

1 At the Lamb's high feast we sing praise to
2 Praise we Christ, whose blood was shed, Pas - chal
3 Might - y vic - tim from the sky, hell's fierce
4 Now no more can death ap - pall, now no
5 Eas - ter tri - umph, Eas - ter joy, this a -

1 our vic - to - rious King, who has washed us
2 vic - tim, Pas - chal bread. With sin - cer - i -
3 pow'rs be - neath you lie. You have con - quered
4 more the grave en - thrall. You have o - pened
5 lone can sin de - stroy. From sin's pow'r, Lord,

1 in the tide flow - ing from his pierc - ed side.
2 ty and love eat we man - na from a - bove.
3 in the fight, you have brought us life and light. Al - le - lu - ia.
4 par - a - dise, and in you your saints shall rise.
5 set us free, new-born souls in you to be.

Text: anonymous, *Ad coenam agni providi*, ca. 6th c.; tr. Robert Campbell, *Hymns and Anthems for … St. Andrew's …*, 1850, alt.
Music: German folk melody, 15th c., *Kirchengeseng*, 1566

The strife is o'er

263

VICTORY 888 with alleluias

Al-le - lu - ia! Al-le - lu - ia! Al-le - lu - ia!

1 The strife is o'er, the bat - tle done,
2 The pow'rs of death have done their worst,
3 The three sad days have quick - ly sped.
4 Lord, by the stripes which wound - ed thee,

the vic - to - ry of life is won.
but Christ their le - gions hath dis - persed.
He ris - es glo - rious from the dead.
from death's dread sting thy ser - vants free,

D.S.

The song of tri - umph has be - gun: Al-le - lu - ia!
Let shouts of ho - ly joy out - burst: Al-le - lu - ia!
All glo - ry to our ris - en Head! Al-le - lu - ia!
that we may live and sing to thee: Al-le - lu - ia!

Text: anonymous, "Finita jam sunt praelia," *Symphonia Sirenum Selectarum,* 1695; tr. Francis Pott, *Hymns Fitted to the Order of Common Prayer,* 1861
Music: Giovanni P. da Palestrina, *Magnificat in the Third Mode,* 1591; adapted by William H. Monk, *Hymns Ancient and Modern,* 1861

264 Come, ye faithful, raise the strain

ST. KEVIN 76. 76D

1 Come, ye faith - ful, raise the strain of tri - um - phant glad - ness!
2 'Tis the spring of souls to - day; Christ has burst his pris - on.
3 "Al - le - lu - ia!" now we cry to our King im - mor - tal,

God has brought forth Is - ra - el in - to joy from sad - ness.
From the frost and gloom of death light and life have ris - en.
who, tri - um - phant, burst the bars of the tomb's dark por - tal;

Now re - joice, Je - ru - sa - lem, and with true af - fec - tion
All the win - ter of our sins, long and dark, is fly - ing
"Al - le - lu - ia!" with the Son, God the Fa - ther prais - ing;

wel - come in un - wea - ried strains Je - sus' res - ur - rec - tion.
from his light, to whom we give thanks and praise un - dy - ing.
"Al - le - lu - ia!" yet a - gain to the Spir - it rais - ing.

Text: St. John of Damascus (Greek hymn), *First Ode of Canon for the Sunday after Easter*, 8th c.; tr. John M. Neale,
Christian Remembrancer, 1859, alt.
Music: Arthur S. Sullivan, *The Hymnary*, 1872

Come, ye faithful, raise the strain 265

AVE VIRGO VIRGINUM (GAUDEAMUS PARITER) 76. 76D

1 Come, ye faith-ful, raise the strain   of   tri - um - phant glad - ness!
2 'Tis   the spring of souls to - day;   Christ hath burst his pris - on,
3 Now the queen of sea-sons, bright   with   the   day   of splen - dor,
4 Nei - ther might the gates of death,   nor   the tomb's dark por - tal,

God hath brought forth Is - ra - el   in - to   joy from sad - ness,
and from three days' sleep in death   as   a   sun hath ris - en.
with   the   roy - al   feast of feasts,   comes its   joy   to ren - der;
nor   the watch-ers,   nor the seal   hold thee   as   a mor - tal.

loosed   from Pha-raoh's bit - ter yoke   Ja - cob's sons and daugh - ters,
All   the win - ter of our sins,   long and dark, is   fly - ing
comes   to glad Je - ru - sa - lem,   who with true   af - fec - tion
But   to - day   a - midst the twelve   thou didst stand, be - stow - ing

led   them with   un - moist - ened foot   through the Red Sea wa - ters.
from   his light,   to whom we give   laud and praise un - dy - ing.
wel - comes in   un - wea - ried strains   Je - sus' res - ur - rec - tion.
thy   true peace which ev - er - more   pass - es   hu - man know - ing.

Text: St. John of Damascus (Greek hymn), *First Ode of Canon for the Sunday after Easter*, 8th c.; tr. John M. Neale,
    Christian Remembrancer, 1859, alt.

Music: Johann Horn, *Ein Gesangbuch der Brüder im Behemen und Merherrn*, 1544; revised in *Catholicum Hymnologium Germanicum*, 1584

266 They crucified my Savior

ASCENSIUS Irregular

1 They cru-ci-fied my Sav-ior and nailed him to the
2 Jo-seph begged his bod-y and laid it in the
3 Ma-ry, she came run-ning, a - look-ing for my
4 An an-gel came from heav-en and rolled the stone a -

cross. They cru-ci-fied my Sav-ior and nailed him to the cross.
tomb. Jo-seph begged his bod-y and laid it in the tomb.
Lord. Ma-ry, she came run-ning, a - look-ing for my Lord.
way. An an-gel came from heav-en and rolled the stone a - way.

cross, and the Lord will bear my spir - it home.
tomb, and the Lord will bear my spir - it home.
Lord, and the Lord will bear my spir - it home.
way, and the Lord will bear my spir - it home.

Text: African-American spiritual
Music: African-American spiritual

267 Christ has arisen

99. 99 with refrain

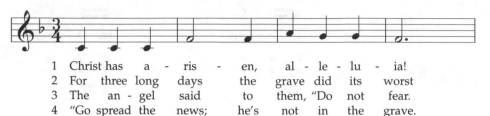

1 Christ has a - ris - en, al - le - lu - ia!
2 For three long days the grave did its worst
3 The an - gel said to them, "Do not fear.
4 "Go spread the news; he's not in the grave.
5 Christ has a - ris - en to set us free.
6 Je - sus is liv - ing, let the earth sing.

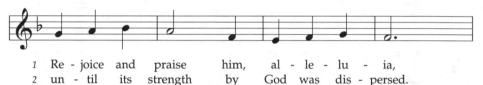

1 Re - joice and praise him, al - le - lu - ia,
2 un - til its strength by God was dis - persed.
3 You look for Je - sus who is not here.
4 He has a - ris - en, mor - tals to save."
5 Al - le - lu - ia, to him prais - es be!
6 He reigns tri - um - phant, e - ter - nal King,

1 for our re - deem - er burst from the tomb,
2 Christ who gives life did death un - der - go,
3 See for your - selves, the tomb is all bare.
4 Je - sus' re - deem - ing la - bors are done.
5 The pow'r of Sa - tan no long - er binds,
6 and he has prom - ised those who be - lieve

1 e - ven from death, dis - pel - ling its gloom.
2 and in its con - quest his might did show.
3 On - ly the grave - clothes are ly - ing there.
4 E - ven the bat - tle with sin is won.
5 nor can en - slave the thoughts of our minds.
6 in - to his king - dom he will re - ceive.

Text: Bernard Kyamanywa; tr. Howard S. Olson, 1969
Music: Haya melody (Tanzania)
        Text and music copyright ©1977 Lutheran World Federation

Refrain

Let us sing praise to him with end-less joy. Death's fear-ful

sting he has come to de-stroy, our sins for-giv - ing,

al - le - lu - ia. Christ has a - ris - en, al - le - lu - ia!

See the splendor of the morning 268

TINMINAGO Irregular

All

Hal - le, hal - le - lu - jah, hal - le - lu - jah!

Group 1

1 See the splen-dor of the morn-ing full of won - der,
2 Wel - come, hail the Prince of glo - ry, our Re - deem - er.
3 Fill our hearts with faith and joy of sal - va - tion,
4 Be u - nit - ed in the name of Christ our Sav - ior,

Group 2

hear the good news: Christ is ris - en, Christ is ris - en!
Shout with joy, for he has freed us, he has freed us.
that with Je - sus we may tri - umph in true glo - ry.
and pro - claim through - out the world his res - ur - rec - tion.

All

Hal - le - lu - jah, hal - le - lu, hal - le - lu - jah!

Text: Francisco F. Feliciano, 1977, *Hymns from the Four Winds,* 1983
Music: Francisco F. Feliciano, 1977, *Hymns from the Four Winds,* 1983
Text and music copyright ©1983 Francisco F. Feliciano

269 Thine is the glory

JUDAS MACCABEUS 55. 65. 65. 65 with refrain

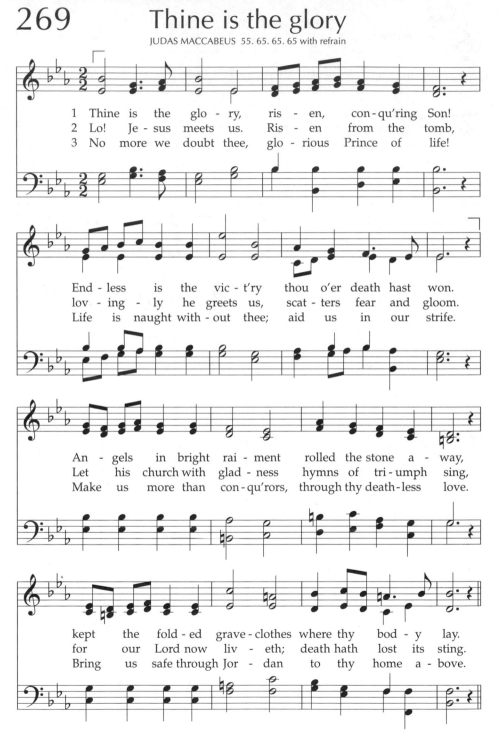

1 Thine is the glo - ry, ris - en, con - qu'ring Son!
2 Lo! Je - sus meets us. Ris - en from the tomb,
3 No more we doubt thee, glo - rious Prince of life!

End - less is the vic - t'ry thou o'er death hast won.
lov - ing - ly he greets us, scat - ters fear and gloom.
Life is naught with - out thee; aid us in our strife.

An - gels in bright rai - ment rolled the stone a - way,
Let his church with glad - ness hymns of tri - umph sing,
Make us more than con - qu'rors, through thy death - less love.

kept the fold - ed grave - clothes where thy bod - y lay.
for our Lord now liv - eth; death hath lost its sting.
Bring us safe through Jor - dan to thy home a - bove.

Text: Edmond L. Budry, "A toi la gloire, O Ressuscité," *Chants Evangéliques,* 1885; tr. Richard B. Hoyle, *Cantate Domino,* 1925
Music: George Frederick Handel, *Joshua,* 1748

Refrain

Thine is the glo - ry, ris - en, con - qu'ring Son!

End - less is the vic - t'ry thou o'er death hast won.

Who are these 270

OTO SĄ BARANKI Irregular

Who are these who are be - liev - ers now? These are

they who have been shout-ing, "Al - le - lu - ia!" They have seen the Sav - ior

and have been filled with splen - dor. Al - le - lu - ia, al - le - lu - ia!

Text: anonymous, *Ad coenam agni providi*, ca. 6th c.
           Translation copyright©1991 The Hymnal Project
Music: Jacek Gałuszka, O.P., 1989
           Copyright ©1989 Jacek Gałuszka, O.P.

271

Christ is arisen

CHRIST IST ERSTANDEN Irregular

Christ is a - ris - en from the grave's dark pris - on. We now re - joice

with glad - ness; Christ will end all sad - ness. Lord, have mer - cy.

All our hopes were end - ed had Je - sus not as - cend - ed

from the grave tri - um - phant - ly. For this, Lord Christ, we wor - ship thee.

Lord, have mer - cy. Al - le - lu - ia! Al - le - lu - ia!

Al - le - lu - ia! We now re - joice with glad - ness;

Christ will end all sad - ness. Lord, have mer - cy.

Text: *"Christ ist erstanden, von der Marter alle,"* ca.1100, Klug's *Gesangbuch,* Wittenberg, 1529; tr. William G. Polack, 1939,
The Lutheran Hymnal, 1941
Translation copyright ©1941 Concordia Publishing House
Music: German melody, 12th c., Klug's *Gesangbuch,* Wittenberg, 1529

Christ is risen! Shout hosanna 272

LADUE CHAPEL 87. 87D

1 Christ is ris - en! Shout ho - san - na! Cel - e - brate
2 Christ is ris - en! Raise your spir - its from the cav -
3 Christ is ris - en! Earth and heav - en nev - er - more

this day of days. Christ is ris - en! Hush in
erns of de - spair. Walk with glad - ness in the
shall be the same. Break the bread of new cre -

won - der, all cre - a - tion is a - mazed.
morn - ing. See what love can do and dare.
a - tion where the world is still in pain.

In the de - sert all - sur - round - ing, see, a spread-
Drink the wine of res - ur - rec - tion, not a ser -
Tell its grim, de - mon - ic cho - rus, "Christ is ris -

ing tree has grown. Heal - ing leaves of grace a -
vant, but a friend; Je - sus is our strong com -
en! Get you gone!" God, the First and Last, is

bound - ing bring a taste of love un - known.
pan - ion — joy and peace shall nev - er end.
with us. Sing ho - san - na, ev - 'ry - one!

Text: Brian Wren, 1984, *Praising a Mystery*, 1986
          Copyright ©1986 Hope Publishing Co.
Music: Ronald Arnatt, 1968, *More Hymns and Spiritual Songs*, 1971
          Copyright © Walton Music Corporation

273 Low in the grave he lay

CHRIST AROSE 11 10 with refrain

1 Low in the grave he lay, Je-sus, my Sav-ior! Wait-ing the com-ing day,
2 Vain-ly they watch his bed, Je-sus, my Sav-ior! Vain-ly they seal the dead,
3 Death can-not keep its prey, Je-sus, my Sav-ior! He tore the bars a-way,

Je-sus, my Lord!

Refrain

Up from the grave he a-rose, with a
he a-rose,

might-y tri-umph o'er his foes! He a-rose a vic-tor from the
He a-rose!

dark do-main, and he lives for-ev-er with his saints to reign! He a-
rose! He a-rose! Al-le-lu-ia! Christ a-rose!
He a-rose! He a-rose!

Text: Robert Lowry, 1874, *Brightest and Best,* 1875
Music: Robert Lowry, 1874, *Brightest and Best,* 1875

O sons and daughters, let us sing 274

GELOBT SEI GOTT 888 with alleluias

1 O sons and daugh-ters, let us sing! The King of heav'n, the
2 That Sun-day morn, at break of day, the faith-ful wom-en
3 An an-gel clad in white they see, who sat and spake un-
4 How bless'd are they who have not seen, and yet whose faith hath
5 On this most ho-ly day of days, to God your hearts and

1 glo-rious King, o'er death to-day rose tri-umph-ing.
2 went their way to seek the tomb where Je-sus lay.
3 to the three, "Your Lord doth go to Gal-i-lee."
4 con-stant been, for they e-ter-nal life shall win.
5 voic-es raise in laud, and ju-bi-lee, and praise.

Al-le-lu - ia! Al-le-lu - ia! Al-le-lu - ia!

Text: Jean Tisserand, *O Filii et Filiae*, 1518-1536; tr. John M. Neale, *Medieval Hymns and Sequences*, 1851, alt., *Hymns Ancient and Modern*, 1861
Music: Melchior Vulpius, *Ein schön geistlich Gesangbuch*, 1609

275 Lift your glad voices

RESURRECTION 11 11. 11 11 (Irregular)

1 Lift your glad voic - es in tri - umph on high,
2 He burst from the fet - ters of dark - ness that bound him,
3 Glo - ry to God, in full an - thems of joy;
4 But Je - sus hath cheered the dark val - ley of sor - row,

for Je - sus hath ris - en, and we shall not die.
re - splen - dent in glo - ry, to live and to save.
the be - ing he gave us, death can - not de - stroy.
and bade us, im - mor - tal, to heav - en as - cend.

Vain were the ter - rors that gath - ered a - round him,
Loud was the cho - rus of an - gels on high,
Sad were the life we may part with to - mor - row,
Lift then your voic - es in tri - umph on high,

and short the do - min - ion of death and the grave.
the Sav - ior hath ris - en, and we shall not die.
if tears were our birth - right, and death were our end.
for Je - sus hath ris - en, and we shall not die.

Text: Henry Ware, Jr., *Christian Disciple,* 1817, alt.
Music: John E. Gould, *Methodist Hymnal with Tunes – Special Edition,* ca. 1878

This joyful Eastertide

VRUECHTEN 67. 67 with refrain

1 This joy-ful Eas-ter-tide a - way with sin and sor - row!
My love, the Cru-ci-fied, hath sprung to life this mor - row.
2 My flesh in hope shall rest, and for a sea-son slum - ber,
till trump from East to West shall wake the dead in num - ber.
3 Death's flood hath lost its chill, since Je-sus crossed the riv - er,
Lov - er of souls, from ill my pass-ing soul de-li - er.

Refrain

Had Christ that once was slain, ne'er burst his three-day pris - on,

our faith had been in vain. But now hath Christ a - ris - en, a -

ris - en, a - ris - en, a - ris - en.

Text: George R. Woodward, *Carols for Easter and Ascension*, 1894
Music: *David's Psalmen*, 1685; harmonized by Alice Parker
Harmonization copyright ©1966 Alice Parker

277 I know that my Redeemer lives

SHOUT ON, PRAY ON LM with refrains

1 I know that my Re - deem - er lives,
2 He lives to bless me with his love, glo - ry, hal - le - lu - jah!
3 He lives, all glo - ry to his name, lu - jah!

What com - fort this sweet sen - tence gives,
He lives to plead for me a - bove, glo - ry, hal - le - lu - jah!
He lives, my Sav - ior, still the same, lu - jah!

Shout on, pray on, we're gain - ing ground,
He lives, my hun - gry soul to feed, glo - ry, hal - le - lu - jah!
What joy the bless'd as - sur - ance gives,
O pray on, we're gain - ing ground,
yes, he lives, my soul to feed,
joy the bless'd as - sur - ance gives,

The dead's a - live and the lost is found,
He lives to help in time of need, glo - ry, hal - le - lu - jah!
I know that my Re - deem - er lives, lu - jah!
dead's a - live, the lost is found,
lives to help in time of need,
know that my Re - deem - er lives,

Text: Samuel Medley, *Psalms and Hymns*, 1775, alt.
Music: American folk melody, *Sacred Harp*, 2nd ed., 1850; harmonized by Alice Parker
         Harmonization copyright ©1988 Alice Parker

Christ is alive! Let Christians sing 278

TRURO LM

1 Christ is a-live! Let Chris-tians sing! His cross stands
2 Christ is a-live! No long-er bound to dis-tant
3 Christ is a-live! His Spir-it burns through this and

emp-ty to the sky. Let streets and homes with
years in Pal-es-tine, he comes to claim the
ev-'ry fu-ture age, till all cre-a-tion

prais-es ring. His love in death shall nev-er die.
here and now and con-quer ev-'ry place and time.
lives and learns his joy, his jus-tice, love, and praise.

Text: Brian Wren, 1968, *New Church Praise*, 1975
         Copyright ©1975 Hope Publishing Co.
Music: anonymous, *Psalmodia Evangelica, Part II*, 1789

I know that my Redeemer lives 279

TRURO

1 I know that my Redeemer lives;
  what joy the bless'd assurance gives!
  He lives, he lives, who once was dead.
  He lives, my everlasting Head!

2 He lives to bless me with his love.
  He lives to plead for me above.
  He lives, my hungry soul to feed.
  He lives to help in time of need.

3 He lives, all glory to his name.
  He lives, my Savior, still the same.
  What joy the bless'd assurance gives;
  I know that my Redeemer lives!

Text: Samuel Medley, *Psalms and Hymns*, 1775, alt.
Music: anonymous, *Psalmodia Evangelica, Part II*, 1789

280 Christ the Lord is risen today

EASTER HYMN 77. 77 with alleluias

1 Christ the Lord is ris'n to - day!
2 Love's re - deem-ing work is done,
3 Lives a - gain our glo-rious King, Al — le - lu - ia!
4 Soar we now where Christ has led,
5 King of glo - ry, soul of bliss,

1 All cre - a - tion joins to say:
2 fought the fight, the bat - tle won.
3 where, O death, is now thy sting? Al — le - lu - ia!
4 fol - l'wing our ex - alt - ed Head.
5 ev - er - last - ing life is this:

1 Raise your joys and tri - umphs high:
2 Death in vain for - bids him rise,
3 Dy - ing once, he all doth save, Al — le - lu - ia!
4 Made like him, like him we rise,
5 Thee to know, thy pow'r to prove,

Text: Charles Wesley, *Hymns and Sacred Poems, Part II*, 1739, alt.
Music: anonymous, *Lyra Davidica*, 1708

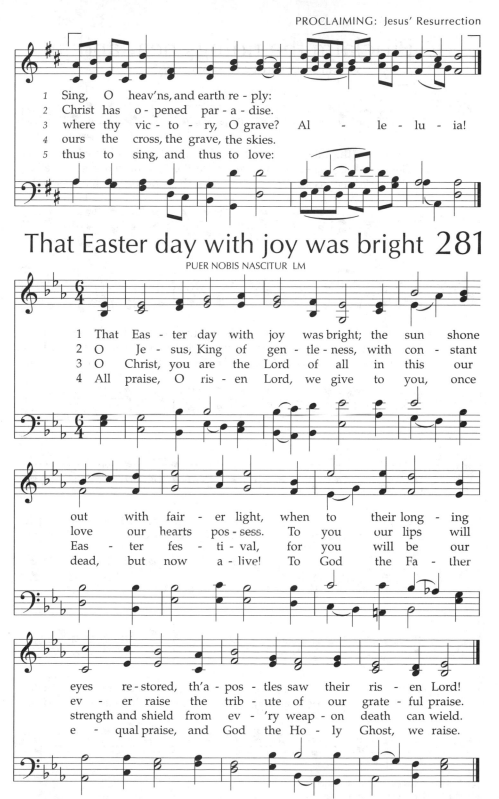

1 Sing, O heav'ns, and earth re - ply:
2 Christ has o - pened par - a - dise.
3 where thy vic - to - ry, O grave? Al - le - lu - ia!
4 ours the cross, the grave, the skies.
5 thus to sing, and thus to love:

That Easter day with joy was bright 281

PUER NOBIS NASCITUR LM

1 That Eas - ter day with joy was bright; the sun shone
2 O Je - sus, King of gen - tle - ness, with con - stant
3 O Christ, you are the Lord of all in this our
4 All praise, O ris - en Lord, we give to you, once

out with fair - er light, when to their long - ing
love our hearts pos - sess. To you our lips will
Eas - ter fes - ti - val, for you will be our
dead, but now a - live! To God the Fa - ther

eyes re - stored, th'a - pos - tles saw their ris - en Lord!
ev - er raise the trib - ute of our grate - ful praise.
strength and shield from ev - 'ry weap - on death can wield.
e - qual praise, and God the Ho - ly Ghost, we raise.

Text: anonymous, *Aurora lucis rutilat* – Part III, from *Claro Paschali gaudio*, 4th or 5th c.; tr. John M. Neale, *The Hymnal Noted*, 1851, alt.

Music: *Christliches Gesangbüchlein*, 1568

282 Proclaim the tidings near and far

SING GLORY, HALLELUJAH 87. 87 with refrain

1 Pro - claim the tid - ings near and far, go tell the bless-ed sto - ry;
2 The Lord is ris - en! O re - joice, the joy-ful cho-rus swell-ing,
3 The Lord is ris - en! O re - joice, the God of life has spo-ken.

the grave has giv - en up its dead – the Lord of life and glo - ry.
and sing glad songs with heart and voice, the won-drous sto - ry tell - ing.
For - ev - er-more through Christ's dear name the pow'r of death is bro-ken.

Refrain

Sing glo - ry, glo - ry, glo-ry, hal-le - lu - jah!
Sing glo-ry, glo-ry, glo-ry, glo-ry, glo-ry, hal-le - lu - jah!

Sing glo - ry, glo - ry, glo-ry, hal-le - lu - jah!
Sing glo-ry, glo-ry, glo-ry, glo-ry, glo-ry, hal-le - lu - jah!

Text: Fronia S. Smith, *Gems and Jewels*, 1890
Music: J. H. Fillmore, *Gems and Jewels*, 1890
        Text and music copyright ©1920 The Fillmore Brothers Co.

Christ who left his home in glory 283

CHRIST IS RISEN 87. 87 with refrain

1 Christ who left his home in glo - ry, and up - on the
2 While the world in peace was sleep - ing, ear - ly on that
3 Christ, our lov - ing me - di - a - tor, now with God for

cross was slain, now is ris'n! O tell the sto - ry
Eas - ter day, came the faith - ful wom - en, weep - ing,
you and me in - ter - cedes, and our Cre - a - tor

Refrain

that the Sav - ior lives a - gain. Hail him!
but the stone was rolled a - way. Hail to the King, the
hears and an - swers ev - 'ry plea.

Hail him! Tell the sto - ry.
might - y Re - deem - er! Hail him who robbed the grave of its pow'r!

Hail! all hail! Je - sus lives for - ev - er - more.
Tell ev - 'ry na - tion, all is well,

Text: Abram B. Kolb, 1896, *Church and Sunday School Hymnal*, 1902
Music: Abram B. Kolb, 1896, *Church and Sunday School Hymnal*, 1902

284 Come away to the skies

EXULTATION 669. 669

1 Come a - way to the skies, my be - lov - ed, a - rise
2 Now with sing - ing and praise, let us spend all the days
3 For the glo - ry we were first cre - at - ed to share,
4 We with thanks do ap - prove the de - sign of that love

and re - joice in the day you were born.
by our gra - cious Cre - a - tor be - stowed,
both the na - ture and king - dom di - vine,
which has joined us to Je - sus' name.

On this fes - ti - val day, come ex - ult - ing a - way,
while in grace we re - ceive from earth's boun - ty we live
now cre - at - ed a - gain that our lives may re - main
So u - nit - ed in heart, let us nev - er - more part,

and with sing - ing to Zi - on re - turn.
to the hon - or and glo - ry of God.
through - out time and e - ter - ni - ty thine.
till we meet at the feast of the Lamb.

Text: anonymous, based on a hymn by Charles Wesley, *Southern Harmony*, 1835, alt.
Music: *Southern Harmony*, 1835; harmonized by The Hymnal Project
Harmonization copyright ©1991 The Hymnal Project

All hail the power of Jesus' name 285

DIADEM CM extended

1 All hail the pow'r of Je - sus' name! Let an - gels pros - trate
2 Ye cho - sen seed of Is - rael's race, ye ran - somed of the
3 Let ev - 'ry kin - dred, ev - 'ry tribe, on this ter - res - trial
4 Oh, that with yon - der sa - cred throng we at his feet may

fall, let an - gels pros - trate fall. Bring forth the roy - al
fall, ye ran - somed of the fall, hail him who saves you
ball, on this ter - res - trial ball, to him all maj - es -
fall, we at his feet may fall! We'll join the ev - er -

di - a - dem, and crown _____ him,
by his grace,
ty as - cribe,
last - ing song, and crown him, crown him, crown him, crown him,

crown _____

crown him, crown him, crown him, and crown him Lord of all.

him, and crown him Lord of all.

Text: Edward Perronet, *Gospel Magazine*, 1779-1780; revised by John Rippon, *Selection of Hymns*, 1787
Music: James Ellor, ca. 1838

286

Look, you saints

BRYN CALFARIA 87. 87. 84. 77

1 Look, you saints, the sight is glo-rious! See the Man of sor-rows
2 Crown the Sav-ior, an-gels, crown him! Rich the tro-phies Je - sus
3 Sin - ners in de - ri-sion crowned him, mocked the dy - ing Sav-ior's

now from the fight re - turned vic - to - rious; ev - 'ry
brings. In the seat of pow'r en - throne him while the
claim. Saints and an - gels crowd a - round him, sing his

knee to him shall bow. Crown him, crown him, crown him,
vault of heav - en rings. crown him, crown him,
tri - umph, praise his name.

crown him, crown him, crown him. Crowns be - fit the
crown him, crown him, crown him, crown him, Crown the Sav - ior
Spread a - broad the

Text: based on Revelation 7:9-15, Thomas Kelly, *Hymns on Various Passages of Scripture,* 3rd ed., 1809, alt.
Music: William Owen, *Y Perl Cerddorol (The Pearl of Music),* Vol. II, 1886; version from *Welsh Hymns and Their Tunes,* 1990

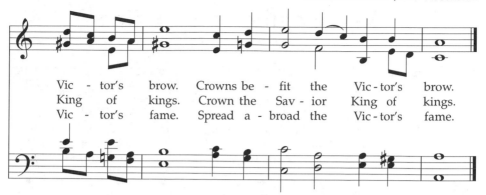

Vic - tor's brow. Crowns be - fit the Vic - tor's brow.
King of kings. Crown the Sav - ior King of kings.
Vic - tor's fame. Spread a - broad the Vic - tor's fame.

Sing we triumphant hymns 287

DEO GRACIAS LM

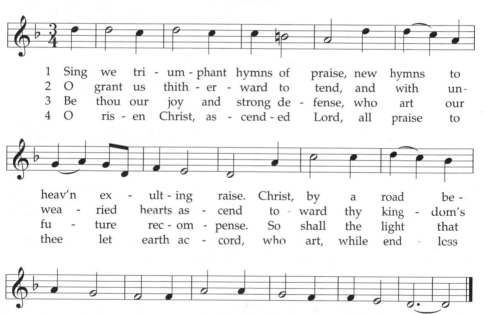

1 Sing we tri - um - phant hymns of praise, new hymns to
2 O grant us thith - er - ward to tend, and with un-
3 Be thou our joy and strong de - fense, who art our
4 O ris - en Christ, as - cend - ed Lord, all praise to

heav'n ex - ult - ing raise. Christ, by a road be -
wea - ried hearts as - cend to - ward thy king - dom's
fu - ture rec - om - pense. So shall the light that
thee let earth ac - cord, who art, while end - less

fore un - trod, as - cend - eth to the throne of God.
throne, where thou, as is our faith, art seat - ed now.
springs from thee be ours through all e - ter - ni - ty.
ag - es run, with Fa - ther and with Spir - it one.

Text: The Venerable Bede, *Hymnum canamus gloriae,* 11th c.; tr. Benjamin Webb, *The Hymnal Noted,* 1851
Music: English melody, 15th c.

288 Rejoice, the Lord is King

DARWALL'S 148th 66. 66. 88

1 Re - joice, the Lord is King! Your Lord and King a -
2 Je - sus the Sav - ior reigns, the God of truth and
3 His king-dom can-not fail, he rules o'er earth and
4 Re - joice in glo-rious hope, Je - sus the judge shall

dore! Mor - tals, give thanks and sing and tri - umph
love. When he had purged our stains he took his
heav'n. The keys of death and hell to Je - sus
come and take his ser - vants up to their e -

ev - er - more. Lift up your heart, lift
seat a - bove. Lift up your heart, lift
now are giv'n. Lift up your heart, lift
ter - nal home. We soon shall hear th'arch-

up your voice, re - joice, a - gain I say, re - joice.
up your voice, re - joice, a - gain I say, re - joice.
up your voice, re - joice, a - gain I say, re - joice.
an - gel's voice, the trump of God shall sound, re - joice!

Text: Charles Wesley, *Moral and Sacred Poems*, 1744
Music: John Darwall, *New Universal Psalmodist*, 1770

Filled with the Spirit's power 289
BIRMINGHAM (CUNNINGHAM) 10 10. 10 10

1 Filled with the Spir - it's pow'r, with one ac - cord the
2 Now with the mind of Christ set us on fire, that
3 Wid - en our love, good Spir - it, to em - brace the

in - fant church con - fessed its ris - en Lord.
u - ni - ty may be our great de - sire.
peo - ple of all lands and ev - 'ry race.

O Ho - ly Spir - it, in the church to - day a -
Give joy and peace, give faith to hear your call, and
Like wind and fire, with life a - mong us move, till

gain your pow'r of fel - low - ship dis - play.
read - i - ness in each to work for all.
we are known as Christ's and Chris - tians prove.

Text: J. R. Peacey, 1967, *100 Hymns for Today*, 1969
Copyright ©1978 Hope Publishing Co.
Music: Joseph Funk's *Genuine Church Music*, 1st ed., 1832

290 Spirit, come, dispel our sadness

O MEIN JESU, ICH MUSS STERBEN 87. 87D

1 Spir-it, come, dis-pel our sad-ness, pierce the clouds of
2 Au-thor of the new cre-a-tion, come, a-noint us

na-ture's night. Come, O Source of joy and glad-ness, breathe your
with your pow'r. Make our hearts your hab-i-ta-tion, with your

life, and spread your light. From the height which knows no mea-sure,
grace our spir-its show'r. Hear, O hear our sup-pli-ca-tion,

as a gra-cious show'r de-scend, bring-ing down the
bless-ed Spir-it, God of peace! Rest up-on this

rich-est trea-sure we can wish, or God can send.
con-gre-ga-tion with the full-ness of your grace.

Text: Paul Gerhardt, 1648; tr. John C. Jacobi, ca. 1725, alt.
Music: *Geistliche Volkslieder*, ca. 1858

O Holy Spirit, by whose breath 291

ST. BARTHOLOMEW LM

1 O Ho - ly Spir - it, by whose breath life ris - es
2 You are the seek - er's sure re - source, of burn - ing
3 In you God's en - er - gy is shown. To us your
4 Flood our dull sens - es with your light. In mu - tual
5 From in - ner strife grant us re - lease. Turn na - tions
6 Praise our Cre - a - tor, Christ the Word, and praise the

1 vi - brant out of death, come to cre - ate, re - new,
2 love the liv - ing source, pro - tec - tor in the midst
3 var - ied gifts make known. Teach us to speak, teach us
4 love our hearts u - nite. Your pow'r the whole cre - a -
5 to the ways of peace. To full - er life your peo -
6 Spir - it, God the Lord, to whom all hon - or, glo -

1 in - spire. Come, kin - dle in our hearts your fire.
2 of strife, the giv - er and the Lord of life.
3 to hear; yours is the tongue and yours the ear.
4 tion fills; con - firm our weak, un - cer - tain wills.
5 ple bring, that as one bod - y we may sing:
6 ry be both now and for e - ter - ni - ty.

Text: attributed to Rabanus Maurus, *Veni Creator Spiritus*, 9th c.; tr. John W. Grant, *Hymn Book*, 1971, alt.
Copyright ©1971 John Webster Grant
Music: Henry Duncalf, *Parochial Harmony*, 1762

292 Away with our fears

ARDWICK 555. 11

1 A - way with our fears, our trou - bles and
2 Our ad - vo - cate there by his death and his
3 Our glo - ri - fied Lord has giv - en his
4 Our heav - en - ly guide with us shall a -
5 The heart that be - lieves his king - dom re -

1 tears! The Spir - it is come, the wit - ness of
2 prayer the gift has ob - tained; for us he has
3 word that his Spir - it will stay, and nev - er a -
4 bide, his com - forts im - part, and set up his
5 ceives, his pow'r and his peace, his life, and his

1 Je - sus re - turned to his home.
2 prayed and the Com - for - ter gained.
3 gain will be tak - en a - way.
4 king - dom of love in our heart.
5 joy's ev - er - last - ing in - crease.

Text: Charles Wesley, *Hymns of Petition and Thanksgiving for the Promise of the Father*, 1746
Music: Henry J. Gauntlett, *Tunes New and Old*, 1864

God sends us the Spirit 293

NATOMAH 669D with refrain

1 God sends us the Spir - it to be-friend and help us,
2 Dark-ened roads are clear - er, heav - y bur - dens light - er,
3 Now we are God's peo - ple, bond - ed by God's pres - ence,

re - cre - ate and guide us, Spir-it-Friend. Spir - it who en - liv - ens,
when we're walk-ing with our Spir-it-Friend. Now we need not fear the
a - gents of God's pur-pose, Spir-it-Friend. Lead us for-ward ev - er,

sanc - ti - fies, en - light-ens, sets us free, is now our Spir-it-Friend.
pow - ers of the dark-ness. None can o - ver-come our Spir-it-Friend.
slip - ping back-ward nev - er, to your re-made world, our Spir-it-Friend.

Refrain

Spir-it of our Mak-er, Spir-it-Friend.
Spir-it of our Je - sus, Spir-it-Friend. Spir-it of God's peo-ple, Spir-it-Friend.

Text: Tom Colvin, 1969, alt.
Music: Gonja folk melody (Ghana); adapted by Tom Colvin and C. J. Natomah
Text and music copyright ©1969 Hope Publishing Co.

Dona nobis pacem Domine 294

Ostinato Am C Dm E sus E
mp
Do - na no - bis pa - cem Do - mi - ne.*

*Translation: Lord, grant us peace.

Music: Jacques Berthier and the Taizé community, Music from Taizé, Vol. II, 1982, 1983, 1984
Copyright ©1982, 1983, 1984 Les Presses de Taizé (France). Used by permission of G.I.A. Publications, Inc.

295 Christ is coming! Let creation

UNSER HERRSCHER (NEANDER) 87. 87. 87

1 Christ is com - ing! Let cre - a - tion from its groans and tra - vail cease. Let the glo - rious proc - la - ma - tion hope re - store and faith in - crease: Christ is com - ing! Christ is com - ing! Come, thou bless - ed Prince of peace.

2 Earth can now but tell the sto - ry of the bit - ter cross and pain. We shall yet be - hold the glo - ry, when thou com - est back to reign: Christ is com - ing! Christ is com - ing! Let each heart re - peat the strain.

3 Long thine ex - iles have been pin - ing, far from rest, and home, and thee. But, in heav'n - ly ves - tures shin - ing, soon they shall thy glo - ry see! Christ is com - ing! Christ is com - ing! Haste the joy - ous ju - bi - lee!

4 With that bless - ed hope be - fore us, let no harp re - main un - strung. Let the might - y ad - vent cho - rus on - ward roll from tongue to tongue: "Christ is com - ing! Christ is com - ing! Come, Lord Je - sus, quick - ly come!"

Text: John R. MacDuff, *Altar Stones*, 1853, alt.
Music: Joachim Neander, *Alpha und Omega, Glaub- und Liebesübung*, 1680

Here from all nations

296

O QUANTA QUALIA 11 10. 11 10

1 Here from all na-tions, all tongues and all peo-ples,
2 These have come out of the great trib-u-la-tion,
3 Gone is their thirst and no more shall they hun-ger.
4 Christ will go with them to clear, liv-ing wa-ter
5 Bless-ing and glo-ry and wis-dom and pow-er

1 count-less the crowd but their voic-es are one.
2 now they may stand in the pres-ence of God,
3 God is their shel-ter and pow-er at their side.
4 flow-ing from springs which his mer-cy sup-plies.
5 be to the Sav-ior a-gain and a-gain.

1 Vast is the sight and ma-jes-tic their sing-ing.
2 serv-ing their Lord day and night in the tem-ple,
3 Sun shall not pain them, no burn-ing will tor-ture.
4 Gone is their grief, and their tri-als are o-ver.
5 Might and thanks-giv-ing and hon-or for-ev-er

1 "God has the vic-t'ry and reigns from the throne!"
2 ran-somed and cleansed by the Lamb's pre-cious blood.
3 Je-sus, the Lamb, is their shep-herd and guide.
4 God wipes a-way ev-'ry tear from their eyes.
5 be to our God: Al-le-lu-ia! A-men.

Text: based on Revelation 7:9-17, Christopher Idle, 1972, *Psalm Praise*, 1973
        Copyright ©1973 Hope Publishing Co.
Music: *Paris Antiphoner*, 1681; adapted by François de la Feillée, *Méthode du plain-chant*, 1808, harmonized by David Evans
        Harmonization copyright © Oxford University Press, London

297 Jesus came – the heavens adoring

BENEDIC ANIMA 87. 87. 87

1 Je - sus came – the heav'ns a - dor - ing – came with
2 Je - sus comes to us in mer - cy, when our
3 Je - sus comes to hearts re - joic - ing – all the
4 Je - sus comes in joy and sor - row, shares a -
5 Je - sus comes on clouds tri - um - phant, when the

1 peace from realms on high. Je - sus came for our re -
2 hearts are bowed with care. Je - sus comes in pow'r to
3 past he now for - gives. Je - sus comes to share his
4 like our hopes and fears. Je - sus comes, what - e'er be -
5 heav'ns shall pass a - way. Je - sus comes a - gain in

1 demp - tion, hum - bly came on earth to die. Al - le - lu - ia!
2 an - swer ev - 'ry ear - nest, heart - felt prayer. Al - le - lu - ia!
3 king - dom with the sin - ners he re - ceives. Al - le - lu - ia!
4 fall us, glads our hearts, and dries our tears. Al - le - lu - ia!
5 glo - ry; let us then our hom - age pay. Al - le - lu - ia!

1 Al - le - lu - ia! came in deep hu - mil - i - ty.
2 Al - le - lu - ia! comes to save us from de - spair.
3 Al - le - lu - ia! Death is con - qu'red – Je - sus lives!
4 Al - le - lu - ia! cheer - ing e'en our fail - ing years.
5 ev - er sing - ing till the dawn of end - less day.

Text: Godfrey Thring, Chope's *Hymnal,* 1864; revised in *Hymns for Today's Church* (Sts. 1-3,5), 1982
         Revision (Sts. 1-3,5) copyright ©1982 Hope Publishing Co.
Music: John Goss, *The Supplemental Hymn and Tune Book,* 1869

Veni Sancte Spiritus

298

VENI SANCTE SPIRITUS Irregular

Ostinato

pp Ve - ni Sanc - te Spir - i - tus.*

Leader

1 Come, Ho - ly Spir - it, from heav-en shine forth with your glo-rious

light. Ve - ni Sanc - te Spir - i - tus. 2 Come from the four winds, O Spir - it,

come breath of God; dis - perse the shad - ows o - ver us, re -

new and strength-en your peo - ple. Ve - ni Sanc - te Spir - i - tus.

3 You are our on - ly com - fort - er, peace of the

soul. In the heat you shade us; in our la - bor you re -

fresh us, and in trou - ble you are our strength. Ve - ni Sanc - te

Spir - i - tus. 4 Kin - dle in our hearts the flame of your love that in the dark-

ness of the world it may glow and reach to all for - ev - er. Ve - ni ...

*Translation: Come, Holy Spirit.

Text: based on Latin sequence, 13th c., Taizé community, *Music from Taizé*, Vol. I, 1978, 1980, 1981
Music: Jacques Berthier, 1978, *Music from Taizé*, Vol. I, 1978, 1980, 1981

299 New earth, heavens new

ALEXANDRA 56. 56. 56 with refrain

1 New earth, heav - ens new, Spir - it of God
2 New love, mer - cies new, Spir - it of God
3 New minds, wis - dom new, Spir - it of God
4 New earth, heav - ens new, Spir - it of God

mov - ing; new seed, crea - tures new,
mov - ing; new strength, hope - ful - ness new,
mov - ing; new law, cov - e - nant new,
mov - ing; new birth, crea - tures new,

Spir - it of life mov - ing; new man,
Spir - it of life mov - ing; new hearts,
Spir - it of life mov - ing; new name,
Spir - it of life mov - ing; new men,

wom-an new, im - age of God mov - ing.
spir - its new, im - age of God mov - ing.
na - ture new, im - age of God mov - ing.
wom-en new, im - age of God mov - ing.

Refrain

Sing a new song to the One who has said, "Be - hold, I make all things

1-3 new."

4 new."

O Holy Spirit, making whole 300

MELITA 88. 88. 88

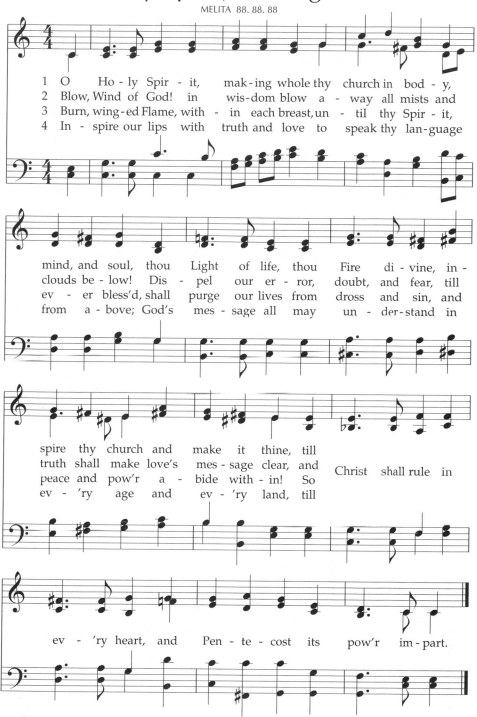

1 O Ho-ly Spir-it, mak-ing whole thy church in bod-y,
2 Blow, Wind of God! in wis-dom blow a-way all mists and
3 Burn, wing-ed Flame, with-in each breast, un-til thy Spir-it,
4 In-spire our lips with truth and love to speak thy lan-guage

mind, and soul, thou Light of life, thou Fire di-vine, in-
clouds be-low! Dis-pel our er-ror, doubt, and fear, till
ev-er bless'd, shall purge our lives from dross and sin, and
from a-bove; God's mes-sage all may un-der-stand in

spire thy church and make it thine, till
truth shall make love's mes-sage clear, and   Christ shall rule in
peace and pow'r a-bide with-in! So
ev-'ry age and ev-'ry land, till

ev-'ry heart, and Pen-te-cost its pow'r im-part.

Text: Henry H. Tweedy, *Christian Worship and Praise*, 1939, alt.
Copyright ©1939 A. S. Barnes & Co., Inc.; renewed 1967 Gordon B. Tweedy
Music: John B. Dykes, *Hymns Ancient and Modern*, 1861

301 Joys are flowing like a river

87. 87 with refrain

1 Joys are flow - ing like a riv - er since the
2 Bring - ing life and health and glad - ness all a -
3 Like the rain that falls from heav - en, like the
4 See, a fruit - ful field is grow - ing, bless - ed
5 What a won - der - ful sal - va - tion, where we

1 Com - fort - er has come, who a - bides with us for -
2 round, this heav'n - ly Guest ban - ished un - be - lief and
3 sun - light from the sky, so the Ho - ly Ghost is
4 fruit of right - eous - ness, and the streams of life are
5 al - ways see God's face! What a per - fect hab - i -

1 ev - er, makes the trust - ing heart a home.
2 sad - ness, changed our wea - ri - ness to rest.
3 giv - en, com - ing on us from on high.
4 flow - ing in the lone - ly wil - der - ness.
5 ta - tion, what a qui - et rest - ing place!

Refrain

Bless - ed qui - et - ness, ho - ly qui - et - ness — what a s -

Text: Manie P. Ferguson, alt.
Music: W. S. Marshall; adapted by James M. Kirk

sur - ance in my soul! On the storm - y sea speak - ing

peace to me – how the bil - lows cease to roll!

Come, divine Interpreter 302

SPANISH CHANT 77. 77. 77

Come, di - vine In - ter - pre - ter, bring us eyes thy book to read,

ears the mys - tic words to hear, words which did from thee pro - ceed,

words that end - less bliss im - part, kept in an o - be - dient heart.

Text: Charles Wesley, *Short Hymns on Select Passages of Holy Scripture,* 1762
Music: Burgoyne's *Collection,* 1827; arranged by Benjamin Carr

303 Come, gracious Spirit

BACA LM extended

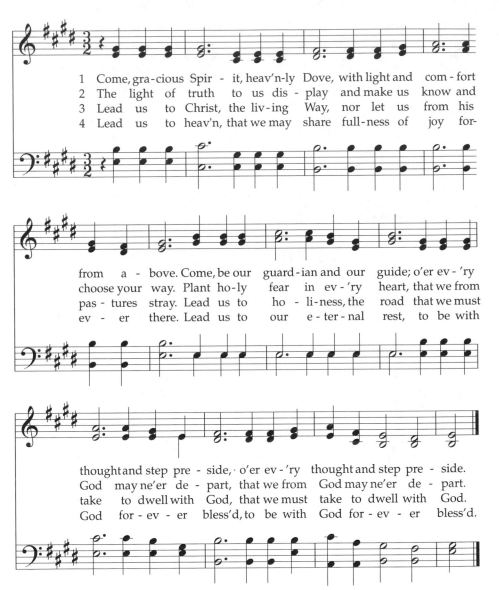

1 Come, gra-cious Spir - it, heav'n-ly Dove, with light and com - fort
2 The light of truth to us dis - play and make us know and
3 Lead us to Christ, the liv-ing Way, nor let us from his
4 Lead us to heav'n, that we may share full-ness of joy for-

from a - bove. Come, be our guard-ian and our guide; o'er ev - 'ry
choose your way. Plant ho-ly fear in ev - 'ry heart, that we from
pas - tures stray. Lead us to ho - li-ness, the road that we must
ev - er there. Lead us to our e - ter-nal rest, to be with

thought and step pre - side, · o'er ev-'ry thought and step pre - side.
God may ne'er de - part, that we from God may ne'er de - part.
take to dwell with God, that we must take to dwell with God.
God for - ev - er bless'd, to be with God for - ev - er bless'd.

Text: Simon Browne and others, *Hymns and Spiritual Songs,* 1720, alt.
Music: William B. Bradbury, *The Jubilee ...,* 1858

There are many gifts

304

MANY GIFTS Irregular with refrain

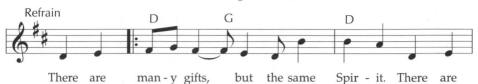

Refrain

There are man-y gifts, but the same Spir-it. There are

man-y works, but the same God, and the Spir-it gives each as it

choos-es. Praise the Lord. Praise God.

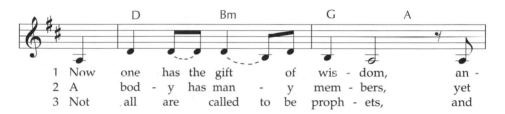

1 Now   one   has the gift   of wis - dom,   an -
2 A   bod - y has man   -   y   mem - bers,   yet
3 Not   all   are called to be   proph - ets, and

oth - er the call - ing to speak,   one the a - bil - i - ty to
all work in u - ni -   ty. The church is the bod - y of
not all are called to   preach, but all should aim   for the

com - fort, an - oth - er the call - ing to teach. There are
Christ,   his arms, ears and eyes, hands and feet. There are
best gifts and love is the great - est of these.

Text: based on 1 Corinthians 12, Patricia Shelly, 1976, *Many Gifts*, 1977
Music: Patricia Shelly, 1976, *Many Gifts*, 1977
        Text and music copyright ©1977 Patricia Shelly

305 Where charity and love prevail

CHESHIRE CM

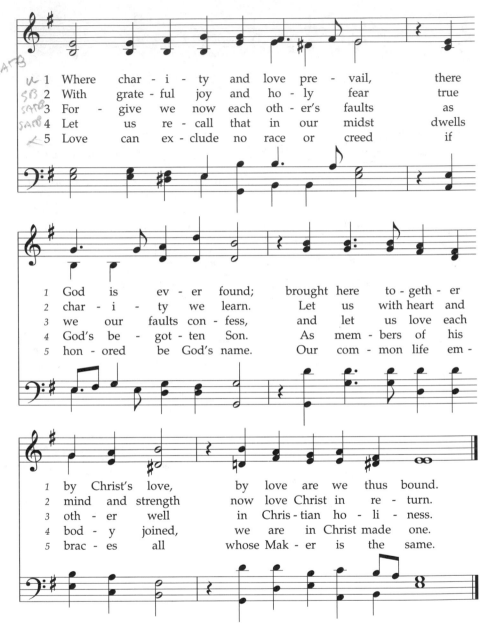

1 Where char - i - ty and love pre - vail, there God is ev - er found; brought here to - geth - er by Christ's love, by love are we thus bound.

2 With grate - ful joy and ho - ly fear true char - i - ty we learn. Let us with heart and mind and strength now love Christ in re - turn.

3 For - give we now each oth - er's faults as we our faults con - fess, and let us love each oth - er well in Chris - tian ho - li - ness.

4 Let us re - call that in our midst dwells God's be - got - ten Son. As mem - bers of his bod - y joined, we are in Christ made one.

5 Love can ex - clude no race or creed if hon - ored be God's name. Our com - mon life em - brac - es all whose Mak - er is the same.

Text: anonymous, *Ubi caritas et amor,* 9th c.; tr. Omer Westendorf, *The People's Mass Book,* 1961, alt.
          Translation copyright ©1961 World Library Publications, Inc.
Music: *The Whole Booke of Psalmes ...,* 1592

In Christ there is no East or West 306

ST. PETER CM

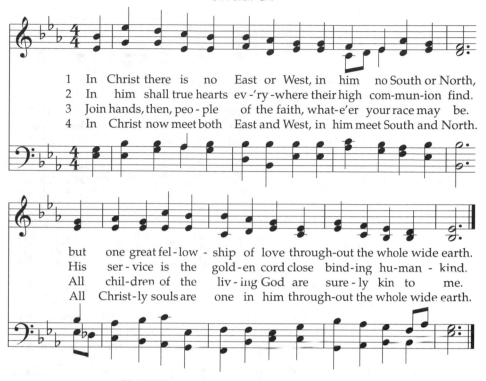

1 In Christ there is no East or West, in him no South or North,
2 In him shall true hearts ev-'ry-where their high com-mun-ion find.
3 Join hands, then, peo-ple of the faith, what-e'er your race may be.
4 In Christ now meet both East and West, in him meet South and North.

but one great fel-low-ship of love through-out the whole wide earth.
His ser-vice is the gold-en cord close bind-ing hu-man-kind.
All chil-dren of the liv-ing God are sure-ly kin to me.
All Christ-ly souls are one in him through-out the whole wide earth.

SPANISH

Oriente ni occidente hay en Cristo y su bondad;
incluída en su amor está la entera humanidad.

En Dios los fieles al Señor su comunión tendrán,
y con los lazos de su amor al mundo ligarán.

¡De razas no haya distinción, obreros de la fe!
El que, cual hijo, sirve a Dios, hermano nuestro es.

Oriente y occidente en él se encuentran, y su amor
las almas une por la fe en santa comunión.

KOREAN

Joo Yesu ane dong seona nambuki itsurya
On seikye modun minjoki da hyungje aninga.

Joo Yesu kyesin Gotmada chamsarang saeuri
Moot bakseong hamkke mookyoseo hangajog irune.

Dakachi soneul matjabjo han abeojimite
Geotmoyang injong daruna han janyo doedoda.

Joo Yesu ane dongseowa nambuki hapayeo
Joo Yesu sarang aneseo dahana daedoda.

Text: John Oxenham, 1908, *Bees in Amber*, 1913, alt.
         Copyright © Estate of John Oxenham
Music: Alexander R. Reinagle, *Psalm Tunes for the Voice and Pianoforte*, ca. 1836

307 Will you let me be your servant

THE SERVANT SONG 87. 87

1,6 Will you let me be your ser-vant,   let me
2 We are pil-grims on a jour-ney,   we are
3 I will hold the Christ-light for you   in the
4 I will weep when you are weep-ing,   when you
5 When we sing to God in heav-en,   we shall

1,6 be as Christ to you?   Pray that I may have the
2 trav-'lers on the road.   We are here to help each
3 night-time of your fear.   I will hold my hand out
4 laugh I'll laugh with you.   I will share your joy and
5 find such har-mon-y,   born of all we've known to-

1,6 grace to let you be my ser - vant too.
2 oth-er walk the mile and bear the load.
3 to you, speak the peace you long to hear.
4 sor-row till we've seen this jour - ney through.
5 geth-er of Christ's love and ag - o - ny.

*Guitar chords for unison singing only

Text: Richard Gillard, 1976, alt.
Music: Richard Gillard, 1976; adapted by Betty Pulkingham
        Text and music copyright ©1977 Scripture in Song

I love thy kingdom, Lord   308

BEALOTH SMD

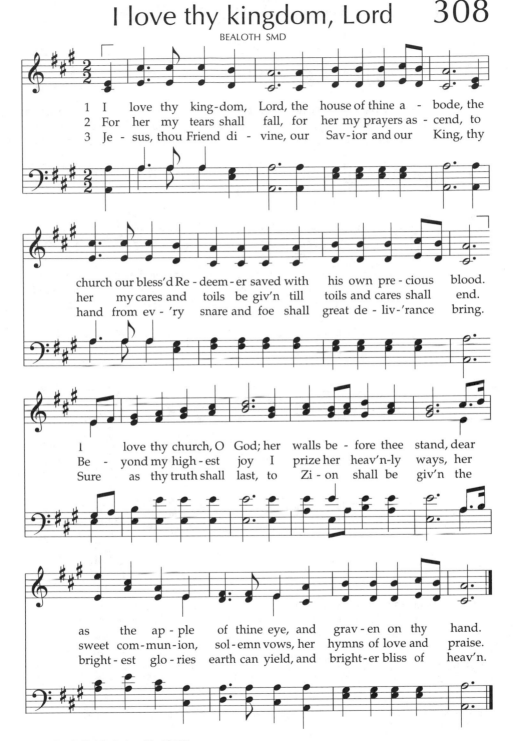

1 I love thy king-dom, Lord, the house of thine a - bode, the
2 For her my tears shall fall, for her my prayers as - cend, to
3 Je - sus, thou Friend di - vine, our Sav-ior and our King, thy

church our bless'd Re - deem - er saved with his own pre - cious blood.
her my cares and toils be giv'n till toils and cares shall end.
hand from ev - 'ry snare and foe shall great de - liv-'rance bring.

I love thy church, O God; her walls be - fore thee stand, dear
Be - yond my high - est joy I prize her heav'n-ly ways, her
Sure as thy truth shall last, to Zi - on shall be giv'n the

as the ap - ple of thine eye, and grav - en on thy hand.
sweet com-mun-ion, sol-emn vows, her hymns of love and praise.
bright - est glo - ries earth can yield, and bright-er bliss of heav'n.

Text: Timothy Dwight, *Psalms of David,* 1801
Music: Lowell Mason, *Sacred Hymns,* 1842

309 Built on the Rock

KIRKEN DEN ER ET GAMMELT HUS 88. 88. 888

1 Built on the Rock the church doth stand, e - ven when
2 Sure - ly in tem - ples made with hands, God, the Most
3 Now we may gath - er with our King e'en in the

stee - ples are fall - ing. Crum - bled have spires in
High, is not dwell - ing. High a - bove earth God's
low - li - est dwell - ing. Prais - es to God we

ev - 'ry land, bells still are chim - ing and call - ing,
tem - ple stands, all earth - ly tem - ples ex - cel - ling.
there may bring, the won - drous mer - cy forth - tell - ing.

call - ing the young and old to rest, but a - bove all the
The One whom heav'ns can - not con - tain chose here a - mong us
Je - sus his grace to us ac - cords. Spir - it and life are

Text: Nikolai F. S. Grundtvig, "Kirken den er et gammelt Hus," *Sang-Värk til den Danske Kirke,* 1837; tr. Carl Döving, 1909,
          The Lutheran Hymnary, 1913
          Translation copyright ©1958 *Service Book and Hymnal*
Music: Ludvig M. Lindeman, *Christelige Psalmer,* 1840

soul dis-tressed, long-ing for rest ev-er-last - ing.
to re-main, built in our bod-ies a tem - ple.
all his words. His truth doth hal-low the tem - ple.

How good a thing it is 310

VENICE SM

1 How good a thing it is, how
2 As per-fume, by its scent, breathes
3 And like re-fresh-ing dew that
4 God grants the choic-est gifts to

pleas - ant to be - hold, when all God's peo - ple
fra - grance all a - round, so life it - self will
falls up - on the hills, true un - ion sheds its
those who live in peace; to them such bless - ings

live as one, the law of love up - hold!
sweet - er be where u - ni - ty is found.
gen - tle grace, and deep - er love in - stills.
shall a - bound and ev - er - more in - crease.

Text: based on Psalm 133, J. E. Seddon, *Hymns for Today's Church*, 1982
Copyright ©1982 Hope Publishing Co.
Music: W. Amps, *Selection of Psalm and Hymn Tunes*, 1853

311 The church's one foundation

AURELIA 76. 76D

1 The church's one foun - da - tion is Je - sus Christ her Lord.
2 E - lect from ev - 'ry na - tion yet one o'er all the earth,
3 Though with a scorn-ful won - der the world sees her op - pressed,
4 'Mid toil and trib - u - la - tion, and tu - mult of her war,
5 Yet she on earth hath un - ion with God the Three-in - One,

1 She is his new cre - a - tion by wa - ter and the word.
2 her char - ter of sal - va - tion: one Lord, one faith, one birth.
3 by schisms rent a - sun - der, by her - e - sies dis - tressed,
4 she waits the con-sum - ma - tion of peace for - ev - er - more,
5 and mys - tic sweet com - mun-ion with those whose rest is won.

1 From heav'n he came and sought her to be his ho - ly bride;
2 One ho - ly name she bless - es, par - takes one ho - ly food,
3 yet saints their watch are keep-ing, their cry goes up, "How long?"
4 till with the vi - sion glo-rious her long-ing eyes are bless'd,
5 Oh, hap - py ones and ho - ly! Lord, give us grace that we,

1 with his own blood he bought her, and for her life he died.
2 and to one hope she press - es, with ev - 'ry grace en - dued.
3 And soon the night of weep-ing shall be the morn of song.
4 and the great church vic - to - rious shall be the church at rest.
5 like them, the meek and low - ly, on high may dwell with thee.

Text: Samuel J. Stone, *Lyra Fidelium*, 1866, alt.
Music: Samuel S. Wesley, *Selection of Psalms and Hymns*, 1864

Lamp of our feet

312

GRÄFENBURG (NUN DANKET ALL') CM

1 Lamp of our feet, where - by we trace our path when wont to stray; stream from the fount of heav'n-ly grace, brook by the trav - 'ler's way;

2 bread of our souls, where - on we feed, true man - na from a - bove, our guide and chart, where - in we read of God's un - end - ing love;

3 pil - lar of fire, through watch - es dark, or ra - diant cloud by day; when waves would 'whelm our toss - ing bark, our an - chor and our stay;

4 word of the ev - er - liv - ing God, will of the glo - rious Son; with - out thee how could earth be trod, or heav'n it - self be won?

5 Lord, grant us all a - right to learn the wis - dom it im - parts, and to its heav - 'nly teach - ing turn, with sim - ple, child - like hearts.

Text: Bernard Barton, *The Reliquary*, 1836
Music: Johann Crüger, *Praxis Pietatis Melica*, 5th ed., 1653

313 Rejoice, rejoice in God

REJOICE IN GOD 86. 88

1 Re - joice, re - joice in God, our Lord, all Chris-tians ev-'ry-
2 O peo-ple ev-'ry-where, ac-cept the truth that Scrip-ture
3 O Je - sus Christ, the Son of God, our friend, the liv-ing
4 Praise God, praise God for - ev-er-more, all Chris-tians ev-'ry-
5 God's word will stand e - ter - nal-ly; in that we are se -

1 where, for now in na - tions far and wide rings
2 brings. A - ban - don self - made ways; re - ly on
3 Word, don't let us turn a - way from you but
4 where. The word of Love has spread a - broad. We
5 cure. So now we all sing joy - ful - ly: A -

1 out, rings out God's might - y word.
2 God, on God the faith - ful guide.
3 from, but from this tempt - ing world.
4 trust, we trust that Love a - lone.
5 men! A - men! God's love is sure.

rings out, rings out

Text: Balthasar Hubmaier, ca. 1520; tr. Ruth Naylor, alt.
Translation copyright ©1983 Ruth Naylor
Music: James W. Bixel, *Assembly Songs,* 1983
Copyright ©1983 James W. Bixel

The word of God is solid ground 314

THE WORD OF GOD 87. 87D

1 The word of God is sol - id ground, our con-stant firm con-
2 What pow - ers can our faith con-strain? What i - ron-clad re-
3 What God-word brings, may we em - brace; suc - cess and suf-f'ring

fes - sion, no source of free - dom more pro - found, no
stric - tions? No self - de - ceiv - ing rule can chain our
greet us; con - front - ing e - vil face to face, as

pur - er a pro - fes - sion. All stead - fast strength, all
con - science and con - vic - tions. Our God a - lone is
scorn and an - ger meet us. For free - dom's sake we

breadth and length of truth, from God's word spring - ing shall
on the throne, and we are sub - jects will - ing. Our
bend, we break, a sign to ev - 'ry na - tion that

we em-ploy to speak our joy, this world our wit-ness bring-ing.
lives o - bey God's high - er way; our love God's law ful - fill - ing.
we have found a sol - id ground; God's word our sure foun - da - tion.

Text: anonymous, ca. 1550, *Ausbund*, 1564; adapted by Harris J. Loewen, *Assembly Songs*, 1983
        Adaptation copyright ©1983 Harris J. Loewen
Music: J. Harold Moyer, *Assembly Songs*, 1983
        Copyright ©1983 Faith and Life Press/Mennonite Publishing House

315 This is a story full of love

PRIMROSE CM

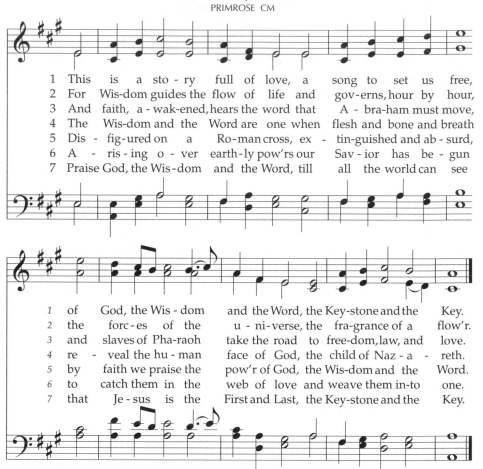

1 This is a sto-ry full of love, a song to set us free,
2 For Wis-dom guides the flow of life and gov-erns, hour by hour,
3 And faith, a-wak-ened, hears the word that A-bra-ham must move,
4 The Wis-dom and the Word are one when flesh and bone and breath
5 Dis-fig-ured on a Ro-man cross, ex-tin-guished and ab-surd,
6 A-ris-ing o-ver earth-ly pow'rs our Sav-ior has be-gun
7 Praise God, the Wis-dom and the Word, till all the world can see

1 of God, the Wis-dom and the Word, the Key-stone and the Key.
2 the forc-es of the u-ni-verse, the fra-grance of a flow'r.
3 and slaves of Pha-raoh take the road to free-dom, law, and love.
4 re-veal the hu-man face of God, the child of Naz-a-reth.
5 by faith we praise the pow'r of God, the Wis-dom and the Word.
6 to catch them in the web of love and weave them in-to one.
7 that Je-sus is the First and Last, the Key-stone and the Key.

Text: Brian Wren, 1985, *Praising a Mystery,* 1986
Copyright ©1986 Hope Publishing Co.
Music: Amzi Chapin or Lucius Chapin, 1811 or 1812, in John Wyeth's *Repository of Sacred Music, Part Second,* 1813

316 In this world abound scrolls

MŌSŌ 57. 57. 78

1 In this world a-bound scrolls of wis-dom num-ber-less,
2 Stud-y as we may, nev-er can we grasp there-by

Text: Saichirō Yuya; tr. Esther Hibbard, 1962, alt.
Copyright © Japanese Hymnal Committee
Music: Japanese melody of Chinese origin, *Sambika,* 1954

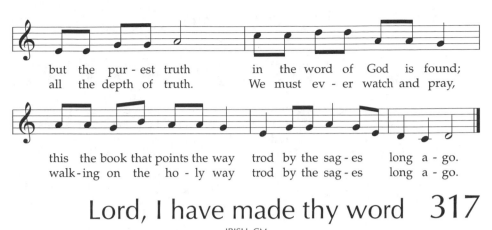

but the pur - est truth in the word of God is found;
all the depth of truth. We must ev - er watch and pray,

this the book that points the way trod by the sag - es long a - go.
walk-ing on the ho - ly way trod by the sag - es long a - go.

Lord, I have made thy word 317

IRISH CM

1 Lord, I have made thy word my choice, my
2 I'll read the his - t'ries of thy love, and
3 In this broad land of wealth un - known, where

last - ing her - i - tage. There shall my no - blest
keep thy laws in sight, while through thy prom - is -
springs of life a - rise, im - mor - tal seeds of

pow'rs re - joice, my warm - est thoughts en - gage.
es I rove, with ev - er - fresh de - light.
bliss are sown, and hid - den glo - ry lies.

Text: based on Psalm 119, Isaac Watts, *Psalms of David ...*, 1719
Music: *A Collection of Hymns and Sacred Poems*, 1749

318
Joy to the world

ANTIOCH CM extended

1 Joy to the world, the Lord is come! Let earth re - ceive her
2 Joy to the earth, the Sav - ior reigns! Let all their songs em -
3 No more let sins and sor - rows grow, nor thorns in - fest the
4 He rules the world with truth and grace, and makes the na - tions

King; let ev - 'ry heart pre - pare him room, and
ploy while fields and floods, rocks, hills, and plains, re -
ground. He comes to make his bless - ings flow far
prove the glo - ries of his right - eous - ness, and

heav'n and na - ture sing, and heav'n and na - ture
peat the sound - ing joy, re - peat the sound - ing
as the curse is found, far as the curse is
won - ders of his love, and won - ders of his

and heav'n and na - ture sing, and

sing, and heav'n, and heav'n and na - ture sing.
joy, re - peat, re - peat the sound - ing joy.
found, far as, far as the curse is found.
love, and won - ders, won - ders of his love.

heav'n and na - ture sing,

Text: based on Psalm 98, Isaac Watts, *Psalms of David ...*, 1719, alt.
Music: Lowell Mason, *Occasional Psalm and Hymn Tunes*, 1836

Jesus shall reign

DUKE STREET LM

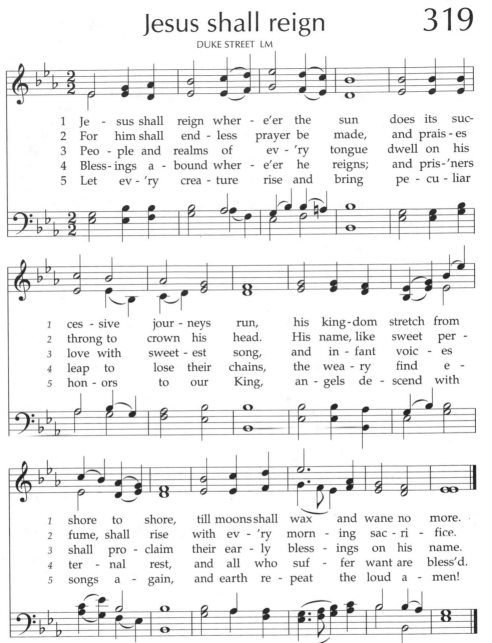

1 Je - sus shall reign wher - e'er the sun does its suc-
2 For him shall end - less prayer be made, and prais - es
3 Peo - ple and realms of ev - 'ry tongue dwell on his
4 Bless - ings a - bound wher - e'er he reigns; and pris-'ners
5 Let ev - 'ry crea - ture rise and bring pe - cu - liar

1 ces - sive jour - neys run, his king-dom stretch from
2 throng to crown his head. His name, like sweet per -
3 love with sweet - est song, and in - fant voic - es
4 leap to lose their chains, the wea - ry find e -
5 hon - ors to our King, an - gels de - scend with

1 shore to shore, till moons shall wax and wane no more.
2 fume, shall rise with ev - 'ry morn - ing sac - ri - fice.
3 shall pro - claim their ear - ly bless - ings on his name.
4 ter - nal rest, and all who suf - fer want are bless'd.
5 songs a - gain, and earth re - peat the loud a - men!

Text: based on Psalm 72, Isaac Watts, *Psalms of David*, 1719, alt.
Music: attributed to John Hatton, *Psalm and Hymn Tunes*, 1793

320 Oh, holy city seen of John

MORNING SONG (CONSOLATION) 86. 86. 86

1 Oh, ho-ly cit - y seen of John, where Christ, the Lamb, shall reign,
2 Oh, shame to us who rest con - tent while lust and greed for gain
3 Give us, O God, the strength to build the cit - y that has stood
4 Al - read-y in the mind of God that cit - y ris - es fair.

with - in whose four-square walls shall come no night, nor need, nor pain,
in street and shop and ten - e -ment wring gold from hu - man pain,
too long a dream, whose laws are love, whose ways are ser - vant -hood,
Lo, how its splen-dor chal-len - ges the souls that great - ly dare,

and where the tears are wiped from eyes that shall not weep a - gain.
and bit-ter lips in blind de - spair cry, "Christ has died in vain!"
and where the sun bright shin-ing is your grace for hu - man good.
yea, bids us seize the whole of life and build its glo - ry there.

Text: Walter R. Bowie, 1909, *Hymns of the Kingdom of God,* 1910
Music: anonymous, 1811 or 1812, in John Wyeth's *Repository of Sacred Music, Part Second,* 1813
Arrangement copyright ©1992 The Hymnal Project

Lift high the cross

321

CRUCIFER 10 10 with refrain

Refrain/Unison

Lift high the cross, the love of Christ pro - claim

till all the world a - dore his sa - cred name.

Harmony

1 O Lord, once lift - ed on the tree of pain,
2 From north and south, from east and west, we raise
3 Let ev - 'ry race and ev - 'ry lan - guage tell
4 Set up your throne, that earth's de - spair may cease

draw all the world to seek you once a - gain.
in grow - ing u - ni - son our song of praise.
of him who saves our lives from death and hell.
be - neath the shad - ow of its heal - ing peace.

Text: George W. Kitchin, 1887; revised by Michael R. Newbolt, *Hymns Ancient and Modern*, 1916, alt.
Music: Sydney H. Nicholson, *Hymns Ancient and Modern*, 1916

322 For we are strangers no more

STRANGERS NO MORE 11 10. 11 10 with refrain

For we are stran-gers no more, but mem-bers of one fam - i - ly; stran-gers no more, but part of one hu - man - i - ty; stran-gers no more, we're neigh-bors to each oth-er now; stran-gers no more, we're sis-ters and we're broth-ers now.

1 Come, walk with me, we'll praise the Lord to - geth - er,
2 Where dif - f'ring cul - tures meet we'll serve to - geth - er.
3 There is a love that binds the world to - geth - er;

as we join song to song and prayer to prayer.
Where ha - tred rag - es we will strive for peace.
a love that seeks the last, the lost, the least.

Come, take my hand, and we will work to - geth - er by
Come, take my hand, and we will pray to - geth - er that
One day that love will bring us all to - geth - er in

lift - ing all the bur - dens we can share.
jus - tice come and strife and war - fare cease.   For we are
Christ from south and north, from west and east.

323 Beyond a dying sun

ENGLE 14 10. 14 10 with refrain

1 Be - yond a dy - ing sun I saw a vi - sion on the sea
2 For God at last shall wipe a - way the tears from ev - 'ry eye.
3 Though ha-tred rag - es on the wind and wars de-file the land,

of gold-en sails full bil-lowed on the wind. (on the wind.)
The sting of death shall pierce the heart no more. (heart no more.)
I see those gold - en sails still com-ing strong, (com-ing strong,)

And ech - o - ing a - bove the waves a voice called af - ter me,
When griev-ing turns to laugh-ter all the pain from us shall fly,
for through the eyes of faith still shines the vi - sion of the Lamb,

"God's dwell-ing place is with you till the end." (till the end.)
and form - er ways lie bleached up - on the shore. (on the shore.)
and o'er a wea-ry earth there rings this song. (rings this song.)

Text: Steve Engle, 1970; revised 1984
Music: Steve Engle, 1970; harmonized by Donald R. Frederick and Steve Engle

Refrain

I see a new world com-ing when ev-'ry-one is free! And

all shall be God's peo-ple in jus-tice, love, and peace.

Seek ye first the kingdom of God 324

SEEK YE FIRST Irregular

Canon

1 Seek ye first the king - dom of God
2 Ask, and it shall be giv - en un - to you.

and his right - eous - ness, and all these things shall be
Seek, and ye shall find. Knock, and the door shall be

add - ed un - to you. Al - le - lu, al - le - lu - ia!
o - pened un - to you. Al - le - lu, al - le - lu - ia!

Al - le - lu - ia,

al - le - lu - ia, al - le -

lu - ia, al - le - lu, al - le - lu - ia!

Text: based on Matthew 6:33 and 7:7, Karen Lafferty, 1972
Music: Karen Lafferty, 1972

325 Creating God, your fingers trace

DEUS TUORUM MILITUM LM

1 Cre - at - ing God, your fin - gers trace the bold de-
2 Sus - tain - ing God, your hands up - hold earth's mys - t'ries
3 Re - deem - ing God, your arms em - brace all now op-
4 In - dwell - ing God, your gos - pel claims one fam - 'ly

signs of far - thest space. Let sun and moon and
known or yet un - told. Let wa - ter's fra - gile
pressed for creed or race. Let peace, de - scend - ing
with a bil - lion names. Let ev - 'ry life be

stars and light and what lies hid - den praise your might.
blend with air, en - a - bling life, pro - claim your care.
as the dove, make known on earth your heal - ing love.
touched by grace un - til we praise you face to face.

Text: Jeffery W. Rowthorn, 1974, *The Hymn,* 1979
         Copyright ©1979 The Hymn Society
Music: French church melody, *Grenoble Antiphoner,* 1753

O Love of God

326

ALFRETON LM

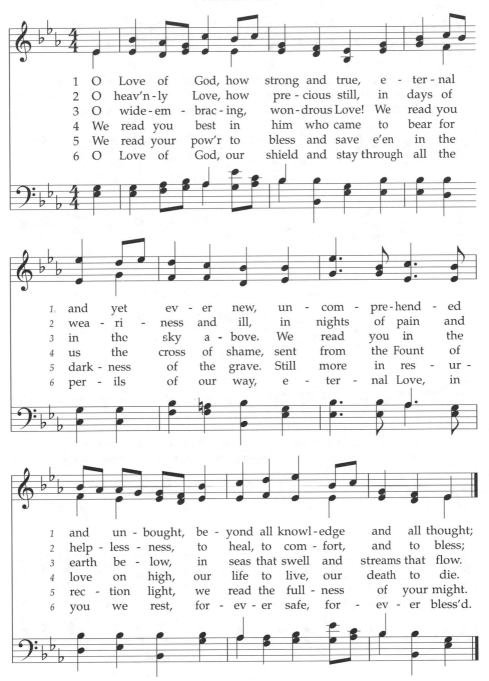

1 O Love of God, how strong and true, e - ter - nal
2 O heav'n-ly Love, how pre - cious still, in days of
3 O wide - em - brac - ing, won-drous Love! We read you
4 We read you best in him who came to bear for
5 We read your pow'r to bless and save e'en in the
6 O Love of God, our shield and stay through all the

1 and yet ev - er new, un - com - pre - hend - ed
2 wea - ri - ness and ill, in nights of pain and
3 in the sky a - bove. We read you in the
4 us the cross of shame, sent from the Fount of
5 dark - ness of the grave. Still more in res - ur -
6 per - ils of our way, e - ter - nal Love, in

1 and un - bought, be - yond all knowl-edge and all thought;
2 help - less - ness, to heal, to com - fort, and to bless;
3 earth be - low, in seas that swell and streams that flow.
4 love on high, our life to live, our death to die.
5 rec - tion light, we read the full - ness of your might.
6 you we rest, for - ev - er safe, for - ev - er bless'd.

Text: Horatius N. Bonar, *Hymns of Faith and Hope, Second Series*, 1861, alt.
Music: William Beastall, *New York Selection of Sacred Music*, 1818

327 Great is thy faithfulness

FAITHFULNESS 11 10. 11 10 with refrain

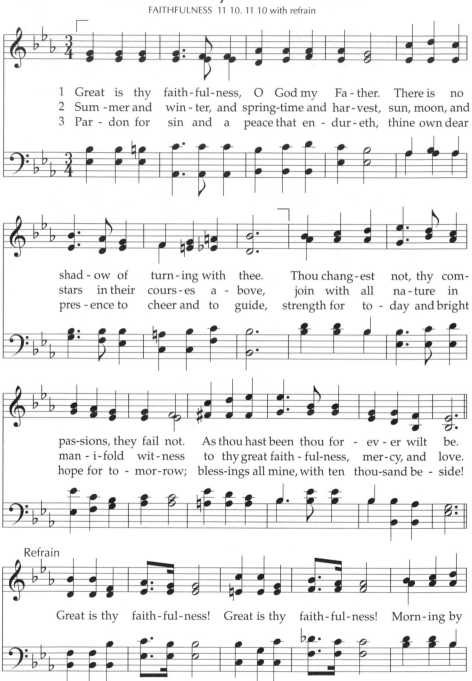

1 Great is thy faith-ful-ness, O God my Fa-ther. There is no
2 Sum-mer and win-ter, and spring-time and har-vest, sun, moon, and
3 Par-don for sin and a peace that en-dur-eth, thine own dear

shad-ow of turn-ing with thee. Thou chang-est not, thy com-
stars in their cours-es a-bove, join with all na-ture in
pres-ence to cheer and to guide, strength for to-day and bright

pas-sions, they fail not. As thou hast been thou for-ev-er wilt be.
man-i-fold wit-ness to thy great faith-ful-ness, mer-cy, and love.
hope for to-mor-row; bless-ings all mine, with ten thou-sand be-side!

Refrain

Great is thy faith-ful-ness! Great is thy faith-ful-ness! Morn-ing by

Text: Thomas O. Chisholm, *Songs of Salvation and Service,* 1923
Music: William M. Runyan, *Songs of Salvation and Service,* 1923
Text and music copyright ©1923, renewal 1951 Hope Publishing Co.

morn-ing new mer-cies I see. All I have need-ed thy

hand hath pro - vid-ed. Great is thy faith-ful-ness! Lord, un-to me!

O God, our help in ages past 328
ST. ANNE CM

1 O God, our help in ag-es past, our hope for years to come,
2 un - der the shad-ow of thy throne thy saints have dwelt se - cure.
3 Be - fore the hills in or-der stood, or earth re-ceived her frame,
4 A thou-sand ag-es in thy sight are like an eve-ning gone,
5 Time, like an ev - er -roll-ing stream, soon bears us all a - way.
6 O God, our help in ag-es past, our hope for years to come,

1 our shel-ter from the storm-y blast, and our e - ter-nal home;
2 Suf - fi-cient is thine arm a - lone, and our de-fense is sure.
3 from ev - er - last-ing thou art God, to end-less years the same.
4 short as the watch that ends the night be - fore the ris-ing sun.
5 We fly for - got - ten, as a dream dies at the op'n-ing day.
6 be thou our guard while trou-bles last, and our e - ter-nal home.

Text: based on Psalm 90, Isaac Watts, *Psalms of David ...*, 1719, alt.
Music: attributed to William Croft, *Supplement to the New Version of the Psalms by Dr. Brady and Mr. Tate,* 6th ed., 1708

329 A mighty fortress is our God

EIN FESTE BURG 87. 87. 555. 67

1 A   might - y   for - tress is   our   God,
2 No   strength of   ours   can match his   might.
3 Though hordes of   dev - ils fill   the   land
4 God's word   for - ev - er   shall a -   bide,

a   sword and   shield vic - to   -   rious.
We would be   lost,   re - ject -   ed.
all threat - 'ning to   de - vour _____ us,
no thanks to   foes, who fear _____ it;

He breaks the   cruel op - pres -   sor's rod
But now   a   cham - pion comes to   fight,
we   trem - ble   not,   un - moved we   stand;
for God   him - self   fights by   our   side

and wins   sal - va - tion glo   -   rious.
whom God   him - self   e - lect -   ed.
they can - not   o - ver - pow'r _____ us.
with weap - ons of   the   Spir -   it.

Text: based on Psalm 46, Martin Luther, 1527-1529, "Ein feste Burg ist unser Gott," *Geistliche Lieder*, 1529, 1531
         Translation copyright ©1978 *Lutheran Book of Worship*
Music: Martin Luther, 1529, *Geistliche Lieder*, 1529, 1531

The old e - vil foe, sworn to
Ask who this may be: Lord of
This world's prince may rage, in fierce
If they take our house, goods, fame,

work us woe, with dread craft and might
hosts is he! Je - sus Christ, our Lord,
war en - gage. He is doomed to fail.
child, or spouse, wrench our life a - way,

he arms him - self to fight. On earth
God's on - ly Son, a - dored. He holds
God's judg - ment must pre - vail! One lit -
they can - not win the day. The king -

he has no e - qual.
the field vic - to - rious.
tle word sub - dues him.
dom's ours for - ev - er!

330
I believe in God

NASADIKI

1 I be - lieve in God the Al - might - y, Ni - na - sa - di - ki,*
   and in Je - sus, the Son from heav - en,

who cre - at - ed earth and the heav - ens, Ni - na - sa - di - ki.
of e - ter - nal love was be - got - ten.

Refrain

Na - sa - di - ki, na - sa - di - ki, Ni - na - sa - di - ki.

Na - sa - di - ki, na - sa - di - ki, Ni - na - sa - di - ki.

*Translation: I believe

2 And conceived by the Holy Spirit …
   he was born of the virgin Mary …
   To the earth he came as a baby …
   born for us, and for our salvation …
   (Refrain)

3 On the earth he lived much as we do …
   and he suffered much under Pilate …
   He was crucified, died, and buried …
   he descended down into hell …
   (Refrain)

Text: based on Nicene creed, 4th c.; composite translation
Music: S. C. Ochieng' Okeyo, *Kariobangi Mass* (Kenya), 1988
          Text and music copyright © S. C. Ochieng' Okeyo

4 On the third day, he rose triumphant …
  as was prophesied in the Scriptures …
  He ascended then up to heaven …
  and shall come again in great glory …
  (Refrain)

5 He shall come once more then to judge us …
  and his kingdom shall have no ending …
  I believe in the Holy Spirit …
  I believe in one holy church …
  (Refrain)

6 I acknowledge one holy baptism …
  I believe in forgiving sinners …
  I expect one great resurrection …
  and the life of the world to come …
  (Refrain)

If Christ is mine

331

LOBT GOTT, IHR CHRISTEN CM extended

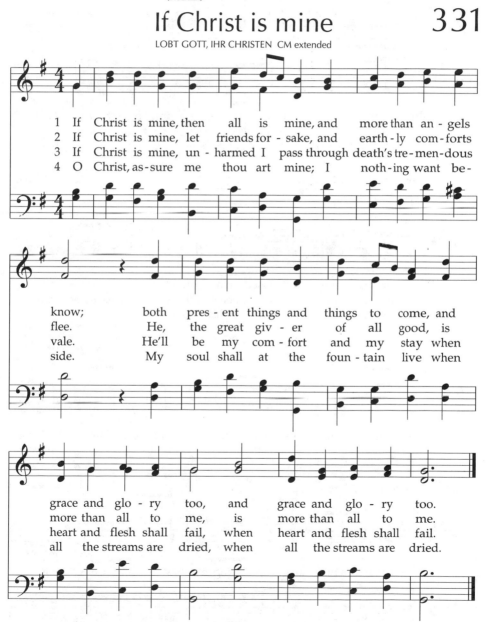

1 If Christ is mine, then all is mine, and more than an - gels
2 If Christ is mine, let friends for - sake, and earth - ly com - forts
3 If Christ is mine, un - harmed I pass through death's tre - men - dous
4 O Christ, as - sure me thou art mine; I noth - ing want be -

know;   both pres - ent things and things to come, and
flee.   He, the great giv - er of all good, is
vale.   He'll be my com - fort and my stay when
side.   My soul shall at the foun - tain live when

grace and glo - ry too, and grace and glo - ry too.
more than all to me, is more than all to me.
heart and flesh shall fail, when heart and flesh shall fail.
all the streams are dried, when all the streams are dried.

Text: Benjamin Beddome, 1776, *Hymns …*, 1817
Music: Nicolaus Hermann, *Ein Christlicher Abentreien*, 1554

332 Blessed assurance

BLESSED ASSURANCE 9 10. 99 with refrain

1 Bless-ed as - sur-ance, Je - sus is mine! Oh, what a fore-taste of
2 Per - fect sub - mis-sion, per-fect de - light, vi-sions of rap-ture now
3 Per - fect sub - mis-sion, all is at rest. I in my Sav - ior am

glo - ry di - vine! Heir of sal - va - tion, pur-chase of God,
burst on my sight. An - gels de - scend - ing bring from a - bove
hap - py and bless'd, watch-ing and wait - ing, look - ing a - bove,

Refrain

born of his Spir - it, washed in his blood. This is my sto - ry,
ech - oes of mer - cy, whis-pers of love.
filled with his good - ness, lost in his love.

this is my song, prais-ing my Sav - ior all the day long. This is my

sto - ry, this is my song, prais-ing my Sav - ior all the day long.

Text: Fanny J. Crosby, *Gems of Praise*, 1873
Music: Phoebe Palmer Knapp, *Gems of Praise*, 1873

Christ, who is in the form of God 333

SONG 34 LM

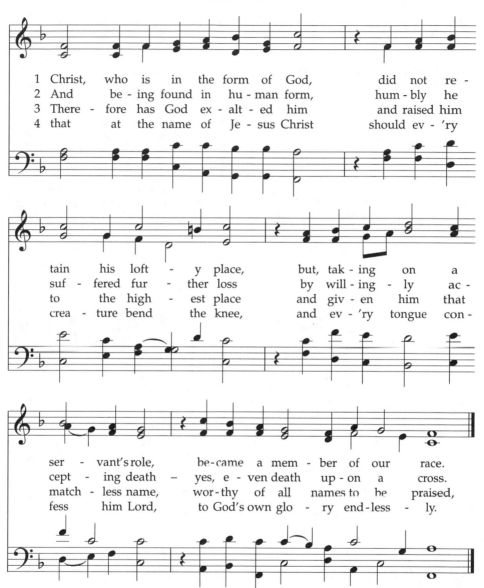

1 Christ, who is in the form of God, did not re-
2 And be-ing found in hu-man form, hum-bly he
3 There-fore has God ex-alt-ed him and raised him
4 that at the name of Je-sus Christ should ev-'ry

tain his loft-y place, but, tak-ing on a
suf-fered fur-ther loss by will-ing-ly ac-
to the high-est place and giv-en him that
crea-ture bend the knee, and ev-'ry tongue con-

ser-vant's role, be-came a mem-ber of our race.
cept-ing death – yes, e-ven death up-on a cross.
match-less name, wor-thy of all names to be praised,
fess him Lord, to God's own glo-ry end-less-ly.

Text: based on Philippians 2:5-11, David T. Koyzis, 1985, *Psalter Hymnal,* 1989
Copyright ©1985 David T. Koyzis
Music: Orlando Gibbons, *Hymnes and Songs of the Church,* 1623

334 Christ is the world's true light

ST. JOAN 67. 67. 66. 66

1 Christ is the world's true light, its cap-tain of sal-
2 In Christ all rac - es meet, their an - cient feuds for -
3 One Lord, in one great Name u - nite us all who

va - tion, the day - star clear and bright of ev - 'ry
get - ting, the whole round world com - plete, from sun - rise
own you. Cast out our pride and shame that hin - der

race and na - tion. New life, new hope a -
to its set - ting. When Christ is throned as
to en - throne you. The world has wait - ed

wakes, for all who own his sway; free - dom her
Lord all shall for - sake their fear, to plow - share
long, has la - bored long in pain. To heal its

Text: George W. Briggs, *Enlarged Songs of Praise,* 1931, alt.
         Copyright ©1931 Oxford University Press, London
Music: Percy E. B. Coller, 1941, *The Hymnal 1940*
         Copyright ©1940 The Church Pension Fund

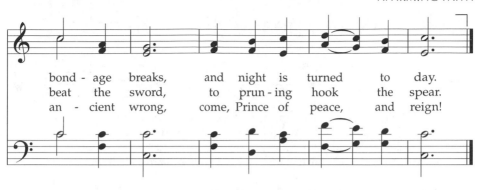

bond - age breaks, and night is turned to day.
beat the sword, to prun - ing hook the spear.
an - cient wrong, come, Prince of peace, and reign!

This is the threefold truth 335

ACCLAMATIONS 12 12. 12

1 This is the three-fold truth on which our faith de - pends,
2 Made sa - cred by long use, new - mint - ed for our time,
3 By this we are up - held when doubt or grief as - sails
4 This is the three-fold truth which, if we hold it fast,

and with this joy - ful cry wor - ship be - gins and ends:
our lit - ur - gies sum up the hope we have in him:
our Chris - tian for - ti - tude, and on - ly grace pre - vails:
chang - es the world and us and brings us home at last:

Christ has died! Christ is ris - en! Christ will come a - gain!

Text: Fred Pratt Green, *Hymns of Faith*, 1980
Music: Jack Schrader, *Hymns of Faith*, 1980
       Text and music copyright ©1980 Hope Publishing Co.

336 When peace, like a river

VILLE DU HAVRE 11 8. 11 9 with refrain

1 When peace, like a riv - er, at - tend - eth my way, when
2 Though Sa - tan should buf - fet, though tri - als should come, let
3 Re - deemed! Oh, the bliss of this glo - ri - ous thought, my
4 And, Lord, haste the day when my faith shall be sight, the

sor - rows like sea bil-lows roll, what - ev - er my lot, thou hast
this bless'd as - sur-ance con - trol, that Christ hath re - gard -ed my
sin – not in part, but the whole – is nailed to his cross, and I
clouds be rolled back as a scroll, the trum-pet shall sound, and the

taught me to say, it is well, it is well with my soul.
help - less es - tate, and hath shed his own blood for my soul.
bear it no more, praise the Lord, praise the Lord, O my soul!
Lord shall de - scend, "E - ven so," it is well with my soul.

Refrain

It is well _____ with my soul, _____
It is well with my

Text: Horatio G. Spafford, *Gospel Hymns, No. 2*, 1876, alt.
Music: Philip P. Bliss, *Gospel Hymns, No. 2*, 1876

soul, it is well, it is well with my soul.

Ask ye what great thing I know 337

HENDON 77. 77. 7

1 Ask ye what great thing I know that de-lights and
2 Who de-feats my fierc-est foes? Who con-soles my
3 Who is life in life to me? Who the death of
4 This is that great thing I know; this de-lights and

stirs me so? What the high re-ward I win? Whose the
sad-dest woes? Who re-vives my faint-ing heart, heal-ing
death will be? Who will place me on his right, with the
stirs me so: faith in him who died to save, him who

Name I glo-ry in?
all its hid-den smart?
count-less hosts of light?   Je-sus Christ, the   cru-ci-fied.
tri-umphed o'er the grave,

Text: Johann C. Schwedler, *Hirschberger Gesangbuch*, 1741; tr. Benjamin H. Kennedy, *Hymnologia Christiana*, 1863
Music: Henri A. C. Malan, 1827; *Carmina Sacra*, 1841

338 I know not why God's wondrous

EL NATHAN CM with refrain

1 I know not why God's won-drous grace to me he
2 I know not how this sav-ing faith to me he
3 I know not how the Spir-it moves, con-vinc-ing
4 I know not when my Lord may come, at night or

hath made known, nor why, with mer-cy, Christ in love re-
did im-part, nor how be-liev-ing in his word wrought
us of sin, re-veal-ing Je-sus through the word, cre-
noon-day fair, nor if I'll walk the vale with him, or

deemed me for his own.
peace with-in my heart.
at-ing faith in him.
meet him in the air.

Refrain

But I know whom I have be-

liev-ed, and am per-suad-ed that he is a-ble to

Text: Daniel W. Whittle, *Gospel Hymns, No. 5*, 1887, alt.
Music: James McGranahan, *Gospel Hymns, No. 5*, 1887

keep that which I've com - mit - ted un - to him a - gainst that day.

Thou art the way 339

RICHMOND CM

1 Thou art the way – to thee a - lone from
2 Thou art the truth – thy word a - lone true
3 Thou art the life – the rend - ing tomb pro -
4 Thou art the way, the truth, the life – grant

sin and death we flee, and they who would the
wis - dom can im - part. Thou on - ly canst in -
claims thy con - qu'ring arm, and those who put their
us that way to know, that truth to keep, that

Fa - ther seek, must seek him, Lord, by thee.
form the mind and pur - i - fy the heart.
trust in thee nor death nor hell can harm.
life to win, whose joys e - ter - nal flow.

Text: George W. Doane, *Songs by the Way, Chiefly Devotional*, 1824, alt.
Music: Thomas Haweis, *Carmina Christo*, ca. 1792

340 'Tis so sweet to trust in Jesus

TRUST IN JESUS 87. 87 with refrain

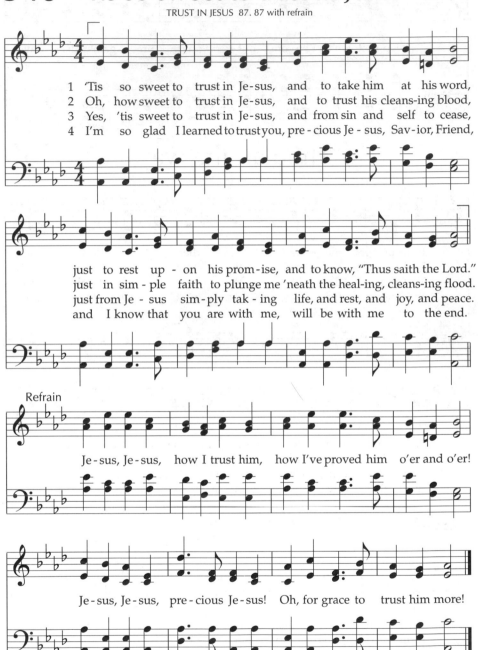

1 'Tis so sweet to trust in Je-sus, and to take him at his word,
2 Oh, how sweet to trust in Je-sus, and to trust his cleans-ing blood,
3 Yes, 'tis sweet to trust in Je-sus, and from sin and self to cease,
4 I'm so glad I learned to trust you, pre-cious Je-sus, Sav-ior, Friend,

just to rest up-on his prom-ise, and to know, "Thus saith the Lord."
just in sim-ple faith to plunge me 'neath the heal-ing, cleans-ing flood.
just from Je-sus sim-ply tak-ing life, and rest, and joy, and peace.
and I know that you are with me, will be with me to the end.

Refrain

Je-sus, Je-sus, how I trust him, how I've proved him o'er and o'er!

Je-sus, Je-sus, pre-cious Je-sus! Oh, for grace to trust him more!

Text: Louisa M. R. Stead, *Songs of Triumph*, 1882, alt.
Music: William J. Kirkpatrick, *Songs of Triumph*, 1882

Jesus loves me

JESUS LOVES ME 77. 77 with refrain

Je-sus loves me! this I know, for the Bi-ble tells me so. Lit-tle ones to him be-long, they are weak, but he is strong. Yes, Je-sus loves me.

Refrain

Yes, Je-sus loves me. Yes, Je-sus loves me; the Bi-ble tells me so.

SPANISH

Cristo me ama, me ama a mí.
Su palabra dice así.
Niños pueden ir a él,
Quien es nuestro amigo fiel.

Sí, Cristo me ama.
Sí, Cristo me ama.
Sí, Cristo me ama,
La Biblia dice así.

HAUSA

Yesu yana kaunarmu,
Wannan na sakankance.
Gaskiyarsa ta tabbata,
Allah ne ya shaida shi.

I, yana sonmu, i, yana sonmu,
I, yana sonmu, Yesu Mai Centonmu.

KOREAN

Yesu sarang Hasiman
Georukhasin marilsei
Wooridrn Yakana
Yesu gwonsei mantoda.

Nal sarang hasim
Nal sarang hasim
Nal sarang hasim
Seong gyongei sseoitne.

NAVAJO

Jesus ayóó'ashó'ní,
Binaaltsoos yee shił halne',
Álchíníigi ánísht'é,
Doo sidziil da, Ei bidziil.

Jesus ayóó'ashó'ní,
Jesus ayoo'ashó'ní,
Jesus ayóó'ashó'ní,
Bizaad yee shił halne'.

Text: Anna B. Warner, 1859
Music: William B. Bradbury, *The Golden Shower*, 1862

342 At the name of Jesus

KING'S WESTON 65. 65D

1 At the name of Je - sus ev-'ry knee shall bow,
2 At his voice cre - a - tion sprang at once to sight,
3 Hum-bled for a sea - son, to re-ceive a name
4 In your hearts en - throne him; there let him sub - due
5 Chris-tians, this Lord Je - sus shall re-turn a - gain,

1 ev - 'ry tongue con - fess him King of glo-ry now.
2 all the an - gel fac - es, all the hosts of light,
3 from the lips of sin - ners un - to whom he came,
4 all that is not ho - ly, all that is not true.
5 with his Fa - ther's glo - ry, with his an - gel train,

1 'Tis the Fa - ther's plea - sure we should call him Lord,
2 thrones and dom - i - na - tions, stars up - on their way,
3 faith - ful - ly he bore it spot-less to the last,
4 Crown him as your cap - tain in temp - ta - tion's hour;
5 for all wreaths of em - pire meet up - on his brow,

1 who from the be - gin-ning was the might - y Word.
2 all the heav'n-ly or - ders, in their great ar - ray.
3 brought it back vic - to - rious, when from death he passed.
4 let his will en - fold you in its light and pow'r.
5 and our hearts con - fess him King of glo - ry now.

Text: Caroline M. Noel, *The Name of Jesus and Other Verses for the Sick and Lonely, Enlarged Edition,* 1870, alt.
Music: Ralph Vaughan Williams, *Songs of Praise,* 1925; arranged for *The Hymnbook,* 1955
Copyright ©1931 Oxford University Press, London

My hope is built on nothing less 343

SOLID ROCK LM with refrain

1 My hope is built on noth-ing less than Je-sus' blood and
2 When dark-ness veils his lov-ing face, I rest up-on un-
3 His oath, his cov-e-nant, and blood, sup-port me in the
4 Not earth, nor hell, my soul can move; I rest up-on un-
5 When he shall come with trum-pet sound, oh, may I then in

1 right-eous-ness. I dare not trust the sweet-est frame, but whol-ly
2 chang-ing grace. In ev-'ry rough and storm-y gale, my an-chor
3 'whelm-ing flood. When all a-round my soul gives way, he then is
4 chang-ing love. I trust his right-eous char-ac-ter, his coun-sel,
5 him be found, dressed in his right-eous-ness a-lone, fault-less to

Refrain

1 lean on Je-sus' name.
2 holds with-in the vale.
3 all my hope and stay. On Christ, the sol-id rock, I stand; all
4 prom-ise, and his pow'r.
5 stand be-fore the throne.

oth-er ground is sink-ing sand, all oth-er ground is sink-ing sand.

Text: Edward Mote, ca. 1834, *Spiritual Magazine*, alt.
Music: William B. Bradbury, 1863, *Devotional Hymn and Tune Book*, 1864

344 I will sing of my Redeemer

MY REDEEMER 87. 87 with refrain

1 I will sing of my Re - deem - er and his
2 I will tell the won - drous sto - ry, how, my
3 I will praise my dear Re - deem - er, his tri -
4 I will sing of my Re - deem - er, and his

won - drous love to me. On the cru - el cross he
lost es - tate to save, in his bound - less love and
um - phant pow'r I'll tell, how the vic - to - ry he
heav'n - ly love to me. He from death to life hath

suf - fered from the curse to set me free.
mer - cy, he the ran - som free - ly gave.
giv - eth o - ver sin and death and hell.
brought me, Son of God, with him to be.

Text: Philip P. Bliss, *Welcome Tidings …*, 1877
Music: James McGranahan, *Welcome Tidings …*, 1877

Refrain

Sing, oh, sing of my Re - deem - er, with his
Sing, oh, sing of my Re-deem-er, sing, oh, sing of my Re-deem-er, with his

blood he pur - chased me, on the
blood he pur-chased me, with his blood he pur-chased me, on the

cross he sealed my par - don, paid the
cross he sealed my par-don, on the cross he sealed my par-don, paid the

debt and made me free.
debt and made me free, and made me free.

345 God sent his Son

BECAUSE HE LIVES* 98. 9 12 with refrain

God sent his Son, they called him Je - sus,

he came to love, heal, and for - give.

He lived and died to buy my par - don,

an emp - ty grave is there to prove my Sav - ior lives.

Be - cause he lives I can face to - mor - row,

*Original title

Text: Gloria and William J. Gaither, 1971
Music: William J. Gaither
        Text and music copyright ©1971 William J. Gaither

because he lives all fear is gone;

because I know he holds the fu-ture,

and life is worth the liv-ing just be-cause he lives.

Dona nobis pacem 346

DONA NOBIS PACEM

Canon

Do-na no-bis pa-cem,* pa-cem. Do-na no-bis

pa-cem. Do-na no-bis pa-cem.

Do-na no-bis pa-cem. Do-na

no-bis pa-cem. Do-na no-bis pa-cem.

*Translation: Grant us peace.

Music: anonymous

347 Through our fragmentary prayers

WORDLESS 77.77

1 Through our frag-men-tar-y prayers and our si-lent, heart-hid
2 Deep-er than the pul-se's beat is the Spir-it's speech-less
3 Let our jab-ber-ings give way to the hum-mings in the
4 Search and sound our mind and heart, Breath and Flame and Wind and

sighs, word-less-ly the Spir-it bears our pro-
groan, mak-ing hu-man prayers com-plete through the
soul, as we yield our lives this day to the
Dove, let your prayer in us im-part strength to

found-est needs and cries: (hum) _____
prayer that is God's own:
God who makes us whole:
do the work of love. (Alleluia or Amen on last stanza)

(hum) _____

Text: Thomas H. Troeger, 1985, *New Hymns for the Life of the Church,* 1991
Music: Carol Doran, 1985, *New Hymns for the Life of the Church,* 1991
        Text and music copyright ©1989 Oxford University Press, Inc.

348   O Lord, hear my prayer

Em   Am/C   D

O   Lord, hear my prayer.   O   Lord, hear my prayer.

Text: based on Psalm 102:1-2, *Music from Taizé,* Vol. II, 1982, 1983, 1984
Music: Jacques Berthier, *Music from Taizé,* Vol. II, 1982, 1983, 1984
        Text and music copyright ©1982 Les Presses de Taizé (France). Used by permission of G.I.A. Publications, Inc.

Spirit of the living God 349

Text: Daniel Iverson, 1926, *Revival Songs*, 1929
Music: Daniel Iverson, 1926, *Revival Songs*, 1929; arranged by Herbert G. Tovey
        Text and music copyright ©1935, renewal 1963 Birdwing Music and BMG Songs, Inc.

350 Lord, teach us how to pray aright

DAYTON CM

1 Lord, teach us how to pray a - right with rev-'rence
2 We per - ish if we cease from prayer; O, grant us
3 O God of love, be - fore your face we come with
4 faith in the on - ly Sac - ri - fice that can for
5 pa - tience to watch and weep and wait, what - ev - er
6 Give these, and then your will be done; thus strength-ened

1 and with fear. Though dust and ash - es
2 pow'r to pray, and when to meet you
3 con - trite heart to ask from you these
4 sin a - tone; to found our hopes, to
5 you may send; cour - age that will not
6 with all might, we, through your Spir - it

1 in your sight, we may, we must draw near.
2 we pre - pare, Lord, meet us by the way.
3 gifts of grace – truth in the in - ward part;
4 fix our eyes on Christ, and Christ a - lone;
5 hes - i - tate to trust you to the end.
6 and your Son, shall pray, and pray a - right.

Text: James Montgomery, 1818, in Thomas Cotterill's *Selection of Psalms and Hymns*, 1819
Music: *The Brethren's Tune and Hymn Book*, 1872; harmonized by The Hymnal Project
         Harmonization copyright ©1991 The Hymnal Project

Our Father who art in heaven 351

Irregular

Our Fa-ther who art in heav-en, hal-low-ed be thy name.

Thy king - dom come, thy will be done on

earth, as it is in heav-en. And give us this day our

dai-ly bread. For - give us our debts, as we for-give our

debt - ors. And lead us not in-to temp - ta - tion,

but de - liv - er us from e - vil, for thine is the king-dom and the

pow - er and the glo - ry for - ev - er - more, for-

ev - er - more. A - men   For - ev - er - more. A - men

Text: Matthew 6:9-13
Music: Jabani P. Mambula
        Copyright ©1974 Church of the Brethren General Board

352 Gentle Shepherd, come and lead us

GENTLE SHEPHERD Irregular

Gen-tle Shep-herd, come and lead us, for we

need you to help us find our way. Gen-tle Shep-herd,

come and feed us, for we need your strength from day to

day. There's no oth-er we can turn to who can

help us face an-oth-er day. Gen-tle Shep-herd, come and

Text: Gloria Gaither, ca. 1974
Music: William J. Gaither, ca. 1974
        Text and music copyright ©1974 William J. Gaither

lead us,   for we   need you to   help us find our   way.

Lord, listen to your children 353

CHILDREN PRAYING 98. 99

Lord,   lis-ten to your chil-dren   pray - ing,

Lord,   send your   Spir-it   in   this   place.

Lord,   lis-ten to your chil-dren   pray - ing,   send us

love,   send us   pow'r,   send us   grace!

Text: Ken Medema, 1970
Music: Ken Medema, 1970
        Text and music copyright ©1973 Hope Publishing Co.

354 Fount of love, our Savior God

MAN-CHIANG-HUNG 77. 77. 77 with refrain

1 Fount of love, our Sav - ior God, Light on baf - fling
2 In this age of sore dis - tress hid - den dan - gers
3 In this chang - ing world of care dreams like bub - bles
4 Man - y paths be - fore us lie, man - y voic - es
5 To this earth of gloom and night, you did bring true

1 ways we've trod, your cross is our com - pass sure,
2 'round us press. Life's true way we can - not find,
3 burst in air. Hu - man hopes are emp - ty things,
4 to us cry. Which of all these shall we choose?
5 free - dom's light. While life's wind - ing roads we tread,

1 your love keeps our vi - sion pure. Lord, we thank you
2 dis - il - lu - sion fills the mind. Sav - ior, give us
3 like dead trees and dried-up springs. Help us, Christ our
4 Here find peace or there all lose? Je - sus, take our
5 Shep - herd Christ, lead on a - head. Guide us through the

1 for your grace; dark - ness flees be - fore your face.
2 eyes to see your great king - dom that will be.
3 Lord, we pray, send us new life ev - 'ry day.
4 hands, we pray, show us your di - vine true way.
5 nar - row door to your joy for - ev - er - more.

Refrain

Fount of love, our Sav - ior God, be our guide.

Text: Ernest Y. L. Yang, 1934, *Hymns of Universal Praise*, 1977; tr. Frank W. Price, 1953, alt.
Music: Chinese verse melody; adapted by Ernest Y. L. Yang, 1933
           Text and music copyright ©1977 The Chinese Christian Literature Council, Ltd.

Savior, like a shepherd lead us 355

BRADBURY 87. 87. 87 extended

1 Sav - ior, like a shep-herd lead us,   much we need thy ten-der care.
2 We are thine, do thou be - friend us,   be the guard-ian of our way.
3 Ear - ly let us seek thy fa - vor,   ear-ly let us do thy will.

In thy pleas-ant pas-tures feed us,   for our use thy folds pre - pare.
Keep thy flock, from sin de -fend us,   seek us when we go a - stray.
Bless - ed Lord and on - ly Sav - ior,   with thy love our spir-its fill.

Bless - ed Je-sus! Bless-ed Je-sus! thou hast bought us, thine we are.
Bless - ed Je-sus! Bless-ed Je-sus! hear, O hear, us when we pray.
Bless - ed Je-sus! Bless-ed Je-sus! thou hast loved us, love us still.

Bless-ed Je - sus! Bless-ed Je-sus! thou hast bought us, thine we are.
Bless-ed Je - sus! Bless-ed Je-sus! hear, O hear, us when we pray.
Bless-ed Je - sus! Bless-ed Je-sus! thou hast loved us, love us still.

Text: anonymous, *Hymns for the Young*, 1836
Music: William B. Bradbury, *Oriola*, 1859

356 Breathe on me, breath of God

TRENTHAM SM

1 Breathe on me, breath of God. Fill me with life a-new,
2 Breathe on me, breath of God, un-til my heart is pure,
3 Breathe on me, breath of God, till I am whol-ly thine,
4 Breathe on me, breath of God, so shall I nev-er die,

that I may love what thou dost love, and do what thou wouldst do.
un-til with thee I will one will, to do and to en-dure.
till all this earth-ly part of me glows with thy fire di-vine.
but live with thee the per-fect life of thine e-ter-ni-ty.

Text: Edwin Hatch, *Between Doubt and Prayer,* 1878, alt.
Music: Robert Jackson, *Fifty Sacred Leaflets,* 1888

357 O Master, let me walk with thee

MARYTON LM

1 O Mas-ter, let me walk with thee in low-ly
2 Help me the slow of heart to move by some clear,
3 Teach me thy pa-tience, still with thee in clos-er,
4 in hope that sends a shin-ing ray far down the

Text: Washington Gladden, *Sunday Afternoon,* 1879
Music: H. Percy Smith, *Church Hymns with Tunes,* 1874

paths of ser - vice free. Tell me thy se - cret,
win - ning word of love. Teach me the way - ward
dear - er com - pa - ny, in work that keeps faith
fu - ture's broad - 'ning way, in peace that on - ly

help me bear the strain of toil, the fret of care.
feet to stay, and guide them in the home - ward way.
sweet and strong, in trust that tri - umphs o - ver wrong,
thou canst give; with thee, O Mas - ter, let me live.

Oyenos, mi Dios 358

Irregular

Em   Am⁷   D   G maj⁷

O - ye - nos, mi Dios,*   ó - ye - nos, mi Dios.

C maj⁷   D♯dim⁷   B⁷   Em

Lis - ten to your peo - ple.   O - ye - nos, mi Dios.

*Translation: Hear us, my God.

Text: Owen Alstott; tr. Mary F. Reza (Spanish)
Music: Bob Hurd and Owen Alstott
Text and music copyright ©1988, 1990 Bob Hurd. Published by OCP Publications

359 Lead us, O Father

ELLERS 10 10. 10 10

1 Lead us, *O Fa - ther, in the paths of peace;
2 Lead us, *O Fa - ther, in the paths of truth;
3 Lead us, *O Fa - ther, in the paths of right;
4 Lead us, *O Fa - ther, to thy heav'n - ly rest,

with - out thy guid - ing hand we go a - stray,
un - helped by thee, in er - ror's maze we grope,
blind - ly we stum - ble when we walk a - lone,
how - ev - er rough and steep the path may be,

and doubts ap - pall, and sor - rows still in - crease.
while pas - sion stains and fol - ly dims our youth,
in - volved in shad - ows of a mor - tal night.
through joy or sor - row, as thou deem - est best,

Lead us, through Christ, the true and liv - ing way.
and age comes on un - cheered by faith and hope.
On - ly with thee we jour - ney safe - ly on.
un - til our lives are per - fect - ed in thee.

*Alternate words: St. 1, O Wisdom ... St. 2, O Teacher ... St. 3, O Guardian ... St. 4, O Shepherd ...

Text: William H. Burleigh, *The New Congregational Hymn Book*, 1859
Music: Edward J. Hopkins, *Supplemental Tune and Hymn Book*, 1869

Break thou the bread of life 360

BREAD OF LIFE 64. 64D

1 Break thou the bread of life, dear Lord, to me,
2 Bless thou the truth, dear Lord, now un - to me,

as thou didst break the loaves be - side the sea.
as thou didst bless the bread by Gal - i - lee.

Be - yond the sa - cred page I seek thee, Lord;
Then shall all bond - age cease, all fet - ters fall,

my spir - it pants for thee, O liv - ing Word.
and I shall find my peace, my All - in - all.

Text: Mary A. Lathbury, *Chautauqua Carols*, 1877
Music: William F. Sherwin, 1877, *The Calvary Selection of Spiritual Songs*, 1878

361 O Spirit of the living God

PLAINFIELD CMD extended

1 O Spir-it of the liv-ing God, thou Light and Fire di-
2 Blow, Wind of God! with wis-dom blow, un - til our minds are
3 Teach us to ut - ter liv-ing words of truth which all may
4 So shall we know the pow'r of Christ who came this world to

vine, de - scend up-on thy church once more and make it tru - ly
free from mists of er - ror, clouds of doubt, which blind our eyes to
hear, the lan-guage all may un - der-stand when love speaks, loud and
save. So shall we rise with him to life which soars be - yond the

thine! Fill it with love and joy and pow'r, with
thee. Burn, wing - ed Fire! In - spire our lips with
clear, till ev - 'ry age and race and clime shall
grave, and earth shall win true ho - li - ness, which

right-eous-ness and peace, till Christ shall dwell in hu - man hearts and
flam - ing love and zeal, to preach to all thy great good news, God's
blend their creeds in one, and earth shall form one fam - i - ly by
makes thy chil-dren whole, till, per - fect - ed by thee, we reach cre-

Text: Henry H. Tweedy, 1933, *The Methodist Hymnal,* 1935, alt.
Music: Jacob Kimball, 1800

sin and sor - row cease, and sin and sor - row cease.
glo - rious com - mon - weal, God's glo - rious com - mon - weal.
whom thy will is done, by whom thy will is done.
a - tion's glo - rious goal, we reach cre - a - tion's goal!

Help us to help each other 362

BALERMA CM

1 Help us to help each oth - er, Lord, each
2 Help us to build each oth - er up, your
3 To - geth - er make us free in - deed – your
4 Drawn by the mag - net of your love we

oth - er's load to bear, that all may live in
strength with - in us prove. In - crease our faith, con -
life with - in us show, and in - to you, our
find our hearts made new. Near - er each oth - er

true ac - cord, our joys and pains to share.
firm our hope, and fill us with your love.
liv - ing Head, let us in all things grow.
let us move, and near - er still to you.

Text: Charles Wesley, *Hymns and Sacred Poems,* 1742; revised in *Hymns for Today's Church,* 1982
        Copyright ©1982 Hope Publishing Co.
Music: François H. Barthélémon; adapted by Robert Simpson, *A Collection of Original ... Sacred Music,* 1833

363 Renew your church

ALL IS WELL 10 6. 10 6. 88. 86

1 Re - new your church, its min - is - tries re - store, both to serve
2 Teach us your word, re - veal its truth di - vine; on our path
3 Teach us to pray, for you are al - ways near. Your still voice
4 Teach us to love with heart and mind and soul. You, O Christ,

and a - dore. Make it a - gain as salt through-out the land
let it shine. Tell of your works, your might - y acts of grace;
let us hear. Our souls are rest - less till they rest in you,
be our goal. Break down old walls of prej - u - dice and hate.

and as light from a stand. 'Mid som - ber shad - ows
from each page show your face. As you have loved us,
where we find strength a - new. Be - fore your pres - ence
Leave us not to our fate. As you have loved and

of the night where greed and ha - tred spread their blight, O
sent your Son, and our sal - va - tion now is won, O
keep us still that we may find for us your will and
giv'n your life to end hos - til - i - ty and strife, O

Text: originally "Renew thy church," K. L. Cober, 1960, alt.
Copyright ©1960 K. L. Cober, copyright ©1985 Judson Press
Music: American folk melody, 1842, adapted from *Sacred Harp*, 1844

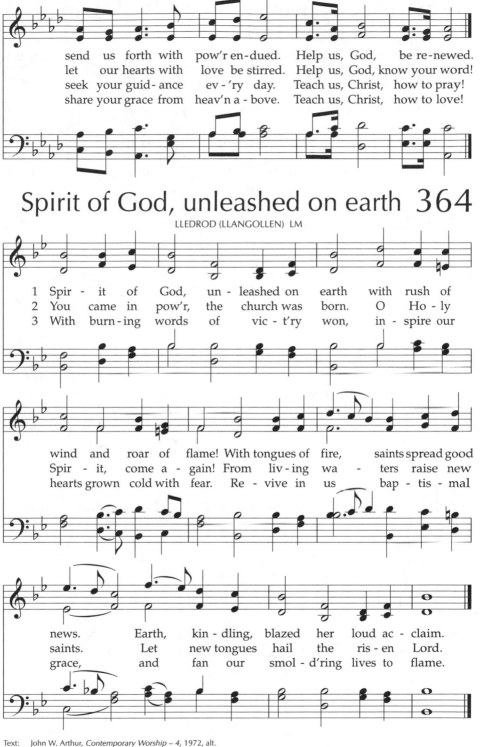

send us forth with pow'r en-dued. Help us, God, be re-newed.
let our hearts with love be stirred. Help us, God, know your word!
seek your guid-ance ev-'ry day. Teach us, Christ, how to pray!
share your grace from heav'n a-bove. Teach us, Christ, how to love!

Spirit of God, unleashed on earth 364

LLEDROD (LLANGOLLEN) LM

1 Spir-it of God, un-leashed on earth with rush of
2 You came in pow'r, the church was born. O Ho-ly
3 With burn-ing words of vic-t'ry won, in-spire our

wind and roar of flame! With tongues of fire, saints spread good
Spir-it, come a-gain! From liv-ing wa-ters raise new
hearts grown cold with fear. Re-vive in us bap-tis-mal

news. Earth, kin-dling, blazed her loud ac-claim.
saints. Let new tongues hail the ris-en Lord.
grace, and fan our smol-d'ring lives to flame.

Text: John W. Arthur, *Contemporary Worship – 4*, 1972, alt.
Copyright © John W. Arthur
Music: Welsh melody, *Llyfr Tonau Cynulleidfaol*, 1859

365 Christ, from whom all blessings

SONG 13 77.77

1 Christ, from whom all bless - ings flow, per - fect-
2 Join us, in one spir - it join, let us
3 Clos - er knit to thee, our Head, nour - ish
4 Man - y are we now, and one, we who
5 Love, like death, hath all de - stroyed, ren - dered

1 ing the saints be - low, hear us, who thy na - ture
2 still re - ceive of thine, still for more on thee we
3 us, O Christ, and feed. Let us dai - ly growth re -
4 Je - sus have put on. There is nei - ther bond nor
5 all dis - tinc - tions void. Names and sects and par - ties

1 share, who thy mys - tic bod - y are:
2 call; thee, who fill - est all in all.
3 ceive, more and more in thee to live.
4 free, male nor fe - male, Lord, in thee.
5 fall. Thou, O Christ, art All - in - all!

Text: Charles Wesley, *Hymns and Sacred Poems*, 1740, alt.
Music: Orlando Gibbons, *Hymnes and Songs of the Church*, 1623

God of grace and God of glory 366

CWM RHONDDA 87. 87. 87 extended

1 God of grace and God of glo - ry, on thy peo - ple
2 Lo! the hosts of e - vil 'round us scorn thy Christ, as -
3 Cure thy chil - dren's war - ring mad - ness; bend our pride to
4 Save us from weak res - ig - na - tion to the e - vils

pour thy pow'r. Crown thine an - cient church's sto - ry, bring her
sail his ways! From the fears that long have bound us, free our
thy con - trol. Shame our wan - ton, self - ish glad - ness, rich in
we de - plore. Let the search for thy sal - va - tion be our

bud to glo - rious flow'r. Grant us wis - dom, grant us cour - age,
hearts to faith and praise. Grant us wis - dom, grant us cour - age,
things and poor in soul. Grant us wis - dom, grant us cour - age,
glo - ry ev - er - more. Grant us wis - dom, grant us cour - age,

for the fac - ing of this hour, for the fac - ing of this hour.
for the liv - ing of these days, for the liv - ing of these days.
lest we miss thy king - dom's goal, lest we miss thy king - dom's goal.
serv - ing thee whom we a - dore, serv - ing thee whom we a - dore.

Text: Harry Emerson Fosdick, 1930, *Praise and Service*, 1932
Music: John Hughes, 1905 or 1907, *The Voice of Thanksgiving, No. 4*, 1928

367 For the healing of the nations

REGENT SQUARE 87. 87. 87

1 For the heal-ing of the na-tions, Lord, we pray with
2 Lead your peo-ple in - to free-dom. From de-spair your
3 All that kills a - bun-dant liv-ing, let it from the
4 You, Cre - a - tor - God, have writ - ten your great name on

one ac - cord, for a just and e - qual shar - ing
world re - lease, that, re - deemed from war and ha - tred,
earth be banned: pride of sta - tus, race, or school-ing,
hu - man - kind. For our grow-ing in your like - ness,

of the things that earth af - fords. To a life of
all may come and go in peace. Show us how, through
dog - mas that ob - scure your plan. In our com - mon
bring the life of Christ to mind, that by our re -

love in ac - tion help us rise and pledge our word.
care and good - ness, fear will die and hope in - crease.
quest for jus - tice may we hal - low life's brief span.
sponse and ser - vice earth its des - ti - ny may find.

Text: Fred Kaan, 1965, alt.
         Copyright ©1968 Hope Publishing Co.
Music: Henry T. Smart, *Psalms and Hymns for Divine Worship,* 1867

O God of love, O Power of peace 368

TALLIS' CANON LM

1 O God of love, O Pow'r of peace, make
2 Whom shall we trust but you, O Lord, where
3 Where saints and an - gels dwell a - bove, all

wars through-out the world to cease. The wrath of hu - man
rest but on your faith - ful word? None ev - er called on
hearts are joined in ho - ly love. O bind us in that

sin re - strain –
you in vain – give peace, O God, give peace a - gain!
heav'n-ly chain –

Text: Henry W. Baker, *Hymns Ancient and Modern,* 1861, alt.; adapted by Ruth C. Duck (St. 1), 1980
        Adaptation (St. 1) copyright ©1980 Ruth Duck
Music: Thomas Tallis, *The Whole Psalter Translated into English Metre,* ca. 1567

369 Lord, whose love in humble service

BEACH SPRING 87. 87D

1 Lord, whose love in hum-ble ser-vice bore the weight of hu-man
2 Still your chil-dren wan-der home-less, still the hun-gry cry for
3 As we wor-ship, grant us vi-sion, till your love's re-veal-ing

need, who up-on the cross, for-sak-en, worked your
bread. Still the cap-tives long for free-dom, still in
light in its height and depth and great-ness dawns up-

mer-cy's per-fect deed; we, your ser-vants, bring the
grief we mourn our dead. As you, Lord, in deep com-
on our quick-ened sight, mak-ing known the needs and

wor-ship not of voice a-lone, but heart, con-se-
pas-sion, healed the sick and freed the soul, by your
bur-dens your com-pas-sion bids us bear, stir-ring

Text: Albert F. Bayly, *Seven New Social Welfare Hymns*, 1961, alt.
Copyright ©1961 Oxford University Press, London
Music: attributed to B. F. White, *Sacred Harp*, 1844; harmonized by Joan A. Fyock
Harmonization copyright ©1989 Joan A. Fyock

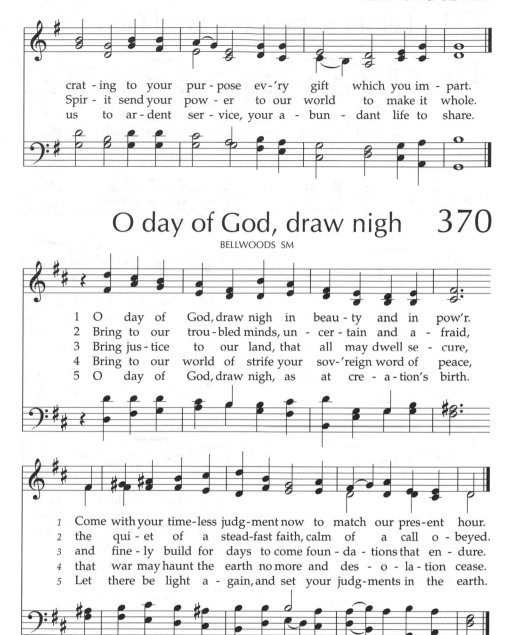

crat - ing to your pur - pose ev-'ry gift which you im - part.
Spir - it send your pow - er to our world to make it whole.
us to ar-dent ser - vice, your a - bun - dant life to share.

O day of God, draw nigh 370

BELLWOODS SM

1 O day of God, draw nigh in beau - ty and in pow'r.
2 Bring to our trou - bled minds, un - cer - tain and a - fraid,
3 Bring jus - tice to our land, that all may dwell se - cure,
4 Bring to our world of strife your sov-'reign word of peace,
5 O day of God, draw nigh, as at cre - a - tion's birth.

1 Come with your time-less judg-ment now to match our pres-ent hour.
2 the qui - et of a stead-fast faith, calm of a call o - beyed.
3 and fine - ly build for days to come foun - da - tions that en - dure.
4 that war may haunt the earth no more and des - o - la - tion cease.
5 Let there be light a - gain, and set your judg-ments in the earth.

Text: Robert B. Y. Scott, 1937, *Hymns for Worship,* 1939, alt.
        Copyright © Emmanuel College of Victoria University
Music: James Hopkirk, *Book of Common Praise,* 1938
        Copyright ©1938 Estate of James Hopkirk

371 Let there be light, Lord God

MISSIONARY CHANT LM

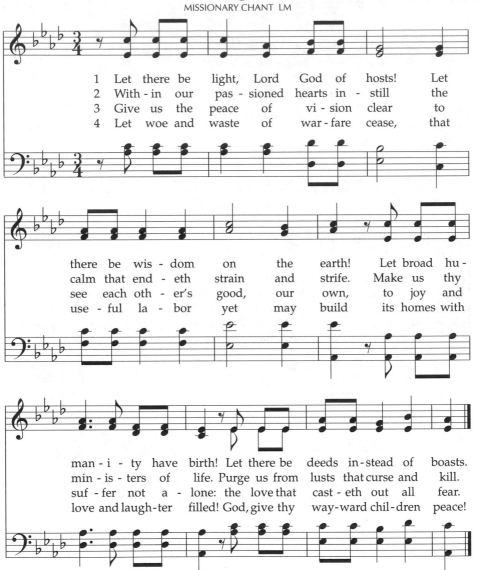

1 Let there be light, Lord God of hosts! Let there be wis-dom on the earth! Let broad hu-man-i-ty have birth! Let there be deeds in-stead of boasts.

2 With-in our pas-sioned hearts in-still the calm that end-eth strain and strife. Make us thy min-is-ters of life. Purge us from lusts that curse and kill.

3 Give us the peace of vi-sion clear to see each oth-er's good, our own, to joy and suf-fer not a-lone: the love that cast-eth out all fear.

4 Let woe and waste of war-fare cease, that use-ful la-bor yet may build its homes with love and laugh-ter filled! God, give thy way-ward chil-dren peace!

Text: William M. Vories, 1908, *Advocate of Peace,* 1909, alt.
Music: Charles H. C. Zeuner, *American Harp,* 1832

O healing river

372

Irregular

1 O heal - ing riv - er, send down your
2 This land is parch - ing, this land is
3 Let the seed of free - dom a - wake and

wa - ters, send down your wa - ters
burn - ing, no seed is grow - ing
flour - ish, let the deep roots nour - ish,

up - on this land. O heal - ing
in the bar - ren ground. O heal - ing
let the tall stalks rise. O heal - ing

riv - er, send down your wa - ters, and wash the
riv - er, send down your wa - ters, O heal - ing
riv - er, send down your wa - ters, O heal - ing

blood from off the sand.
riv - er, send your wa - ters down.
riv - er, from out of the skies.

Text: anonymous
Music: traditional North American hymn melody

373 Thou true Vine, that heals

PLEADING SAVIOR 87. 87D

1 Thou true Vine, that heals the na-tions, Tree of life, thy
2 Noth-ing can we do with-out thee; on thy life de-

branch-es we. They who leave thee fade and with-er,
pends each one. If we keep thy words and love thee,

none bear fruit ex-cept in thee. Cleanse us, make us sane and
all we ask for shall be done. May we, lov-ing one an-

sim-ple, till we merge our lives in thine, gain our-
oth-er, ra-diant in thy light a-bide; so through

selves in thee, the Vin-tage, give our-selves through thee, the Vine.
us, made fruit-ful by thee, shall our God be glo-ri-fied.

Text: Percy Dearmer, *Songs of Praise*, 1925
Music: American folk hymn, *Christian Lyre*, 1830; harmonized by Ralph Vaughan Williams, *The English Hymnal*, 1906
Text and harmonization copyright © Oxford University Press, London

O young and fearless Prophet 374

BLAIRGOWRIE 13 13. 13 13

1 O young and fear-less Proph-et of an-cient Gal-i-lee,
2 We mar-vel at the pur-pose that held you to your course,
3 O help us stand un-swerv-ing a-gainst war's blood-y way,
4 Cre-ate in us the splen-dor that dawns when hearts are kind,
5 O young and fear-less Proph-et, we need your pres-ence here,

1 your life is still a sum-mons to serve hu-man-i-ty,
2 while ev-er on the hill-top be-fore you loomed the cross.
3 where hate and lust and false-hood hold back your ho-ly sway.
4 that knows not race nor sta-tion as boun-d'ries of the mind;
5 a-mid our pride and glo-ry to see your face ap-pear;

1 to make our thoughts and ac-tions less prone to please the crowd,
2 Your stead-fast face set for-ward where love and du-ty shone,
3 For-bid false love of coun-try, that blinds us to your call
4 that learns to val-ue beau-ty, in heart, or mind, or soul,
5 once more to hear your chal-lenge a-bove our nois-y day,

1 to stand with hum-ble cour-age for truth with hearts un-cowed.
2 while we be-tray so quick-ly and leave you there a-lone.
3 who lifts a-bove the na-tions the u-ni-ty of all.
4 and longs to bind God's chil-dren in-to one per-fect whole.
5 a-gain to lead us for-ward a-long God's ho-ly way.

Text: S. Ralph Harlow, 1930-1931, *The Methodist Hymnal,* 1935, alt.
Music: John B. Dykes, 1872

375 Heal us, Immanuel, here we are

DUNFERMLINE CM

1 Heal us, Im - man - uel, here we are – we wait to
2 Our faith is fee - ble, we con - fess, we faint - ly
3 Re - mem - ber him who once ap - plied with trem - bling
4 She, too, who touched thee in the press, and heal - ing
5 Like her, with hopes and fears we come to touch thee

1 feel thy touch. Deep - wound - ed souls to
2 trust thy word; but wilt thou pit - y
3 for re - lief: "Lord, I be - lieve," with
4 vir - tue stole, was an - swered, "Daugh - ter,
5 if we may. O send us not de -

1 thee re - pair, and, Sav - ior, we are such.
2 us the less? Be that far from thee, Lord!
3 tears he cried, "O help my un - be - lief."
4 go in peace. Thy faith hath made thee whole."
5 spair - ing home; send none un - healed a - way.

Text: William Cowper, *Olney Hymns, Book I,* 1779
Music: *The CL Psalmes of David,* 1615

O God, thou faithful God 376

O GOTT, DU FROMMER GOTT (DARMSTADT) 67. 67. 66. 66

1 O God, thou faith-ful God, thou Foun-tain ev-er flow-ing,
2 And grant me, Lord, to do, with read-y heart and will-ing,
3 When dan-gers gath-er 'round, still keep me calm and fear-less.

with-out whom noth-ing is, all per-fect gifts be-stow-ing,
what-e'er thou shalt com-mand, my call-ing here ful-fill-ing;
Help me to bear the cross when life is dark and cheer-less,

grant me a health-y frame, and give me, Lord, with-in,
and do it when I ought, with zeal and joy-ful-ness,
to o-ver-come my foe with words and ac-tions kind;

a con-science free from blame, a soul un-hurt by sin.
and bless the work I've wrought, for thou wilt give suc-cess.
when coun-sel I would know, good coun-sel let me find.

Text: Johann Heermann, "O Gott, du frommer Gott," *Devoti Musica Cordis*, 1630; tr. Catherine Winkworth, *Lyra Germanica*,
        Series II, 1858, alt.
Music: *Himmels-Lust und Welt-Unlust*, 1679; harmonized by J. S. Bach, Cantata No. 45, 1726

377 Healer of our every ill

Heal-er of our ev-'ry ill, Light of each to-mor-row,

give us peace be-yond our fear, and hope be-yond our sor-row.

1 You who know our fears and sad-ness, grace us with your
2 In the pain and joy be-hold-ing, how your grace is
3 Give us strength to love each oth-er, ev-'ry sis-ter,
4 You who know each thought and feel-ing, teach us all your

peace and glad-ness. Spir-it of all com-fort, fill our hearts.
still un-fold-ing, give us all your vi-sion, God of love.
ev-'ry broth-er. Spir-it of all kind-ness, be our guide.
way of heal-ing. Spir-it of com-pas-sion, fill each heart.

Text: Marty Haugen, 1986, *Gather,* 1988
Music: Marty Haugen, 1986, *Gather,* 1988
        Text and music copyright ©1987 G.I.A. Publications, Inc.

By Peter's house

378

HEALING HEM LM with refrain

1 By Pe - ter's house in vil - lage fair, you met the sick
2 On qui - et pool your shad - ow fell to bless, to heal,
3 In syn - a - gogue, by tem - ple wall, the blind found sight,
4 You met their need. O hear our call from bed and chair,

and healed them there. Down crowd - ed path the wom - an trod
to make folk well. On moun - tain or where waves washed wide,
the lame stood tall. "Your faith has healed," you said, and then
in room and hall. O give to us the faith they knew,

Refrain

to touch the robe of the Son of God.
the throngs found whole - ness at your side.
the faint grew strong, deaf heard a - gain. O Je - sus of
the strength to trust, to come to you!

the heal - ing hem and hand and heart, heal us as them!

Text: Anne Metzler Albright, *Messenger*, 1963
       Copyright ©1963 Anne Metzler Albright
Music: Bradley P. Lehman
       Copyright ©1991 Bradley P. Lehman

379 O Christ, the healer

TYRANT HEROD LM

1 O Christ, the heal - er, we have come to pray for health,
2 From ev - 'ry ail - ment flesh en - dures our bod - ies clam -
3 In con - flicts that de - stroy our health we rec - og - nize
4 Grant that we all, made one in faith, in your com - mu -

to plead for friends. How can we fail to be re -
or to be freed, yet in our hearts we would con -
the world's dis - ease; our com - mon life de - clares our
ni - ty may find the whole - ness that, en - rich - ing

stored when reached by love that nev - er ends?
fess that whole - ness is our deep - est need.
ills. Is there no cure, O Christ, for these?
us, shall reach and pros - per hu - man - kind.

Text: Fred Pratt Green, 1967, *Hymns and Songs*, 1969
    Copyright ©1969 Hope Publishing Co.
Music: David N. Johnson, *Hymnal for the Hours*, 1989
    Copyright ©1989 G.I.A. Publications, Inc.

Let us pray

PETITIONS LITANY

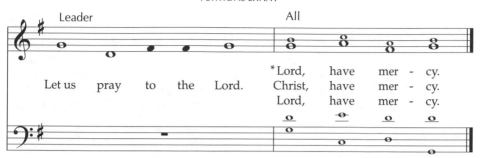

Leader

All

Let us pray to the Lord.

*Lord, have mer - cy.
Christ, have mer - cy.
Lord, have mer - cy.

*Alternate phrase: Lord, hear our prayer.

Music: Byzantine chant
Copyright ©1984 G.I.A. Publications, Inc.

Amen (Dresden)

A - men, a - men.

Music: attributed to Johann G. Naumann, 18th c.

Amen (Threefold)

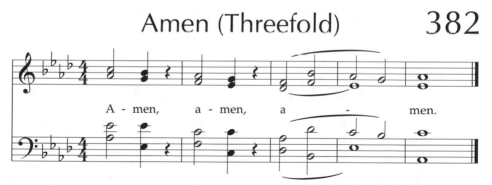

A - men, a - men, a - men.

Music: attributed to Danish origin

383 God, whose giving

HYFRYDOL 87. 87D

1 God, whose giv - ing knows no end - ing from your
2 Skills and time are ours for press - ing toward the
3 Trea - sure, too, you have en - trust - ed, gain through

rich and end - less store – na - ture's won - der, Je - sus'
goals of Christ your Son: all at peace in health and
pow'rs your grace con - ferred – ours to use for home and

wis - dom, cost - ly cross, grave's shat - tered door –
free - dom, rac - es joined, the church made one.
kin - dred, and to spread the gos - pel word.

gift - ed by you, we turn to you, of - f'ring
Now di - rect our dai - ly la - bor, lest we
O - pen wide our hands in shar - ing, as we

Text: Robert L. Edwards, *Ten New Stewardship Hymns,* 1961
Copyright ©1961, renewal 1989 The Hymn Society
Music: Rowland H. Prichard, ca. 1830, *Cyfaill y Cantorion,* 1844; arranged by Ralph Vaughan Williams, *The English Hymnal,* 1906,
adapted 1951, *BBC Hymn Book*
Arrangement copyright ©1951 Oxford University Press, London

up   our - selves   in   praise.   Thank - ful   song   shall
strive   for   self   a - lone.   Born   with   tal - ents,
heed   Christ's age - less call,   heal - ing,   teach - ing,

rise   for - ev - er,   gra - cious Do - nor   of   our   days.
make   us   ser - vants fit   to   an - swer at   your   throne.
and   re - claim - ing, serv - ing you   by serv - ing   all.

We give thee but thine own 384

SCHUMANN SM

1 We give thee but thine own, what - e'er the gift may   be.
2 May we thy boun-ties thus   as   stew-ards true re - ceive,
3 To com-fort and to   bless, to   find a balm for   woe,
4 The cap-tive to re - lease, to   God the lost to   bring,
5 And we be-lieve thy word, though dim our faith may   be,

1 All   that we have is   thine a-lone, a   trust, O Lord, from thee.
2 and glad-ly, as thou bless-est us, to thee our first-fruits give.
3 to   tend the lone and   fa - ther-less, is an - gels' work be - low.
4 to   teach the way of   life and peace; that is a Christ-like thing.
5 what-e'er for thine we   do, O Lord, we do it un - to thee.

Text: William W. How, 1858, *Psalms and Hymns*, 1864
Music: *Cantica Laudis*, 1850

385 What gift can we bring

ANNIVERSARY SONG 11 11. 11 11

1 What gift can we bring, what pres - ent, what to - ken?
2 Give thanks for the past, for those who had vi - sion,
3 Give thanks for to - mor - row, full of sur - pris - es,
4 This gift we now bring, this pres - ent, this to - ken,

What words can con - vey it – the joy of this day?
who plant - ed and wa - tered so dreams could come true.
for know - ing what - ev - er to - mor - row may bring,
these words can con - vey it – the joy of this day!

When grate - ful we come, re - mem - b'ring, re - joic - ing,
Give thanks for the now, for stud - y, for wor - ship,
we're giv - en God's word that al - ways, for - ev - er,
When grate - ful we come, re - mem - b'ring, re - joic - ing,

what song can we of - fer in hon - or and praise?
for mis - sion that bids us turn prayer in - to deed.
we rest in God's keep - ing and live in God's love.
this song we now of - fer in hon - or and praise!

Text: Jane Marshall, *Hymnal Supplement II*, 1987, alt.
Music: Jane Marshall, *Hymnal Supplement II*, 1987
Text and music copyright ©1982 Hope Publishing Co.

As saints of old

REGWAL CMD

1 As saints of old their first-fruits brought of or-chard, flock, and
2 A world in need now sum-mons us to la-bor, love, and
3 In grat-i-tude and hum-ble trust we bring our best to-

field to God, the giv-er of all good, the source of boun-teous
give, to make our life an of-fer-ing to God, that all may
day to serve your cause and share your love with all a-long life's

yield, so we to-day first-fruits would bring, the wealth of this good
live. The church of Christ is call-ing us to make the dream come
way. O God, who gave your-self to us in Je-sus Christ your

land, of farm and mar-ket, shop and home, of mind and heart and hand.
true: a world re-deemed by Christ-like love; all life in Christ made new.
Son, teach us to give our-selves each day un-til life's work is done.

Text: Frank von Christierson, *Ten New Stewardship Hymns*, 1961, alt.
          Copyright ©1961, renewal 1989 The Hymn Society
Music: Leland B. Sateren, 1963, *Sing!* 1970
          Copyright ©1963 Augsburg Publishing House

387 Lord, thou dost love

PLEADING SAVIOR 87. 87D

1 Lord, thou dost love the cheer-ful giv-er, who with
2 We are thine, thy mer-cy sought us, found us,
3 Bless'd by thee with gifts and grac-es, may we
4 Sav-ior, thou hast free-ly giv-en all the

o - pen heart and hand bless-es free-ly,
in death's dread-ful way, to the fold in
heed thy church's call, glad-ly in all
bless-ings we en-joy: earth-ly store and

as a riv-er that re-fresh-es all the
safe-ty brought us, nev-er-more from thee to
times and plac-es give to thee who giv-est
bread of heav-en, love and peace with-out al -

land. Grant us, then, the grace of giv-ing
stray. Thine own life thou free-ly gav-est
all. Thou hast bought us, and no long-er
loy. Hum-bly now we bow be-fore thee,

Text: Robert Murray, *Scottish Church Hymnary,* 1898
Music: American folk melody, *Christian Lyre,* 1830; this arrangement from *The Plymouth Collection of Hymns and Tunes,* 1855

with a spir - it large and free, that our life and
as an of - f'ring on the cross for each sin - ner
can we claim to be our own. Ev - er free and
and our all to thee re - sign, for the king - dom,

all our liv - ing we may con - se - crate to thee.
whom thou sav - est from e - ter - nal shame and loss.
ev - er strong - er, we shall serve thee, Lord, a - lone.
pow'r, and glo - ry are, O Lord, for - ev - er thine.

Grant us, Lord, the grace 388
STUTTGART 87. 87

Grant us, Lord, the grace of giv - ing, with a spir - it large and free,

that our-selves and all our liv - ing we may of - fer un - to thee.

Text: anonymous
Music: attributed to C. F. Witt, *Psalmodia Sacra*, 1715; adapted by Henry J. Gauntlett, *Hymns Ancient and Modern*, 1861

389 Take my life

HENDON 77. 77 extended

1 Take my life, and let it be con-se-crat-ed,
2 Take my hands, and let them move at the im-pulse
3 Take my voice, and let me sing, al-ways, on-ly
4 Take my sil-ver and my gold; not a mite would
5 Take my will, and make it thine; it shall be no
6 Take my love; my Lord, I pour at thy feet its

1 Lord, to thee. Take my mo-ments and my days; let them
2 of thy love. Take my feet, and let them be swift and
3 for my King. Take my lips, and let them be filled with
4 I with-hold. Take my in-tel-lect and use ev-'ry
5 long-er mine. Take my heart, it is thine own, it shall
6 trea-sure store. Take my-self, and I will be ev-er,

1 flow in cease-less praise, let them flow in cease-less praise.
2 beau-ti-ful for thee, swift and beau-ti-ful for thee.
3 mes-sag-es from thee, filled with mes-sag-es from thee.
4 pow'r as thou shalt choose, ev-'ry pow'r as thou shalt choose.
5 be thy roy-al throne, it shall be thy roy-al throne.
6 on-ly, all for thee, ev-er, on-ly, all for thee.

Text: Frances R. Havergal, *Songs of Grace and Glory*, Appendix, 1874
Music: Henri A. C. Malan, 1827; *Carmina Sacra*, 1841

God of the fertile fields

390

MILTON ABBAS 664. 6664

1 God of the fer - tile fields, Lord of the
earth that yields our dai - ly bread, forth from thy
boun - teous hand come gifts thy love has planned,
that all, in ev - 'ry land, be clothed and fed.

2 We would thy stew - ards be, hold - ing in
trust from thee all thou dost give. Help us in
love to share, teach us like thee to care,
that earth may all be fair, and all may live.

3 As grows the hid - den seed to fruit that
serves our need, thy king - dom grows. So let our
toil be used, no gift of thine a - bused,
no hum - blest task re - fused, thy love be - stows.

4 God of the coun - try - side, dear to our
Lord who died to make us one, we pledge our
lives to thee, to serve thee faith - ful - ly,
till in e - ter - ni - ty our day is done.

Text: Georgia Harkness, *Fourteen New Rural Hymns,* 1955, alt.
        Copyright ©1955, renewal 1983 The Hymn Society
Music: Eric H. Thiman, *Congregational Praise,* 1951
        Copyright © Estate of Eric H. Thiman

391 God, whose farm is all creation

STUTTGART 87. 87

1 God, whose farm is all cre - a - tion,
2 Take our plow - ing, seed - ing, reap - ing,
3 All our la - bor, all our watch - ing,

take the grat - i - tude we give. Take the fin - est
hopes and fears of sun and rain, all our think - ing,
all our cal - en - dar of care in these crops of

of our har - vest, crops we grow that all may live.
plan - ning, wait - ing, rip - ened in this fruit and grain.
your cre - a - tion, take, O God; they are our prayer.

Text: John Arlott, *BBC Hymn Book,* 1951
          Copyright © Estate of John Arlott
Music: attributed to C. F. Witt, *Psalmodia Sacra,* 1715; adapted by Henry J. Gauntlett, *Hymns Ancient and Modern,* 1861

392 Heart and mind, possessions, Lord

TANA MANA DHANA Irregular

1 Heart and mind, pos - ses - sions, Lord, I of - fer un - to thee;
2 Heart and mind, pos - ses - sions, Lord, I of - fer un - to thee;

Text: Krishnarao Rathnaji Sangle; tr. Alden H. Clark
Music: Indian melody; adapted by Marion J. Chute
          Text and music copyright ©1958 United Church Press

all   these were thine, Lord,   thou didst give them all to me.
thou   art   the way,   the   truth,   thou   art the life.

Won - drous are thy do - ings un - to me.   Plans   and my thoughts and
Sin - ful, I com - mit my - self to thee.   Je - sus Christ is   fill - ing

ev - 'ry - thing I ev - er do   are de - pen - dent on   thy
all   the   heart of me.   He can give me vic - t'ry o'er

will   and love a - lone.   I com - mit my spir - it un - to thee.
all   that threat - ens me.   Je - sus Christ is fill - ing all my heart.

A charge to keep I have   393

BOYLSTON SM

1 A   charge to keep I   have, a   God to glo - ri - fy,   a
2 To   serve the pres - ent   age, my   call - ing to ful - fill, oh,
3 Arm   me with zeal - ous   care, as   in thy sight to   live, and,
4 Help   me to watch and   pray, and   on thy - self re - ly,   as -

nev - er - dy - ing   soul to save, and   fit it   for the   sky.
may it all   my   pow'rs en - gage, to   do my Mas - ter's   will!
oh, thy ser - vant, Lord, pre - pare a   strict ac - count to   give.
sured if I   my   trust be - tray, I   shall for - ev - er   die.

Text: Charles Wesley, *Short Hymns on Select Passages of Holy Scripture, Vol. 1*, 1762
Music: Lowell Mason, *The Choir, or Union Collection of Church Music*, 1832

394 How buoyant and bold the stride

LIBERATION 10 10. 11 11

1 How buoy-ant and bold the stride of Christ's friends,
2 Not slowed by the bulk and drag of great loads,
3 Christ sent them in twos in-stead of a-lone
4 Ap-proach-ing a town or high cit-y wall,
5 Lord, grant us a faith so brave and so bright

1 when swept by his words like high-lift-ing winds,
2 to cit-ies and towns, on path-ways and roads,
3 to tell the good news, wher-ev-er un-known,
4 they won-dered what soul a-wait-ed Christ's call
5 that we too shall dare to trav-el as light

1 they set out to preach and to heal in the land
2 they car-ried the glad ur-gent gos-pel of grace
3 and lift up each oth-er when hurt and con-fused
4 and who would re-act with dis-in-t'rest or scorn
5 as those who took noth-ing but what they would need

1 with noth-ing to take but a staff in their hand!
2 that beat in their hearts and that drummed in their pace.
3 be-cause what they of-fered was mocked and re-fused.
4 and how man-y oth-ers by doubt would be torn.
5 to bring peace and heal-ing with grace and with speed.

Text: Thomas H. Troeger, 1983, *New Hymns for the Lectionary,* 1986
Music: Carol Doran, 1983, *New Hymns for the Lectionary,* 1986
        Text and music copyright ©1983 Oxford University Press, Inc.

Here I am, Lord

77. 74D with refrain

1 I, the Lord of sea and sky,
I have heard my people cry.
All who dwell in dark and sin
my hand will save.
I who made the stars of night,
I will make their darkness bright.
Who will bear my light to them?
Whom shall I send?
(Refrain)

2 I, the Lord of snow and rain,
I have borne my people's pain.
I have wept for love of them.
They turn away.
I will break their hearts of stone,
give them hearts for love alone.
I will speak my word to them.
Whom shall I send?
(Refrain)

3 I, the Lord of wind and flame,
I will tend the poor and lame.
I will set a feast for them.
My hand will save.
Finest bread I will provide,
till their hearts be satisfied.
I will give my life to them.
Whom shall I send?
(Refrain)

Text: based on Isaiah 6, Daniel L. Schutte, 1980, *Lord of Light*, 1981
Music: Daniel L. Schutte; arranged by Michael Pope, S.J., and John Weissrock
          Text and music copyright ©1981 Daniel L. Schutte and New Dawn Music

396 The work is thine, O Christ

DIE SACH' IST DEIN 86. 86. 88. 88. 46

1 The work is thine, O Christ our Lord, the cause for which we
2 Through suf-f'ring thou, O Christ, didst go un - to thy throne a-
3 Thou hast, O Sav-ior, led the way through ag - o - ny and

stand, and be - ing thine, 'twill o - ver-come its foes on ev - 'ry
bove, and lead-est now the self-same way those true in faith and
death. O give, we pray, yet more and more thy Spir-it's liv - ing

hand. Yet grains of wheat, be - fore they grow, are
love. So lead us, then, though suf - f'rings wait, to
breath! Send mes - sen - gers o'er land and sea to

bur - ied in the earth be-low. All that is old doth
share thy king-dom's heav'n - ly state. Thy death has bro - ken
bring thy chil - dren all to thee. Thy name can save, thy

Text: Samuel Preiswerk (Sts. 1-2), Felician von Zaremba (St. 3), *Die Sach' ist dein;* tr. Julius H. Horstmann, *Christian Hymns,* 1908
Music: J. Michael Haydn, 18th c., *Hier liegt vor deiner Majestät*

per - ish there to form a life both new and fair. So
Sa - tan's might, and leads the faith - ful to the light, e -
name makes free! We con - se - crate our - selves to thee as

too are we from self and sin made free.
ter - nal light, from dark - ness in - to light.
ser - vants true, as work - ers brave and true.

God loves all his many people 397

85. 85 with refrain

1 God loves all his man - y peo - ple with sur - pass - ing love,
2 God wants you to come to him now, wants you as his child.
3 In the Lord is our sal - va - tion, in the Lord is love.

bless - es all as his own chil - dren, cares for ev - 'ry one.
Come, my friend, do not re - fuse him; he is Lord of all.
Come, my friend, do not re - fuse him; come, re - ceive his joy.

Refrain

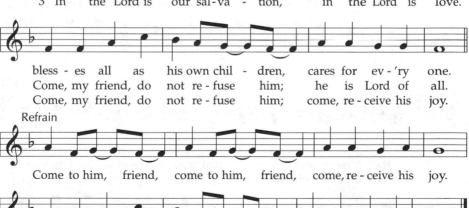

Come to him, friend, come to him, friend, come, re - ceive his joy.

Earth - ly things don't last for - ev - er, come, re - ceive his joy.

Text: Lubunda Mukungu; tr. revised by Anna Juhnke, *International Songbook*, Mennonite World Conference, 1978, alt.
         Translation copyright ©1978, 1990 Mennonite World Conference
Music: Tshiluba melody (Zaire), *International Songbook*, Mennonite World Conference, 1978

398 I love to tell the story

HANKEY 76. 76D with refrain

1 I love to tell the sto - ry of un - seen things a - bove,
2 I love to tell the sto - ry. 'Tis pleas - ant to re - peat
3 I love to tell the sto - ry, for those who know it best

of Je - sus and his glo - ry, of Je - sus and his love.
what seems, each time I tell it, more won - der - ful - ly sweet.
seem hun - ger - ing and thirst - ing to hear it, like the rest.

I love to tell the sto - ry, be - cause I know 'tis true.
I love to tell the sto - ry, for some have nev - er heard
And when, in scenes of glo - ry, I sing the new, new song,

It sat - is - fies my long - ings as noth - ing else could do.
the mes - sage of sal - va - tion from God's own ho - ly word.
'twill be the old, old sto - ry that I have loved so long.

Text: Catherine Hankey, 1866, refrain by William G. Fischer, 1869, *Joyful Songs Nos. 1-3 Combined*, 1869
Music: William G. Fischer, *Joyful Songs Nos. 1-3 Combined*, 1869

I love to tell the sto - ry, 'twill be my theme in glo - ry,

to tell the old, old sto - ry of Je - sus and his love.

Now go forward 399

Irregular

Now go for - ward, press t'ward the goal.

Plen - ti - ful har - vest waits for you. Faith - ful ser - vants,

fear not death, toil and la - bor for the Lord.

Come, be - hold, your days pass a - way. Look a - head, the

cross leads the way. While you have breath

on this day, give your - self. For - ward go!

Text: anonymous; tr. Evelyn Chiu, 1986
    Translation copyright ©1986 Evelyn Chiu
Music: traditional Chinese melody

400 Santo, santo, santo (Holy, holy, holy)

SANTO Irregular

1 San - to, san - to, san - to, san - to, san - to, san - to_es nues - tro
2 San - to, san - to, san - to, san - to, san - to, san - to_es nues - tro
1 Ho - ly, ho - ly, ho - ly, ho - ly, ho - ly, ho - ly is our
2 Ho - ly, ho - ly, ho - ly, ho - ly, ho - ly, ho - ly is our

Dios, Se - ñor de to - da la tie - rra. San - to,
Dios, Se - ñor de to - da la his - to - ria. San - to,
God, God, the Lord of earth and heav - en. Ho - ly,
God, God, the Lord of all of his - t'ry. Ho - ly,

san - to_es nues - tro Dios. San - to, Que a - com - pa - ña a nues - tro
san - to_es nues - tro Dios. Ben - di - tos los que_en su
ho - ly is our God. Ho - ly, Who ac - com - pan - ies our
ho - ly is our God. Bless - ed those who in the

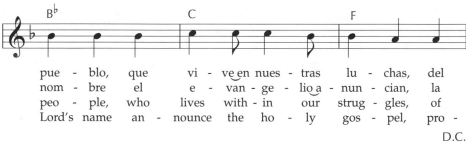

pue - blo, que vi - ve_en nues - tras lu - chas, del
nom - bre el e - van - ge - lio_a - nun - cian, la
peo - ple, who lives with - in our strug - gles, of
Lord's name an - nounce the ho - ly gos - pel, pro -

u - ni - ver - so_en - te - ro el ú - ni - co Se - ñor.
bue - na y gran no - ti - cia de la li - be - ra - ción.
all the earth and heav - en the one and on - ly Lord.
claim - ing the good news that our lib - er - a - tion comes.

Text: Guillermo Cuellar, 1980, *Misa Popular Salvadoreña*; tr. Linda McCrae
Music: Guillermo Cuellar, 1980, *Misa Popular Salvadoreña*
Text and music copyright ©1980 Guillermo Cuellar, Nicaragua

This little light of mine

401

LATTIMER Irregular

1 This lit-tle light of mine,
2 Ev - 'ry - where I go, I'm goin'-a let it shine,
3 All through the night,

this lit-tle light of mine,
ev - 'ry - where I go, I'm goin'-a let it shine,
all through the night,

this lit-tle light of mine,
ev - 'ry - where I go, I'm goin'-a let it shine,
all through the night,

let it shine, let it shine, let it shine. (let it shine)

Text: African-American spiritual
Music: African-American spiritual; adapted by William F. Smith, 1987
Adaptation copyright ©1989 The United Methodist Publishing House

402 Christian, let your burning light

BURNING LIGHT 77. 77 with refrain

1 Chris-tian, let your burn-ing light   shine on all with lus-ter bright.
2 As   you jour-ney here be-low,   shed a ray wher - e'er you go.
3 That your light may guide you through, bright-ly let it   shine a-new.

Let your words and deeds be pure.   All for Christ you must en-dure.
Find in   this your pure de-light,   let your light shine clear and bright.
Keep up cour-age – nev-er fail   till you're safe with - in the vail.

Refrain

Chris - tian, let your light   shine   all a - long your way.

You may guide   a wan - d'rer   to e - ter - nal day.

You may save from end-less night   if you let your lamp burn bright.

Text: E. G. Coleman, 1898, *Gospel Songs and Hymns No. 1*, 1899
Music: E. G. Coleman, 1898, *Gospel Songs and Hymns No. 1*, 1899

The church of Christ, in every age 403

DICKINSON COLLEGE LM

1 The church of Christ, in ev - 'ry age be - set by
2 A - cross the world, a - cross the street, the vic - tims
3 Then let the ser - vant church a - rise, a car - ing
4 For he a - lone, whose blood was shed, can cure the
5 We have no mis - sion but to serve in full o -

1 change but Spir - it - led, must claim and test
2 of in - jus - tice cry for shel - ter and
3 church that longs to be a part - ner in
4 fe - ver in our blood, and teach us how
5 be - dience to our Lord, to care for all,

1 its her - i - tage and keep on ris - ing from the dead.
2 for bread to eat, and nev - er live un - til they die.
3 Christ's sac - ri - fice, and clothed in Christ's hu - man - i - ty.
4 to share our bread and feed the starv - ing mul - ti - tude.
5 with - out re - serve, and spread his lib - er - at - ing word.

Text: Fred Pratt Green, 1969, *26 Hymns,* 1971
         Copyright ©1971 Hope Publishing Co.
Music: Lee H. Bristol, Jr., 1962, *More Hymns and Spiritual Songs,* 1971
         Copyright ©1962 Theodore Presser Co.

404 O Jesus Christ, may grateful hymns

CITY OF GOD 11 10. 11 10

1 O Je-sus Christ, may grate-ful hymns be ris - ing
2 Grant us new cour - age, sac - ri - fi - cial, hum - ble,
3 Show us your Spir - it, brood-ing o'er each cit - y

in ev - 'ry cit - y for your love and care.
strong in your strength to ven - ture and to dare,
as you once wept a - bove Je - ru - sa - lem,

In - spire our wor - ship, grant the glad sur - pris - ing
to lift the fall - en, guide the feet that stum - ble,
seek - ing to gath - er all in love and pit - y,

that your bless'd Spir - it rous - es ev - 'ry - where.
seek out the lone - ly and God's mer - cy share.
and heal - ing those who touch your gar - ment's hem.

Text: Bradford G. Webster, *Five New Hymns of the City,* 1954, alt.
Copyright ©1954, renewal 1982 The Hymn Society
Music: Daniel Moe, 1956
Copyright ©1957 Augsburg Publishing House

Where cross the crowded ways 405

GERMANY LM

1 Where cross the crowd-ed ways of life, where sound the
2 In haunts of wretch-ed-ness and need, on shad-owed
3 From ten-der child-hood's help-less-ness, from wom-an's
4 The cup of wa-ter giv'n for you still holds the
5 O Mas-ter, from the moun-tain-side, make haste to
6 till all the world shall learn your love, and fol-low

1 cries of race and clan, a-bove the noise of
2 thresh-olds dark with fears, from paths where hide the
3 grief, man's bur-dened toil, from fam-ished souls, from
4 fresh-ness of your grace. Yet long these mul-ti-
5 heal these hearts of pain. A-mong these rest-less
6 where your feet have trod, till glo-rious from your

1 self-ish strife, we hear your voice, O Son of Man!
2 lures of greed, we catch the vi-sion of your tears.
3 sor-row's stress, your heart has nev-er known re-coil.
4 tudes to view the sweet com-pas-sion of your face.
5 throngs a-bide – O tread the cit-y's streets a-gain,
6 heav'n a-bove shall come the cit-y of our God.

Text: Frank M. North, *Christian City*, 1903, alt.
Music: W. Gardiner's *Sacred Melodies*, Vol. 2, 1815

406 And is the gospel peace and love

FARMINGTON LM

1 And is the gos - pel peace and love! Such
2 When - e'er the an - gry pas - sions rise, and
3 Oh, how be - nev - o - lent and kind, how

let our con - ver - sa - tion be; the ser - pent blend - ed with the
tempt our thoughts and tongues to strife, to Je - sus let us lift our
mild! how read - y to for - give! Be this the tem - per of our

dove, wis - dom and meek sim - plic - i - ty.
eyes, bright pat - tern of the Chris - tian life.
mind, and these the rules by which we live.

Text: Anne Steele, *Poems on Subjects Chiefly Devotional*, Vol. 1, 1760
Music: adapted from Joseph Funk's *Genuine Church Music*, 1st ed., 1832

We are people of God's peace 407

AVE VIRGO VIRGINUM (GAUDEAMUS PARITER) 76. 76D

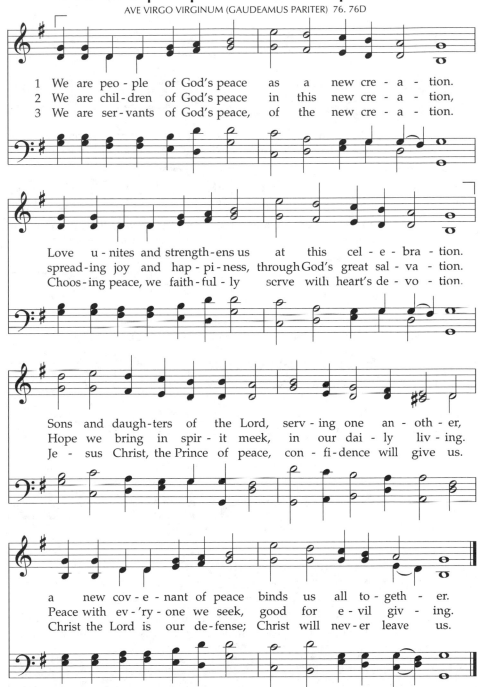

1 We are peo-ple of God's peace as a new cre - a - tion.
2 We are chil-dren of God's peace in this new cre - a - tion,
3 We are ser-vants of God's peace, of the new cre - a - tion.

Love u - nites and strength-ens us at this cel - e - bra - tion.
spread-ing joy and hap - pi - ness, through God's great sal - va - tion.
Choos-ing peace, we faith-ful - ly serve with heart's de - vo - tion.

Sons and daugh-ters of the Lord, serv - ing one an - oth - er,
Hope we bring in spir - it meek, in our dai - ly liv - ing.
Je - sus Christ, the Prince of peace, con - fi - dence will give us.

a new cov - e - nant of peace binds us all to - geth - er.
Peace with ev - 'ry - one we seek, good for e - vil giv - ing.
Christ the Lord is our de - fense; Christ will nev - er leave us.

Text: Menno Simons, 1552; tr. Esther C. Bergen, *International Songbook*, Mennonite World Conference, 1990
          Translation copyright ©1990 Mennonite World Conference
Music: Johann Horn, *Ein Gesangbuch der Brüder im Behemen und Merherrn*, 1544; revised in *Catholicum Hymnologium
          Germanicum*, 1584

408

O day of peace

JERUSALEM LMD

1 O day of peace that dim-ly shines through all our
2 Then shall the wolf dwell with the lamb nor shall the

hopes and prayers and dreams, guide us to jus-tice, truth, and
fierce de-vour the small. As beasts and cat-tle calm-ly

love, de-liv-ered from our self-ish schemes. May swords of
graze, a lit-tle child shall lead them all. Then en-e-

hate fall from our hands, our hearts from en-vy find re-
mies shall learn to love, all crea-tures find their true ac-

lease, till by God's grace our war-ring world shall see Christ's
cord. The hope of peace shall be ful-filled, for all the

Text: Carl P. Daw, Jr., *The Hymnal 1982*, 1985
Copyright ©1982 Hope Publishing Co.
Music: Charles H. H. Parry, 1916; harmonized by Richard Proulx, 1986
Harmonization copyright ©1986 G.I.A. Publications, Inc.

prom - ised reign of peace.
earth shall know the Lord.

What does the Lord require 409

MICAH 66. 66. 66

1 What does the Lord re - quire for praise and of - fer - ing?
2 Peo - ple of earth, give ear! Should you not jus - tice know?
3 Still down the ag - es ring the proph-et's stern com-mands.
4 How shall our life ful - fill God's law so hard and high?

What sac - ri - fice, de - sire, or trib - ute bid you bring? Do
Will God your plead - ing hear, while crime and cruel - ty grow? Do
To mer - chant, work - er, king, he brings God's high de - mands. Do
Let Christ en - due our will with grace to for - ti - fy. Then

just - ly, love mer - cy, walk hum - bly with your God.
just - ly, love mer - cy, walk hum - bly with your God.
just - ly, love mer - cy, walk hum - bly with your God.
just - ly, in mer - cy, we'll hum - bly walk with God.

Text: based on Micah 6:6-8, Albert F. Bayly, 1949, *Rejoice, O People*, 1950
        Copyright © Oxford University Press, London
Music: Larry Warkentin, 1990
        Copyright ©1990 Larry Warkentin

410 Lord of light, your name outshining

EBENEZER 87. 87D

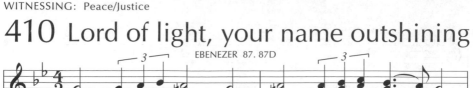

1 Lord of light, your name out - shin - ing
2 By the toil of faith - ful work - ers
3 Grant that knowl - edge, still in - creas - ing,
4 By the prayers of faith - ful watch - ers,

all the stars and suns of space, use our tal - ents
in some far out - ly - ing field, by the cour - age,
at your feet may low - ly kneel. With your grace our
nev - er si - lent day or night, by the cross of

in your king - dom as the ser - vants of your grace.
where the ra - diance of the cross is still re - vealed,
tri - umphs hal - low, with your char - i - ty our zeal.
Je - sus, bring - ing peace to all and heal - ing light,

Use us to ful - fill your pur - pose in the gift of
by the vic - to - ries of meek-ness, through re - proach and
Lift the na - tions from the shad - ows to the glad - ness
by the love that pass - es knowl-edge, mak - ing all your

Text: Howell E. Lewis, *The Congregational Hymnary*, 1916, alt.
Music: Thomas J. Williams, 1896, *Baptist Book of Praise*, 1901

Christ your Son.
suf - f'ring won, Lord of light, as in high - est heav - en,
of the sun —
chil - dren one,

so on earth your will be done.

I bind my heart this tide   411

UNION 67. 77

1 I bind my heart this tide to the Gal - i - le-an's side, to the
2 I bind my soul this day to the neigh-bor far a - way, and the
3 I bind my heart in thrall to the God, the Lord of all, to the
4 I bind my-self to peace, to make strife and en-vy cease. God,

wounds of Cal - va - ry, to the Christ who died for me.
stran-ger near at hand, in this town, and in this land.
God, the poor one's friend, and the Christ whom he did send.
knit thou sure the cord of my thrall-dom to my Lord! A-men

Text: Lauchlan M. Watt, *The Tryst, A Book of the Soul*, 1907, alt.
Music: J. Randall Zercher, 1965, *The Mennonite Hymnal*, 1969
        Copyright ©1965 J. Randall Zercher

412 We shall walk through the valley

Irregular

1 We shall walk through the val - ley of the shad - ow of death,
2 There will be no sor - row - ing there,
3 (Hum) -

(melody)

we shall walk through the val - ley in peace!
there will be no sor - row - ing there.
(Hum) -

And if Je - sus him - self will be our lead -
And if Je - sus him - self will be our lead -
And if Je - sus him - self will be our lead -

(melody)

er, we shall walk through the val - ley in peace!
er, we shall walk through the val - ley in peace!
er, we shall walk through the val - ley in peace!

Text: African-American spiritual
Music: African-American spiritual; adapted by W. Appling
      Adaptation copyright ©1970 World Library Publications, Inc.

Faith of the martyrs

ST. CATHERINE LM with refrain

1 *Faith of the mar - tyrs, liv - ing still in spite of dun - geon, fire, and sword, oh, how our hearts beat high with joy when-e'er we hear that glo - rious word! Faith of the mar - tyrs, ho - ly faith, we will be true to thee till death.

2 The mar - tyrs chained in pris - ons dark, were still in heart and con - science free, and bless'd would be their chil - dren's fate, if they, like them, should die for thee! Faith of the mar - tyrs, ho - ly faith, we will be true to thee till death.

3 Faith of the mar - tyrs, we will love both friend and foe in all our strife, and preach thee, too, as love knows how, by sav - ing word and faith - ful life! Faith of the mar - tyrs, ho - ly faith, we will be true to thee till death.

*Alternate phrases: "Faith of our fathers" or "Faith of our mothers"

Text: Frederick W. Faber, *Jesus and Mary,* 1849, alt.
Music: Henri F. Hemy, *Crown of Jesus Music,* 1864; adapted by James G. Walton, *Plainsong Music for the Holy Communion Office,* 1874

414
God, who stretched

HOLY MANNA 87. 87D

1 God, who stretched the span - gled heav - ens, in - fi - nite in time and place, flung the suns in burn - ing ra - diance through the si - lent fields of space; we, your chil - dren in your like - ness, share in - ven - tive pow'rs with you. Great Cre - a - tor,

2 We have ven - tured worlds un-dreamed of since the child-hood of our race, known the ec - sta - sy of wing - ing through un - trav - eled realms of space, probed the se - crets of the a - tom, yield-ing un - im - ag - ined pow'r, fac - ing us with

3 As each far ho - ri - zon beck - ons, may it chal - lenge us a - new, chil - dren of cre - a - tive pur - pose serv - ing oth - ers, hon - 'ring you. May our dreams prove rich with prom - ise, each en - deav - or well be - gun. Great Cre - a - tor,

Text: Catherine Cameron, 1967, *Contemporary Worship I,* 1969, alt.
        Copyright ©1967 Hope Publishing Co.
Music: *The Columbian Harmony,* 1825

still cre - at - ing, show us what we yet may do.
life's de - struc - tion or our most tri - um - phant hour.
give us guid - ance till our goals and yours are one.

Forth in thy name

415

KEBLE LM

1 Forth in thy name, O Lord, I go, my dai - ly
2 The task thy wis - dom hath as - signed, oh, let me
3 Thee may I set at my right hand, whose eyes mine
4 Give me to bear thine eas - y yoke, and ev - 'ry
5 for thee de - light - ful - ly em - ploy what - e'er thy

1 la - bor to pur - sue; thee, on - ly thee, re -
2 cheer - ful - ly ful - fill, in all my works thy
3 in - most sub - stance see, and la - bor on at
4 mo - ment watch and pray, and still to things e -
5 boun - teous grace hath giv'n, and run my course with

1 solved to know in all I think, or speak, or do.
2 pres - ence find, and prove thy good and per - fect will.
3 thy com - mand, and of - fer all my works to thee.
4 ter - nal look, and has - ten to thy glo - rious day;
5 e - ven joy, and close - ly walk with thee to heav'n.

Text: Charles Wesley, *Hymns and Sacred Poems, Part II*, 1749
Music: John B. Dykes, *Hymns Ancient and Modern*, 1875

416   For Christ and the church

FOR CHRIST AND THE CHURCH 10 12. 11 11 with refrain

1 For Christ and the church let our voic-es ring, let us hon-or the
2 For Christ and the church be our ear-nest prayer, let us fol-low his
3 For Christ and the church, will-ing of-f'rings make, time and tal-ents and
4 For Christ and the church let us cast a-side, by his con-quer-ing

name of our own bless-ed King. Let us work with a will in the
ban-ner, the cross dai-ly bear. Let us yield, whol-ly yield, to his
gold, for the dear Mas-ter's sake. We'll re-mem-ber the best we can
grace, chains of self, fear, and pride. May our lives be en-riched by an

strength of youth, and loy-al-ly stand for the king-dom of truth.
Spir-it's power, and faith-ful-ly serve him in life's bright-est hour.
bring to him, the heart's wealth of love that will nev-er grow dim.
aim so grand, then hap-py the call to the Sav-ior's right hand.

Refrain

For Christ, our dear Re-deem-er, for Christ, who died to save,
For Christ, for Christ,

Text: Eliza E. Hewitt, *Living Hymns*, 1890
Music: William J. Kirkpatrick, *Living Hymns*, 1890

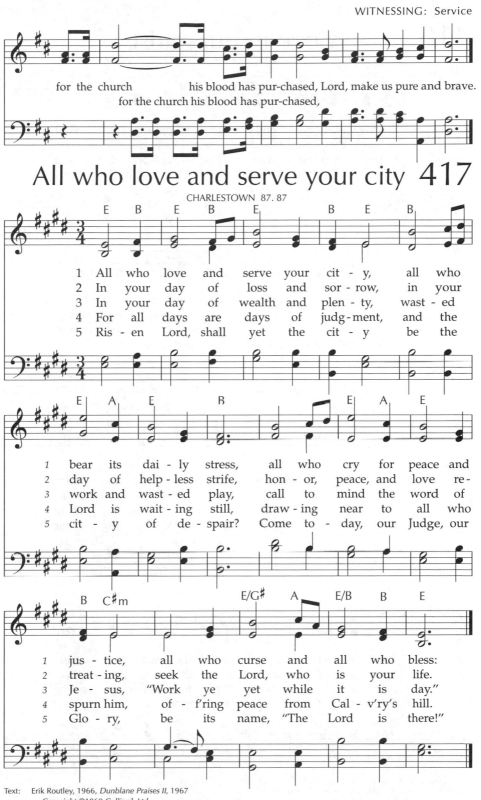

for the church   his blood has pur-chased, Lord, make us pure and brave.
for the church his blood has pur-chased,

All who love and serve your city 417

CHARLESTOWN 87. 87

E	B	E	B	E		B	E	B

1 All   who   love   and   serve   your   cit - y,   all   who
2 In   your   day   of   loss   and   sor - row,   in   your
3 In   your   day   of   wealth   and   plen - ty,   wast - ed
4 For   all   days   are   days   of   judg - ment,   and   the
5 Ris - en   Lord,   shall   yet   the   cit - y   be   the

E	A	E		B		E	A	E

1 bear   its   dai - ly   stress,   all   who   cry   for   peace and
2 day   of   help - less   strife,   hon - or,   peace, and   love re-
3 work and   wast - ed   play,   call   to   mind   the   word of
4 Lord   is   wait - ing   still,   draw - ing   near   to   all who
5 cit - y   of   de - spair?   Come to - day,   our   Judge,   our

B	C#m			E/G#	A	E/B	B	E

1 jus - tice,   all   who   curse   and   all   who   bless:
2 treat - ing,   seek   the   Lord,   who   is   your   life.
3 Je - sus,   "Work   ye   yet   while   it   is   day."
4 spurn him,   of - f'ring   peace   from   Cal - v'ry's   hill.
5 Glo - ry,   be   its   name,   "The   Lord   is   there!"

Text: Erik Routley, 1966, *Dunblane Praises II*, 1967
           Copyright ©1969 Galliard, Ltd.
Music: *United States Sacred Harmony*, 1799

418 Move in our midst

PINE GLEN 99. 99

1 Move in our midst, thou Spir - it of God.
2 Touch thou our hands to lead us a - right.
3 Strike from our feet the fet - ters that bind.
4 Kin - dle our hearts to burn with thy flame.

Go with us down from thy ho - ly hill.
Guide us for - ev - er, show us thy way.
Lift from our lives the weight of our wrong.
Raise up thy ban - ners high in this hour.

Walk with us through the storm and the calm.
Trans - form our dark - ness in - to thy light.
Teach us to love with heart, soul, and mind.
Stir us to build new worlds in thy name.

Spir - it of God, go thou with us still.
Spir - it of God, lead thou us to - day.
Spir - it of God, thy love makes us strong.
Spir - it of God, O send us thy pow'r!

Text: Kenneth I. Morse, 1942, 1949, *The Brethren Hymnal*, 1951
Music: Perry L. Huffaker, 1950, *The Brethren Hymnal*, 1951

Lead on, O cloud of Presence 419

LANCASHIRE 76. 76D

1 Lead on, O cloud of Pres - ence, the ex - o - dus is come.
2 Lead on, O fier - y Pil - lar, we fol - low yet with fears,
3 Lead on, O God of free - dom, and guide us on our way,

In wil - der - ness and des - ert our tribe shall make its home.
but we shall come re - joic - ing though joy be born of tears.
and help us trust the prom - ise through strug - gle and de - lay.

Our slav - 'ry left be - hind us, new hopes with - in us grow.
We are not lost, though wan - d'ring, for by your light we come,
We pray our sons and daugh - ters may jour - ney to that land

We seek the land of prom - ise where milk and hon - ey flow.
and we are still God's peo - ple. The jour - ney is our home.
where jus - tice dwells with mer - cy, and love is law's de - mand.

Text: Ruth C. Duck, *Because We Are One People,* 1974, alt.
        Copyright ©1974 Ruth Duck
Music: Henry T. Smart, 1835, *Psalms and Hymns for Divine Worship,* 1867

420 Heart with loving heart united

O DU LIEBE MEINER LIEBE 87. 87D

1 Heart with lov - ing heart u - nit - ed, met to know God's ho - ly will.
2 May we all so love each oth - er and all self - ish claims de - ny,
3 Since, O Lord, you have de - mand - ed that our lives your love should show,

Let his love in us ig - nit - ed more and more our spir - its fill.
so that each one for the oth - er will not hes - i - tate to die.
so we wait to be com - mand - ed forth in - to your world to go.

He the head, we are his mem - bers, we re - flect the light he is.
E - ven so our Lord has loved us, for our lives he gave his life.
Kin - dle in us love's com - pas - sion so that ev - 'ry - one may see

He the Mas - ter, we dis - ci - ples, he is ours and we are his.
Still he grieves and still he suf - fers, for our self - ish - ness and strife.
in our fel - low - ship the prom - ise of a new hu - man - i - ty.

Text: Nicolaus L. von Zinzendorf, *Herz und Herz vereint zusammen*, 1723, *Die letzten Reden unseres Herrn*, 1725; tr. Walter
         Klaassen, 1965
         Translation copyright ©1969, 1983 Walter Klaassen
Music: *Manuscript Chorale Book*, 1735

Bless'd be the tie that binds

DENNIS SM

1 Bless'd be the tie that binds our hearts in
2 Be - fore our Fa - ther's throne we pour our
3 We share each oth - er's woes, each oth - er's
4 When we a - sun - der part, it gives us
5 This glo - rious hope re - vives our cour - age
6 From sor - row, toil, and pain, and sin we

1 Chris - tian love. The fel - low - ship of
2 ar - dent prayers; our fears, our hopes, our
3 bur - dens bear, and of - ten for each
4 in - ward pain, but we shall still be
5 by the way, while each in ex - pec -
6 shall be free, and per - fect love and

1 kin - dred minds is like to that a - bove.
2 aims are one, our com - forts and our cares.
3 oth - er flows the sym - pa - thiz - ing tear.
4 joined in heart, and hope to meet a - gain.
5 ta - tion lives and longs to see the day.
6 friend - ship reign through all e - ter - ni - ty.

Text: John Fawcett, *Hymns Adapted to the Circumstances of Public Worship …*, 1782, alt.
Music: arranged from Johann G. Nägeli by Lowell Mason, *The Psaltery,* 1845

422
Bwana awabariki
(May God grant you a blessing)

Irregular

1 Bwa - na   a - wa - ba - ri - ki,   Bwa - na   a - wa - ba - ri - ki,
2 May   God   grant you a bless-ing,   may   God   grant you a bless-ing,

Bwa - na   a - wa - ba - ri - ki   mi - le - le.
may   God   grant you a bless-ing   ev - er - more.

U - ki - mcha Bwa - na.   Bwa - na   a - wa - ba - ri - ki.
Re - vere the Lord.   May   God   grant you a bless-ing.

Text: Swahili folk hymn
Music: Swahili melody

423 May the grace of Christ our Savior

FELLOWSHIP 87. 87

1 May   the grace   of   Christ   our Sav - ior,   and   the Fa - ther's
2 Thus   may we   a - bide   in un - ion   with   each oth - er

Text: John Newton, *Olney Hymns, Book III*, 1779
Music: Conrad G. Lint

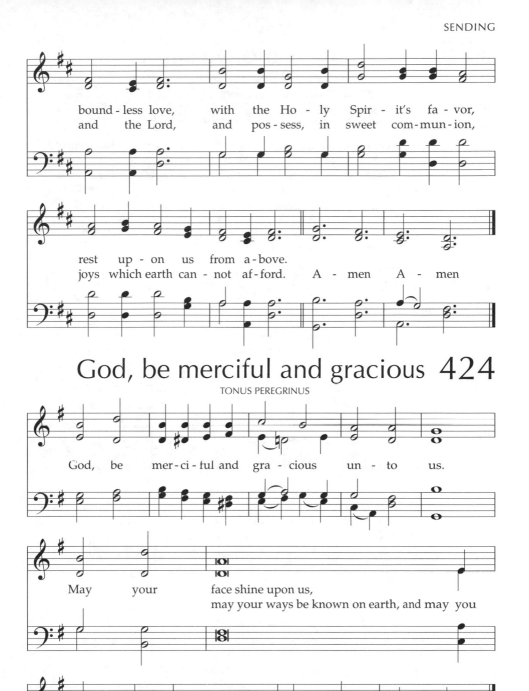

bound - less love, with   the Ho - ly Spir - it's fa - vor,
and   the Lord,   and   pos - sess, in sweet com - mun - ion,

rest up - on us from a - bove.
joys which earth can - not af - ford.   A - men   A - men

God, be merciful and gracious 424
TONUS PEREGRINUS

God, be   mer - ci - ful and gra - cious   un - to   us.

May   your   face shine upon us,
            may your ways be known on earth, and may you

grant   us   peace.   A - men   A - men

Text: based on Psalm 67
Music: Psalm tone, pre-16th c.; harmonized by J. S. Bach

425 Come, come, ye saints

ALL IS WELL 10 6. 10 6. 88. 86

1 Come, come, ye saints, no toil nor la-bor fear, but with joy
2 The world of care is with us ev-'ry day; let it not
3 We'll find the rest which God for us pre-pared, when at last

wend your way. Though hard to you the jour-ney may ap-pear,
this ob-scure: Here we can serve the Mas-ter on the way,
he will call. Where none will come to hurt or make a-fraid,

grace shall be as your day. We have a liv - ing
and in him be se-cure. Gird up your loins, fresh
he will reign o - ver all. We will make the air with

Lord to guide, and we can trust him to pro-vide. Do
cour-age take, our God will nev - er us for-sake. And
mu - sic ring, shout praise to God our Lord and King. Oh,

Text: William Clayton, 1846; altered by Joseph F. Green, *Broadman Songs for Men, No. 2*, 1960
            Copyright ©1960, 1988 The Broadman Press
Music: American folk melody; adapted from *Sacred Harp*, 1844

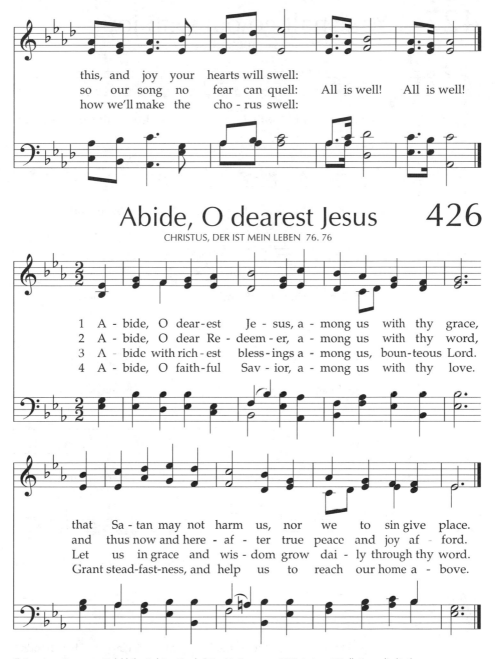

this, and joy your hearts will swell:
so our song no fear can quell: All is well! All is well!
how we'll make the cho - rus swell:

Abide, O dearest Jesus   426
CHRISTUS, DER IST MEIN LEBEN 76. 76

1 A - bide, O dear-est Je - sus, a - mong us with thy grace,
2 A - bide, O dear Re - deem - er, a - mong us with thy word,
3 A - bide with rich - est bless - ings a - mong us, boun-teous Lord.
4 A - bide, O faith-ful Sav - ior, a - mong us with thy love.

that Sa - tan may not harm us, nor we to sin give place.
and thus now and here - af - ter true peace and joy af - ford.
Let us in grace and wis - dom grow dai - ly through thy word.
Grant stead-fast-ness, and help us to reach our home a - bove.

Text: Josua Stegmann, "Ach bleib mit deiner Gnade," *Suspiria Temporum*, 1628; tr. August Crull, *Evangelical Lutheran Hymn Book*, 1982
Translation copyright ©1941 Concordia Publishing House
Music: Melchior Vulpius, *Ein schön geistlich Gesangbuch*, 1609

427 You shall go out with joy

THE TREES OF THE FIELD Irregular

You shall go out with joy and be led forth with peace.

The moun-tains and the hills will break forth be-

fore you. There'll be shouts of joy and all the trees of the

field will clap, will clap their hands.

And all the trees of the field will clap their hands,

the trees of the field will clap their hands.

The trees of the field will clap their hands,

while you go out with joy.

Text: based on Isaiah 55:12; adapted by Steffi Geiser Rubin
Music: Stuart Dauermann, 1975

Lord, let us now depart in peace 428

DISMISSAL 88. 86

Lord, let us now de - part in peace, who in thy name are
gath - ered here. Dis - close the bright - ness
of thy face, and be for - ev - er near. A - men

Text: anonymous
Music: George Whelpton

Go now in peace 429

Canon

GO NOW IN PEACE

Go now in peace, go now in peace, may the love of
God sur - round you ev - 'ry - where, ev - 'ry - where
you may go. Coda (ad lib) Go now in peace, go now in peace.

Text: Natalie Sleeth, *Sunday Songbook*
Music: Natalie Sleeth, *Sunday Songbook*

430 God be with you

RANDOLPH 98 89

1 God be with you till we meet a - gain; lov - ing
2 God be with you till we meet a - gain; un - seen
3 God be with you till we meet a - gain; when life's
4 God be with you till we meet a - gain; keep love's

coun - sels guide, up - hold you, may the Shep - herd's
wings, pro - tect - ing, hide you, dai - ly man - na
per - ils thick con - found you, put un - fail - ing
ban - ner float - ing o'er you, smite death's threat - 'ning

care en - fold you; God be with you till we meet a - gain.
still pro - vide you; God be with you till we meet a - gain.
arms a - round you; God be with you till we meet a - gain.
wave be - fore you; God be with you till we meet a - gain.

Text: Jeremiah E. Rankin, *Gospel Bells*, 1880, alt.
Music: Ralph Vaughan Williams, *The English Hymnal*, 1906
        Copyright © Oxford University Press, London

God be with you

1 God be with you till we meet again;
by his counsels guide, uphold you,
with his sheep securely fold you;
God be with you till we meet again.

2 God be with you till we meet again;
'neath his wings protecting hide you,
daily manna still provide you;
God be with you till we meet again.

Text: Jeremiah E. Rankin, *Gospel Bells*, 1880

With all my heart I offer

BENEDICTION 10 10. 10 10

1 With all my heart I of - fer thanks to God. Ma - jes - tic are the
2 Al - le - lu - ia, al - le - lu - ia, a - men. Al - le - lu - ia, al -

won - ders of our Lord, whose mer - cies nev - er fail from day to day,
le - lu - ia, a - men. Al - le - lu - ia, al - le - lu - ia, a - men.

whose right - eous hand will lead us all the way.
Al - le - lu - ia, al - le - lu - ia, a - men. A - men

whose hand
A - men

Text: Carol Ann Weaver, *Jericho*, 1979
Music: Carol Ann Weaver, *Jericho*, 1979

433
Go, my children

AR HYD Y NOS 12 12. 88. 12

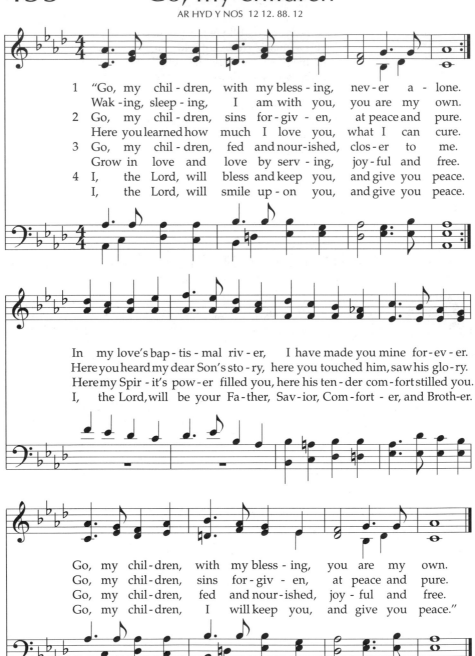

1 "Go, my chil - dren, with my bless - ing, nev - er a - lone.
  Wak -ing, sleep - ing, I am with you, you are my own.
2 Go, my chil - dren, sins for - giv - en, at peace and pure.
  Here you learned how much I love you, what I can cure.
3 Go, my chil - dren, fed and nour - ished, clos - er to me.
  Grow in love and love by serv - ing, joy - ful and free.
4 I, the Lord, will bless and keep you, and give you peace.
  I, the Lord, will smile up - on you, and give you peace.

In my love's bap - tis - mal riv - er, I have made you mine for - ev - er.
Here you heard my dear Son's sto - ry, here you touched him, saw his glo - ry.
Here my Spir - it's pow - er filled you, here his ten - der com - fort stilled you.
I, the Lord, will be your Fa - ther, Sav - ior, Com - fort - er, and Broth - er.

Go, my chil - dren, with my bless - ing, you are my own.
Go, my chil - dren, sins for - giv - en, at peace and pure.
Go, my chil - dren, fed and nour - ished, joy - ful and free.
Go, my chil - dren, I will keep you, and give you peace."

Text: Jaroslav J. Vajda
      Copyright ©1983 Jaroslav J. Vajda
Music: Welsh folk melody

Thuma mina

THUMA MINA Irregular

Text: South African text
Music: South African melody

435 May the Lord, mighty God

WEN-TI Irregular

May the Lord, might - y God, bless and

keep you for - ev - er, grant you peace, *Fine*

per - fect peace, cour - age in ev - 'ry en - deav - or.

I (melody)
Lift your eyes and see God's face, full of

II
Lift your eyes and see God's face, full of

grace for - ev - er. May the Lord,

grace for - ev - er. May the Lord,

D.C.
might - y God, bless and keep you for - ev - er.

might - y God, bless and keep you for - ev - er.

Text: based on Numbers 6:24-26
Music: Chinese melody; adapted from Pao-chen Li's "Wen-Ti"

All who believe and are baptized 436

LOBT GOTT DEN HERREN 87. 87. 887

1 All who be-lieve and are bap-tized shall see the
Lord's sal-va - tion. Bap-tized in - to the death of
Christ, each is a new cre-a - tion. Through Christ's re-
demp - tion we shall stand a-mong the glo - rious heav'n - ly
band of ev - 'ry tribe and na - tion.

2 With one ac - cord, O God, we pray, grant us your
Ho - ly Spir - it. Help us in our in - fir - mi-
ty through Je - sus' blood and mer - it. Grant us to
grow in grace each day that, as is prom - ised here, we
may e - ter - nal life in - her - it.

Text: Thomas Kingo, "Enhver, som tror og bliver döbt," *Hymnal Prepared for the Danish Church*, 1689; tr. George A. T. Rygh, 1909,
       The Lutheran Hymnary, 1913
Music: Melchior Vulpius, *Ein schön geistlich Gesangbuch*, 1609

437 Count well the cost

MACH'S MIT MIR 87. 87. 88

1 "Count well the cost," Christ Je-sus says, "when you lay the foun-
2 In - to Christ's death be bur-ied now through bap-tism's joy-ous
3 With-in the church's warm em-brace the child of God is
4 In Chris-tian growth we are ma-tured, of fruit-ful vines a

da - tion." Are you re-solved, though all seem lost, to
un - ion. No claim of self dare you al-low if
mold - ed. God's Spir-it lights the in-fant face and
to - ken. That this good growth may be as-sured oft-

risk your rep-u-ta - tion, your self, your wealth, for
you de-sire com-mun-ion with Christ's true church, his
in God's grace is fold - ed. With child-like steps, Christ's
times to us is bro - ken the bread of fel-low-

Christ the Lord as you now give your sol-emn word?
will-ing bride, which, through his word, he has sup-plied.
plan we trace, till we grow up in god-ly grace.
ship re-plete when Christ's re-deemed to-geth-er meet.

Text: Alexander Mack, Sr., "Überschlag die Kost," *Geistreiches Gesang-Buch …*, 1720; tr. Ora W. Garber, *European Origins of the Brethren*, 1958, alt.

Music: Johann H. Schein, 1628

I sing with exultation

NUN WEND IHR HÖREN SAGEN 75. 75. 76. 76

1 I sing with ex - ul - ta - tion, all my heart's de - light
2 God sends him as ex - am - ple, light and liv - ing guide.
3 Sing praise to Christ our Sav - ior, who, in grace in - clined,
4 Christ bids us, none com - pel - ling, to his glo - rious throne.

is God who brings sal - va - tion, frees from death's dread might.
Be - fore my end he bids me in his realm a - bide,
to us re - veals his na - ture: pa - tient, lov - ing, kind.
They on - ly who are will - ing Christ as Lord to own,

I praise thee, Christ of heav - en, who ev - er shall en - dure,
that I may love and cher - ish his right - eous - ness di - vine,
His love di - vine out - pour - ing, dis - played to ev - 'ry - one,
they are as - sured of heav - en, who will right faith pur - sue,

who takes a - way my sor - row, keeps me safe and se - cure.
that I with him for - ev - er bliss e - ter - nal may find.
is fash - ioned like his Fa - ther's as no oth - er has done.
with hearts made pure do pen - ance, sealed in bap - tism true.

Text: Felix Manz, ca. 1526, "Mit Lust so will ich singen," *Ausbund*, 1564; tr. Marion Wenger, 1966, *The Mennonite Hymnal*, 1969,
        altered by Harris J. Loewen
        Translation copyright ©1966 Marion Wenger
        Alteration copyright ©1990 Harris J. Loewen
Music: *Im Bentzenauer Ton*, 1540

439 I want Jesus to walk with me

Irregular

1　　I want Je - sus　　　to walk with　me.
2　　In my tri - als,　　　Lord, walk with　me.
3 When I'm in trou - ble,　Lord, walk with　me.

I want Je - sus　　　to walk with　me.
In my tri - als,　　　Lord, walk with　me.
When I'm in trou - ble,　Lord, walk with　me.

All a - long my　　pil - grim jour - ney,
When my heart is　　al - most break - ing,
When my head is　　bowed in sor - row,

Lord, I want Je - sus　to walk with　me.
Lord, I want Je - sus　to walk with　me.
Lord, I want Je - sus　to walk with　me.

Text:　African-American spiritual
Music:　African-American spiritual

I believe in you, Lord Jesus 440

MUNICH 86. 76. 76. 76

1 I be - lieve in you, Lord Je - sus, as God's be - lov - ed Son.
2 Let me take your way, Lord Je - sus, and keep your cross in view,
3 I be - lieve and I will fol - low through ev - 'ry day and hour.

I trust you for sal - va - tion, your great a - tone - ment's done.
be bur - ied in your like - ness, and rise to walk with you.
Bap - tize me with your Spir - it, with ho - li - ness and pow'r.

Help me for - sake sin's plea - sures and all its e - vil ways.
O wash me in the foun - tain that flows for ev - 'ry race.
Yes, I be - lieve, Lord Je - sus. Your fol - l'wer I will be,

I prom - ise to be faith - ful to you through all my days.
Re - deem and cleanse and par - don, and save me by your grace.
and while your Spir - it guides me I'll serve you loy - al - ly.

Text: Mary Stoner Wine, *The Brethren Hymnal*, 1951, alt.
Music: anonymous, *Neu-vermehrtes ... Gesangbuch*, 1693; harmonized by Felix Mendelssohn, 1846

441 I bind unto myself today

ST. PATRICK LMD

1 I bind un - to my - self to - day the
2 I bind this day to me for - ev'r by
3 I bind un - to my - self to - day the
4 I bind un - to my - self to - day the
6 I bind un - to my - self the Name, the

1 strong name of the Trin - i - ty, by
2 pow'r of faith Christ's in - car - na - tion, his
3 vir - tues of the star - lit heav'n, the
4 pow'r of God to hold and lead, an
6 strong name of the Trin - i - ty, by

1 in - vo - ca - tion of the same, the
2 bap - tism in the Jor - dan Riv - er, death
3 glo - rious sun's life - giv - ing ray, the
4 eye to watch, the might to stay, an
6 in - vo - ca - tion of the same, the

Return to beginning for St. 2

1 Three - in - One, and One - in - Three.
2 on the cross for my sal - va - tion,
3 white - ness of the moon at e - ven,
4 ear to heark - en to my need;
6 Three - in - One, and One - in - Three,

Text: attributed to St. Patrick, *Irish Liber Hymnorum*, 1897; tr. Cecil F. Alexander, 1889, *Writings of St. Patrick*, 1889, alt.
Music: traditional Irish melody, *Collection of Irish Music*, 1902; harmonization adapted from Charles V. Stanford, 1902

2 his burst - ing from the spic - ed
3 the flash - ing of the light - ning
4 the wis - dom of my God to
6 of whom all na - ture hath cre -

2 tomb, his rid - ing up the heav'n - ly
3 free, the whirl - ing wind's tem - pes - tuous
4 teach, a hand to guide, a shield to
6 a - tion, e - ter - nal Mak - er, Spir - it,

2 way, his com - ing at the day of
3 shocks, the sta - ble earth, the deep salt
4 ward; the word of God to give me
6 Word. Praise to the God of my sal -

(St. 5 next page)

2 doom I bind un - to my - self to - day.
3 sea, a - round the old e - ter - nal rocks.
4 speech, the heav'n - ly host to be my guard.
6 va - tion; sal - va - tion is of Christ the Lord!

Christ be with me

DEIRDRE LMD

5 Christ be with me, Christ with-in me, Christ be-
Christ be-neath me, Christ a-bove me, Christ in

hind me, Christ be-fore me, Christ be-side me, Christ to
qui-et, Christ in dan-ger, Christ in hearts of all that

After repeat, return to previous hymn.

win me, Christ to com-fort and re-store me;
love me, Christ in mouth of friend and stran-ger.

Text: attributed to St. Patrick, *Irish Liber Hymnorum,* 1897; tr. Cecil F. Alexander, 1889, *Writings of St. Patrick,* 1889
Music: traditional Irish melody, *Ancient Music of Ireland,* 1840; adapted for *The English Hymnal,* 1906
     Adaptation copyright © Oxford University Press, London

We know that Christ is raised 443

ENGELBERG 10 10 10 4

1 We know that Christ is raised and dies no more. Em-braced by
2 We share by wa - ter in his sav - ing death. Re-born, we
3 The God of splen-dor clothes the Son with life. The Spir-it's
4 A new cre - a - tion comes to life and grows as Christ's new

death, he broke its fear-ful hold, and our de - spair he turned to
share with him an Eas-ter life as liv - ing mem-bers of our
fis-sion shakes the church of God. Bap-tized, we live with God the
bod - y takes on flesh and blood. The u - ni - verse, re-stored and

1-3

blaz - ing joy. Hal - le - lu - jah!
Sav - ior Christ. Hal - le - lu - jah!
Three - in - One. Hal - le - lu - jah!

4

whole, will sing: hal - le - lu - jah!

Text: based on Romans 6, John B. Geyer, 1967, *Hymns and Songs,* 1969, alt.
          Copyright ©1969 John B. Geyer
Music: Charles V. Stanford, *Hymns Ancient and Modern,* 1904

444 Lord, I want to be a Christian

LORD, I WANT TO BE Irregular

1 Lord, I want to be a Chris-tian in my heart, in my
heart. Lord, I want to be a Chris-tian in my heart.
In my heart, in my heart,
Lord, I want to be a Chris-tian in my heart.

2 Lord, I want to be more loving …
3 Lord, I want to be more holy …
4 Lord, I want to be like Jesus …

Text: African-American spiritual, *Folk Songs of the American Negro,* 1907
Music: African-American spiritual, *Folk Songs of the American Negro,* 1907

445 Come, Holy Spirit, Dove divine

MARYTON LM

1 Come, Ho-ly Spir-it, Dove di-vine, on these bap-
2 We sink be-neath the wa-ter's face, and thank you
3 And as we rise with you to live, O let the

tis - mal wa-ters shine, and teach our hearts, in
for your sav-ing grace. We die to sin and
Ho - ly Spir-it give the seal of bless-ing

Text: Adoniram Judson, ca. 1829, *Collection,* 1832, alt.
Music: H. Percy Smith, *Church Hymns with Tunes,* 1874

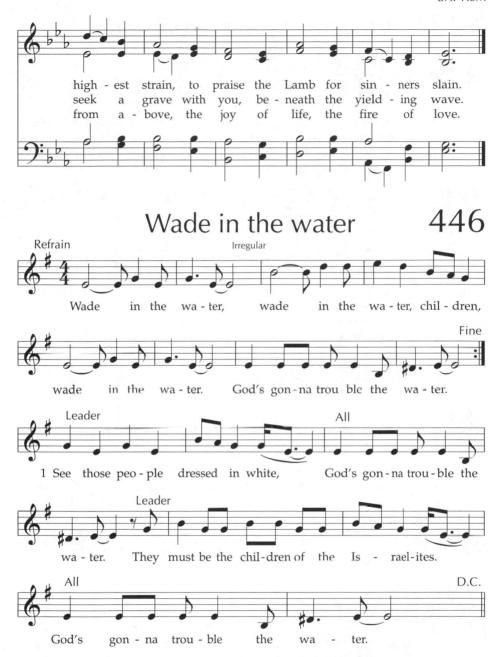

high - est strain, to praise the Lamb for sin - ners slain.
seek a grave with you, be - neath the yield - ing wave.
from a - bove, the joy of life, the fire of love.

Wade in the water 446

Refrain   Irregular

Wade in the wa - ter, wade in the wa - ter, chil - dren,

Fine

wade in the wa - ter. God's gon - na trou - ble the wa - ter.

Leader   All

1 See those peo - ple dressed in white, God's gon - na trou - ble the

Leader

wa - ter. They must be the chil - dren of the Is - rael - ites.

All   D.C.

God's gon - na trou - ble the wa - ter.

2 See those people dressed in black ...   They come a long way and they ain't turning back.
3 See those people dressed in blue ...   They look like my people coming through.
4 See those people dressed in red ...   They must be the children that Moses led.
5 Some say Peter, some say Paul ...   There ain't but one God made them all.

Text: African-American spiritual
Music: African-American spiritual

447 O Jesus, I have promised

ANGEL'S STORY 76. 76D

1 O Je-sus, I have prom-ised to serve thee to the end.
2 O let me feel thee near me, the world is ev-er near;
3 O let me hear thee speak-ing in ac-cents clear and still,
4 O Je-sus, thou hast prom-ised to all who fol-low thee

Be thou for-ev-er near me, my Mas-ter and my friend.
I see the sights that daz-zle, the tempt-ing sounds I hear.
a-bove the storms of pas-sion, the mur-murs of self-will.
that where thou art in glo-ry there shall thy ser-vant be.

I shall not fear the bat-tle if thou art by my side,
My foes are ev-er near me, a-round me and with-in,
O speak to re-as-sure me, to has-ten or con-trol,
And, Je-sus, I have prom-ised to serve thee to the end.

nor wan-der from the path-way if thou wilt be my guide.
but, Je-sus, draw thou near-er, and shield my soul from sin.
O speak, and make me lis-ten, thou Guard-ian of my soul.
O give me grace to fol-low, my Mas-ter and my friend.

Text: John E. Bode, 1868, *Psalms and Hymns, Appendix,* 1869
Music: Arthur H. Mann, *The Methodist Sunday School Hymn Book,* 1881

Awake, awake, fling off the night 448

HILARY LM

1 A - wake, a - wake, fling off the night! for God has
2 A - wake and rise, like those re - newed, those with the
3 A - wake, and rise up from the dead, and Christ his
4 Then sing for joy, and use each day. Give thanks for

sent a glo - rious light, and we who live in
Spir - it's pow'r en - dued. The light of life in
light on you will shed. Its pow'r will wrong de -
ev - 'ry - thing al - way. Lift up your hearts! with

Christ's new day must works of dark - ness put a - way.
us must glow, and fruits of truth and good - ness show.
sires de - stroy, and your whole na - ture fill with joy.
one ac - cord praise God through Je - sus Christ our Lord.

Text: based on Ephesians 5:6-20, J. R. Peacey, *100 Hymns for Today,* 1969, alt.
        Copyright ©1991 Hope Publishing Co.
Music: Lawrence F. Bartlett, 1974, *The Australian Hymn Book,* 1977
        Copyright ©1977 Lawrence F. Bartlett

449 Jesus took a towel

JESUS TOOK A TOWEL Irregular

Je - sus took a tow - el and he gird - ed him - self, then he

washed my feet, yes, he washed my feet. Je - sus took a ba - sin and he

knelt him - self down, and he washed, yes, he washed my feet.

1 The heav - ens are the Lord's and the earth is his, the
2 The hour had come, the feast was near;

clouds are his char - iot, glo - ry his cloak. He
Je - sus loved his own, loved them to the end. O

made the moun - tains, set the lim - its of the sea, and he
Lord, let me see, let me un - der - stand why you

stooped and washed my feet.
stooped and washed my feet.

Text: based on John 13, Chrysogonus Waddell, O.C.S.O., 1968, *Worship III*, 1986
Music: Chrysogonus Waddell, O.C.S.O., 1968, *Worship III*, 1986
Text and music copyright © Gethsemani Abbey

Here in our upper room   450

HOLLEY LM

1 Here in our up-per room with you, a-round your
2 As you, our bless'd Ex - am - ple, taught, we kneel to
3 We share with you the feast of love as hearts are
4 With heart, and not with hands a - lone, we keep the

hal - lowed ta - ble, Lord, may we with deep hu -
serve our neigh - bor's need, the cleans-ing of your
knit in one ac - cord. Oh, may your Spir - it
or - di - nance a - new, and through these sa - cred

mil - i - ty ful - fill the pre - cepts of your word.
Spir - it sought in heart and mind, in thought and deed.
in us move our wills to love you more, dear Lord.
sym - bols prove in serv-ing oth - ers we serve you.

Text: Paul M. Robinson, 1949, *The Brethren Hymnal,* 1951, revised 1990
Copyright ©1951, 1990 Church of the Brethren General Board
Music: George Hews, *Boston Academy's Collection of Church Music,* 3rd ed., 1835

451 How pleasant is it

KOMMT HER ZU MIR 88.7D

1 How pleas-ant is it and how good that fol-low-
2 'Tis pre-cious and of hon-ored worth, that Christ our
3 Then let us give our clear-est thought in this our
4 Who thus en-gag-es in this rite must note how
5 And now, Lord Je-sus, fi-nal-ly may your good

1 ers of Je-sus should, in faith and love u-nit - ing,
2 Lord, while here on earth, di-vine love dem-on-strat - ing,
3 time, as ser-vants ought, un-to this new ab-lu - tion,
4 Christ did it that night in deep hu-mil-i-a - tion,
5 Spir-it out-poured be, your grace and might dis-play - ing,

1 like ser-vants wash each oth-er's feet when at the
2 in true hu-mil-i-ty of heart stooped down to
3 so that we too in it may share in hum-ble
4 and al-so see that be-ing whole re-quires the
5 and thus shall we in this hour start to live like

1 feast of love they meet, in fel-low-ship de-light - ing.
2 play the ser-vant's part, this prac-tice con-se-crat - ing.
3 love as we pre-pare for cer-tain per-se-cu - tion.
4 cleans-ing of the soul through Christ's out-poured sal-va - tion.
5 you, with a whole heart, your ho-ly love o-bey - ing.

Text: attributed to Wilhelm Knepper, Freylinghausen's *Geistreiches Gesang-Buch* ..., 1720; tr. Ora W. Garber, *European Origins of the Brethren*, 1958, alt.
Music: Freylinghausen's *Geistreiches Gesang-Buch* ..., 1741; harmonized by Hedwig T. Durnbaugh.
Harmonization copyright ©1983 Hedwig T. Durnbaugh.

Ubi caritas et amor
452

UBI CARITAS Irregular

U - bi ca - ri - tas ___ et a - mor,
et a - mor,
(melody in tenor) et a - mor,

u - bi ca - ri - tas, De - us i - bi est.*

*Translation: Where charity and love are found, God is there.

Text: Ubi caritas et amor, 9th c.
Music: Jacques Berthier, *Music from Taizé*, Vol. I, 1978, 1980, 1981
        Copyright © Les Presses de Taizé (France). Used by permission of G.I.A. Publications, Inc.

Let us break bread together   453

COMMUNION SPIRITUAL 10 10 with refrain

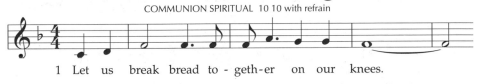

1 Let us break bread to - geth - er on our knees.

Let us break bread to - geth - er on our knees.

Refrain

When I fall on my knees with my face to the ris - ing

sun, O Lord have mer - cy on me.

2 Let us drink wine together …
3 Let us praise God together …

Text: African-American spiritual
Music: African-American spiritual

454 Seed, scattered and sown

EKKLESIA Irregular with refrain

Seed, scat-tered and sown, wheat, gath-ered and grown,

bread, bro-ken and shared as one, the liv-ing Bread of God.

Vine, fruit of the land, wine, work of our hands, one cup that is

shared by all, the liv-ing Cup, the liv-ing Bread of God.

1 Is not the bread we break, a shar-ing in our Lord?
2 The seed which falls on rock will with-er and will die.
3 As wheat up-on the hills was gath-ered and was grown,

Text: based on *Didache 9,* 1 Corinthians 10, and Mark 4:3-6, Dan Feiten, 1987, *Gather,* 1988
Music: Dan Feiten, 1987, *Gather,* 1988; harmonized by Marilyn Houser Hamm
Text and music copyright ©1987 Ekklesia Music
Harmonization copyright ©1990 Marilyn Houser Hamm

D.C.

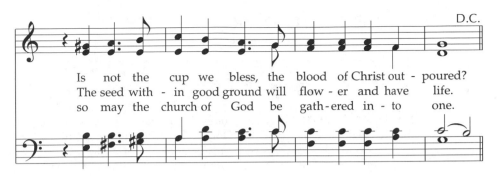

Is not the cup we bless, the blood of Christ out - poured?
The seed with - in good ground will flow - er and have life.
so may the church of God be gath - ered in - to one.

Bread of life 455

ROHRER 87. 87

1 Bread of life, whose bod - y, bro - ken, feeds the
2 Let these hands now calm - ly fold - ing speak my
3 Lord, I wel - come you to ta - ble; grace my

hun - ger of my heart, may the thanks that you have
grat - i - tude for grace, lest the trea - sure I am
sup - per ev - er new. With your feast of love en -

spo - ken bless each loaf I break a - part.
hold - ing dis - ap - pear be - fore my face.
a - ble ev - 'ry guest to live for you.

Text: Kenneth I. Morse, *Gospel Messenger*, 1955, alt.
Music: Wilbur E. Brumbaugh, *Gospel Messenger*, 1955

456 Shepherd of souls, refresh

CAITHNESS CM

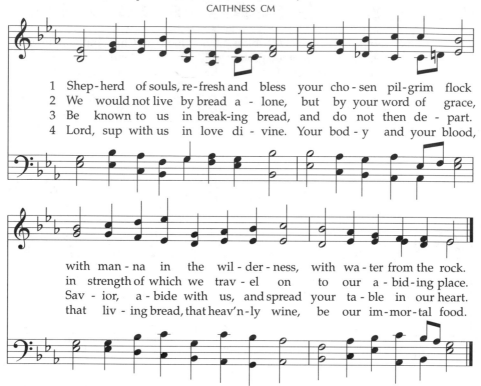

1 Shep-herd of souls, re-fresh and bless your cho-sen pil-grim flock
2 We would not live by bread a - lone, but by your word of grace,
3 Be known to us in break-ing bread, and do not then de - part.
4 Lord, sup with us in love di - vine. Your bod-y and your blood,

with man - na in the wil - der - ness, with wa - ter from the rock.
in strength of which we trav - el on to our a - bid-ing place.
Sav - ior, a - bide with us, and spread your ta - ble in our heart.
that liv - ing bread, that heav'n-ly wine, be our im-mor-tal food.

Text: anonymous, *Collection of Hymns … of the United Brethren* (Sts. 1-2), 1832, alt., James Montgomery (Sts. 3-4), *Christian Psalmist,* 1825
Music: *The Psalmes of David in Prose and Meeter,* 1635; harmonization from *The English Hymnal,* 1906
Harmonization copyright © Oxford University Press, London

457 Be present at our table, Lord

OLD HUNDREDTH LM

1 Be pre - sent at our ta - ble, Lord. Be
2 We thank thee, Lord, for this, our food, for

Text: John Cennick, *Sacred Hymns for the Children of God …,* 1741
Music: Louis Bourgeois, *Genevan Psalter,* 1551

here and ev - 'ry - where a - dored. These mer - cies bless and
life, and health, and ev - 'ry good. Let man - na to our

grant that we *may feast in par - a - dise with thee.
souls be giv'n – the Bread of life sent down from heav'n.

*Alternate last phrase: … may live and work today with thee.

Great God, the giver of all good 458

RETREAT LM

Great God, the giv - er of all good, ac -

cept our thanks and bless this food. Grace, health, and strength to

us af - ford, through Je - sus Christ, our ris - en Lord.

Text: James Skinner, *Daily Service Hymnal*, 1863, alt.
Music: Thomas Hastings, *Juvenile Songs*, 1841

459 I come with joy to meet my Lord

DOVE OF PEACE CM extended

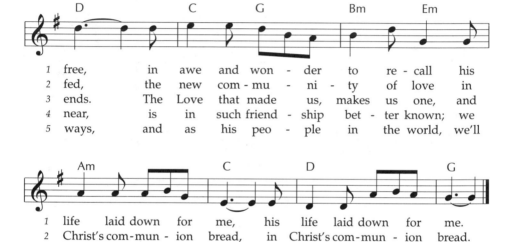

	G	C/G	G		G	Em

1 I come with joy to meet my Lord, for - giv - en, loved, and
2 I come with Chris-tians far and near to find, as all are
3 As Christ breaks bread and bids us share, each proud di - vi - sion
4 And thus with joy we meet our Lord. His pres - ence, al - ways
5 To - geth - er met, to - geth - er bound, we'll go our dif - f'rent

D		C	G	Bm	Em

1 free, in awe and won - der to re - call his
2 fed, the new com - mu - ni - ty of love in
3 ends. The Love that made us, makes us one, and
4 near, is in such friend - ship bet - ter known; we
5 ways, and as his peo - ple in the world, we'll

Am		C	D		G

1 life laid down for me, his life laid down for me.
2 Christ's com-mun - ion bread, in Christ's com-mun - ion bread.
3 stran - gers now are friends, and stran - gers now are friends.
4 see and praise him here, we see and praise him here.
5 live and speak his praise, we'll live and speak his praise.

Text: Brian Wren, 1968, revised 1977, *The Hymnbook* (Canada), 1971
              Copyright ©1971 Hope Publishing Co.
Music: American folk melody, *Southern Harmony,* 1854

Una espiga
(Sheaves of summer)

460

UNA ESPIGA Irregular

1 U - na es - pi - ga do - ra - da por el sol, el ra-
2 Com - par - ti - mos la mis - ma co - mun - ión, so - mos
1 Sheaves of sum - mer turned gold - en by the sun, grapes in
2 We are shar - ing the same com - mun - ion meal, we are

ci - mo que cor - ta el vi - ña - dor, se con-
tri - go del mis - mo Sem - bra - dor, un mo-
bunch - es cut down when ripe and red, are con-
wheat by the same great Sow - er sown. Like a

vier - ten a - ho - ra en pan y vi - no de a - mor,
li - no a la vi - da nos tri - tu - ra con do - lor,
vert - ed in - to the bread and wine of God's love
mill - stone, life grinds us down with sor - row and pain,

en el cuer - po y la san - gre del Se - ñor.
Dios nos ha - ce pue - blo nue - vo en el a - mor.
in the bod - y and blood of our dear Lord.
but God makes us new peo - ple bound by love.

3 Como granos que han hecho el mismo pan,
   como notas que tejen un cantar,
   como gotas de agua que se funden en el mar,
   los cristianos un cuerpo formarán.

3 Like the grains which become one same whole loaf,
   like the notes that are woven into song,
   like the droplets of water that are blended in the sea,
   we, as Christians, one body shall become.

4 En la mesa de Dios se sentarán,
   como hijos su pan compartirán,
   una misma esperanza caminando cantarán,
   en la vida como hermanos se amarán.

4 At God's table together we shall sit.
   As God's children, Christ's body we will share.
   One same hope we will sing together as we walk along.
   Brothers, sisters, in life, in love, we'll be.

Text: Cesáreo Gabaraín, 1973; tr. George Lockwood IV
        Translation (English) copyright ©1989 The United Methodist Publishing House
Music: Cesáreo Gabaraín, 1973
        Text (Spanish) and music copyright ©1973 Cesáreo Gabaraín. Published by OCP Publications

461 In the quiet consecration

STENKA RAZIN 87. 87

1 In the qui - et con - se - cra - tion of this
2 Here we learn through sa - cred sym - bol all your
3 Christ, the liv - ing bread of heav - en, Christ, whose
4 By your death for sin a - ton - ing, by your
5 while a - far in sol - emn ra - diance shines the

1 glad com - mun - ion hour, here we rest in you, Lord
2 grace can be and do by this won - der - ful in -
3 blood is drink in - deed, here by faith and with thanks-
4 res - ur - rec - tion - life, hold us fast in joy - ful
5 feast that is to come — af - ter con - flict, heav - en's

1 Je - sus, taste your love and touch your pow'r.
2 dwell - ing – you in us, and we in you.
3 giv - ing in our hearts on you we feed.
4 un - ion, strength - en us to face the strife;
5 glo - ry, your great feast of love and home.

Text: Constance Coote, 1910, *At His Table*, 1913
Music: Russian folk melody; harmonized by Esther Wiebe
        Harmonization copyright ©1992 Esther Wiebe

Now the silence

462

NOW Irregular

Now the si - lence, now the peace, now the emp - ty hands up -

lift - ed. Now the kneel - ing, now the plea, now the Fa - ther's

arms in wel - come. Now the hear - ing, now the pow'r,

now the ves - sel brimmed for pour - ing. Now the bod - y,

now the blood, now the joy - ful cel - e - bra - tion.

Now the wed - ding, now the songs, now the heart, for - giv - en, leap - ing.

Now the Spir - it's vis - i - ta - tion, now the Son's e - piph - a - ny,

now the Fa - ther's bless - ing, now, now, now.

Text: Jaroslav J. Vajda, *This Day,* 1968
Music: Carl F. Schalk, *Worship Supplement to the Lutheran Hymnal,* 1969
Text and music copyright ©1969 Hope Publishing Co.

463 Let all mortal flesh keep silence

PICARDY 87. 87. 87

1 Let all mor-tal flesh keep si - lence, and with fear and
2 King of kings, yet born of Ma - ry, as of old on
3 Rank on rank the host of heav - en spreads its van-guard
4 At his feet the six - winged ser - aph, cher - u - bim with

trem - bling stand. Pon-der noth-ing earth - ly mind - ed,
earth he stood, Lord of lords in hu - man ves - ture,
on the way, as the Light of light de - scend-eth
sleep - less eye, veil their fac - es to the Pres - ence,

for with bless-ing in his hand Christ our God to earth dein the bod - y and the blood, he will give to all the
from the realms of end - less day, that the pow'rs of hell may
as with cease-less voice they cry, "Al - le - lu - ia! Al - le-

scend - eth, our full hom-age to de - mand.
faith - ful his own self for heav'n - ly food.
van - ish, as the dark-ness clears a - way.
lu - ia! Al - le - lu - ia, Lord Most High!"

Text: *Liturgy of St. James of Jerusalem* (Greek hymn), 5th c.; tr. Gerard Moultrie, *Lyra Eucharistica*, 2nd ed., 1864, alt.
Music: French carol, *Chansons populaires des provinces de France*, 1860

Let the hungry come to me 464

ADORO TE DEVOTE 12 12. 11 11

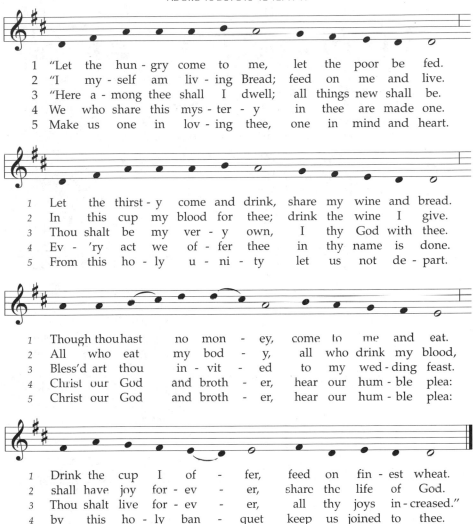

1 "Let the hun-gry come to me, let the poor be fed.
2 "I my-self am liv-ing Bread; feed on me and live.
3 "Here a-mong thee shall I dwell; all things new shall be.
4 We who share this mys-ter-y in thee are made one.
5 Make us one in lov-ing thee, one in mind and heart.

1 Let the thirst-y come and drink, share my wine and bread.
2 In this cup my blood for thee; drink the wine I give.
3 Thou shalt be my ver-y own, I thy God with thee.
4 Ev-'ry act we of-fer thee in thy name is done.
5 From this ho-ly u-ni-ty let us not de-part.

1 Though thou hast no mon-ey, come to me and eat.
2 All who eat my bod-y, all who drink my blood,
3 Bless'd art thou in-vit-ed to my wed-ding feast.
4 Christ our God and broth-er, hear our hum-ble plea:
5 Christ our God and broth-er, hear our hum-ble plea:

1 Drink the cup I of-fer, feed on fin-est wheat.
2 shall have joy for-ev-er, share the life of God.
3 Thou shalt live for-ev-er, all thy joys in-creased."
4 by this ho-ly ban-quet keep us joined to thee.
5 by this ho-ly ban-quet keep us joined to thee.

Text: Delores Dufner, O.S.B. (Sts. 1-3), alt., Adoro te devote, latens Deitas (Sts. 4-5), 13th or 14th c.;
        tr. Melvin L. Farrell, S.S. (Sts. 4-5)
        Text (Sts. 1-3) copyright ©1985 The Sisters of Saint Benedict
        Translation (Sts. 4-5) copyright ©1955, 1961, 1964 World Library Publications, Inc.
Music: Plainsong, Processionale, 1697

465 Here, O my Lord, I see thee

KINGSBORO 10 10. 10 10

1 Here, O my Lord, I see thee face to face.
2 Here would I feed up - on the bread of God,
3 This is the hour of ban - quet and of song,
4 Too soon we rise; the sym - bols dis - ap - pear.
5 Feast af - ter feast thus comes and pass - es by,

1 Here would I touch and han - dle things un - seen,
2 here drink with thee the roy - al wine of heav'n.
3 this is the heav'n - ly ta - ble spread for me.
4 The feast, though not the love, is past and gone.
5 yet, pass - ing, points to the glad feast a - bove,

1 here grasp with firm - er hand e - ter - nal grace,
2 Here would I lay a - side each earth - ly load,
3 Here let me feast, and feast - ing, still pro - long
4 The bread and wine re - move, but thou art here,
5 giv - ing sweet fore - taste of the fes - tal joy,

Text: Horatius N. Bonar, 1855, *Hymns of Faith and Hope,* 1857
Music: M. Lee Suitor, 1975, *Hymnal Supplement,* 1984; harmonized by Marilyn Houser Hamm and M. Lee Suitor
Copyright ©1991 M. Lee Suitor
Harmonization copyright ©1990 Marilyn Houser Hamm and M. Lee Suitor

D | **D Maj⁷** | **Bm** | **Em⁷** | **A** | **D**

1 and all my wea - ri - ness up - on thee lean.
2 here taste a - fresh the calm of sin for-giv'n.
3 the brief, bright hour of fel - low-ship with thee.
4 near - er than ev - er, still my shield and sun.
5 the Lamb's great brid - al feast of bliss and love.

Jesus, sun and shield art thou 466

COLDREY 76. 76. 77

1 Je - sus, sun and shield art thou, sun and shield for - ev - er!
2 Je - sus, peace and joy art thou, joy and peace for - ev - er!
3 Je - sus, song and strength art thou, strength and song for - ev - er!
4 Je - sus, bread and wine art thou, bread and wine for - ev - er!

Nev - er canst thou cease to shine, cease to guard us nev - er.
Joy that fades not, chang - es not, peace that leaves us nev - er.
Strength that nev - er can de - cay, song that ceas - eth nev - er.
Nev - er canst thou cease to feed or re - fresh us, nev - er.

Cheer our steps as on we go; come be - tween us and the foe.
Joy and peace we have in thee, now and through e - ter - ni - ty.
Still to us this strength and song through e - ter - nal days, pro - long.
Feed us still on bread di - vine, drink we still of heav'n - ly wine.

Text: Horatius N. Bonar, *Hymns of Faith and Hope, Second Series*, 1861
Music: Henry T. Smart, *Psalms and Hymns for Divine Worship*, 1867

467 Author of life divine

ST. JOHN 66. 66. 88

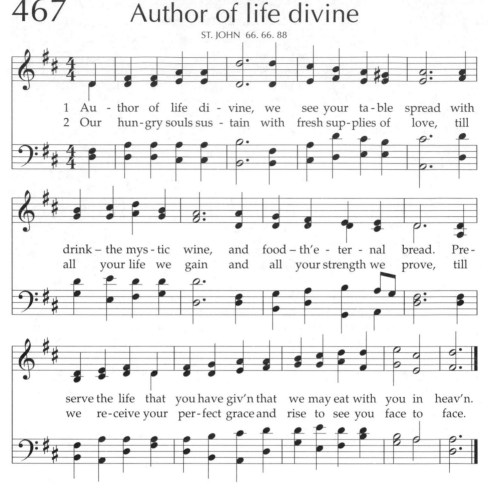

1 Au - thor of life di - vine, we see your ta - ble spread with
2 Our hun-gry souls sus - tain with fresh sup-plies of love, till

drink – the mys - tic wine, and food – th'e - ter - nal bread. Pre-
all your life we gain and all your strength we prove, till

serve the life that you have giv'n that we may eat with you in heav'n.
we re-ceive your per-fect grace and rise to see you face to face.

Text: John Wesley and Charles Wesley, *Hymns on the Lord's Supper*, 1745; revised in *Hymns for Today's Church*, 1982
        Copyright ©1982 Hope Publishing Co.
Music: *The Parish Choir, Vol. 3*, 1851

468 O Bread of life, for sinners broken

SHENG EN 99. 99

1 O Bread of life, for sin - ners bro - ken,
2 For all we seek your grace sus - tain - ing.
3 Now may your life to us de - scend - ing

of God's own love the dear - est to - ken,
Your love shines, though your strength is wan - ing,
en - ter our lives, all veils thus rend - ing,

Text: Timothy T'ing Fang Lew, *Hymns of Universal Praise*, 1936; tr. Frank W. Price, alt.
        Translation copyright © Estate of Frank W. Price
Music: Su Yin-Lan, *Hymns of Universal Praise*, 1936

we hear the words so gent - ly spo - ken,
thus by your death our life ob - tain - ing.
Im - man - u - el, our joy un - end - ing.

"Do this for me in my re - mem - brance."
"Come un - to me, you hea - vy - lad - en."
"I am with you, this day and ev - er."

Bread of the world 469

LES COMMANDEMENS DE DIEU 98. 98

1 Bread of the world in mer - cy bro - ken,
2 Look on the heart by sor - row bro - ken,

Wine of the soul in mer - cy shed, by whom the
look on the tears by sin - ners shed, and be your

words of life were spo - ken, and in whose death our sins are dead:
feast to us the to - ken that by your grace our souls are fed.

Text: Reginald Heber, *Hymns written and adapted to … the Church Year*, 1827
Music: *La forme des prières …*, 1545; harmonization adapted from Claude Goudimel, *Les Pseaumes …*, 1565

470

Christ Jesus lay

CHRIST LAG IN TODESBANDEN 87. 87. 78. 74

1 Christ Je-sus lay in death's strong bands for our of-fens - es
2 It was a strong and dread-ful strife when life and death con-
3 Then let us feast this ho - ly day on Christ, the bread of

giv - en, but now at God's right hand he stands and
tend - ed. The vic-to-ry re-mained with life, the
heav - en. The Word of grace has purged a - way the

brings us life from heav - en. There-fore let us
reign of death was end - ed. Ho - ly Scrip - ture
old and e - vil leav - en. Christ a - lone our

joy - ful be and sing to God right thank-ful-ly loud
plain - ly says that death is swal-lowed up by death, its
souls will feed, he is our meat and drink in - deed; faith

Text: Martin Luther, "Christ lag in Todesbanden," *Eyn Enchiridion*, 1524; tr. Richard Massie, *Martin Luther's Spiritual Songs,* 1854, alt.
Music: *Gesangbüchlein*, Wittenberg, 1524; adapted from CHRIST IST ERSTANDEN and harmonized by J. S. Bach, from Cantata No. 4, ca. 1708

songs of hal - le - lu - jah!
sting is lost for - ev - er. Hal - le - lu - jah!
lives up - on no oth - er!

Eat this bread 471

Eat this bread, drink this cup, come to me and nev - er be hun - gry. Eat this bread, drink this cup, trust in me and you will not thirst.

Text: based on John 6:35, Robert Batastini and the Taizé community, 1983, *Music from Taizé*, Vol. II, 1982, 1983, 1984
Music: Jacques Berthier, *Music from Taizé*, Vol. II, 1982, 1983, 1984

472 I am the Bread of life

I AM THE BREAD OF LIFE Irregular with refrain

1 I am the Bread of life. You who
2 The bread that I will give is my
3 Un - less you eat of the
4 I am the res - ur - rec - tion,
5 Yes, Lord, I be - lieve that

1 come to me shall not hun - ger, and who be -
2 flesh for the life of the world, and if you
3 flesh of the Son of Man and
4 I am the life. If you be -
5 you are the Christ, the

1 lieve in me shall not thirst. No one can come to
2 eat of this bread, you shall live for -
3 drink of his blood, and drink of his
4 lieve in me, e - ven though you
5 Son of God, who has

1 me un - less the Fa - ther beck - ons.
2 ev - er, you shall live for - ev - er.
3 blood, you shall not have life with - in you.
4 die, you shall live for - ev - er.
5 come in - to the world.

Refrain

And I will raise you up, and I will raise you

Text: based on John 6, Suzanne Toolan, *Music for the Requiem Mass*, 1966; tr. Sara Claassen (Spanish)
Music: Suzanne Toolan, *Music for the Requiem Mass*
Text (English) and music copyright ©1970 G.I.A. Publications, Inc.

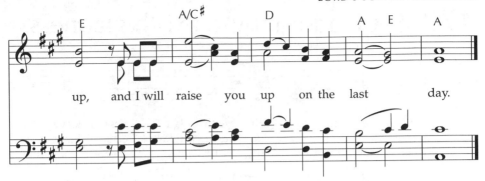

up, and I will raise you up on the last day.

1 Yo soy el pan de vida.
Los que a mí vienen no tendrán hambre;
los que en mí creen nunca tendrán sed.
Nadie vendrá a mí
si no me lo da el Padre.

Estribillo:
Y les resucitaré,
y les resucitaré,
y les resucitaré en el día final.

2 El pan que doy es mi carne;
lo doy por la vida del mundo.
Si uno come de este pan,
vivirá para siempre, vivirá para siempre.
(Estribillo)

3 Si no coméis
de la carne del Hijo del Hombre
y bebéis de su sangre,
y bebéis de su sangre,
no tenéis vida en vosotros.
(Estribillo)

4 Yo soy la resurrección,
yo soy la vida.
Los que creen en mí,
aunque mueran,
tendrán vida eterna.
(Estribillo)

5 Señor, sí, creemos
que tú eres el Cristo,
el Hijo de Dios,
que has venido
a este mundo.
(Estribillo)

473 Soul, adorn thyself with gladness

SCHMÜCKE DICH, O LIEBE SEELE LMD

1 Soul, a-dorn thy-self with glad - ness, leave the
2 Sun, who all my life dost bright - en; Light, who
3 Je - sus, Bread of life, I pray thee, let me

gloom - y haunts of sad - ness. Come in - to the
dost my soul en - light - en; Joy, the best that
glad - ly here o - bey thee. Nev - er to my

day - light's splen - dor, there with joy thy prais-es ren - der
an - y know - eth; Fount, whence all my be - ing flow - eth:
hurt in - vit - ed, be thy love with love re - quit - ed.

un - to him whose grace un - bound - ed hath this
at thy feet I cry, my Mak - er, let me
From this ban - quet let me mea - sure, Lord, how

Text: Johann Franck (St. 1), "Schmücke dich, O liebe Seele," *Geistliche Kirchen-Melodien*, 1649, Crüger-Runge's *Gesangbuch*
         (Sts. 2-3), 1653; tr. Catherine Winkworth, *Chorale Book for England*, 1863, alt.
Music: Johann Crüger, *Geistliche Kirchen-Melodien*; harmonized by J. S. Bach, from Cantata No. 180, ca. 1724

won - drous ban - quet found - ed. High o'er all the
be a fit par - tak - er of this bless - ed
vast and deep its trea - sure. Through the gifts thou

heav'ns he reign - eth, yet to dwell with thee he deign - eth.
food from heav - en, for our good, thy glo - ry giv - en.
here dost give me, as thy guest in heav'n re - ceive me.

I hunger and I thirst 474

IBSTONE 66. 66

1 I hun - ger and I thirst; Je - sus, my man - na be!
2 O bruised and bro - ken Bread, my life - long needs sup - ply.
3 O true life - giv - ing Vine, let me your good - ness prove.
4 Rough paths my feet have trod since first their course be - gan.
5 For still the de - sert lies be - hind me and be - fore:

1 O liv - ing Wa - ters, burst out of the rock for me!
2 As liv - ing souls are fed, so feed me, or I die.
3 By your life sweet - en mine, re - fresh my soul with love.
4 Re - new me, Bread of God, re - store me, Son of Man.
5 O liv - ing Wa - ters, rise with - in me ev - er - more!

Text: John S. B. Monsell, *Hymns of Love and Praise,* 2nd ed., 1866, alt.
Music: Maria Tiddeman, *Hymns Ancient and Modern,* 1875, alt.

475 Become to us the living Bread

GELOBT SEI GOTT 888 with alleluias

1 Be - come to us the liv - ing Bread by which the
2 Be - come the nev - er - fail - ing wine, the spring of
3 May Chris - tians all with one ac - cord u - nite a -

Chris - tian life is fed, re - newed, and great - ly
joy that shall in - cline our hearts to bear the
round the sa - cred board to praise your ho - ly

com - fort - ed.
cov - 'nant sign. Al - le - lu - ia! _____
name, O Lord.

Al - le - lu - ia! _____ Al - le - lu - ia!

Text: based on John 6:35-58, Miriam Drury, 1970, *The Worshipbook: Services and Hymns,* 1972
Copyright ©1972 The Westminster Press
Music: Melchior Vulpius, *Ein schön geistlich Gesangbuch,* 1609

This is the feast of victory   476

FESTIVAL CANTICLE Irregular with refrain

This is the feast _____ of vic-to-ry for our God. Al-le-

1-5 | Final ending

lu - ia! Al-le - lu - ia! Al-le - lu - ia!   lu - ia!

1 (♩)	Wor - thy	is	Christ, the	Lamb	who	was	slain,		whose
2	Pow	- er,	rich - es,	wis - dom,	and		strength,		and
3	Sing	with	all	the	peo - ple	of	God,		and
4	Bless	- ing,	hon - or,	glo - ry,	and		might	be	to
5	For	the	Lamb _____		who	was	slain	has	be -

D.C.

1	blood	set	us	free	to	be	peo - ple of God.
2	hon	- or,		bless - ing, and	glo	- ry	are his.
3	join	in	the	hymn of	all	cre - a	- tion.
4	God	and	the	Lamb for - ev - er.	A		- men.
5	gun	his		reign.	Al - le - lu		- ia!

Text: based on Revelation 5:12-13, John W. Arthur, 1970, *Lutheran Book of Worship,* 1978
Music: Richard Hillert, *Lutheran Book of Worship,* 1978
Copyright ©1978 Richard Hillert

477 For the bread

KINGDOM 87. 87

1 For the bread which you have bro - ken, for the
2 By this prom - ise that you love us, by your
3 In your ser - vice, Lord, de - fend us, in our

wine which you have poured, for the words which you have
gift of peace re - stored, by your call to heav'n a -
hearts keep watch and ward; in the world to which you

spo - ken, now we give you thanks, O Lord.
bove us, hal - low all our lives, O Lord.
send us, let your king - dom come, O Lord.

Text: Louis F. Benson, 1924, *Hymns, Original and Translated*, 1925, alt.
Music: V. Earle Copes, 1959, *The Methodist Hymnal*, 1966
Copyright ©1959 Abingdon Press

478 Sent forth by God's blessing

ASH GROVE 66 11. 66 11D

1 Sent forth by God's bless - ing, our true faith con - fess - ing,
2 With praise and thanks - giv - ing to God ev - er liv - ing

the peo - ple of God from this dwell - ing take leave.
the tasks of our ev - 'ry - day life we will face.

The sup-per is end-ed. Oh, now be ex-tend-ed
Our faith ev-er shar-ing, in love ev-er car-ing,

the fruits of this ser-vice in all who be-lieve.
em-brac-ing the chil-dren of each tribe and race.

Harmony

The fruit of Christ's teach-ing, re-cep-tive souls reach-ing,
With your feast you feed us, with your light now lead us,

shall blos-som in ac-tion for God and for all.
u-nite us as one in this life that we share.

Unison

His grace did in-vite us, his love shall u-nite us
Then may all the liv-ing with praise and thanks-giv-ing

to work for God's king-dom and an-swer his call.
give hon-or to Christ and his name that we bear.

Text: Omer Westendorf, *People's Mass Book*, 1964, alt.
        Copyright ©1964 World Library Publications, Inc.
Music: Welsh folk melody; harmonized by Gerald H. Knight
        Harmonization copyright © The Royal School of Church Music

479 Lord of our growing years

NEWTON 66. 66 with refrain

1 Lord of our grow-ing years, with us from in-fan-cy,
2 Lord of our strong-est years, stretch-ing our youth-ful pow'rs,
3 Lord of our mid-dle years, giv-er of stead-fast-ness,
4 Lord of our old-er years, steep though the road may be,
5 Lord of our clos-ing years, al-ways your prom-ise stands.

Refrain

1 laugh-ter and quick-dried tears, fresh-ness and en-er-gy:
2 lov-ers and pi-o-neers when all the world seems ours:
3 cour-age that per-se-veres when there is small suc-cess: Your
4 rid us of fool-ish fears, bring us se-ren-i-ty.
5 Hold us when death ap-pears, safe-ly with-in your hands.

grace sur-rounds us all our days – for all your gifts we bring our praise.

Text: David Mowbray, *Hymns for Today's Church,* 1982
    Copyright ©1982 Hope Publishing Co.
Music: J. Harold Moyer, 1990
    Copyright ©1991 The Hymnal Project

Shepherd of tender youth 480

HUMMEL STREET 664. 6664

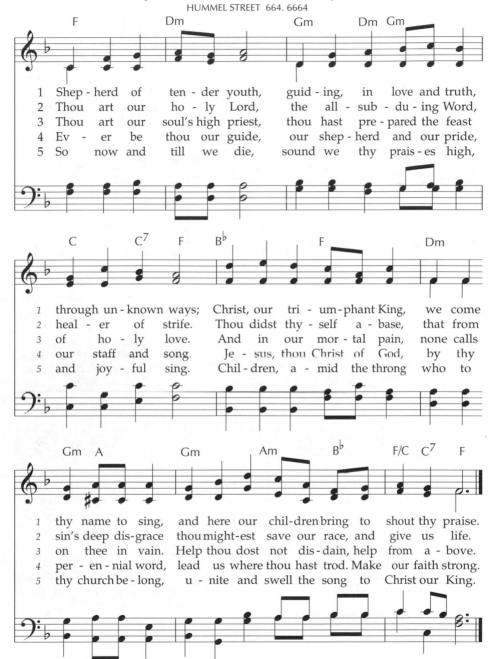

1 Shep-herd of ten-der youth, guid-ing, in love and truth,
2 Thou art our ho-ly Lord, the all-sub-du-ing Word,
3 Thou art our soul's high priest, thou hast pre-pared the feast
4 Ev-er be thou our guide, our shep-herd and our pride,
5 So now and till we die, sound we thy prais-es high,

1 through un-known ways; Christ, our tri-um-phant King, we come
2 heal-er of strife. Thou didst thy-self a-base, that from
3 of ho-ly love. And in our mor-tal pain, none calls
4 our staff and song. Je-sus, thou Christ of God, by thy
5 and joy-ful sing. Chil-dren, a-mid the throng who to

1 thy name to sing, and here our chil-dren bring to shout thy praise.
2 sin's deep dis-grace thou might-est save our race, and give us life.
3 on thee in vain. Help thou dost not dis-dain, help from a-bove.
4 per-en-nial word, lead us where thou hast trod. Make our faith strong.
5 thy church be-long, u-nite and swell the song to Christ our King.

Text: Clement of Alexandria, 2nd or 3rd c.; tr. Henry M. Dexter, *The Congregationalist,* 1849
Music: Richard D. Brode, 1990
Copyright ©1990 Richard D. Brode

481 O God, your constant care

WAREHAM LM

1 O God, your con-stant care and love are shed up-
2 We thank you, Lord, for dreams of youth, for wis - dom
3 All time is yours, O Lord, to give. May we, in
4 Let not the pass - ing of the years rob us of

on us from a - bove, through-out our lives in
lead - ing on to truth, for mem - 'ries gath - ered
all the years we live, find that each day of
joy or cause us fears, and make our faith, O

ev - 'ry stage, from in - fan - cy to lat - er age.
through the years, and faith that grows from joys and tears.
life is new, a cel - e - bra - tion, Lord, with you.
Lord, hold true, that we may al - ways rest in you.

Text: H. Glen Lanier, *Ten New Hymns on Aging and the Later Years,* 1976
Copyright ©1976 The Hymn Society
Music: William Knapp, *A Sett of New Psalm Tunes and Anthems,* 1738

Mothering God, you gave me birth 482

MOTHERING GOD LM extended

1 Moth-er-ing God, you gave me birth in the bright morn-ing of this world. Cre-a-tor, Source of ev-'ry breath, you are my rain, my wind, my sun; you are my rain, my wind, my sun.

2 Moth-er-ing Christ, you took my form, of-fer-ing me your food of light, grain of life, and grape of love, your ver-y bod-y for my peace; your ver-y bod-y for my peace.

3 Moth-er-ing Spir-it, nur-t'ring one, in arms of pa-tience hold me close, so that in faith I root and grow un-til I flow'r, un-til I know; un-til I flow'r, un-til I know.

Text: based on the writings of Julian of Norwich, Jean Janzen, 1991
Copyright ©1991 Jean Wiebe Janzen
Music: Janet Peachey, 1991
Copyright ©1991 Janet Peachey

483 O God, who gives us life

GRACIOUS GIFT CMD

1 O God, who gives us life and breath, who shapes us
2 O God, who calls your peo - ple out to ven - ture
3 O God of cov - e - nant and law, re - vealed in

in the womb, who guards our lives from birth to death,
and to dare, to plumb the bleak a - byss of doubt
cloud and flame, your might - y deeds e - voke our awe;

then leads us from the tomb: De - liv - er us from
and find you e - ven there: When we de - spair in
we dare not speak your name. Yet we by faith are

fears that kill the life we have from you. Help us to
wan - der - ing through wastes of emp - ty lies, re - fresh us
drawn to you and will your peo - ple prove, as on our

Text: Carl P. Daw, Jr., 1989, *A Year of Grace,* 1990
        Copyright ©1990 Hope Publishing Co.
Music: Jonathan Shively, 1991
        Copyright ©1991 Jonathan Shively

know your Spir-it still is mak-ing all things new.
with the liv-ing spring of hope that nev—er dies.
hearts you write a-new the cov-e-nant of love.

From time beyond my memory 484

TRUSTING MERCY LM extended

1 From time be-yond my mem-o-ry your love has been my
2 But now the years are pass-ing by when friends de-part and
3 Sing prais-es to the Ho-ly One, pro-claim-ing love from

rock, O Lord. Since child-hood days I trust-ed you, and in my
spir-its fail. O God, come quick-ly to my side, that in your
day to day, ex-alt-ing tri-umphs to the skies, and trust-ing

youth de-clared your word, and in my youth de-clared your word.
strength I may pre-vail, that in your strength I may pre-vail.
mer-cy, come what may, and trust-ing mer-cy, come what may.

Text: based on Psalm 71, Michael Perry, 1989, *Psalms for Today*, 1990
Copyright ©1990 Hope Publishing Co.
Music: John L. Horst, 1990
Copyright ©1990 John L. Horst

485 Teach me the measure of my days

MORTALITY CM

1 Teach me the mea - sure of my days, thou
2 A span is all that we can boast, an
3 See the vain race of mor - tals move like
4 What should I wish or wait for then, from
5 Now I for - bid my car - nal hope, my

1 Mak - er of my frame. I would sur - vey life's
2 inch or two of time. We are but van - i -
3 shad - ows o'er the plain. They rage and strive, de -
4 crea - tures, earth, and dust? They make our ex - pec -
5 fond de - sires re - call. I give my mor - tal

1 nar - row space, and learn how frail I am.
2 ty and dust in all our flow'r and prime.
3 sire and love, but all the noise is vain.
4 ta - tions vain, and dis - ap - point our trust.
5 in - t'rest up, and make my God my all.

Text: based on Psalm 39, Isaac Watts, *Psalms of David* ..., 1719, alt.
Music: *The Brethren's Tune and Hymn Book,* 1872

God of our life

486

SANDON 10 4. 10 4. 10 10

1 God of our life, through all the cir-cling years, we trust in
2 God of our past, our times are in thy hand; with us a-
3 God of the com - ing years, through paths un - known we fol - low

thee. In all the past, through all our hopes and fears, thy
bide. Lead us by faith to hope's true prom - ised land; be
thee. When we are strong, Lord, leave us not a - lone; our

hand we see. With each new day, when morn - ing lifts the
thou our guide. With thee to bless, the dark - ness shines as
ref - uge be. Be thou for us in life our dai - ly

veil, we own thy mer - cies, Lord, which nev - er fail.
light, and faith's fair vi - sion chang - es in - to sight.
bread, our heart's true home when all our years have sped.

Text: Hugh T. Kerr, *The Church School Hymnal*, 1928
         Copyright ©1928 F. M. Braselman, renewed 1956 Presbyterian Board of Christian Education
Music: Charles H. Purday, *Church and Home Metrical Psalter and Hymnal*, 1860

487 Teach me, O Lord

BISHOP LM

1 Teach me, O Lord, thy way of truth, and from it
2 In thy com - mand - ments make me walk, for in thy
3 Turn thou my eyes from van - i - ty, and cause me
4 Turn thou a - way re - proach and fear. Thy right-eous

I will not de - part; that I may stead - fast -
law my joy shall be. Give me a heart that
in thy ways to tread. O let thy ser - vant
judg - ments I con - fess. To know thy pre - cepts

ly o - bey, give me an un - der - stand - ing heart.
loves thy will, from dis-con - tent and en - vy free.
prove thy word, and thus to god - ly fear be led.
I de - sire. Re - vive me in thy right-eous - ness.

Text: based on Psalm 119:33-40, *Psalter*, 1912
Music: Joseph P. Holbrook, *The Presbyterian Hymnal*, 1874

Strong Son of God, immortal Love 488

ST. CRISPIN LM

1 Strong Son of God, im - mor - tal Love, whom we, that
2 thou seem - est hu - man and di - vine, the high - est,
3 Our lit - tle sys - tems have their day – they have their
4 We have but faith – we can - not know, for knowl-edge
5 Let knowl-edge grow from more to more, but more of

1 have not seen thy face, by faith, and faith a -
2 ho - liest One art thou. Our wills are ours, we
3 day and cease to be. They are but bro - ken
4 is of things we see, and yet we trust it
5 rev - 'rence in us dwell, that mind and soul, ac -

1 lone, em - brace, be - liev-ing where we can - not prove;
2 know not how – our wills are ours, to make them thine.
3 lights of thee, and thou, O Lord, art more than they.
4 comes from thee, a beam in dark - ness – let it grow.
5 cord - ing well, may make one mu - sic as be - fore.

Text: Alfred Tennyson, Prologue to *In Memoriam*, 1850, alt.
Music: George J. Elvey, 1862, *A Selection of Psalm and Hymn Tunes*, 1863

489 O little children, gather

BEAUTIFUL FLOWER 87. 12 7

1 O lit-tle chil-dren, gath-er near and learn of Je-sus'
2 Let Je-sus Christ your teach-er be, your thoughts to him ad-
3 Then quick-ly come, all chil-dren dear, in Je-sus' school en-
4 How good it is, and ex-cel-lent to see the chil-dren
5 So, chil-dren, fol-low in his ways, and pray-ing, read-ing,

1 glo-ry. Now come and of his good-ness hear, his
2 dress-ing. He calls: "O come now un-to me and
3 roll-ing. Here sit and learn, his judg-ment fear, his
4 turn-ing to right-eous ways, o-be-di-ent and
5 sing-ing, seek heav-en all your earth-ly days, and

1 love and pow'r; come list-en to his sto-ry.
2 joy-ful be. I'll give you ev-'ry bless-ing."
3 truth re-vere, his wis-dom great ex-tol-ling.
4 in-no-cent, in Je-sus' school of learn-ing.
5 shout his praise, to him all hon-or bring-ing.

Text: Christopher Dock, *Ach Kinder, wollt ihr lieben*, ca. 1770; tr. Alice Parker, 1962, *Come Let Us Join*, 1966, alt.
Music: *The Philharmonia*, 1875; arranged by Alice Parker, *Come Let Us Join*, 1966
Translation and music arrangement copyright ©1991 Alice Parker

Lord of the home

HURSLEY LM

490

1 Lord of the home, your on - ly Son re-ceived a
2 Help us, O Lord, our homes to make your Ho - ly
3 Pray we that all who with us dwell, your love and
4 Teach us to keep our homes so fair, that were our
5 Lord, may your Spir - it sanc - ti - fy each house-hold

1 moth - er's ten - der love, and from an earth - ly
2 Spir - it's dwell - ing place. Our hands' and hearts' de -
3 joy and peace may know; and while our lips your
4 Lord a child once more, he might be glad our
5 du - ty we ful - fill. May we our Mas - ter

1 fa - ther won his vi - sion of your home a - bove.
2 vo - tion take to be the ser - vants of your grace.
3 prais - es tell, may faith - ful lives your glo - ry show.
4 hearth to share, and find a wel - come at our door.
5 glo - ri - fy in glad o - be - dience to your will.

Text: Albert F. Bayly, 1947, *Rejoice, O People*, 1950, alt.
         Copyright © Oxford University Press, London
Music: adapted from GROSSER GOTT, WIR LOBEN DICH, *Katholisches Gesangbuch*, ca. 1774

491 Softly and tenderly Jesus is calling

THOMPSON 11 7. 11 7 with refrain

1 Soft - ly and ten - der - ly Je - sus is call - ing,
2 Why should we tar - ry when Je - sus is plead - ing,
3 Oh, for the won - der - ful love he has prom - ised,

call - ing for you and for me. See, on the por - tals he's
plead - ing for you and for me? Why should we lin - ger and
prom - ised for you and for me! Though we have sinned, he has

wait - ing and watch - ing, watch - ing for you and for me.
heed not his mer - cies, mer - cies for you and for me?
mer - cy and par - don, par - don for you and for me.

Refrain

"Come home, come home! You who are
come home, Come home!

Text: Will L. Thompson, *Sparkling Gems Nos. 1 & 2 Combined*, 1880
Music: Will L. Thompson, *Sparkling Gems Nos. 1 & 2 Combined*, 1880

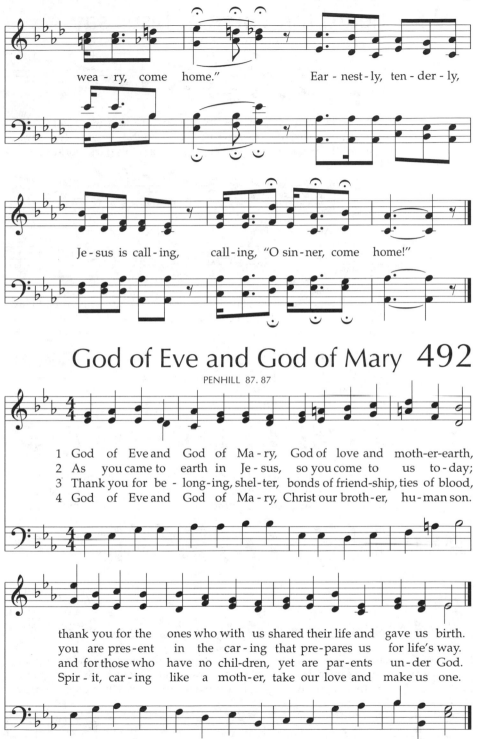

wea - ry, come home." Ear - nest - ly, ten - der - ly,

Je - sus is call - ing, call - ing, "O sin - ner, come home!"

God of Eve and God of Mary 492

PENHILL 87. 87

1 God of Eve and God of Ma - ry, God of love and moth-er-earth,
2 As you came to earth in Je - sus, so you come to us to - day;
3 Thank you for be - long-ing, shel - ter, bonds of friend-ship, ties of blood,
4 God of Eve and God of Ma - ry, Christ our broth-er, hu-man son.

thank you for the ones who with us shared their life and gave us birth.
you are pres-ent in the car - ing that pre-pares us for life's way.
and for those who have no chil-dren, yet are par-ents un - der God.
Spir - it, car - ing like a moth-er, take our love and make us one.

Text: Fred Kaan, 1987
        Copyright ©1989 Hope Publishing Co.
Music: Pamela Ward, *New Songs of Praise 4*, 1988
        Copyright ©1988 Oxford University Press, London

493 I heard the voice of Jesus say

KINGSFOLD CMD

1 I heard the voice of Je-sus say, "Come un-to me and rest.
2 I heard the voice of Je-sus say, "Be - hold, I free - ly give
3 I heard the voice of Je-sus say, "I am this dark world's light.

Lay down, O wea - ry one, lay down your head up - on my breast."
the liv - ing wa - ter, thirst-y one; stoop down and drink and live."
Look un - to me, your morn shall rise, and all your day be bright."

I came to Je - sus as I was, so wea - ry, worn, and sad.
I came to Je - sus, and I drank of that life - giv - ing stream.
I looked to Je - sus, and I found in him my star, my sun,

I found in him a rest - ing place, and he has made me glad.
My thirst was quenched, my soul re - vived, and now I live in him.
and in that light of life I'll walk till tra-v'ling days are done.

Text: Horatius N. Bonar, *Hymns Original and Selected,* 1846, alt.

Music: English folk melody, *English County Songs,* 1893; adapted and harmonized by Ralph Vaughan Williams, *The English Hymnal,* 1906, alt.

Harmonization copyright © Oxford University Press, London

Christian, do you hear the Lord? 494

ORIENTIS PARTIBUS 77. 77

1 Chris - tian, do you hear the Lord? Je - sus
2 "I de - liv - ered you when bound, and when
3 "Can a moth - er's ten - der - ness for her
4 "Mine is an un - chang - ing love, high - er
5 "You shall see my glo - ry soon, when the
6 Lord, it is my chief com - plaint that my

1 speaks his gra - cious word. Gent - ly sounds the
2 bleed - ing healed your wound. Saw you wan - d'ring,
3 own dear child grow less? Though she may for -
4 than the heights a - bove, deep - er than the
5 work of grace is done. Crowned with splen - dor
6 love is weak and faint. Yet, I love you,

1 Sav - ior's call, "Do you love me best of all?
2 set you right, turned your dark - ness in - to light.
3 get - ful be, you are al - ways dear to me.
4 depths be - neath, free and faith - ful, strong as death.
5 you shall be. Chris - tian, come and fol - low me!"
6 and a - dore – oh, for grace to love you more!

Text: William Cowper, *New Appendix* to Maxwell's *Collection*, 1768; revised in *Hymns for Today's Church*, 1982
Copyright ©1982 Hope Publishing Co.
Music: Pierre de Corbeil; harmonized by Richard Redhead, *Church Hymn Tunes, Ancient and Modern*, 1853

495 O let all who thirst

COME TO THE WATER* Irregular

1 O let all who thirst, let them come to the wa-ter. (let them come) And let all who have noth-ing, let them come to the Lord: (to the Lord) with-out mon-ey,

2 And let all who seek, let them come to the wa-ter. And let all who have noth-ing, let them come to the Lord: with-out mon-ey,

3 And let all who toil, let them come to the wa-ter. And let all who are wea-ry, let them come to the Lord: all who la-bor

4 And let all the poor, let them come to the wa-ter. Bring the all who are lad-en, bring them all to the Lord. Bring the chil-dren

*Original title

Text: based on Isaiah 55:1-2 and Matthew 11:28-30, John B. Foley, S.J., 1974, *Wood Hath Hope*, 1978
Music: John B. Foley, S.J.; harmonization revised 1991

with-out price; why should you pay the price,
with-out strife; why should you spend your life,
with-out rest; how can your soul find rest,
with-out might; eas - y the load and light –

ex-cept for the Lord? _____ (for the Lord?)
ex-cept for the Lord? _____ (for the Lord?)
ex-cept for the Lord? _____ (for the Lord?)
come to the Lord. _____ (to the Lord.)

Like Noah's weary dove   496

SM

1 Like No - ah's wea - ry dove, that soared the earth a - round,
2 O cease, my wan-dering soul, on rest - less wing to roam.
3 Be - hold the ark of God, be - hold the o - pen door.
4 There, safe thou shalt a - bide. There, sweet shall be thy rest,
5 And, when the waves of ire a - gain the earth shall fill,

1 but not a rest - ing place a - bove the cheer-less wa-ters found;
2 All the wide world to ei - ther pole, has not for thee a home.
3 Has - ten to gain that dear a - bode, and rove, my soul, no more.
4 and ev - 'ry long-ing sat - is - fied, with full sal - va - tion bless'd.
5 the ark shall ride the sea of fire, then rest on Zi - on's hill.

Text: William A. Muhlenberg, *Prayer Book Collection,* 1826
Music: John H. Hopkins, Jr., 1882

497 Come, ye disconsolate

CONSOLATOR (CONSOLATION) 11 10. 11 10

1 Come, ye dis - con - so - late, wher - e'er ye lan - guish,
2 Joy of the des - o - late, light of the stray - ing,
3 Here see the Bread of life; see wa - ters flow - ing

come to the mer - cy seat, fer - vent - ly kneel.
hope of the pen - i - tent, fade - less and pure!
forth from the throne of God, pure from a - bove.

Here bring your wound - ed hearts, here tell your an - guish.
Here speaks the Com - fort - er, ten - der - ly say - ing,
Come to the feast of love, come, ev - er know - ing

Earth has no sor - rows that Heav'n can - not heal.
"Earth has no sor - rows that Heav'n can - not cure."
earth has no sor - rows but Heav'n can re - move.

Text: Thomas Moore (Sts. 1-2), *Sacred Songs, Duets and Trios*, 1816, alt., Thomas Hastings (St. 3), *Spiritual Songs for Social Worship*, 1831
Music: Samuel Webbe, Sr., *A Collection of Motetts and Antiphons*, 1792

He comes to us as one unknown 498

REPTON 86. 88. 6 extended

1 He comes to us as one un-known, a
2 He comes when souls in si - lence lie and
3 He comes to us in sound of seas, the
4 He comes in love as once he came by
5 He comes in truth when faith is grown – be -

1 breath un - seen, un - heard, as though with - in a
2 thoughts of day de - part, half - seen up - on the
3 o - cean's fume and foam, yet small and still up -
4 flesh and blood and birth, to bear with - in our
5 lieved, o - beyed, a - dored; the Christ in all the

1 heart of stone, or shriv - eled seed in dark-ness sown, a
2 in - ward eye, a fall - ing star a - cross the sky of
3 on the breeze, a wind that stirs the tops of trees, a
4 mor - tal frame a life, a death, a sav - ing name, for
5 Scrip - tures shown, as yet un-seen, but not un - known, our

1 pulse of be - ing stirred, a pulse of be - ing stirred.
2 night with - in the heart, of night with - in the heart.
3 voice to call us home, a voice to call us home.
4 ev - 'ry child of earth, for ev - 'ry child of earth.
5 Sav - ior and our Lord, our Sav - ior and our Lord.

Text: Timothy Dudley-Smith, 1982, *On the Move*, 1983
         Copyright ©1984 Hope Publishing Co.
Music: Charles H. H. Parry, *Judith*, 1888, *Hymns Ancient and Modern*, 1904

499 Lord, speak to me

CANONBURY LM

1 Lord, speak to me, that I may speak in
2 O lead me, Lord, that I may lead the
3 O strength-en me, that while I stand firm
4 O teach me, Lord, that I may teach the
5 O fill me with thy full-ness, Lord, un-
6 O use me, Lord, use e-ven me, just

1 liv-ing ech-oes of thy tone. As thou hast sought, so
2 wan-d'ring and the wav-'ring feet. O feed me, Lord, that
3 on the Rock, and strong in thee, I may stretch out a
4 pre-cious things thou dost im-part, and wing my words, that
5 til my ver-y heart o'er-flow in kin-dling thought and
6 as thou wilt, and when and where, un-til thy bless-ed

1 let me seek thine err-ing chil-dren lost and lone.
2 I may feed thy hun-g'ring ones with man-na sweet.
3 lov-ing hand to wres-tlers with the trou-bled sea.
4 they may reach the hid-den depths of many a heart.
5 glow-ing word, thy love to tell, thy praise to show.
6 face I see, thy rest, thy joy, thy glo-ry share.

Text: Frances R. Havergal, 1872, *Under the Surface*, 1874
Music: adapted from Robert Schumann, *Hymnal with Tunes, Old and New*, 1872

As the hart with eager yearning 500

GENEVA 42 (FREU DICH SEHR) 87. 87. 77. 88

1 As the hart with ea - ger yearn - ing seeks the cool - ing
2 Day and night in grief and an - guish bit - ter tears have

wa - ter - course, so my soul with ar - dor burn - ing
been my meat, while my long - ing soul may lan - guish

longs for God, its heav'n - ly source. When shall I be - hold God's
to par - take of man - na sweet. O my soul, be not dis-

face? When shall I re - ceive God's grace? When shall I, God's
mayed. Trust in God, who is our aid. Hope and joy God's

prais - es voic - ing, come be - fore our God re - joic - ing?
love pro - vides you, 'tis God's hand a - lone that guides you.

Text: based on Psalm 42, Christine T. Curtis, 1939, *The Hymnal* (Evangelical and Reformed), 1941, alt.
Music: Louis Bourgeois, *Genevan Psalter,* 1551; harmonization adapted from Claude Goudimel, *Les Pseaumes ...,* 1565

501 Come down, O Love divine

DOWN AMPNEY 66 11. 66 11

1 Come down, O Love di - vine, seek thou this soul of mine,
2 O let it free - ly burn, till earth - ly pas - sions turn
3 Let ho - ly char - i - ty mine out - ward ves - ture be,
4 And so the yearn - ing strong, with which the soul will long,

and vis - it it with thine own ar - dor glow - ing.
to dust and ash - es in its heat con - sum - ing.
and low - li - ness be - come mine in - ner cloth - ing;
shall far out - pass the pow'r of hu - man tell - ing;

O Com - fort - er, draw near, with - in my heart ap - pear,
And let thy glo - rious light shine ev - er on my sight,
true low - li - ness of heart which takes the hum - bler part,
for none can guess its grace, till love cre - ates a place

and kin - dle it, thy ho - ly flame be - stow - ing.
and clothe me 'round, the while my path il - lum - ing.
and o'er its own short - com - ings weeps with loath - ing.
where - in the Ho - ly Spir - it makes a dwell - ing.

Text: Bianco da Siena, ca. 1367, *Laudi Spirituali del Bianco da Siena*, 1851; tr. Richard F. Littledale, *People's Hymnal*, 1867, alt.
Music: Ralph Vaughan Williams, *The English Hymnal*, 1906

Spirit of God! descend

502

MORECAMBE 10 10. 10 10

1 Spir - it of God! de - scend up - on my heart.
2 I ask no dream, no proph - et ec - sta - sies,
3 Hast thou not bid us love thee, God and King?
4 Teach me to feel that thou art al - ways nigh.
5 Teach me to love thee as thine an - gels love,

1 Wean it from earth, through all its puls - es move.
2 no sud - den rend - ing of the veil of clay,
3 All, all thine own, soul, heart, and strength, and mind;
4 Teach me the strug - gles of the soul to bear,
5 one ho - ly pas - sion fill - ing all my frame;

1 Stoop to my weak - ness, might - y as thou art,
2 no an - gel vis - i - tant, no op - 'ning skies,
3 I see thy cross, there teach my heart to cling.
4 to check the ris - ing doubt, the reb - el sigh;
5 the bap - tism of the heav'n - de - scend - ed Dove,

1 and make me love thee as I ought to love.
2 but take the dim - ness of my soul a - way.
3 O let me seek thee, and O let me find!
4 teach me the pa - tience of un - an - swered prayer.
5 my heart an al - tar, and thy love the flame.

Text: George Croly, *Lyra Britannica,* 1867
Music: Frederick C. Atkinson, 1870, *Congregational Church Hymnal,* 1887

503 Come, O thou Traveler unknown

VERNON 88. 88. 88

1 Come, O thou Trav-el - er un-known, whom still I hold, but can-not see! My com-pa-ny be - fore is gone, and I am left a - lone with thee. With thee all night I mean to stay and wres-tle till the break of day.

2 I need not tell thee who I am,
my misery and sin declare.
Thyself has called me by my name,
look on thy hands and read it there.
But who, I ask thee, who art thou?
Tell me thy name, and tell me now.

3 In vain thou strugglest to get free;
I never will unloose my hold.
Art thou the Man that died for me?
The secret of thy love unfold.
Wrestling, I will not let thee go,
till I thy name, thy nature know.

4 Wilt thou not yet to me reveal
thy new, unutterable name?
Tell me, I still beseech thee, tell,
to know it now resolved I am.
Wrestling, I will not let thee go,
till I thy name, thy nature know.

5 'Tis all in vain to hold thy tongue
or touch the hollow of my thigh.
Though every sinew is unstrung,
out of my arms thou shalt not fly.
Wrestling, I will not let thee go,
till I thy name, thy nature know.

6 What though my shrinking flesh complain
and murmur to contend so long,
I rise superior to my pain;
when I am weak then I am strong,
and when my all of strength shall fail
I shall with the God-man prevail.

7 My strength is gone, my nature dies,
I sink beneath thy weighty hand,
faint to revive, and fall to rise.
I fall, and yet by faith I stand,
I stand and will not let thee go,
till I thy name, thy nature know.

8 Yield to me now – for I am weak
but confident in self-despair!
Speak to my heart, in blessing speak,
be conquered by my instant prayer.
Speak, or thou never hence shalt move,
and tell me if thy name is Love.

9 'Tis Love! 'tis Love! thou diedst for me,
I hear thy whisper in my heart.
The morning breaks, the shadows flee,
pure, universal Love thou art.
To me, to all, thy mercies move –
thy nature, and thy name is Love.

Text:	based on Genesis 32:24-32, Charles Wesley, *Hymns and Sacred Poems*, 1742
Music:	American folk melody, *The Christian Harmony*, 1805

10 My prayer hath power with God; the grace
   unspeakable I now receive!
   Through faith I see thee face to face,
   I see thee face to face, and live!
   In vain I have not wept and strove –
   thy nature, and thy name is Love.

11 Contented now upon my thigh
   I halt, till life's short journey end.
   All helplessness, all weakness I
   on thee alone for strength depend,
   nor have I power from thee to move.
   Thy nature, and thy name is Love!

Note: Because of source problems for "Come, O thou Traveler unknown," the stanza order was incorrect in earlier
printings of *Hymnal: A Worship Book.* It is corrected here. For more information, see *Hymnal Companion.*

Have thine own way 504

ADELAIDE 54. 54D

1 Have thine own way, Lord! Have thine own way! Thou art the
2 Have thine own way, Lord! Have thine own way! Search me and
3 Have thine own way, Lord! Have thine own way! Wound-ed and
4 Have thine own way, Lord! Have thine own way! Hold o'er my

pot-ter, I am the clay. Mold me and make me aft-er thy
try me, Mas-ter, to-day! Wash me just now, Lord, wash me just
wea-ry, help me, I pray! Pow-er – all pow-er – sure-ly is
be-ing ab-so-lute sway! Fill with thy Spir-it till all shall

will, while I am wait-ing, yield-ed and still.
now, as in thy pres-ence hum-bly I bow.
thine! Touch me and heal me, Sav-ior di-vine!
see Christ on-ly, al-ways, liv-ing in me!

Text: Adelaide A. Pollard, *Northfield Hymnal with Alexander's Supplement,* 1907, alt.
Music: George C. Stebbins, *Northfield Hymnal with Alexander's Supplement,* 1907

505 I am thine, O Lord

I AM THINE 10 7. 10 7 with refrain

1 I am thine, O Lord, I have heard thy voice, and it
2 Oh, the pure de-light of a sin-gle hour that be-
3 Con-se-crate me now to thy ser-vice, Lord, by the

told thy love to me. But I long to rise in the arms of faith,
fore thy throne I spend, when I kneel in prayer, and with thee, my God,
pow'r of grace di - vine. Let my soul look up with a stead-fast hope,

Refrain

and be clos-er drawn to thee.
I com - mune as friend with friend! Draw me near - er,
and my will be lost in thine.
near - er, near - er,

near - er, bless-ed Lord, to the cross where thou hast died. Draw me

near - er, near - er, near-er, bless-ed Lord, to thy pre-cious bleed-ing side.

Text: Fanny J. Crosby, *Brightest and Best*, 1875
Music: William H. Doane, *Brightest and Best*, 1875

I sought the Lord

506

FAITH 10 10. 10 6

1 I sought the Lord, and af-ter-ward I knew he moved my
2 Thou didst reach forth thy hand and mine en-fold, I walked and
3 I find, I walk, I love, but, oh, the whole of love is

soul to seek him, seek-ing me. It was not I that
sank not on the storm-vexed sea. 'Twas not so much that
but my an-swer, Lord, to thee! For thou wert long be-

found, O Sav-ior true, no, I was found of thee.
I on thee took hold as thou, dear Lord, on me.
fore-hand with my soul, al-ways thou lov-edst me.

Text: *Holy Songs, Carols, and Sacred Ballads,* 1880
Music: J. Harold Moyer, 1965, *The Mennonite Hymnal,* 1969

507 Gracious Spirit, dwell with me

REDHEAD NO. 76 (GETHSEMANE) 77. 77. 77

1 Gra - cious Spir - it, dwell with me: I my - self would
2 Truth - ful Spir - it, dwell with me: I my - self would
3 Si - lent Spir - it, dwell with me: I my - self would
4 Might - y Spir - it, dwell with me: I my - self would
5 Ho - ly Spir - it, dwell with me: I my - self would

1 gra - cious be, and, with words that help and heal,
2 truth - ful be, and, with wis - dom kind and clear,
3 si - lent be, qui - et as the grow - ing blade,
4 might - y be, might - y so as to pre - vail
5 ho - ly be, break from sin and choose the good,

1 would thy life in mine re - veal, and, with ac - tions
2 let thy life in mine ap - pear, and, with ac - tions
3 which through earth its way has made, si - lent - ly, like
4 where un - aid - ed I must fail, ev - er, by a
5 cher - ish what my Sav - ior would, and what - ev - er

1 bold and meek, would for Christ my Sav - ior speak.
2 lov - ing - ly speak my Lord's sin - cer - i - ty.
3 morn - ing light, put - ting mists and chills to flight.
4 might - y hope, press - ing on and bear - ing up.
5 I can be, give to him who gave me thee.

Text: Thomas T. Lynch, *The Rivulet: A Contribution to Sacred Song*, 1855, alt.
Music: Richard Redhead, *Church Hymn Tunes, Ancient and Modern*, 1853

Holy Spirit, Truth divine   508

MERCY 77.77

1 Ho - ly Spir - it, Truth di - vine, dawn up-
2 Ho - ly Spir - it, Love di - vine, glow with-
3 Ho - ly Spir - it, Pow'r di - vine, fill and
4 Ho - ly Spir - it, Law di - vine, reign with-
5 Ho - ly Spir - it, Peace di - vine, still this
6 Ho - ly Spir - it, Joy di - vine, glad - den

1 on this soul of mine. Voice of God, and
2 in this heart of mine. Kin - dle ev - 'ry
3 nerve this will of mine. Bold - ly may I
4 in this soul of mine. Be my law and
5 rest - less heart of mine. Speak to calm this
6 now this heart of mine. In the des - ert

1 in - ward Light, wake my spir - it, clear my sight.
2 high de - sire, pur - i - fy me with your fire.
3 al - ways live, brave - ly serve and glad - ly give.
4 I shall be firm - ly bound, for - ev - er free.
5 toss - ing sea, grant me your tran - quil - i - ty.
6 ways I sing, spring, O liv - ing Wa - ter, spring!

Text: Samuel Longfellow, *Hymns of the Spirit,* 1864
Music: arranged from Louis M. Gottschalk, "The Last Hope," 1854; adapted by Edwin P. Parker

509   The tree of life

APPLE TREE LM

1 The tree of life my soul hath seen,   lad - en with
2 His beau - ty doth all things ex - cel.   By faith I
3 For hap - pi - ness I long have sought,   and plea - sure
4 I'm wea - ry with my for - mer toil.   Here I will
5 This fruit doth make my soul to thrive.   It keeps my

1 fruit and al - ways green.   The trees of
2 know, but ne'er can tell   the glo - ry
3 dear - ly I have bought.   I missed of
4 sit and rest a - while.   Un - der the
5 dy - ing faith a - live,   which makes my

1 na - ture fruit - less be com - pared with Christ the
2 which I now can see in Je - sus Christ the
3 all – but now I see – 'tis found in Christ the
4 shad - ow I will be of Je - sus Christ the
5 soul in haste to be with Je - sus Christ the

1-4 | 5

1 ap - ple tree.   (2 His)
2 ap - ple tree.   (3 For)
3 ap - ple tree.   (4 I'm)
4 ap - ple tree.   (5 This)
5 ap - ple tree.

Text: anonymous, *Divine Hymns*, 1784
Music: Alice Parker, 1989
         Copyright ©1989 Alice Parker

O Christ, in thee my soul   510

NONE BUT CHRIST CM with refrain

1 O Christ, in thee my soul hath found, and found in thee a - lone,
2 I sighed for rest and hap-pi-ness, I yearned for them, not thee.
3 I tried the bro-ken cis-terns, Lord, but ah! the wa-ters failed!
4 The plea-sures lost I sad-ly mourned, but nev-er wept for thee,

the peace, the joy I sought so long, the bliss till now un - known.
But while I passed my Sav-ior by, his love laid hold on me.
E'en as I stooped to drink they fled, and mock'd me as I wailed.
till grace my sight-less eyes re-ceived, thy love-li-ness to see.

Refrain

Now none but Christ can sat-is-fy, none oth-er name for me!

There's love, and life, and last - ing joy, Lord Je - sus, found in thee.

Text: anonymous, *Gospel Hymns, No. 4*, 1883
Music: James McGranahan, *Gospel Hymns, No. 4*, 1883

511 God, who touches earth

EARTHRISE 85. 85

1 God, who touch - es   earth with beau - ty,
2 Like your springs and   run - ning wa - ters,
3 Like your danc - ing   waves in sun - light,
4 Like the arch - ing   of the heav - ens,
5 God, who touch - es   earth with beau - ty,

1 make my heart a - new.   With your Spir - it   re - cre - ate me
2 make me crys - tal pure.   Like your rocks   of   tow'r - ing gran-deur,
3 make me glad and free.   Like the straight-ness   of   the pine trees
4 lift my thoughts a - bove.   Turn my dreams to   no - ble ac - tion,
5 make my heart a - new.   Keep me ev - er,   by your Spir - it,

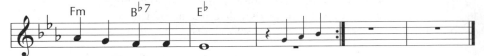

1 pure and strong and   true.
2 make me strong and   sure.
3 let me up - right   be.
4 min - is - tries of   love.
5 pure and strong and   true.

Text: Mary S. Edgar, 1925, alt.
           Copyright ©1939 J. W. Gilchrist
Music: Alfred V. Fedak, 1988
           Copyright ©1989 Sacred Music Press

512 If all you want, Lord

FIRST COMMAND CM

1 If all you want, Lord, is my heart, my heart is yours a - lone –
2 If all you want, Lord, is my mind, my mind be - longs to you,
3 If heart and mind would both suf - fice, while I kept strength and soul,
4 But since, O God, you want them all to shape with your own hand,

Text: Thomas H. Troeger, The Hymn, 1987
Music: Carol Doran, The Hymn, 1987
           Text and music copyright ©1987 Oxford University Press, Inc.

pro-vid-ing   I may set a - part my   mind to be my   own.
but let my heart re - main in - clined to   do what it would   do.
at least I   would not sac-ri - fice com - plete - ly my con - trol.
I   pray for grace to heed your call to   live your first com - mand.

To go to heaven   513

10 10. 10 10

Leader

1 To   go   to heav - en   my heart is long - ing.
2 The peace of heav - en   all else ex - cel - ling;
3 The God who loves   us   as no one oth - er
4 Why de - lay long - er? This is the best day

How shall   I   get   there   with - out pro - long - ing?
the place ce - les - tial   where God is dwell - ing.
has sent   us Je - sus   to be our broth - er.
to choose to fol - low   Je - sus, the true   way.

All

The way is Je - sus.   He chang - es nev - er.

The Sav - ior wants   you   with him for - ev - er.

Text: Ndilivako Ndelwa; tr. Howard S. Olson
Music: Kinga melody (Tanzania)

514 Lord, I am fondly, earnestly

OPEN THE WELLS 10 9. 10 9 with refrain

1 Lord, I am fond - ly, ear - nest - ly long - ing in - to thy
2 Dead to the world would I be, O Fa - ther, dead un - to
3 I would be thine, and serve thee for - ev - er, filled with thy

ho - ly like - ness to grow, thirst - ing for more and deep - er com -
sin, a - live un - to thee. Cru - ci - fy all the earth - ly with -
Spir - it, lost in thy love. Come to my heart, Lord, come with a -

Refrain

mun - ion, yearn - ing thy love more full - y to know.
in me, emp - tied of sin and self may I be. O - pen the
noint - ing, show - ers of grace send down from a - bove.

wells of grace and sal - va - tion, pour the rich
O - pen the wells of grace and sal - va - tion,

Text: Elisha A. Hoffman, *Church and Sunday School Hymnal*, 1902
Music: Charles E. Pollock, *Church and Sunday School Hymnal*, 1902

Jesus, Rock of ages 515

Text: M. Gerald Derstine, 1973
Music: M. Gerald Derstine, 1973; harmonized by Marilyn Houser Hamm and M. Gerald Derstine
Text and music copyright ©1973 M. Gerald Derstine
Harmonization copyright ©1991 Marilyn Houser Hamm and M. Gerald Derstine

516 Just as I am, without one plea

WOODWORTH LM

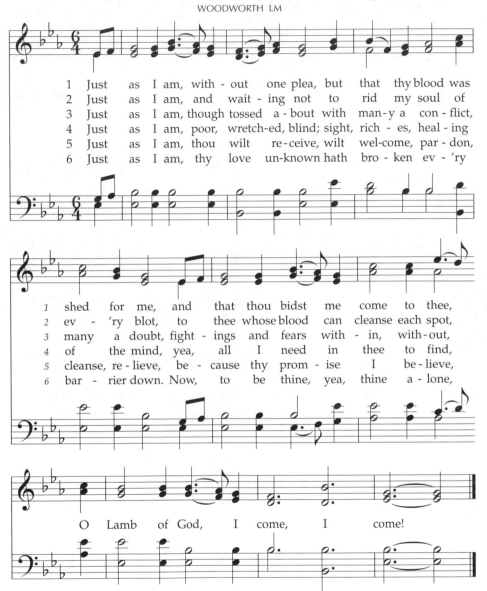

1 Just as I am, with-out one plea, but that thy blood was
2 Just as I am, and wait-ing not to rid my soul of
3 Just as I am, though tossed a-bout with man-y a con-flict,
4 Just as I am, poor, wretch-ed, blind; sight, rich-es, heal-ing
5 Just as I am, thou wilt re-ceive, wilt wel-come, par-don,
6 Just as I am, thy love un-known hath bro-ken ev-'ry

1 shed for me, and that thou bidst me come to thee,
2 ev-'ry blot, to thee whose blood can cleanse each spot,
3 many a doubt, fight-ings and fears with-in, with-out,
4 of the mind, yea, all I need in thee to find,
5 cleanse, re-lieve, be-cause thy prom-ise I be-lieve,
6 bar-rier down. Now, to be thine, yea, thine a-lone,

O Lamb of God, I come, I come!

Text: Charlotte Elliott, 1834, *Invalid's Hymn Book*, 1836
Music: William B. Bradbury, *The Mendelssohn Collection or ... Third Book of Psalmody*, 1849

Open my eyes, that I may see 517

OPEN MY EYES 88. 98. 88. 84

1 O-pen my eyes, that   I may see glimps-es of truth thou hast for me.
2 O-pen my ears, that   I may hear voic-es of truth thou send-est clear,
3 O-pen my mouth, and let me bear glad-ly the warm truth ev-'ry-where.
4 O-pen my mind, that   I may read more of thy love in word and deed.

Place in my hands the   won-der-ful key   that shall un-clasp, and
and while the wave notes fall on my ear,   ev-'ry-thing false will
O-pen my heart, and   let me pre-pare   love with thy chil-dren
What shall I   fear while yet thou dost lead? On-ly for light from

set   me free. Si-lent-ly now I   wait for thee, read-y, my God, thy
dis-ap-pear. Si-lent-ly now I   wait for thee, read-y, my God, thy
thus   to share. Si-lent-ly now I   wait for thee, read-y, my God, thy
thee   I plead. Si-lent-ly now I   wait for thee, read-y, my God, thy

will   to see. O-pen my eyes, il - lu-mine me, Spir-it di - vine!
will   to see. O-pen my ears, il - lu-mine me, Spir-it di - vine!
will   to see. O-pen my heart, il - lu-mine me, Spir-it di - vine!
will   to see. O-pen my mind, il - lu-mine me, Spir-it di - vine!

Text: Clara H. Scott, *Best Hymns, No. 2*, 1895
Music: Clara H. Scott, *Best Hymns, No. 2*, 1895

518 Eternal Light, shine in my heart

JACOB LM

1 E - ter - nal Light, shine in my heart. E - ter - nal
2 E - ter - nal Life, raise me from death. E - ter - nal
3 un - til by your most cost - ly grace, in - vit - ed

Hope, lift up my eyes. E - ter - nal Pow'r, be
Bright - ness, help me see. E - ter - nal Spir - it,
by your ho - ly word, at last I come be -

my sup - port. E - ter - nal Wis - dom, make me wise.
give me breath. E - ter - nal Sav - ior, come to me,
fore your face to know you, my e - ter - nal God.

Text: based on a prayer by Alcuin, Christopher Idle, 1977, *Hymns for Today's Church*, 1982
           Copyright ©1982 Hope Publishing Co.
Music: Jane Marshall, *The Hymnal 1982*, 1985
           Copyright ©1984 G.I.A. Publications, Inc.

Shepherd me, O God

519

Irregular

Refrain

Shep-herd me, O God, be - yond my wants, be - yond my fears, from death in - to life.

1 God is my shepherd, so nothing shall I want,
   I rest in the meadows of faithfulness and love,
   I walk by the quiet waters of peace.
   (Refrain)

2 Gently you raise me and heal my weary soul,
   you lead me by pathways of righteousness and truth;
   my spirit shall sing the music of your name.
   (Refrain)

3 Though I should wander the valley of death,
   I fear no evil, for you are at my side,
   your rod and your staff, my comfort and my hope.
   (Refrain)

4 You have set me a banquet of love in the face of hatred,
   crowning me with love beyond my power to hold.
   (Refrain)

5 Surely your kindness and mercy follow me
   all the days of my life;
   I will dwell in the house of my God forevermore.
   (Refrain)

Text: based on Psalm 23, Marty Haugen, 1985, *Gather*, 1988
Music: Marty Haugen, *Gather*, 1988
        Text and music copyright ©1986 G.I.A. Publications, Inc.

520 Oh, for a closer walk with God

CAITHNESS CM

1 Oh, for a clos-er walk with God, a calm and heav'n-ly frame,
2 Where is the bless-ed-ness I knew when first I saw the Lord?
3 What peace-ful hours I once en-joyed, how sweet their mem-'ry still.
4 Re-turn, O ho-ly Dove, re-turn, sweet Mes-sen-ger of rest.
5 The dear-est i-dol I have known, what-e'er that i-dol be,
6 So shall my walk be close to God, calm and se-rene my frame;

1 a light to shine up-on the road that leads me to the Lamb!
2 Where is the soul-re-fresh-ing view of Je-sus and his word?
3 But they have left an ach-ing void the world can nev-er fill.
4 I hate the sins that made thee mourn, and drove thee from my breast.
5 help me to tear it from thy throne, and wor-ship on-ly thee.
6 so pur-er light shall mark the road that leads me to the Lamb.

Text: William Cowper, *A Collection of Psalms and Hymns*, 2nd ed., 1772
Music: *The Psalmes of David in Prose and Meeter*, 1635; harmonized in *The English Hymnal*, 1906
Harmonization copyright © Oxford University Press, London

521 Come, thou fount

NETTLETON 87. 87D

1 Come, thou fount of ev-'ry bless-ing, tune my heart to
2 Here I raise my Eb-en-e-zer, hith-er by thy
3 Oh, to grace how great a debt-or dai-ly I'm con-

Text: Robert Robinson, 1758, *A Collection of Hymns ...*, 1759
Music: American folk melody, in John Wyeth's *Repository of Sacred Music, Part Second*, 1813

sing thy grace. Streams of mer - cy, nev - er ceas - ing, call for
help I'm come, and I hope, by thy good plea - sure, safe - ly
strained to be! Let that grace now, like a fet - ter, bind my

songs of loud - est praise. Teach me some me - lo - dious
to ar - rive at home. Je - sus sought me when a
wan - d'ring heart to thee. Prone to wan - der, Lord, I

son - net, sung by flam - ing tongues a - bove. Praise the
stran - ger, wan - d'ring from the fold of God. He, to
feel it, prone to leave the God I love. Here's my

mount, I'm fixed up - on it, mount of God's un - chang - ing love.
res - cue me from dan - ger, in - ter - posed his pre - cious blood.
heart, O take and seal it, seal it for thy courts a - bove.

522 My Jesus, I love thee

GORDON 11 11. 11 11

1 My Je - sus, I love thee, I know thou art mine.
2 I love thee, be - cause thou hast first lov - ed me,
3 In man - sions of glo - ry and end - less de - light

For thee all the fol - lies of sin I re - sign.
and pur - chased my par - don on Cal - va - ry's tree.
I'll ev - er a - dore thee in heav - en so bright.

My gra - cious Re - deem - er, my Sav - ior art thou.
I love thee for wear - ing the thorns on thy brow.
I'll sing with the glit - ter - ing crown on my brow.

If ev - er I loved thee, my Je - sus, 'tis now.

Text: William R. Featherstone, ca. 1862, *Primitive Methodist Magazine,* 1862
Music: Adoniram J. Gordon, 1872, *The Service of Song for Baptist Churches,* 1876

Dear Lord and Father of mankind 523

REST (WHITTIER) 86. 886

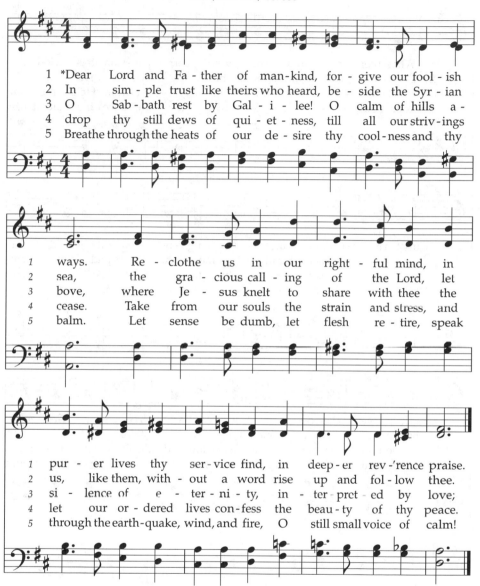

1 *Dear Lord and Fa - ther of man-kind, for - give our fool - ish
2 In sim - ple trust like theirs who heard, be - side the Syr - ian
3 O Sab-bath rest by Gal - i - lee! O calm of hills a -
4 drop thy still dews of qui - et - ness, till all our striv-ings
5 Breathe through the heats of our de - sire thy cool-ness and thy

1 ways. Re - clothe us in our right - ful mind, in
2 sea, the gra - cious call - ing of the Lord, let
3 bove, where Je - sus knelt to share with thee the
4 cease. Take from our souls the strain and stress, and
5 balm. Let sense be dumb, let flesh re - tire, speak

1 pur - er lives thy ser - vice find, in deep - er rev -'rence praise.
2 us, like them, with - out a word rise up and fol - low thee.
3 si - lence of e - ter - ni - ty, in - ter - pret - ed by love;
4 let our or - dered lives con-fess the beau - ty of thy peace.
5 through the earth-quake, wind, and fire, O still small voice of calm!

*Alternate phrase: Dear Lord, thou life of humankind

Text: John Greenleaf Whittier, *The Atlantic Monthly,* 1872
Music: Frederick C. Maker, *Congregational Church Hymnal,* 1887

524 What mercy and divine compassion

MIR IST ERBARMUNG 98. 98. 88 extended

1 What mer - cy and di - vine com - pas-sion has God in
2 E - ter - nal wrath should be my por - tion. The Lamb of
3 Great God, ac - cept my ad - o - ra-tion. Help me your
4 Your boun-teous grace is my as - sur-ance, the blood of

Christ re - vealed to me! My haugh-ty spir - it would not
God, for sin - ners slain, re-moved the curse and con - dem-
mer - cy to con - fess. In Je - sus Christ is my sal -
Christ my on - ly plea, your heart of love my con - so -

ask it, yet he be - stowed it, full and free. In God my
na - tion, his blood a - toned for ev - 'ry stain. God's love in
va - tion, he is my hope in life and death. His blood, his
la - tion un - til your glo - rious face I see. My theme, through

heart does now re - joice. I praise his grace with
Christ on Cal - v'ry's tree from guilt and shame has
right - eous - ness a - lone I claim be - fore your
nev - er - end - ing days, shall be your great re -

Text: Philipp F. Hiller, "Mir ist Erbarmung widerfahren," *Geistliches Liederkästlein,* Part II, 1767; tr. Frieda Kaufman, 1938,
         The Mennonite Hymnary, 1940, alt.
         Translation copyright ©1940 Board of Publications of the General Conference Mennonite Church of North America
Music: *Allgemeines Choral-Buch,* 1819

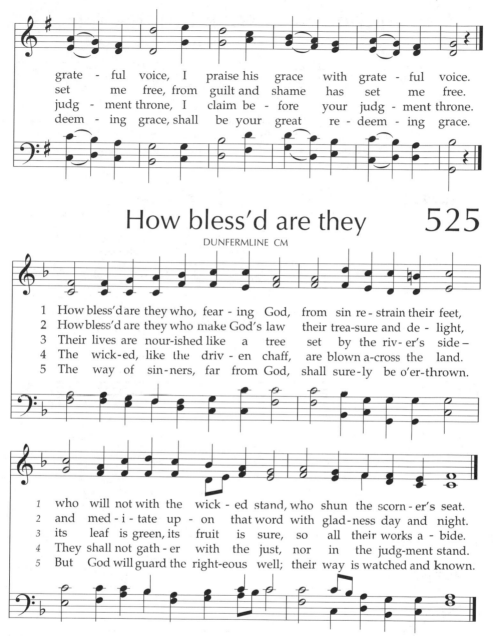

grate - ful voice, I praise his grace with grate - ful voice.
set me free, from guilt and shame has set me free.
judg - ment throne, I claim be - fore your judg - ment throne.
deem - ing grace, shall be your great re - deem - ing grace.

How bless'd are they 525

DUNFERMLINE CM

1 How bless'd are they who, fear - ing God, from sin re - strain their feet,
2 How bless'd are they who make God's law their trea-sure and de - light,
3 Their lives are nour-ished like a tree set by the riv - er's side –
4 The wick-ed, like the driv - en chaff, are blown a-cross the land.
5 The way of sin-ners, far from God, shall sure-ly be o'er-thrown.

1 who will not with the wick - ed stand, who shun the scorn - er's seat.
2 and med - i - tate up - on that word with glad-ness day and night.
3 its leaf is green, its fruit is sure, so all their works a - bide.
4 They shall not gath - er with the just, nor in the judg-ment stand.
5 But God will guard the right-eous well; their way is watched and known.

Text: based on Psalm 1, *Psalter*, 1912, alt.
Music: *The CL Psalmes of David,* 1615

526 In the rifted Rock I'm resting

RIFTED ROCK 87. 87 with refrain

1 In the rift - ed Rock I'm rest - ing, safe - ly
2 Long pur - sued by sin and Sa - tan, wea - ry,
3 Peace which pass - eth un - der - stand - ing, joy the
4 In the rift - ed Rock I'll hide me, till the

shel - tered, I a - bide. There no foes nor storms mo -
sad, I longed for rest. Then I found this heav'n - ly
world can nev - er give, now in Je - sus, I am
storms of life are past, all se - cure in this bless'd

lest me, while with - in the cleft I hide.
shel - ter, o - pened in my Sav - ior's breast.
find - ing; in his smiles of love I live.
ref - uge, heed - ing not the fierc - est blast.

Refrain

Now I'm rest - ing, sweet - ly rest - ing, in the

Text: Mary Dagworthy James, *The Chautauqua Collection*, 1875
Music: W. Warren Bentley, *The Chautauqua Collection*, 1875

cleft once made for me. Je-sus, bless-ed Rock of

ag - es, I will hide my - self in thee.

Lord Jesus, think on me 527

SOUTHWELL SM

1 Lord Je-sus, think on me, and purge a - way my sin. From
2 Lord Je-sus, think on me, with anx - ious cares op-pressed. Let
3 Lord Je-sus, think on me, nor let me go a-stray. Through
4 Lord Je-sus, think on me, when flows the tem-pest high. When
5 Lord Je-sus, think on me, that, when the flood is past, I

1 earth-born pas-sions set me free, and make me pure with - in.
2 me thy lov-ing ser-vant be, and taste thy prom-ised rest.
3 dark-ness and per - plex - i - ty point out the heav'n-ly way.
4 daunt-ed by the en - e - my, O Sav - ior, be thou nigh.
5 may th'e-ter - nal bright-ness see, and share thy joy at last.

Text: Synesius of Cyrene, ca. 400, *Tenth Ode by Synesius*; tr. Allen W. Chatfield, *Songs and Hymns of the Earliest Greek Christian Poets*, 1876
Music: W. Damon's *Psalmes of David*, 1579

528 I stand amazed in the presence

HOW MARVELOUS 87. 87 with refrain

1 I stand a-mazed in the pres - ence of
2 For me it was in the gar - den he
3 He took my sins and my sor - rows, he
4 When with the ran-somed in glo - ry his

Je - sus the Naz - a - rene, and won-der how he could
prayed, "Not my will, but thine." He had no tears for his
made them his ver - y own. He bore the bur - den to
face I at last shall see, 'twill be my joy through the

love me, a sin - ner con-demned, un - clean.
own griefs, but sweat drops of blood for mine.
Cal - v'ry, and suf - fered and died a - lone.
ag - es to sing of his love for me.

Refrain

How mar-vel-ous! How won-der-ful!
Oh, how mar-vel-ous! Oh, how won-der-ful! And my song shall ev - er be:

Text: Charles H. Gabriel (Sts. 1-3), *Praises*, 1905, anonymous (St. 4), *Praises*, 1905
Music: Charles H. Gabriel, *Praises*, 1905

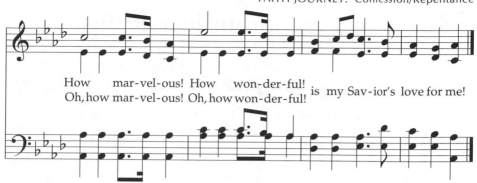

How mar-vel-ous! How won-der-ful!
Oh, how mar-vel-ous! Oh, how won-der-ful! is my Sav-ior's love for me!

Father, I stretch my hands to thee 529

MARTYRDOM CM

1 Fa - ther, I stretch my hands to thee, no oth -
2 What did thine on - ly Son en - dure, be - fore
3 Sure - ly thou canst not let me die! O speak
4 Au - thor of faith! to thee I lift my wea -

er help I know. If thou with - draw thy - self
I drew my breath! What pain, what la - bor to
and I shall live, and here I will un - wea -
ry, long - ing eyes. O let me now re - ceive

from me, ah! whith - er shall I go?
se - cure my soul from end - less death!
ried lie, till thou thy Spir - it give.
that gift! My soul with - out it dies.

Text: Charles Wesley, *Psalms and Hymns*, 1741
Music: Hugh Wilson; lined by J. Jefferson Cleveland and Verolga Nix, 1979
        Arrangement copyright ©1979 J. Jefferson Cleveland and Verolga Nix

530 What wondrous love is this

WONDROUS LOVE 12 9. 12. 12 9

1 What won-drous love is this, O my soul, O my
2 When I was sink-ing down, sink-ing down, sink-ing
3 To God and to the Lamb I will sing, I will
4 And when from death I'm free I'll sing on, I'll sing

soul? What won-drous love is this, O my soul?
down, when I was sink-ing down, sink-ing down,
sing, to God and to the Lamb I will sing,
on, and when from death I'm free, I'll sing on,

What won-drous love is this that caused the Lord of
when I was sink-ing down be - neath God's right - eous
to God and to the Lamb who is the great I
and when from death I'm free, I'll sing and joy - ful

bliss to bear the dread-ful curse for my soul, for my
frown, Christ laid a - side his crown for my soul, for my
Am, while mil-lions join the theme, I will sing, I will
be, and through e - ter - ni - ty I'll sing on, I'll sing

Text: *Cluster of Spiritual Songs ... and Sacred Poems,* 3rd ed., 1823
Music: American folk hymn, *Southern Harmony,* 1840; harmonized by Alice Parker
Harmonization copyright ©1966 Alice Parker

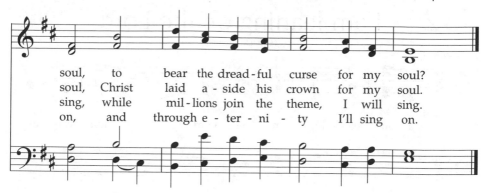

soul, to bear the dread-ful curse for my soul?
soul, Christ laid a-side his crown for my soul.
sing, while mil-lions join the theme, I will sing.
on, and through e-ter-ni-ty I'll sing on.

Ah, what shame I have to bear 531

IMAYŌ 75.75

1 Ah, what shame I have to bear,
2 In this hut I sleep and wake,
3 Tat - tered sleeves are wet with dew

for I left my home to pur - sue an
tak - ing care of swine. No one has pit -
when I think of home. Wak - ing from my

emp - ty dream, spent my life in vain!
y on me. Loud blows the chill - y wind.
fool - ish dreams, to my home I'll go.

Text: Sōgo Matsumoto, 1895; tr. Esther Hibbard, 1962
        Copyright © Japanese Hymnal Committee
Music: Japanese melody, 12th c.

532 I am leaning on the Lord

TURNER Irregular

Refrain

I am lean-ing on the Lord, I am lean-ing on the Lord, I am lean-ing on the Lord, who died on Cal-va-ry.

Fine

Leader

1 Tell me, how did you feel when you
2 Did you love ev-'ry-bod-y when you
3 Did your soul feel hap-py when you

Text: African-American spiritual
Music: African-American spiritual; adapted and arranged by William F. Smith, 1986
Adaptation and arrangement copyright ©1989 The United Methodist Publishing House

come out,
come out,
come out,
All
come out   the wil - der - ness,   come out   the wil - der - ness,

Leader
Tell   me,   how   did you feel   when you
Did   you   love   ev - 'ry - bod - y   when you
Did   your   soul   feel   hap - py when you

come out   the wil - der - ness?

D.C.
come out,
come out,
come out,
All   D.C.
come out   the wil - der - ness,   lean - ing   on   the   Lord?

533 Jesus, my Lord, my God, my all

ADORO (ST. CHRYSOSTOM) 88. 88. 88

1 Je-sus, my Lord, my God, my all, hear me, bless'd Sav - ior,
2 Je-sus, too late I thee have sought. How can I love thee
3 Je-sus, what didst thou find in me that thou hast dealt so
4 Je-sus, of thee shall be my song. To thee my heart and

when I call. Hear me, and from thy dwell - ing place pour
as I ought? And how ex - tol thy match - less fame, the
lov - ing - ly? How great the joy that thou hast brought! oh,
soul be - long. All that I am or have is thine, and

down the rich - es of thy grace.
glo - rious beau - ty of thy name?
far ex - ceed - ing hope or thought! Je-sus, my Lord, I
thou, my Sav - ior, thou art mine.

thee a - dore. Oh, may I love thee more and more.

Text: Henry Collins, *Hymns for Missions*, 1854
Music: Joseph Barnby, *Musical Times*, 1871

Prince of peace, control my will 534

OYER 77. 77

1 Prince of peace, con - trol my will. Bid this strug - gling
2 Thou hast bought me with thy blood, o - pened wide the
3 May thy will, not mine, be done. May thy will and
4 Sav - ior, at thy feet I fall, thou my life, my

heart be still. Bid my fears and doubt - ing cease,
gate to God. Peace I ask, but peace must be,
mine be one. Chase these doubt - ings from my heart,
God, my all! Let thy hap - py ser - vant be

hush my spir - it in - to peace.
Lord, in be - ing one with thee.
now thy per - fect peace im - part.
one for - ev - er more with thee.

Text: Mary A. Serrett Barber, *Hymns for the Use of the Methodist Episcopal Church, Revised Edition*, 1853
Music: Bradley P. Lehman, 1984
            Copyright ©1984 Bradley P. Lehman

535 Who now would follow Christ

WARUM BETRÜBST DU DICH, MEIN HERZ 886. 86

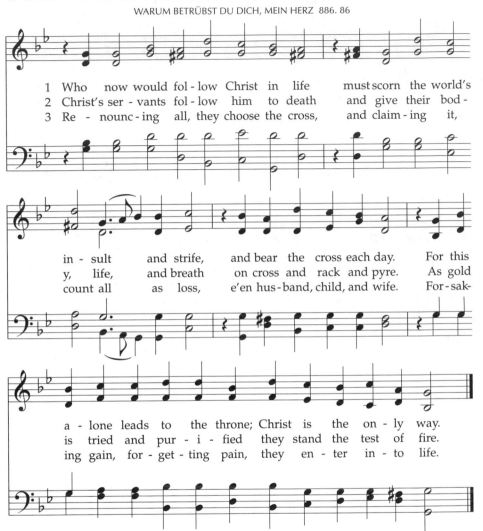

1 Who now would fol-low Christ in life   must scorn the world's
2 Christ's ser-vants fol-low him to death   and give their bod-
3 Re-nounc-ing all, they choose the cross,   and claim-ing it,

in - sult   and strife,   and bear the cross each day.   For this
y, life,   and breath   on cross and rack and pyre.   As gold
count all   as loss,   e'en hus-band, child, and wife.   For-sak-

a - lone leads to the throne; Christ is the on - ly way.
is tried and pur - i - fied they stand the test of fire.
ing gain, for - get - ting pain, they en - ter in - to life.

Text: "Wer Christo jetzt will folgen nach," *Ausbund,* 1564; tr. David Augsburger, 1962, *The Mennonite Hymnal,* 1969, revised 1983
       Translation copyright ©1969, 1983 David Augsburger
Music: Bartholomeus Monoetius, 1565; harmonized by J. Harold Moyer, 1965
       Harmonization copyright ©1969 Faith and Life Press/Mennonite Publishing House

Take up your cross

536

KEDRON LM

1 "Take up your cross," the Sav - ior said, "if
2 Take up your cross, let not its weight fill
3 Take up your cross, nor heed the shame, and
4 Take up your cross then, in his strength, and
5 Take up your cross, and fol - low on, nor

1 you would my dis - ci - ple be. Take up your cross, with
2 your weak soul with vain a - larm. His strength shall bear your
3 let your fool - ish pride be still. The Lord for you ac -
4 calm - ly sin's temp - ta - tions brave. It guides you to a
5 think till death to lay it down, for on - ly they who

1 will - ing heart, and hum - bly fol - low af - ter me."
2 spir - it up, and brace your heart and nerve your arm.
3 cept - ed death up - on a cross on Cal - v'ry's hill.
4 bet - ter home, and points to glo - ry o'er the grave.
5 bear the cross may hope to wear the glo - rious crown.

Text: Charles W. Everest, *Visions of Death and Other Poems,* 1833, alt.
Music: American folk melody, Joseph Funk's *Genuine Church Music,* 1st ed., 1832; harmonized by The Hymnal Project
        Harmonization ©1989 The Hymnal Project

537 En medio de la vida
(You are the God within life)

1 En me-dio de la   vi - da   es-tás pre-sen-te_oh Dios,
2 Tú_es-tás en la_a - le-grí - a   y_es-tás en el do - lor,
1 You are the God with - in life, pres-ent where-e'er we live,
2 We   feel you in our suf - f'ring, and in our hap - pi - ness,

mas cer - ca que mi_a - lien - to,   sus - ten - to de mi   ser.
com - par - tes con tu   pue - blo   la lu - cha por el   bien.
clos - er than all our sigh - ing, sus - tain - ing pow'r you give.
fight-ing for hu - man wel - fare, shar-ing with ev - 'ry - one.

Tú_im-pul - sas en mis ve - nas   mi san-gre_al pal - pi - tar
En   Cris - to_tú has ve - ni - do   la vi - da_a re - di - mir
In - side our ver - y   bod - ies, you pump the blood of life;
In   Christ, the In - car - na - tion, you have re-deemed our lives,

y_el rit - mo de la   vi - da   vas dan-do_al co - ra - zón.
y_en pren - da de tu   rei - no   el mun-do_a con - ver - tir.
rhy - thm in ev - 'ry heart - beat drums out the pulse of life.
pledg-ing to us your king - dom, you came, the world to change.

Estribillo (Refrain)

Oh Dios de cie - lo_y   tie - rra, te sir - vo des - de_a - quí:
O God of earth and   heav - en, we serve you where we   are.

Text: Mortimer Arias, *Celebremos, Segundo Parte,* 1983; tr. George Lockwood IV
Music: Antonio Auza, *Celebremos, Segundo Parte,* 1983; arranged by Homero Perera
    Text and music copyright © Mortimer Arias

te a - mo en mis her - ma - nos, te a - do - ro en la cre a - ción.
We love you in all peo - ple, we praise you in your world!

Lead me, Lord 538

Lead me, Lord, lead me in thy right-eous-ness. Make thy way

plain be - fore my face. For it is thou, Lord, thou, Lord,

on - ly that mak-est me dwell in safe - ty. A - men

Text: based on Psalms 5:8 and 4:8
Music: Samuel S. Wesley, "Lead Me, Lord" (anthem), 1861

539 Make me a captive, Lord

LEOMINSTER SMD

1 Make me a cap-tive, Lord, and then I shall be free.
2 My heart is weak and poor till it a mas-ter find.
3 My pow'r is faint and low till I have learned to serve.
4 My will is not my own till thou hast made it thine.

Force me to ren-der up my sword, and I shall con-qu'ror be.
It has no spring of ac-tion sure – it var-ies with the wind.
It wants the need-ed fire to glow, it wants the breeze to nerve.
If it would reach a mon-arch's throne it must its crown re - sign.

I sink in life's a - larms when by my - self I stand. Im-
It can - not free - ly move till thou hast wrought its chain. En-
It can - not drive the world un - til it - self be driv'n. Its
It on - ly stands un - bent, a - mid the clash - ing strife, when

pris - on me with - in thine arms, and strong shall be my hand.
slave it with thy match-less love, and death-less it shall reign.
flag can on - ly be un-furled when thou shalt breathe from heav'n.
on thy bo-som it has leant, and found in thee its life.

Text: George Matheson, *Sacred Songs*, 1890
Music: George W. Martin, *The Journal of Part Music, Vol. II,* 1862; harmonized by Arthur S. Sullivan, *Church Hymns with Tunes,* 1874

Strong, righteous man of Galilee 540

MELITA 88. 88. 88

1 Strong, right-eous man of Gal-i-lee, robed with thy peace we
2 Firm, peace-ful man of Gal-i-lee, girt with thy strength we
3 Calm, suf-f'ring man of Gal-i-lee, clad in thy grace we
4 God's peace-ful man of Gal-i-lee, Love's tri-umph, we shall

fol-low thee — in tem-ple court, thy cleans-ing rod
fol-low thee — not to re-venge, but heal and pray,
fol-low thee — love at the well, share Mar-tha's loss,
fol-low thee — to crum-ble ev-'ry boun-d'ry wall,

on greed and lies, the wrath of God. Robed with thy peace we
to turn the cheek, and trib-ute pay. Girt with thy strength we
for-give the nails, and take the cross. Clad in thy grace we
build high-ways to the hearts of all. Love's tri-umph, we shall

fol-low thee, strong, right-eous man of Gal-i-lee.
fol-low thee, firm, peace-ful man of Gal-i-lee.
fol-low thee, calm, suf-f'ring man of Gal-i-lee.
fol-low thee, God's peace-ful man of Gal-i-lee.

Text: Harry W. Farrington, 1921
          Copyright © Mrs. Harry Webb Farrington
Music: John B. Dykes, *Hymns Ancient and Modern*, 1861

541 How clear is our vocation, Lord

REPTON 86. 88. 66

1 How clear is our vo - ca - tion, Lord, when
2 But if, for - get - ful, we should find your
3 We mar - vel how your saints be - come in
4 In what you give us, Lord, to do, to -

once we heed your call: to live ac - cord - ing
yoke is hard to bear; if world - ly pres - sures
hin - dranc - es more sure, whose joy - ful vir - tues
geth - er or a - lone, in old rou - tines and

to your word, and dai - ly learn, re -
fray the mind, and love it - self can -
put to shame the ca - sual way we
ven - tures new, may we not cease to

freshed, re - stored, that you are Lord of
not un - wind its tan - gled skein of
wear your name, and by our faults ob -
look to you, the cross you hung up -

all, and will not let us fall.
care, our in - ward life re - pair.
scure your pow'r to cleanse and cure.
on - all you en - deav - ored done.

Text: Fred Pratt Green, 1981, *The Hymns and Ballads of Fred Pratt Green,* 1982
        Copyright ©1982 Hope Publishing Co.
Music: Charles H. H. Parry, *Judith,* 1888

Holy Spirit, gracious Guest 542

ANDERSON 77.75

1 Ho - ly Spir - it, gra - cious Guest,
2 Faith that moun - tains could re - move,
3 Though I as a mar - tyr bleed,
4 Love is kind and suf - fers long,
5 Proph - e - cy will fade a - way,
6 Faith and hope and love we see,

1 hear and grant our heart's re - quest for that gift su -
2 tongues of earth or heav'n a - bove, knowl - edge, all things,
3 give my goods the poor to feed, all is vain if
4 love is pure and thinks no wrong, love than death it -
5 melt - ing in the light of day. Love will ev - er
6 join - ing hand in hand a - gree — but the great - est

1 preme and best: ho - ly, heav'n - ly love.
2 emp - ty prove if I have no love.
3 love I need; there - fore, give me love.
4 self more strong; there - fore, give us love.
5 with us stay; there - fore, give us love.
6 of the three, and the best, is love.

Text: based on 1 Corinthians 13, Christopher Wordsworth, *The Holy Year,* 1862; revised in *Hymns for Today's Church,* 1982
         Copyright ©1982 Hope Publishing Co.
Music: Jane Marshall, 1985, *Hymnal Supplement II,* 1987
         Copyright ©1985 Hope Publishing Co.

543 I long for your commandments

76. 76. 876

1 I long for your com-mand - ments; your judg-ments all are good.
2 With-out your lamp to guide me I wan - der from the way.
3 Oh, how I love your knowl - edge, more pre - cious than pure gold.

With - in your word is wis - dom; your teach-ings un - der-stood
With-out your laws and pre - cepts, I stum - ble in the dark.
It sat - is - fies like hon - ey, a sweet-ness on my tongue.

are com - fort to my spir - it's need and in the night my
Your un - der-stand-ings are my hope that I may run in
It leads me to sal - va-tion's door where you have spread your

so - lace. Your stat - utes are my song.
free - dom. Your ways are my re - lease.
ta - ble. O lead me to your home.

Text: based on Psalm 119:131-135, Jean Janzen, 1991
        Copyright ©1991 Jean Wiebe Janzen
Music: Heinrich Schütz, *Psalmen Davids* ..., revised and enlarged ed., 1661

When we walk with the Lord 544

TRUST AND OBEY 669D with refrain

1 When we walk with the Lord in the light of his word, what a
2 Not a bur-den we bear, not a sor-row we share, but our
3 But we nev-er can prove the de-lights of his love, un-til
4 Then in fel-low-ship sweet we will sit at his feet, or we'll

glo - ry he sheds on our way! While we do his good will, he a -
toil he doth rich-ly re- pay. Not a grief nor a loss, not a
all on the al-tar we lay, for the fa-vor he shows, and the
walk by his side in the way. What he says we will do, where he

bides with us still, and with all who will trust and o - bey.
frown nor a cross, but is bless'd if we trust and o - bey.
joy he be - stows, are for them who will trust and o - bey.
sends we will go, nev - er fear, on - ly trust and o - bey.

Refrain

Trust and o - bey, for there's no oth - er way to be

hap - py in Je - sus, but to trust and o - bey.

Text: John H. Sammis, *Hymns Old and New*, 1887
Music: Daniel B. Towner, *Hymns Old and New*, 1887

545 Be thou my vision

SLANE 10 10. 9 10

1 Be thou my vi - sion, O Lord of my heart;
2 Be thou my wis - dom, be thou my true word;
3 Be thou my buck - ler, my sword for the fight.
4 Rich - es I heed not, nor vain, emp - ty praise;
5 High King of heav - en, when vic - t'ry is won

1 naught be all else to me save that thou art.
2 I ev - er with thee, and thou with me, Lord.
3 Be thou my dig - ni - ty, thou my de - light,
4 thou mine in - her - i - tance, now and al - ways.
5 may I reach heav - en's joys, O bright heav'n's Sun!

1 Thou my best thought, by day or by night,
2 Thou my great Fa - ther, thy child may I be,
3 thou my soul's shel - ter, thou my high tower.
4 Thou and thou on - ly, first in my heart,
5 Heart of my heart, what - ev - er be - fall,

1 wak - ing or sleep - ing, thy pres - ence my light.
2 thou in me dwell - ing, and I one with thee.
3 Raise thou me heav'n - ward, O Pow'r of my pow'r.
4 high King of heav - en, my trea - sure thou art.
5 still be my vi - sion, O Rul - er of all.

Text: Ancient Irish, *Rob tu mo bhoile, a Comdi cride;* tr. Mary Elizabeth Byrne, *Erin,* Vol. II, 1905, versified by Eleanor Hull
Music: Irish melody, *Old Irish Folk Music and Songs,* 1909; harmonized by Martin Shaw, *Enlarged Songs of Praise,* 1931, alt.
Harmonization copyright © Oxford University Press, London

Guide my feet

546

GUIDE MY FEET Irregular

1,6 Guide my feet while I run this race, yes, my Lord!

Guide my feet while I run this race, yes, my Lord!

Guide my feet while I run this race, for I don't want to run this race in vain! (race in vain!)

2 Hold my hand ...
3 Stand by me ...
4 I'm your child ...
5 Search my heart ...

Text: African-American spiritual
Music: African-American spiritual; harmonized by Wendell Whalum
    Harmonization copyright © Wendell Whalum

547 My dear Redeemer and my Lord

SOCIAL BAND LMD

1 My dear Re - deem - er and my Lord, I read my du - ty in thy
2 Cold moun - tains and the mid - night air wit - nessed the fer - vor of your

word. But in thy life the law ap - pears drawn out in
prayer. The des - ert thy temp - ta - tions knew, thy con - flict

liv - ing char - ac - ters. Such was thy truth, and such thy
and thy vic - t'ry too. Be thou my pat - tern; make me

zeal, such def - 'rence to thy Fa - ther's will, such love, and
bear more of thy gra - cious im - age here. Then God the

Text: Isaac Watts, *Hymns and Spiritual Songs*, Book II, 1707-1709, alt.
Music: American folk melody, *The Christian Harmony*, 1805; harmonized by J. Harold Moyer, 1965
Harmonization copyright ©1969 Faith and Life Press/Mennonite Publishing House

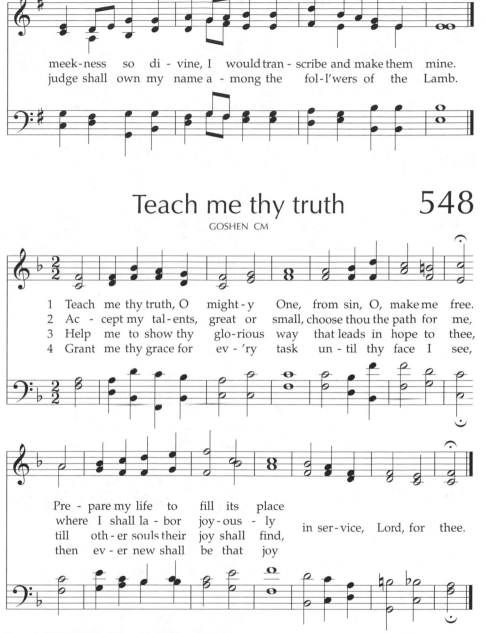

meek-ness so di - vine, I would tran - scribe and make them mine.
judge shall own my name a - mong the fol-l'wers of the Lamb.

Teach me thy truth

548

GOSHEN CM

1 Teach me thy truth, O might-y One, from sin, O, make me free.
2 Ac - cept my tal-ents, great or small, choose thou the path for me,
3 Help me to show thy glo-rious way that leads in hope to thee,
4 Grant me thy grace for ev - 'ry task un - til thy face I see,

Pre - pare my life to fill its place
where I shall la - bor joy-ous - ly   in ser-vice, Lord, for thee.
till oth - er souls their joy shall find,
then ev - er new shall be that joy

Text: Edith Witmer, 1937, *Life Songs No. 2*, 1938
Music: Walter E. Yoder, *Life Songs No. 2*, 1938

549 Savior of my soul

JOHN NAAS 55. 88. 55

1 Sav-ior of my soul, let me choose thy goal. Self to thee I would sur-ren-der, choose thy cross, be thy con-ten-der. Let me choose thy goal, Sav-ior of my soul.

2 Christ, ex-tend thy hand, for I can-not stand. Thy soul's pow'r, O share with me, and I thy fol-l'wer close will be. I am too weak to stand; Christ, ex-tend thy hand.

3 Je-sus, grant me grace so to run my race, that I may vic-to-rious be. Thy fa-vor show and pros-per me. So as I run my race, Je-sus, grant me grace.

Text: John (Johannes) Naas, "Heiland meiner Seel'," *Die Kleine Harfe*, 1792; tr. Lillian Grisso
Music: William Beery, 1944, *The Brethren Hymnal*, 1951

Living and dying with Jesus 550

SMJET ZIVJET KRISTU 10 10. 10 9 extended

1 Liv - ing and dy-ing with   Je - sus our Lord,   no great - er
2 Free - ly to own   the   Mar - tyr's   shame;   glo - ry
3 Life lived for Je - sus   yet while it's day,   sad low-'ring

joy can the whole world af-ford.   Wheth-er in suf-f'ring, e - ven while
crowns e'en the suf-f'rer's pain,   ev - er with Je - sus   in heav'n-ly
dark-ness   can't long hold sway. Fer - vent-ly serv - ing, los - ing heart

dy - ing,   joy be-yond mea-sure is our re-ward. Wheth-er in suf-f'ring,
plac-es,   for - ev - er home with God to re-main.   Ev - er with Je - sus
nev - er, God's lav-ish grace guards all on the way.   Fer - vent-ly serv - ing,

e - ven while dy-ing,   joy be-yond mea - sure   is our re-ward.
in heav'n-ly plac-es,   for - ev - er home with God to re-main.
los - ing heart nev-er, God's lav-ish grace guards all on the way.

Text: Croatian hymn, *Duhovne Pjesme*, ca. 1950; tr. Sara Wenger Shenk
         Translation copyright ©1990 Sara Wenger Shenk
Music: Slavic melody, *Duhovne Pjesme*, ca. 1950

551 In the stillness of the evening

I DE SENE TIMERS STILLHET 88. 88. 88

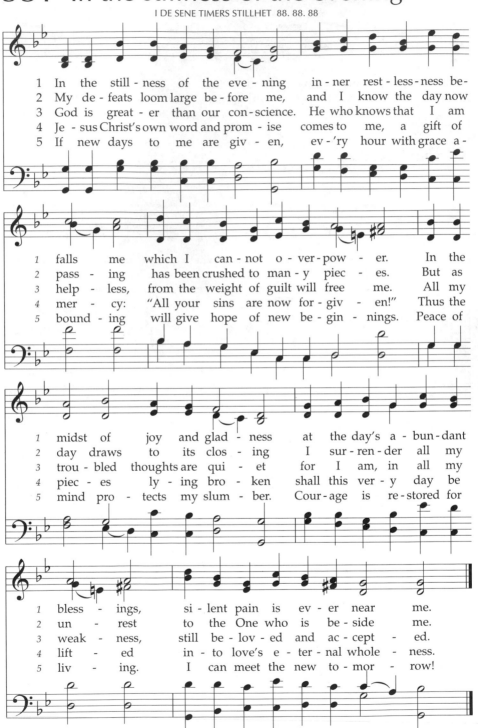

1 In the still-ness of the eve-ning in-ner rest-less-ness be-
2 My de-feats loom large be-fore me, and I know the day now
3 God is great-er than our con-science. He who knows that I am
4 Je-sus Christ's own word and prom-ise comes to me, a gift of
5 If new days to me are giv-en, ev-'ry hour with grace a-

1 falls me which I can-not o-ver-pow-er. In the
2 pass-ing has been crushed to man-y piec-es. But as
3 help-less, from the weight of guilt will free me. All my
4 mer-cy: "All your sins are now for-giv-en!" Thus the
5 bound-ing will give hope of new be-gin-nings. Peace of

1 midst of joy and glad-ness at the day's a-bun-dant
2 day draws to its clos-ing I sur-ren-der all my
3 trou-bled thoughts are qui-et for I am, in all my
4 piec-es ly-ing bro-ken shall this ver-y day be
5 mind pro-tects my slum-ber. Cour-age is re-stored for

1 bless-ings, si-lent pain is ev-er near me.
2 un-rest to the One who is be-side me.
3 weak-ness, still be-lov-ed and ac-cept-ed.
4 lift-ed in-to love's e-ter-nal whole-ness.
5 liv-ing. I can meet the new to-mor-row!

Text: Svein Ellingsen, *I de sene timers stillhet*, 1971; tr. Hedwig T. Durnbaugh, *Praises Resound!*, 1991
Translation copyright ©1990 Hedwig T. Durnbaugh
Music: Harald Herresthal, 1977
Original text and music copyright ©1978 Norsk Musikforlag, A/S, Oslo

By gracious powers

552

INTERCESSOR 11 10. 11 10

1 By gra-cious pow'rs so won-der-ful-ly shel-tered,
2 Yet is this heart by its old foe tor-ment-ed,
3 And when this cup you give is filled to brim-ming
4 Yet when a-gain in this same world you give us

and con-fi-dent-ly wait-ing come what may,
still e-vil days bring bur-dens hard to bear.
with bit-ter sor-row, hard to un-der-stand,
the joy we had, the bright-ness of your sun,

we know that God is with us night and morn-ing,
O give our fright-ened souls the sure sal-va-tion,
we take it thank-ful-ly and with-out trem-bling,
we shall re-mem-ber all the days we lived through,

and nev-er fails to greet us each new day.
for which, O Lord, you taught us to pre-pare.
out of so good and so be-lov'd a hand.
and our whole life shall then be yours a-lone.

Text: based on Ephesians 5:20, Dietrich Bonhöffer, 1945, *The Cost of Discipleship*, 2nd ed., 1959; tr. Fred Pratt Green, 1972, *Cantate Domino*, 1974
Translation copyright ©1974 Hope Publishing Co.
Music: Charles H. H. Parry, *Hymns Ancient and Modern*, 1904

553 I am weak and I need thy strength

LEAD ME, GUIDE ME* Irregular with refrain

1 I am weak and I need thy strength and pow'r to help me o - ver my weak - est hour. Help me through the dark - ness thy face to see. Lead me, O Lord, lead me.

2 Help me tread in the paths of right - eous - ness. Be my aid when Sa - tan and sin op - press. I am put - ting all my trust in thee. Lead me, O Lord, lead me.

3 I am lost if you take your hand from me. I am blind with - out thy light to see. Lord, just al - ways let me thy ser - vant be. Lead me, O Lord, lead me.

*Original title

Text: Doris M. Akers
Music: Doris M. Akers

Refrain

Lead me, guide me, a - long the way,

for if you lead me, I can - not stray.

Lord, let me walk each day with thee.

Lead me, O Lord, lead me.

Our Father who art in heaven 554
(Pater noster qui es in coelis)

Irregular

Ostinato

Fine

Our__ Fa - ther who art in heav - en, our__
Pa - ter nos - ter qui es in coe - lis, Pa - ter

555   I need thee every hour

NEED 64. 64 with refrain

1 I need thee ev-'ry hour, most gra - cious Lord.
2 I need thee ev-'ry hour, stay thou near - by.
3 I need thee ev-'ry hour, in joy or pain.
4 I need thee ev-'ry hour, teach me thy will,
5 I need thee ev-'ry hour, most ho - ly One.

1 No ten - der voice like thine can peace af - ford.
2 Temp - ta - tions lose their pow'r when thou art nigh.
3 Come quick - ly and a - bide, or life is vain.
4 and thy rich prom - is - es in me ful - fill.
5 O make me thine in - deed, thou bless - ed Son.

Refrain

I need thee, oh, I need thee, ev - 'ry hour I need thee.

O bless me now, my Sav - ior, I come to thee.

Text: Annie S. Hawks, 1872, *Royal Diadem for the Sunday School*, 1873
Music: Robert Lowry, 1872, *Royal Diadem for the Sunday School*, 1873

Lord, thou hast searched me 556

TENDER THOUGHT LM

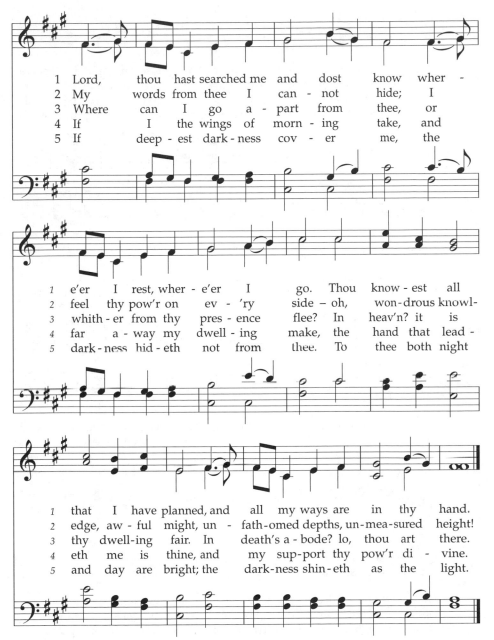

1 Lord, thou hast searched me and dost know wher-
2 My words from thee I can-not hide; I
3 Where can I go a-part from thee, or
4 If I the wings of morn-ing take, and
5 If deep-est dark-ness cov-er me, the

1 e'er I rest, wher-e'er I go. Thou know-est all
2 feel thy pow'r on ev-'ry side – oh, won-drous knowl-
3 whith-er from thy pres-ence flee? In heav'n? it is
4 far a-way my dwell-ing make, the hand that lead-
5 dark-ness hid-eth not from thee. To thee both night

1 that I have planned, and all my ways are in thy hand.
2 edge, aw-ful might, un- fath-omed depths, un-mea-sured height!
3 thy dwell-ing fair. In death's a-bode? lo, thou art there.
4 eth me is thine, and my sup-port thy pow'r di-vine.
5 and day are bright; the dark-ness shin-eth as the light.

Text: based on Psalm 139, *The Psalter Hymnal,* 1927
Music: Ananias Davisson, *Kentucky Harmony,* 1816; harmonized by The Hymnal Project
        Harmonization copyright ©1991 The Hymnal Project

557 O God, in restless living

RUTHERFORD 76. 76. 76. 75

1 O God, in rest-less liv-ing we lose our spir-it's peace.
2 Teach us, be-yond our striv-ing, the rich re-wards of rest.
3 Re-cep-tive make our spir-its, our need is to be still.
4 We grow not wise by strug-gling, we gain but things by strain.

Calm our un-wise con-fu-sion, bid thou our clam-or cease.
Who does not live se-rene-ly is nev-er deep-ly bless'd.
As dawn fades flick-'ring can-dle, so dim our anx-ious will.
We cease to wa-ter gar-dens, when comes thy plen-teous rain.

Let anx-ious hearts grow qui-et, like pools at eve-ning still,
O tran-quil, ra-diant Sun-light, bring thou our lives to flow'r,
Re-veal thy ra-diance through us, thine am-ple strength re-lease.
O, beau-ti-fy our spir-its in rest-ful-ness from strife,

till thy re-flect-ed heav-ens all our spir-its fill.
less wea-ried with our ef-fort, more a-ware of pow'r.
Not ours, but thine the tri-umph in the pow'r of peace.
en-rich our souls in se-cret with a-bun-dant life.

Text: Harry Emerson Fosdick, 1931
Music: Edward F. Rimbault, *Psalms and Hymns for Divine Worship*, 1867

When the storms of life are raging 558

STAND BY ME 83. 83. 77. 83

1 When the storms of life are rag - ing,
2 In the midst of trib - u - la - tion,
3 In the midst of faults and fail-ures, stand by me; (stand by me)
4 In the midst of per - se - cu - tion,
5 When I'm grow-ing old and fee - ble,

1 when the storms of life are rag - ing,
2 in the midst of trib - u - la - tion,
3 in the midst of faults and fail-ures, stand by me. (stand by me)
4 in the midst of per - se - cu - tion,
5 when I'm grow - ing old and fee - ble,

1 When the world is toss-ing me, like a ship up-on the sea,
2 When the hosts of hell as-sail, and my strength be-gins to fail,
3 When I've done the best I can, and my friends mis-un-der-stand,
4 When my foes in war ar-ray, un-der - take to stop my way,
5 When my life be-comes a bur-den, and I'm near-ing chill-y Jor-dan,

1 thou who rul - est wind and wa - ter,
2 thou who nev - er lost a bat-tle,
3 thou who know-est all a-bout me, stand by me. (stand by me)
4 thou who sav - ed Paul and Si - las,
5 O thou Lil - y of the Val-ley,

Text: Charles A. Tindley, ca. 1906
Music: Charles A. Tindley, ca. 1906; arranged by William F. Smith, *The United Methodist Hymnal*, 1989

559 O thou, in whose presence

ZION'S PILGRIM 11 8. 11 8D

1 O thou, in whose pres-ence my soul takes de-light, on whom in af-
2 Oh, why should I wan-der an al-ien from thee, or cry in the

flic-tion I call, my com-fort by day, and my song in the night,
des-ert for bread? Thy foes will re-joice when my sor-rows they see,

my hope, my sal-va-tion, my all: Where dost thou, dear Shep-herd, re-
and smile at the tears I have shed. He looks, and ten thou-sands of

sort with thy sheep? To feed in the pas-tures of love? Say, why in the
an-gels re-joice, and myr-i-ads wait for his word. He speaks, and e-

val-ley of death should I weep, or lone in the wil-der-ness rove?
ter-ni-ty, filled with his voice, re-ech-oes the praise of the Lord.

Text: Joseph Swain, *Redemption, a Poem in Five Books*, 1791
Music: *Christian Lyre*, 1831; harmonized by J. Harold Moyer, 1965
        Harmonization copyright ©1969 Faith and Life Press/Mennonite Publishing House

In lonely mountain ways

560

GOLDEN HILL SM

1 In lone - ly moun - tain ways of
2 My jour - ney may be long, the
3 And though when eve - ning falls, a

this world's trial and care, my heart knows naught of
path - way rough and steep. Suf - fi - cient for each
stone my pil - low shapes, the vi - sion of our

fear - scarred days; the Mas - ter's hand is there!
day my song; my way the Lord does keep.
king - dom calls and here a Beth - el makes.

Text: Sugao Nishimura, 1903; tr. Paul R. Gregory
        Translation copyright ©1983 Paul R. Gregory
Music: Aaron Chapin, 1805, *Kentucky Harmony*, 1816

561 Give to the winds thy fears

HANTS SM extended

1 Give to the winds thy fears. Hope and be un - dis-
2 Through waves and clouds and storms, God gent - ly clears ___ thy
3 What though thou rul - est not, yet heav'n and earth ___ and
4 Thine ev - er - last - ing truth, O God, thy cease - less

mayed. God hears thy sighs and counts thy tears. God
way. Wait thou the time, so shall this night soon
hell pro - claim God sit - teth on the throne, and
love, sees all thy chil - dren's wants, and knows what

shall lift up thy head, ___ God shall lift up thy head.
end in joy - ous day, ___ soon end in joy - ous day.
rul - eth all things well, ___ and rul - eth all things well.
best for each will prove, ___ what best for each will prove.

Text: Paul Gerhardt, "Befiehl du deine Wege," *Praxis Pietatis Melica*, 1656; tr. John Wesley, *Hymns and Sacred Poems*, 1739, alt.
Music: Joseph Funk's *Harmonia Sacra* (new name for *Genuine Church Music* after four editions), 5th ed., 1851; harmonized by Alice Parker
        Harmonization copyright ©1991 Alice Parker

562 Nada te turbe

Na - da te tur - be, na - da te es - pan - te.

Quien a Dios tie - ne na - da le fal - ta. Na - da te tur - be,

na - da te_es - pan - te. Só - lo Dios bas - ta.*

*Translation: Let nothing trouble you, let nothing frighten you.
Whoever has God lacks nothing. God alone is enough.

Text: Santa Teresa de Jesus
Music: Jacques Berthier, *Songs and Prayers from Taizé*, 1991

I to the hills will lift mine eyes 563
DUNDEE CM

1 I   to the hills will lift mine eyes. From whence doth come mine aid?
2 Thy   foot he'll not let slide, nor will   he   slum-ber that thee keeps.
3 The   Lord thee keeps, the Lord thy shade   on   thy right hand doth stay.
4 The   Lord shall keep thy soul. He shall   pre - serve thee from all   ill.

My   safe - ty com - eth from the Lord,   who heav'n and earth hath made.
Be - hold, he that keeps Is - ra - el,   he   slum-bers   not, nor sleeps.
The   moon by night thee shall not smite,   nor   yet   the   sun by   day.
Hence-forth thy go - ing out and in   God keep for - ev - er   will.

Text: based on Psalm 121, *The Psalms of David in Meeter*, 1650
Music: *The CL Psalmes of David*, 1615

564 I am trusting thee, Lord Jesus

87. 87D

1 I am trust-ing thee, Lord Je - sus, I am trust-ing
2 I am trust-ing thee for par - don; hum-bly at thy
3 I am trust-ing thee for cleans-ing, spot-less in the
4 I am trust-ing thee to guide me; gent-ly thou a -

on - ly thee; trust-ing thee for full sal - va-tion, full sal-
feet I bow, for thy grace and ten-der mer - cy, for thy
crim-son flood; trust-ing thee to make me ho-ly by thine
lone dost lead, ev - 'ry day and hour sup - ply-ing gra-cious-

va - tion great and free.
peace I trust thee now.
own life - giv - ing blood. I am trust-ing thee, Lord Je - sus,
ly my ev - 'ry need.

my Re - deem - er and my God. I am trust-ing

Text: adapted from Frances R. Havergal, 1874, *Loyal Responses,* 1878
Music: Julius Dietrich, *Gemeinschaftsliederbuch,* Offenbach, 1894

thee, Lord Je - sus, to sus - tain me by thy word.

My faith looks up to thee 565

OLIVET 664. 6664

1 My faith looks up to thee, thou Lamb of Cal - va - ry,
2 May thy rich grace im - part strength to my faint-ing heart,
3 While life's dark maze I tread, and griefs a - round me spread,
4 When ends life's tran-sient dream, when death's cold, sul - len stream

Sav - ior di - vine. Now hear me while I pray, take all my
my zeal in - spire. As thou hast died for me, oh, may my
be thou my guide. Bid dark-ness turn to day, wipe sor-row's
shall o'er me roll, bless'd Sav - ior, then, in love, fear and dis-

guilt a - way, oh, let me from this day be whol - ly thine.
love to thee – pure, warm, and change -less be, a liv - ing fire.
tears a - way, nor let me ev - er stray from thee a - side.
trust re-move. Oh, bear me safe a-bove, a ran-somed soul.

Text: Ray Palmer, 1830, *Spiritual Songs for Social Worship*, 1832
Music: Lowell Mason, *Spiritual Songs for Social Worship*, 1832

566 In the cross of Christ I glory

RATHBUN 87. 87

1 In the cross of Christ I glo - ry, tow - 'ring
2 When the woes of life o'er - take me, hopes de -
3 When the sun of bliss is beam-ing light and
4 Bane and bless - ing, pain and plea-sure, by the

o'er the wrecks of time. All the light of sa - cred
ceive and fears an - noy, nev - er shall the cross for -
love up - on my way, from the cross the ra - diance
cross are sanc - ti - fied. Peace is there that knows no

sto - ry, gath - ers 'round its Head sub - lime.
sake me; lo! it glows with peace and joy.
stream-ing, adds more lus - ter to the day.
mea - sure, joys that through all time a - bide.

Text: John Bowring, *Hymns*, 1825
Music: Ithamar Conkey, 1849, *Collection of Psalms and Hymn Tunes*, 1851

How firm a foundation 567

FOUNDATION (BELLEVUE) 11 11. 11 11

1 How firm a foun-da-tion, ye saints of the Lord,
2 "Fear not, I am with thee; O be not dis-mayed,
3 "When through the deep wa-ters I call thee to go,
4 "When through fi-ery tri-als thy path-way shall lie,
5 "The soul that on Je-sus still leans for re-pose,

1 is laid for your faith in his ex-cel-lent Word!
2 for I am thy God, and will still give thee aid.
3 the riv-ers of sor-row shall not o-ver-flow,
4 my grace, all-suf-fi-cient, shall be thy sup-ply.
5 I will not, I will not de-sert to its foes.

1 What more can he say than to you he hath said,
2 I'll strength-en thee, help thee, and cause thee to stand,
3 for I will be with thee, thy trou-bles to bless,
4 The flame shall not hurt thee. I on-ly de-sign
5 That soul, though all hell should en-deav-or to shake,

1 to you who for ref-uge to Je-sus have fled?
2 up-held by my right-eous, om-ni-po-tent hand.
3 and sanc-ti-fy to thee thy deep-est dis-tress.
4 thy dross to con-sume, and thy gold to re-fine.
5 I'll nev-er, no nev-er, no nev-er for-sake!"

Text: "K" in Rippon's *Selection of Hymns,* 1787
Music: American folk melody, in Joseph Funk's *Genuine Church Music,* 1st ed., 1832

568 As spring the winter doth succeed

PSALM 9 LM

1 As spring the win - ter doth suc - ceed, and leaves the
2 My win - ter's past, my storms are gone, and for - mer
3 I have a Shel - ter from the storm, a Shad - ow
4 My Sun's re - turned with heal - ing wings; my soul and

na - ked trees do dress, the earth, once dead, is clothed in
clouds seem now all fled. But, if they must e - clipse a -
from the faint - ing heat. I have ac - cess un - to the
bod - y doth re - joice. My heart ex - ults and prais - es

green; at sun - shine each their joy ex - press.
gain, I'll run where I was nour - ish - ed.
throne where God doth dwell, so won - drous great.
sings to God who heard my wail - ing voice.

Text: Anne Bradstreet, 1657, alt.
Music: Henry Lawes, *A Paraphrase upon the Divine Poems*, 1638

569 Day by day, dear Lord

Irregular

Day by day, dear Lord, of thee three things I pray:

to see thee more clear - ly, love thee more dear - ly,

to see thee, love thee,

fol - low thee more near - ly, day by day.

Text: St. Richard of Chichester, 13th c.
Music: Harold W. Friedell, *Eight Orisons*
Copyright ©1960 H. W. Gray Co., Inc., c/o CPP/Belwin

We walk by faith 570

SHANTI CM

1,5 We walk by faith, and not by sight; no
2 We may not touch his hands and side, nor
3 Help then, O Lord, our un - be - lief, and
4 that when our life of faith is done, in

gra - cious words we hear of him who spoke as
fol - low where he trod, yet in his prom - ise
may our faith a - bound to call on you when
realms of clear - er light we may be - hold you

none e'er spoke, but we be - lieve him near.
we re - joice, and cry, "My Lord and God!"
you are near, and seek where you are found:
as you are in full and end - less sight.

Text: Henry Alford, *Psalms and Hymns*, 1844
Music: Marty Haugen, 1983, *Mass of Creation*, 1984
Copyright ©1984 G.I.A. Publications, Inc.

571 'Tis not with eyes of flesh we see

ST. PETERSBURG 88. 88. 88

1 'Tis not with eyes of flesh we see that Christ is
2 O Christ, you have the words of life – un - to no
3 Be - liev - ing thus, O Son of God, we walk with

God's a - noint - ed one. With eyes of faith we know that he
oth - er can we go. None but your - self can calm our strife,
you a - long life's way. We fol - low where your feet have trod

is God's be - lov - ed on - ly Son – e - ter - nal King en-
and none but you our hopes can know. Since you have walked this
un - to the realms of glo - rious day. O fill our hearts with

throned a - bove, re - veal - er of God's grace and love.
way be - fore, you are to us the on - ly door.
joy - ous song! Sus - tain our faith and make us strong!

Text: Ora W. Garber, *The Brethren Hymnal,* 1951, alt.
Music: Dimitri S. Bortniansky, *Choralbuch,* 1825, alt.

Prayer is the soul's sincere desire 572

DORKING CM

1 Prayer is the soul's sin - cere de - sire,
2 Prayer is the bur - den of a sigh,
3 Prayer is the sim - plest form of speech
4 Prayer is the Chris - tian's vi - tal breath,
5 O Christ, by whom we come to God,

1 un - utter - ed or ex - pressed, the mo - tion of a
2 the fall - ing of a tear, the up - ward glanc - ing
3 that in - fant lips can try; prayer the sub - lim - est
4 the Chris - tian's na - tive air, the watch-word at the
5 the life, the truth, the way; the path of prayer that

1 hid - den fire that trem - bles in the breast.
2 of an eye, when none but God is near.
3 strains that reach the Maj - es - ty on high.
4 gates of death while en - t'ring heav'n with prayer.
5 you have trod, Lord, teach us how to pray.

Text: James Montgomery, 1818, alt.
Music: Stephanie Martin, 1990
Copyright ©1990 Stephanie Martin

573 What a friend we have in Jesus

BLAENWERN 87. 87D

1 What a friend we have in Je - sus, all our sins and griefs to bear! What a priv - i - lege to car - ry ev - 'ry - thing to God in prayer! Oh, what peace we of - ten for - feit, oh, what need - less pain we bear, all be - cause we do not car - ry ev - 'ry - thing to God in prayer.

2 Have we tri - als and temp - ta - tions? Is there trou - ble an - y - where? We should nev - er be dis - cour-aged – take it to the Lord in prayer! Can we find a friend so faith - ful, who will all our sor - rows share? Je - sus knows our ev - 'ry weak - ness – take it to the Lord in prayer!

3 Are we weak and heav - y - lad - en, 'cum - bered with a load of care? Pre-cious Sav - ior, still our ref - uge, take it to the Lord in prayer! Do thy friends de - spise, for - sake thee? Take it to the Lord in prayer! In his arms he'll take and shield thee – thou wilt find a so - lace there.

Text: Joseph M. Scriven, ca. 1855, *Spirit Minstrel: A Collection of Hymns and Music*, 1857, alt.
Music: William P. Rowlands, *Can a moliant*, 1916

(What a friend we have in Jesus) 574

ERIE (CONVERSE) 87. 87D

HAUSA

Yesu yana jin addu'a,
Yesu Ubangijinmu,
masu sonsa, masu binsa,
su ne nasa cetattu.
Yawan sonsu a wurinsa!
su ne tasa dukiya,
Yana zuba musu ido,
Yana ba su daraja.

Yesu yana yin addu'a,
aikin ceto nasa ne,
masu roko wurin Allah
sai a cikin sunansa.
Shi ja gora ne gare mu,
ganin Allah sai da shi,
Yesu, shugaban sujadar
da mutane za su yi.

Mu ma sai mu yi addu'a,
Almasihu yana nan.
Kalma tasa ta tabbata,
shi zai yarda da rokon.
Ya riga ya yi alheri,
ya yi mana gafara.
Kyautarsa ta wadace mu
har iyakar duniya.

SPANISH

¡Oh qué amigo nos es Cristo!
El llevó nuestro dolor,
y nos manda que llevemos
todo a Dios en oración.
¿Vive el hombre desprovisto
de paz, gozo y santo amor?
Esto es porque no llevamos
todo a Dios en oración.

¿Vives débil y cargado
de cuidados y temor?
A Jesús, refugio eterno,
dile todo en oración.
¿Te desprecian tus amigos?
Dilo a Cristo en oración.
En sus brazos gozo tierno
hallará tu corazón.

Jesucristo es nuestro amigo:
de esto pruebas él nos dió
al sufrir el cruel castigo
que el culpable mereció.
Y su pueblo redimido
hallará seguridad
fiando en este amigo eterno
y esperando en su bondad.

KOREAN

Joejm matteun uri goojoo,
ŏtji jo-eun chingooji
Geogjeong geunsim moogeounjim
uri jookke makkise.
Jookke goham ŏm neun go ro
bokeul batji mottane
Saramdri ŏtjikayeo
aroeljurul marulga.
Sikeom gugjeong modeun geogrom.

Omnun saram nugunga
Bujirubsi nagsimmalgo
gidodryo aroese.
Irun jinsilhasin chingoo
chazabolsu itsulkka
Uri yakham asioni
otji ani aroelkka.

Geunsim geokjeong moogeounjim
anijinja nugunga
Pinancheoneun uri
Yesu jookke gidodrise
Seisang chingu myeolsihago
neorul jorong hayeodo
Yesu pume ankiŏseo
chamdoen wiro batketne.

CREE

Kototeminaw Ciisas Karayst
Enaayaahtomaakoyak
Ekiitawinak kaakike
Tanaataayak Manitoo.
Moosak kakwatakihtawin
Pikwantaw kitaayaanaw
Aayis nama kinaataanaw
Ciisas pemaacihiwet.

Ihtakwan ci aymisiwin
Kiwaneyihtenaanaw
Ekawihkaac iyimotaan
Kita' ayamihaayaak.
Kimositestaamakonaw
Saapo wiicewikonaw
Nakaacihtaw esayayaak
Moosak naataayaan Ciisas.

Kinesowisinaanaw cii
Kosikwan neyaahtamak
Naatamoostawataak Ciisas
Kakeskimiwewinihk.
Kinakatikonawak cii
Askiihk kitotemnawak
Karayst kaototemikonaw
Kinatomikonaanaw.

Music: Charles C. Converse, 1868, *Silver Wings*, 1870

575 Precious Lord, take my hand

PRECIOUS LORD Irregular

1 Pre - cious Lord, take my hand, lead me on, let me
2 When my way grows drear, pre - cious Lord, lin - ger
3 When the dark - ness ap - pears and the night draws

stand, I am tired, I am weak, I am worn.
near, when my life is al - most gone,
near, and the day is past and gone,

Through the storm, through the night, lead me on to the
hear my cry, hear my call, hold my hand lest I
at the riv - er I stand, guide my feet, hold my

light, take my hand, pre - cious Lord, lead me home.
fall. Take my hand, pre - cious Lord, lead me home.
hand. Take my hand, pre - cious Lord, lead me home.

Text: Thomas A. Dorsey, 1932
Music: George N. Allen, *The Oberlin Social and Sabbath School Hymn Book,* 1844; adapted by Thomas A. Dorsey, 1932
Text and music copyright ©1938 Hill and Range Songs, Inc. Copyright renewed, assigned to Unichappell Music, Inc.

If you but trust in God

576

WER NUR DEN LIEBEN GOTT LÄSST WALTEN 98. 98. 88

1 If you but trust in God to guide you and place your
2 What gain is there in fu - tile weep - ing, in help - less
3 In pa - tient trust a - wait his lei - sure, in cheer - ful
4 Sing, pray, and keep his ways un - swerv - ing. Of - fer your

con - fi - dence in him, you'll find him al - ways there be -
an - ger and dis - tress? If you are in his care and
hope, with heart con - tent, to take what - e'er your Fa - ther's
ser - vice faith - ful - ly, and trust his word. Though un - de -

side you, to give you hope and strength with - in, for those who
keep - ing, in sor - row will he love you less? For he who
plea - sure and all - dis - cern - ing love have sent. Doubt not your
serv - ing, you'll find his prom - ise true to be. God nev - er

trust God's change - less love build on the Rock that will not move.
took for you a cross will bring you safe through ev - 'ry loss.
in - most wants are known to him who chose you for his own.
will for - sake in need the soul that trusts in him in - deed.

Text: Georg Neumark, "Wer nur den lieben Gott lässt walten," *Fortgepflanzter musikalisch-poetischer Lustwald,* 1657;
          tr. Catherine Winkworth (Sts. 1,3-4), *Chorale Book for England,* 1863, alt., Jaroslav J. Vajda (St. 2), *Lutheran Book
          of Worship,* 1978
          Translation (St. 2) copyright ©1978 *Lutheran Book of Worship*
Music: Georg Neumark, *Fortgepflanzter musikalisch-poetischer Lustwald,* 1657

577 O Love that will not let me go

ST. MARGARET 88. 886

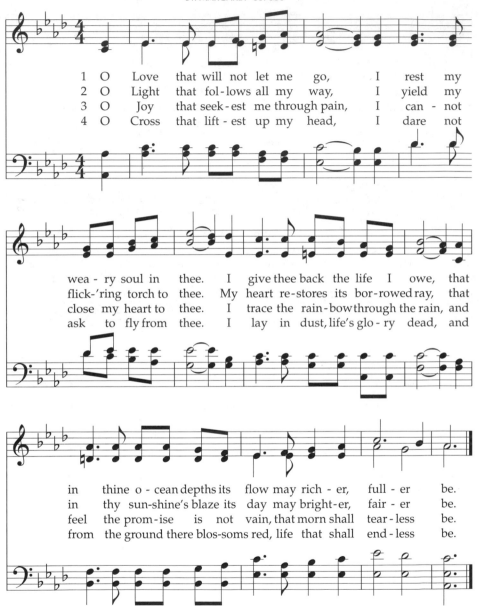

1 O Love that will not let me go,
I rest my weary soul in thee.
I give thee back the life I owe,
that in thine ocean depths its flow
may richer, fuller be.

2 O Light that follows all my way,
I yield my flick'ring torch to thee.
My heart restores its borrowed ray,
that in thy sunshine's blaze its day
may brighter, fairer be.

3 O Joy that seekest me through pain,
I cannot close my heart to thee.
I trace the rainbow through the rain,
and feel the promise is not vain,
that morn shall tearless be.

4 O Cross that liftest up my head,
I dare not ask to fly from thee.
I lay in dust, life's glory dead,
and from the ground there blossoms red,
life that shall endless be.

Text: George Matheson, 1882, *Life and Work* ..., 1883
Music: Albert L. Peace, 1884, *Scottish Hymnal*, 1885

The Lord's my shepherd 578

CRIMOND CM

1 The Lord's my shep - herd, I'll not want. He
2 My soul he doth re - store a - gain, and
3 Yea, though I walk in death's dark vale, yet
4 My ta - ble thou hast fur - nish - ed in
5 Good - ness and mer - cy all my life shall

1 makes me down to lie in pas - tures green, he
2 me to walk doth make with - in the paths of
3 will I fear none ill, for thou art with me
4 pres - ence of my foes. My head thou dost with
5 sure - ly fol - low me, and in God's house for -

1 lead - eth me the qui - et wa - ters by.
2 right - eous - ness, e'en for his own name's sake.
3 and thy rod and staff me com - fort still.
4 oil a - noint, and my cup o - ver - flows.
5 ev - er - more my dwell - ing place shall be.

Text: based on Psalm 23, *The Psalms of David in Meeter*, 1650
Music: Jessie S. Irvine; adapted and harmonized by David Grant, *The Northern Psalter*, 1872

579 Lift every voice and sing

ANTHEM 66 10. 66 10. 14 14 66 10

1 Lift ev-'ry voice and sing, till earth and heav - en ring,
2 Ston-y the road we trod, bit - ter the chas - t'ning rod,
3 God of our wea - ry years, God of our si - lent tears,

ring with the har - mo - nies of lib - er - ty.
felt in the days when hope un - born had died,
thou who hast brought us thus far on the way,

Let our re - joic - ing rise high as the lis - t'ning skies,
yet with a stead - y beat, have not our wea - ry feet
thou who hast by thy might, led us in - to the light,

let it re - sound loud as the roll - ing sea.
come to the place for which our peo - ple sighed?
keep us for - ev - er in the path, we pray.

Text: J. Rosamond Johnson, 1899
Music: J. Rosamond Johnson, 1899

Sing a song full of the faith that the dark past has taught us.
We have come o - ver a way that with tears has been wa - tered.
Lest our feet stray from the plac - es, our God, where we met thee,

Sing a song full of the hope that the pres - ent has brought
We have come, tread-ing our path thro' the blood of the slaugh -
lest, our hearts drunk with the wine of the world, we for - get

us. Fac - ing the ris - ing sun of our new day be -
tered, out from the gloom - y past till now we stand at
thee, shad-owed be - neath thy hand, may we for - ev - er

gun, let us march on till vic - to - ry is won.
last where the bright gleam of our bright star is cast.
stand, true to our God, true to our na - tive land.

580

My life flows on

HOW CAN I KEEP FROM SINGING 87. 87 with refrain

1 My life flows on in end-less song, a-bove earth's lam-en-ta-tion.
2 Through all the tu-mult and the strife, I hear that mu-sic ring-ing.
3 What though my joys and com-forts die? The Lord my Sav-ior liv-eth.
4 The peace of Christ makes fresh my heart, a foun-tain ev-er spring-ing!

I catch the sweet, though far-off hymn that hails a new cre-a-tion.
It finds an ech-o in my soul. How can I keep from sing-ing?
What though the dark-ness gath-er 'round? Songs in the night he giv-eth.
All things are mine since I am his! How can I keep from sing-ing?

Refrain

No storm can shake my in-most calm while to that Rock I'm cling-ing.

Since Love is Lord of heav'n and earth, how can I keep from sing-ing?

Text: Robert Lowry's *Bright Jewels for the Sunday School*, 1869, alt.
Music: Robert Lowry's *Bright Jewels for the Sunday School*, 1869; arranged by The Hymnal Project
Arrangement copyright ©1989 The Hymnal Project

Take thou my hand, O Father 581

SO NIMM DENN MEINE HÄNDE 74. 74D

1 Take thou my hand, O Fa-ther, and lead thou me, un-til my jour-ney end-eth e-ter-nal-ly. A-lone I will not wan-der one sin-gle day. Be thou my true com-pan-ion and with me stay.

2 O cov-er with thy mer-cy my poor, weak heart! Let ev-'ry thought re-bel-lious from me de-part. Per-mit thy child to lin-ger here at thy feet, and full-y trust thy good-ness with faith com-plete.

3 Though naught of thy great pow-er may move my soul, with thee through night and dark-ness I reach the goal. Take, then, my hand, O Fa-ther, and lead thou me, un-til my jour-ney end-eth e-ter-nal-ly.

1 So nimm denn meine Hände
und führe mich
bis an mein selig Ende
und ewiglich!
Ich kann allein nicht gehen,
nicht einen Schritt;
wo du wirst gehn und stehen,
da nimm mich mit.

2 In deine Gnade hülle
mein schwaches Herz,
und mach es endlich stille
in Freud und Schmerz.
Lass ruhn zu deinen Füssen
dein schwaches Kind;
es will die Augen schliessen
und folgen blind.

3 Wenn ich auch gar nichts fühle
von deiner Macht,
du bringst mich doch zum Ziele
auch durch die Nacht.
So nimm denn meine Hände
und führe mich
bis an mein selig Ende
und ewiglich!

Text: Julie K. Hausmann, "So nimm denn meine Hände," *Maiblumen, Lieder einer Stillen im Lande*, Vol. 1, 1862; tr. Herman Brückner, *Wartburg Hymnal for Church, School, and Home*, 1918
Music: Friedrich Silcher, *Kinderlieder*, Vol. III, 1842

582 Guide me, O thou great Jehovah

CWM RHONDDA 87. 87. 87 extended

1 Guide me, O thou great Je - ho - vah, pil - grim through this
2 O - pen now the cry - stal foun - tain whence the heal - ing
3 When I tread the verge of Jor - dan, bid my anx - ious

bar - ren land. I am weak, but thou art might - y; hold me with thy
wa - ters flow. Let the fi - ery, cloud - y pil - lar lead me all my
fears sub - side. Death of death and hell's de - struc - tion, land me safe on

pow'r - ful hand. Bread of heav - en, Bread of heav - en,
jour - ney through. Strong De - liv'r - er, strong De - liv'r - er,
Ca - naan's side. Songs of prais - es, songs of prais - es,

feed me till I want no more, feed me till I want no more.
be thou still my strength and shield, be thou still my strength and shield.
I will ev - er give to thee, I will ev - er give to thee.

Text: William Williams, "Arglwydd arwain trwy'r anialwch," Aleluia, 1745; tr. Peter Williams and William Williams, Hymns on
        Various Subjects, 1771
Music: John Hughes, 1905 or 1907, The Voice of Thanksgiving, No. 4, 1928

Ndikhokele, O Jehova 583
(Guide me, O thou great Jehovah)
XHOSA HYMN 87. 87

1 Ndi - kho - ke - le, O Je - ho - va,
U - na - man - dla a - ndi - na - wo,
O msi - ndi - si, O msi - ndi - si,

ndi - ngum - ha - mbi Nko - si yam.
u - no - bu - tha - tha - ka ndim.
Ngu - we o - li - kha - ka lam.

Text: William Williams, "Arglwydd arwain trwy'r anialwch," *Aleluia,* 1745; Xhosa language transcription by Edith W. Ming
Music: Xhosa melody (South Africa)
Text and music copyright © African Methodist Episcopal Church, Nashville, Tenn.

They that wait upon the Lord 584

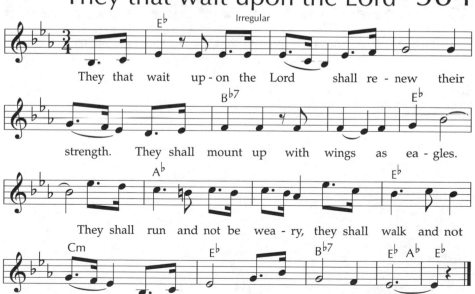

They that wait up - on the Lord shall re - new their
strength. They shall mount up with wings as ea - gles.
They shall run and not be wea - ry, they shall walk and not
faint. Teach me, Lord, teach me, Lord, to wait.

Text: based on Isaiah 40:31, Stuart Hamblen, 1953 (chorus of song "Teach me, Lord, to wait")
Music: Stuart Hamblen, 1953
Text and music copyright ©1953, renewed 1981 Hamblen Music Co.

585

In your sickness

Irregular

In your sick-ness, your suf-f'rings, your trials, and pains, he is

with you all the time. Per-se-cu-tion, temp-ta-tions, and

lone-li-ness, he is with you all the time. He is there with you,

he is there with you, he is with you all the time. He is

there with you, he is there with you, he is with you all the time.

Text: adapted from the Twi language, *Asempa Hymns*
Music: Ghanaian melody, from *Ghana Praise*
          Text and music copyright © Asempa Publishers

Cast thy burden upon the Lord 586

BIRMINGHAM (MENDELSSOHN)

Cast thy bur-den up-on the Lord, and he shall sustain thee. He nev-er will suf-fer the
right-eous to fall. He is at thy right hand. Thy
mer-cy, Lord, is great, and far a-bove the heav'ns. Let
none be made a-sham-ed, that wait up-on thee.

Text: Julius Schubring, *Wirf dein Anliegen auf den Herrn*; tr. William Bartholomew, *Elijah*, 1846
Music: *Neu-vermehrtes Gesangbuch*, 1693; adapted by Felix Mendelssohn, *Elijah*, 1846

587 Come, my Way, my Truth, my Life

THE CALL 77. 77

1 Come, my Way, my Truth, my Life: such a
2 Come, my Light, my Feast, my Strength: such a
3 Come, my Joy, my Love, my Heart: such a

way as gives us breath; such a truth as ends all
light as shows a feast; such a feast as mends in
joy as none can move; such a love as none can

strife; such a life as kill - eth death.
length; such a strength as makes _____ his guest.
part; such a heart as joys _____ in love.

Text: George Herbert, *The Temple,* 1633
Music: Ralph Vaughan Williams, 1911, *Five Mystical Songs, No. 4*; adapted in *Hymnal for Colleges and Schools,* 1956
Copyright ©1911 Stainer & Bell, Ltd., London

Jesus, the very thought of thee 588

ST. AGNES CM

1 Je - sus, the ver - y thought of thee
2 Nor voice can sing, nor heart can frame,
3 O Hope of ev - 'ry con - trite heart!
4 But what to those who find? Ah, this
5 Je - sus! our on - ly joy be thou,

1 with sweet-ness fills my breast; but sweet-er far thy
2 nor can the mind re - call a sweet-er sound than
3 O Joy of all the meek! To those who fal - ter
4 nor tongue nor pen can show! The love of Je - sus —
5 as thou our prize wilt be; Je - sus! be thou our

1 face to see and in thy pres - ence rest.
2 thy dear name, O Sav - ior of us all.
3 thou art kind! How good to those who seek!
4 what it is, none but his loved ones know.
5 glo - ry now, and through e - ter - ni - ty.

Text: attributed to St. Bernard of Clairvaux, *Jesu dulcis memoria*, 12th c.; tr. Edward Caswall, *Lyra Catholica*, 1849, alt.
Music: John B. Dykes, *Hymnal for Use in the English Church*, 1866

589 My Shepherd will supply my need

RESIGNATION CMD

1 My Shep-herd will sup-ply my need; Je-ho-vah
2 When I walk through the shades of death thy pres-ence
3 The sure pro-vi-sions of my God at-tend me

is his name. In pas-tures fresh he makes me feed, be-
is my stay. One word of thy sup-port-ing breath drives
all my days. Oh, may thy house be mine a-bode, and

side the liv-ing stream. He brings my wan-d'ring spir-it
all my fears a-way. Thy hand, in sight of all my
all my work be praise. There would I find a set-tled

back, when I for-sake his ways, and leads me,
foes, doth still my ta-ble spread. My cup with
rest, while oth-ers go and come, no more a

Text: based on Psalm 23, Isaac Watts, *Psalms of David* ..., 1719
Music: American folk melody, ca. 1828, version from Joseph Funk's *Genuine Church Music,* 1st ed., 1832; harmonized by
J. Harold Moyer, 1965
Harmonization copyright ©1969 Faith and Life Press/Mennonite Publishing House

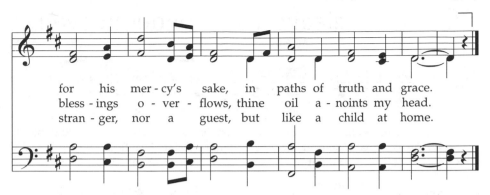

for his mer - cy's sake, in paths of truth and grace.
bless - ings o - ver - flows, thine oil a - noints my head.
stran - ger, nor a guest, but like a child at home.

The care the eagle gives her young 590

CRIMOND CM

1 The care the ea - gle gives her young, safe
2 As when the time to ven - ture comes, she
3 And if we flut - ter help - less - ly, as

in her loft - y nest, is like the ten - der
stirs them out to flight, so we are pressed to
fledg - ling ea - gles fall, be - neath us lift God's

love of God for us made man - i - fest.
bold - ly try, to strive for dar - ing height.
might - y wings to bear us, one and all.

Text: based on Deuteronomy 32:11, R. Deane Postlethwaite
Music: Jessie S. Irvine; adapted and harmonized by David Grant, *The Northern Psalter*, 1872

591 Lo, a gleam from yonder heaven

JUNIATA 87. 87 with refrain

1 Lo,   a gleam from yon-der heav-en breaks up-on our star-less night.
2 When we're tossed on trou-bled wa-ters, on temp-ta-tion's o-cean wide,
3 Out of   sin, and out of   weak-ness, this fair   light still beck-ons   on,

Like a   kind-ly hand it   beck-ons, "Walk in   me; I am   the   Light."
like a   sil-ver flood de-scend-ing, he our   souls will safe-ly   guide.
through the val-ley of all   shad-ows, to his   own re-splen-dent dawn.

Refrain

Je-sus,   light se-rene, e-ter-nal! Glo-rious   sun of right-eous-ness!

Morn-ing   star of all the   ag-es, with thy   beams our spir-its   bless.

Text: Adaline H. Beery, 1896, *Brethren Hymnal*, 1901
Music: William Beery, 1896, *Brethren Hymnal*, 1901

Love divine, all loves excelling 592

BEECHER 87. 87D

1 Love di - vine, all loves ex - cel - ling, Joy of heav'n, to earth come down,
2 Breathe, O breathe thy lov-ing Spir - it in - to ev-'ry trou-bled breast.
3 Come, Al-might - y, to de - liv - er, let us all thy life re - ceive.
4 Fin - ish, then, thy new cre - a - tion; pure and spot-less let us be.

fix in us thy hum-ble dwell-ing, all thy faith-ful mer - cies crown.
Let us all in thee in - her - it, let us find the prom-ised rest.
Sud - den-ly re - turn, and nev - er, nev - er-more thy tem - ples leave.
Let us see thy great sal - va-tion per-fect-ly re - stored in thee.

Je - sus, thou art all com - pas-sion, pure, un-bound-ed love thou art.
Take a - way the love of sin-ning; Al-pha and O - me - ga be.
Thee we would be al-ways bless-ing, serve thee as thy hosts a - bove,
Changed from glo-ry in - to glo - ry, till in heav'n we take our place,

Vis - it us with thy sal - va-tion; en - ter ev - 'ry trem-bling heart.
End of faith, as its be - gin-ning, set our hearts at lib - er - ty.
pray, and praise thee with-out ceas-ing, glo-ry in thy per - fect love.
till we cast our crowns be - fore thee, lost in won-der, love, and praise.

Text: Charles Wesley, *Hymns for those that seek ...*, 1747
Music: John Zundel, *Christian Heart Songs*, 1870

593   O Power of love

ST. PETERSBURG 98. 98. 99

1 O Pow'r of love, all else tran-scend-ing, in Je-sus
2 Thou art my rest; no earth-ly trea-sure can sat-is-
3 To thee my heart and life be giv-en; thou art in

pres-ent ev-er-more, I wor-ship thee, in hom-age bend-ing,
fy my yearn-ing heart, and naught can give to me the plea-sure
truth my high-est good. For me thy sa-cred side was riv-en,

thy name to hon-or and a-dore. Yea, let my soul, in
I find in thee, my cho-sen part. Thy love, so ten-der,
for me was shed thy pre-cious blood. O thou who art the

deep de-vo-tion, bathe in love's might-y bound-less o-cean.
so pos-sess-ing, is joy to me, and ev-'ry bless-ing.
world's sal-va-tion, be thine my love and ad-o-ra-tion.

Text: Gerhard Tersteegen, *Ich bete an die Macht der Liebe*, 1757, revised in *Sammlung*, 1825; tr. Herman Brückner, *Wartburg Hymnal for Church, School, and Home*, 1918, alt.
Music: Dimitri S. Bortniansky, *Choralbuch*, 1825

Lord, you sometimes speak 594

CLEVELAND 87. 87. 9

1 Lord, you some-times speak in won - ders,
2 Lord, you some-times speak in whis - pers,
3 Lord, you some-times speak in si - lence,
4 Lord, you sure - ly speak in Scrip - ture –
5 Lord, you al - ways speak in Je - sus,

1 un - mis - tak - a - ble and clear; might - y
2 still and small and scarce - ly heard; on - ly
3 through our loud and nois - y day. We can
4 words that sum - mon from the page, shown and
5 al - ways new yet still the same. Teach us

1 signs to prove your pres - ence, o - ver - com - ing doubt and fear. O
2 those who want to lis - ten catch the all - im - por - tant word. O
3 know and trust you bet - ter when we quiet - ly wait and pray. O
4 taught us by your Spir - it with fresh light for ev - 'ry age. O
5 now more of our Sav - ior; make our lives dis - play his name. O

1 Lord, you some-times speak in won - ders.
2 Lord, you some-times speak in whis - pers.
3 Lord, you some-times speak in si - lence.
4 Lord, you sure - ly speak in Scrip - ture.
5 Lord, you al - ways speak in Je - sus.

Text: Christopher Idle, 1966, *Youth Praise 2*, 1969
        Copyright ©1969 Hope Publishing Co.
Music: Christopher Johnson, 1987, *New Songs of Praise 4*, 1988
        Copyright © Christopher Johnson

595 Jesus, priceless treasure

JESU, MEINE FREUDE 665. 665. 786

1 Je - sus, price - less trea - sure, source of pur - est plea - sure, tru - est friend to me, long my heart hath pant - ed, till it well - nigh faint - ed, thirst - ing af - ter thee. Thine I am, O spot - less Lamb; I will suf - fer

2 In thine arm I rest me; foes who would mo - lest me can - not reach me here. Though the earth be shak - ing, ev - 'ry heart be quak - ing, Je - sus calms my fear. Sin and hell in con - flict fell with their heav - iest

3 Hence, all thoughts of sad - ness! for the Lord of glad - ness, Je - sus, en - ters in. Those who love the Sav - ior, though the storms may gath - er, still have peace with - in. Yea, what - e'er we here must bear, still in thee lies

Text: Johann Franck, "Jesu, meine Freude," *Praxis Pietatis Melica*, 5th ed., 1653; tr. Catherine Winkworth, *Chorale Book for England*, 1863
Music: Johann Crüger, *Praxis Pietatis Melica*, 5th ed., 1653; harmonized by J. S. Bach, Motet No. 3 in E minor, 1723

naught to hide thee, ask for naught be-side thee.
storms as-sail me; Je-sus will not fail me.
pur-est plea - sure, Je-sus, price-less trea - sure!

And I will raise you up 596
ON EAGLE'S WINGS*

"And I will raise you up on ea-gle's wings, bear you on the breath of dawn, make you to shine like the sun, and hold you in the palm of my hand."

*Original title

Text: based on Psalm 91, Michael Joncas, alt.
Music: Michael Joncas
Text and music copyright ©1979 New Dawn Music

597 Oh, how happy are they

NEW CONCORD 669. 669

1 Oh, how hap-py are they who the Sav-ior o-bey,
2 Oh, that com-fort was mine, when the fa-vor di-vine
3 What a heav-en be-low my Re-deem-er to know,
4 Je-sus all the day long was my joy and my song.

and have laid up their trea - sures a - bove!
I first found in the blood of the Lamb.
and the an - gels could do noth - ing more,
Oh, that all his sal - va - tion may see!

Oh, what tongue can ex - press the sweet com - fort and
When my heart it be - lieved, what a joy it re -
than to fall at his feet, and the sto - ry re -
"He has loved me!" I cried. "He has suf - fered and

peace of a soul in its ear - li - est love.
ceived, what a heav - en in Je - sus his name!
peat, and the lov - er of sin - ners a - dore.
died, to re - deem such a reb - el as me!"

Text: Charles Wesley, *Hymns and Sacred Poems*, 1749, alt.
Music: American folk melody, in Joseph Funk's *Genuine Church Music*, 1st ed., 1832; harmonized by J. Harold Moyer, 1965

A wonderful Savior is Jesus 598

KIRKPATRICK 11 8. 11 8 with refrain

1 A won-der-ful Sav-ior is Je-sus my Lord, a won-der-ful
2 A won-der-ful Sav-ior is Je-sus my Lord; he tak-eth my
3 With num-ber-less bless-ings each mo-ment he crowns, and filled with his
4 When clothed in his bright-ness, trans-port-ed I rise to meet him in

Sav-ior to me. He hid-eth my soul in the cleft of the rock, where
bur-den a-way. He hold-eth me up, and I shall not be moved; he
full-ness di-vine, I sing in my rap-ture, "Oh, glo-ry to God for
clouds of the sky, his per-fect sal-va-tion, his won-der-ful love I'll

Refrain

riv-ers of plea-sure I see.
giv-eth me strength as my day. He hid-eth my soul in the cleft of the rock
such a Re-deem-er as mine!"
shout with the mil-lions on high.

that shad-ows a dry, thirst-y land. He hid-eth my life in the depths of his love,

and cov-ers me there with his hand, and cov-ers me there with his hand.

Text: Fanny J. Crosby, *The Finest of the Wheat No. 1*, 1890
Music: William J. Kirkpatrick, *The Finest of the Wheat No. 1*, 1890

599 He leadeth me

HE LEADETH ME LM with refrain

1 He lead-eth me, oh, bless-ed thought! Oh, words with heav'n-ly
2 Some-times 'mid scenes of deep-est gloom, some-times where E - den's
3 Lord, I would clasp thy hand in mine, nor ev - er mur-mur
4 And when my task on earth is done, when by thy grace, the

com-fort fraught! What - e'er I do, wher - e'er I be, still
bow - ers bloom, by wa - ters calm, o'er trou - bled sea, still
nor re - pine; con - tent, what-ev - er lot I see, since
vic - t'ry's won, e'en death's cold wave I will not flee, since

Refrain

'tis God's hand that lead - eth me.
'tis his hand that lead - eth me. He lead - eth me, he
'tis my God that lead - eth me.
God through Jor - dan lead - eth me.

lead - eth me, by his own hand he lead - eth me. His

Text: Joseph H. Gilmore, *Watchman and Reflector,* 1862, alt.
Music: William B. Bradbury, *The Golden Censer,* 1864

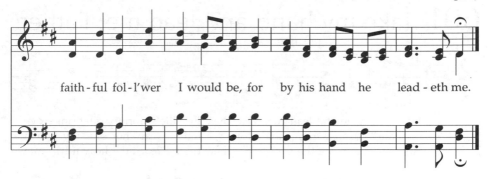

faith-ful fol-l'wer   I would be, for   by his hand   he   lead-eth me.

O bless the Lord, my soul   600

ST. THOMAS (WILLIAMS) SM

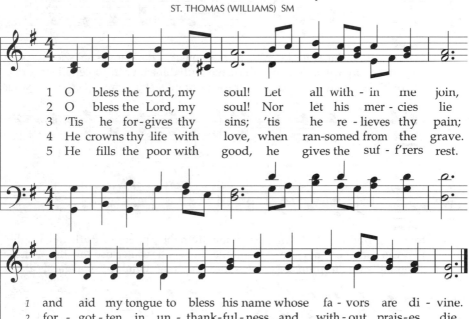

1 O   bless the Lord, my   soul! Let   all with-in   me   join,
2 O   bless the Lord, my   soul! Nor   let his mer-cies   lie
3 'Tis   he for-gives thy   sins; 'tis   he re-lieves thy   pain;
4 He crowns thy life with   love, when   ran-somed from the   grave.
5 He   fills the poor with   good, he   gives the suf-f'rers   rest.

1 and   aid my tongue to   bless his name whose   fa-vors are di-vine.
2 for-got-ten in un-thank-ful-ness, and   with-out prais-es   die.
3 'tis   he that heals thy   sick-ness-es,   and makes thee young a-gain.
4 He   that re-deemed my   soul from hell hath   sov-'reign pow'r to   save.
5 The   Lord hath judg-ments for   the proud, and   jus-tice for th' op-pressed.

Text: based on Psalm 103, Isaac Watts, *Psalms of David ...*, 1719
Music: Aaron Williams, *The Universal Psalmodist*, 1763

601 Take my hand and lead me, Father

HUNTINGDON 87. 87D with refrain

1 Take my hand and lead me, Fa-ther, thro' life's storm-y pil-grim - age.
2 For the road is rough and ston-y, and I can-not see my way.
3 Hold my hand in thine, O Fa-ther, till I reach the heav'n-ly gates.

Let thy light shine bright-er, Fa-ther, on its dark, mys-ter - ious page,
Yet, if thou wilt deign to guide me with thine own re-splen-dent ray,
There I'll leave my cross and bur-den, for my star-gemmed crown a -waits.

for I find my feet oft stray-ing from the path of truth and right,
I can nev-er, nev - er stum-ble, but shall walk close to thy side,
Then I'll sing in strains of rap-ture, in the light of per-fect day,

feel the need of thy pro - tec-tion, and thy light to shine more bright.
with a love so pure and trust-ing that no sin can e'er di - vide.
thou didst deign to guide me, Fa-ther, and hast led me all the way.

Text: Gertrude A. Flory, *Sowing and Reaping,* 1889
Music: William Beery, *Sowing and Reaping,* 1889

602

Lift up your hearts

BOUNDING HEART 10 10. 10 10

1 "Lift up your hearts!" We lift them to the Lord,
2 A - bove the storms that dark - en hu - man life –
3 Then, with the trum - pet call as Christ ap - pears,

and give to God our thanks with one ac - cord.
pride, jeal - ou - sy, and en - vy, rage and strife,
"Lift up your hearts!" rings, peal - ing in our ears.

It is our joy and du - ty all our days
where cold mis - trust holds friend and friend a - part –
Still shall our hearts re - spond with full ac - cord –

to lift our hearts in grate - ful thanks and praise.
O Lord of love, lift ev - 'ry Chris - tian heart!
"We lift them up, we lift them to the Lord!" A - men

Text: Henry M. Butler, *Harrow School Hymn Book,* 1881, alt.
Music: Alvin F. Brightbill, *The Brethren Hymnal,* 1951

Sometimes a light surprises 603

SURPRISE 76. 76D extended

1 Some - times a light sur - pris - es the child of God who
2 In ho - ly con - tem - pla - tion we sweet - ly then pur -
3 It can bring with it noth - ing but he will bear us
4 Though vine and fig tree nei - ther their wont - ed fruit should

sings. _____ It is the Lord who ris - es with heal - ing
sue _____ the theme of God's sal - va - tion, and find it
through. _ Who gives the lil - ies cloth - ing will clothe his
bear, _____ though all the fields should with - er, nor flocks nor

in his wings. _____ When com - forts are de - clin - ing, he
ev - er new. _____ Set free from pres - ent sor - row we
peo - ple, too. _____ Be - neath the spread - ing heav - ens no
herds be there, _____ yet God, the same a - bid - ing, his

grants the soul a - gain a sea - son of clear shin - ing, to
cheer - ful - ly can say, let the un - known to - mor - row bring
crea - ture but is fed, and he who feeds the ra - vens will
praise shall tune my voice, for while in him con - fid - ing I

cheer it af - ter rain, _____ to cheer it af - ter rain.
with it what it may, _____ bring with it what it may.
give his chil - dren bread, _____ will give his chil - dren bread.
can - not but re - joice, _____ I can - not but re - joice.

Text: William Cowper, *Olney Hymns, Book III*, 1779, alt.
Music: Jane Marshall, 1974

604 Jesu, joy of man's desiring

WERDE MUNTER 87. 87. 88. 77

1 *Je - su, joy of man's de - sir - ing, ho - ly wis - dom, love most bright, drawn by thee, our souls as - pir - ing soar to un - cre - at - ed light. Word of God, our flesh that fash - ioned, with the fire of life im - pas - sioned, striv - ing still to truth un - known, soar - ing, dy - ing 'round thy throne.

2 Through the way, where hope is guid - ing, hark, what peace - ful mu - sic rings, where the flock, in thee con - fid - ing, drink of joy from death - less springs. Theirs is beau - ty's fair - est plea - sure. Theirs is wis - dom's ho - liest trea - sure. Thou dost ev - er lead thine own in the love of joys un - known.

*Alternate phrase: Jesu, joy of our desiring
**Numbers in parentheses indicate measures of rest if Bach's accompaniment is used.

Text: Martin Janus, "Jesu, meiner Seelen Wonne," *Christlich Herzens Andacht,* 1665; tr. Robert Bridges
Music: Johann Schop, *Das Dritte Zehn,* 1642; harmonized by J. S. Bach, Cantata No.147, *Herz und Mund und Tat und Leben,* 1716

I love thee, Lord

AL LADO DE MI CABAÑA CM

1 I love thee, Lord, but not be-cause I
2 but for that thou didst all the world up -
3 and griefs and tor - ments num - ber - less, and
4 Then, why, most lov - ing Je - sus Christ, should
5 not with the hope of gain - ing aught, not
6 E'en so I love thee, and will love, and

1 hope for heav'n there - by, nor yet for fear that
2 on the cross em - brace; for us didst bear the
3 sweat of ag - o - ny, e'en death it - self; and
4 I not love thee well, not for the sake of
5 seek - ing a re - ward, but as thy - self hast
6 in thy praise will sing, sole - ly be - cause thou

1 lov - ing not I might for - ev - er die,
2 nails and spear, and man - i - fold dis - grace,
3 all for one who was thine en - e - my.
4 win - ning heav'n nor an - y fear of hell,
5 lov - ed me, O ev - er - lov - ing Lord!
6 art my God and my e - ter - nal King.

Text: Spanish hymn, 17th c.; tr. Edward Caswall, adapted by Percy Dearmer, alt.
        Copyright © Oxford University Press, London
Music: Spanish medieval folk melody; harmonized by The Hymnal Project
        Harmonization copyright ©1991 The Hymnal Project

606 Oh, have you not heard

THE BEAUTIFUL RIVER 11 7. 11 7 with refrain

1 Oh, have you not heard of that beau-ti-ful stream that
2 Its foun-tains are deep and its wa-ters are pure, and
3 This beau-ti-ful stream is the riv-er of life! It
4 Oh, will you not drink of this beau-ti-ful stream, and

flows through the prom-ised land? Its wa-ters gleam bright in the
sweet to the wea-ry soul. It flows from the throne of Je-
flows for all na-tions free! A balm for each wound in its
dwell on its peace-ful shore? The Spir-it says: Come, all ye

heav-en-ly light, and rip-ple o'er gold-en sand.
ho-vah a-lone! O come where its bright waves roll.
wa-ter is found; O sin-ner, it flows for thee!
wea-ry ones, home, and wan-der in sin no more.

Refrain

O seek that beau-ti-ful stream, O seek that

Text: R. Torry, Jr., *Sabbath School Gems*, 1864; tr. Ernst H. Gebhardt (German), *Frohe Botschaft*, 1875, alt.
Music: Asa Hull, *Sabbath School Gems*, 1864, alt.

beau - ti - ful stream. Its wa - ters, so free, are flow - ing for thee, O seek that beau - ti - ful stream.

1 Ich weiss einen Strom, dessen herrliche Flut
   fliesst wunderbar stille durchs Land,
   doch strahlet und glänzt er wie feurige Glut,
   wem ist dieses Wasser bekannt?

Refrain:
O Seele, ich bitte dich: Komm!
   und such diesen herrlichen Strom!
Sein Wasser fliesst frei und mächtiglich,
   O glaub's, es fliesset für dich!

2 Wohin dieser Strom sich nur immer ergiesst,
   da jubelt und jauchzet das Herz,
   das nunmehr den köstlichsten Segen geniesst,
   erlöset von Sorgen und Schmerz.
   (Refrain)

3 Der Strom ist gar tief und sein Wasser ist klar,
   es schmecket so lieblich und fein;
   es heilet die Kranken und stärkt wunderbar,
   ja machet die Unreinsten rein.
   (Refrain)

4 Wen dürstet, der komme und trinke sich satt,
   so rufet der Geist und die Braut,
   nur wer in dem Strome gewaschen sich hat,
   das Angesicht Gottes einst schaut.
   (Refrain)

607

Today I live

HEARTBEAT 10 11. 10 11

1 To - day I live, but once shall come my death.
2 How I shall die, or when, I do not know,
3 When earth - ly life shall close, as close it must,
4 Mean - while I live and move and I am glad,

One day shall still my laugh - ter and my cry - ing,
nor where, for end - less is the world's ho - ri - zon;
let Je - sus be my broth - er and my mer - it.
en - joy this life and all its in - ter - weav - ing.

bring to a halt my heart - beat and my breath. Lord,
but save me, Lord, from thoughts that lay me low, from
Let me with - out re - gret re - call the past, then,
Each giv - en day, as I take up the thread, let

give me faith for liv - ing and for dy - ing.
mor - bid fears that freeze my pow'r of rea - son.
Lord, in - to your hands com - mit my spir - it.
love sug - gest my mode, my mood of liv - ing.

Text: Fred Kaan, 1975
        Copyright ©1975 Hope Publishing Co.
Music: Jane Marshall, 1980
        Copyright ©1980 Hope Publishing Co.

If death my friend and me divide 608

CHAPEL 886. 886 extended

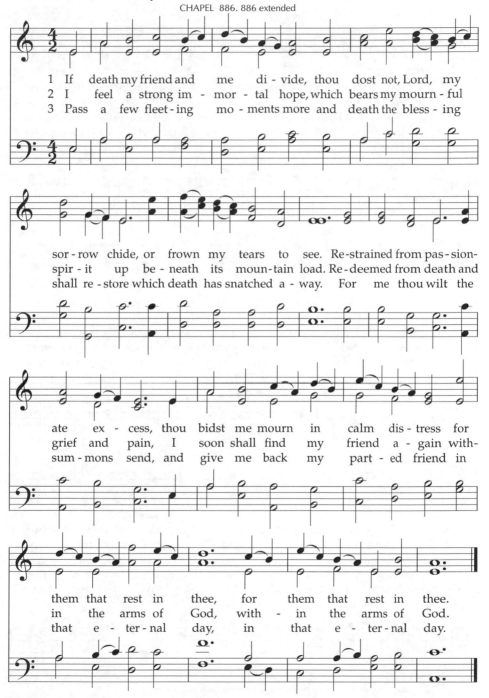

1 If death my friend and me divide, thou dost not, Lord, my
2 I feel a strong im-mor-tal hope, which bears my mourn-ful
3 Pass a few fleet-ing mo-ments more and death the bless-ing

sor-row chide, or frown my tears to see. Re-strained from pas-sion-
spir-it up be-neath its moun-tain load. Re-deemed from death and
shall re-store which death has snatched a-way. For me thou wilt the

ate ex-cess, thou bidst me mourn in calm dis-tress for
grief and pain, I soon shall find my friend a-gain with-
sum-mons send, and give me back my part-ed friend in

them that rest in thee, for them that rest in thee.
in the arms of God, with-in the arms of God.
that e-ter-nal day, in that e-ter-nal day.

Text: Charles Wesley, *Short Hymns on Select Passages of Holy Scripture*, 1762
Music: Joseph Funk's *Genuine Church Music*, 1st ed., 1832; harmonized by The Hymnal Project
Harmonization copyright ©1992 The Hymnal Project

609
Awake, my soul

CHRISTMAS CM extended

1 A - wake, my soul, stretch ev - 'ry nerve, and press with vig - or
2 A cloud of wit - ness - es a - round holds thee in full sur -
3 'Tis God's all- an - i - mat - ing voice that calls thee from on
4 that prize, with peer-less glo - ries bright which shall new lus - ter
5 Bless'd Sav - ior, in - tro - duced by thee have I my race be -

1 on! A heav'n - ly race de - mands thy zeal, and
2 vey. For - get the steps al - read - y trod, and
3 high. 'Tis God's own hand pre - sents the prize to
4 boast, when vic - tors' wreaths and mon - archs' gems shall
5 gun, and crowned with vic - t'ry at thy feet I'll

1 an im - mor - tal crown, and an im - mor - tal crown.
2 on - ward urge thy way, and on - ward urge thy way.
3 thine as - pir - ing eye, to thine as - pir - ing eye;
4 blend in com - mon dust, shall blend in com - mon dust.
5 lay my hon - ors down, I'll lay my hon - ors down.

Text: Philip Doddridge, *Hymns ...*, 1755
Music: George Frederick Handel, *Siroe*, 1728; adapted in James Hewitt's *Harmonia Sacra*, 1812

On Jordan's stormy banks I stand 610

BOUND FOR THE PROMISED LAND CM with refrain

1 On Jor-dan's storm-y banks I stand, and cast a wish-ful eye
2 There gen-'rous fruits that nev-er fail, on trees im-mor-tal grow.
3 All o'er those wide ex-tend-ed plains shines one e-ter-nal day.
4 When shall I reach that hap-py place, and be for-ev-er bless'd?
5 Filled with de-light, my rap-tured soul can here no long-er stay.

1 to Ca-naan's fair and hap-py land, where my pos-ses-sions lie.
2 There rocks and hills and brooks and vales with milk and hon-ey flow.
3 There God the sun for-ev-er reigns, and scat-ters night a-way.
4 When shall I see my Fa-ther's face, and in his bo-som rest?
5 Though Jor-dan's waves a-round me roll, fear-less I'd launch a-way.

Refrain

I'm bound for the prom-ised land, I'm bound for the prom-ised land.

Oh, who will come and go with me? I'm bound for the prom-ised land.

Text: Samuel Stennett, *A Selection of Hymns from the Best Authors,* 1787
Music: American folk melody, *Southern Harmony,* 1835; harmonized by J. Harold Moyer, 1965
Harmonization copyright ©1969 Faith and Life Press/Mennonite Publishing House

611 Soon and very soon

Irregular

1 Soon and ver-y soon, we are goin' to see the King,
2 No more cry-in' there, we are goin' to see the King,
3 No more dy-in' there, we are goin' to see the King,
4 Soon and ver-y soon, we are goin' to see the King,

soon and ver-y soon, we are goin' to see the King,
no more cry-in' there, we are goin' to see the King,
no more dy-in' there, we are goin' to see the King,
soon and ver-y soon, we are goin' to see the King,

soon and ver-y soon, we are goin' to see the King,
no more cry-in' there, we are goin' to see the King,
no more dy-in' there, we are goin' to see the King,
soon and ver-y soon, we are goin' to see the King,

hal-le-lu-jah, hal-le-lu-jah, we're goin' to see the King!

Text: based on Revelation 21:4, Andraé Crouch
Music: Andraé Crouch
          Text and music copyright ©1973 BudJohn Songs, Inc. (Crouch Music/BudJohn/ASCAP)

Steal away

612

STEAL AWAY TO JESUS 57 87 with refrain

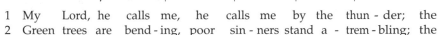

Refrain

Steal a-way, steal a-way, steal a-way to Je-sus!

Fine

Steal a-way, steal a-way home, I ain't got long to stay here.

Leader

1 My Lord, he calls me, he calls me by the thun-der; the
2 Green trees are bend-ing, poor sin-ners stand a-trem-bling; the
3 My Lord, he calls me, he calls me by the light-ning; the

All   D.C.

trum-pet sounds with-in my soul; I ain't got long to stay here.

Text: African-American spiritual
Music: African-American spiritual

613 In heavenly love abiding

HEAVENLY LOVE 76. 76D extended

1 In heav'n-ly love a - bid-ing, no change my heart shall fear, and
2 Wher - ev - er he may guide me, no want shall turn me back. My
3 Green pas-tures are be - fore me, which yet I have not seen. Bright

safe is such con - fid-ing, for noth-ing chang - es here. The storm may
shep-herd is be - side me, and noth-ing can I lack. His
skies will soon be o'er me, where dark - est clouds have been. My

storm may roar with - out me,

roar with - out me, my heart may low be laid, but
wis-dom ev - er wak - eth, his sight is nev-er dim, he
hope I can-not mea - sure, my path to life is free, my

God is 'round a - bout me, and can I be dis - mayed? But
knows the way he tak - eth, and I will walk with him. He
Sav - ior has my trea - sure, and he will walk with me. My

Text: Anna L. Waring, *Hymns and Meditations*, 1850
Music: Felix Mendelssohn, *Sechs Lieder*, Opus 59, No. 3, 1843

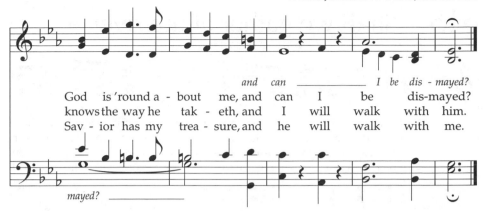

and can _____ I be dis-mayed?

God is 'round a - bout me, and can I be dis-mayed?
knows the way he tak - eth, and I will walk with him.
Sav - ior has my trea - sure, and he will walk with me.

mayed? _____

In the bulb there is a flower 614

PROMISE 87. 87D

1 In the bulb there is a flow - er; in the seed, an ap - ple tree;
2 There's a song in ev - 'ry si - lence, seek - ing word and mel - o - dy.
3 In our end is our be - gin - ning; in our time, in fin - i - ty;

in co - coons, a hid - den prom - ise: But - ter - flies will soon be free!
There's a dawn in ev - 'ry dark - ness, bring - ing hope to you and me.
in our doubt there is be - liev - ing; in our life, e - ter - ni - ty.

In the cold and snow of win - ter there's a spring that waits to be,
From the past will come the fu - ture; what it holds, a mys - ter - y,
In our death, a res - ur - rec - tion; at the last, a vic - to - ry,

un - re - vealed un - til its sea - son, some - thing God a - lone can see.

Text: Natalie Sleeth, 1985
Music: Natalie Sleeth, 1985
        Text and music copyright ©1986 Hope Publishing Co.

615 Shall we gather at the river

BEAUTIFUL RIVER 87. 87 with refrain

1 Shall we gath-er at the riv-er, where bright an-gel feet have
2 On the mar-gin of the riv-er, wash-ing up its sil-ver
3 Ere we reach the shin-ing riv-er, lay we ev-'ry bur-den
4 Soon we'll reach the shin-ing riv-er, soon our pil-grim-age will

trod, with its crys-tal tide for-ev-er flow-ing
spray, we will walk and wor-ship ev-er, all the
down. Grace our spir-its will de-liv-er, and pro-
cease, soon our hap-py hearts will quiv-er with the

Refrain

by the throne of God?
hap-py gold-en day. Yes, we'll gath-er at the riv-er,
vide a robe and crown.
mel-o-dy of peace.

the beau-ti-ful, the beau-ti-ful riv-er, gath-er with the

Text: Robert Lowry, 1864, *Happy Voices*, 1865
Music: Robert Lowry, *Happy Voices*, 1865

saints at the riv-er that flows by the throne of God.

Children of the heavenly Father 616

SANDELL LM

D   A

1 Chil - dren of the heav'n - ly Fa - ther safe - ly
2 God his own doth tend and nour - ish, in his
3 Nei - ther life nor death shall ev - er from the
4 Though he giv - eth or he tak - eth, God his

A⁷   D   G

in his bo - som gath - er. Nes - tling bird nor star in
ho - ly courts they flour - ish. From all e - vil things he
Lord his chil - dren sev - er. Un - to them his grace he
chil - dren ne'er for - sak - eth. His the lov - ing pur - pose

D   B⁷   Em   A   A⁷   D

heav - en such a ref - uge e'er was giv - en.
spares them, in his might - y arms he bears them.
show - eth, and their sor - rows all he know - eth.
sole - ly to pre - serve them pure and ho - ly.

Text: Caroline V. S. Berg, "Tryggare kan ingen vara," *Andeliga Daggdroppar,* 1855; tr. Ernst W. Olson, *The Hymnal,* 1925
Translation copyright ©1925, 1953 Board of Publication, Lutheran Church in America
Music: Swedish melody, *Song Book for Sunday School,* 1871

617 Jesus, keep me near the cross

NEAR THE CROSS 76. 76 with refrain

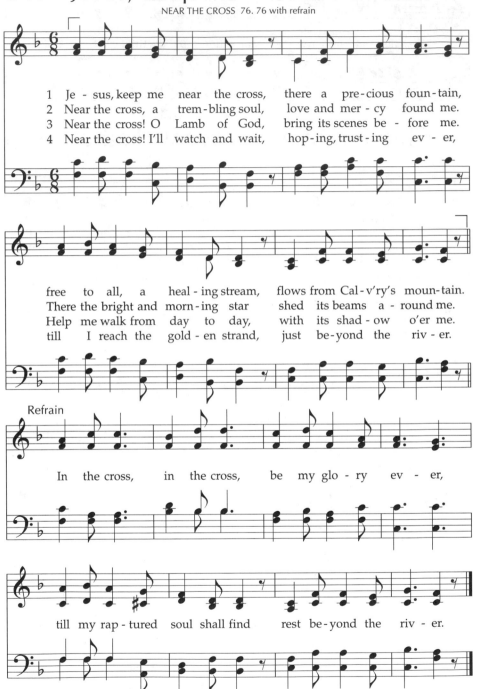

1 Je - sus, keep me near the cross, there a pre - cious foun - tain,
2 Near the cross, a trem - bling soul, love and mer - cy found me.
3 Near the cross! O Lamb of God, bring its scenes be - fore me.
4 Near the cross! I'll watch and wait, hop - ing, trust - ing ev - er,

free to all, a heal - ing stream, flows from Cal - v'ry's moun - tain.
There the bright and morn - ing star shed its beams a - round me.
Help me walk from day to day, with its shad - ow o'er me.
till I reach the gold - en strand, just be - yond the riv - er.

Refrain

In the cross, in the cross, be my glo - ry ev - er,

till my rap - tured soul shall find rest be - yond the riv - er.

Text: Fanny J. Crosby, *Bright Jewels for the Sunday School*, 1869
Music: William H. Doane, *Bright Jewels for the Sunday School*, 1869

Jesus, lover of my soul 618

ABERYSTWYTH 77.77D

1 Je - sus, lov - er of my soul, let me to thy bo - som fly,
2 Oth - er ref - uge have I none; hangs my help-less soul on thee.
3 Thou, O Christ, art all I want, more than all in thee I find –
4 Plen-teous grace with thee is found, grace to cov - er all my sin.

while the near - er wa-ters roll, while the tem-pest still is high.
Leave, ah, leave me not a - lone, still sup - port and com-fort me.
raise the fall - en, cheer the faint, heal the sick, and lead the blind.
Let the heal-ing streams a-bound, make and keep me pure with-in.

Hide me, O my Sav - ior, hide, till the storm of life is past,
All my trust on thee is stayed, all my help from thee I bring.
Just and ho - ly is thy name; I am all un - right-eous-ness.
Thou of life the foun-tain art, free-ly let me take of thee.

safe in - to the ha-ven guide, O re - ceive my soul at last.
Cov - er my de-fense-less head with the shad-ow of thy wing.
False and full of sin I am; thou art full of truth and grace.
Spring thou up with - in my heart, rise to all e - ter - ni - ty.

Text: Charles Wesley, *Hymns and Sacred Poems*, 1740
Music: Joseph Parry, *Ail Llyfr Tonau ac Emynau*, 1879

619 Glorious things of thee are spoken

AUSTRIAN HYMN 87. 87D

1 Glo - rious things of thee are spo - ken, Zi - on, cit - y
2 See, the streams of liv - ing wa - ters spring - ing from e -
3 'Round each hab - i - ta - tion hov - 'ring, see the cloud and
4 Sav - ior, if of Zi - on's cit - y I, through grace, a

of our God. He whose word can - not be bro - ken formed thee
ter - nal love, well sup - ply thy sons and daugh - ters, and all
fire ap - pear for a glo - ry and a cov - 'ring, show - ing
mem - ber am, let the world de - ride or pit - y, I will

for his own a - bode. On the Rock of ag - es found - ed,
fear of want re - move. Who can faint while such a riv - er
that the Lord is near. Thus de - riv - ing from their ban - ner
glo - ry in thy name. Fad - ing are the world - lings' plea - sures,

what can shake thy sure re - pose? With sal - va - tion's
ev - er flows, their thirst t'as - suage — grace, which like the
light by night and shade by day, safe they feed up -
all their boast - ed pomp and show, sol - id joys and

Text: John Newton, *Olney Hymns, Book I*, 1779, alt.
Music: Franz Joseph Haydn, 1797, *Sacred Music*, 1802

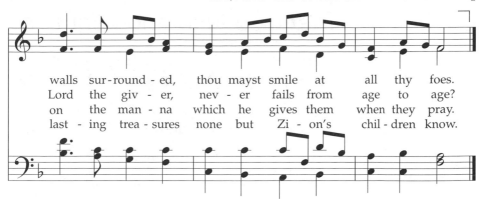

walls sur-round-ed, thou mayst smile at all thy foes.
Lord the giv-er, nev-er fails from age to age?
on the man-na which he gives them when they pray.
last-ing trea-sures none but Zi-on's chil-dren know.

Child of blessing, child of promise 620

STUTTGART 87. 87

1 Child of bless-ing, child of prom-ise,
2 Child of joy, our dear-est trea-sure,
3 Child of God, your lov-ing Par-ent,

love's cre-a-tion, love in-deed! Fresh from God, re-
God's you are, from God you came. Back to God we
learn to know whose child you are. Grow to laugh and

fresh our spir-its, in-to joy and laugh-ter lead.
hum-bly give you, bless-ing you in Je-sus' name.
sing and wor-ship, trust and love God more than all.

Text: Ronald S. Cole-Turner, *Everflowing Streams*, 1981, alt.
         Copyright ©1981 Ronald S. Cole-Turner
Music: attributed to C. F. Witt, *Psalmodia Sacra …*, 1715; adapted by Henry J. Gauntlett, *Hymns Ancient and Modern*, 1861

621 Jesus, friend so kind and gentle

SICILIAN MARINERS 87. 87. 87

1 Je - sus, friend so kind and gen - tle, lit - tle ones we
2 Thou who didst re - ceive the chil - dren to thy - self so

bring to thee. Grant to them thy dear - est bless - ing,
ten - der - ly, give to all who teach and guide them,

let thine arms a - round them be. Now en - fold them
wis - dom and hu - mil - i - ty, vi - sion true to

in thy good - ness, from all dan - ger keep them free.
keep them no - ble, love to serve them faith - ful - ly.

Text: Philip E. Gregory, 1948, *The Hymnbook* (Presbyterian), 1955
Copyright ©1948 Philip E. Gregory
Music: *The European Magazine and London Review*, 1792

Wonder of wonders

622

LOVELLE 10 9. 10 9. 10 9

1 Won - der of won - ders, life is be - gin - ning, frag - ile as
2 Now with re - joic - ing make cel - e - bra - tion; joy full of
3 Lord of cre - a - tion, dy - ing and liv - ing, Fa - ther and

blos - som, strong as the earth. Shaped in a per - son,
prom - ise, laugh - ter through tears. Nam - ing and bless - ing
Moth - er, Part - ner and Friend, lov - er of chil - dren,

love has new mean - ing. Par - ents and peo - ple sing at his* birth.
bring ded - i - ca - tion hum - ble in pur - pose o - ver the years.
lift all our lov - ing in - to your king - dom, world with - out end.

Won - der of won - ders, life is be - gin - ning,

frag - ile as blos - som, strong as the earth!

*Alternate words: "her" or "their"

Text: Brian Wren, 1974, *Faith Looking Forward*, 1983
          Copyright ©1983 Hope Publishing Co.
Music: Larry Warkentin, 1988
          Copyright ©1990 Larry Warkentin

623　When love is found

O WALY WALY LM

1　When love is　found　　　　and hope comes home,
2　When love has flower'd　　in trust　and　care
3　When love is　tried　　　　as loved ones change,
4　When love is　torn　　　　and trust　be - trayed,
5　Praise God for　love,　　　praise God for　life,

1　When love is　found　　　　and hope comes
2　When love has flower'd　　in trust　and
3　When love is　tried　　　　as loved ones
4　When love is　torn　　　　and trust　be -
5　Praise God for　love,　　　praise God for

1　sing and be　glad　　　　that two are　one.
2　build both each day　　　that love may　dare
3　hold still to　hope　　　　though all seems strange,
4　pray strength to love　　till tor-ments　fade,
5　in　age　or　youth,　　　in hus-band,　wife.

1　home,　　　　sing and be　glad　　　　that two are
2　care　　　　　build both each day　　　that love may
3　change,　　　hold still to　hope　　　　though all seems
4　trayed,　　　pray strength to love　　till tor - ments
5　life,　　　　in　age　or　youth,　　　in hus-band,

Text:　Brian Wren, 1978, *Faith Looking Forward*, 1983
　　　　Copyright ©1983 Hope Publishing Co.
Music:　traditional English melody; harmonized by Alice Parker
　　　　Harmonization copyright ©1989 Alice Parker

1 When love ex - plodes   and fills the   sky,
2 to   reach be - yond   home's warmth and light,
3 till   ease re - turns   and love grows   wise
4 till   lov - ers keep   no score of   wrong,
5 Lift   up your hearts!   Let love be   fed

1 one.   When love ex - plodes   and fills the
2 dare   to   reach be - yond   home's warmth and
3 strange,   till   ease re - turns   and love grows
4 fade,   till   lov - ers keep   no score of
5 wife.   Lift   up your hearts!   Let love be

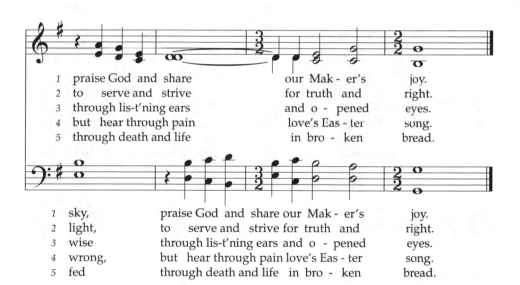

1 praise God and share   our Mak - er's   joy.
2 to   serve and strive   for truth and   right.
3 through lis-t'ning ears   and o - pened   eyes.
4 but hear through pain   love's Eas - ter   song.
5 through death and life   in bro - ken   bread.

1 sky,   praise God and share our Mak - er's   joy.
2 light,   to   serve and strive for truth and   right.
3 wise   through lis-t'ning ears and o - pened   eyes.
4 wrong,   but hear through pain love's Eas - ter song.
5 fed   through death and life in bro - ken   bread.

624 O perfect Love

SANDRINGHAM 11 10. 11 10

1 O per-fect Love, all hu-man thought tran-scend-ing,
2 O per-fect Life, be thou their full as-sur-ance
3 Grant them the joy which bright-ens earth-ly sor-row.

low-ly we kneel in prayer be-fore thy throne,
of ten-der char-i-ty and stead-fast faith,
Grant them the peace which calms all earth-ly strife,

that theirs may be the love which knows no end-ing,
of pa-tient hope, and qui-et, brave en-dur-ance,
and to life's day the glo-rious, un-known mor-row

whom thou for-ev-er-more dost join in one.
with child-like trust that fears not pain nor death.
that dawns up-on e-ter-nal love and life.

Text: Dorothy F. B. Gurney, 1883, *Supplement to Hymns Ancient and Modern*, 1889
Music: Joseph Barnby, 1889, *Church Hymnary*, 1898

Your love, O God, has called us 625

CORNISH LM

1 Your love, O God, has called us here, for all love
2 O gra-cious God, you con-se-crate all that is
3 O God of love, in-spire our life, re-veal your

finds its source in you, the per-fect love that
love-ly, good, and true. Bless those who in your
will in all we do. Join ev-'ry hus-band,

casts out fear, the love that Christ makes ev-er new.
pres-ence wait and ev-'ry day their love re-new.
ev-'ry wife in mu-tual love and love for you.

Text: Russell Schulz-Widmar, 1981, *The Hymnal 1982,* 1985
            Copyright ©1982 Hope Publishing Co.
Music: M. Lee Suitor, ca. 1975, *The Hymnal 1982,* 1985
            Copyright ©1984 M. Lee Suitor

626 Hear us now, O God our Maker

HYFRYDOL 87. 87D

1 Hear us now, O God our Ma - ker, send your
2 Give them joy to light - en sor - row, give them

Spir - it from a - bove on this Chris - tian man and
hope to bright - en life. Go with them to face the

wom - an who here make their vows of love!
mor - row, stay with them in ev - 'ry strife.

Bind their hearts in true de - vo - tion end - less
As your word has prom - ised, ev - er fill them

Text: Harry N. Huxhold, 1971, *Lutheran Book of Worship*, 1978, alt.
         Copyright ©1978 *Lutheran Book of Worship*
Music: Rowland H. Prichard, 1830, *Cyfaill y Cantorion,* 1844; arranged by Ralph Vaughan Williams, *The English Hymnal,* 1906,
         adapted 1951, *BBC Hymn Book*
         Arrangement copyright © Oxford University Press, London

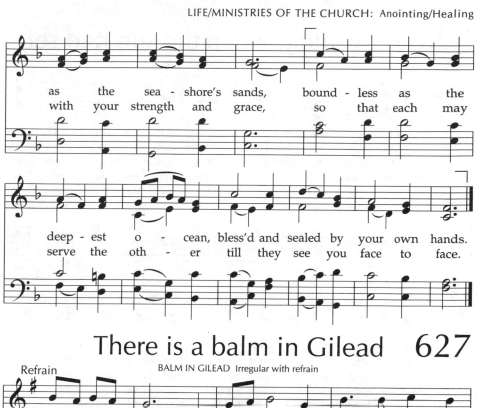

as   the   sea - shore's   sands,   bound - less   as   the
with   your   strength   and   grace,   so   that   each   may

deep - est   o -   cean,   bless'd and sealed by   your   own   hands.
serve   the   oth -   er   till   they   see   you   face   to   face.

There is a balm in Gilead   627

BALM IN GILEAD Irregular with refrain

Refrain

There   is   a   balm   in   Gil - e - ad   to   make   the wound - ed

whole,   there   is   a   balm   in   Gil - e - ad   to

Fine

heal   the   sin - sick   soul.   1 Some - times   I   feel   dis -
2 If   you   can - not preach like

cour - aged   and   think   my   work's   in   vain,   but
Pe - ter,   if you   can - not   pray   like   Paul,   you can

D.C.

then   the   Ho - ly   Spir - it   re - vives   my   soul   a - gain.
tell   the love of   Je - sus   and   say, "He died for   all."

Text: African-American spiritual
Music: African-American spiritual

628 At evening, when the sun had set

ANGELUS (WHITSUN HYMN) LM

1 At eve-ning, when the sun had set, the sick, O
2 Once more the Heal-er comes, and we, op-pressed with
3 O Sav-ior Christ, our fears dis-pel — for some are
4 And none, O Lord, have per-fect rest, for none are
5 O Sav-ior Christ, the Son of Man, you have been
6 Your touch has still its an-cient pow'r; no word from

1 Lord, a-round you lay. In what dis-tress and
2 var-ious ills, draw near. And though your form we
3 sick and some are sad, and some have nev-er
4 whol-ly free from sin; and those who long to
5 trou-bled, test-ed, tried. Your kind but search-ing
6 you can fruit-less fall. Meet with us in this

1 pain they met, but in what joy they went a-way!
2 can-not see, we know and feel that you are here.
3 loved you well, and some have lost the love they had.
4 serve you best are con-scious most of wrong with-in.
5 glance can scan the ver-y wounds that shame would hide.
6 sa-cred hour and in your mer-cy heal us all!

Text: Henry Twells, *Hymns Ancient and Modern, Appendix,* 1868; revised in *Hymns for Today's Church,* 1982, alt.
Copyright ©1982 Hope Publishing Co.
Music: attributed to Georg Joseph, *Heilige Seelenlust,* 1657; altered in *Cantica Spiritualia,* 1847

Immortal Love, forever full   629

SERENITY CM

1 Im - mor - tal Love, for - ev - er full, for - ev - er flow - ing free, for - ev - er shared, for - ev - er whole, a nev - er - ebb - ing sea!

2 Up - on our lips we bear the Name all oth - er names a - bove; yet Love a - lone knows whence it came, that all - em - brac - ing Love.

3 We may not climb the heav'n - ly steeps to bring the Lord Christ down. In vain we search the low - est deeps, for him no depths can drown.

4 But warm, sweet, ten - der, e - ven yet a pres - ent help is he, and faith has still its Ol - i - vet, and love its Gal - i - lee.

5 The mar - gin of his robe we feel through sor - row and through pain. We touch the Lord whose love can heal, and we are whole a - gain.

Text: John Greenleaf Whittier, *The Independent*, 1866; revised in *Hymns for Today's Church*, 1982
Copyright ©1982 Hope Publishing Co.
Music: William V. Wallace; adapted by Uzziah C. Burnap from "Ye winds that waft …," 1856

630 Silence! frenzied, unclean spirit

AUTHORITY 87. 87D

1 "Si - lence! fren - zied, un - clean spir - it,"
2 Lord, the de - mons still are thriv - ing
3 Si - lence, Lord, the un - clean spir - it,

cried God's heal - ing, ho - ly One. "Cease your rant - ing!
in the grey cells of the mind: ty - rant voic - es,
in our mind and in our heart. Speak your word that

Flesh can't bear it. Flee as night be -
shrill and driv - ing, twist - ed thoughts that
when we hear it all our de - mons

fore the sun." At Christ's voice the de - mon trem - bled,
grip and bind, doubts that stir the heart to pan - ic,
shall de - part. Clear our thought and calm our feel - ing,

from its vic - tim mad - ly rushed, while the crowd that
fears dis - tort - ing rea - son's sight, guilt that makes our
still the frac - tured, war - ring soul. By the pow - er

was as - sem - bled stood in won - der, stunned and hushed.
lov - ing fran - tic, dreams that cloud the soul with fright.
of your heal - ing make us faith - ful, true and whole.

Text: based on Mark 1:21-28 and Luke 4:31-37, Thomas H. Troeger, *New Hymns for the Lectionary,* 1986
Music: Carol Doran, *New Hymns for the Lectionary,* 1986
Text and music copyright ©1984 Oxford University Press, Inc.

Anoint us, Lord

631

ANOINT US, LORD Irregular

1,4 A - noint us, Lord, we feel the need of your
2 A - noint us, Lord, we are sick and a -
3 A - noint us, Lord, we want to give our-selves to

strength. Flow through our lives with your love.
lone. Lone - ly and lost, we seek re - lief.
you, strengths and weak-ness-es a - like.

Pour your cool-ing oils down, give us sound - ness of
Pour your cool-ing oils down, while prayers of faith we
Pour your cool-ing oils down, and con - se-crate our

breath. Bring your Spir - it like a dove.
raise. New life we shall re - ceive.
lives. We give our - selves to you.

Text: John David Bowman, *The Brethren Songbook,* 1979
Music: John David Bowman, *The Brethren Songbook,* 1979, alt.

632 God the Spirit, Guide and Guardian

HYFRYDOL 87.87D

1 God the Spir - it, Guide and Guard - ian, wind - sped
2 Christ our Sav - ior, Sov - 'reign, Shep - herd, Word - made -

Flame and hov - 'ring Dove, Breath of life and Voice of
flesh, Love cru - ci - fied, Teach - er, Heal - er, suf - f'ring

proph - ets, Sign of bless - ing, Pow - er of love:
Ser - vant, Friend of sin - ners, Foe of pride:

Give to those who lead your peo - ple fresh a -
In your tend - ing may all min - is - ters learn and

noint - ing of your grace. Send them forth as
live a shep - herd's care. Grant them cour - age

Text: Carl P. Daw, Jr., 1987, *The United Methodist Hymnal*, 1989
         Copyright ©1989 Hope Publishing Co.
Music: Rowland H. Prichard, ca. 1830, *Cyfaill y Cantorion*, 1844; arranged by Ralph Vaughan Williams, *The English Hymnal*, 1906,
         adapted 1951, *BBC Hymn Book*
         Arrangement copyright © Oxford University Press, London

bold a - pos - tles to your church in ev - 'ry place.
and com - pas - sion shown through word and deed and prayer.

Whom shall I send? 633

DEUS TUORUM MILITUM LM

1 Whom shall I send? our Mak - er cries; and man - y,
2 For who can serve a God so pure, or claim to
3 And yet, be - liev - ing God who calls knows what we
4 Those who are called God pur - i - fies, and dai - ly

when they hear God's voice, are sure where their vo -
speak in such a name, while doubt makes ev - 'ry
are and still may be, our past de - feats, our
gives us strength to bend our thoughts, our skills, our

ca - tion lies, but man - y shrink from such a choice.
step un - sure, and self con - fus - es ev - 'ry aim?
fu - ture falls, we dare to an - swer, "Lord, send me!"
en - er - gies, and life it - self to this one end.

Text: Fred Pratt Green, *26 Hymns*, 1971
         Copyright ©1971 Hope Publishing Co.
Music: French church melody, *Grenoble Antiphoner*, 1753

634 Let hope and sorrow now unite

MIT FREUDEN ZART 87. 87. 887

1 Let hope and sor-row now u-nite to con-se-crate
2 With faith, or doubt, or o-pen mind we whis-per life's
3 Be glad for life, in age or youth; its worth is past

life's end - ing, and praise good friends now gone from sight,
great ques - tion. The ebb and flow of space and time
con - ceiv - ing. And stand by jus - tice, love, and truth

though grief and loss are rend - ing. The sto - ry in
sur - pass our small per - cep - tion. Yet knowl-edge grows
as pat - terns for be - liev - ing. Give thanks for all

a well-loved face, the years and days our thoughts re - trace,
with joy - ful gains and finds out won - ders far more strange
each per - son gives – as faith comes true, and Je - sus lives,

Text: Brian Wren, 1979, *Faith Looking Forward*, 1983, alt.
Copyright ©1983 Hope Publishing Co.
Music: adapted from GENEVA 138, *Genevan Psalter*, 1547, Bohemian Brethren's *Kirchengeseng*, 1566

are   trea - sures worth   de - fend - ing.
than   hopes   of   res - ur - rec - tion.
there'll   be   an   end   to   griev - ing.

O Lord of life, wherever they be 635

VICTORY 888 with alleluia

1 O   Lord   of   life,   wher - e'er   they   be,
2 All souls are thine,   and,   here   or   there,
3 Thy word   is   true,   thy   ways   are   just;
4 Oh, hap - py   they   in   God   who   rest,

safe in thine   own   e - ter - ni - ty,   our dead are
they rest with - in   thy   shel - t'ring care.   One prov - i -
a - bove the   re - quiem, "Dust to dust,"   shall rise our
no more by   fear   and   doubt   op - pressed;   liv - ing or

liv - ing   un - to   thee.
dence a - like   they share.
psalm of grate - ful trust.   Al - le - lu - ia!
dy - ing, they are bless'd.

Text: Frederick L. Hosmer, 1888, "Chicago Unity," *The Thoughts of God in Hymns and Poems*, 2nd series, 1894
Music: Giovanni P. da Palestrina, *Magnificat in the Third Mode*, 1591; adapted by William H. Monk, *Hymns Ancient and Modern*, 1861

636
For all the saints

SINE NOMINE 10 10 10 with alleluias

1 For all the saints, who from their la - bors rest, who
2 Thou wast their rock, their for - tress, and their might, __
3 Oh, may thy peo - ple, faith - ful, true, and bold, __
7 But lo! there breaks a yet more glo - rious day; the
8 From earth's wide bounds, from o - cean's far - thest coast, through

1 thee by faith be - fore the world con - fessed, thy
2 thou, Lord, their cap - tain in the well-fought fight, __
3 fight as the saints who no - bly fought of old, and
7 saints tri - um - phant rise in bright ar - ray, the
8 gates of pearl streams in the count - less host, __

1 name, O Je - sus, be for - ev - er bless'd.
2 thou, in the dark - ness drear, the one true light.
3 win, with them, the glo - rious crown of gold.
7 King of glo - ry pass - es on his way.
8 sing - ing to Fa - ther, Son, and Ho - ly Ghost,

Harmony

4 Oh, bless'd com-mun-ion, fel-low-ship di - vine! We fee-bly strug-gle,
5 And when the strife is fierce, the suf-f'ring long, steals on the ear the
6 The gold-en eve-ning bright-ens in the West. Soon, soon to faith-ful

they in glo-ry shine, yet all are one in thee, for all are
dis-tant tri-umph song, and hearts are brave a - gain, and arms are
ser-vants com-eth rest. _____ Sweet is the calm of par - a - dise the

thine.
strong. Al - le - lu - ia, al - le - lu - ia!
bless'd.

Text: William W. How, *Hymns for Saints' Days, and Other Hymns,* 1864, alt.
Music: Ralph Vaughan Williams, *The English Hymnal,* 1906
        Copyright © Oxford University Press, London

637

When grief is raw

RYAN 10 4 10 4 8 10

1 When grief is raw and mu - sic goes un - heard
2 When time gives room for grat - i - tude and tears,
3 The height and breadth of what your love pre - pares
4 All shall be judged, the great - est and the least,

and thought is numb, we have no pol - ished phras - es to re - cite.
Lord, make us free to grieve, re - mem - ber, hon - or and de - light.
soar out of time be - yond our spec - u - la - tion and our sight.
and all be loved till ev - 'ry hurt is healed, all wrong set right.

You are our Lord. In faith we grasp fa - mil - iar
Let love be strong to bear re - grets and ban - ish
The cross re - mains to earth the prom - ise that it
Sing and be glad! The Lamb pre - pares his wed - ding

words: "I am the res - ur - rec - tion, I am life."
fears – "I am the res - ur - rec - tion, I am life."
bears: "I am the res - ur - rec - tion, I am life."
feast and in the midst of death we are in life.

Text: Brian Wren, 1976, *Faith Looking Forward*, 1983
        Copyright ©1983 Hope Publishing Co.
Music: Larry Warkentin, 1989
        Copyright ©1990 Larry Warkentin

God is working his purpose out 638

PURPOSE Irregular

1 God is work-ing his pur-pose out as year suc-
2 From ut-most east to ut-most west, where hu-man
3 March we forth in the strength of God, with the ban-ner of
4 All we can do is noth-ing worth un - less God

ceeds to year. God is work - ing his
feet have trod, by the mouth of man - y
Christ un - furled, that the light of the glo - rious
bless-es the deed. Vain - ly we hope for the

pur-pose out, and the time is draw-ing near. Near-er and
mes - sen - gers goes forth the voice of God, "Give ear to
gos - pel of truth may shine through-out the world. Fight we the
har - vest - tide till God gives life to the seed. Yet near-er and

near - er draws the time, the time that shall sure - ly be,
me, ye con - ti-nents, ye isles, give ear to me,
fight with sor-row and sin to set the cap-tives free,
near - er draws the time, the time that shall sure - ly be,

when the earth shall be filled with the glo - ry of God
that the earth may be filled with the glo - ry of God
that the earth may be filled with the glo - ry of God
when the earth shall be filled with the glo - ry of God

1-3   4

as the wa-ters cov-er the sea.
as the wa-ters cov-er the sea."
as the wa-ters cov-er the sea.
as the wa-ters cov-er the sea.

Text: Arthur C. Ainger, 1894, *Church Missionary Hymn Book*, 1899, alt.
Music: Martin Shaw, *Enlarged Songs of Praise*, 1931
Copyright © Oxford University Press, London

639 Great God, we sing

WAREHAM LM

1 Great God, we sing that might-y hand, by which sup-
2 With grate-ful hearts the past we own. The fu-ture,
3 In scenes ex-alt-ed or de-pressed, thou art our

port-ed, still we stand. The o-p'ning year thy mer-cy
all to us un-known, we to thy guard-ian care com-
joy, and thou our rest. Thy good-ness all our hopes shall

shows; that mer-cy crowns it, till it close.
mit, and, peace-ful, leave be-fore thy feet.
raise, a-dored through all our chang-ing days.

Text: Philip Doddridge, *Hymns Founded on Various Texts in Holy Scriptures,* 1755
Music: William Knapp, *A Sett of New Psalm Tunes and Anthems,* 1738

This is a day of new beginnings 640

NEW BEGINNINGS 98. 98

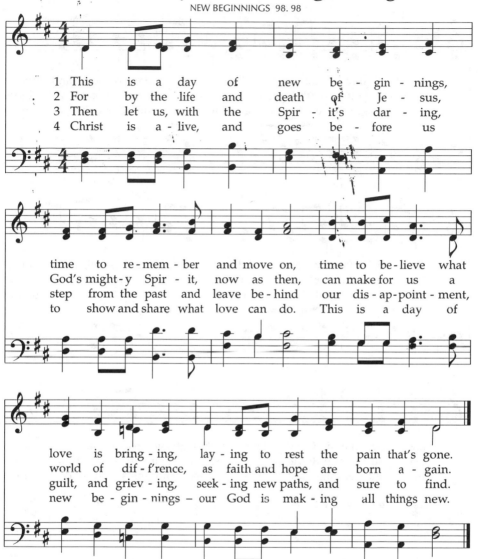

1 This is a day of new be - gin - nings,
2 For by the life and death of Je - sus,
3 Then let us, with the Spir - it's dar - ing,
4 Christ is a - live, and goes be - fore us

time to re - mem - ber and move on, time to be - lieve what
God's might - y Spir - it, now as then, can make for us a
step from the past and leave be - hind our dis - ap - point - ment,
to show and share what love can do. This is a day of

love is bring - ing, lay - ing to rest the pain that's gone.
world of dif - f'rence, as faith and hope are born a - gain.
guilt, and griev - ing, seek - ing new paths, and sure to find.
new be - gin - nings – our God is mak - ing all things new.

Text: Brian Wren, 1978, *Faith Looking Forward*, 1983, alt.
            Copyright ©1983, 1987 Hope Publishing Co.
Music: Richard D. Brode
            Copyright ©1991 Richard D. Brode

641 O day of rest and gladness

MENDEBRAS 76. 76D

1 O   day of rest and   glad-ness, O   day of joy and   light,
2 On   you, at earth's cre - a - tion, the   light first had its   birth.
3 New   grac-es ev - er   gain-ing from   this our day of   rest,

O   balm for care and   sad-ness, most   beau - ti - ful, most   bright;
On   you, for our   sal - va - tion, Christ   rose from depths of   earth.
we   reach the rest   re - main-ing to   spir - its of the   bless'd.

on   you, the high and   low - ly through ag - es   joined in   tune,
On   you, our Lord vic - to - rious, the   Spir - it   sent from heav'n,
In   shouts of high - est   prais - es, the   chur-ch's   voice is   heard,

sing   "Ho - ly, ho - ly,   ho - ly," to   the great   God   Tri - une.
and   thus on you most   glo-rious, a   three-fold   light   was   giv'n.
the   Three - in - One a - dor - ing: Cre - a - tor,   Spir - it,   Word.

Text: Christopher Wordsworth, *Holy Year ...,* 1862, alt.
Music: German melody, adapted by Lowell Mason, *Modern Psalmist,* 1839

This is the day the Lord has made 642

ARLINGTON CM

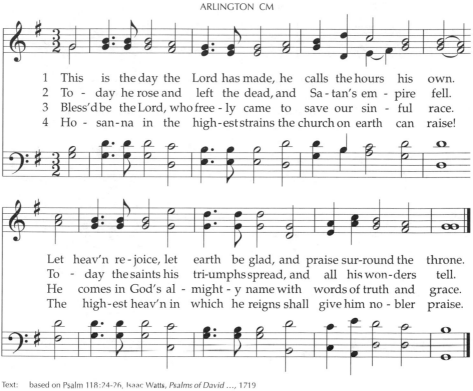

1 This is the day the Lord has made, he calls the hours his own.
2 To - day he rose and left the dead, and Sa - tan's em - pire fell.
3 Bless'd be the Lord, who free - ly came to save our sin - ful race.
4 Ho - san - na in the high - est strains the church on earth can raise!

Let heav'n re - joice, let earth be glad, and praise sur - round the throne.
To - day the saints his tri - umphs spread, and all his won - ders tell.
He comes in God's al - might - y name with words of truth and grace.
The high - est heav'n in which he reigns shall give him no - bler praise.

Text: based on Psalm 118:24-26, Isaac Watts, *Psalms of David …*, 1719
Music: Thomas A. Arne 1762; adapted by Ralph Harrison, *Sacred Harmony*, Vol. I, 1784

Amen 643

Canon

A - men, a - men, a - men.

A - men, a - men, a - men, a - men.

A - men, a - men, a - men.

Music: Richard Proulx, 1982, "Eucharistic Prayer for Children II," 1986
Copyright ©1986 G.I.A. Publications, Inc.

644 When morning gilds the skies

LAUDES DOMINI 666. 666

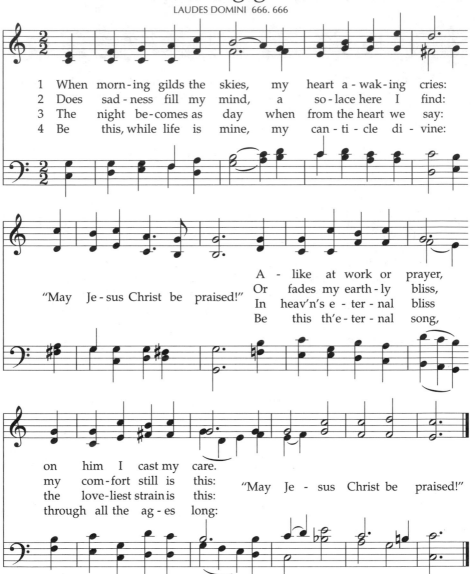

1 When morn-ing gilds the skies, my heart a-wak-ing cries:
2 Does sad-ness fill my mind, a so-lace here I find:
3 The night be-comes as day when from the heart we say:
4 Be this, while life is mine, my can-ti-cle di-vine:

"May Je-sus Christ be praised!"

A - like at work or prayer,
Or fades my earth-ly bliss,
In heav'n's e-ter-nal bliss
Be this th'e-ter-nal song,

on him I cast my care.
my com-fort still is this:
the love-liest strain is this:
through all the ag-es long:

"May Je - sus Christ be praised!"

Text: *Katholisches Gesangbuch*, 1828; tr. Edward Caswall, *Catholic Hymns*, 1854, *Masque of Mary*, 1858, revised 1873, alt.
Music: Joseph Barnby, *Hymns Ancient and Modern*, Appendix, 1868

Each morning brings us

ALL MORGEN IST GANZ FRISCH LM

1 Each morn - ing brings us fresh out - poured the
2 O God, thou Star of dawn - ing day, give
3 to walk as by the light of day, that

1 Each morn - ing brings us fresh out - poured the
2 O God, thou Star of dawn - ing day, give
3 to walk as by the light of day, that

lov-ing-kind-ness of the Lord. It ends not as the
us that light for which we pray. Make thou thy flame in
we may ev - er, come what may, in our faith strong, un -

lov-ing-kind-ness of the Lord. It ends not as the day
us that light for which we pray. Make thou thy flame in us
we may ev - er, come what may, in our faith strong, un-wav-

day goes past, but gives us strength while life shall last.
us to glow, that we no lack of grace may know;
wav-'ring be, a - bid - ing stead-fast one with thee.

goes past, but gives us strength while life shall last.
to glow, that we no lack of grace may know;
'ring be, a - bid - ing stead - fast one with thee.

Text: Johannes Zwick, *All Morgen ist ganz frisch und neu*, ca. 1536, *Nüw Gesangbüchle*, 3rd ed., 1545; tr. Margaret Barclay, 1951,
        Cantate Domino, 1951
Music: *Wittenbergisch Gesangbüchli*, 1537; adapted by Johann Walther

646 O Splendor of God's glory bright

SPLENDOR PATERNAE LM

1	O Splen-dor of God's glo-ry bright,	from light e-ter-nal
2	Come, ver-y Sun of heav-en's love,	in last-ing ra-diance
3	Con-firm our will to do the right,	and keep our hearts from
4	Be hal-low'd this and ev-'ry day;	let meek-ness be our
5	O Lord, with each re-turn-ing morn	thine im-age to our

1	bring-ing light,	thou Light of lights, light's liv-ing spring,
2	from a-bove,	and pour the Ho-ly Spir-it's ray
3	en-vy's blight.	Let faith her ea-ger fires re-new,
4	morn-ing ray,	and faith-ful love our noon-day light,
5	hearts is borne.	Oh, may we ev-er clear-ly see

1	true day, all days il-lu-min-ing:	
2	on all we think or do	to-day.
3	and hate the false and love	the true.
4	our hope, our sun-set, calm	and bright.
5	our Sav-ior and our God	in thee. A-men

Text: Ambrose of Milan, *Splendor paternae gloriae*, 4th c.; composite translation
Music: Sarum plainsong, *Sarum Antiphonal*

647 Por la mañana (At break of day)

		C Irregular
1	Por la mañ-a-na* yo di-ri-jo mi a-la-ban-za
2	Cuan-do la no-che sea-prox-i-ma, ten-e-bro-sa,
1	At break of day I raise my voice in ad-o-ra-tion
2	When shades of night de-scend and threat-en to op-press us,

	a Dios que ha si-do y es mi ú-ni-ca es-per-an-za.
	en el e-var-le mi o-ra-ción mi al-ma se go-za;
	to God who is my on-ly hope and my sal-va-tion.
	my soul in prayer re-joic-ing-ly God's name con-fess-es.

*Original title: Pero Queda Cristo

Por la mañ - a - na yo le in - vo - co con el al - ma
sien - to su paz in - a - go - ta - ble, dul - ce y gra - ta
At break of day my long - ing soul in - vokes Christ's mer - it,
A peace so great and won - der - ful be - yond de - scrip - tion

y le su - pli - co que me dé su dul - ce cal - ma.
por - que te - mor - es y an - sie - dad Cris - to los ma - ta.
know - ing his grace will bring peace to my rest - less spir - it.
is mine, for Christ re - moves all wor - ry and af - flic - tion.

Y él nos es - cu - cha pues nos a - ma tan - to,
Tam - bién el - e - vo mi can - tar al cie - lo
Be - cause of his great love he hears our prayers,
I al - so raise my voice in ad - o - ra - tion

y nos a - li - via de cual - quier que - bran - to.
cuan - do a la tie - rra ba - ja ne - gro ve - lo.
grant - ing re - lief from all our fears and cares.
when all the world is suf - f'ring trib - u - la - tion.

Nos da su ma - no po - der - o - sa y fuer - te,
El sol se o - cul - ta, pe - ro que - da Cris - to,
His might - y hand up - holds us with his pow - er,
The sun goes down, with night its shad - ow cast - ing,

pa - ra li - brar - nos de la mis - ma muer - te.
a quien mis o - jos en el sue - lo han vis - to.
e - ven de - liv - er - ing us in death's hour.
but Christ re - mains. His love is ev - er - last - ing.

Text: Alfredo Colom M.; tr. Mary B. Valencia
Translation ©1978, 1990 Mennonite World Conference
Music: Alfredo Colom M.
Text (Spanish) and music copyright ©1954 Singspiration Music

648 Morning has broken

BUNESSAN 10 9. 10 9

1 Morn-ing has bro - ken   like the first morn - ing;
2 Sweet the rain's new   fall,   sun - lit from heav - en,
3 Mine is the sun - light,   mine is the morn - ing,

black-bird has spo - ken   like the first bird.   Praise for the sing - ing,
like the first dew - fall   on the first grass.   Praise for the sweet - ness
born of the one light   E - den saw play.   Praise with e - la - tion,

praise for the morn - ing,   praise for them, spring - ing   fresh from the Word.
of the wet gar - den,   sprung in com - plete - ness   where his feet pass.
praise ev-'ry morn - ing,   God's re - cre - a - tion   of the new day.

Text: Eleanor Farjeon, *Enlarged Songs of Praise,* 1931, alt.
    Copyright ©1957 Eleanor Farjeon
Music: Gaelic melody, *Songs and Hymns of the Gael,* 1888; harmonized by Martin Shaw, alt.
    Harmonization copyright © Oxford University Press, London

On the radiant threshold 649

BE THOU OUR GUIDE 65. 65 with refrain

1 On the ra-diant thresh-old of this dawn-ing day,
2 Lo! the Sav-ior bids us come to seek his aid,
3 Keep us from temp - ta-tion, bless in ev - 'ry need.

in the sa-cred still-ness, we will pause and pray.
of - fers help and guid-ance till the eve-ning's shade.
Lead us, gen-tle Shep-herd, where thy flocks do feed.

Refrain

In the morn-ing, noon, and eve-ning, we would seek thy side.

O do thou, dear Lord, be-friend us, O be thou our guide.

Text: Albert C. Wieand, *Gospel Songs and Hymns, No. 1*, 1898, alt.
Music: George B. Holsinger, *Gospel Songs and Hymns, No. 1*, 1898

650 Father, we praise thee

CHRISTE SANCTORUM 11 11 11 5

1 Fa - ther, we praise thee, now the night is o - ver.
Ac - tive and watch - ful, stand we all be - fore thee.
Sing - ing, we of - fer prayer and med - i - ta - tion — thus we a - dore thee.

2 Mon - arch of all things, fit us for thy man - sions.
Ban - ish our weak - ness, health and whole - ness send - ing.
Bring us to heav - en, where thy saints u - nit - ed joy with - out end - ing.

3 All - ho - ly Fa - ther, Son, and e - qual Spir - it, Trin - i - ty bless - ed,
send us thy sal - va - tion. Thine is the glo - ry, gleam - ing and re - sound - ing through all cre - a - tion.

Text: attributed to Gregory the Great, *Nocte surgentes vigilemus omnes*, 6th c.; tr. Percy Dearmer, *The English Hymnal*, 1906
Translation copyright © Oxford University Press, London
Music: French church melody, *Paris Antiphoner*, 1681

I owe the Lord a morning song   651

GRATITUDE CM

1 I owe the Lord a morn - ing song of
2 He kept me safe an - oth - er night; I
3 Keep me from dan - ger and from sin, help
4 Keep me till thou wilt call me hence, where

grat - i - tude and praise, for the kind mer - cy
see an - oth - er day. Now may his Spir - it,
me thy will to do, so that my heart be
nev - er night can be, and save me, Lord, for

he has shown in length - 'ning out my days.
as the light, di - rect me in his way.
pure with - in, and I thy good - ness know.
Je - sus' sake; he shed his blood for me.

Text: Amos Herr, *Hymns and Tunes …*, 1890
Music: Amos Herr, *Hymns and Tunes …*, 1890
        Text and music copyright ©1927 Mennonite Publishing House

652 The day you gave us, Lord

ST. CLEMENT 98. 98

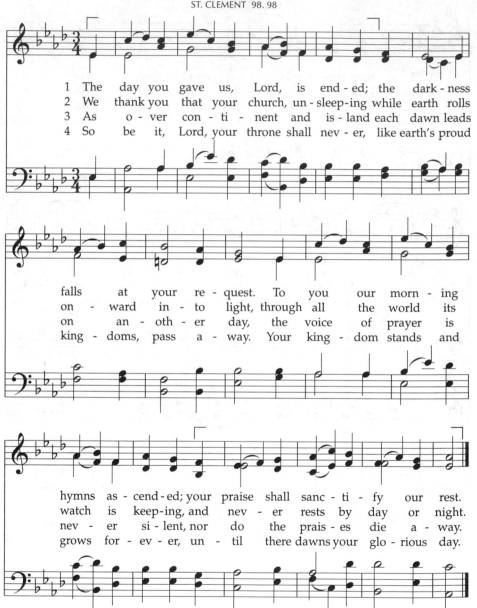

1 The day you gave us, Lord, is end-ed; the dark-ness
2 We thank you that your church, un-sleep-ing while earth rolls
3 As o-ver con-ti-nent and is-land each dawn leads
4 So be it, Lord, your throne shall nev-er, like earth's proud

falls at your re-quest. To you our morn-ing
on-ward in-to light, through all the world its
on an-oth-er day, the voice of prayer is
king-doms, pass a-way. Your king-dom stands and

hymns as-cend-ed; your praise shall sanc-ti-fy our rest.
watch is keep-ing, and nev-er rests by day or night.
nev-er si-lent, nor do the prais-es die a-way.
grows for-ev-er, un-til there dawns your glo-rious day.

Text: John Ellerton, 1870, *Church Hymns*, 1871, alt.
Music: Clement C. Scholefield, *Church Hymns with Tunes*, 1874

Abide with me

EVENTIDE 10 10. 10 10

1 A - bide with me! fast falls the e - ven - tide.
2 Swift to its close ebbs out life's lit - tle day.
3 I need thy pres - ence ev - 'ry pass - ing hour.
4 I fear no foe, with thee at hand to bless.
5 Hold then thy cross be - fore my clos - ing eyes.

1 The dark - ness deep - ens; Lord, with me a - bide.
2 Earth's joys grow dim, its glo - ries pass a - way.
3 What but thy grace can foil the temp - ter's pow'r?
4 Ills have no weight, and tears no bit - ter - ness.
5 Shine through the gloom, and point me to the skies.

1 When oth - er help - ers fail, and com - forts flee,
2 Change and de - cay in all a - round I see.
3 Who like thy - self my guide and stay can be?
4 Where is death's sting? where, grave, thy vic - to - ry?
5 Heav'n's morn - ing breaks, and earth's vain shad - ows flee;

1 Help of the help - less, O a - bide with me.
2 O thou who chang - est not, a - bide with me.
3 Through cloud and sun - shine, O a - bide with me.
4 I tri - umph still, if thou a - bide with me.
5 in life and death, O Lord, a - bide with me.

Text: Henry F. Lyte, 1847, *Remains of Henry Francis Lyte*, 1850
Music: William H. Monk, *Hymns Ancient and Modern*, 1861

654

Sun of my soul

HURSLEY LM

1 Sun of my soul, thou Sav - ior dear, it is not
2 A - bide with me from morn till eve, for with - out
3 Watch by the sick, en - rich the poor with bless - ings
4 Come near and bless us when we wake, ere through the

night if thou be near. Oh, may no earth - born
thee I can - not live. A - bide with me when
from thy bound - less store. Be ev - 'ry mourn - er's
world our way we take, till in the o - cean

cloud a - rise to hide thee from thy ser - vant's eyes.
night is nigh, for with - out thee I dare not die.
sleep to - night, like in - fants' slum - bers, pure and light.
of thy love we lose our - selves in heav'n a - bove.

Text: John Keble, 1820, *Christian Year*, 1827
Music: adapted from GROSSER GOTT, WIR LOBEN DICH, *Katholisches Gesangbuch*, ca. 1774

Now, on land and sea descending 655

VESPER HYMN 87. 87. 86. 87

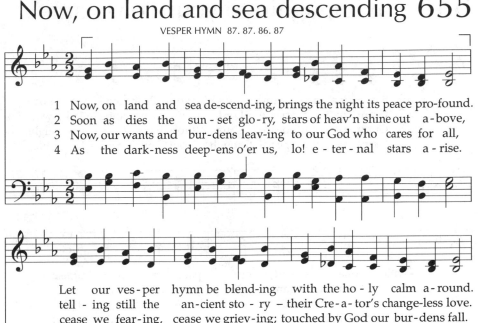

1 Now, on land and sea de-scend-ing, brings the night its peace pro-found.
2 Soon as dies the sun - set glo-ry, stars of heav'n shine out a - bove,
3 Now, our wants and bur-dens leav-ing to our God who cares for all,
4 As the dark-ness deep-ens o'er us, lo! e - ter - nal stars a - rise.

Let our ves-per hymn be blend-ing with the ho - ly calm a-round.
tell - ing still the an-cient sto - ry – their Cre-a-tor's change-less love.
cease we fear-ing, cease we griev-ing; touched by God our bur-dens fall.
Hope and faith and love rise glo-rious, shin-ing in the Spir - it's skies.

Ju - bi - la - te! Ju - bi - la - te! Ju - bi - la - te! A - men!

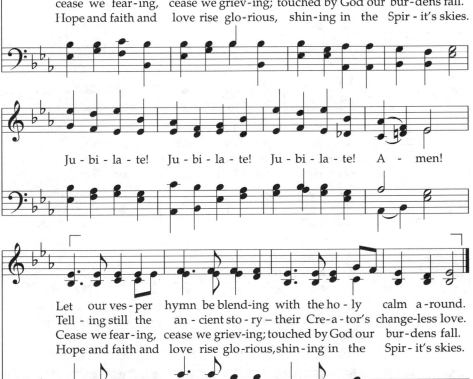

Let our ves - per hymn be blend-ing with the ho - ly calm a-round.
Tell - ing still the an - cient sto - ry – their Cre-a-tor's change-less love.
Cease we fear-ing, cease we griev-ing; touched by God our bur-dens fall.
Hope and faith and love rise glo-rious, shin-ing in the Spir - it's skies.

Text: Samuel Longfellow, *Vespers*, 1859
Music: John A. Stevenson, *A Selection of Popular National Airs*, 1818

656 Savior, again to your dear name

ELLERS 10 10. 10 10

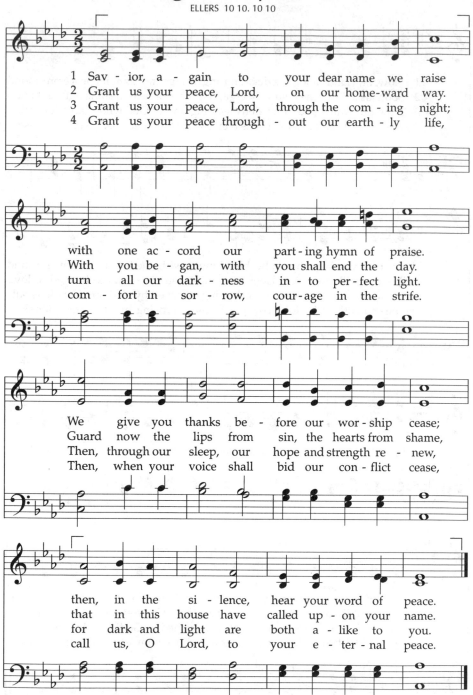

1 Sav - ior, a - gain to your dear name we raise
2 Grant us your peace, Lord, on our home-ward way.
3 Grant us your peace, Lord, through the com - ing night;
4 Grant us your peace through - out our earth - ly life,

with one ac - cord our part - ing hymn of praise.
With you be - gan, with you shall end the day.
turn all our dark - ness in - to per - fect light.
com - fort in sor - row, cour - age in the strife.

We give you thanks be - fore our wor - ship cease;
Guard now the lips from sin, the hearts from shame,
Then, through our sleep, our hope and strength re - new,
Then, when your voice shall bid our con - flict cease,

then, in the si - lence, hear your word of peace.
that in this house have called up - on your name.
for dark and light are both a - like to you.
call us, O Lord, to your e - ter - nal peace.

Text: John Ellerton, 1866, *Hymns Ancient and Modern, Appendix*, 1868, alt.
Music: Edward J. Hopkins, 1866, *Supplemental Tune and Hymn Book*, 1869

Now all the woods are sleeping 657

O WELT, ICH MUSS DICH LASSEN 776. 778

1 Now all the woods are sleep-ing, through fields the shad-ows
2 The ra-diant sun has van-ished, its gold-en rays are
3 Now all the heav'n-ly splen-dor breaks forth in star-light
4 Though long our an-cient blind-ness has missed God's lov-ing-

creep-ing, and cit-ies sink to rest. Let
ban-ished from dark-'ning skies of night. But
ten-der from myr-iad worlds un-known. And
kind-ness and plunged us in-to strife, one

us, as night is fall-ing, up-on our Mak-er
Christ the sun of glad-ness, dis-pel-ling all our
we, this mar-vel see-ing, for-get our self-ish
day when life is o-ver shall death's fair night un-

call-ing, give thanks to God, who loves us best.
sad-ness, shines down on us in warm-est light.
be-ing, for joy of beau-ty not our own.
cov-er the fields of ev-er-last-ing life.

Text: Paul Gerhardt, "Nun ruhen alle Wälder," *Praxis Pietatis Melica,* 1648; composite translation by Inter-Lutheran Commission on Worship, 1978
Translation copyright ©1978 *Lutheran Book of Worship,* alt. Used by permission of Augsburg Fortress
Music: attributed to Heinrich Isaac, *Ein Auszug guter alter und neuer Teutschen Liedlein,* 1539

658 All praise to thee, my God

Unison when sung in canon   TALLIS' CANON LM

1 All praise to thee, my God, this night, for all the bless-ings of the light. Keep me, O keep me, King of kings, be-neath thine own al-might-y wings.

2 For-give me, Lord, for thy dear Son, the ill that I this day have done, that with the world, my-self, and thee, I, ere I sleep, at peace may be.

3 Oh, may my soul on thee re-pose, and with sweet sleep my eye-lids close, sleep that shall me more vig-'rous make to serve my God when I a-wake.

4 Praise God, from whom all bless-ings flow. Praise him, all crea-tures here be-low. Praise him a-bove, ye heav'n-ly host. Praise Fa-ther, Son, and Ho-ly Ghost.

Text: Thomas Ken, 1694, *A Manual of Prayers ...*, 1695
Music: Thomas Tallis, *The Whole Psalter Translated into English Metre*, ca. 1567

INTRODUCTION TO WORSHIP RESOURCES

The worship resources and scripture readings were selected according to four principles: (1) congregational readability; (2) suitability for a variety of worship settings and seasons of the church year; (3) expression of essential themes in Anabaptist and Pietist practice; and (4) representation of various eras of Christian history.

Each reading has been formatted to help worship leaders and congregations grasp its movement of thought. Designations of "Leader," "People," and "ALL" have been given in many instances where such divisions are important for clarity. Where no designations are offered, parts may be assigned at the discretion of the worship leader, or the piece may be read in unison.

The prayers and readings have been organized under the same categories as the hymns. The page banners serve as guides. However, the scripture readings follow the biblical sequence.

All of the resources are indexed topically and by scriptural allusion to aid the search for particular themes or readings appropriate for specific worship settings.

Worship Resources

GATHERING

659

Leader: Grace unto you and peace from God,
who was and who is
and who is to come,

People: **and from Jesus Christ, the faithful witness,**
the first born of the dead,
ruler above all rulers of the earth.

Leader: In love Jesus Christ suffered death to free us from our sins,

People: **making all who confess Christ a nation of priests**
set aside for God's service.

ALL: *To Jesus Christ be glory and power forever and ever!*

660

Leader: The Lord be with you.

People: **And also with you.**

Leader: Lift up your hearts.

People: **We lift them to the Lord.**

Leader: Let us give thanks to the Lord our God.

People: **It is right to give our thanks and praise.**

661

Leader: We gather as pilgrims
on a journey of faith.

People: **We come seeking the cloud of your presence**
as we travel the way.
We come seeking your pillar of fire
to light our darkness.

ALL: *Shine in our hearts, O God,*
with the light of your love.
Make your presence known
through Jesus the Christ. AMEN

662

Leader: Come, let us worship,

People: **for we are the people of God's pasture.**

Leader: Come, let us worship and bow down,

People: **for we are the sheep of God's hand.**

Leader: Come, let us worship and bow down
before the Lord, our Maker.

ALL: *For the Lord is our God,*
and God desires our worship!

663

Leader: The Lord is my light and my salvation;

People: **whom shall I fear?**

Leader: The Lord is the stronghold of my life;

People: **of whom shall I be afraid?**

ALL: *One thing I ask of you, O Lord,*
and that I will pursue:
to live in your house
all the days of my life,
to behold your beauty
and to seek you in your temple.

664

Leader: Watch! Wait!
The day of God is at hand!

People: **Like the bud on a tree,**
God's possibilities are about to blossom!

Leader: Stay awake!
The reign of God is very near.

People: **We are here,**
watching and waiting with hope.

ALL: *May God bring justice to all people*
on this day.
May God's reign come on earth
as in heaven.

665

Leader: Glory to God in the highest

People: **and peace to all people on earth!**

ALL: *Today a Savior is born to us –*
Christ the Lord.
Let all the earth rejoice
in God's great gift.

666

Leader: Call a solemn assembly
and gather the people.
Let all the inhabitants of the land
tremble before our God.

People: **God knows all the secrets of our hearts**
and understands all our ways.

Leader: The day of God is coming;
      it is near –
    a day of clouds and shadows,
    a day of darkness and great gloom.
People: **God's judgments are blameless and sure,**
    but God's grace is sufficient for all our needs.
Leader: Rend your hearts and not your garments;
    come to God with fasting,
    come with weeping and mourning.
People: **We will worship God**
    with pure and loving hearts.
    We will seek to be faithful
    to the One who has called us here.

667

Left: He's coming,
Right: **he's coming,**
ALL: *line his pathway again with palms!*
Left: He's coming,
Right: **he's coming,**
ALL: *clear the pathway; raise the palms!*
He's coming:
    Son of David,
    Suffering Servant,
    Savior,
    Risen Lord!

668

Leader: This is the day that the Lord has made.
    Let us rejoice and be glad in it.
People: **This is the day that the stone is cast aside**
    and the mantle of darkness is torn away.
Leader: God has swallowed up death forever
    and brushed our tears away.
People: **This is the day of salvation.**
Leader: Be glad and rejoice –
    the Lord of Light has come and reigns forever.
    Christ is risen!
People: **Christ is risen indeed!**
ALL: *Alleluia! Alleluia!*

669

Leader: A mighty wind has blown,
People: **and tongues of fire have danced!**
Leader: The Spirit is with us,
People: **just as Jesus promised.**
Leader: God's Spirit moves among us
    and gathers us together.
People: **God's Spirit gives us power**
    and calls us to serve the world.
ALL: *God's Spirit is poured out upon us.*
Worship God with joy!

670

Leader: Our God,
    we gather to worship you, the One who creates all things.
People: For the gift of creation, we give thanks.
Leader: We gather to worship you,
    the One who brings salvation through Jesus Christ.
People: For the gift of redemption, we give thanks.
Leader: We gather to worship you,
    the One who sustains us by the Spirit.
People: For the gift of your presence, we give thanks.
Leader: We bring to you our offerings of thanks and praise
    for all your gifts.
ALL: We worship you – our Creator, Redeemer, and Sustainer. AMEN

671

Leader: O God,
    we come seeking you in our worship together.
We come to you for truth
    because we are untrue.
We come to you for strength
    because we are weak.
We come to you for wisdom
    because we are unwise.
People: Move in our midst;
    show us your truth, your strength, and your wisdom,
    through our Savior, Jesus Christ. AMEN

672

With all your saints across the generations
    we gather, Holy God,
    to approach your mystery and hear your judgment.
We come seeking the faith of those who have gone before us
    in righteousness and truth.
Lead us by your Word
    to walk in your ways
    and observe your commandments. AMEN

673

O God, author of eternal light,
    lead us in our worshipping this day:
        that our lips may praise you,
        our lives may bless you,
        and our meditations glorify you,
        through Christ our Lord. AMEN

674

Dear God, our friend,
    we come to worship you today.
We come to sing, pray, and listen.
You always hear us.
Help us to hear you. AMEN

675

Come, Lord,
　work upon us,
　set us on fire and clasp us close;
　be fragrant to us,
　draw us to your loveliness;
　let us love,
　let us run to you. AMEN

676

O God,
　you withdraw from our sight
　　that you may be known by our love.
Help us to enter the cloud where you are hidden
　　and surrender all our certainty
　　to the darkness of faith
　　in Jesus Christ. AMEN

677

O living Christ,
　come to us in the glory of your risen power;
　come to us in the humility of your wondrous love.
Come and reign among us!
Let new life course through our veins,
　new love bind us together,
　and new vision spur us on to follow you forever.
Even so, come Lord Jesus. AMEN

678

Come, Child of Bethlehem,
　make your presence known to us
　and dwell in our midst as we worship.
Come, servant King,
　teach us the ways of your kingdom
　and make our hearts your throne.
Come, Brother of all,
　show us the meaning of our humanity.
　Go before us and lead us to God;
　bring us to the fullness of your kingdom. AMEN

679

Leader: Holy Spirit, Creating Presence,
　　　　as in the beginning you hover over the waters;
　　　　you breathe life into all creatures;
　　　　without you every living creature dies and returns to nothing.
People: **Come, Holy Spirit.**
Leader: Holy Spirit, Comforter,
　　　　by you we are born again as children of God;
　　　　you make us living temples of your presence;
　　　　you pray within us prayers too deep for words.
People: **Come, Holy Spirit.**

(continued)

Leader: Holy Spirit, Lord and Giver of life,
           you are light; you bring us light;
           you are goodness and the source of all goodness.

People: Come, Holy Spirit.

Leader: Holy Spirit, Breath of life,
           you sanctify and breathe life into the whole body of the church;
           you dwell in each of us
           and will one day give new life to our mortal bodies.

ALL: Come, Holy Spirit.

PRAISING/ADORING

680

God of all life,
  we thank you
    for the signs of your love that surround us,
      for sun and warmth and all that comes to life
        within creation,
      for all that sleeps within the earth awaiting birth.
We praise you
  for the wisdom of your care,
  water on the earth,
  sunlight on our spirits,
  hands on blinded eyes.

Continue to touch us.
Reach out to us with compassion and forgiveness
  that we may receive your gifts,
  that we may know your love and grace
    and rise to new life in Jesus Christ. AMEN

681

Leader: Clap your hands, all you nations;
           shout to God with cries of joy!

**People: How majestic is the Lord Most High;
           how mighty is the great Sovereign over all the earth!**

Leader: Sing praises to God;
           sing psalms in God's honor.

**People: God reigns over the nations;
           God is exalted over all.**

*ALL: Praise the Lord, all people;
           praise God's everlasting name!*

682

May ground below
    air above
    sea around
  be hallowed
  filled with the Three-in-One
    God of life
    Christ of love
    Spirit of peace.

May all cry "GLORY!"
  before the Three-in-One
    God of life
    Christ of love
    Spirit of peace.

683

Praise the One who hears the cry of the poor,
  who lifts up the weak and gives them strength.
Praise the One who feeds the hungry
  and satisfies the longing of those in need.
Praise the One who holds with tenderness the orphan and widow
  and gives the stranger a land and a home.

684

Praise God from the heavens;
  praise God in the heights;
praise God, all you angels;
  praise God, all you heavenly hosts.
Praise God, sun and moon;
  praise God, all you shining stars.
Praise God, you highest heavens,
  and you waters above the heavens.

Let all praise the name of God,
  who commanded and they were created.

God established them forever and ever
  and gave a decree which shall not pass away.
Praise God, all the earth,
  you sea monsters and all depths,
  fire and hail, snow and frost,
  stormy winds that fulfill God's word.
Praise God, you mountains and all hills,
  fruit trees and all cedars,
  wild beasts and all tame animals,
  creeping things and flying birds.
Let the rulers of the earth and all peoples
  and all the judges of the earth –
  men and women alike,
  old and young together –
let them praise the name of God
  whose name alone is exalted;
  whose majesty is above earth and heaven,
  and who has raised the fortunes of the people.

May this God be praised by all the faithful ones,
  by the children of Israel, the people close to God.
Alleluia! Praise God!

685

Blessed be the God and Father of our Lord Jesus Christ,
   who chose us in Christ before the foundation of the world,
   who destined us for adoption,
   who forgave us our trespasses,
   who made known the mystery of the divine will,
   who marked us with the seal of the Spirit.
Blessed be God's name!

686

O God, you are my God.
I seek you, my soul thirsts for you;
   my flesh faints for you,
      as in a dry and weary land
      where there is no water.
So I have looked upon you in the sanctuary,
   beholding your power and glory.
Because your steadfast love is better than life,
   my lips will praise you.
So I will bless you as long as I live;
   I will lift up my hands and call on your name. AMEN

687

Sing to God a new song,
   sing praise from the ends of the earth,
   you who go down to the sea, and all that is in it,
   you islands, and all who live in them.
Let the desert and its towns raise their voices;
   let them give glory and praise to God.

688

Praise the Holy One!
Praise, O servants of God,
   praise the name of the Holy One of Israel.
Let that name be praised,
   both now and forevermore.
From the rising of the sun to its setting
   the name of the Holy One is to be praised.

689

Then I looked, and I heard the voice of many angels surrounding the throne
   and the living creatures and the elders;
      they numbered myriads of myriads and thousands of thousands,
         singing with full voice,
"Worthy is the Lamb that was slain
   to receive power and wealth, wisdom and might,
   honor and glory and blessing!"
Then I heard every creature in heaven
   and on earth and under the earth and in the sea,
      and all that is in them, singing,
"To the One seated on the throne and to the Lamb
   be blessing and honor and glory and might
   forever and ever!"

690

Leader: Have mercy on us, O God,
    according to your unfailing love;

People: **Blot out all our transgressions,**
    according to your great compassion;

Leader: Wash away all our iniquities
    and cleanse us from our sin.

People: **For we know our transgressions,**
    and our sin is always before us.

Leader: We have sinned against you
    and have done what is evil in your sight.

ALL: *As a sacrifice we bring our broken and contrite hearts.*

— PAUSE FOR SILENCE. —

Leader: God will create in each of us a pure heart.
God will not take the Holy Spirit from us.
God will restore to us the joy of salvation
    and grant us willing spirits to sustain us.

ALL: *Praise to the God of mercy who loves and forgives us.*

691

Leader: Almighty God, Spirit of purity and grace,
    whose dwelling is with the humble and contrite heart,
        hear your children's confession of sin and grant us mercy.
For all that has been evil in our lives;
    for unholy thoughts and impure motives,
    for any scorn of goodness, trifling with truth,
        and indifference to beauty,
    for being petty when we could have been gracious,

People: **forgive us, O God.**

Leader: For lack of love toward you,
    whose love has never failed;
    for doubt in your providence,
    for acts of ingratitude,
    and for disobedience to visions we have been able to see,

People: **forgive us, O God.**

Leader: For the wrong we have done to our neighbors;
    for silence in the face of war,
    for neglect of charity and failure in justice,
    for forgetfulness of others' pain,
    and for advantage taken of another's weakness,

People: **forgive us, O God.**

Leader: For our faulty following of the Master;
    our slow faith in his power to save,
    our timid, hesitant answers to his call for service,
    our insensibility to the meaning of the cross;
    for all that mars our discipleship
    and makes it difficult for others to believe in him,

People: **forgive us, O God.**

Leader: May God, who is almighty and merciful,
    forgive our sins,
    empower us to overcome temptation,
    and enable us to love as Jesus loved.

People: **AMEN**

692

O God,
   you rule the world from end to end
      and for all time.
You alone are God. In you alone we hope.

Forgive our sins.
Heal our diseases.
Save our lives from destruction.

We repent of our stubbornness and pride.
We desire to yield ourselves more fully to your will.

Keep us in your presence
   that we might serve and witness in the world,
   through Jesus Christ, our Lord. AMEN

693

Father,
   I have sinned against heaven and before you.
I am not worthy to be called your child
   because I have not carried out your will.
But speak a word of comfort and my soul shall be healed.
God, be merciful to me, a sinner. AMEN

694

Forgiving God,
   you do not deal with us according to our sins,
   nor repay us according to our iniquities.
For as the heavens are high above the earth,
    so great is your steadfast love toward those who fear you;
   as far as the east is from the west,
    so far you remove our transgressions from us. AMEN

695

Our lives are cluttered, Lord Jesus,
   by too many things
   and too much to do.
We are driven by the need to succeed
   and distracted by our service.
We have often lost our way.
Forgive us.

Let us, like Mary,
   find the one thing that is needed
   and sit at your feet. AMEN

696

God of love and justice,
   we long for peace within and peace without.
We long for harmony in our families,
   for serenity in the midst of struggle,
   and for commitment to each other's growth.

We long for the day when our homes
will be a dwelling place for your love.

Yet we confess that we are often anxious;
we do not trust each other,
and we harbor violence.
We are not willing to take the risks
and make the sacrifices that love requires.

Look upon us with kindness and grace.
Rule in our homes and in all the world;
show us how to walk in your paths,
through the mercy of our Savior. AMEN

697

Leader: O Prince of peace,
from peace that is no peace,
from the grip of all that is evil,
from a violent righteousness . . .
People: **deliver us.**
Leader: From paralysis of will,
from lies and misnaming,
from terror of truth . . .
People: **deliver us.**
Leader: From hardness of heart,
from trading in slaughter,
from the worship of death . . .
People: **deliver us.**
Leader: By the folly of your gospel,
by your choosing our flesh,
by your nakedness and pain . . .
People: **heal us.**
Leader: By your weeping over the city,
by your refusal of the sword,
by your facing of horror . . .
People: **heal us.**
Leader: By your bursting from the tomb,
by your coming in judgment,
by your longing for peace . . .
People: **heal us.**
ALL: *Grant us peace. AMEN*

698

Forgive me my sins, O Lord.
Forgive me the sins of my youth
and the sins of my age,
the sins of my soul
and the sins of my body,
my secret and my whispering sins,
the sins I have done to please myself
and the sins I have done to please others.

(continued)

Forgive those sins which I know
and the sins which I do not know.
Forgive them, Lord;
forgive them all in your great goodness,
through Jesus Christ, our Lord. AMEN

699

Lord, our God,
great, eternal, wonderful,
utterly to be trusted:
you give life to us all,
you help those who come to you,
you give hope to those who cry to you.
Forgive our sins, secret and open,
and rid us of every habit of thought
that stands against the gospel.
Set our hearts at peace,
so we may live our lives before you
confidently and without fear,
through Jesus Christ, our Lord. AMEN

700

Lord Jesus,
blind I am, do thou enlighten me;
naked I am, do thou clothe me;
wounded, do thou heal me;
dead, do thou quicken me.
I know of no light,
no physician,
no life, except thee. AMEN

701

Dear Jesus,
it is hard to forgive people
when they hurt us and our friends.
We want to hit back –
and sometimes we do.
But you teach us to love our enemies
no matter what they do.
Forgive us, Lord Jesus,
when we do not forgive others.
Help us to understand why people hurt others,
and let our hearts be filled with love for them. AMEN

702

Jesus, Lamb of God, have mercy on us.
Jesus, Bearer of our sins, have mercy on us.
Jesus, Redeemer of the world, grant us peace.

703

Gracious God, hear our confession.
Our faith is uncertain,
   our forgiveness slow,
   our conviction weak,
   our compassion wavering.
We have exalted the proud and powerful,
   put down the weak,
   saturated the rich with good things,
   neglected the poor,
   sent the hungry away empty-handed.
We have helped ourselves.

Show us your mercy.
Help us show mercy,
   through your Son, our Savior. AMEN

704

Seek God who may be found,
   call upon God who is near;
   let the wicked forsake their ways
   and the unrighteous their thoughts;
let them return to the Sovereign One,
   who will have mercy on them,
   and to our God, who will abundantly pardon.

705

People: **Christ has set us free from the burden of sin and guilt.**
Leader: Stand fast, therefore, and do not submit again to a yoke of slavery.
   ALL: *Rejoice! We are indeed set free!*

706

Leader: Because of God's great love for you
   and God's rich mercy for all,
   you are fully forgiven.
People: **We will live as those who are truly loved**
   and truly forgiven
   through the gift of God's grace.

707

Leader: This is the message we have heard from Jesus Christ
   and proclaim to you,
   that God is light and in God is no shadow at all.
People: **If we live in the light, as God is in the light,**
   then we share a common life with one another,
   and the blood of Jesus, God's Son, cleanses us from all sin.

708

May God, who is almighty and merciful,
   forgive our sins,
   heal our diseases,
   and bring us to eternal life,
     through Jesus Christ, our Lord.

709

> There is therefore now no condemnation
>   for those who are in Christ Jesus.
> For the law of the Spirit of life in Christ Jesus
>   has set us free from the law of sin and death.

AFFIRMING FAITH

710

Leader: We affirm that the God of Abraham, Isaac, and Jacob,
  Miriam, Hannah, and Mary is our God.

People: **We affirm that God has come to us in our likeness,
  taking the form of a servant in Jesus of Nazareth.**

Leader: We believe that God, in Christ, suffered the pain and agony
  of the cross to provide for our salvation.

People: **We believe that God demonstrated power over sin and death
  by raising Jesus from the dead
  and declaring that the risen Christ is Lord.**

Leader: God has given us new life and freedom in the fullness of the Holy Spirit,
  who is the guide and power of the community of believers.

ALL: *We believe that in the end, God's rule of peace and justice
  will be fully established
  and that Jesus Christ will reign forever and ever.*

711

Leader: Jesus taught us to speak of hope as the coming of God's kingdom.

ALL: *We believe that God is at work in our world,
  turning hopeless and evil situations into good.
We believe that goodness and justice and love
  will triumph in the end
  and that tyranny and oppression cannot last forever.
One day all tears will be wiped away;
  the lamb will lie down with the lion,
  and justice will roll down like a mighty stream.*

Leader: True peace and true reconciliation are not only desired,
  they are assured and guaranteed in Christ.

ALL: *This is our faith.
This is our hope.*

712

> I believe in God, the Father almighty,
>   creator of heaven and earth.
> I believe in Jesus Christ, God's only Son, our Lord,
>   who was conceived by the Holy Spirit,
>   born of the Virgin Mary,
>   suffered under Pontius Pilate,
>   was crucified, died, and was buried;
>   he descended to the dead.
>   On the third day he rose again;
>   he ascended into heaven,
>   he is seated at the right hand of the Father,
>   and he will come again to judge the living and the dead.

I believe in the Holy Spirit,
    the holy catholic* church,
    the communion of saints,
    the forgiveness of sins,
    the resurrection of the body,
    and the life everlasting.

*universal

713

We believe in Jesus Christ,
    who was promised to the people of Israel,
    who came in the flesh to dwell among us,
    who announced the coming of the rule of God,
    who gathered disciples and taught them,
    who died on the cross to free us from sin,
    who rose from the dead to give us life and hope,
    who reigns in heaven at the right hand of God,
    who comes to judge and bring justice to victory.

We believe in God,
    who raised Jesus from the dead,
    who created and sustains the universe,
    who acts to deliver God's people in times of need,
    who desires everyone everywhere to be saved,
    who rules over the destinies of people and nations,
    who continues to love us even when we turn away.

We believe in the Holy Spirit,
    who is the form of God present in the church,
    who moves us to faith and obedience,
    who is the guarantee of our deliverance,
    who leads us to find God's will in the word,
    who assists those who are renewed in prayer,
    who guides us in discernment,
    who impels us to act together.

We believe God has made us a people,
    to invite others to follow Christ,
    to encourage one another to deeper commitment,
    to proclaim forgiveness of sins and hope,
    to reconcile people to God through word and deed,
    to bear witness to the power of love over hate,
    to proclaim Jesus the Ruler of all,
    to meet the daily tasks of life with purpose,
    to suffer joyfully for the cause of right,
        to the ends of the earth,
        to the end of the age,
        to the praise of Christ's glory.

He was the Son of God.
He was the Son of Man.
He came down from heaven.
He was born in a stable.
Kings came to his cradle.
His first home was a cave.
He was born to be a king.
He was a child of Mary.
He was the greatest among rulers.
He was the least among servants.
He was loved and honored.
He was despised and rejected.
He was gentle and loving.
He made many enemies.
He counseled perfection.
He was a friend of sinners.
He was a joyful companion.
He was a man of sorrows.
He said, "Rejoice."
He said, "Repent."
"Love God with all your heart."
"Love your neighbor as yourself."
"Don't be anxious."
"Count the cost."
"Deny yourself."
"Ask and receive."
In him was life.
He died on a cross.
He was a historic person.
He lives today.
He was Jesus of Nazareth.
He is Christ the Lord.

715

Leader: My soul proclaims your greatness, O my God,
and my spirit rejoices in you, my Savior,
for your regard has blessed me,
an ordinary woman, who serves you.

People: **From this day all generations**
will call me blessed,
for you who are mighty have made me great.
Most holy be your name.

Leader: Your mercy is on those who fear you
throughout all generations.
You have shown strength with your arm.
You have scattered the proud in their hearts' fantasy.

People: **You have put down the mighty from their seat**
and have lifted up the powerless.
You have filled the hungry with good things
and have sent the rich empty away.

ALL: *You, remembering your mercy,*
have helped your people Israel,
as you promised Abraham and Sarah
mercy to their children forever.

716

No one can lay any foundation other than the one already laid,
   which is Jesus Christ.
In Christ the whole building is joined together
   and rises to become a holy temple in the Lord.
And in Christ we too are being built together
   to become a dwelling in which God lives by the Spirit.
As we come to Christ, the living Stone –
   rejected by builders but chosen by God –
we also, like living stones,
   are being built into a spiritual house to be a holy priesthood,
   offering spiritual sacrifices acceptable to God through Jesus Christ.
So then we are no longer foreigners and aliens,
   but citizens with God's people and members of God's household,
   built on the foundation of the apostles and prophets,
   with Christ Jesus as the chief cornerstone.

717

I believe in God,
      the giver of grain and bread,
   and in Jesus Christ,
      the bread of life broken for us,
   and in the Holy Spirit,
      God's nourishing power in every grain and loaf.
I believe that Christ is to be leaven in us,
   so that we may offer the bread of life
   to the hungers of every human heart.

PRAYING

718

Leader: Eternal God,
      we give you thanks for the founders of your church,
         for those whom you called and formed in the image of your Son,
         for those who suffered and died for their faith.
People: **We thank you for the cloud of witnesses.**
Leader: We give you thanks for the reformers of your church:
      for their rediscovery of truth,
      for their eagerness to live simply,
      for their faithful study of your word,
      for their endeavor to serve their neighbors.
People: **We thank you for the cloud of witnesses.**
  ALL: *God of our forebears,*
      give us the courage and wisdom
         of the saints who have gone before us;
      form us in the image of your Son;
         renew your Holy Spirit's work in our generation.
   May we live and serve under the rule of Jesus Christ
      until your reign comes. AMEN

719

Holy God,
you know all about me –
    you know how I feel, when I'm happy or sad;
    you know what I say, when I'm kind or rude;
    you know what I do, when I'm good or bad.
Thank you, God, for knowing all about me
    and still loving me. AMEN

720

ALL: *Listening God,*
       you hear our prayers before we speak,
         yet welcome our praying;
       therefore we come with confidence
         to lay our requests before you.

Leader: We pray for Christians everywhere,
       for our denomination and our congregation,
       for faithfulness and strength to persevere in righteousness.
     We pray for the whole people of God.

People: **Lord, hear our prayer.**

Leader: We pray for the nations of the world,
       for all leaders
     and for those who make policy decisions.
     We pray for the commonwealth of our global community.

People: **Lord, hear our prayer.**

Leader: We pray for those who are overcome by violence,
       for victims of injustice or oppression,
       and for those in poverty or pain.
     We pray for all who need healing and peace.

People: **Lord, hear our prayer.**

Leader: We pray for those who endure trials,
       for those who are dying,
       and for those who mourn.
     We pray for all who need comfort and hope.

People: **Lord, hear our prayer.**

Leader: You have heard the prayers of your people, O God.
     We rest in the comfort of your care,
       as we pray in Jesus' name.

ALL: **AMEN**

721

Almighty God,
   from whom comes each good gift of life,
     we remember your loving-kindness and your uncounted mercies
       as we join in grateful praise.
For all your gifts to us and to our human race;
   for our life and the world in which we live,
     we give you thanks, O God.
For the order and constancy of nature;
   for the beauty and bounty of the world;
   for day and night, summer and winter, seed-time and harvest;
   for the varied joys which every season brings,
     we give you thanks, O God.

For the work we are enabled to do,
    and the truth we are permitted to discover;
    for whatever good there has been in our past,
    and for all the hopes which lead us on toward better things,
    we give you thanks, O God.
For all the joys and comforts of life;
    for homes and families;
    for our friends;
    for the love, sympathy, and goodwill of persons near and far,
    we give you thanks, O God.
For all cultures, wise government, and just laws which order our common life;
    for education and all the treasures of literature, science, and art,
    we give you thanks, O God.
For the discipline of life;
    for the tasks and trials which train us to know ourselves
    and which bring us to accept one another,
    we give you thanks, O God.
For the desire and power to help others;
    for every opportunity of serving our generation in ways large or small,
    we give you thanks, O God.
For the gift of Jesus Christ, and everything which is ours as his disciples;
    for the presence and inspiration of your Holy Spirit throughout our days,
    we give you thanks, O God.
For the tender ties which bind us to the unseen world;
    for the faith which dispels the shadows of earth
    and fills the closing years of life with the light of hope,
    we give you thanks, O God.

ALL: *God of all grace and love,*
    we have praised you with our lips
    for all the richness and meaning that life holds for us.
    Now send us into the world to praise you with our lives,
    through Jesus Christ, our Lord. AMEN

722   — PAUSE FOR SILENCE AFTER EACH INTERCESSION. SPECIFIC REQUESTS MAY BE ADDED. —

Leader: Merciful God,
    your love for us makes us bold to join our prayers
    with all who need your help.
    We bring our prayers to you:

    For those who suffer pain;
    For those who struggle with limits of body and soul;
    For those who are satisfied with less than the life
      for which they were created;
    For those who know their guilt and their need
      but do not know of Jesus;
    For those who know that they must shortly die
      and for those who cannot wait to die.

ALL: *Come, Redeeming God,*
    take all these sufferings upon yourself and transform them.
    Be merciful also to us, who offer these prayers,
    so that we might enter the sufferings of others
    and become agents of your healing love,
    through Jesus Christ, our Lord. AMEN

723

God our healer,
   whose mercy is like a refining fire,
touch us with your judgment,
   and confront us with your tenderness;
   that, being comforted by you,
   we may reach out to a troubled world,
   through Jesus Christ. AMEN

724

Lord God,
   in whom I find life, health, and strength,
   through whose gifts I am clothed and fed,
   through whose mercy I have been forgiven and cleansed,
  be for me Guide, Strength, Savior, and Lord,
   all the days of my life.
I offer my prayers through Christ. AMEN

725

God of guidance,
   quicken your Holy Spirit
    in our hearts and minds
    so we may follow what is right.
Give us direction so we may know
   which way to choose and which to refuse;
   which course to claim and which to reject;
   which action to take and which to avoid.
Enlighten our minds,
   purify our hearts,
   strengthen our wills,
   and lead us to live as faithful followers of Jesus
    all the days of our lives. AMEN

726

Gracious and eternal God,
   we thank you for the bonds of love we share within your church.
We thank you for Jesus Christ,
   who has joined us into one living body.
Enable us, by your Spirit,
   to walk together in unity of love and purpose,
   to help one another by work and example,
   to live in faithful obedience to your will.
By the justice and mercy we show one another,
   may your name be praised,
   through Jesus Christ, our Lord. AMEN

727

Merciful and loving Father,
   we ask you with all our hearts
    to bountifully pour out on our enemies
     whatever will be for their good.

Above all, give them a sound and uncorrupt mind
    with which they might honor and love you
       and also love us.
Do not let their hating us turn to their harm.
Lord, we desire their amendment and our own.
Do not separate them from us by punishing them;
    deal gently with them and join them to us.
Help us to see that we have all been called to be citizens
       of the everlasting city;
    let us begin to love each other now
       because love is the end we seek. AMEN

728

Almighty God,
    you have given us grace at this time with one accord
       to make our common supplications to you,
    and you have promised through your well-beloved Son
       that when two or three are gathered together
       you will hear their requests.
Fulfill now our desires and petitions,
    as may be best for us,
    granting us in this world
       knowledge of your truth,
    and in the age to come
       eternal life,
       through Jesus Christ, our Lord. AMEN

729

Spirit of peace,
    quiet our hearts,
    heal our anxious thoughts,
    free us from our fretful ways.
Breathe on us your holy calm
    so that in the stillness of your presence
    we may open ourselves to trust
    and be transformed. AMEN

730

Most gracious God,
    protect us from worry about the concerns of this life,
       so that we will not become entangled by them;
    from the needs of our bodies
       so that we will not be enslaved by desires;
    and from any hindrance to our spirits,
       so that we will not be defeated by troubles.
Give us strength to resist,
    patience to endure
    and steadfastness to persevere,
    for the sake of Jesus Christ, our Lord. AMEN

731

Our Father in heaven,
    hallowed be your name,
    your kingdom come,
    your will be done,
    on earth as in heaven.
Give us today our daily bread.
Forgive us our sins
    as we forgive those who sin against us.
Save us from the time of trial
    and deliver us from evil.
For the kingdom, the power, and the glory are yours
    now and forever. AMEN

732

Liberating God,
    your Son taught us to pray
        for your kingdom to come on earth
        as it is in heaven.
Let your kingdom come;
    let justice roll like a river
    and righteousness like a never-ending stream.
Let your will be done;
    let those who mourn be comforted
    and those in bondage be set free.
Strengthen our hope in you, O God,
    for we long for your everlasting reign. AMEN

733

Lord,
    make me an instrument of your peace.
Where there is hatred, let me sow love;
    where there is injury, pardon;
    where there is doubt, faith;
    where there is despair, hope;
    where there is darkness, light;
    where there is sadness, joy.
O divine Master,
    grant that I may not so much seek
        to be consoled, as to console;
        to be understood, as to understand;
        to be loved, as to love.
For it is in giving that we receive;
    it is in pardoning that we are pardoned;
    it is in dying that we are born to eternal life. AMEN

734

Savior of the earth's children,
    you came as a little child
    to lead us to wisdom and love.
When you grew up,
    you welcomed the children
    and told us the kingdom belongs to them.
Call us to a child's tenderness,
    humility, energy, and love,
        for Jesus' sake. AMEN

735

Transforming God,
   you come to us in expected and unexpected ways,
      desiring to be known yet remaining a mystery.
Make your presence known among us.
Confront us.
Wrestle with us.
Change us, through Jesus Christ, our Lord. AMEN

736

God of community,
   whose call is more insistent
     than ties of family or blood;
   may we so respect and love
     those whose lives are linked with ours
     that we fail not in loyalty to you,
     but make choices according to your will,
     through Jesus Christ. AMEN

737

Almighty God,
   in whom we live and move and have our being,
you have made us for yourself,
   so that our hearts are restless
     until they rest in you.
Grant us purity of heart and strength of purpose,
   that no selfish passion may hinder us from knowing your will,
   no weakness from doing it;
   but that in your light we may see light clearly,
     and in your service find our perfect freedom,
     through Jesus Christ, our Lord. AMEN

738

God be in my head
   and in my understanding;
God be in my eyes
   and in my looking;
God be in my mouth
   and in my speaking;
God be in my heart
   and in my thinking;
God be at my end
   and at my departing. AMEN

739

Almighty God,
   to you all hearts are open,
   all desires are known,
   and from you no secrets are hidden.
Cleanse the thoughts of our hearts
   by the inspiration of your Holy Spirit
   that we may perfectly love you
   and worthily magnify your holy name,
   through Christ, our Lord. AMEN

740

God our lover,
    in whose arms we are held,
    and by whose passion we are known,
  require of us also that love
    which is filled with longing,
    delights in the truth,
    and costs not less than everything,
    through Jesus Christ. AMEN

741

Almighty God,
  to those chosen to see,
  you revealed your beloved Son,
    transfigured in glory on the holy mount.
In your great mercy, help us to see;
    deliver us from this world's darkness,
    change us from glory to glory into his likeness,
      through Jesus Christ, our Lord,
        who lives and reigns with you and the Holy Spirit,
        one God, now and forever. AMEN

742

Most holy God,
    the source of all good desires,
    all right judgments,
    and all just works:
  Give to us, your servants,
    that peace which the world cannot give,
      so that our minds may be fixed on the doing of your will,
      and that we, being delivered from the fear of all enemies,
      may live in peace and quietness;
      through the mercies of Christ Jesus, our Savior. AMEN

743

Merciful and everlasting God,
  you have not spared your only Son,
    but delivered him up for all of us
    that he might bear our sins on the cross.
Grant that our hearts may be so fixed on him
    that we need not fear the power of any adversaries
    through the same Jesus Christ, your Son, our Savior. AMEN

744

God our creator,
    you have made us one with this earth,
    to tend it and to bring forth fruit.
May we so respect and cherish
    all that has life from you,
    that we may share in the labor of all creation
    to give birth to your hidden glory,
    through Jesus Christ. AMEN

745

Hidden God,
in mystery and silence
you are present in our lives,
bringing new life out of death,
hope out of despair.
We thank you that you do not leave us alone
but labor to make us whole.
Help us to perceive your unseen hand
in the unfolding of our lives,
and to attend to the gentle guidance of your Spirit,
that we may know the joy of your love
and rest in your peace. AMEN

746

Tender and compassionate God,
you long to gather us in your arms
as a hen gathers her chicks.
Draw us to yourself in love,
surround us with your grace,
and keep us in the shelter of your wings
so that in our time of testing
we may not fall away. AMEN

747

God of resurrection and life,
the shadows of Good Friday have been dispersed
by the light of Easter.
We rejoice in your power
that turns sorrow into joy,
despair into hope,
defeat into victory,
and evil into goodness.
Set us free on this day of resurrection
to burst out of the tombs that have trapped us.
Let new life spring forth and bring grace to all,
through Jesus Christ, the Risen One. AMEN

OFFERING

748

Dear God,
I offer you my praise.
I offer you my heart.
I offer you my money.
I offer you my life.
Thank you for everything you give to me. AMEN

749

O God,
our offerings proclaim
that work and worship are one,
that life is undivided.
Use these gifts for your church's ministries
of reconciliation, service, and mercy. AMEN

750

Gracious God,
    we thank you for gifts that belong not to us alone,
        but to all our sisters and brothers,
            since they, too, are created in your image.
Let their need become our need;
    let their hunger become our hunger;
        and grant to us also a portion of their pain,
            so that in sharing ourselves,
            we discover the Christ who walks
            with our brothers and sisters. AMEN

751

Generous God,
    you gave us life;
    now we give our lives back to you.
We present ourselves:
    our work and play,
    our joys and sorrows,
    our thoughts and deeds,
    our gifts and resources,
    to be used by you
        for the sake of all people everywhere,
        through Jesus Christ, our Lord. AMEN

WITNESSING

752

Gracious God,
    grant that the words we have heard this day
    may be so grafted within our hearts
    that they bring forth fruit
    to the honor and praise of your name,
    through Jesus Christ, our Lord. AMEN

753

ALL: *With what shall I come before the Lord,*
and bow myself before God on high?

People: **Shall I come before God with burnt offerings,**
with calves a year old?

Leader: Will the Lord be pleased with thousands of rams,
with ten thousands of rivers of oil?

People: **Shall I give my firstborn for my transgression,**
the fruit of my body for the sin of my soul?

ALL: *God has told you, O mortal, what is good;*
and what does the Lord require of you
but to do justice,
and to love kindness,
and to walk humbly with your God?

754

Leader: Very truly, I tell you,
    unless a grain of wheat falls into the earth and dies,
    it remains just a single grain;
    but if it dies,
    it bears much fruit.

People: **Those who love their life will lose it,**
    and those who hate their life in this world
        will keep it for eternal life.

ALL: *Whoever serves me must follow me,*
    and where I am,
        there will my servant be also.

755

Leader: Speak to all the world
    of the Child by whose word the universe is held together!

People: **We can hardly speak for ourselves;**
    how can we speak in the name of the Son of God?

Leader: "Whom shall I send?" God asks us. "Who will go?"
    If those to whom God has shown love have no words,
        who can tell the world that God's reign is among us?

People: **Send us the Advocate,**
    the Holy Spirit to teach us,
    to remind us of everything Jesus proclaimed.

Leader: Show us how to bring your presence to others –

People: **when to keep silence,**
    when to act in secret,
    when to openly name the Name.

Leader: Free our hearts, our hands, our voices to confess Christ,
    to give people the reason for the hope that is in us.

ALL: *Glory be to you, Lord Jesus Christ.*
    You took the form of a servant.
    You preached peace.
    You healed the oppressed.
    You died for us.
    We will tell the world
        that you are the author of our salvation.
    Here we are; send us!

756

O God,
    for too long the world
    has called us to war,
    and our dead lie sprawled
    across the bleeding centuries.
But you
    break the bow and shatter the spear,
    calling us to sow the seeds of peace
    in the midst of despair.
In tenderness,
    may we take the tiniest sprouts
    and plant them
    where they can safely grow
    into blossoms of hope. AMEN

757

Savior God,
    through your grace
    we hold a treasure in earthen vessels:
        the living presence of Jesus Christ.
Let us bear your good news with joy
    till grace overflows in the earth
    and salvation comes to all.
For yours is the power
    and yours the glory,
        now and forever. AMEN

758

Leader: We follow Christ
People: **who says, "Take up your cross."**
Leader: We follow Christ
People: **who bids us come and die.**
Leader: We follow Christ
People: **who summons us to new life.**
   ALL: *The One who calls is faithful*
            and will keep us.

759

God,
    I'm worried about people:
        forgotten older people,
        children without mothers or fathers,
        prisoners of war,
        workers without jobs,
        people who have no homes,
            who are hungry or cold,
        people who live with problems
            that wind up tight inside.
Show me how I can help them.
Give me the right words
    to tell them of your love,
        for Jesus' sake. AMEN

760

God our security,
    who alone can defend us
    against the principalities and powers
    that rule this present age;
    may we trust in no weapons
        except the whole armor of faith,
        that in dying we may live,
        and, having nothing, we may own the world,
            through Jesus Christ. AMEN

761

Empower us
    to nurture those newborn in faith,
    to search for those still scattered
    on the hillsides of the world
    waiting for shepherd love.

Empower us
    to gather together
    your other sheep
    in our communities
    and to the ends of the earth.
Empower us, Lord,
    to tend your flock. AMEN

SENDING

762

ALL: *Come, Holy Spirit.*
Left: Come as Holy Fire and burn in us.
Right: **Come as Holy Wind and cleanse us within.**
Left: Come as Holy Light and lead us in our darkness.
Right: **Come as Holy Truth and dispel our ignorance.**
Left: Come as Holy Power and overcome our weakness.
Right: **Come as Holy Life and dwell in us.**
ALL: *Send us, abide with us, use us,*
    that the Father may be glorified
    and our joy be made full. AMEN

763

Leader: We came to worship.
People: **We go now to serve.**
Leader: We have been given the light.
People: **We go now to let it shine.**
Leader: We have been blessed by God's love.
People: **We go now to share it.**
Leader: We are Christ's disciples.
People: **We go now to witness to all.**

764

Leader: Go in love,
People: **for love alone endures.**
Leader: Go in peace,
People: **for it is the gift of God.**
Leader: Go in safety,
People: **for we cannot go where God is not.**

765

Gentle God,
    you have come near to us
        and have shown us your patience,
        compassion, and love.
As we go, O God,
    give us patience when people are indifferent to your Word,
    give us compassion for the needs of the world,
    and give us love which reflects your forgiveness and grace,
    through Jesus Christ, our Savior. AMEN

766

Leader: Now may the Lord Jesus bless your soul
and strengthen your faith.
Let this hour of worship grow within you
and bear fruit which will remain for life eternal.

People: **We will together praise and glorify our God forever.**

767

Ever-present God,
in Christ Jesus you never leave or forsake us.
Teach us to be faithful to your call,
to persevere in commitment,
and beyond all else,
to know the strength and joy
of being near to you,
in the name of our Savior. AMEN

768

Eternal Lord,
as we leave this place of worship and communion,
may we go, knowing that you never leave or forsake us.
Help us to go with the song of faith in our hearts,
the peace of Christ in our lives,
the protection of the Spirit beside us,
and the security of your presence beneath us. AMEN

769

Guide us, O Lord,
by your Word and Holy Spirit,
that in your light we may see light,
in your truth find freedom,
and in your will discover peace,
through Jesus Christ, our Lord. AMEN

770

The blessing of the God of Sarah and of Abraham,
the blessing of the Son, born of Mary,
the blessing of the Holy Spirit,
who broods over us as a mother over her children,
be with us all. AMEN

771

Master,
now you are dismissing your servant in peace,
according to your word;
for my eyes have seen your salvation,
which you have prepared in the presence of all peoples,
a light for revelation to the Gentiles
and for glory to your people Israel.

772

May God bless and keep you.
May the very face of God shine on you
    and be gracious to you.
May God's presence embrace you
    and give you peace.

773

May our Lord Jesus Christ himself and God our Father,
        who has shown us such love,
    and in his grace has given us
        such unfailing encouragement
        and so sure a hope,
    still encourage and strengthen you
        in every good deed and word.

774

May the God of steadfastness and encouragement
        grant you to live in harmony with one another,
        in accordance with Christ Jesus,
    so that together you may with one voice
        glorify the God and Father of our Lord Jesus Christ.

BAPTISM

775

Congregational covenant

We declare anew our covenant:
    to repent of our sinful and evil ways;
    to accept Jesus Christ as authority and example
        for our life;
    to live by grace in God's holy community,
        according to Christ's rule and way.

Candidates' covenant

We join with these members of Christ's body
        by declaring our covenant:
        to repent of our sinful and evil ways;
        to accept Jesus Christ as authority and example
            for our life;
        to live by grace in God's holy community,
            according to Christ's rule and way.

Congregational prayer

Gracious God,
    you have given baptism as a sign of the washing away
        of our sins by the blood of Christ.
    You have called these people and moved their hearts.
    Wash them inwardly with your Holy Spirit
        so they might be holy and pure.
    Make them strong to walk in new life,
        so that no suffering or temptation might draw them away,
        in the name of Jesus Christ. AMEN

776

Leader: God our deliverer,
    we remember how, by your loving hand,
    you led the sons and daughters of Abraham and Sarah
        through the deep waters from bondage to freedom
        and marked them a holy people
            through the blood of the everlasting covenant.

People: **We rejoice that in the fullness of time**
    you gave us Jesus, the child of Mary and Joseph,
      your beloved Son, our Lord and Christ.

Leader: We remember John baptizing him in the water of the Jordan,
    the Spirit descending upon him like a dove,
    and the offering of himself to free us from sin and death
    and to lead us to everlasting life.

People: **We thank you that by the washing with water**
    and the outpouring of the Holy Spirit
  we are baptized into the covenant of your grace,
    made one with Christ and his church,
    and commissioned to show forth his love in word and deed. AMEN

Leader: Once we were no people!
People: **Now we are God's people!**
  ALL: *Blessing and honor and glory and power*
    be unto our God forever and ever!

777

As we now receive you into the fellowship of the church,
    we make this covenant with you
    as we renew our own covenant with God:
        to bear each others' burdens,
        to assist in times of need,
        to share our gifts and possessions,
        to forgive as Christ has forgiven us,
        to support each other in joy and sorrow,
           and in all things to work for the common good,
        thus making known Christ's presence among us
           to the glory of God.
As we unite with each other now,
    may we all be joined with Christ, our Lord.

778

Leader: Through baptism we are united to Jesus Christ
    and given part in Christ's ministry of reconciliation.
Baptism is the visible sign of an invisible event:
    the reconciliation of people to God.
Baptism shows the death of the old self and the rising to life of a new self.
It shows also the pouring out of the Holy Spirit
    on those whom God has chosen.
Baptism declares God's forgiveness;
    it seals the gift of the Spirit
    and joins the believer to the body of Christ.

People: **This is the water of baptism.**
Out of this water we rise with new life,
    forgiven of sin,
    and one in Christ,
    members of Christ's body.

779

O God,
  you brooded over the water at creation.
Be present now at this baptism, a symbol of re-creation.
You love all you have made and desire their salvation.
By your Spirit you have drawn these people to Christ.
In baptism seal your mercy's work in their lives.
Let it lead them to the secret of the cross:
  to be crucified with Christ so Christ may rise to life in them.
Bring them into the companionship of your church.
Set them on the narrow way.
Draw them deeper into your love.
Give them the joy of their salvation,
  for the sake of your Son, our Savior. AMEN

AT THE LAYING ON OF HANDS

780

People: **All-powerful God,**
  grant _____(name)_____ the fullness of the Holy Spirit:
    a clean heart,
    a right spirit,
    the joy of salvation.
  Make her/him one in whom Christ is seen to live again.
  Release the gifts you gave her/him in creation
    and redeemed in Christ.
Leader: May the God of peace sanctify you wholly.
  May your spirit and soul and body be kept sound and blameless
    until the coming of our Lord Jesus Christ.
  ALL: *The One who calls you is faithful and will do it. AMEN*

LORD'S SUPPER PREPARATION

781

How can we discern our errors, O God?

Clear us from hidden faults.
Let the words of our mouths
  and the meditations of our hearts
  be acceptable in your sight,
  O Lord, our rock and redeemer.
Look graciously on our remorse;
  help us to turn from evil.
We offer you ourselves,
  body and soul, to be cleansed.

As we drink the cup,
  give us assurance of forgiveness
  through the blood of Christ.
Accept our promise to be true to you
  and give us power to fulfill it.
Let us find strength in the breaking of the bread
  to live and to die,
  for Jesus' sake. AMEN

782

Leader: O Eternal Wisdom, O Vulnerable God,
    we praise you and give you thanks,
        because you laid aside your power as a garment
        and took upon you the form of a slave.

**People: You became obedient unto death,
    even death on a cross,
    receiving authority and comfort
    from the hands of a woman;
  for God chose what is weak in the world
    to shame the strong,
  and God chose what is low and despised in the world,
    even things that are not,
    to bring to nothing things that are.**

*ALL: Therefore, with the woman who gave you birth,
    the women who befriended you and fed you,
    the woman who anointed you for death,
    the women who met you, risen from the dead,
  we praise you.*

Leader: Blessed is our brother Jesus,
    who on this night, before Passover,
    rose from supper, laid aside his garments,
    took a towel and poured water,
    and washed his disciples' feet, saying to them:
      "If I, your Lord and Teacher,
        have washed your feet,
        you also ought to wash one another's feet.
      If you know these things,
        blessed are you if you do them.
      If I do not wash you,
        you have no part in me."

**People: Lord, not my feet only
    but also my hands and my head.**

*ALL: Come now, tender Spirit of our God,
    wash us and make us one body in Christ;
    that, as we are bound together
      in this gesture of love,
    we may no longer be in bondage
      to the principalities and powers
        that enslave creation,
    but may know your liberating peace
      such as the world cannot give. AMEN*

783

Lord Jesus,
  we have knelt before each other
    as you once knelt before your disciples,
    washing another's feet.
We have done what words stammer to express.
Accept this gesture of love as a pledge
  of how we mean to live our lives.
Bless us, as you promised,
  with joy and perseverance in the way of the cross. AMEN

784

May the body and blood of Christ,
     which alone can satisfy our hunger and quench our thirst,
     fill us with peace.
May God bless us tomorrow with daily manna for strength
     and sweet water for refreshment
     so that we may live with joy.

785

Leader: Blessed are you, O God.
     You made bread to strengthen us.
     You set aside this bread
          as a sign of your Son's broken body.
     In breaking it, may we participate
          in the reconciliation of Christ.
People: **May Christ's body be the bread of our souls,**
     to give us strength to continue our pilgrimage,
     being made worthy to sit with all the redeemed
          at the marriage feast of the Lamb.
ALL: *Hear us, O God, through our mediator, Jesus Christ. AMEN*

Leader: Blessed are you, O God.
     You made the vine to strengthen us.
     You set aside this cup
          as a sign of your Son's shed blood.
     In drinking the cup,
          may we participate in the blood of Christ.
People: **May Christ's blood make us strong**
     to drink the cup of suffering
          without complaint, for Jesus' sake,
     in the hope that we shall drink new wine
          in your kingdom.
ALL: *Hear us, O God, for the sake of your eternal love. AMEN*

786

O God,
     your steadfast love has been ours for generations.
Through Christ, you brought us out of the abyss of death
     and into the light of eternal love.
With joy and thanksgiving, we proclaim our salvation,
     remembering Christ's death and resurrection,
          until he comes again.
As we break bread and share the cup together,
     may Christ be present with us,
     and may the Spirit bind us together
          as Christ's body in this world. AMEN

787

Almighty, merciful, and loving Father,
   we are gathered in your presence
   to celebrate the memorial of the broken body
      and shed blood of your Son.
Make us worthy to sit at Christ's table as his friends.
In this supper, let our hungry souls be fed
   with the body and blood of your beloved Son
      through the gift of the Holy Spirit.
May Christ live in us and we in him.
Give us assurance through the breaking of bread
   that we are partakers of your covenant.
May we grow in faith, love, and willingness
   to carry the cross of Christ.
In his name we pray. AMEN

788

Blessed are you, God of heaven and earth.
In mercy for our fallen world you gave your only Son,
   that all those who believe in him should not perish
   but have eternal life.
We give thanks to you for the salvation
   you have prepared for us through Jesus Christ.
Send now your Holy Spirit into our hearts,
   that we may receive our Lord with a living faith
   as he comes to us in his holy supper.

— MAY BE CONCLUDED WITH THE LORD'S PRAYER —

789

Almighty and loving God,
   we thank you that through your great love
      you have fed us from our Lord's table
      and have assured us that your goodness to us never fails.
We give you thanks that we are members of the body of Christ,
   heirs with Christ, and brothers and sisters in your family.
By your grace assist us in our pilgrimage
   that we may go forth strong and faithful in our witness,
   through Jesus Christ, our Lord. AMEN

790

Blessed are you, O God.
You set aside
   this bread as a sign of your Son's broken body,
   this cup as a sign of his shed blood,
   this basin as a sign of his servanthood.
Through them you have made us partakers of Christ
   and of one another.
As we go forth, give us grace
   to count others better than ourselves,
   to love our enemies,
   to seek peace.
Send the Spirit of truth to keep alive in us
   what Jesus taught and did,
   who lives and reigns with you and the Holy Spirit,
   one God, forever and ever. AMEN

791

You have offered your child
  to the strong and tender providence of God.
We rejoice with you and give thanks
  for the gift of your child.
We promise, with humility and seriousness,
  to share in your child's nurture and well-being.
We will support, by our example and words,
    your efforts to provide a loving and caring home,
    where trust in God grows and Christ's way is chosen.
Our prayers will be with you and for you.
May our shared life and witness
  help make your task both joyful and fruitful.

792

Maker of galaxies and planets,
      yet also of the hairs on our heads,
    we magnify your name
      for our creation and for all the blessings of this life.
Especially are we glad for the birth
  of _____ (name) _____ .
We claim the same assurance for her/him
    that Jesus gave to the children he took into his arms:
    that they belong to your kingdom.
Give the parents grace to raise their child to your glory.
Let this child come to her/his own faith in Christ crucified.
Protect her/him against misfortune and mishap.
Let the love that ____ (name) ____ receives and gives know no limits.
In the end, grant her/him eternal life,
    for Jesus' sake. AMEN

793

We commit ourselves to follow Jesus Christ,
    through whom God has made friends with the world
    and in whose name we share the work of reconciliation.
We commit ourselves to the way of the cross,
    living a life of simplicity, self-denial, and prayer.
We commit ourselves to love each other,
    serving the church,
    and sharing our time, talents, and possessions.
We commit ourselves to care for the world,
    bringing good news to the poor,
    setting free the oppressed,
    and proclaiming Jesus as Liberator and Lord.
In this commitment we find joy, peace, and new life.

794

Leader: These persons now presented to you
have witnessed to their faith in Jesus Christ
and offer themselves as companions in our obedience to Christ.
It is our privilege and joy to welcome them into our family of faith.

People: **We freely receive you, even as Christ has received us.**
We open ourselves to fellowship with you
in worship, study, service, and discipline.
We pledge our willingness to give and receive counsel,
to offer and accept forgiveness in the redeemed community.
We joyfully accept you as partners,
both in the care of our spiritual family,
and in our mission to the world.

795

People: **In company with your faithful people in every age,**
we have called out those with gifts for your service, O God.
Fill them with the love of Christ
and the power of the Spirit
as they carry out the church's ministry.

Those commissioned:
Grant us wisdom, patience, and hope when we falter.
Give us joy in serving your church
and keep us faithful to this calling.

ALL: *For the ministries taking form within us*
and for all the callings yet to be,
we praise your name, O Lord! AMEN

796

As God's Spirit calls and the church commissions,
the servants of Christ are scattered in places of need
throughout the world.
We accept your service as an extension of this congregation
and pledge our support of your ministry.
We join with you in seeking first the kingdom of God.
Consider your assignment as God at work in you,
ministering to human need.
May you be given a deep love for those among whom you will live,
and may Christ be known through you in word and deed.
Our prayers will continually support you
while you are absent from us.

797

Leader: As __(husband)__'s and __(wife)__'s community(ies) of faith,
will you now pledge your support to them in their marriage?
People: **__(husband)__ and __(wife)__ ,**
we are thankful for God's love and grace that brings you together.

We are witnesses to the vows you have made to each other,
 and we commit ourselves to help you fulfill your vows.
We pledge to you our prayers, our counsel, and our continued friendship.
May God grant us strength as we strive to be faithful to each other
 and to Christ, our Lord.

798

God of all life,
 in you we live and move and have our being.

Bless ___(husband)___ and ___(wife)___ with your grace.
May they keep the vows they have made,
 and always know the joy of this day.

Bless them with your love.
May their love for each other grow deeper
 and their love for you shine forth.

Bless them with your mercy.
May they be patient and forgiving
 and share each other's burdens,
 whatever life might bring.

Bless them with your peace.
May they be calm and confident
 and live in harmony among all people.

Bless them with your presence.
May Christ abide in their hearts and home,
 and may they offer praise and thanksgiving through all their life,
 in the name of Christ, and to your glory. AMEN

ANOINTING/HEALING

799

ALL: *O God,*
       we come to you at this moment
        because you love us.
       You know us more deeply than we know ourselves.
       You desire wholeness for each of your children,
        broken though we are in body, mind, and spirit.
       As we come before you, we pray for healing in each of our lives.

— PAUSE FOR SILENCE. —

Leader: Now we offer you our <u>sister/brother</u>.
         Embrace <u>her/him</u> with your love.
         As we anoint <u>her/him</u> with oil, anoint <u>her/him</u> with the Spirit.
ALL: *Restore <u>her/him</u> according to your will,*
        through the One who suffered and conquered for us,
        even Jesus Christ. AMEN

800

We accept your confession of failure
   to fulfill your Christian commitment.
We also confess that we have failed
   to provide the companionship
      which keeps the conscience alert
      and the will strong to resist temptation.
Forgive us our failure to surround you with resources
   to draw you from the mastery of sin.
We promise to be a forgiving community
   in which you are loved, accepted, and encouraged.
We will seek to be a healing fellowship –
   forgetting the past
   and continuing our quest to follow Christ.
Having been freely pardoned ourselves
   and having received your confession,
   we declare you forgiven for the sake of Christ
   and commend you to the keeping of the Holy Spirit.

801

Everlasting God,
   you are our refuge and strength,
   a helper close at hand, a shelter in time of need.
Help us, O God, to hear your words of comfort,
   so that by faith our fears might be dispelled,
   our loneliness eased,
   and our hope revived.
May your Holy Spirit carry us through our sorrow
   into the comfort of your presence which endures
      for all eternity,
      in Jesus' name. AMEN

802

Eternal Light,
   shine into our hearts.
Eternal Goodness,
   deliver us from evil.
Eternal Power,
   be our support.
Eternal Wisdom,
   scatter the darkness of our ignorance.
Eternal Pity,
   have mercy upon us,
   that with all our heart and mind and soul and strength
      we may seek your face
      and be brought by infinite mercy
      to your holy presence,
      through Jesus Christ, our Lord. AMEN

803

ALL: *O God, Sovereign of the universe,*
without you nothing is true, nothing is just.
In your Word you reveal the way of love.
By your Spirit you make it possible.

Leader: From greed and selfishness,
from a society in which the rich get richer
and the poor get poorer,

People: compassionate God, deliver us.

Leader: From racial prejudice and religious intolerance,
from a society which makes its weakest
and most recent members into scapegoats,

People: compassionate God, deliver us.

Leader: From indifference to the needs of other countries,
from the delusion that you love any other nation less
than you love us,

People: compassionate God, deliver us.

Leader: From self-indulgence and indifference,
from a society in which fidelity
and responsibility have little place,

People: compassionate God, deliver us.

ALL: *Author of life,*
give us hearts set on the coming of your reign;
give us wise, just, and humble leaders;
give all who live in this land a will to live in peace,
through Jesus Christ, the One who is above all powers
and dominions. AMEN

804

Leader: Lord of all creation, provider of every good thing,
you reveal yourself to us
as creator and sustainer of the world.
You offer us the earth for our pleasure and care.

People: We offer our labor to you
to sustain the goodness of your creation.

Leader: Hear our prayer for those who invest, risk, and employ.

People: Use their ingenuity for the common good.

Leader: Hear our prayer for those who build, repair, and produce.

People: Make them competent as they practice their skill.

Leader: Hear our prayer for those who create, teach, and heal.

People: Grant them understanding and compassion.

Leader: Hear our prayer for those who tend, love, and care.

People: Give them open hearts and generous spirits.

Leader: Hear our prayer for those who have completed their labors
and for those who cannot work.

People: Grant them peace and purpose in living.

ALL: *Maker of heaven and earth,*
pour your creating power through all we do.
Make us fruitful laborers in your vineyard,
through Jesus Christ. AMEN

805

Leader:
Eternal God,
    before you the generations pass.
Your character is love,
    your way is compassion,
    your name is everlasting.

Today we remember those who lived, labored, and loved among us.
Because of their lives, we know better how to live.
Because of their suffering, we find greater strength.
Because of their death, we better understand
    what is important in life.

People: **We sorrow, but not as those who have no hope.**
We grieve, but not as those who center their thoughts on death.
We sense loneliness, but not as those who are left alone.
We thank you, God, that even in separation,
    we experience love, peace, and hope.

Leader: We praise you, God,
    for light which arises out of darkness,
    for comfort which is constant in the midst of confusion,
    for hope which springs out of sorrow.

People: **We thank you, God, for sending a Savior who says:**
    "I am the resurrection and the life;
    those who believe in me . . . shall never die."

ALL: *O God,*
    grant us grace to affirm in life, as in death,
    that we are yours.
Our help is in you.
Our hope is in your promise,
    through Jesus Christ, our loving Lord. AMEN

Scripture Readings

806 *Genesis 1:1-3,6-7,9,11,14,20,24,26-28,31*

In the beginning when God created the heavens and the earth, the earth was a
formless void and darkness covered the face of the deep, while a wind from
God swept over the face of the waters.
Then God said, "Let there be light"; and there was light.
    And God said, "Let there be a dome in the midst of the waters, and let it
    separate the waters from the waters." So God made the dome and
    separated the waters that were under the dome from the waters that were
    above the dome.
And God said, "Let the waters under the sky be gathered together into one
place, and let the dry land appear."
    Then God said, "Let the earth put forth vegetation: plants yielding seed,
    and fruit trees of every kind on earth that bear fruit with the seed in it."
And God said, "Let there be lights in the dome of the sky to separate the day
from the night; and let them be for signs and for seasons and for days and
years . . . "

And God said, "Let the waters bring forth swarms of living creatures, and let birds fly above the earth across the dome of the sky."

And God said, "Let the earth bring forth living creatures of every kind: cattle and creeping things and wild animals of the earth of every kind."

Then God said, "Let us make humankind in our image, according to our likeness; and let them have dominion over the fish of the sea, and over the birds of the air, and over the cattle, and over all the wild animals of the earth, and over every creeping thing that creeps upon the earth."

So God created humankind in his image, in the image of God he created them; male and female he created them.

God blessed them, and God said to them, "Be fruitful and multiply, and fill the earth and subdue it."

God saw everything that he had made, and indeed, it was very good.

807   *Exodus 20:1-5a,6-10a,11-17,22,24b*

God spoke all these words, saying:

"I am the Lord your God who brought you out of the land of Egypt, the house of slavery. You shall have no other gods before me.

You shall not make for yourself an idol, whether in the form of anything that is in heaven above, or on the earth below, or that is in the waters under the earth.

You shall not bow down to them or worship them.

You shall not make wrongful use of the name of the Lord your God, for the Lord will not acquit anyone who misuses his name.

Remember the sabbath day, and keep it holy. Six days you shall labor and do all your work, but the seventh day is a sabbath of the Lord your God; you shall not do any work.

For in six days the Lord made heaven and earth, the sea, and all that is in them, but rested the seventh day; therefore the Lord blessed the sabbath day and consecrated it.

Honor your father and your mother, so that your days may be long in the land that the Lord your God is giving you.

You shall not commit murder.

You shall not commit adultery.

You shall not steal.

You shall not bear false witness against your neighbor.

You shall not covet your neighbor's house; you shall not covet your neighbor's wife, or male or female slave, or ox, or donkey, or anything that belongs to your neighbor."

The Lord said to Moses: Thus you shall say to the Israelites: "You have seen for yourselves that I spoke with you from heaven. In every place where I cause my name to be remembered I will come to you and bless you."

808 *Deuteronomy 6:4-15*

Hear, O Israel: The Lord is our God, the Lord alone. You shall love the Lord your God with all your heart, and with all your soul, and with all your might.
Keep these words that I am commanding you today in your heart. Recite them to your children and talk about them when you are at home and when you are away, when you lie down and when you rise.
  Bind them as a sign on your hand, fix them as an emblem on your forehead, and write them on the doorposts of your house and on your gates.
When the Lord your God has brought you into the land that he swore to your ancestors, to Abraham, to Isaac, and to Jacob, to give you – a land with fine, large cities that you did not build, houses filled with all sorts of goods that you did not fill, hewn cisterns that you did not hew, vineyards and olive groves that you did not plant – and when you have eaten your fill, take care that you do not forget the Lord, who brought you out of the land of Egypt, out of the house of slavery.
  The Lord your God you shall fear; him you shall serve, and by his name alone you shall swear. Do not follow other gods, any of the gods of the peoples who are all around you, because the Lord your God, who is present with you, is a jealous God. The anger of the Lord your God would be kindled against you and he would destroy you from the face of the earth.

809 *Joshua 24:14-18*

"Now therefore revere the Lord, and serve him in sincerity and in faithfulness; put away the gods that your ancestors served beyond the River and in Egypt, and serve the Lord. Now if you are unwilling to serve the Lord, choose this day whom you will serve, whether the gods your ancestors served in the region beyond the River or the gods of the Amorites in whose land you are living; but as for me and my household, we will serve the Lord."
  Then the people answered, "Far be it from us that we should forsake the Lord to serve other gods; for it is the Lord our God who brought us and our ancestors up from the land of Egypt, out of the house of slavery, and who did those great signs in our sight. He protected us along all the way that we went, and among all the peoples through whom we passed; and the Lord drove out before us all the peoples, the Amorites who lived in the land. Therefore we also will serve the Lord, for he is our God."

810 *Job 10:1-3a,8-9,18-22; 23:8-9,3,7*

"I loathe my life;
    I will give free utterance to my complaint;
    I will speak in the bitterness of my soul.

I will say to God, Do not condemn me;
  let me know why you contend against me.
Does it seem good to you to oppress,
  to despise the work of your hands?

Your hands fashioned and made me;
  and now you turn and destroy me.
Remember that you fashioned me like clay;
  and will you turn me to dust again?
Why did you bring me forth from the womb?
  I wish I had died before any eye saw me.
If only I had never come into being,
  or had been carried straight from the womb to the grave!
Are not the days of my life few?
Let me alone, that I may find a little comfort
    before I go, never to return,
    to the land of gloom and deep darkness,
    to the land of gloom and chaos,
    where light is like darkness.
If I go forward, he is not there;
  or backward, I cannot perceive him;
  on the left he hides, and I cannot behold him;
  I turn to the right, but I cannot see him.

Oh, that I knew where I might find him,
  that I might come even to his dwelling!
There an upright person could reason with him,
  and I should be acquitted forever by my judge."

811   *Psalm 1*

Blessed are those
  who do not follow the advice of the wicked,
    or take the path that sinners tread,
    or sit in the seat of scoffers;
  but their delight is in the law of the Lord,
    and on his law they meditate day and night.
They are like trees planted by streams of water,
    which yield their fruit in its season,
    and their leaves do not wither.
In all that they do, they prosper.

The wicked are not so,
  but are like chaff that the wind drives away.
Therefore the wicked will not stand in the judgment,
    nor sinners in the congregation of the righteous;
    for the Lord watches over the way of the righteous,
    but the way of the wicked will perish.

812 *Psalm 8:1,3-9*

O Lord, our Sovereign,
how majestic is your name in all the earth!
You have set your glory above the heavens.
When I look at your heavens, the work of your fingers,
the moon and the stars that you have established;
what are human beings that you are mindful of them,
mortals that you care for them?
Yet you have made them a little lower than God,
and crowned them with glory and honor.
You have given them dominion over the works of your hands;
you have put all things under their feet,
all sheep and oxen,
and also the beasts of the field,
the birds of the air, and the fish of the sea,
whatever passes along the paths of the seas.
O Lord, our Sovereign,
how majestic is your name in all the earth!

813 *Psalm 19:7-11*

The law of the Lord is perfect,
reviving the soul;
the decrees of the Lord are sure,
making wise the simple;
the precepts of the Lord are right,
rejoicing the heart;
the commandment of the Lord is clear,
enlightening the eyes;
the fear of the Lord is pure,
enduring forever;
the ordinances of the Lord are true
and righteous altogether.
More to be desired are they than gold,
even much fine gold;
sweeter also than honey,
and drippings of the honeycomb.
Moreover by them is your servant warned;
in keeping them there is great reward.

814 *Psalm 23*

The Lord is my shepherd, I shall not want;
  he makes me lie down in green pastures.
He leads me beside still waters;
  he restores my soul.
He leads me in paths of righteousness
  for his name's sake.

Even though I walk through the valley of the shadow of death,
    I fear no evil;
  for thou art with me;
  thy rod and thy staff,
    they comfort me.

Thou preparest a table before me
    in the presence of my enemies;
  thou anointest my head with oil,
    my cup overflows.
Surely goodness and mercy shall follow me
    all the days of my life;
  and I shall dwell in the house of the Lord forever.

815 *Psalm 24*

The earth is the Lord's and all that is in it,
  the world, and those who live in it;
  for he has founded it on the seas,
    and established it on the rivers.
Who shall ascend the hill of the Lord?
And who shall stand in his holy place?
  Those who have clean hands and pure hearts,
    who do not lift up their souls to what is false,
    and do not swear deceitfully.
They will receive blessing from the Lord,
    and vindication from the God of their salvation.
  Such is the company of those who seek him,
    who seek the face of the God of Jacob.
Lift up your heads, O gates!
  and be lifted up, O ancient doors!
    that the King of glory may come in.
Who is the King of glory?
  The Lord, strong and mighty,
    the Lord, mighty in battle.
Lift up your heads, O gates!
  and be lifted up, O ancient doors!
    that the King of glory may come in.
Who is this King of glory?
  The Lord of hosts,
    he is the King of glory.

816 *Psalm 42*

As the deer pants for streams of water,
    so my soul pants for you, O God.
My soul thirsts for God, for the living God.
When shall I come and behold the face of God?
My tears have been my food day and night,
    while people say to me continually,
    "Where is your God?"
These things I remember as I pour out my soul:
    how I used to go with the multitude,
        leading the procession to the house of God,
        with shouts of joy and thanksgiving
        among the festive throng.
Why are you downcast, O my soul?
Why so disturbed within me?
Put your hope in God,
    for I will yet praise him, my Savior and my God.
My soul is downcast within me;
    therefore I will remember you
        from the land of the Jordan,
        the heights of Hermon – from Mount Mizar.
Deep calls to deep in the roar of your waterfalls;
    all your waves and breakers have swept over me.
By day the Lord directs his love,
    at night his song is with me –
        a prayer to the God of my life.
I say to God my Rock,
    "Why have you forgotten me?
Why must I go about mourning,
    oppressed by the enemy?"
My bones suffer mortal agony as my foes taunt me,
    saying to me all day long, "Where is your God?"
Why are you downcast, O my soul?
Why so disturbed within me?
Put your hope in God,
    for I will yet praise him, my Savior and my God.

817 *Psalm 46:8-11*

Come, behold the works of the Lord;
    see what desolations he has brought on the earth.

He makes wars cease to the end of the earth;
    he breaks the bow, and shatters the spear;
    he burns the shields with fire.

"Be still, and know that I am God!
  I am exalted among the nations,
  I am exalted in the earth."

The Lord of hosts is with us;
  the God of Jacob is our refuge.   ·

818   *Psalm 51:1-12,15-17*

Have mercy on me, O God,
    according to your steadfast love;
    according to your abundant mercy
      blot out my transgressions.
Wash me thoroughly from my iniquity,
    and cleanse me from my sin.

For I know my transgressions,
    and my sin is ever before me.
Against you, you alone, have I sinned,
    and done what is evil in your sight,
    so that you are justified in your sentence
      and blameless when you pass judgment.
Indeed, I was born in the midst of iniquity;
    in the midst of sin my mother conceived me.

You desire truth in the inward being;
    therefore teach me wisdom in my secret heart.
Purge me with hyssop, and I shall be clean;
    wash me, and I shall be purer than snow.
Let me hear joy and gladness;
    let the bones that you have crushed rejoice.
Hide your face from my sins,
    and blot out all my iniquities.

Create in me a clean heart, O God,
    and put a new and right spirit within me.
Do not cast me away from your presence,
    and do not take your holy spirit from me.
Restore to me the joy of your salvation,
    and sustain in me a willing spirit.

O Lord, open my lips,
    and my mouth will declare your praise.
For you have no delight in sacrifice;
    if I were to give a burnt offering, you would not be pleased.
The sacrifice acceptable to God is a broken spirit;
    a broken and contrite heart, O God, you will not despise.

819 *Psalm 90:1-6,9-10,12-14*

Lord, you have been our dwelling place
    in all generations.
Before the mountains were brought forth,
    or ever you had formed the earth and the world,
    from everlasting to everlasting you are God.
You turn us back to dust,
    and say, "Turn back, you mortals."
For a thousand years in your sight
    are like yesterday when it is past,
    or like a watch in the night.
You sweep them away; they are like a dream,
    like grass that is renewed in the morning;
    in the morning it flourishes and is renewed;
    in the evening it fades and withers.
For all our days pass away under your wrath;
    our years come to an end like a sigh.
The days of our life are seventy years,
    or perhaps eighty, if we are strong;
    even then their span is only toil and trouble;
    they are soon gone, and we fly away.
So teach us to count our days
    that we may gain a wise heart.
Turn, O Lord! How long?
Have compassion on your servants!
Satisfy us in the morning with your steadfast love,
    so that we may rejoice and be glad all our days.

820 *Psalm 96:1-3,9-13*

Sing to the Lord a new song;
    sing to the Lord, all the earth.
Sing to the Lord, praise his name;
    proclaim his salvation day after day.
Declare his glory among the nations,
    his marvelous deeds among all peoples.
Worship the Lord in the splendor of his holiness;
    tremble before him, all the earth.
Say among the nations, "The Lord reigns."
The world is firmly established, it cannot be moved;
    he will judge the peoples with equity.
Let the heavens rejoice, let the earth be glad;
    let the sea resound, and all that is in it;
    let the fields be jubilant, and everything in them.
Then all the trees of the forest will sing for joy;
    they will sing before the Lord, for he comes,
    he comes to judge the earth.
He will judge the world in righteousness
    and the peoples in his truth.

821 *Psalm 100*

Make a joyful noise to the Lord, all the lands!
   Serve the Lord with gladness!
   Come into his presence with singing!
Know that the Lord is God!
It is he that made us, and we are his;
   we are his people, and the sheep of his pasture.
Enter his gates with thanksgiving,
   and his courts with praise!
   Give thanks to him, bless his name!
For the Lord is good;
   his steadfast love endures forever,
   and his faithfulness to all generations.

822 *Psalm 103:1-18*

Bless the Lord, O my soul,
   and all that is within me,
   bless his holy name.
Bless the Lord, O my soul,
   and do not forget all his benefits –
who forgives all your iniquity,
   who heals all your diseases,
who redeems your life from the Pit,
   who crowns you with steadfast love and mercy,
who satisfies you with good as long as you live
   so that your youth is renewed like the eagle's.
The Lord works vindication
   and justice for all who are oppressed.
He made known his ways to Moses,
   his acts to the people of Israel.
The Lord is merciful and gracious,
   slow to anger and abounding in steadfast love.
He will not always accuse,
   nor will he keep his anger forever.
He does not deal with us according to our sins,
   nor repay us according to our iniquities.
For as the heavens are high above the earth,
   so great is his steadfast love toward those who fear him;
as far as the east is from the west,
   so far he removes our transgressions from us.
As a father has compassion for his children,
   so the Lord has compassion for those who fear him.
For he knows how we were made;
   he remembers that we are dust.
As for mortals, their days are like grass;
   they flourish like a flower of the field;
for the wind passes over it, and it is gone,
   and its place knows it no more.

(continued)

But the steadfast love of the Lord is from everlasting to everlasting
    on those who fear him,
      and his righteousness to children's children,
to those who keep his covenant
    and remember to do his commandments.

823   *Psalm 139:1-18*

O Lord, you have searched me
    and you know me.
You know when I sit and when I rise;
    you perceive my thoughts from afar.
You discern my going out and my lying down;
    you are familiar with all my ways.
Before a word is on my tongue
    you know it completely, O Lord.
You hem me in – behind and before;
    you have laid your hand upon me.
Such knowledge is too wonderful for me,
    too lofty for me to attain.
Where can I go from your Spirit?
    Where can I flee from your presence?
If I go up to the heavens, you are there;
    if I make my bed in the depths, you are there.
If I rise on the wings of the dawn,
    if I settle on the far side of the sea,
even there your hand will guide me,
    your right hand will hold me fast.
If I say, "Surely the darkness will hide me
    and the light become night around me,"
even the darkness will not be dark to you;
    the night will shine like the day,
    for darkness is as light to you.
For you created my inmost being;
    you knit me together in my mother's womb.
I praise you because I am fearfully and wonderfully made;
    your works are wonderful,
    I know that full well.
My frame was not hidden from you
    when I was made in the secret place.
When I was woven together in the depths of the earth,
    your eyes saw my unformed body.
All the days ordained for me were written in your book
    before one of them came to be.
How precious to me are your thoughts, O God!
How vast is the sum of them!
Were I to count them,
    they would outnumber the grains of sand.
When I awake,
    I am still with you.

824 *Psalm 145:13b-21*

The Lord is faithful in all his words,
    and gracious in all his deeds.
The Lord upholds all who are falling,
    and raises up all who are bowed down.
The eyes of all look to you,
    and you give them their food in due season.
You open your hand,
    satisfying the desire of every living thing.
The Lord is just in all his ways,
    and kind in all his doings.
The Lord is near to all who call on him,
    to all who call on him in truth.
He fulfills the desire of all who fear him;
    he also hears their cry, and saves them.
The Lord watches over all who love him,
    but all the wicked he will destroy.
My mouth will speak the praise of the Lord,
    and all flesh will bless his holy name forever and ever.

825 *Psalm 146:3-10*

Do not put your trust in princes,
    in mortals, in whom there is no help.
When their breath departs, they return to the earth;
    on that very day their plans perish.
Happy are those whose help is the God of Jacob,
    whose hope is in the Lord their God,
who made heaven and earth,
    the sea, and all that is in them;
who keeps faith forever;
    who executes justice for the oppressed;
    who gives food to the hungry.
The Lord sets the prisoners free;
    the Lord opens the eyes of the blind.
The Lord lifts up those who are bowed down;
    the Lord loves the righteous.
The Lord watches over the strangers;
    he upholds the orphan and the widow,
    but the way of the wicked he brings to ruin.
The Lord will reign forever,
    your God, O Zion, for all generations.
Praise the Lord!

826 *Proverbs 3:1-6*

My child, do not forget my teaching,
    but let your heart keep my commandments;
for length of days and years of life
    and abundant welfare they will give you.
Do not let loyalty and faithfulness forsake you;
    bind them around your neck,
    write them on the tablet of your heart.
So you will find favor and good repute
    in the sight of God and of people.
Trust in the Lord with all your heart,
    and do not rely on your own insight.
In all your ways acknowledge him,
    and he will make straight your paths.

827 *Isaiah 9:2-7*

The people who walked in darkness
    have seen a great light;
those who lived in a land of deep darkness –
    on them light has shined.
You have multiplied the nation,
    you have increased its joy;
they rejoice before you
    as with joy at the harvest,
    as people exult when dividing plunder.
For the yoke of their burden,
    and the bar across their shoulders,
    the rod of their oppressor,
    you have broken as on the day of Midian.
For all the boots of the tramping warriors
    and all the garments rolled in blood
        shall be burned as fuel for the fire.
For to us a child is born,
    to us a son is given;
and the government will be upon his shoulder,
    and his name will be called
        "Wonderful Counselor, Mighty God,
        Everlasting Father, Prince of Peace."
His authority shall grow continually,
    and there shall be endless peace
    for the throne of David and his kingdom.
He will establish and uphold it
    with justice and with righteousness
    from this time onward and forevermore.
The zeal of the Lord of hosts will do this.

828 *Isaiah 40:1-11*

Comfort, O comfort my people, says your God.
Speak tenderly to Jerusalem, and cry to her
  that she has served her term,
  that her penalty is paid,
  that she has received from the Lord's hand
    double for all her sins.
A voice cries out:
  "In the wilderness prepare the way of the Lord,
  make straight in the desert a highway for our God.
Every valley shall be lifted up,
    and every mountain and hill be made low;
  the uneven ground shall become level,
    and the rough places a plain.
Then the glory of the Lord shall be revealed,
  and all people shall see it together,
  for the mouth of the Lord has spoken."
A voice says, "Cry out!"
  And I said, "What shall I cry?"
All people are grass,
  their constancy is like the flower of the field.
The grass withers, the flower fades,
  when the breath of the Lord blows upon it;
  surely the people are grass.
The grass withers, the flower fades;
  but the word of our God will stand forever.
Get you up to a high mountain,
    O Zion, herald of good tidings;
  lift up your voice with strength,
    O Jerusalem, herald of good tidings,
  lift it up, do not fear;
  say to the cities of Judah,
    "Here is your God!"
See, the Lord God comes with might,
  and his arm rules for him;
his reward is with him,
  and his recompense before him.
He will feed his flock like a shepherd,
  he will gather the lambs in his arms,
he will carry them in his bosom,
  and gently lead those that are with young.

829 *Isaiah 53:1-6*

Who has believed what we have heard?
    And to whom has the arm of the Lord been revealed?
For he grew up before him like a young plant,
    and like a root out of dry ground;
he had no form or comeliness that we should look at him,
    and no beauty that we should desire him.
He was despised and rejected;
    a man of sorrows, and acquainted with grief;
and as one from whom we hide our faces
    he was despised, and we esteemed him not.
Surely he has borne our griefs
    and carried our sorrows;
yet we esteemed him stricken,
    smitten by God, and afflicted.
But he was wounded for our transgressions,
    he was bruised for our iniquities;
upon him was the chastisement that made us whole,
    and with his stripes we are healed.
All we like sheep have gone astray;
    we have all turned to our own way,
and the Lord has laid on him
    the iniquity of us all.

830 *Isaiah 58:1-9b*

Shout it aloud, do not hold back.
Raise your voice like a trumpet.
Declare to my people their rebellion
    and to the house of Jacob their sins.
For day after day they seek me out;
    they seem eager to know my ways,
    as if they were a nation that does what is right
    and has not forsaken the commands of its God.
They ask me for just decisions
    and seem eager for God to come near them.
"Why have we fasted," they say,
    "and you have not seen it?
    Why have we humbled ourselves,
    and you have not noticed?"
Yet on the day of your fasting, you do as you please
    and exploit all your workers.
Your fasting ends in quarreling and strife,
    and in striking each other with wicked fists.
You cannot fast as you do today
    and expect your voice to be heard on high.
Is this the kind of fast I have chosen,
    only a day to humble oneself?
Is it only for bowing one's head like a reed
    and for lying on sackcloth and ashes?

Is that what you call a fast,
a day acceptable to the Lord?
Is not this the kind of fasting I have chosen:
    to loose the chains of injustice
        and untie the cords of the yoke,
    to set the oppressed free
        and break every yoke?
Is it not to share your food with the hungry
    and to provide the poor wanderer with shelter –
    when you see the naked, to clothe them,
    and not to turn away from your own flesh and blood?
Then your light will break forth like the dawn,
    and your healing will quickly appear;
    then your righteousness will go before you,
    and the glory of the Lord will be your rear guard.
Then you will call, and the Lord will answer;
    you will cry for help, and he will say:
Here am I.

831   *Lamentations 3:1-8,19-26*

I am one who has seen affliction under the rod of God's wrath;
he has driven and brought me into darkness without any light;
    against me alone he turns his hand,
    again and again, all day long.
He has made my flesh and my skin waste away,
    and broken my bones;
he has besieged and enveloped me
    with bitterness and tribulation;
he has made me sit in darkness
    like the dead of long ago.
He has walled me about so that I cannot escape;
he has put heavy chains on me;
    though I call and cry for help, he shuts out my prayer.

The thought of my affliction and my homelessness
    is wormwood and gall!
My soul continually thinks of it and is bowed down within me.
But this I call to mind, and therefore I have hope:
The steadfast love of the Lord never ceases,
    his mercies never come to an end;
    they are new every morning; great is your faithfulness.
"The Lord is my portion," says my soul,
    "therefore I will hope in him."
The Lord is good to those who wait for him,
    to the soul that seeks him.
It is good that one should wait quietly
    for the salvation of the Lord.

832 *Daniel 9:4b-6a,7-8,15,18-19 (portions omitted)*

Great and awesome God,
keeping covenant and steadfast love with those who love you
and keep your commandments,
we have sinned and done wrong,
acted wickedly and rebelled,
turning aside from your commandments and ordinances.
We have not listened to your servants the prophets,
who spoke in your name.
Righteousness is on your side, O Lord,
but open shame falls on us because we have sinned against you.
Now, O Lord our God,
who brought your people out of the land of Egypt
with a mighty hand,
we have done wickedly.
Incline your ear, O my God, and hear.
Open your eyes and look at our desolation.
We do not present our supplication before you
on the ground of our righteousness,
but on the ground of your great mercies.
O Lord, hear; O Lord, forgive;
O Lord, listen and act and do not delay!
For your own sake, O my God,
because your people bear your name!

833 *Micah 4:1-4*

In days to come the mountain of the Lord's house
shall be established as the highest of the mountains,
and shall be raised up above the hills.
Peoples shall stream to it,
and many nations shall come and say:
"Come, let us go up to the mountain of the Lord,
to the house of the God of Jacob;
that he may teach us his ways
and that we may walk in his paths."
For out of Zion shall go forth instruction,
and the word of the Lord from Jerusalem.
He shall judge between many peoples,
and shall arbitrate between strong nations far away;
they shall beat their swords into plowshares,
and their spears into pruning hooks;
nation shall not lift up sword against nation,
neither shall they learn war any more;
but they shall all sit under their own vines
and under their own fig trees,
and no one shall make them afraid;
for the mouth of the Lord of hosts has spoken.

834 *Matthew 5:1-16*

When Jesus saw the crowds, he went up the mountain; and after he sat down, his disciples came to him. Then he began to speak, and taught them, saying:
"Blessed are the poor in spirit, for theirs is the kingdom of heaven.
   Blessed are those who mourn, for they will be comforted.
Blessed are the meek, for they will inherit the earth.
   Blessed are those who hunger and thirst for righteousness, for they will be filled.
Blessed are the merciful, for they will receive mercy.
   Blessed are the pure in heart, for they will see God.
Blessed are the peacemakers, for they will be called children of God.
   Blessed are those who are persecuted for righteousness' sake, for theirs is the kingdom of heaven.
Blessed are you when people revile you and persecute you and utter all kinds of evil against you falsely on my account.
   Rejoice and be glad, for your reward is great in heaven, for in the same way they persecuted the prophets who were before you.
You are the salt of the earth; but if salt has lost its taste, how can its saltiness be restored? It is no longer good for anything, but is thrown out and trampled under foot.
   You are the light of the world. A city built on a hill cannot be hid.
No one after lighting a lamp puts it under the bushel basket, but on the lampstand, and it gives light to all in the house.
In the same way, let your light shine before others, so that they may see your good works and give glory to your Father in heaven."

835 *Matthew 6:25-33*

"Therefore I tell you, do not worry about your life, what you will eat or what you will drink, or about your body, what you will wear.
   Is not life more than food, and the body more than clothing?
Look at the birds of the air; they neither sow nor reap nor gather into barns, and yet your heavenly Father feeds them. Are you not of more value than they?
   And can any of you by worrying add a single hour to your span of life?
   And why do you worry about clothing?
Consider the lilies of the field, how they grow; they neither toil nor spin, yet I tell you, even Solomon in all his glory was not clothed like one of these.
   But if God so clothes the grass of the field, which is alive today and tomorrow is thrown into the oven, will he not much more clothe you – you of little faith?
Therefore do not worry, saying, 'What will we eat?' or 'What will we drink?' or 'What will we wear?'
   For it is the Gentiles who strive for all these things; and indeed your heavenly Father knows that you need all these things.
But strive first for the kingdom of God and his righteousness, and all these things will be given to you as well."

836 *Matthew 9:35-38*

And Jesus went about all the cities and villages, teaching in their synagogues, and proclaiming the good news of the kingdom, and healing every disease and every infirmity.

When Jesus saw the crowds, he had compassion for them because they were harassed and helpless, like sheep without a shepherd. Then he said to his disciples,

"The harvest is plentiful, but the laborers are few; therefore ask the Lord of the harvest to send out laborers into the harvest."

837 *Matthew 18:15-20*

— MATTHEW 18:12-14 AND 18:21-22 MIGHT BE READ BY THE WORSHIP LEADER. —

"If another member of the church sins against you, go and point out the fault when the two of you are alone. If the member listens to you, you have regained that one.

But if you are not listened to, take one or two others along with you, so that every word may be confirmed by the evidence of two or three witnesses.

If the member refuses to listen to them, tell it to the church; and if the offender refuses to listen even to the church, let such a one be to you as a Gentile and a tax collector.

Truly I tell you, whatever you bind on earth will be bound in heaven, and whatever you loose on earth will be loosed in heaven.

Again, truly I tell you, if two of you agree on earth about anything you ask, it will be done for you by my Father in heaven. For where two or three are gathered in my name, I am there among them."

838 *Mark 8:34-38*

— MARK 8:27-33 MIGHT BE READ BY THE WORSHIP LEADER. —

He called the crowd with his disciples, and said to them, "If any want to become my followers, let them deny themselves and take up their cross and follow me.

For those who want to save their life will lose it, and those who lose their life for my sake, and for the sake of the gospel, will save it. For what will it profit them to gain the whole world and forfeit their life?

Indeed, what can they give in return for their life?

Those who are ashamed of me and of my words in this adulterous and sinful generation, of them the Son of Man will also be ashamed when he comes in the glory of his Father with the holy angels."

839 *Mark 10:13-16*

People were bringing little children to him in order that he might touch them; and the disciples spoke sternly to them. But when Jesus saw this, he was indignant and said to them,

"Let the little children come to me; do not stop them; for it is to such as these that the kingdom of God belongs. Truly I tell you, whoever does not receive the kingdom of God as a little child will never enter it."

And he took them up in his arms, laid his hands on them, and blessed them.

840 *Luke 1:46-55*

My soul proclaims the greatness of the Lord,
   my spirit rejoices in God my Savior;
   for he has looked with favor on his lowly servant.
From this day all generations will call me blessed;
   the Almighty has done great things for me,
   and holy is his name.
He has mercy on those who fear him
   in every generation.
He has shown the strength of his arm,
   he has scattered the proud in their conceit.
He has cast down the mighty from their thrones,
   and has lifted up the lowly.
He has filled the hungry with good things,
   and the rich he has sent away empty.
He has come to the help of his servant Israel,
   for he has remembered his promise of mercy,
   the promise he made to our fathers,
   to Abraham and his children forever.

841 *John 1:1-5,10-14*

In the beginning was the Word, and the Word was with God, and the Word was God. He was in the beginning with God. All things came into being through him, and without him not one thing came into being. What has come into being in him was life, and the life was the light of all people. The light shines in the darkness, and the darkness did not overcome it.

He was in the world, and the world came into being through him; yet the world did not know him. He came to what was his own, and his own people did not accept him. But to all who received him, who believed in his name, he gave power to become children of God, who were born, not of blood or of the will of the flesh or of the will of man, but of God.

And the Word became flesh and lived among us, and we have seen his glory, the glory as of a father's only son, full of grace and truth.

842 *John 3:1-17*

Now there was a Pharisee named Nicodemus, a leader of the Jews. He came to Jesus by night and said to him, "Rabbi, we know that you are a teacher who has come from God; for no one can do these signs that you do apart from the presence of God."

Jesus answered him, "Very truly, I tell you, no one can see the kingdom of God without being born from above."

Nicodemus said to him, "How can anyone be born after having grown old? Can one enter a second time into the mother's womb and be born?"

Jesus answered, "Very truly, I tell you, no one can enter the kingdom of God without being born of water and Spirit. What is born of the flesh is flesh, and what is born of the Spirit is spirit. Do not be astonished that I said to you, 'You must be born from above.' The wind blows where it chooses, and you hear the sound of it, but you do not know where it comes from or where it goes. So it is with everyone who is born of the Spirit."

Nicodemus said to him, "How can these things be?"

Jesus answered him, "Are you a teacher of Israel, and yet you do not understand these things?

"Very truly, I tell you, we speak of what we know and testify to what we have seen; yet you do not receive our testimony. If I have told you about earthly things and you do not believe, how can you believe if I tell you about heavenly things? No one has ascended into heaven except the one who descended from heaven, the Son of Man. And just as Moses lifted up the serpent in the wilderness, so must the Son of Man be lifted up, that whoever believes in him may have eternal life.

"For God so loved the world that he gave his only Son, so that everyone who believes in him may not perish but may have eternal life. Indeed, God did not send the Son into the world to condemn the world, but in order that the world might be saved through him."

843 *John 13:2b-17*

And during supper Jesus, knowing that the Father had given all things into his hands, and that he had come from God and was going to God, got up from the table, took off his outer robe, and tied a towel around himself. Then he poured water into a basin and began to wash the disciples' feet and to wipe them with the towel that was tied around him.

Jesus came to Simon Peter, who said to him, "Lord, are you going to wash my feet?"

Jesus answered, "You do not know now what I am doing, but later you will understand."

Peter said to him, "You will never wash my feet."

Jesus answered, "Unless I wash you, you have no share with me."

Simon Peter said to him, "Lord, not my feet only but also my hands and my head!"

Jesus said to him, "One who has bathed does not need to wash, except for the feet, but is entirely clean. And you are clean, though not all of you." For he knew who was to betray him; for this reason he said, "Not all of you are clean."

After he had washed their feet, had put on his robe, and had returned to the table, he said to them, "Do you know what I have done to you? You call me Teacher and Lord – and you are right, for that is what I am. So if I, your Lord and Teacher, have washed your feet, you also ought to wash one another's feet. For I have set you an example, that you also should do as I have done to you.
Very truly, I tell you, servants are not greater than their master, nor are messengers greater than the one who sent them. If you know these things, you are blessed if you do them."

844 *John 14:1-6,15-19*

"Set your troubled hearts at rest. Trust in God always; trust also in me. There are many dwelling places in my Father's house; if it were not so I should have told you; for I am going to prepare a place for you.
And if I go and prepare a place for you, I shall come again and take you to myself, so that where I am you may be also; and you know the way I am taking."
Thomas said, "Lord, we do not know where you are going, so how can we know the way?"
Jesus replied, "I am the way, the truth, and the life; no one comes to the Father except by me."

"If you love me you will obey my commands; and I will ask the Father, and he will give you another to be your advocate, who will be with you forever – the Spirit of truth.
The world cannot accept him, because the world neither sees nor knows him; but you know him, because he dwells with you and will be in you.
I will not leave you bereft; I am coming back to you. In a little while the world will see me no longer, but you will see me; because I live, you too will live."

845 *John 15:9-11*

— JOHN 15:1-5 MIGHT BE READ BY THE WORSHIP LEADER. —

"As the Father has loved me, so I have loved you; abide in my love. If you keep my commandments, you will abide in my love, just as I have kept my Father's commandments and abide in his love. I have said these things to you so that my joy may be in you, and that your joy may be complete."

846   *John 15:12-17*

"This is my commandment, that you love one another as I have loved you.
No one has greater love than this, to lay down one's life for one's friends. You
are my friends if you do what I command you.
> **I do not call you servants any longer, because the servant does not know
> what the master is doing; but I have called you friends, because I have
> made known to you everything that I have heard from my Father.**
You did not choose me but I chose you. And I appointed you to go and bear
fruit, fruit that will last, so that the Father will give you whatever you ask him
in my name.
> **I am giving you these commands so that you may love one another."**

847   *Romans 6:1-11*

What then are we to say? Should we continue in sin in order that grace may
abound?
> **By no means! How can we who died to sin go on living in it? Do you not
> know that all of us who have been baptized into Christ Jesus were
> baptized into his death?**
*Therefore we have been buried with him by baptism into death, so that, just
as Christ was raised from the dead by the glory of the Father, so we too might
walk in newness of life.*
For if we have become identified with him in his death, we shall also be
identified with him in his resurrection.
> **We know that our old self was crucified with him so that the body of sin
> might be destroyed, and we might no longer be enslaved to sin.**
For whoever has died is freed from sin.
> **But if we have died with Christ, we believe that we will also live with
> him.**
*We know that Christ, being raised from the dead, will never die again; death
no longer has dominion over him. The death he died, he died to sin, once for
all; but the life he lives, he lives to God. So you also must consider yourselves dead to sin and alive to God in Christ Jesus.*

848   *Romans 8:18-27*

I consider that the sufferings of this present time are not worth comparing
with the glory about to be revealed to us.
> **For the creation waits with eager longing for the revealing of the children
> of God; for the creation was subjected to futility, not of its own will but
> by the will of the one who subjected it, in hope that the creation itself
> will be set free from its bondage to decay and will obtain the freedom of
> the glory of the children of God.**
We know that the whole creation has been groaning in labor pains until now;
and not only the creation, but we ourselves, who have the first fruits of the
Spirit, groan inwardly while we wait for adoption, the redemption of our
bodies. For in hope we were saved.
> **Now hope that is seen is not hope. For who hopes for what is seen? But
> if we hope for what we do not see, we wait for it with patience.**

Likewise the Spirit helps us in our weakness; for we do not know how to pray as we ought, but that very Spirit intercedes with sighs too deep for words. **And God, who searches the heart, knows what is the mind of the Spirit, because the Spirit intercedes for the saints according to the will of God.**

849 *Romans 8:28-39*

For we know that in all things God works toward a good end with those who love God, who are called according to God's design.
For God has always known his own and has established that they are to be conformed to the image of God's Son, so that Christ is but the first-born child among a whole multitude of sisters and brothers.
For those whom God has thus established, God has also called; and those whom God has called, have indeed been fully accepted; and those whom God has accepted, God has also clothed in splendor.
What then shall we say about these things? If God be for us, who can stand against us?
For indeed, God did not spare his own Son, but gave him up for us all. How will he not with Christ lavish upon us every other good gift?
Who will bring any charge against those whom God has called? God has accepted. Who, then, can condemn?
It is Christ Jesus, who died, rather, who was raised, who is at the right hand of God, who indeed intercedes for us.
Who shall separate us from the love of Christ? Will affliction or anguish or persecution or hunger or nakedness or danger or sword?
As it is written, "For your sake we are being killed all day long; we are considered sheep to be slaughtered."
But in all these things through the love of Christ we have surpassed the need to conquer.
For I am confident that neither death nor life, nor angels nor rulers, nor things present, nor things to come, nor powers, nor height, nor depth, nor any other created thing will be able to separate us from the love of God which is in Christ Jesus our Lord.

850 *Romans 12:9-21*

Let love be genuine; hate what is evil, hold fast to what is good; love one another with mutual affection; outdo one another in showing honor.
Do not lag in zeal, be ardent in spirit, serve the Lord.
Rejoice in hope, be patient in suffering, persevere in prayer.
Contribute to the needs of the saints; extend hospitality to strangers.
Bless those who persecute you; bless and do not curse them.
Rejoice with those who rejoice, weep with those who weep.
Live in harmony with one another; do not be haughty, but associate with the lowly; do not claim to be wiser than you are.
Do not repay anyone evil for evil, but take thought for what is noble in the sight of all.

(continued)

If it is possible, so far as it depends on you, live peaceably with all.
**Beloved, never avenge yourselves, but leave room for the wrath of God;
for it is written, "Vengeance is mine, I will repay, says the Lord."**
No, "if your enemies are hungry, feed them; if they are thirsty, give them
something to drink; for by doing this you will heap burning coals on their
heads."
Do not be overcome by evil, but overcome evil with good.

851 *1 Corinthians 12:4-13*

*Now there are varieties of gifts, but the same Spirit; and there are varieties of
services, but the same Lord; and there are varieties of activities, but it is the
same God who activates all of them in everyone. To each is given the
manifestation of the Spirit for the common good.*
To one is given through the Spirit the utterance of wisdom, and to another the
utterance of knowledge according to the same Spirit,
**to another faith by the same Spirit, to another gifts of healing by the one
Spirit, to another the working of miracles,**
to another prophecy, to another the discernment of spirits,
**to another various kinds of tongues,
to another the interpretation of tongues.**
All these are activated by one and the same Spirit, who allots to each one
individually just as the Spirit chooses.
**For just as the body is one and has many members, and all the members
of the body, though many, are one body, so it is with Christ.**
*For in the one Spirit we were all baptized into one body – Jews or Greeks,
slaves or free – and we were all made to drink of one Spirit.*

852 *1 Corinthians 15:50-58*

What I am saying, brothers and sisters, is this: flesh and blood cannot inherit
the kingdom of God, nor does the perishable inherit the imperishable. Listen,
I will tell you a mystery! We will not all die, but we will all be changed, in a
moment, in the twinkling of an eye, at the last trumpet.
**For the trumpet will sound, and the dead will be raised imperishable,
and we will be changed.**
For this perishable body must put on imperishability, and this mortal body
must put on immortality. When this perishable body puts on imperishability,
and this mortal body puts on immortality, then the saying that is written will
be fulfilled:
**"Death has been swallowed up in victory."
"Where, O death, is your victory?
Where, O death, is your sting?"**
The sting of death is sin, and the power of sin is the law.
**But thanks be to God,
who gives us the victory through our Lord Jesus Christ.**
Therefore, my beloved, be steadfast, immovable, always excelling in the work
of the Lord, because you know that in the Lord your labor is not in vain.

853   *2 Corinthians 5:17-21*

If anyone is in Christ, there is a new creation:
everything old has passed away;
see, everything has become new!
All this is from God,
    who reconciled us to himself through Christ,
    and has given us the ministry of reconciliation;
    that is, God was in Christ reconciling the world to himself,
        not counting their trespasses against them,
        and entrusting the message of reconciliation to us.
So we are ambassadors for Christ,
    since God is making his appeal through us;
    we entreat you on behalf of Christ, be reconciled to God.
For our sake he made him to be sin who knew no sin,
    so that in him we might become the righteousness of God.

854   *Ephesians 4:1b-6*

Lead a life worthy of the calling to which you have been called,
    with all humility and gentleness,
    with patience, bearing with one another in love,
    making every effort to maintain the unity of the Spirit
        in the bond of peace.
There is one body and one Spirit,
    just as you were called to the one hope of your calling,
        one Lord, one faith, one baptism,
        one God and Father of all,
        who is above all and through all and in all.

855   *Philippians 2:5-11*

Have this mind among yourselves, which you have in Christ Jesus,
    who, though he was in the form of God,
    did not regard equality with God as something to be exploited,
but emptied himself,
    taking the form of a slave,
    being born in human likeness.
And being found in human form, he humbled himself
and became obedient to the point of death –
    even death on a cross.

Therefore God also highly exalted him
    and gave him the name that is above every name,
so that at the name of Jesus every knee should bend,
    in heaven and on earth and under the earth,
and every tongue should confess that Jesus Christ is Lord,
    to the glory of God the Father.

856 *Colossians 3:1-4,12-15a*

So if you have been raised with Christ, seek the things that are above, where Christ is, seated at the right hand of God.
Set your minds on things that are above, not on things that are on earth, for you have died, and your life is hidden with Christ in God.
When Christ who is your life is revealed, then you also will be revealed with him in glory.

As God's chosen ones, holy and beloved, clothe yourselves with compassion, kindness, humility, meekness, and patience.
Bear with one another and, if anyone has a complaint against another, forgive each other; just as the Lord has forgiven you, so you also must forgive.
Above all, clothe yourselves with love, which binds everything together in perfect harmony. And let the peace of Christ rule in your hearts.

857 *James 5:13-16*

Are any among you suffering?
They should pray.
Are any cheerful?
They should sing songs of praise.
Are any among you sick?
They should call for the elders of the church
 and have them pray over them,
 anointing them with oil in the name of the Lord.
The prayer of faith will save the sick,
 and the Lord will raise them up;
 and anyone who has committed sins will be forgiven.
Therefore confess your sins to one another,
 and pray for one another, so that you may be healed.
The prayer of the righteous is powerful and effective.

858 *1 Peter 2:4-5, 9-10*

Come to him, a living stone, though rejected by mortals yet chosen and precious in God's sight, and like living stones, let yourselves be built into a spiritual house, to be a holy priesthood, to offer spiritual sacrifices acceptable to God through Jesus Christ.
You are a chosen race, a royal priesthood, a holy nation, God's own people, in order that you may proclaim the mighty acts of him who called you out of darkness into his marvelous light.
Once you were not a people,
but now you are God's people;
once you had not received mercy,
but now you have received mercy.

859 *1 John 4:18-21*

There is no fear in love, but perfect love casts out fear; for fear has to do with punishment, and whoever fears has not reached perfection in love. We love because he first loved us.

Those who say, "I love God," and hate their brothers or sisters, are liars; for those who do not love a brother or sister whom they have seen, cannot love God whom they have not seen.

The commandment we have from him is this: those who love God must love their brothers and sisters also.

860 *Revelation 21:1-4*

Then I saw a new heaven and a new earth; for the first heaven and the first earth had passed away, and the sea was no more. And I saw the holy city, the new Jerusalem, coming down out of heaven from God, prepared as a bride adorned for her husband. And I heard a loud voice from the throne saying,

"See, the home of God is among mortals.
He will dwell with them as their God;
they will be his people,
and God himself will be with them;
he will wipe every tear from their eyes.
Death will be no more;
mourning and crying and pain will be no more,
for the first things have passed away."

861 *Revelation 22:1-5*

Then the angel showed me the river of the water of life, bright as crystal,
   flowing from the throne of God and of the Lamb
      through the middle of the street of the city.
On either side of the river is the tree of life
   with its twelve kinds of fruit,
      producing its fruit each month;
   and the leaves of the tree are for the healing of the nations.
No longer will there be any curse.
But the throne of God and of the Lamb will be in the city,
   and his servants will worship him;
they will see his face,
   and his name will be on their foreheads.
And there will be no more night;
   they will need no light of lamp or sun,
for the Lord God will be their light,
   and they will reign forever and ever.

ACKNOWLEDGMENTS

Church of the Brethren, General Conference Mennonite, or Mennonite Church congregations may reproduce for worship and educational purposes any single item from *Hymnal: A Worship Book* for one-time use, as in a bulletin, special program, or lesson resource, provided that: (1) the item bears only a Brethren Press, Church of the Brethren General Board, Faith and Life Press, Mennonite Publishing House, Herald Press, or Hymnal Project copyright notice, or is in the public domain; (2) the copyright notice as shown on the page is included on the reproduction; and (3) *Hymnal: A Worship Book* is acknowledged as the source. Permission requests for use of more than one item belonging to these copyright holders should be addressed to the publishing house.

Material in the public domain does not have copyright information on the hymnal page, nor does it have a listing in the acknowledgments in this book.

Permissions have been obtained for *Hymnal: A Worship Book* with the restriction that its distribution is limited to the United States of America, its possessions and territories, and Canada. Some items showing no copyright information may have copyright protection in other countries. Every effort has been made to trace the owner(s) and/or administrator(s) of each copyright. The Publishers regret any omission and will, upon written notice, make the necessary correction(s) in subsequent printings.

Scripture, unless otherwise indicated, is from the *New Revised Standard Version Bible*, copyright 1989 by the Division of Christian Education of the National Council of Churches of Christ in the USA, 475 Riverside Dr., New York, NY 10115, (212) 870-2271. Used by permission.

Additional Scripture is taken from (1) *The Holy Bible, New International Version*, copyright ©1973, 1978, 1984 International Bible Society, and is used by permission of Zondervan Bible Publishers, 1415 Lake Drive, S.E., Grand Rapids, MI 49506, (616) 459-6900; (2) *The Holy Bible, Revised Standard Version*, copyright ©1946, 1952, 1971 National Council of Churches of Christ in the USA, and is used by permission of the Division of Education and Ministry of the National Council of Churches of Christ in the USA, 475 Riverside Dr., New York, NY 10115, (212) 870-2271; and (3) *The Revised English Bible*, copyright ©1989 Cambridge University Press, and is used by permission of Cambridge University Press, Edinburgh Building, Shaftsbury Ave., Cambridge CB2 2RU United Kingdom, (0223) 312393.

Addresses of Copyright Holders

The addresses of copyright holders with three or more items in the book are listed below. Other addresses are given in the succeeding index.

ABINGDON PRESS, 201 Eighth Ave., S., P.O. Box 801, Nashville, TN 37202, (615) 749-6422

AUGSBURG FORTRESS PUBLISHERS, 426 S. Fifth St., Box 1209, Minneapolis, MN 55440, (800) 328-4648

BRETHREN PRESS, 1451 Dundee Ave., Elgin, IL 60120, (800) 323-8039, fax (847) 742-6103

CHURCH OF THE BRETHREN GENERAL BOARD (see BRETHREN PRESS)

CHURCH PENSION FUND, THE, 800 Second Ave., New York, NY 10017, (800) 223-6602

CONCORDIA PUBLISHING HOUSE, 3558 S. Jefferson Ave., St. Louis, MO 63118, (314) 268-1000

CROSSROAD/CONTINUUM PUBLISHING COMPANY, 370 Lexington Ave., New York, NY 10017, (212) 532-3650

ENGLISH LANGUAGE LITURGICAL CONSULTATION, 1275 K St., N.W., Suite 1202, Washington, D.C., 20005-4097, (202) 347-0800

FAITH AND LIFE PRESS, P.O. Box 347, Newton, KS 67114, (316) 283-5100

FYOCK, JOAN A., c/o Lititz Church of the Brethren, 300 W. Orange St., Lititz, PA 17543, (717) 626-2131

GEISER, LINEA REIMER, 610 Revere Dr., Goshen, IN 46526, (219) 533-2629

G.I.A. Publications, 7404 S. Mason Ave., Chicago, IL 60638, (708) 496-3800

HAMM, MARILYN HOUSER, Box 1887, Altona, Manitoba R0G 0B0 Canada, (204) 324-5438

HAL LEONARD PUBLISHING CORPORATION, 777 W. Bluemound Rd., P.O. Box 13819, Milwaukee, WI 53213, (414) 774-3630

HOPE PUBLISHING COMPANY, 380 S. Main Pl., Carol Stream, IL 60188, (630) 665-3200

HYMN SOCIETY, THE (see HOPE PUBLISHING COMPANY)

HYMNAL PROJECT, THE (see BRETHREN PRESS)

JANZEN, JEAN, 5508 E. Lane, Fresno, CA 93727, (209) 251-9006

KROPF, MARLENE, Mennonite Board of Congregational Ministries, Box 1245, Elkhart, IN 46515-1245, (219) 294-7523

LEHMAN, BRADLEY P., 251 W. Gay St., Harrisonburg, VA 22801

LION PUBLISHING CORPORATION, Peter's Way, Sandy Lane West, Oxford OX4 5HG England, (44) 01865-747550

LOEWEN, HARRIS J., c/o Music Department, Brock University, St. Catharines, Ontario L2S 3A1 Canada, (416) 688-5550

MENNONITE PUBLISHING HOUSE, 616 Walnut Ave., Scottdale, PA 15683, (412) 887-8500

MENNONITE WORLD CONFERENCE, 50 Kent Ave., Kitchener, Ontario N2G 3R1 Canada, (519) 571-0060, fax (519) 571-1980

MOREHOUSE PUBLISHING, 871 Ethan Allen Highway, Ridgefield, CT 06877, (203) 431-3927

NEW DAWN MUSIC, P.O. Box 13248, Portland, OR 97213-0248, (800) 243-3296

OCP PUBLICATIONS, 5536 N.E. Hassalo, Portland, OR 97213, (800) 547-8992

OXFORD UNIVERSITY PRESS, INC., 200 Madison Ave., New York, NY 10016, (212) 679-7300

OXFORD UNIVERSITY PRESS, 3 Park Rd., London NW1 6XN England, (071) 233-5455

PARKER, ALICE, 801 West End Ave., 9-D, New York, NY 10025, (212) 663-1165

PILGRIM PRESS/UNITED CHURCH PRESS, 700 Prospect Ave. E., Cleveland, OH 44115, (216) 736-3700

REFORMED CHURCH IN AMERICA, RCA Distribution Center, 4500 60th St., S.E., Grand Rapids, MI 49512, (800) 968-7221

REMPEL, JOHN D., c/o Faith and Life Press

SCHIRMER, G., 257 Park Ave. S., New York, NY 10010, (212) 254-2100, fax (212) 254-2013

SCM PRESS, LTD., 26-30 Tottenham Rd., London, N1 4BZ England

UNICHAPPELL MUSIC, INC. (see HAL LEONARD PUBLISHING CORPORATION)

UNITED CHURCH PRESS (see PILGRIM PRESS)

UNITED METHODIST PUBLISHING HOUSE, THE (see ABINGDON PRESS)

WARKENTIN, LARRY, c/o Fresno Pacific College, 1717 S., Chestnut Ave., Fresno, CA 93702 (209) 251-8053

WESTMINSTER/JOHN KNOX PRESS, 100 Witherspoon St., Louisville, KY 40202-1396, (502) 569-5052

WIEBE, ESTHER, c/o Canadian Mennonite Bible College, 600 Shaftesbury Blvd., Winnipeg, Manitoba R3P 0M4 Canada, (204) 888-6781

WORLD LIBRARY PUBLICATIONS, 3815 N. Willow Rd., Schiller Park, IL 60176, (847) 678-0621

Index of Copyright Holders

168   Refr: © Philip K. Clemens, 17716 R. 89, Corry, PA 16047, (814) 664-9102. Used by permission
      Music: ©1983 Philip K. Clemens. Used by permission
171   Text: ©1991 Jean Wiebe Janzen. Used by permission
173   Trans. (Sts. 3-4): ©1969 Concordia Publishing House. Used by permission from CPH
174   Text: ©1973 by Hope Publishing Co. All rights reserved. Used by permission
175   Trans: ©1965 Martin L. Seltz, c/o Helen L. Seltz, 416 N. 19th Ave., South St. Paul, MN 55075. Used by permission
      Harm: ©1964 Esther Wiebe. Used by permission
177   Text: from The Hymnal 1982 ©1985 The Church Pension Fund. Used by permission
178   Arr: © Oxford University Press, London. Reprinted by permission
179   Text: ©1963 Ladies of the Grail. Used by permission of G.I.A. Publications, Inc. All rights reserved
      Music: © Trappist Abbey of Tamié, 73200 Plancherine, FRANCE. Used by permission
180   Text and music arr: ©1961 H. Freeman & Co./International Music Publications
181   Text: ©1987 by Hope Publishing Co. All rights reserved. Used by permission
      Music: J. Harold Moyer, ©1991 The Hymnal Project
184   Harm: © 1969 Faith and Life Press/Mennonite Publishing House. All rights reserved. Used by permission
186   Trans: ©1978 Lutheran Book of Worship. Reprinted by permission of Augsburg Fortress
187   ©1977 John B. Foley, S.J., and OCP Publications. All rights reserved. Used with permission
188   Trans: ©1982 by Hope Publishing Co. All rights reserved. Used by permission
190   English words by J. E. Middleton. Used by permission of The Frederick Harris Music Co., Ltd., 529 Speers Rd., Oakville, Ontario L6K 2G9 CANADA. All rights reserved
192   Trans. and arr: ©1924 J. Curwen & Sons, Ltd. (London). All rights for the U.S. and Canada controlled by G. Schirmer, Inc. (New York). International copyright secured. All rights reserved
194   Arr: ©1989 Joan A. Fyock. Used by permission
198   Setting: ©1978 Lutheran Book of Worship. Reprinted by permission of Augsburg Fortress
200   Music: ©1989 Joan A. Fyock. Used by permission
202   ©1945 by Boosey & Co., Ltd.; copyright renewed. Reprinted by permission of Boosey & Hawkes, Inc., 24 E. 21st St., New York, NY 10010-7200
203   Trans. (Sts. 2-3): ©1989 by Hope Publishing Co. All rights reserved. Used by permission
204   Music: ©1979 Les Presses de Taizé. Used by permission of G.I.A. Publications, Inc., exclusive agent. All rights reserved
205   Trans: ©1978 Lutheran Book of Worship. Reprinted by permission of Augsburg Fortress
206   Harm: © Rosalind Rusbridge, Bristol Churches Housing Assoc., Ltd., 7 York Ct., Wilder St., Bristol, BS2 8QH ENGLAND.
207   Trans: ©1989 The United Methodist Publishing House. Reprinted from The United Methodist Hymnal by permission
208   Text: ©1982 by Hope Publishing Co. All rights reserved. Used by permission
209   Text: ©1990 by Hope Publishing Co. All rights reserved. Used by permission
      Arr: ©1953, renewed G. Schirmer, Inc. International copyright secured. All rights reserved. Used by permission
217   Trans. (St. 1): ©1971 The Hymn Book of the Anglican Church of Canada and the United Church of Canada. Used by permission
219   Trans: ©1958 Service Book and Hymnal. Reprinted by permission of Augsburg Fortress
221   Harm: ©1990 Alice Parker. Used by permission
222   Trans: ©1978 Lutheran Book of Worship. Reprinted by permission of Augsburg Fortress
223   Text: ©1983 by Hope Publishing Co. All rights reserved. Used by permission
      Music: ©1990 by Marilyn Houser Hamm. Used by permission
224   ©1987 by Hope Publishing Co. All rights reserved. Used by permission
225   Trans: © Oxford University Press, London. Reprinted by permission
226   ©1986 by G.I.A. Publications, Inc. All rights reserved. Used by permission
227   Text: ©1986 by G.I.A. Publications, Inc. All rights reserved. Used by permission
      Music: ©1970 by G.I.A. Publications, Inc. All rights reserved. Used by permission
229   Text (Spanish) and music: ©1979 Cesáreo Gabaraín. Published by OCP Publications. All rights reserved. Used with permission
      Trans: ©1989 The United Methodist Publishing House. Reprinted from The United Methodist Hymnal by permission

230   Text: ©1990 Mennonite World Conference. Used by permission
231   Harm: ©1985 by G.I.A. Publications, Inc. All rights reserved. Used by permission
232   Text: ©1977 by Hope Publishing Co. All rights reserved. Used by permission
      Music: ©1984 Bradley P. Lehman. Used by permission
233   Text: ©1989 by Hope Publishing Co. All rights reserved. Used by permission
      Music: ©1991 Philip K. Clemens, 17716 R. 89, Corry, PA 16047, (814) 664-9102. Used by permission
235   Text: ©1982 by Hope Publishing Co. All rights reserved. Used by permission
      Music: ©1925 John Ireland Trust, 35 St. Mary's Mansions, St. Mary's Terrace, London, W2 1SQ ENGLAND. Used by permission
239   Text: ©1982 by Hope Publishing Co. All rights reserved. Used by permission
242   Music: ©1982 Les Presses de Taizé. Used by permission of G.I.A. Publications, Inc., exclusive agent. All rights reserved
243   Trans: © F. E. Pilcher, 94 Willington Blvd., Toronto, Ontario M8X 2H7 CANADA. Used by permission
      Music: ©1977 Lawrence F. Bartlett, 2 New South Head Rd., Vaucluse NSW 2030 AUSTRALIA. Used by permission
244   Trans: from The Hymnal 1982 ©1938 The Church Pension Fund. Used by permission
245   Arr: © Oxford University Press, London. Reprinted by permission
246   Text: ©1981 W. L. Wallace, 215A Mt. Pleasant Rd., Mt. Pleasant, Christchurch 8008, NEW ZEALAND. Used by permission
      Music: ©1983 Taihei Sato, 9-2-20-1402, Takashimadaira, Itabashi-ku, Tokyo 175, JAPAN. Used by permission
247   ©1981 Les Presses de Taizé. Used by permission of G.I.A. Publications, Inc., exclusive agent. All rights reserved
248   Music: ©1982 The Church Pension Fund. Used by permission
251   Text: ©1990 by Hope Publishing Co. All rights reserved. Used by permission
255   Text: © J. W. Shore, 158 Hilltop Dr., Kirkholt, Rochdale, Lancashire, OL11 2RZ ENGLAND. Used by permission
256   Trans. (Sts. 2,4-5): ©1982 The Church Pension Fund. Used by permission
261   Text: ©1990 by Hope Publishing Co. All rights reserved. Used by permission
267   ©1977 Lutheran World Federation, P.O. Box 2100, 1211 Geneva 2, SWITZERLAND. Used by permission
268   ©1983 Francisco F. Feliciano, A.I.L.M., P.O. Box 3167, Manila, 1099, PHILIPPINES. Used by permission
270   Trans: ©1991 The Hymnal Project
      Music: ©1989 Jacek Gałuszka, Dominican House of Studies, Holy Trinity Priory, ul. Stolarska 12, 31-043 Krakow, POLAND. Used by permission
271   Trans: ©1941 Concordia Publishing House. Used by permission from CPH
272   Text: ©1986 by Hope Publishing Co. All rights reserved. Used by permission
      Music: © Walton Music Corporation, c/o Stanley Ashare, CPA PC, 220 E. 57th St., Ste. 2K, New York, NY 10022. Used by permission
276   Harm: ©1966 Alice Parker. Used by permission
277   Harm: ©1988 Alice Parker. Used by permission
278   Text: ©1975 by Hope Publishing Co. All rights reserved. Used by permission
282   ©1920 The Fillmore Brothers Co.
284   Harm: ©1991 The Hymnal Project
289   Text: ©1978 by Hope Publishing Co. All rights reserved. Used by permission
291   Trans: ©1971 John Webster Grant, Apt. 1002, 86 Gloucester St., Toronto, Ontario M4Y 2S2 CANADA. Used by permission
293   ©1969 by Hope Publishing Co. All rights reserved. Used by permission
294   Music: ©1982, 1983, 1984 Les Presses de Taizé. Used by permission of G.I.A. Publications, Inc., exclusive agent. All rights reserved
296   Text: ©1973 by Hope Publishing Co. All rights reserved. Used by permission
      Harm: © Oxford University Press, London. Reprinted by permission
297   Text: ©1982 by Hope Publishing Co. All rights reserved. Used by permission
298   ©1979 Les Presses de Taizé. Used by permission of G.I.A. Publications, Inc., exclusive agent. All rights reserved
299   ©1992 by Hope Publishing Co. All rights reserved. Used by permission
300   Text: ©1939 by A. S. Barnes & Co., Inc.; copyright © renewed 1967 by Gordon B. Tweedy. Reprinted by permission of HarperCollins Publishers, Inc., 10 E. 53rd St., New York, NY 10022
304   ©1977 by Patricia Shelly, Box 41, North Newton, KS 67117. Used by permission

305 Trans: ©1961 by World Library Publications, Inc. All rights reserved. Used with permission
306 Text: © Estate of John Oxenham. By permission of Desmond Dunkerley, 23 Haslemere Rd., Southsea, Portsmouth, Hants, P04 8BB ENGLAND
307 ©1977 Scripture in Song (admin. by Maranatha! Music, Inc., c/o The Copyright Company, 40 Music Square E., Nashville, TN 37203). All rights reserved. International copyright secured. Used by permission
309 Trans: ©1958 *Service Book and Hymnal*. Reprinted by permission of Augsburg Fortress
310 Text: ©1982 by Hope Publishing Co. All rights reserved. Used by permission
313 Trans: ©1983 by Ruth Naylor, 123 Villanova Dr., Bluffton, OH 45817. Used by permission
Music: ©1983 James W. Bixel. Used by permission
314 Text adpt: ©1983 Harris J. Loewen. Used by permission
Music: ©1983 by Faith and Life Press/Mennonite Publishing House. All rights reserved. Used by permission
315 Text: ©1986 by Hope Publishing Co. All rights reserved. Used by permission
316 Text: © Japanese Hymnal Committee, UCC in Japan, 2-3-18 Nishiwaseda, Shinjuku-ku, Tokyo 169, JAPAN. Used by permission
320 Arr: ©1992 The Hymnal Project
321 ©1974 by Hope Publishing Co. All rights reserved. Used by permission
322 Text: ©1979 Church of the Brethren General Board. Used by permission
Music: ©1979 by Dianne Huffman Morningstar, 2950 Gettysburg Rd., Camp Hill, PA 17011. Used by permission
323 ©1970 Steve Engle, 223 E. Third St., Waynesboro, PA 17268, and the Church of the Brethren, LaVerne, Calif. Used by permission
324 ©1972 Maranatha! Music, Inc. (admin. by The Copyright Company, 40 Music Square E., Nashville, TN 37203). All rights reserved. International copyright secured. Used by permission
325 Text: ©1979 by The Hymn Society. All rights reserved. Used by permission
327 ©1923, renewal 1951 by Hope Publishing Co. All rights reserved. Used by permission
329 Trans: ©1978 *Lutheran Book of Worship*. Reprinted by permission of Augsburg Fortress
330 © S. C. Ochieng' Okeyo, Kenyatta University, Faculty of Arts, Music Department, P.O. Box 43884, Nairobi, KENYA. Used by permission
333 Text: ©1985 by David T. Koyzis, 499 Stone Church Rd. W., Hamilton, Ontario L9B 1A5 CANADA. Used by permission
334 Text: ©1931 Oxford University Press, London. Reprinted by permission
Music: from *The Hymnal 1982*, ©1940 The Church Pension Fund. Used by permission
335 ©1980 by Hope Publishing Co. All rights reserved. Used by permission
342 Music: ©1931 Oxford University Press, London. Reprinted by permission
345 ©1971 by William J. Gaither (Gaither Music Co., Box 300, Alexandria, IN 46001). All rights reserved. Used by permission
347 ©1989 Oxford University Press, Inc. Used by permission
348 ©1982 Les Presses de Taizé. Used by permission of G.I.A. Publications, Inc., exclusive agent. All rights reserved
349 ©1935, renewal 1963 Birdwing Music. Admin. by EMI Christian Publishers, P.O. Box 5085, Brentwood, TN 37024-5085, (615) 371-4300. All rights reserved. International copyright secured. Used by permission
350 Harm: ©1991 The Hymnal Project
351 ©1974 Church of the Brethren General Board. Used by permission
352 ©1974 by William J. Gaither (Gaither Music Co., Box 300, Alexandria, IN 46001). All rights reserved. Used by permission
353 ©1973 by Hope Publishing Co. All rights reserved. Used by permission
354 ©1977 The Chinese Christian Literature Council, Ltd.
358 ©1988, 1990 Bob Hurd. Published by OCP Publications. All rights reserved. Used with permission
362 Text: ©1982 by Hope Publishing Co. All rights reserved. Used by permission
363 Text: ©1960 K. L. Cober, ©1985 by Judson Press, P.O. Box 851, Valley Forge, PA 19482-0851. Used by permission
364 Text: © John W. Arthur
367 Text: ©1968 by Hope Publishing Co. All rights reserved. Used by permission
368 Adpt. (St. 1): ©1980 Ruth Duck, Garrett-Evangelical Theological Seminary, 2121 Sheridan Rd., Evanston, IL 60201. Used by permission
369 Text: ©1961 Oxford University Press, London. Reprinted by permission
Harm: ©1989 Joan A. Fyock. Used by permission

370 Text: © Emmanuel College, 75 Queen's Park Crescent E., Toronto, Ontario M5S 1K7 CANADA. Used by permission
Music: ©1938 Estate of James Hopkirk, c/o Arthur E. B. Armstrong, 131 Branda Cres., Scarborough, Ontario M1K 3C8 CANADA. Used by permission
373 Text and harm: © Oxford University Press, London. Reprinted by permission
377 ©1987 by G.I.A. Publications, Inc. All rights reserved. Used by permission
378 Text: ©1963 by Anne Metzler Albright, 919 Darlow Dr., McPherson, KS 67460. Used by permission
Music: ©1991 Bradley P. Lehman. Used by permission
379 Text: ©1969 by Hope Publishing Co. All rights reserved. Used by permission
Music: ©1989 by G.I.A. Publications, Inc. All rights reserved. Used by permission
380 Music: ©1984 by G.I.A. Publications, Inc. All rights reserved. Used by permission
383 Text: ©1961, renewal 1989 by The Hymn Society. All rights reserved. Used by permission
Arr: ©1951 Oxford University Press, London. Reprinted by permission
385 ©1982 by Hope Publishing Co. All rights reserved. Used by permission
386 Text: ©1961, renewal 1989 by The Hymn Society. All rights reserved. Used by permission
Tune and setting: ©1963 by Augsburg Publishing House. Reprinted by permission of Augsburg Fortress
390 Text: ©1955, renewal 1983 by The Hymn Society. All rights reserved. Used by permission
Music: © Estate of Eric H. Thiman, c/o Royal Academy of Music, Marylebone Rd., London, NW1 5HT ENGLAND. Used by permission
391 Text: © Estate of John Arlott
392 ©1958 United Church Press. Reprinted with the permission of The Pilgrim Press
394 ©1983 Oxford University Press, Inc. Used by permission
395 ©1981 Daniel L. Shutte and OCP. All rights reserved. Used with permission
397 Trans: ©1978, 1990 Mennonite World Conference. Used by permission
399 Trans: ©1986 Evelyn Chiu, c/o Conference of Mennonites in British Columbia, 31414 Marshall Rd., Clearbrook, British Columbia V2T 3X8 CANADA. Used by permission
400 © Guillermo Cuellar, Residencial el Cortijo, Senda B2, Avenue Montes Urales, Colonia Montebello, San Salvador, EL SALVADOR. Phone and fax 011-503-274-9070. Used by permission
401 Music adpt: ©1989 The United Methodist Publishing House. Reprinted from *The United Methodist Hymnal* by permission
403 Text: ©1971 by Hope Publishing Co. All rights reserved. Used by permission
Music: ©1962 Theodore Presser Co., Presser Pl., Bryn Mawr, PA 19010. Used by permission
404 Text: ©1954, renewal 1982 by The Hymn Society. All rights reserved. Used by permission
Tune and setting: ©1957 Augsburg Publishing House. Reprinted by permission of Augsburg Fortress
407 Trans: ©1990 Mennonite World Conference. Used by permission
408 Text: ©1982 by Hope Publishing Co. All rights reserved. Used by permission
Harm: ©1986 by G.I.A. Publications, Inc. All rights reserved. Used by permission
409 Text: © Oxford University Press, London. Reprinted by permission
Music ©1990 Larry Warkentin. Used by permission
411 Music: ©1965 by J. Randall Zercher, Westbury United Methodist Church, 5200 Willowbend Blvd., Houston, TX 77096. Used by permission
412 Music adpt: ©1970 by World Library Publications, Inc. All rights reserved. Used with permission
414 Text: ©1967 by Hope Publishing Co. All rights reserved. Used by permission
417 Text: ©1969 by Galliard, Ltd. All rights reserved. Used by permission of Galaxy Music Corp., c/o E. C. Schirmer, 138 Ipswich St., Boston, MA 02215
419 Text: ©1974 Ruth Duck, Garrett-Evangelical Theological Seminary, 2121 Sheridan Rd., Evanston, IL 60201. Used by permission
420 Trans: ©1969, 1983 by Walter Klaassen, Site 12-A, C. 23, R.R. 7, Vernon, British Columbia, V1T 7Z3 CANADA. Used by permission
425 Text: ©1960, 1988 by Broadman Press, 127 Ninth Ave. N., Nashville, TN 37234. Used by permission
426 Trans: ©1941 Concordia Publishing House. Reprinted by permission
427 ©1975 by Lillenas Publishing Co., Box 419527, Kansas City, MO 64141. All rights reserved. Used by permission
429 ©1976 Hinshaw Music, Inc., P.O. Box 470, Chapel Hill, NC 27514. Used by permission

554 ©1980 Les Presses de Taizé. Used by permission of G.I.A. Publications, Inc., exclusive agent. All rights reserved

556 Harm: ©1991 The Hymnal Project

558 Arr: ©1989 The United Methodist Publishing House. Reprinted from *The United Methodist Hymnal* by permission

559 Harm: ©1969 Faith and Life Press/Mennonite Publishing House. All rights reserved. Used by permission

560 Trans: ©1983 Paul R. Gregory, Homestead Village, Inc., 1800 Village Circle, Apt. 145, Lancaster, PA 17603. Used by permission

561 Harm: ©1991 Alice Parker. Used by permission

562 Music: © Les Presses de Taizé. Used by permission of G.I.A. Publications, Inc., exclusive agent. All rights reserved

569 Music: ©1960 H. W. Gray Co., Inc., c/o CPP/Belwin, Inc., P.O. Box 4340, Miami, FL 33014. Used with permission. All rights reserved

570 Music: ©1984 by G.I.A. Publications, Inc. All rights reserved. Used by permission

572 Music: ©1990 by Stephanie Martin, 2-890 Castle Field Ave., Toronto, Ontario M6B 1C8 CANADA. Used by permission

575 ©1938 Hill and Range Songs, Inc. Copyright renewed, assigned to Unichappell Music, Inc. (Rightsong Music, Publisher). International copyright secured. All rights reserved. Unauthorized copying, arranging, adapting, recording or public performance is an infringement of copyright. Infringers are liable under the law

576 Trans. (St. 2): ©1978 *Lutheran Book of Worship*. Reprinted by permission of Augsburg Press

579 ©1921 Edward B. Marks Music Company (div. of Hal Leonard Pub. Corp.). Copyright renewed. International copyright secured. All rights reserved. Used by permission

580 Arr: ©1989 The Hymnal Project

583 © African Methodist Episcopal Church, 500 8th Ave. S., Nashville, TN 37203. Used by permission

584 ©1953, renewed 1981 Hamblen Music Co., c/o Cohen and Luckenbacher, 740 N. La Brea, Los Angeles, CA 90038. ASCAP, International copyright secured. All rights reserved. Used by permission. Sheet music available

585 © Asempa Publishers, Box 919, Accra, GHANA, West Africa. Used by permission

587 Music: ©1911 by Stainer & Bell, Ltd., P.O. Box 110, Victoria House, 23 Gruneisen Rd., London, N3 1DZ ENGLAND. Used by permission

589 Harm: ©1969 Faith and Life Press/Mennonite Publishing House. All rights reserved. Used by permission

594 Text: ©1969 by Hope Publishing Co. All rights reserved. Used by permission
Music: © Christopher Johnson. Used by permission

596 ©1979 New Dawn Music. All rights reserved. Used with permission

597 Harm: ©1969 Faith and Life Press/Mennonite Publishing House. All rights reserved. Used by permission

603 Music: ©1974 by Carl Fischer, Inc., 62 Cooper Square, New York, NY 10003. International copyright secured. All rights reserved. Reprinted by permission

605 Trans: © Oxford University Press, London. Reprinted by permission
Harm: ©1991 The Hymnal Project

607 Text: ©1975 by Hope Publishing Co. All rights reserved. Used by permission
Music: ©1980 by Hope Publishing Co. All rights reserved. Used by permission

608 Harm: ©1992 The Hymnal Project

610 Harm: ©1969 Faith and Life Press/Mennonite Publishing House. All rights reserved. Used by permission

611 ©1973 BudJohn Songs, Inc. (Crouch Music/BudJohn/ ASCAP). Admin. by EMI Christian Publishers, P.O. Box 5085, Brentwood, TN 37024-5085, (615) 371-4300. International copyright secured. All rights reserved. Used by permission

614 ©1986 by Hope Publishing Co. All rights reserved. Used by permission

616 Trans: ©1925, 1953 Board of Publication, Lutheran Church in America. Reprinted by permission of Augsburg Fortress

620 Text: ©1981 by Ronald S. Cole-Turner, Memphis Theological Seminary, 168 East Parkway South, Memphis, TN 38104. Used by permission

621 Text: ©1948 Philip E. Gregory

622 Text: ©1983 by Hope Publishing Co. All rights reserved. Used by permission
Music: ©1990 Larry Warkentin. Used by permission

623 Text: ©1983 by Hope Publishing Co. All rights reserved. Used by permission
Harm: ©1989 Alice Parker. Used by permission

625 Text: ©1982 by Hope Publishing Co. All rights reserved. Used by permission
Music: ©1984 M. Lee Suitor, 3730A N. 55th St., Milwaukee, WI 53216, (414) 445-8580. Used by permission

626 Text: ©1978 *Lutheran Book of Worship*. Reprinted by permission of Augsburg Fortress
Arr: © Oxford University Press, London. Reprinted by permission

628 Text: ©1982 by Hope Publishing Co. All rights reserved. Used by permission

629 Text: ©1982 by Hope Publishing Co. All rights reserved. Used by permission

630 ©1984 Oxford University Press, Inc. Used by permission

631 ©1979 The Glade Valley Church of the Brethren, 2 Chapel Pl., Walkersville, MD 21793. Used by permission

632 Text: ©1989 by Hope Publishing Co. All rights reserved. Used by permission
Arr: © Oxford University Press, London. Reprinted by permission

633 Text: ©1971 by Hope Publishing Co. All rights reserved. Used by permission

634 Text: ©1983 by Hope Publishing Co. All rights reserved. Used by permission

636 Music: © Oxford University Press, London. Reprinted by permission

637 Text: ©1983 by Hope Publishing Co. All rights reserved. Used by permission
Music: ©1990 Larry Warkentin. Used by permission

638 Music: ©1931 Oxford University Press, London. Reprinted by permission

640 Text: ©1983, 1987 by Hope Publishing Co. All rights reserved. Used by permission
Music: ©1991 Richard D. Brode, c/o Brethren Press. Used by permission

643 Music: ©1986 by G.I.A. Publications, Inc. All rights reserved. Used by permission

647 Text (Spanish) and music: ©1954 Singspiration Music. All rights reserved. Used by permission of Benson Music Group, Inc., 365 Great Circle Rd., Nashville, TN 37228
Trans: ©1978, 1990 Mennonite World Conference. Used by permission

648 Text: ©1957 by Eleanor Farjeon. Reprinted by permission of Harold Ober Associates, Inc., 425 Madison Ave., New York, NY 10017
Harm: © Oxford University Press, London. Reprinted by permission

650 Trans: © Oxford University Press, London. Reprinted by permission

651 ©1927 Mennonite Publishing House. Used by permission

657 Trans: ©1978 *Lutheran Book of Worship*. Reprinted by permission of Augsburg Fortress

659 Revelation 1:4-6, adapted from *Revised Standard Version* by Ruth C. Duck, *Bread for the Journey*, ed. Ruth C. Duck, copyright ©1981, altered. Reprinted with the permission of The Pilgrim Press

660 English translation of Sursum Corda, prepared by the English Language Liturgical Consultation (ELLC), copyright ©1988. Used by permission

661 Ruth C. Duck, *Flames of the Spirit*, ed. Ruth C. Duck, copyright ©1985, altered. Reprinted with the permission of The Pilgrim Press

662 Earle W. Fike, Jr., *We Gather Together*, copyright ©1979 Brethren Press. Used by permission

663 Psalm 27:1,4, adapted from *New Revised Standard Version*

664 Sandra E. Graham, *Flames of the Spirit*, ed. Ruth C. Duck, copyright ©1985, altered. Reprinted with the permission of The Pilgrim Press

665 Copyright ©1992 The Hymnal Project, based on Luke 2:11,14, *New Revised Standard Version*

666 Lavon Bayler, *Refreshing Rains of the Living Word*, copyright ©1988, altered. Reprinted with the permission of The Pilgrim Press

667 Adapted from the poem "He's Coming," by Linea Reimer Geiser, copyright ©1990 Linea Reimer Geiser. Used by permission

668 Altered from *All the Seasons of Mercy*, by Diane Karay, copyright ©1987 Diane Karay. Used by permission of Westminster/John Knox Press

669 Wheadon United Methodist Church Worship Commission, Evanston, Ill., *Bread for the Journey*, ed. Ruth C. Duck, copyright ©1981, altered. Reprinted with the permission of The Pilgrim Press

670 Copyright ©1988 Ruth A. Yoder, 26175 Woodridge Dr., Elkhart, IN 46517. Used by permission

671 Mervin Cripe, *We Gather Together*, copyright ©1979 Brethren Press, adapted. Used by permission

672 Lavon Bayler, *Refreshing Rains of the Living Word*, copyright ©1988, altered. Reprinted with the permission of The Pilgrim Press

673 Sarum missal, 11th c.

674 Copyright ©1992 The Hymnal Project

675 St. Augustine of Hippo, North Africa, ca. 400

676 Janet Morley, *All Desires Known*, copyright ©1988 Morehouse Publishing. Used by permission

677 The Iona Community, Scotland, *The New Book of Christian Prayers*, copyright ©1986 Tony Castle. Edited by Tony Castle. Crossroad/Continuum Publishing Company. Used by permission

678 Rebecca J. Slough, copyright ©1992 The Hymnal Project

679 Taizé community, 20th c., Taizé, France, copyright © Ateliers et Presses de Taizé, F-71250 Taizé-Communaute, FRANCE, altered. Used by permission

680 Adapted from *More Than Words*, Pat Kozak, C.S.J., and Janet Schaffran, C.D.P. First edition copyright ©1986 Pat Kozak, C.S.J., and Janet Schaffran, C.D.P.; second revised edition copyright ©1988. Crossroad/Continuum Publishing Company. Used with permission

681 Psalm 47:1-2,6-9, adapted from *Revised Standard Version*

682 Copyright ©1988 Linea Reimer Geiser. Used by permission

683 Psalm 146:7-9, adapted from *More Than Words*, Pat Kozak, C.S.J., and Janet Schaffran, C.D.P. First edition copyright ©1986 Pat Kozak, C.S.J., and Janet Schaffran, C.D.P.; second revised edition copyright ©1988. Crossroad/Continuum Publishing Company. Also adapted from *New Revised Standard Version*

684 Psalm 148, adapted from *Psalms Anew*, edited/paraphrased by Nancy Schreck and Maureen Leach, copyright ©1984 Saint Mary's Press, 702 Torrance Heights, Winona, MN 55927. Used by permission. Also adapted from *New Revised Standard Version*

685 Ephesians 1:3-14, adapted from *New Revised Standard Version*, copyright ©1992 The Hymnal Project

686 Psalm 63:1-4, adapted from *New Revised Standard Version*

687 Isaiah 42:10-12, adapted from *New International Version*

688 Copyright ©1992 The Hymnal Project

689 Revelation 5:11-13, adapted from *New Revised Standard Version*

690 Copyright ©1988 Ruth A. Yoder, 26175 Woodridge Dr., Elkhart, IN 46517. Used by permission

691 Adapted from a litany of repentance, Edward K. Ziegler, *The Adventurous Future*, ed. Paul H. Bowman, copyright ©1959 Brethren Press. Used by permission

692 Ernest Fremont Tittle, adapted from *A Book of Pastoral Prayers*, Abingdon-Cokesbury Press, New York and Nashville, copyright ©1951 for *The Mennonite Hymnal*, copyright ©1969. Further revised by The Hymnal Project, copyright ©1992

693 Balthasar Hubmaier, 16th c., based on Luke 15:18-19,21 and 18:13. Translation copyright ©1991 John D. Rempel. Used by permission

694 Psalm 103:10-12, adapted from *New Revised Standard Version*

695 Copyright ©1992 Marlene Kropf. Used by permission

696 Ruth C. Duck, *Flames of the Spirit*, ed. Ruth C. Duck, copyright ©1985, altered. Reprinted with the permission of The Pilgrim Press

697 Peace litany, 20th c., source unknown

698 Lancelot Andrewes, ca. 1600, *The New Book of Christian Prayers*, copyright ©1986 Tony Castle. Edited by Tony Castle. Crossroad/Continuum Publishing Company

699 Based on a prayer from The Liturgy of St. Basil of Caesarea, 4th c., adapted from *Contemporary Prayers for Public Worship*, ed. Caryl Micklem

700 Menno Simons, 16th c., "Meditation on the 25th Psalm," *The Complete Writings of Menno Simons*, translated by Leonard Verduin, ed. J. C. Wenger, copyright ©1956 Herald Press, Scottdale, PA 15683. Used by permission

701 Adapted from *365 Children's Prayers*, written and compiled by Carol Watson, copyright ©1989 Lion Publishing Corporation. Used by permission

702 English translation of Agnus Dei, prepared by the English Language Liturgical Consultation (ELLC), copyright ©1988. Used by permission

703 Adapted from the musical "Prayer Phrases" by Harris J. Loewen, copyright ©1986 Harris J. Loewen. Used by permission

704 Isaiah 55:6-7, *An Inclusive Language Lectionary: Year A*, copyright ©1982. Reprinted with the permission of The Pilgrim Press

705 Copyright ©1992 The Hymnal Project, based on Galatians 5:1,13, *New Revised Standard Version*

706 Copyright ©1988 Marlene Kropf. Used by permission

707 1 John 1:5,7, adapted from *New Revised Standard Version* and *Revised English Bible*, copyright ©1992 The Hymnal Project

708 Mass of the Roman Rite

709 Romans 8:1-2, adapted from *New Revised Standard Version*

710 Adapted from a liturgy of baptism by Assembly Mennonite Church, Goshen, Ind., *Baptism and Church Membership*, Worship Series 3, ed. James H. Waltner, copyright ©1979 Faith and Life Press/Mennonite Publishing House. Used by permission

711 South African creed, 20th c., used with the permission of Canadian Catholic Organization for Development and Peace, Toronto, Ontario, CANADA

712 English translation of The Apostles' Creed, prepared by the English Language Liturgical Consultation (ELLC), copyright ©1988. Used by permission

713 Affirmation of faith, 20th c., adapted from *The Mennonite Hymnal*, copyright ©1969 Faith and Life Press/Mennonite Publishing House. Used by permission

714 Adapted from *We Gather Together*, Kenneth I. Morse, copyright ©1979 Brethren Press. Used by permission

715 Luke 1:46-55, Mother Thunder Mission, from *Language About God in Liturgy and Scripture*, copyright ©1980 The Geneva Press, Philadelphia, Pa. (since taken over by Westminster/John Knox Press); used by permission. Original version from *A Daily Office*, copyright ©1976 Mother Thunder Mission

716 Copyright ©1992 The Hymnal Project, based on 1 Corinthians 3:11, 1 Peter 2:4-5, and Ephesians 2:19-22, *New Revised Standard Version*

717 Adapted from *We Gather Together*, Alvin Franz Brightbill, copyright ©1979 Brethren Press. Used by permission

718 Adapted from "Litany of Thanksgiving," Edward K. Ziegler, *The Adventurous Future*, ed. Paul H. Bowman, copyright ©1959 Brethren Press. Used by permission

719 Adapted from *365 Children's Prayers*, written and compiled by Carol Watson, copyright ©1989 Lion Publishing Corporation. Used by permission

720 Copyright ©1992 The Hymnal Project

721 *The Hymnal of the United Church of Christ*, copyright ©1974. Reprinted with the permission of United Church Press, 700 Prospect Ave. E., Cleveland, OH 44115-1100

722 Adapted from *Contemporary Prayers for Public Worship*, ed. Caryl Micklem, copyright ©1967 SCM Press, Ltd. Used by permission

723 Janet Morley, *All Desires Known*, copyright ©1988 Morehouse Publishing. Used by permission

724 *A Guide to Prayer for Ministers and Other Servants*, copyright ©1983 The Upper Room, 1908 Grand Ave., Nashville, TN 37202-0189. Used by permission

725 Adapted from *Prayers for the Christian Year*, William Barclay, copyright ©1964 SCM Press, Ltd. Used by permission

726 Adapted from "Reception into Communicant Membership," *Worship the Lord*, ed. James R. Esther and Donald J. Bruggink, copyright ©1987 The Reformed Church in America. Used by permission

727 Elizabethan prayer, 16th c., adapted from *God of a Hundred Names*, 1962, collected and arranged by Barbara Greene and Victor Gollancz. Published by Victor Gollancz, Ltd., 14 Henrietta St., London, WC2E 8QJ ENGLAND

728 Attributed to St. John Chrysostom, 4th c., adapted

729 Copyright ©1992 Marlene Kropf. Used by permission

730 Thomas à Kempis, *A Manual of Worship and Polity*, copyright ©1955 House of the Church of the Brethren, alt. Used by permission

731 English translation of The Lord's Prayer, prepared by the English Language Liturgical Consultation (ELLC), copyright ©1988. Used by permission

732 Copyright ©1982 Arlene Martin Mark, 29222 Frailey Dr., Elkhart, IN 46514. Adaptation used by permission

733 Attributed to St. Francis of Assisi, 13th c.

734 Adapted from *All the Seasons of Mercy*, by Diane Karay, copyright ©1987 Diane Karay. Used by permission of Westminster/John Knox Press

735 Rebecca J. Slough, adaptation copyright ©1992 The Hymnal Project

736 Janet Morley, *All Desires Known*, copyright ©1988 Morehouse Publishing. Used by permission

737 St. Augustine of Hippo, North Africa, ca. 400

738 Sarum primer, ca. 11th c.

739 Leonine missal, 7th c.

740 Janet Morley, *All Desires Known*, copyright ©1988 Morehouse Publishing. Used by permission

741 Copyright ©1992 The Hymnal Project

742 Adaptation of a collect for peace based on the Gelasian Sacramentary, 8th c., translated from Latin by Thomas Cranmer, 16th c., *The Book of Common Prayer*

743 Adapted and reprinted from *Prayers of the Reformers*, ed. Clyde Manschreck, copyright ©1958 Muhlenberg Press. Used by permission of Augsburg Fortress

744 Janet Morley, *All Desires Known*, copyright ©1988 Morehouse Publishing. Used by permission

745 Ruth C. Duck, *Bread for the Journey*, ed. Ruth C. Duck, copyright ©1981, altered. Reprinted with the permission of The Pilgrim Press

746 Copyright ©1992 The Hymnal Project

747 Robert H. Midgley, *Flames of the Spirit*, ed. Ruth C. Duck, copyright ©1985, altered. Reprinted with the permission of The Pilgrim Press

748 Copyright ©1992 The Hymnal Project

749 Anne Neufeld Rupp, *Prayers for Corporate Worship*, copyright ©1981 Faith and Life Press/Mennonite Publishing House. Used by permission

750 Kenneth I. Morse, *We Gather Together*, copyright ©1979 Brethren Press. Used by permission

751 First University United Methodist Church, Minneapolis, Minn. Adapted from *Ventures in Worship, Vol. 1*, ed. David J. Randolph, copyright ©1969 Abingdon Press. Reprinted by permission

752 Adapted from "Order of Worship," *Worship the Lord*, ed. James R. Esther and Donald J. Bruggink, copyright ©1987 The Reformed Church in America. Used by permission
753 Micah 6:6-8, adapted from *New Revised Standard Version*
754 John 12:24-26, adapted from *New Revised Standard Version*
755 Copyright ©1991 John D. Rempel. Used by permission
756 Copyright ©1988 Linea Reimer Geiser. Used by permission
757 Copyright ©1992 Marlene Kropf. Used by permission
758 Mary Susan Gast, *Flames of the Spirit*, ed. Ruth C. Duck, copyright ©1985, altered. Reprinted with the permission of The Pilgrim Press
759 Reprinted from *Just a Minute, Lord*, by Lois Waldrif Johnson. Copyright ©1973 Augsburg Publishing House. Used by permission of Augsburg Fortress
760 Janet Morley, *All Desires Known*, copyright ©1988 Morehouse Publishing. Used by permission
761 Copyright ©1988 Linea Reimer Geiser. Used by permission
762 Ancient prayer, source unknown, adapted by Charles F. Whiston, 20th c., *A Prayer Companion*. Last paragraph by The Hymnal Project, which revised Whiston's adaptation, copyright ©1992 The Hymnal Project
763 Jimmy R. Ross, *We Gather Together*, copyright ©1979 Brethren Press, adapted. Used by permission
764 Earle W. Fike, Jr., *Book of Worship*, copyright ©1964 Brethren Press. Used by permission
765 Copyright ©1992 The Hymnal Project, based on a prayer from *Contemporary Prayers for Public Worship*, ed. Caryl Micklem.
766 Alexander Mack, Sr., 18th c., *Rites and Ordinances*, 1713, translated in *European Origins of the Brethren*, copyright ©1958 Brethren Press. Used by permission
767 Copyright ©1992 The Hymnal Project
768 Harold Z. Bomberger, *We Gather Together*, copyright ©1979 Brethren Press. Used by permission
769 Adapted from "Order of Worship," *Worship the Lord*, ed. James R. Esther and Donald J. Bruggink, copyright ©1987 The Reformed Church in America. Used by permission
770 Lois M. Wilson, *Jesus Christ–the Life of the World: A Worship Book*, copyright ©1983 WCC Publications, World Council of Churches, 150, route de Ferney, P.O. Box 2100, 1211 Geneva 2, SWITZERLAND. Used by permission
771 Luke 2:29-32, *New Revised Standard Version*
772 Numbers 6:24-26, adapted from *New Revised Standard Version*, copyright ©1992 The Hymnal Project
773 2 Thessalonians 2:16-17, adapted from *Revised English Bible*
774 Romans 15:5-6, *New Revised Standard Version*
775 First two paragraphs adapted from a liturgy of baptism by Assembly Mennonite Church, Goshen, Ind., *Baptism and Church Membership*, Worship Series 3, ed. James H. Waltner, copyright ©1979 Faith and Life Press/Mennonite Publishing House. Used by permission. Last paragraph copyright ©1991 John D. Rempel, based on the writings of Reinhard Rahusen, 18th c. Used by permission
776 Adapted from *Worship Vessels: Resources for Renewal*, by F. Russell Mitman, Harper & Row, San Francisco, Calif., copyright ©1987
777 Adapted from *The Mennonite Hymnal*, copyright ©1969 Faith and Life Press/Mennonite Publishing House, based on Anabaptist baptismal vows, 16th c. Used by permission
778 Adapted by permission from *Book of Worship of the United Church of Christ*, copyright ©1986 United Church of Christ, Office for Church Life and Leadership, 700 Prospect Ave. E., Cleveland, OH 44115-1100
779 Copyright ©1991 John D. Rempel, based on the writings of Pilgram Marpeck, 16th c. Used by permission
780 Copyright ©1991 John D. Rempel. Used by permission
781 From Johann (John) Wichert's collection of prayers, 20th c., based on the prayers of Jacob Janzen, translation and adaptation copyright ©1991 John D. Rempel. Used by permission
782 Janet Morley, *All Desires Known*, copyright ©1988 Morehouse Publishing. Used by permission
783 Copyright ©1991 John D. Rempel. Used by permission
784 Copyright ©1986 Florence Schloneger, c/o Faith and Life Press. Adaptation used by permission
785 Reinhard Rahusen, 18th c., translation copyright ©1992 John D. Rempel. Used by permission
786 Copyright ©1992 The Hymnal Project
787 Leenaerdt Clock, ca. 1600, translation and adaptation copyright ©1991 John D. Rempel. Used by permission
788 Copyright ©1978 *Lutheran Book of Worship*, c/o Augsburg Fortress. Used by permission
789 *Pastor's Manual*, copyright ©1978 Brethren Press. Used by permission

790 Copyright ©1991 John D. Rempel. Used by permission
791 John H. Mosemann, adapted from *The Mennonite Hymnal*, copyright ©1969 Faith and Life Press/Mennonite Publishing House. Used by permission
792 Copyright ©1991 John D. Rempel, based on the writings of Pilgram Marpeck, 16th c. Used by permission
793 Copyright ©1977 Mennonite Church of the Servant, 1505 Fairview, Wichita, KS 67203. Used by permission
794 John H. Mosemann, adapted from *The Mennonite Hymnal*, copyright ©1969 Faith and Life Press/Mennonite Publishing House. Used by permission
795 Copyright ©1992 The Hymnal Project. Last paragraph by Gail Anderson Ricciuti, adapted from "Litany of Praise and Hope," *Women's Prayer Services*; ed. Iben Gjerding and Katherine Kinnamon, copyright ©1983 World Council of Churches, published in a North American edition, 1987, by Twenty-Third Publications, P.O. Box 180, Mystic, CT 06355. Used by permission
796 John H. Mosemann, adapted from *The Mennonite Hymnal*, copyright ©1969 Faith and Life Press/Mennonite Publishing House. Used by permission
797 Copyright ©1990 Nadine Pence Frantz, c/o Bethany Theological Seminary, 615 National Rd. W., Richmond, IN 47374-4095. Adapted and used by permission
798 Adapted from "Order of Worship for Christian Marriage," *Worship the Lord*, ed. James R. Esther and Donald J. Bruggink, copyright ©1987 The Reformed Church in America. Used by permission
799 Adapted from *Pastor's Manual*, copyright ©1978 Brethren Press. Used by permission. Later revised for *Minister's Manual*, copyright ©1983 Faith and Life Press/Mennonite Publishing House. Used by permission. Further revised by The Hymnal Project, copyright ©1992.
800 John H. Mosemann, adapted from *The Mennonite Hymnal*, copyright ©1969 Faith and Life Press/Mennonite Publishing House. Used by permission
801 Adapted from *Contemporary Prayers for Public Worship*, ed. Caryl Micklem, copyright ©1967 SCM Press, Ltd., for *Minister's Manual*, copyright ©1983 Faith and Life Press/Mennonite Publishing House. Used by permission. Further revised by The Hymnal Project, copyright ©1992.
802 Alcuin, 8th c.
803 Copyright ©1991 John D. Rempel. Used by permission
804 Copyright ©1992 The Hymnal Project
805 Copyright ©1982 Mennonite Publishing House. Used by permission

In the following section, all Scripture, unless otherwise indicated, is from the *New Revised Standard Version*.

807 Verses 1,2b,4c,9,10a from *Tanakh*, copyright ©1985 The Jewish Publication Society, 1930 Chestnut St., Philadelphia, PA 19103. Used by permission
810 Verses 18b-19 from *New International Version*
811 Verse 1a from *Revised Standard Version*
814 *Revised Standard Version*
816 Verses 1,4-11 from *New International Version*
818 Verses 5,7 copyright ©1991 Eugene F. Roop, c/o Bethany Theological Seminary, 615 National Rd. W., Richmond, IN 47374-4095. Used by permission
820 *New International Version*
821 *Revised Standard Version*
823 *New International Version*
827 Verse 6 from *Revised Standard Version*
828 Verse 11 from *Revised Standard Version*
829 Verses 1-5 from *Revised Standard Version* with alterations
830 Verses 1-5a,5c-9a from *New International Version*
836 *Revised Standard Version* with alterations
840 English translation of Magnificat, prepared by International Consultation on English Texts (ICET), later known as the English Language Liturgical Consultation (ELLC), copyright ©1975. Used by permission
843 Verse 6 altered
844 *Revised English Bible*
847 Verse 5 from *Revised English Bible*
849 Copyright ©1991 Virginia Wiles, Muhlenberg College, 2400 Chew St., Allentown, PA 18104. Used by permission
853 Verse 19 altered
855 Verse 5 from *Revised Standard Version*
861 Verse 3a from *New International Version;* verses 3b,5 altered
853 Verse 19 altered
855 Verse 5 from *Revised Standard Version*
861 Verse 3a from New International Version; Verses 3b,5 altered

TOPICAL INDEX

Numbers in parentheses refer to the worship resources and Scripture readings. First lines have been abbreviated to allow space for more entries.

Jesus Christ: Life of

Hark! the glad sound, 184
O love, how deep, 236
Sing, my tongue, 256
When Christ's appearing, 217

(712,713,714,776,782)

Jesus Christ: Lordship of

All glory, laud, and honor, 237
All hail the power, 106, 285
At the name of Jesus, 342
Blessed Jesus, at, 13
Blessing and honor, 108
Christ is alive, 278
Christ is coming, 295
Christ the Lord is risen, 280
Come, come, ye saints, 425
Come, thou long-expected, 178
Creator of the stars, 177
Crown him with many, 116
Fairest Lord Jesus, 117
Fling wide the door, 186
From all that dwell, 49
Hail to the Lord's, 185
I sing with exultation, 438
Jesus shall reign, 319
Jesus, thou mighty Lord, 115
Joy to the world, 318
Let all mortal flesh, 463
Let the heavens, 187
Lift high the cross, 321
Look, you saints, 286
O Holy Spirit, making whole, 300
Of the Father's love, 104
Rejoice, the Lord is King, 288
Ride on, ride on, 239
Silence! frenzied, 630
Sing we triumphant hymns, 287
The work is thine, 396
This is the feast, 476
What Child is this, 215

(677,710,714,803,827,855,861)

Jesus Christ: Love of

Alas! and did my Savior, 253
At break of day, 647
Christ is alive, 278
Christian, do you hear, 494
Come, O thou Traveler, 503
How brightly beams, 222
How shallow former shadows, 251
I heard the voice, 493
I love to tell, 398
I stand amazed, 528
Jesus, friend so kind, 621
Jesus, lover of my soul, 618
Jesus loves me, 341
Jesus, Rock of ages, 515
Jesus, the very thought, 588
Jesus took a towel, 449
Love divine, all loves, 592
My song is love, 235
O love, how deep, 236
O Power of love, 593
Oh, how shall I receive, 182
Por la mañana, 647
Open are the gifts, 255
Savior, like a shepherd, 355
Softly and tenderly, 491
'Tis so sweet, 340

What wondrous love, 530
When I survey, 259, 260
When Jesus wept, 234
Where cross the crowded, 405
Why has God forsaken, 246

Jesus Christ: Names of

Abide, O dearest Jesus, 426
All who love and serve, 417
Blessed Savior, we adore, 107
Bread of life, 455
Christ who left his home, 283
Come, O thou Traveler, 503
Fairest Lord Jesus, 117
Gentle Shepherd, 352
Hark! the herald angels, 201
I will praise the Lord, 109
Jesu, joy, 604
Jesus, keep me near, 617
Look, you saints, 286
Man of sorrows, 258
Morning Star, 214
O Christ, the healer, 379
Prince of peace, 534
Rejoice, the Lord is King, 288
See the splendor, 268
To us a Child of hope, 189

(667,689,702)

Jesus Christ: Presence of

Away in a manger, 194
Away with our fears, 292
Blessed are the persecuted, 230
Christ be with me, 442
Here, O my Lord, 465
Jesus Christ, God's only, 40
Jesus, stand among us, 25
Jesus, the very thought, 588
Let the hungry come, 464
Lord Jesus, think on me, 527
Shepherd of souls, 456
To go to heaven, 513
What a friend we have, 573, 574

(678,757,786,787)

Jesus Christ: Teachings of

Blessed are the persecuted, 230
Blessed Jesus, at your word, 13
How pleasant is it, 451
Oh, blessed are, 231
Our Father/Pater noster, 554
Our Father who art, 228, 351
Renew your church, 363
The kingdom of God, 224

(714,835)

Joy

Cantemos al Señor, 55
Christ is arisen, 271
Come, we that love, 14
From all that dwell, 49
From heaven above, 205
God loves all, 397
Good Christian friends, 210
How brightly beams, 222
I am leaning, 532
I come with joy, 459
I know that my Redeemer
  lives, 277, 279

Jesu, joy, 604
Joy to the world, 318
Joyful, joyful, 71
Joys are flowing, 301
Jubilate Deo, 103
Let our gladness, 198
Let's sing unto the Lord, 55
Lord, with devotion, 79
My life flows on, 580
O Christ, in thee, 510
Oh, how happy are they, 597
Oh, how joyfully, 209
Rejoice, rejoice in God, 313
Rejoice, the Lord is King, 288
Still, I search, 88
Teach me thy truth, 548
You shall go out, 427

(767,784)

Judgment

Come, ye faithful, 264, 265
How bless'd are they, 525
O day of God, 370
When grief is raw, 637

(666,723,811,820)

Justice

All who love and serve, 417
Beyond a dying sun, 323
Brothers and sisters, 142
Christ is alive, 278
En medio de la vida, 537
For the fruit, 90
For the healing, 367
For we are strangers no more, 322
Hail to the Lord's anointed, 185
Hark! the glad sound, 184
I bind my heart, 411
I'll praise my Maker, 166
My soul proclaims, 181
O bless the Lord, 80, 600
O day of God, 370
O young and fearless Prophet, 374
Oh, holy city seen of John, 320
To us a Child of hope, 189
What does the Lord require, 409
You are salt, 226
You are the God, 537

(664,683,703,711,715,720,732,
750,753,803,824,830,840)

Kingdom

Blessed Savior, we adore, 107
Christ is the world's, 334
En medio de la vida, 537
Glorious things, 619
Hail to the Lord's anointed, 185
Here from all nations, 296
I love thy kingdom, 308
It came upon a midnight, 195
Jesus shall reign, 319
Joy to the world, 318
Lift high the cross, 321
Lord of light, your name, 410
O day of God, 370
O day of peace, 408
O Savior, rend, 175
Oh, blessed are, 231
Oh, holy city seen of John, 320

Let our gladness, 198
Lord, I am fondly, 514
Lord Jesus, think on me, 527
Love divine, all loves, 592
Marvelous grace, 151
My song is love, 235
Now the silence, 462
O Bread of life, 468
O Christ, in thee, 510
O Lamb of God, 146
O Power of love, 593
Oh, for a thousand, 81, 110
Oh, how happy are they, 597
Oh, how joyfully, 209
Oh, how wondrous, 147
Por la mañana, 647
Savior, like a shepherd, 355
See the splendor, 268
Sing, my tongue, 256
Sing we triumphant hymns, 287
The Lord is King, 69
This is the day, 58, 642
Thou art the way, 339
What mercy and divine
  compassion, 524
What wondrous love, 530
Wonderful grace, 150
You shall go out, 427

(663,665,668,685,727,755,757,
776,779,786,788,827,842)

Sanctification

(See Regeneration)

Scripture

Break thou the bread, 360
In this world abound, 316
Jesus loves me, 341
Lamp of our feet, 312
Lord, I have made, 317
Renew your church, 363
Teach me, O Lord, 487
The word of God, 314

Seasons

All beautiful the march, 159
All things bright, 156
As spring the winter, 568
Come, ye faithful, 264, 265
Come, ye thankful, 94
Lord, should rising whirlwinds, 92
Praise to God, 91
Sing to the Lord, 98

Second Coming

At the name, 342
Blessed Savior, we adore, 107
Come, thou long-expected, 178
Fling wide the door, 186
For all the saints, 636
Hail to the Lord's anointed, 185
Hark! the glad sound, 184
Here from all nations, 296
I know not why, 338
Jesus came–the heavens, 297
Joy to the world, 318
Let all mortal flesh, 463
Lift up your hearts, 602
Look, you saints, 286
Man of sorrows, 258

My hope is built, 343
O Savior, rend, 175
Praise him, praise him, 100
Rejoice, the Lord is King, 288
Sleepers, wake, 188
Soon and very soon, 611
This is the threefold truth, 335

(677,697)

Seeking God

As the hart, 500
Go, my children, 433
How lovely is your dwelling, 171
I sought the Lord, 506
O thou, in whose presence, 559
Oh, for a closer walk, 520
O let all who thirst, 495
Prayer is the soul's, 572

(663,671,686,737,802,816)

Service

A charge to keep, 393
As saints of old, 386
Brothers and sisters, 142
Dear Lord and Father, 523
For Christ and the church, 416
For the bread, 477
For the fruit, 90
For the healing, 367
Forth in thy name, 415
Here in our upper room, 450
How buoyant and bold, 394
How pleasant is it, 451
I bind my heart, 411
Je louerai l'Eternel, 76
Jesus took a towel, 449
Jubilate Deo, 103
Living and dying, 550
Lord of light, your name, 410
Lord, speak to me, 499
Lord, whose love, 369
Lord, you have come, 229
O God of mystery, 130
O Jesus Christ, may, 404
O Master, let me walk, 357
O young and fearless Prophet, 374
Praise, I will praise, 76
Sent forth by God's, 478
Teach me thy truth, 548
The church of Christ, 403
Tú has venido, 229
Will you let me be, 307

(669,683,717,723,733,750,751,754,
755,763,790,793,796,843,850)

Sin

Alas! and did my Savior, 253
Holy Spirit, Storm of love, 132
It came upon a midnight, 195
Joys are flowing, 301
Lord, thou dost love, 387
Marvelous grace, 151
O Christ, the Lamb, 153
Open, Lord, my inward ear, 140
Silence! frenzied, 630
Who are these, 270

(690,691,693,694,698,
775,800,818,847,852)

Social Concern

(See also Justice, Peace,
  Service)

Here I am, Lord, 395
Jesus took a towel, 449
O Jesus Christ, may, 404
The church of Christ, 403

(803)

Sorrow

(See also Grief)

Before the cock crew, 243
Come, ye disconsolate, 497
If death my friend, 608
Stay with me, 242
When grief is raw, 637
When Jesus wept, 234

(801,805,816)

Steadfastness

Awake, my soul, 609
Built on the Rock, 309
Cast thy burden, 586
Christian, let your burning, 402
For God so loved, 167
Great God, how infinite, 82
Great God, we sing, 639
Great is the Lord, 87
Great is thy faithfulness, 327
How firm a foundation, 567
I to the hills, 169, 563
If you but trust, 576
Immortal, invisible, 70
Jesus, thou mighty Lord, 115
Let all creation bless, 61
Lord of our growing, 479
Lord, should rising whirlwinds, 92
Lord, thou hast searched, 556
Lord, with devotion, 79
Make music, 73
My God, my God, 248
My hope is built, 343
Now, on land and sea, 655
Now thank we all our God, 85, 86
O God, our help, 328
Praise, my soul, 63, 65
Praise to God, 91
Sometimes a light, 603
We give thanks unto you, 161

(774)

Stewardship

As saints of old, 386
Come and give thanks, 57
God of the fertile fields, 390
God, whose giving, 383
Heart and mind, 392
Lord, thou dost love, 387
We give thee but thine, 384

(744,804)

Suffering

Babylon streams, 134
By the waters, 148
Faith of the martyrs, 413
Holy Spirit, Storm of love, 132
My God, my God, 248

USES IN WORSHIP INDEX

This index lists items that are related to worship in specific times or places; worship themes are found in the topical index. First lines are abbreviated to allow space for more entries. Cross-references are abbreviated according to the major headings in the hymnal: PROC (PROCLAIMING); FJ (FAITH JOURNEY); L/M (LIFE/MINISTRIES); and D/L (DAYS OF LIFE). Cross references with no numbers listed refer to other categories in the topical and uses in worship indexes.

Adoring

(See PRAISING/ADORING 46-127)

Advent

(See PROC: Jesus, Advent 172-188)

Christ is coming, 295

(664,678,714,715,815, 827,828,833,841)

Affirming Faith

(See AFFIRMING FAITH 325-345)

A mighty fortress, 165, 329
A wonderful Savior, 598
All hail the power, 106,285
All who believe, 436
At break of day, 647
At the Lamb's high feast, 262
Bless'd be the God, 174
Break forth, O beauteous, 203
Built on the Rock, 309
Christ has arisen, 267
Christ is alive, 278
Christ is arisen, 271
Christ is our cornerstone, 43
Christ Jesus lay, 470
Christ the Lord is risen, 280
Come, come, ye saints, 425
Come, O thou Traveler, 503
Creating God, your fingers, 168, 325
En medio de la vida, 537
Fairest Lord Jesus, 117
God is working, 638
Great is the Lord, 87
He comes to us, 498
He leadeth me, 599
Here from all nations, 296
Holy God, we praise, 121
I believe in you, 440
I bind unto myself, 441
I heard the voice, 493
I know that my Redeemer lives, 277, 279
I long for your commandments, 543
I sing the mighty power, 46
I sing with exultation, 438
I stand amazed, 528
I'll praise my Maker, 166
In the cross, 566
In the stillness, 551
In thee is gladness, 114
In your sickness, 585
Jesus shall reign, 319
Jesus, sun and shield, 466
Jesus, the very thought, 588
Lamp of our feet, 312
Let hope and sorrow, 634
Let our gladness, 198
Lift your glad voices, 275

Lord, should rising whirlwinds, 92
Lord, you sometimes speak, 594
Low in the grave, 273
Man of sorrows, 258
Marvelous grace, 151
Mothering God, 482
My life flows on, 580
My Shepherd will supply, 589
My song is love, 235
O Christ, in thee, 510
O God, great womb, 155
O God, our help, 328
O Power of love, 593
O sons and daughters, 274
Oh, for a thousand, 81, 110
Oh, how happy, 597
Oh, how wondrous, 147
Oh, love, how deep, 236
Open are the gifts, 255
Out of the depths, 133
Por la mañana, 647
Praise to God, 91
Rejoice, the Lord is King, 288
See the splendor, 268
Shepherd me, O God, 519
Sometimes a light, 603
Strong Son of God, 488
The church's one foundation, 311
The King of love, 170
The Lord's my shepherd, 578
The strife is o'er, 263
The tree of life, 509
The word of God, 314
Thine is the glory, 269
'Tis not with eyes, 571
To us a Child of hope, 189
We know that Christ, 443
We praise thee, O God, 99
We walk by faith, 570
What wondrous love, 530
When morning gilds, 644
Wonderful grace, 150
You are the God, 537

(685,686,710-717,812,814,840,841, 842,848,849,852,853,854,855,860)

All Saints Day

(See L/M: Funeral 634-637; FJ: Death/Eternal Life 606-619)

Anniversaries

Great God, we sing, 639
Lord of our growing, 479
O God, your constant care, 481

Anointing

(See L/M: Anointing 627-631)

By Peter's house, 378
Cast thy burden, 586
Father, I stretch, 529
Heal us, Immanuel, 375

Healer of our every ill, 377
In your sickness, 585
O bless the Lord, 80, 600
O Christ, the healer, 379
The sacrifice you accept, 141
There's a wideness, 145

(690,698,700,708,722, 745,814,848,857)

Ascension

(See PROC: Jesus' Ascension 284-288)

Christ, who is in the form, 333
Crown him with many, 116
Praise him, praise him, 100
Sing hallelujah, praise, 67
This is a story, 315

(676,689,855)

Ash Wednesday

Create in me a clean heart, 128
From the depths, 136
Kyrie eleison, 144
Kyrie (Taizé), 152
Out of the depths, 133
The glory of these forty, 225
The sacrifice you accept, 141

(818,830)

Baptism

(See BAPTISM 436-448)

At the name of Jesus, 342
Breathe on me, breath, 356
Come down, O Love, 501
Come, my Way, 587
Come, thou fount, 521
Create my soul anew, 3
Eternal Light, shine, 518
Gracious Spirit, dwell, 507
Have thine own way, 504
Holy Spirit, Truth divine, 508
I am trusting thee, 564
I believe in God, 330
I bind my heart, 411
I cannot dance, 45
I love thee, Lord, 605
If all you want, 512
If Christ is mine, 331
Jesus, my Lord, 533
Jesus, sun and shield, 466
Just as I am, 516
Living and dying, 550
Lord, I am fondly, 514
Lord, speak to me, 499
Marvelous grace, 151
My Jesus, I love, 522
New earth, 299
O Power of love, 593
Obey my voice, 163
Oh, how happy, 597

Open my eyes, 517
Spirit of God! descend, 502
Take my life, 389
This is a day of new, 640
Who are these, 270
Who now would follow, 535

(685,710,713,716,726,809,847,854)

Blessings

Bwana awabariki, 422
Child of blessing, 620
Go, my children, 433
Go now in peace, 429
God, be merciful, 424
God be with you, 430, 431
Grace to you, 24
Lord, bless the hands, 93
May God grant you, 422
May the grace, 423
May the Lord, mighty, 435

(680,770,772,773,774,784)

Child Blessing

(See L/M: Child Blessing 620-622)

(791,792,839)

Canticles

Bless'd be the God, 174
Blessed be the Lord, 179
From heaven above, 205
Gloria, 204
Let all creation bless, 61
My soul proclaims, 181

(715,771)

Children: Hymns Appropriate for

All creatures of our God, 48
All glory, laud, and honor, 237
All people that on earth, 42
All praise to thee, 658
All things bright, 156
Angels we have heard, 197
Asithi: Amen, 64
Awake, arise, 56
Away in a manger, 194
Be present at our table, 457
Be thou my vision, 545
Blessed are the persecuted, 230
Bright and glorious, 219
Bwana awabariki, 422
By the waters, 148
Children of the heavenly, 616
Christ be with me, 442
Christ has arisen, 267
Christ the Lord, 280
Christ, we do all adore, 105
Christian, do you hear, 494
Come and see, 20
Come, let us all, 12
Come, thou Almighty King, 41
Come, thou long-expected, 178
Come, we that love, 14
Come, ye thankful, 94
Creating God, your fingers, 168, 325
Dona nobis pacem, 346
Ehane he'ama, 78
Fairest Lord Jesus, 117
Faith of the martyrs, 413

Far, far away, 139
Father God, you are holy, 78
Fling wide the door, 186
For God so loved us, 167
For the beauty, 89
From heaven above, 205
From the depths, 136
Gloria, 204
Glory be to the Father, 127
Go, my children, 433
Go now in peace, 429
God created heaven, 160
God loves all, 397
God of many names, 77
God sends us, 293
God, who touches earth, 511
Good Christian friends, 210
Grace to you, 24
Great God, the giver, 458
Great is the Lord, 87
Great is thy faithfulness, 327
Guide me, O thou, 583
Guide my feet, 546
Hark! the glad sound, 184
Hark! the herald angels, 201
He comes to us, 498
Hear us, my God, 358
Heart and mind, 392
Here I am, Lord, 395
Holy God, we praise, 121
Holy, holy, holy, 120
Holy, holy, holy, 400
Hosanna, loud hosanna, 238
I believe in God, 330
I know that my Redeemer lives, 277, 279
I love to tell, 398
I owe the Lord, 651
I sing the mighty power, 46
I want Jesus to walk, 439
I will praise the Lord, 109
Immortal, invisible, 70
In Christ there is no East, 306
In the bulb, 614
In your sickness, 585
Infant holy, 206
It came upon a midnight, 195
Je louerai l'Eternel, 76
Jesus loves me, 341
Jesus took a towel, 449
Jesus, we want, 10
Joy to the world, 318
Joyful, joyful, 71
Jubilate Deo, 103
Let all mortal flesh, 463
Let our gladness, 198
Let the whole creation, 51
Let us break bread, 453
Lift your glad voices, 275
Lo, how a Rose, 211
Lord, bless the hands, 93
Lord, I want to be, 444
Lord, listen to your, 353
Lord, our Lord, 157
Love came down, 208
Low in the grave, 273
Many and great, 35
May God grant you, 422
May the Lord, mighty, 435
Morning has broken, 648
My Shepherd will supply, 589
Ndikhokele, O Jehova, 583

New earth, 299
O come, all ye faithful, 212
O God, our help, 328
O little town, 191
O Lord, hear my prayer, 348
O Lord, our Lord, 112
O Prince of peace, 15
O worship the Lord, 124
Obey my voice, 163
Oh, how joyfully, 209
On this day, 192
Our Father who art, 351
Oyenos, mi Dios, 358
Por la mañana, 647
Praise God from whom, 118, 119
Praise, I will praise, 76
Praise the Lord, 52
Praise the Lord, sing, 50
Praise the Lord, who reigns, 54
Proclaim the tidings, 282
Santo, santo, santo, 400
Savior, like a shepherd, 355
Seek ye first, 324
Silent night, 193
Sing amen, 64
Songs of praise, 60
Steal away, 612
The care the eagle, 590
The first Noel, 199
The God of Abraham, 162
The King of love, 170
The kingdom of God, 224
The virgin Mary, 202
They that wait, 584
This is my Father's world, 154
This little light, 401
Thuma mina, 434
To go to heaven, 513
To us a Child, 189
'Twas in the moon, 190
Two fishermen, 227
We give thanks unto you, 161
Were you there, 257
What a friend we have, 573, 574
What Child is this, 215
When Israel was in, 164
While shepherds watched, 196
With happy voices, 83
You are salt, 226
You shall go out, 427

Children: Readings Appropriate for

*(660,665,667,674,682,687,701,702,
708,714,719,731,738,748,759,
763,764,770,772)*

Christ the King Sunday

All glory, laud, and honor, 237
Blessed Savior, we adore, 107
Blessing and honor, 108
Christ is alive, 278
Christ, we do all adore, 105
Christ, who is in the form, 333
Crown him with many, 116
Hail to the Lord's, 185
Jesus shall reign, 319
Jesus, thou mighty Lord, 115
Joy to the world, 318
Look, you saints, 286
O Prince of peace, 15
Rejoice, the Lord is King, 288

Sing we triumphant hymns, 287
Soon and very soon, 611
The Lord is King, 69
This is the feast, 476

(689,843,855)

Christmas Season

(See PROC: Jesus' Birth 189-215)

As with gladness, 218
Hail the bless'd morn, 221
Joy to the world, 318
Let all mortal flesh, 463
Let the heavens, 187
Of the Father's love, 104
On this day, 192
Oh, how shall I receive, 182
Savior of the nations, come, 173

(665,678,714,715,820,827,841)

Commissioning

Breathe on me, breath, 356
Come, O creator Spirit, 27
For Christ and the church, 416
Forth in thy name, 415
God the Spirit, Guide, 632
Guide my feet, 546
Heart and mind, 392
Heart with loving heart, 420
Here I am, Lord, 395
Holy, holy, holy, 400
How buoyant and bold, 394
How clear is our vocation, 541
Lead on, O cloud, 419
Lord, speak to me, 499
Lord, whose love, 369
Lord, you have come, 229
Move in our midst, 418
Now go forward, 399
O God, thou faithful God, 376
O Holy Spirit, by whose, 291
O Jesus, I have promised, 447
O Spirit of the living God, 361
Santo, santo, santo, 400
Spirit of God, unleashed, 364
Take up your cross, 536
Teach me thy truth, 548
The care the eagle, 590
The church of Christ, 403
The work is thine, 396
There are many gifts, 304
Thuma mina, 434
Tú has venido, 229
Two fishermen, 227
Whom shall I send? 633

(669,671,725,761,851)

Confessing

(See Confessing/Reconciling 128-153; FJ: Confession/Repentance 520-533)

Ah, holy Jesus, 254
All praise to thee, 658
And is the gospel, 406
Before the cock crew, 243
Bread of the world, 469
Come and see, 20
Creator of the stars, 177
Heal us, Immanuel, 375
Just as I am, 516

Man of sorrows, 258
My hope is built, 343
O young and fearless Prophet, 374
Prince of peace, 534
Take thou my hand, 581
We would extol thee, 74
When peace, like a river, 336

(671,781,798,800,818,829,832,853,857)

Covenant Renewal

(775,777,793,809)

Dedications

(See Child Blessing)

Built on the Rock, 309
I love thy kingdom, 308
Lord of the worlds, 39
Unto thy temple, 4
When the morning stars, 34

Doxologies (last stanza)

All creatures of our God, 48
All praise to thee, 658
Blessed be the Lord, 179
Creator of the stars, 177
Father, we praise, 650
Fling wide the door, 186
For God so loved us, 167
Glory be to the Father, 127
Holy God, we praise, 121
O Holy Spirit, by whose, 291
O Love, how deep, 236
On Jordan's banks, 183
Praise God from whom, 118, 119
Praise God, the Source, 95
Sing my tongue, 256
Sing to the Lord, 98
Sing we triumphant hymns, 287
That Easter day, 281
This is a story, 315
To God, with the Lamb, 125
When Christ's appearing, 217

(785)

Easter Season

(See PROC: Jesus' Resurrection 261-283)

All hail the power, 106, 285
Ask ye what great thing, 337
Blessing and honor, 108
Christ Jesus lay, 470
Christ, we do all adore, 105
Crown him with many, 116
God sent his Son, 345
I believe in God, 330
I bind unto myself, 441
In the bulb, 614
Jesus came—the heavens, 297
Lift high the cross, 321
Look, you saints, 286
O Christe Domine, 113
Sing, my tongue, 256
The Lord is King, 69
This is a day, 642
This is a story, 315
This is the day, 640
This is the feast, 476
This is the threefold, 335
We give thanks unto you, 161

We walk by faith, 570
Were you there, 257

*(659,677,710,747,806,
833,852,855,856,858)*

Epiphany

(See PROC: Jesus' Epiphany 216-222)

On this day, 192
The first Noel, 199
The virgin Mary had, 202
What Child is this, 215

Eternity Sunday

(See L/M: Funeral 634-637;
FJ: Death/Eternal Life 606-619)

(672,718,860,861)

Evening

(See D/L: Evening 652-658)

In the stillness, 551
O God, in restless living, 557

Footwashing

(See LORD'S SUPPER:
Footwashing 449-451)

How good a thing, 310
Where charity and love, 305
Will you let me be, 307

(782,843)

Funeral

(See L/M: Funeral 634-637;
FJ: Death/Eternal Life 606-619)

Bless'd be the tie, 421
Christ is arisen, 271
Christ the Lord is risen, 280
God of our life, 486
I heard the voice, 493
Lift your glad voices, 275
Now thank we all, 85, 86
O God, our help, 328
Shepherd me, O God, 519
The church's one foundation, 311
The King of love, 170
This joyful Eastertide, 276
We shall walk, 412
Why has God forsaken, 246

(802,805,816,822,844,849,860,861)

Gathering

(See GATHERING 1-45)

Abide, O dearest Jesus, 426
All creatures of our God, 48
All hail the power, 106, 285
Cantemos al Señor, 55
Come, gracious Spirit, 303
Come, Holy Spirit, 298
Father, we praise, 650
From all that dwell, 49
Heart with loving heart, 420
How good a thing, 310
Joyful, joyful, 71
Let the heavens, 187
Let the whole creation, 51
Let's sing unto the Lord, 55
Lord, with devotion, 79

Morning has broken, 648
Now the silence, 462
O day of rest, 641
O Jesus Christ, may, 404
O worship the King, 66
Obey my voice, 163
Oh, for a thousand, 81, 110
Oh, that I had a thousand, 84
Praise God from whom, 118, 119
Praise him, praise him, 100
Praise, my soul, 63, 65
Praise the Lord, 52
Praise the Lord who reigns, 54
Sing praise to God, 59
Sleepers, wake, 188
They that wait, 584
This is the day, 58
This is the day, 642
Veni Sancte Spiritus, 298
We praise thee, O God, 99
Worship the Lord, 220

(686,687,735,739,815,821)

Good Friday

(See PROC: Jesus' Passion/Death
237-260)

Holy Spirit, Storm of love, 132
In the cross, 566
Jesus, keep me near, 617
My faith looks up, 565
My song is love, 235
O Lamb of God, 146
What wondrous love, 530
When Jesus wept, 234

(743,829)

Healings: Celebration of

At evening, when the sun, 628
In your sickness, 585
O Love of God, 326
There is a balm, 627

Holy Week

(See PROC: Jesus' Passion/Death
237-260)

(746,843)

Installations

(See Commissioning)

How clear is our vocation, 541
May the grace, 423
Teach me thy truth, 548

(777,851)

Lent

(See Discipleship)

Christ, who is in the form, 333
Christian, do you hear, 494
Come down, O Love, 501
Create in me a clean heart, 128
Far, far away, 139
Forgive our sins, 137
From the depths, 136
I bind unto myself, 441
In the cross, 566
Kyrie eleison, 144
Kyrie (Taizé), 152
Lord Jesus, think on me, 527

My faith looks up, 565
My song is love, 235
O Christ, the Lamb, 153
O Love, how deep, 236
Shepherd me, O God, 519
Take up your cross, 536
The glory of these forty, 225
The sacrifice you accept, 141
We give thanks unto you, 161
We walk by faith, 570
What wondrous love, 530
When Jesus wept, 234
Who now would follow, 535

*(661,666,686,690,691,692,695,702,
714,732,739,743,746,807,816,818,
830,834,835,849,853, 855)*

Lord's Day

(See D/L: Lord's Day 641-642)

Awake, arise, 56
Jesus, we want to meet, 10
Morning has broken, 648
O sons and daughters, 274
On the radiant threshold, 649
Songs of praise, 60
The day you gave us, 652
This is a day, 640
What gift can we bring, 385

(668)

Lord's Supper

(See LORD'S SUPPER 452-478;
784-790)

At the Lamb's high feast, 262
Christ, from whom, 365
Christ is risen, 272
Come, my Way, 587
Come, ye disconsolate, 497
Count well the cost, 437
For we are strangers, 322
Heart with loving heart, 420
Here in our upper room, 450
Here in this place, 6
How good a thing, 310
In thy holy place, 2
Lift up your hearts, 602
Like the murmur, 29
Lord Jesus Christ, 22
Open are the gifts, 255
Open now thy gates, 19
The King of love, 170
The Lord's my shepherd, 578
What is this place, 1
Where charity and love, 305

(660,768,781,784-790)

Love Feast

(See LORD'S SUPPER 452-461)

All praise to our redeeming, 21
Bless'd be the tie, 421
Count well the cost, 437
Forgive our sins, 137
Heart with loving heart, 420
Help us to help, 362
Here in our upper room, 450
Here in this place, 6
How pleasant is it, 451
I hunger and I thirst, 474
Jesus took a towel, 449

Lord Jesus Christ, 22

*(698,699,713,714,716,717,768,
781,785,786,787,788,843)*

Maundy Thursday

Alone thou goest forth, 244
Before the cock crew, 243
Calvary, 249
Go to dark Gethsemane, 240
In the quiet consecration, 461
Jesus took a towel, 449
Stay with me, 242
'Tis midnight, 241

Memorials

(See Eternity Sunday)

Morning

(See D/L: Morning 644-651)

Awake, arise, 56
Awake, awake, fling off, 448
By gracious powers, 552
Christ, whose glory fills, 216
Fairest Lord Jesus, 117
Great is thy faithfulness, 327
Holy, holy, holy, 120
Jesus shall reign, 319
Make music, 73
Morning Star, 214
Songs of praise, 60
This is my Father's world, 154

National Holidays

(720,803,817,833)

New Year

(See L/M: Special Days 638-640)

All beautiful the march, 159
From heaven above, 205
Great God, how infinite, 82
O God, our help, 328
What gift can we bring, 385

(819)

Offering

(See OFFERING 383-393)

For Christ and the church, 416
Lord, speak to me, 499
Teach me thy truth, 548
We plow the fields, 96
Worship the Lord, 220

(670)

Ordination

(See L/M: Ordination 632-633)

All praise to our redeeming, 21
Be thou my vision, 545
Breathe on me, breath, 356
Come down, O Love, 501
Eternal Light, shine, 518
Forth in thy name, 415
Heart and mind, 392
Here I am, Lord, 395
Holy, holy, holy, 400
How clear is our vocation, 541
I am weak, 553
I love thy kingdom, 308
Lord, speak to me, 499

Lord, you have come, 229
O God, thou faithful God, 376
O Jesus, I have promised, 447
Open my eyes, 517
Santo, santo, santo, 400
Spirit of the living God, 349
Take my life, 389
Take up your cross, 536
Teach me thy truth, 548
The work is thine, 396
There are many gifts, 304
Thuma mina, 434
Tú has venido, 229

(716,725,738,761,795,851)

Palm Sunday/Passion Sunday

All glory, laud, and honor, 237
All hail the power, 106, 285
Alone thou goest forth, 244
Fling wide the door, 186
Hail to the Lord's anointed, 185
Hosanna, loud hosanna, 238
Jesus shall reign, 319
Ride on, ride on, 239

(667,855)

Peace Sunday

(See PRAYING: For the World
367-374; WITNESSING: Peace/
Justice 403-412)

Christ is the world's, 334
Dona nobis pacem, 346
Dona nobis pacem Domine, 294
For we are strangers no more,
322
Here, O Lord, your servants, 7
How good a thing, 310
In Christ there is no East, 306
O Prince of peace, 15

*(683,711,720,727,732,733
742,756,760,803,833)*

Pentecost

(See PROC: Jesus' Presence in
Spirit 289-294; PROC: Activity
of the Spirit 298-304)

Breathe on me, breath, 356
Breathe upon us, 28
Come down, O Love, 501
Come, O Creator Spirit, 27
Dona nobis pacem, 346
Fire of God, 129
Holy Spirit, come, 26
Holy Spirit, gracious Guest, 542
Holy Spirit, Truth divine, 508
I cannot dance, 45
Like the murmur, 29
Move in our midst, 418
O Spirit of the living God, 361
Spirit divine, inspire, 30
Spirit of God, unleashed, 364
Spirit of the living God, 349
Wind who makes, 31

(669,679,710,718,762,851)

Praising

(See PRAISING/ADORING 46-
127)

All hail the power, 106, 285

All praise to thee, 658
At break of day, 647
Before Jehovah's aweful, 18
Bless'd be the God, 174
Christ is arisen, 271
Christ is our cornerstone, 43
Christ is risen, 272
Christ upon the mountain, 232
Christ who left his home, 283
Come, thou Almighty King, 41
Come, thou fount, 521
Come, we that love, 14
Come, ye faithful, 264, 265
Gloria, 204
Hosanna, loud hosanna, 238
I sing with exultation, 438
I will sing of my Redeemer, 344
I'll praise my Maker, 166
Let all together, 213
Let our gladness, 198
Let the heavens, 187
Lord Jesus Christ, 22
Many and great, 35
Morning has broken, 648
New earth, 299
Now, on land, 655
O Power of love, 593
O sons and daughters, 274
Oh, how wondrous, 147
On this day, 192
Por la mañana, 647
Proclaim the tidings, 282
Rejoice, the Lord is King, 288
Santo, santo, santo, 400
See the splendor, 268
Sleepers, wake, 188
Soon and very soon, 611
The day you gave, 652
The God of Abraham, 162
Thine is the glory, 269
This is my Father's world, 154
This is the day, 58
This is the day, 642
This is the feast, 476
We give thanks unto you, 161
What mercy and divine
compassion, 524
When in our music, 44
When morning gilds, 644
When the morning stars, 34
With all my heart, 432

*(660,670,681,687,688,689,721,755,
766,795,805,820,821,824,840)*

Praying

(See PRAYING 346-382; 718-747)

Be thou my vision, 545
Bread of the world, 469
Cast thy burden, 586
Create in me a clean heart, 128
Create my soul anew, 3
Dear Lord and Father, 523
Father, I stretch, 529
Fire of God, 129
Forgive our sins, 137
God of our life, 486
God, who stretched, 414
God, who touches earth, 511
God, whose purpose, 135
Gracious Spirit, dwell, 507
Have thine own way, 504

I am weak, 553
Lift every voice, 579
Like the murmur, 29
Lord Jesus Christ, 22
Lord Jesus, think on me, 527
Lord of light, your name, 410
Lord, speak to me, 499
O God, in restless living, 557
O Gott Vater, 33
O Holy Spirit, making, 300
O Lamb of God, 146
On the radiant threshold, 649
Our Father God, thy name, 32
Our Father/Pater noster, 554
Our Father who art, 228, 351
Out of the depths, 133
Precious Lord, 575
Savior of my soul, 549
Shepherd me, O God, 519
Spirit of God! descend, 502
Sun of my soul, 654
Take thou my hand, 581
Teach me thy truth, 548
Teach me, O Lord, 487
Thuma mina, 434
When the storms of life, 558

(679,697,718-747,802,803,804)

Reception of New Members

All praise to our redeeming, 21
For Christ and the church, 416
For we are strangers no more, 322
Heart with loving heart, 420
There are many gifts, 304

(716,726,777)

Reconciliation

Help us to help, 362
How good a thing, 310
We are people, 407
When love is found, 623

(704,800)

Sending

(See SENDING 418-435)

Asithi: Amen, 64
Christian, let your burning, 402
For the bread, 477
For we are strangers, 322
Forth in thy name, 415
How buoyant and bold, 394
Lead me, Lord, 538
Lead us, O Father, 359
Now go forward, 399
Savior, again, 656
Savior of my soul, 549
Sing amen, 64
Take my life, 389

(659,660,721,723,742,752,761)

Special Days

(See L/M: Special Days 638-
640)

Lead on, O cloud, 419
O God, your constant care, 481

(803,804,805)

Table Graces

Be present at our table, 457

Bread of life, 455
For the bread, 477
From the hands, 97
Great God, the giver, 458
Lord, bless the hands, 93
Praise God from whom, 118, 119
Shepherd of souls, 456

Thanksgiving

As saints of old, 386
Come and give thanks, 57
Come, ye thankful, 94
For the beauty, 89
For the fruit, 90
God of the fertile fields, 390
God, whose farm, 391
God, whose giving, 383
Lord, should rising whirlwinds, 92
Now thank we all, 85, 86

Praise the Lord, 54
Praise the Lord, sing, 50
Praise to God, 91
Sing to the Lord, 98
We gather together, 17
We plow the fields, 96

(717,721,744,821)

Transfiguration

Christ upon the mountain, 232

(741)

Wedding

(See L/M: Wedding 623-626)

Come away to the skies, 284
Help us to help, 362
Holy Spirit, gracious Guest, 542

May the grace, 423
Now thank we all, 85, 86
Will you let me be, 307

(798)

Witnessing

(See Mission; Discipleship;
  Service)

World Communion Sunday

(See LORD'S SUPPER 452-478)

Christ is the world's true, 334
For we are strangers no more, 322
Here, O Lord, your servants, 7
In Christ there is no East, 306
O Prince of peace, 15
The church's one foundation, 311

(713,720)

SCRIPTURAL ALLUSIONS/REFERENCES INDEX

Italic numbers refer to worship resources or scripture readings. Numbers in [ ] indicate hymns with
stanzas in the *Accompaniment Handbook* with the allusions or references cited.

HYMN AUTHOR INDEX

HYMN TRANSLATOR INDEX

WORSHIP RESOURCES AUTHOR INDEX

COMPOSER/ARRANGER INDEX

TUNE INDEX

METRICAL INDEX

FIRST LINE INDEX OF WORSHIP RESOURCES
AND SCRIPTURE READINGS

FIRST LINE INDEX OF HYMNS

- Regular-face type indicates the original language of a hymn.
- Italic first lines are given for translations of hymns when the original language also appears, usually as the primary musical setting.
- Upper case is used for titles of hymns that differ from the first line (often a traditional title) and in cases where English words may be used with a musical setting in which a language other than English is given.
- Upper case in parentheses is used for texts that appear twice, each with its own tune name.
- Upper case in brackets indicates first lines of stanzas found in the *Accompaniment Handbook.*
- Lower case in parentheses signifies the origin of a musical treatment of Amens and The Lord's Prayer.